THE JASTA WAR CHRONOLOGY

THE
JASTA WAR
CHRONOLOGY

A COMPLETE LISTING OF CLAIMS AND LOSSES, AUGUST 1916 – NOVEMBER 1918

NORMAN FRANKS, FRANK BAILEY AND RICK DUIVEN

GRUB STREET · LONDON

Published by
Grub Street
The Basement
10 Chivalry Road
London SW11 1HT

A complete record for this book is available from the British Library

ISBN 1 898697 84 1

Typeset by Pearl Graphics, Hemel Hempstead
Printed and bound by Biddles Ltd, Guildford and Ling's Lynn

ACKNOWLEDGEMENTS

The authors are aware of the many friends and historians who have in small ways helped to
formulate information for this book over many years. Once the project was under way much
of this accumulated knowledge was brought to the fore. However, in the final research stage
we have been helped by the following, to whom we acknowledge sincere gratitude and thanks.

Russell Guest, Alan Toelle, Staff of the Public Records Office, Kew, England, and
SHAA. Photographs were received from many people but particular thanks are due to the
Jack Bruce/Stew Leslie collection, and Greg van Wyngarden.

Contents

Introduction

This listing of German Jasta pilot victories for the period August 1916 till 11 November 1918 has come from several sources, and not just from a copy of the listings to be found in the German *Nachrichtenblatt*, virtually the equivalent of the British and French Communiqués.

Historians will know that the Allied communiqués were nothing more than a periodic publication of interesting events with many items not included due to many circumstances. In the *Nachrichtenblatt* too, information on victories was never one hundred percent. One can see in the 'late confirmation' lists that it often took some days if not weeks to confirm a pilot's victory claim, and often even when confirmed it failed to be noted in a future publication.

Study of various German documents, such as the surviving Kofl reports, (Kommandeur de Flieger, CO of aviation of an armee) and Jasta records have added to the listings recorded here, but it is known that some gaps appear, especially in the final weeks of the war, at which time record keeping or the records themselves suffered from the impending defeat of Germany.

However, the lists do show the best that can be found regarding Jasta pilot victories, added to which are many of the *unconfirmed* claims, noted as a '–' in the running pilot totals. These were either victories which failed to receive official confirmation, or they were disputed claims which were subsequently awarded to another pilot, to a two-seater crew, or to flak or ground fire. In general (although there are some questionable events) victory claims were not shared, even if two or more pilots combined to bring down a hostile aeroplane or balloon, unlike the Allied system, where sometimes four or five pilots were credited with a shared kill, each having a 'victory' recorded against his name.

The list also records zlg claims. This stood for 'zur landung gezwungen' – forced to land (on the allied side of the line). In general this was where the allied machine was seen to land but where it either seemed more or less intact, or it could not be shelled by German artillery. The suggestion is therefore that it was not destroyed and would soon be repaired and back in action. Oddly enough, quite a number of allied aircraft that should have been recorded as zlg, were in fact credited as 'kills'. Perhaps it depended on who you were, or who you knew?! Equally, a number of 'victories' that fell on the Allied side of the lines were far from lost to British and French squadrons, but somehow they were confirmed. This is not a book for questions, we merely note the claims and credits.

The running pilot totals shown on the far right of the lists are the chronological number, not necessarily the victory number given by the Germans. This is because a pilot could have, say, his fourth victory confirmed, before his third was made official. For ease of reference we have stuck strictly to date order.

We have generally listed the type of allied aeroplane claimed, although it becomes obvious that the German pilots (indeed allied pilots too) often identified a type which was only similar to that which was actually in action against them. Often the Germans merely quoted a 'type', such as a Sopwith, which could cover almost any single-seater, whether it was a Sopwith or not. A Spad too could be either a single or a two-seater, for instance. Then there is the type claimed that was no longer at the front; several G100 Martinsydes were claimed long after they had been replaced.

We have clarified in most cases the claims for *gitterrumpf* (latticed-tailed 'pusher' machines, such as the DH2, FE8, or FE2) and the *rumff DD*, (fuselaged biplane, ie: type unknown, but not a pusher), and the *einzitzer* and *zwiesitzer* (single or two-seater aeroplanes) for ease of reference.

As to casualties among the Jastas, as far as is known there is no major file of losses of aircraft, and in general, the main casualties recorded are those which resulted in the death or injury of a pilot. Whether such a list ever existed is not known for sure, although one would expect some sort of quartermaster return did exist. Ed Ferko, the late, noted expert on German WW1 airforce matters could offer no knowledge of one. If a pilot merely crashed after a combat and walked away unharmed, there is more often than not no record. Therefore, at a glance it would seem that claims over German fighters by allied pilots were much exaggerated. Some of this, most readers will know, has been referred to in the book *Bloody April, Black September* by Franks, Guest and Bailey (Grub Street 1995). Suffice it to say that overclaiming, generally in good faith (with a few noted exceptions), did go on, but without a finite list of losses, it is impossible to know just how many fighters were shot down where Jasta pilots survived unharmed. Therefore a true 'loss' figure is impossible to record. However, it is not too difficult to see that the German Jastas did not lose as many men as the allied claims might suggest, in any period of the war.

The attempt made to identify the aircraft or balloons claimed by the Jasta pilots can never be wholly correct, but they are our best guess, tempered in many cases by correct information. In all these things, they can still be reassessed by the dedicated air historian. So perhaps they should be taken merely as a guide. It is unfortunate that the French losses are not wholly known either, nor is the fate of those missing, which is why most are noted as merely – MIA (missing in action).

At the beginning of each month we have listed each armee with its attached Jastas. By refering to the map, the location of the 'front' where the actions are fought can be established. This may help to identify the area of combat, especially as most of the place names where either the combat took place or the allied aeroplane fell, are generally spelt the German way, or are noted by a German, whereas a British, French, Belgian or American pilot, may record another nearby spot.

Regarding place names, the authors in many cases have transcribed the original place name entry as noted in the German records where there seemed no good reason to change it (they have also retained 'Wald', 'See', 'Bahnhof' etc. where the reader would know these as wood, lake and station). This is done for a reason. Over the years some historians have corrected spellings wrongly, making a location difficult to identify or reconcile. Moreover, German and Allied spelling often differed, again a potential hazard.

It is the authors' intention that the cross-checking of German pilots and their scores in this chronology, whether ace or not, can be done by referring to *Above the Lines* (for aces), *Jasta Pilots* (for any pilot) and *The Sky Their Battlefield* (for British and some American casualties).

We are rapidly getting to the stage, with this series of books from Grub Street, where the air historian or amateur enthusiast can play to their heart's content to cross refer, dig into, research fully, many of the events of the first air war. With the four volumes of WW1 aces (*Above the Trenches, Over the Front, Above the Lines, Above the War Fronts*, plus *Bloody April, Black September, The Jasta Pilots*, also *The Sky Their Battlefield*, and the recent book on Belgian fighter pilots, *Above Flanders Fields*, (and maybe too, *Under the Guns of the Red Baron*, and *Under the Guns of the German Aces*), a vast area of research can be accessed. A forthcoming Grub Street book on all German airforce fatalities in WW1 will add to the field of Great War aviation research.

Please, therefore, take the enclosed victory listing as a step to further work and research. We cannot claim it is one hundred percent accurate or complete, (nobody can do that) but it is it offered as a step forward along the road of our knowledge of the first air war.

NORMAN FRANKS, SURREY, ENGLAND.
FRANK BAILEY, NEW JERSEY, USA AND RICK DUIVEN, CALIFORNIA, USA.

WWI Jasta Pilot Victories & Casualties
1916

The victory lists are under the headings of pilot's name, his Jasta/Marine Jasta, the allied type claimed, location of crash or combat, time, pilot's running score, and authors' remarks concerning victims under a., b., c., etc.*

---

24 August 1916

OfStv L Reimann	1	Sopwith 2	Metz-en-Couture	1830	1	a.

a.   A890, No 70 Sqn, RFC, 2/Lt AM Vaucour & Lt AJ Bott, shot up and forced to land, neither occcupant harmed.
Losses – Nil

---

25 August 1916

Hptm M Zander	1	FE2b	Gueudecourt		3	a.

a.   4285, No 22 Sqn, RFC, Lt RD Walker & 2/Lt C Smith, departed at 0645, POWs.
Losses – Nil

---

26 August 1916

Vfw H-K Müller	5	Voisin	Verdun Sector		4	a.

a.   Possibly a Caudron from Escadrille C 53, Sgt Mars & S/Lt Humbert, MIAs.
Losses – Nil

---

27 – 28 August 1916

No Claims – No Losses

---

29 August 1916

Obltn H Bethge	1	BE2c	S Auchonvillers	1205	1	a.

a. 4187, No 15 Sqn, RFC, Lt R Burleigh & 2/Lt R C Harry, KIAs.
Losses – Nil

---

30 August 1916

No Claims – No Losses

---

31 August 1916

Ltn H v Keudell	1	G100	Beaumetz	0800	1	a.
Obltn H Bethge	1	G100	Fins	0815	2	a.
Ltn G Leffers	1	G100	Moislains	0840	6	a.
Vfw H-K Müller	5	Balloon	Maasbogen		5	

a.   No 27 Sqn, RFC, lost four Martinsydes that departed at 0620 this date: 7287, 2/Lt MH Strange, POW; 7482, Capt A Skinner, KIA; 7479, 2/Lt AJ O'Bryne, WIA/POW; and 7299 Capt OL Whittle, POW.
Losses – Nil

---

* NOTE: IN THE CASE OF TWO-SEATER OR THREE-SEATER CLAIMS THE FIRST NAMED IS THE PILOT AND THE OTHERS ARE EITHER OBSERVERS, GUNNERS, PHOTOGRAPHERS OR BOMBARDIERS.

Jasta Armee Assignments as of 1 September 1916

1 Armee 1,2	4 Armee 8
2 Armee 3,4	5 Armee 5,6,7
3 Armee –	

1 September 1916

The French Counter-attack on the Verdun Front commenced.

No Claims

Losses:
Vfw Hans Miesegades   3   Killed testing a Fokker biplane near St Quentin.

2 September 1916

Hptm O Boelcke	2	DH2	NE Thiepval	1915	20	a.

a.   7895, No 32 Sqn, RFC, Capt RE Wilson, POW.
Losses – Nil

3 September 1916

Ltn G Leffers	1	FE2b	Mory	0900	7	a.

a.   6934, No 23 Sqn, RFC, 2/Lt FDH Sams & Cpl W Summers, POWs.
Losses – Nil

4 – 5 September 1916

No Claims – No Losses

6 September 1916

Obltn H-J Buddecke	4	FE2b	Chaulnes	1855	8	a.
Ltn O Bernert	4	Caudron	Dompierre		2	

a.   5238, No 25 Sqn, RFC, 2/Lts JL Robertson & EC Kemp, departed at 1530, KIAs.
Losses – Nil

7 September 1916

Ltn W Frankl	4	Nieuport	NE Combles	10	
Ltn H v Keudell	1	Nieuport	NE Miraumont	2	a.

a.   Sgt Guy Grosourdy de Saint Pierre, N 38, flying a Nieuport XI, hit in the lung and came down near Puisieux, S Reims.
Losses – Nil

8 September 1916

Hptm O Boelcke	2	FE2b	Flers	1825	21	a.

a.   4921, No 22 Sqn, RFC. Lt EGA Bowen & Lt RM Stalker, fell in flames north of Le Sars, KIAs.
Losses – Nil

9 September 1916

Hptm O Boelcke	2	DH2	Thiepval, SW Bapaume	1840	22	a.

a.   7842, No 24 Sqn, RFC, Lt NP Manfield, departed at 1615, KIA.
Losses – Nil

10 September 1916

No Claims – No Losses

---

11 September 1916

| Ltn O Bernert | 4 | Nieuport | Allennes | 1100 | 3 |

Losses – Nil

---

12 September 1916

No Claims

Losses:

| Ltn Ewald v Mellenthin | 3 | Killed in action over Pozières. |

---

13 September 1916

No Claims – No Losses

---

14 September 1916

Hptm O Boelcke	2	Sopwith 2	Morval	0915	23	a.
Hptm O Boelcke	2	DH2	Driencourt	1010	24	b.
Ltn K Wintgens	1	Nieuport	Bussu	1100	14	
Ltn K Wintgens	1	Pusher	N of Rancourt	1810	15	

a.   A987, No 70 Sqn, RFC, 2/Lt JH Gale & Pvt JM Strathy, last seen S of Bapaume, MIAs.
b.   7873, No 24 Sqn, RFC, 2/Lt JV Bowring, departed at 0755, WIA/POW.
Losses – Nil

---

15 September 1916

Hptm O Boelcke	2	Sopwith 2	Hesbecourt	0800	25	a.
Hptm O Boelcke	2	Sopwith 2	Eterpigny	0815	26	b.
Ltn K Wintgens	1	BE12	Manancourt	1230	16	c.
Ltn W Frankl	4	Nieuport	Péronne		11	d.

a.   A895, No 70 Sqn, RFC, Capt GL Cruickshank, DSO MC, & Lt RA Preston, last seen at 0640, in combat near Ytres, KIAs.
b.   A1903, No 70 Sqn, RFC, 2/Lt CJ Beatty & Capt FG Glenday, KIAs.
c.   6583, No 21 Sqn, RFC, 2/Lt C Elphinstone, departed at 0930, WIA/POW.
d.   A136, No 60 Sqn, RFC, Capt ASM Summers, departed at 0830 for a balloon attack S of Bapaume, flamed the balloon but went down in flames himself, KIA.
Losses – Nil

---

16 September 1916

| Ltn O Höhne | 2 | FE2b | Manancourt | 1800 | 1 | a. |
| Obltn H-J Buddecke | 4 | Vikkers | Chaulnes | 1855 | 8 | |

a.   6999, No 11 Sqn, RFC, 2/Lt AL Pinkerton & Lt JW Sanders, departed at 1740, last seen W of Marcoing, POWs.
Losses – Nil

---

17 September 1916

Ltn E Böhme	2	Sopwith 2	NW Hervilly	0745	2	a.
Hptm M Zander	1	FE2b	Heudicourt	0900	4	b.
Ltn H Reimann	2	FE2b	S Trescault	1135	2	c.
Hptm O Boelcke	2	FE2b	Equancourt	1135	27	c.
Ltn M v Richthofen	2	FE2b	Villers Plouich	1140	1	c.
Ltn K Wintgens	1	G100	Beaumetz	1200	17	

Ltn W Höhndorf	1	Caudron	Morval	1300	12	
Obltn R Berthold	4	G100	Cambrai		7	d.
Ltn W Frankl	4	FE2b	Equancourt	1135	12	c.

a.   A1913, No 70 Sqn, RFC, 2/Lts O Nixon, KIA, & R Wood, WIA/POW.
b.   4852, No 23 Sqn, RFC, Sgt B Irwin & 2/Lt FG Thierry, departed at 0607, KIAs
c.   No 11 Sqn, RFC, lost four FE2bs this date, all departed at about 0905, two last seen going down W of Marcoing: 7018, 2/Lt LBF Morris & Lt T Rees, KIAs; 7019, Capt D Grey & Lt LB Helder, POWs; and 4844, 2/Lt TPL Molloy & Sgt GJ Morton, POWs; 6994, 2/Lt H Thompson WIA/POW/DOW, & Sgt JE Glover, KIA.
d.   7286, No 27 Sqn, RFC, Lt WHS Chance, departed 0710, POW.
Losses – Nil

18 September 1916

No Claims – No Losses

19 September 1916

| Hptm O Boelcke | 2 | Morane 1 | Grevillerswald | 1930 | 28 | a. |

a.   A204, No 60 Sqn, Capt HC Tower, departed 1730, last seen over Achiet-le-Grand, KIA.
Losses – Nil

20 – 21 September 1916

No Claims – No Losses

22 September 1916

Ltn H Reimann	2	BE12	Le Transloy	0915	2	a.
Ltn A Krönig	3	Sopwith	N Bouchavesnes	0915	1	
Ltn O Höhne	2	BE12	Combles		2	a.
OfStv L Reimann	2	BE12	Sailly-Saillisel		2	a.
Obltn H-J Buddecke	4	FE2b	Combles		9	b.
Obltn R Berthold	4	BE12	Bertincourt		–	a.

a.   No 19 Sqn, RFC, lost three BE12s this date: 6561, 2/Lt RD Herman, WIA/POW/DOW; 6591, 2/Lt RH Edwards, KIA; 6544, 2/Lt G Hedderwick, KIA.
b.   6993, No 25 Sqn, RFC, 2/Lt KF Hunt & 1/AM LO Law, departed at 0640, POWs.
Losses:

| Ltn Winand Grafe | 2 | 2 victories, killed in combat with BE12s of No 19 Sqn, RFC east of Bapaume. |
| Ltn Eberhard Fügner | 4 | Severely wounded in combat SE of Bapaume. |

23 September 1916

Ltn M v Richthofen	2	G100	S Beugny	0950	2	a.
Ltn H Reimann	2	G100	Bus	0950	4	b.
Obltn H-J Buddecke	4	BE12	Sailly	0955	10	c.
Ltn E Böhme	2	G100	Hervilly	0955	–	b.
OfStv A Behling	4	BE2e	Villers-Carbonnel	1900	1	d.

a.   7481, No 27 Sqn, RFC, Sgt H Bellerby, KIA.
b.   No 27 Sqn, RFC, lost three Martinsydes this date, one of which was involved in a mid-air collision, and the one above: 7480, 2/Lt OC Godfrey, KIA; 7475, 2/Lt EJ Roberts, KIA.
c.   6167, No 21 Sqn, RFC, Lt JM Kenny, WIA/POW/DOW.
d.   5814, No 34 Sqn, RFC, 2/Lt PR Pinsent, WIA/DOW, & Lt JAR Butler, WIA, shot down S of Mametz.
Losses:

| Ltn Hans Reimann | 2 | Killed in a collision with Martinsyde A1565 of 2/Lt LF Forbes, No 27 Sqn, RFC, who deliberately rammed him. Forbes survived the crash and went on to become Air Marshal Sir Leslie Forbes. |
| Ltn Werner Lehmann | 9 | Killed in an accident at AFP 3, Somme-Py. |

24 September 1916

Ltn K Wintgens	1	BE12	Flesquières		18	a.
Ltn K Wintgens	1	BE12	Flesquèires		19	a.
Obltn R Berthold	4	Nieuport	Rancourt		–	b.

a. No 19 Sqn, RFC, lost two aircraft this date on an offensive patrol over Havrincourt: 6546, 2/Lt T West, KIA; and 6579, 2/Lt G Edwards, KIA.
b. Possibly a N 103 pilot, Sgts A Steuer and F Roman were both listed as missing while flying Nieuport XVIIs in the Somme Sector.
Losses – Nil

25 September 1916

No Claims

Losses:

Ltn Kurt Wintgens	1	Shot down in flames near Villers- Carbonnel, reportedly by Lt Alfred Heurtaux, of Escadrille N 3, for his 8th victory.

26 September 1916

Ltn W Frankl	4	Caudron	Bancourt	0920	13	a.
Obltn R Berthold	4	Sopwith 2	Bertincourt	1315	8	b.

a. G.4 of Escadrille C 6, Lts Munier and Dellon, MIAs.
b. Probably A1916, No 70 Sqn, RFC, 2/Lt FJN Echlin & 1/AM A Grundy, seen to go down at 1020 SW of Bapaume.
Losses – Nil

27 September 1916

Hptm O Boelcke	2	G100	NE Ervillers	1000	29	a.
Patrol	2	G100	SW Tilloy			b.

a. 1568, No 27 Sqn, RFC, 2/Lt HA Taylor, departed at 0920, KIA.
b. 7495, No 27 Sqn, RFC, 2/Lt S Dendrino, departed at 0920, WIA/POW/DOW.
Losses – Nil

28 – 29 September 1916

No Claims – No Losses

30 September 1916

Ltn M v Richthofen	2	FE2b	Fremicourt	1150	3	a.

a. 6973, No 11 Sqn, RFC, Lt EC Lansdale, WIA/POW/DOW, & Sgt A Clarkson, KIA, departed at 0910, seen to fall in flames at 1045 SE of Bapaume.
Losses:

Ltn Ernst Diener	2	Killed in combat with Nieuports near Bapaume, probably by Lt Albert Ball, No 60 Sqn, RFC, for his 31st victory.

JASTA ARMEE ASSIGNMENTS AS OF 1 OCTOBER 1916

1 Armee 1,2,5	6 Armee 10
2 Armee 3,4,6	7 Armee 12
3 Armee 9	Det 'A' 14
4 Armee 8	Det 'B' 13
5 Armee –	

1 October 1916

Hptm O Boelcke	2	BE2c	NW Flers		30	a.
Uffz A Ulmer	8	Balloon	Oostvleden		1	b.

a.   Possibly A 2533, a DH2 of No 32 Sqn, RFC, Captain HWG Jones, crashed in a shell hole but pilot was not harmed.
b.   Probably Belgian 38th Balloon Company.
Losses:
Ltn Herwarth Phillips   2   Killed by AA fire S Bapaume, at Beaulincourt.

2 – 6 October 1916

No Claims – No Losses

7 October 1916

Obltn H Berr	5	Caudron	Combles	1000	3	
Ltn M v Richthofen	2	BE12	Equancourt	1010	4	a.
Obltn H Berr	5	BE2c	Combles		4	b.
Hptm O Boelcke	2	Nieuport	Morval		31	c.

a.   6618, No 21 Sqn, RFC, 2/Lt WC Fenwick, departed at 0730, KIA.
b.   6564, No 21 Sqn, RFC, Lt JA Stewart, WIA, departed at 0730, aircraft badly shot up.
c.   French Nieuport XIIbis, Cdt Challe & S/Lt Mewius, F 24, missing in the Amiens Sector.
Losses – Nil

8 – 9 October 1916

No Claims – No Losses

10 October 1916

Ltn E Böhme	2	DH2	E Longueval	0950	3	a.
OfStv H Müller	2	DH2	Vraucourt	1100	1	b.
Ltn W Frankl	4	Nieuport	Villers-Carbonnel	1330	14	c.
Hptm M Zander	1	DH2	Beugny	1730	5	d.
Ltn H Imelmann	2	Sopwith 2	Lagnicourt		1	e.
Hptm O Boelcke	2	FE2b	NE Pozières		32	f.
Obltn L Linck	10	Vikkers	Vitry		FTL	g.
Ltn M v Richthofen	2	Vikkers	Roeux	1800	–	h.

a.   A2539, No 32 Sqn, RFC, 2/Lt MJG Mare-Montembault, last seen in combat east of Longueval at 0850, POW.
b.   A 2540, No 24 Sqn, RFC, 2/Lt N Middlebrook, last seen at 1010 in combat over Le Transloy, POW.
c.   A French Nieuport XIV was missing, Sgt R Thuau (P) N 62, & Lt J Billon de Plan (O) N 62, MIAs.
d.   A2556, No 24 Sqn, RFC, Sgt S Cockerell, departed at 1515, forced to land near Meaulte after combat, WIA.
e   A382, No 70 Sqn, RFC, Lt JB Lawton & 2/Lt FM Lawledge, KIAs.
f.   6992, No 11 Sqn, RFC, Sgt E Haxton & Cpl BFG Jeffs, shot down in flames near Morval, had departed at 1440, KIAs.
g.   Possibly 4918, No 23 Sqn, RFC, Capt RN Adams KIA & 2/Lt GJ Ogg OK, departed at 0710, aircraft crash-landed in a shell hole near Meaulte piloted by the observer.
h.   4292, No 25 Sqn, RFC, 2/Lt M Hayne, KIA, & Lt A Copeland, WIA/POW, lost returning from a bombing raid on Oppy. This claim disputed by and awarded to Vzfw Fritz Kosmahl & Oberleutnant Neubürger of FA22.
Losses:
Uffz Julius Heck   Kest 5   Killed near Freiberg.

11 October 1916

No Claims – No Losses

12 October 1916

Ltn E Udet	15	Bréguet	Rustenhart	1530	2	a.
Ltn K Haber	15	Sopwith 2	Offenberg		5	b.
Ltn Pfälzer	15	Bréguet	Bremgarten		1	a.

a. Escadrille BM 120 lost four aircraft this date on the Oberndorf Raid.
b. Possibly #9660 of 3 Wing RNAS, F/S/Lt CH Butterworth, who was shot down and forced to land near Freiburg, WIA/POW.
Losses – Nil

13 – 15 October 1916

No Claims – No Losses

16 October 1916

OfStv L Reimann	2	BE2e	SW Thiepval	1405	3	a.
Hptm O Boelcke	2	BE2d	E Hebuterne	1420	33	b.
Ltn M v Richthofen	2	BE12	Ytres	1700	5	c.
Hptm O Boelcke	2	DH2	Beaulencourt	1745	34	d.
Vfw A Ulmer	8	Morane	Ennetières	1745	2	e.
Vfw H-K Müller	5	Caudron	S Flers	1750	6	
Ltn L Dornheim	5	Caudron	S Le Forêt		1	

a. Probably 5818, No 34 Sqn, RFC, Lt HT Horsfield, OK, & Lt CKM Douglas, WIA, departed at 1215, involved in combat over Warlencourt.
b. 6745, No 15 Sqn, RFC, Sgt F Barton & Lt EM Carre, departed at 1215, KIAs.
c. 6580, No 19 Sqn, RFC, 2/Lt J Thompson, KIA.
d. A2542, No 24 Sqn, RFC, Capt P Langan-Byrne, DSO, departed at 1515, MIA.
e. A137, No 1 Sqn, RFC, 2/Lts C Moore-Kelly, WIA/POW & TGG Sturrock, KIA, departed at 1337, seen to go down NE Courtrai.
Losses:

Gefr Gustav Beerendonk	10	Wounded in combat.

17 October 1916

Ltn G Leffers	1	FE2b	SW Bapaume	1200	8	a.
Hptm O Boelcke	2	FE2b	W Bullecourt	1210	35	a.
Obltn S Kirmaier	2	FE2b	NE Bapaume		4	b.
Ltn R Theiller	5	Vikkers	N Maurepas		3	c.

a. No 11 Sqn, RFC, lost two FE2bs this date: 6965, 2/Lts CL Roberts, WIA/POW, & JL Pulleyn, KIA. Departed at 1010 and last seen going down near Quéant; 7670, Lt WP Bowman and 2/Lt G Clayton, departed at 1011, KIAs.
b. 4866, No 23 Sqn, RFC, 2/Lts JK Parker, WIA/POW, & JC Wilson, KIA, departed at 0857, last seen over Velu.
c. No 18 Sqn, RFC.
Losses – Nil

18 – 19 October 1916

No Claims – No Losses

20 October 1916

Hptm O Boelcke	2	FE2b	W Agny	1030	36	a.
Ltn E Böhme	2	FE2b	NW Monchy	1030	4	a.
Vfw E Clausnitzer	4	FE2b	Barleux	1650	1	
Obltn H Berr	5	FE2b	SE Le Transloy	1700	5	
OfStv M Müller	2	BE12	SE Grevillers Wood	1750	2	b.
Vfw C Kress	6	Morane	S Péronne		3	c.

a. No 11 Sqn, RFC, lost two FE2bs this date: 4867, 2/Lts NR de Pomeroy, KIA, & W Black, WIA/POW, departed at 0815; 7674, Lt RP Harvey, WIA, & 2/Lt GK Welsford, KIA, departed at 0751, brought down near Achicourt.
b. 6608, No 21 Sqn, RFC, 2/Lt CJ Creery, KIA.
c. A French Morane XXI was missing, MdL Lods (P) N 69 & S/Lt Grenay (O) C 27, MIAs.

Losses:

Vfw Paul Piechl	5	Flying Halberstadt DIII 393/16 when killed in combat near Longueval, probably by Capt EW Barrett, No 29 Sqn, RFC.

21 October 1916

Lt O Bernert	4	Caudron	Chaulnes	1620	4	
Vfw Weichel	8	Balloon	Nieppe	1620	1	a.
Ltn A Mohr	3	Nieuport	NW Barleux	1630	1	
Obltn S Kirmaier	2	BE2c	Ecoust St Main		5	b.
OfStv L Reimann	2	BE2c	Courcelette		4	b.

a.   British 9th Balloon Section, one observer, Lt Nops, was killed, and the other Lt Formby of the 19th Heavy Battery, made a safe descent.

b.   2546, No 12 Sqn, RFC, 2/Lt AB Raymond-Barker, departed at 0905, crashed near Bullecourt, POW.

Losses:

Ltn Hans Petersson	3	Killed in combat near Péronne.

22 October 1916

Obltn H Berr	5	Morane	Sailly-Saillisel	1100	6	a.
Ltn W Frankl	4	Sopwith 2	Driencourt	1145	15	
Hptm O Boelcke	2	Sopwith 2	Beaulencourt	1150	37	b.
Ltn E Böhme	2	Sopwith 2	Lesboeufs	1150	5	b.
Vfw H-K Müller	5	DH2	Bapaume	1200	7	c.
Ltn A Frey	9	Nieuport	Tahure	1300	1	d.
OfStv L Reimann	2	BE12	SE Lagnicourt	1400	5	e.
Hptm O Boelcke	2	BE12	SW Grevillers	1540	38	f.
Ltn H Imelmann	2	FE2b	Bailleul	1740	2	g.
Ltn A Träger	8	DH2	Polygonwald		1	
OfStv L Reimann	2	Sopwith 2	–			b.

a.   A247, No 3 Sqn, RFC, 2/Lts FGW Marchant & CC Hann, WIA/DOWs.

b.   No 45 Sqn, RFC, lost three aircraft that departed at 1015 this date: 7777, Capt L Porter & 2/Lt GB Samuels, MIAs; 7786, 2/Lts OJ Wade & WJ Thuell, KIAs; A1061, Sgt P Snowdon and 2/Lt W F H Fullerton, KIAs; and A1066, 2/Lt HH Griffith, OK, and Lt F Surgery, WIA, was badly damaged, had departed at 0840 and shot up at 1045.

c.   5952, No 29 Sqn, RFC, 2/Lt JN Holton, departed at 1000, KIA.

d.   A French Nieuport XI was missing in this sector, Brig C Decorme, N 38.

e.   6180, No 19 Sqn, RFC, 2/Lt R Watts, departed 1200, POW.

f.   6654, No 21 Sqn, RFC, 2/Lt WT Willcox, shot down near Warlencourt, POW.

g.   7684, No 11 Sqn, RFC, 2/Lt ALM Shephard & 1/AM NL Brain, departed at 1410, KIAs.

Losses:

OfStv Leopold Reimann	2	Wounded in combat at 1740 over St Catherine.
Obltn Ludwig Linck	10	Killed in action over Carvin.
OfStv Wilhelm Viereck	10	Wounded in action over Provin.

23 October 1916

Ltn H Kunz	7	Nieuport	Maucourt	1515	1	a.

a.   Escadrille N 76 lost two aircraft this date in the Verdun Sector, MdL Paga flying a Nieuport XVI and S/Lt C Aimard flying a Nieuport XVII. However, probably a Nieuport XVII of N 77 flown by Lt Santa Maria, who landed intact and DoW.

Losses – Nil

24 October 1916

No Claims – No Losses

25 October 1916

Ltn M v Richthofen	2	BE12	SW Bapaume	0950	6	a.
Ltn O Höhne	2	BE2d	Gommecourt	1150	3	b.
Hptm O Boelcke	2	BE2c	Miraumont	1210	39	c.

a.   6629, No 21 Sqn, RFC, 2/Lt AJ Fisher, departed 0745, last seen NE of Maricourt, KIA.
b.   5831, No 7 Sqn, RFC, 2/Lts W Fraser & J Collen, departed at 1010, brought down in flames near Puisieux, KIAs.
c.   2524, No 4 Sqn, RFC, 2/Lts SN Williams & GR Bolitho, departed at 0845, MIAs.
Losses – Nil

26 October 1916

Ltn H v Keudell	1	Nieuport	Bevillers	1540	3	a.
Ltn H Imelmann	2	Nieuport	Serre	1630	3	b.
Hptm O Boelcke	2	BE2c	SW Serre	1645	40	c.
Obltn S Kirmaier	2	DH2	Le Transloy	1650	6	
Obltn S Kirmaier	2	BE2d	N Grandcourt	1720	7	d.
Obltn H Berr	5	FE2b	Le Transloy	1800	7	e.
Obltn H Berr	5	Balloon	S Maurepas	1810	8	
Ltn R Nauck	6	Farman	Omiecourt		1	f.

a.   A133, No 60 Sqn, RFC. Lt WM Carlyle, KIA.
b.   A165, No 60 Sqn, RFC, Capt EL Foot, MC, (5v), crash-landed unharmed.
c.   4205, No 15 Sqn, RFC, 2/Lt LC Fawkner, KIA.
d.   6235, No 7 Sqn, RFC, 2/Lts FG Parsons & GA Palfreyman, departed at 1510, KIAs.
e.   4993, No 18 Sqn, RFC, 2/Lts PF Heppell & HBO Mitchell, departed at 1435, came down W of Le Transloy, POWs.
f.   One Farman of Escadrille F 33 missing in the Amiens Sector, Adj Guilhaumon (P) & Lt Rouch (O).
Losses – Nil

27 October 1916

No Claims – No Losses

28 October 1916

Ltn H v Keudell	1	BE12	Brevillers	0930	4	a.
Ltn F Mallinckrodt	6	Caudron	Villeveque		1	b.

a.   6483, No 21 Sqn, RFC, 2/Lt M Sharpe, KIA.
b.   One Caudron G 4 from Escadrille C 207 missing in the Amiens Sector, Cpl de Sars & S/Lt Resseguier.
Losses:

Hptm Oswald Boelcke	2	Killed, the victim of a mid-air collision with Ltn Erwin Böhme also of Jasta 2 during combat with 24 Sqn RFC, who survived and achieved 24 victories before being killed in combat 29 November 1917.

29 October 1916

Obltn H v Keudell	1	BE12	S Miraumont	0930	4
Ltn R Theiller	5	Pusher	SE Combles	1745	4

Losses – Nil

30 October 1916

No Claims
Losses:

Ltn Hans Wackwitz	3	Wounded in action.

31 October 1916

No Claims – No Losses

Jasta Armee Assignments as of 1 November 1916

1 Armee 1,2,5,21	6 Armee 11
2 Armee 3,4,6,20	7 Armee 9,12
3 Armee –	Det 'A' 17,19
4 Armee 8,18	Det 'B' 15,16
5 Armee 7,10,14	Det 'C' 13

1 November 1916

Ltn R Theiller	5	Nieuport	S Le Transloy	1530	5	
Ltn S Kirmaier	2	BE2e	Le Sars	1540	8	a.
Obltn H Berr	5	Caudron	S Courcelette	1630	9	

a.   6265, No 9 Sqn, RFC, 2/Lts SW Mann & AE Wynn, departed at 1315, brought down about 1430 near Rocquigny, about 10 km E of Le Sars, KIAs.
Losses – Nil

2 November 1916

Vfw C Kress	6	Voisin	Chaulnes		4	

Losses:
Ltn Hermann Göring   5   Wounded in action at 1715 hours.

3 November 1916

Ltn M v Richthofen	2	FE2b	NE Grévillers	1410	7	a.
Ltn O Höhne	2	BE2d	Hebuterne	1435	4	
Ltn R Theiller	5	FE2b	W Le Mesnil	1445	6	b.
OfStv M Müller	2	FE2b	SE Bapaume	1520	3	b.
Ltn E König	2	FE2b	Barestre	1525	1	b.
Ltn H Imelmann	2	Nieuport	Douchy	1645	4	c.
Obltn H Berr	5	BE2c	NW Martinpuich	1745	10	
Rttm J Wulff	6	DD	Vermandovillers		2	d.

a.   7010, No 18 Sqn, RFC, Sgt Cuthbert G Baldwin & 2/Lt GA Bentham, departed at 1135, seen to go down E of Engelbermer, KIAs.
b.   No 22 Sqn, RFC, lost three FE2bs this date: 6374, 2/Lts WE Knowlden & BWA Ordish, departed at 1300, WIA/POWs; 7026, Capt AT Lucas, KIA, & Lt A Anderson, POW, departed at 1337; 5250, Capt AJM Pemberton, KIA, & 2/Lt L CL Cook, POW, departed at 1300. Crashed into a kite balloon on the ground.
c.   A125, No 60 Sqn, RFC, Lt JMJ Spencer, departed at 1505, brought down near Adinfer Woods, WIA/POW/DOW.
d.   A Farman from Escadrille F 24, Adj Saillard & S/Lt Trebout, missing in action in this sector.
Losses – Nil

4 – 8 November 1916

No Claims – No Losses

9 November 1916

Obltn H v Keudell	1	DH2	SE Grévillers	1013	5	a.
Ltn O Bernert	4	DH2	Le Sars	1030	5	b.
Ltn M v Richthofen	2	BE2c	Beugny	1030	8	c.
Ltn O Höhne	2	Nieuport	Flers	1050	5	d
Ltn H Wortmann	2	Nieuport	SW Le Transloy	1055	1	d.
Rttm J Wulff	6	Caudron	S Chaulnes	1215	3	e.

Ltn G Leffers	1	DH2	SW Wancourt	1340	9	f.
Ltn H v Keudell	1	DH2	E Tilloy	1400	6	f.
Ltn E Böhme	2	FE8	Arleux	1510	6	g.
Ltn E Zschunke,	6	Caudron			zlg	h.
Ltn H Imelmann	2	DH2	Haplincourt		5	
Obltn S Kirmaier	2	BE2c	Mory		9	i.
Ltn O Bernert	4	FE8	Martinpuich		6	j.
Ltn O Bernert	4	DH2	Haplincourt		7	k.
Ltn H Baldamus	9	Nieuport			6	

a.   A2543, No 29 Sqn, RFC, 2/Lt I Curlewis, departed at 0830, WIA/POW.
b.   7915, No 29 Sqn, RFC, Capt AC Bolton, departed at 0830, WIA/POW.
c.   2505, No 12 Sqn, RFC, 2/Lt JG Cameron, departed at 0805, last seen near Sapignies, KIA.
d.   Two Nieuports lost this date, not known which pilot got which specific aircraft, both came down in Allied lines: A272, No 60 Sqn, RFC, Lt AD Bell-Irving, 7 victories, wounded and crash-landed. One Nieuport XVII, Caporal L Millot, Escadrille N 103, killed in action in this sector.
e.   Probably an R.4 from Escadrille F 208, Lt Leleu (P), S/Lt Guedon (O) & Sgt Desprats (G), MIAs.
f.   With two claims for the same type aircraft in the same area in the same time frame only one claim can be verified, but which pilot should have been credited cannot be ascertained. 7925, No 29 Sqn, RFC, 2/Lt HA Hallam, departed at 1130, POW.
g.   Possibly 7624, No 40 Sqn, RFC, Capt T Mapplebeck, WIA/POW.
h.   Possibly an R.4 from Escadrille F 208 that was missing, Lt Leleu, S/Lt Guedon and Sgt Desprats, MIAs.
i.   2502, No 12 Sqn, RFC, Lt GF Knight, departed at 0815, seen to go down near Mory, POW.
j.   6409, No 40 Sqn, RFC, 2/Lt HF Evans, departed at 1300, shot down NW of Cambrai, POW.
k.   7915, No 29 Sqn, RFC, Capt AC Boulton, departed at 0830, WIA/POW.
Losses – Nil

10 November 1916

Vfw H Pfeiffer	9	Nieuport	W Suippes	1115	5	
Vfw H Pfeiffer	9	Caudron	Souain	1120	6	a.
Ltn H v Keudell	1	Sopwith 2	Havrincourt Wood	1230	7	b.
Obltn E Hahn	1	DD	Rocquigny	1230	1	c.

a.   A Caudron G4 of Escadrille C 212, Lts de Saint Pern & de Pommereau, killed in combat, in this sector.
b.   A885, No 70 Sqn, RFC, 2/Lt M Allport & Lt TM Bennet, last seen in combat over Havrincourt Wood, KIAs.
c.   Possibly Sgt Roxas-Elias, Escadrille N 73, flying a Nieuport XXI who was missing in this sector.
Losses:
Vfw Christian Kress   6   Killed at 1300 hours over Nesle, probably by S/Lt Georges
                                     Guynemer, N 3, for his 19th victory.

11 November 1916

Ltn H Kunz	7	Nieuport		1730	2

Losses – Nil

12 November 1916

No Claims – No Losses

13 November 1916

No Claims

Losses:
Ltn Bodo Frhr v Lyncker   2   Injured in an accident.

14 November 1916

Ltn H Gontermann	5	FE2b	Morval	1030	1	
Vfw W Göttsch	8	Balloon	Westvledern		1	a.

a.   A Belgian balloon, the observers made safe descents, probably that of the 38th Balloon Company.
Losses – Nil

15 November 1916

No Claims – No Losses

16 November 1916

Ltn H v Keudell	1	Nieuport	Beaucourt, SE Serre	0900	8	a.
Vfw F Loerzer	6	Caudron	SE Pressoire	0935	1	b.
OfStv M Müller	2	BE2c	Flers	1045	4	c.
Ltn A Mohr	3	Nieuport	W Brie	1200	2	d.
Obltn S Kirmaier	2	Sopwith 2	S Bancourt	1545	10	e.
Uffz W Seitz	8	FE2d	Abeele		1	f.
Vfw P Glasmacher	8	FE2b	W Ypern		–	g.

a.   A225, No 60 Sqn, RFC, Lt DH Bacon, departed at 0700, KIA.
b.   Probably a Caudron G4 from Escadrille C 66, Sgt Girard & Adj Laguesse, that was missing in this sector.
c.   2518, No 7 Sqn, RFC, 2/Lts DA MacNeill & RGR Allen, departed at 0905, crashed near Beaumont-Hamel, KIAs.
d.   A135, No 60 Sqn, RFC, 2/Lt HE Martin, KIA.
e.   A3432, No 70 Sqn, RFC, Sgt RS Evans & 2/Lt LP Struben, last seen at 1430, KIAs.
f.   A37, No 20 Sqn, RFC, 2/Lt JW Francis & Lt FRC Cobbold, departed at 1215, engaged in combat and forced to land near Abeele, neither harmed.
g.   Possibly 7003, No 25 Sqn, RFC, 2/Lt H Sellers, OK, & 2/Lt WW Fitzgerald WIA.
Losses:

Ltn Karl Büttner	2	Flying Albatros DI 391/16 'Bü' (G.1) shot down and taken POW by Capt GA Parker & Lt HE Hervey, No 8 Sqn, RFC.
Ltn Albert Krönig	3	Severely injured at 1750 over Thielt airfield.
Ltn Ernst Wever	6	Shot down in flames and killed over Pressoire Wald, probably by Lt Albert Heurtaux, N 3, who claimed a Fokker at Pressoire, at 0950, his 13th victory.
Vfw Otto Augst	12	Wounded in action.

17 November 1916

Ltn O Höhne	2	DH2	SE Bapaume	1130	6	a
Ltn H v Keudell	1	FE2b	Gueudecourt	1200	9	b.
Vfw W Göttsch	8	DH2	SW Ypres		2	c.

a.   A2577, No 24 Sqn, RFC, 2/Lt WC Crawford, departed at 0920, came down near Ligny, about 7 km N of Gueudecourt, KIA.
b.   6950, No 22 Sqn, RFC, 2/Lt MR Helliwell, WIA, & Pte FD Cox, injured, crashed landed near Pozières after a combat.
c.   Two No 29 Sqn, RFC DH2 pilots, A2565, 2/Lt WSF Saundby, and 2555, Capt SE Cowan, collided in mid-air while attacking the same enemy aircraft, KIAs.
Losses:

Lt Wilhelm Schlolaut	9	Killed near Monthois.

18 – 19 November 1916

No Claims – No Losses

20 November 1916

Obltn S Kirmaier	2	BE2d	N Miraumont	0900	11	
Ltn M v Richthofen	2	BE2d	S Grandcourt	0910	9	a.
Ltn M v Richthofen	2	FE2b	Gueudecourt	1615	10	b.

a.   2767, No 15 Sqn, RFC, 2/Lt JC Lees & Lt TH Clark, departed at 0650, last seen over Miraumont at 0845, POWs. It seems this was the enemy aircraft claimed by Kirmaier and von Richthofen.

b.   4848, No 18 Sqn, RFC, 2/Lts GS Hall, WIA//POW & G Doughty, KIA, departed at 1315.
Losses – Nil

21 November 1916

No Claims – No Losses

22 November 1916

Ltn E Böhme	2	Morane	Longueval	1410	7	a.
Ltn H v Keudell	1	DH2	Biefvillers	1415	10	b.
Ltn E König	2	FE2b	Hebuterne	1650	2	c.

a.   A248, No 3 Sqn, RFC, 2/Lt EP Roberts & Capt GL Watson, involved in combat W of Flers, both WIA.
b.   A2607, No 32 Sqn, RFC, Lt R Corbett, downed at 1530 NE of Bapaume, WIA/POW.
c.   7677, No 11 Sqn, RFC, 2/Lts F Crisp & JAV Boddy, who were shot down in a damaged condition near Hebuterne.
Losses:

Obltn Stefan Kirmaier	2	Killed in combat at 1310 over Les Boeufs, by Capt JO Andrews, MC, and 2/Lt K Crawford, No 24 Sqn, RFC.
Ltn Erich Zschunke	6	Wounded in action.
Gefr Robert Michaelis	12	Killed W Gueudecourt.

23 November 1916

Lt D Collin	2	DH2	N Le Sars	1100	1	a.
Ltn F Ray	1	Pup	Haplincourt	1110	1	b.
Ltn A Mohr	3	Nieuport	Brie	1245	3	
Ltn M v Richthofen	2	DH2	S Ligny	1500	11	c.

a.   A2554, No 24 Sqn, RFC, 2/Lt HB Begg, departed at 0950, KIA.
b.   N5190, No 8 Sqn, RNAS, F/S/Lt WH Hope, departed at 0830, last seen over Albert, DoW.
c.   5964, No 24 Sqn, RFC, Major LG Hawker, VC, DSO, 7 victories, departed at 1300, last seen over Achiet-le-Grand, KIA.
Losses – Nil

24 November 1916

Vfw A Schramm	7	Nieuport	Vaux-Teich	1140	1	
Ltn H Baldamus	9	Nieuport 2	Aure	1215	7	a.
Vfw H Pfeiffer	9	Nieuport	Ardeuil		7	

a.   2712, Escadrille C 56.
Losses:

| Uffz Otto Krönert | 14 | Killed in combat near Château-Salins. |

25 – 26 November 1916

No Claims – No Losses

27 November 1916

Ltn W Voss	2	Nieuport	Miraumont	0940	1	a.
OfStv M Müller	2	Nieuport	Miraumont	0940	5	a.
Ltn W Voss	2	DH2/FE2b	S Bapaume	1415	2	b.

a.   Only one Nieuport loss can be confirmed, which pilot's claim is valid is not known. A281, No 60 Sqn, RFC, Capt GA Parker, DSO, MC, departed at 0800, last seen over Bapaume, at 0940, MIA – often assumed to have been Voss's claim.
b.   4915, No 18 Sqn, RFC, Lt FA George, WIA, & 1/AM OW Watts, KIA, shot down in flames.
Losses – Nil

28 – 30 November 1916

No Claims – No Losses

JASTA ARMEE ASSIGNMENTS AS OF 1 DECEMBER 1916

1 Armee 1,2,5,21,22	6 Armee 11,12
2 Armee 3,4,6,20	7 Armee 9
3 Armee –	Det 'A' 17,19,24
4 Armee 8,18	Det 'B' 15,16
5 Armee 7,10,14,	Det 'C' 13,23

1 December 1916

No Claims

Losses:

Ltn Amann	2	Flying an Albatros DI, shot down and taken prisoner.

Battle of the Somme which commenced 14 July 1916 ended on 1 December 1916

2 December 1916

Ltn H Baldamus	9	Caudron	S Aure	8	a.
Ltn H Baldamus	9	Caudron	S Aure	9	a.
Ltn H Pfeiffer	9	Caudron	S Vacquois	8	a.

a.   Two French Caudron G.4s were lost this date in the Châlons Sector: Escadrille C 53 lost Sgt Lanier & Coutand; and Lt Cuvillier & Cpl Ringuet, MIAs. Also one Farman F43 from Escadrille F 50,lost this date, Adj Lachat & S/Lt Louvet, MIAs.

Losses – Nil

3 December 1916

No Claims – No Losses

4 December 1916

Ltn O Splitgerber	12	FE2b	Mercatel	1	a.

a.   7022, No 25 Sqn, RFC, 2/Lt DS Johnson & Lt I Heald, departed at 0905, shot down in the La Bassée – Arras area, KIAs.

Losses:

OfStv Karl Ernthaller	1	Flying Fokker DI 175/16 killed in combat over Pronville.
Vfw Wilhelm Hennebeil	12	Killed in combat S of Bailleul.

5 December 1916

No Claims – No Losses

6 December 1916

No Claims

Losses:

Ltn Hansen	3	Wounded in action.

7 – 10 December 1916

No Claims – No Losses

11 December 1916

Ltn M v Richthofen	2	DH2	Mercatel	1155	12	a.
Ltn A Schulte	12	BE2g	Annequin	1245	1	b.

a.   5986, No 32 Sqn, RFC, Lt Benedict PG Hunt, departed at 0920, POW.
b.   7153, No 10 Sqn, RFC, 2/Lts GW Dampler & HC Barr, KIAs.
Losses – Nil

12 – 13 December 1916
No Claims – No Losses

14 December 1916

Vfw A Schramm	7	Nieuport	Souville	1600	2	a.

a.   Probably a Nieuport XVII French Escadrille N 12, Lt des Vallières, POW.
Losses – Nil

15 December 1916
No Claims – No Losses

16 December 1916
No Claims – No Losses

The French Offensive on the Verdun Front which started on 1 September 1916 ended this date.

17 December 1916

Vfw J Buckler	17	Caudron	Bras	1620	1

Losses – Nil

18 December 1916

Ltn Weitz	15	Nieuport	Niederaspach		1

Losses – Nil

19 December 1916
No Claims – No Losses

20 December 1916

Ltn M v Richthofen	2	DH2	Monchy	1130	13	a.
Obltn H Bethge	1	DH2	Vailly	1150	–	b.
Ltn P Bona	1	FE2b	Mory	1200	–	c.
Ltn M v Richthofen	2	FE2b	Moreuil	1345	14	d.
Ltn H Imelmann	2	FE2b	NE Beugny	1345	6	e.
Ltn H Wortmann	2	FE2b	Sapignies	1405	2	f.
Vfw H-K Müller	5	Caudron	SE Courcelette	1645	8	

a.   7927, No 29 Sqn, RFC, Capt AG Knight, DSO, departed at 0945, last seen over Adfiner Wood, KIA.
b.   Possibly A2552, No 29 Sqn, RFC, 2/Lt HB Hurst, fuel tank hit and forced to land near Beaumetz, pilot not harmed.
c.   Possibly from No 11 Sqn, RFC, Lt WO Boger WIA.
d.   A5446, No 18 Sqn, RFC, Lt Lionel GD'Arcy & Sub/Lt RC Whiteside, RNVR, departed at 1115, last seen over Le Transloy, KIAs.
e.   A5452, No 18 Sqn, RFC, Ltn CH Windrum & JA Hollis, departed at 1125, last seen over Sapignies, going towards Gommecourt, POWs.
f.   4884, No 18 Sqn, RFC, Lt R Smith & 2/Lt H Fiske departed at 1125, last seen at 1255 going down in flames, KIAs.
Losses:
Ltn Kurt Haber   3   Shot down in flames and killed in combat over Péronne at 1545,
                              probably by S/Lt Charles Nungesser, N 65, the Frenchman's 21st victory.

21 December 1916

Ltn W Voss	2	BE2d	Miraumont	1100	3	a.

a.   5782, No 7 Sqn, RFC, Lt DW Davis, WIA/POW & 2/Lt William MV Cotton, KIA.

Losses – Nil

---

22 – 23 December 1916

No Claims – No Losses

---

24 December 1916

Ltn E Udet	15	Caudron	Oberaspach	1100	3	a.
Vfw G Strasser	17	Caudron	NW Ft Douaumont	1640	1	a.

a.   Caudron G.4 of Escadrille C 34, MdL Hourcade & S/Lt Lombart shot down in flames near Aspach, KIAs. Also two Farmans were lost this date: one F43 from Escadrille F 22, MdL Allart & Sol Poussin, MIAs, one F42 from Escadrille F 71, Brig Murel & S/Lt Gavrel, MIAs.

Losses:

Ltn Lothar Erdmann	20	Killed in combat over St Quentin.

---

25 December 1916

No Claims – No Losses

---

26 December 1916

Ltn R Theiller	5	Vikkers	W Sailly	1055	7	a
Ltn E König	2	DH2	Beaulencourt	1115	3	b.
Ltn D Collin	2	DH2	E Morval	1120	2	b.
Ltn L Dornheim	5	BE2c	Weilly	1145	2	
Obltn H Bethge	1	BE2d	Beugny	1210	3	c.
Vfw P Bona	1	BE2c	Sapignies	1210	1	c.
OfStv H-K Müller	5	BE2c	Le Sars	1355	9	
Ltn E Böhme	2	BE2d	Courcelette	1515	8	d.
Vfw A Ulmer	8	Nieuport 2	Hooge		3	e.

a.   A5453, No 18 Sqn, RFC, Capt HLH Owen, OK, & Lt R Mayberry, injured, crash-landed in a shell hole after combat.

b.   Only one claim can be verified, which pilot should be credited is not known, 7885, No 24 Sqn, RFC, 2/Lt E L Lewis, departed at 0935, down in flames at 1015, KIA.

c.   No 5 Sqn, RFC, lost two aircraft that departed at 0915 this date: BE2c 4498, 2/Lt HE Arnold, KIA, and BE2d 6254, 2/Lt FN Insoll, POW.

d.   No 5 Sqn, RFC, 2/L WH Hubbard, the pilot, WIA.

e.   A3924, No 46 Sqn, RFC, Capt JWW Nason & Lt CAF Brown, departed at 1030, KIAs.

Losses:

OfStv Hans Müller	5	Severely wounded in combat by Lt RWP Hall & 2/Lt EFW Smith, No 9 Sqn, RFC (Smith DoW next day).

---

27 December 1916

OfStv W Cymera	1	FE2b	Cherisy	1220	1	a.
Ltn M v Richthofen	2	DH2	Ficheux	1625	15	b.
Ltn J Kintzelmann	7	Farman	Louvemont		1	c.

a.   7666, No 11 Sqn, RFC, Capt JB Quested, OK, & Lt HJH Dicksee, WIA.

b.   5985, No 29 Sqn, RFC, Sgt JTB McCudden MM, CdG, pilot and a/c not harmed.

c.   Probably a Farman F42 from Escadrille F 5, Sgt D Fusier & Lt Thamin, missing in action in the Verdun Sector.

Losses:

Ltn Gustav Leffers	5	Flying an Albatros DII, killed in combat about 1200 near Cerisy by Capt JB Quested & Lt HJH Dicksee of No 11 Sqn, RFC. It was Quested's 7th victory.

28 – 29 December 1916

No Claims – No Losses

30 December 1916

Ltn F Mallinckrodt	6	Caudron	Ablaincourt	–

31 December 1916

No Claims – No Losses

WWI Jasta Pilot Victories & Casualties
1917

JASTA ARMEE ASSIGNMENTS AS OF 1 JANUARY 1917

Western Front

1 Armee 1,2,5,21,22
2 Armee 3,6,20
3 Armee 10
4 Armee 8,18
5 Armee 4,7,14

6 Armee 11
7 Armee 9
Det 'A' 12,17,19,24
Det 'B' 15,16
Det 'C' 13,23

Other Fronts

11 Armee 25   Macedonia

---

1 – 3 January 1917

No Claims – No Losses

---

4 January 1917

Ltn M v Richthofen	B	Pup	Metz-en-Couture	1615	16	a.
Ltn F Mallinckrodt	6	Pup	Neuchâtel		2	b.
Uffz W Hoffmann	5	EA	Clery		1	

a. N5193, No 8 Sqn, RNAS, F/Lt AS Todd, departed at 1430, last seen in combat at 1515 over Bapaume, KIA.
b. A626, No 8 Sqn, RNAS, F/S/Lt JC Croft, departed at 1430, last seen as above, over Bapaume, POW.
Losses: – Nil

---

5 January 1917

Vfw W Göttsch	8	BE2e	S Vormzeele	1100	3	b.
Ltn A Mohr	3	Caudron	Barleux-Flaucourt	1440	4	a.
Vfw F Manschott	7	Voisin	S Douaumont	1620	2	

a. Caudron G.4 of Escadrille C 6, Brig Dinior & S/Lt Philippe, MIAs.
b. 7190, No 6 Sqn, RFC, 2/Lt H Jameson & Lt DW Thomson, departed at 0835, KIAs.
Losses:
Vfw Erwin Kernchen   25   Killed in an accident.

---

6 January 1917

No Claims – No Losses

---

7 January 1917

Ltn E Böhme	B	DH2	Beugny	1230	9	a.
Vfw W Göttsch	8	FE2d	Ypern-Kemmel	1300	4	c.
Lt G Schlenker	3	RE8	NE Péronne	1340	1	b.

a. 7851, No 32 Sqn, RFC, 2/Lt ES Wagner, departed at 1100, KIA.
b. A174, No 52 Sqn, RFC, Maj L Parker, KIA, & 2/Lt FA Mann, POW, departed at 1140, came down between Albert and Allaines.

c.   A39, No 20 Sqn, RFC, Sgt TT Mottershead, VC, INJ/DOI & Lt WE Gower, INJ, aircraft shot up, landed N of Bailleul.
Losses – Nil

8 – 9 January 1917

No Claims – No Losses

10 January 1917

Uffz H Körner	8	Balloon	Dranoutre	1540	1	a.

a.   British balloon 2-5-2 (F 25), Lt C W M Whitlock, OK.
Losses:
Ltn O Höhne   B   6 victories, wounded in combat at 1030 with Sopwith two-seaters.

11 – 14 January 1917

No Claims – No Losses

15 January 1917

Hptm F-K Burckhardt	25	BE2c	Smolari	1	a.

a.   No 47 Sqn, RFC, 2/Lt SMJ White & 2/Lt H Matthews, KIAs.
Losses – Nil

16 – 18 January 1917

No Claims – No Losses

19 January 1917

Ltn O Brauneck	25	Caudron	N Gjevgjeli	5

Losses – Nil

20 January 1917

Ltn O Brauneck	25	Farman	SW Lake Dorian	–
Ltn O Brauneck	25	EA	SW Lake Dorian	–

Losses – Nil

21 January 1917

No Claims – No Losses

22 January 1917

Obltn E Dostler	13	Caudron	Nixeville	1	a.

a.   Caudron G.4 of Escadrille C 224, Sgt Pivard & Cpl Mulot, WIAs, in the Souilly Sector.
Losses:
Ltn Karl Pertz   23   Killed by two Nieuports while trying to land at Puisieux. Probably credited to Adj
                         Gustav Douchy of N 38 who claimed an Albatros for his 3rd victory in this area.

23 January 1917

Ltn M v Richthofen	11	FE8	SW Lens	1610	17	a.
Ltn H Baldamus	9	Caudron	W St Martin	1635	10	b.
Vfw F Manschott	7	Farman	Douaumont		3	
Ltn W v Bülow	18	FE8	Bixschoote		5	c.
Ltn W v Bülow	18	Sopwith 2	Gheluvelt		6	d.

| Ltn J Jacobs | 22 | Caudron | Terny-Sorny – Soissons | | | 1 |

a. 6388, No 40 Sqn, RFC, 2/Lt J Hay, departed at 1312, brought down near Lens at 1505, KIA.
b. Caudron G.4 #2712, Escadrille C 56, Sgt Lyaudet & S/Lt Colle, MIAs, in the Châlons Sector.
c. A1078, No 45 Sqn, RFC, 2/Lt JV Lyle & Bdr A Harrison, departed at 1230, last seen over Dadizeele, headed for Ypres, KIAs.
d. 7613, No 41 Sqn, RFC, 2/Lt SF Cody, departed at 1424, shot down E of Boesinghe, KIA.

Losses:

| Ltn Hans Imelmann | B | 6 victories, killed in combat at 1405 near Miraumont by Capt JC McMillan & 2/Lt Hopkins, No 4 Sqn, RFC. |
| Vfw Paul Ostrop | B | Flying an Albatros DII when killed in combat at 1440 near Miraumont by Lt EC Pashley, No 24 Sqn, RFC. |

24 January 1917

Ltn M v Richthofen	11	FE2b	W Vimy	1215	18	a.
Ltn H v Keudell	1	Pup	Bihucourt	1310	11	b.
Vfw A Ulmer	8	FE8	W Wytschaete	1650	5	c.
Vfw A Ulmer	8	BE2e	N Warneton		4	d.
Vfw P Glasmacher	8	Bréguet	S Boesinghe		1	
Uffz W Hoffmann	5	Caudron	Harbonnières		2	

a. 6997, No 25 Sqn, RFC, Capt O Greig & 2/Lt JE MacLennan, departed at 0950, brought down near Vimy, WIA/POWs.
b. N5198, No 8 Sqn, RNAS, F/Lt CP Mackenzie, departed at 1115, last seen over Bapaume, MIA.
c. 6417, No 41 Sqn, RFC, Sgt C Tooms, departed at 1435, KIA.
d. 6308, No 53 Sqn, RFC, Lts TF Preston & CM Buck, came down near Warneton, KIAs.

Losses:

| OfStv Leopold Reimann | B | 5 victories, killed flying Albatros DIII 526/16 when it broke up in the air. |

25 January 1917

Flgmt G Kinkel	B	FE2b	NE Moislains	1130	1	a.
Obltn K v Grieffenhagen	18	FE2d	SE Bousbecque		1	b.
Vfw W Seitz	8	BE2e	Messines		2	c.
Vfw K Holler	6	Nieuport	SW Roye		1	

a. No 20 Sqn, RFC,
b. A34, No 20 Sqn, RFC, Lts S Adler & RW White, seen to go down near Menin, WIA/POWs. This aircraft also claimed by a flak unit.
c. Probably 6311, No 53 Sqn, RFC, Capt FWH Simpson, OK, 2/Lt J Houghton, WIA.

Losses:

| Flgmt Gustav Kinkel | B | 1 victory; flying Albatros DIII 1982/16 when shot down and taken prisoner by Lt AE McKay, No 24 Sqn RFC. |

26 January 1917

| Ltn W v Bülow | 18 | Sopwith 2 | Reckem | | 7 | a. |

a. A1074, No 45 Sqn, RFC, F/Sgt WG Webb & Cpl RD Fleming, shot down in flames near Halluin, KIAs.

Losses:

| Vzflgmt Max Winkelmann | 5 | Shot down by AA fire and taken prisoner. |
| Ltn Karl Groterjahn | 22 | 3 victories, killed in combat between Trosly and Verneuil. |

27 January 1917

No Claims

Losses:

| Ltn Bruno Kalff | 20 | Killed in combat near Essigny-le-Petit. |

28 January 1917

No Claims – No Losses

29 January 1917

| Ltn G Schuster | | 17 | Caudron | Nomeny | | 1 |

Losses:

| Ltn Georg Simon | 11 | Wounded in action. |
| Ltn Walter Lautz | 20 | Severely wounded in combat over Vendhuille, died of wounds 19 May 1917. |

30 – 31 January 1917

No Claims – No Losses

JASTA ARMEE ASSIGNMENTS AS OF 1 FEBRUARY 1917

Western Front

1 Armee 1,2,5,21,22
2 Armee 3,6,20
3 Armee 10
4 Armee 8,18,28
5 Armee 4,7,14

6 Armee 11,30
7 Armee 9
Det 'A' 12,17,19,24
Det 'B' 15,16,26
Det 'C' 13,23

Other Fronts

11 Armee 25   Macedonia

1 February 1917

Vfw F Manschott	7	Farman	N Esnes	1425	4	
Ltn M v Richthofen	11	BE2d	Vimy	1600	19	a.
Ltn W Voss	B	DH2	Achiet-le-Petit	1730	4	b.
Vfw W Göttsch	8	FE2d	E Moorseele		5	c.
Vfw W Göttsch	8	FE2d	Bondues, N Lille		6	d.
Obflgmstr K Meyer	SFSI	Pup	Breedene-Blankenberghe		6	e.

a.   6742, No 16 Sqn, RFC, Lts PW Murray, POW/DOWs, & DJ McRae, WIA/DOW, departed at 1430.
b.   A2614, No 29 Sqn, RFC, Capt Albert FV Daly, departed at 1530, brought down near Beaumont Hamel, POW.
c.   A1951, No 20 Sqn, RFC, 2/Lts WA Reeves & FH Bronskill, last seen between Roulers and Courtrai, POWs.
d.   A28, No 20 Sqn, RFC, 2/Lt ED Spicer & Capt CM Carbert, MC, last seen between Roulers and Courtrai, KIAs.
e.   N6161, No 3 Sqn, RNAS, F/S/L GL Elliott, POW.

Losses – Nil

2 February 1917

Vfw F Manschott	7	Voisin	Courrières Wood	1425	5	
Vfw P Bona	1	FE2b	SW Hendecourt	1425	2	a.
Ltn H Gutermuth	5	DH2	Gommecourt	1530	1	b.
Ltn H Baldamus	9	Farman	S Cernay		11	c.
Ltn J Wolff	17	Voisin	S Regineville	–		

a.   7705, No 23 Sqn, RFC, 2/Lt RJ Whitney & Lt TG Holley, departed at 1140 last seen at 1315 NE of Bapaume, POWs.
b.   A2570, No 32 Sqn, RFC, 2/Lt H Blythe, departed at 1400, seen to come down E of Puisieux, POW/DOW.

c.   French Escadrille F 71, Lt de Landrain & S/Lt Berger, MIAs.
Losses – Nil

3 February 1917

Ltn A Kuen	14	Caudron	Embermenil	1525	1	a.

a.   Probably G.4 of Escadrille C 22, Cpl Faivre-Pierret & S/Lt Malzac, MIAs.
Losses:

Vfw Walter Göttsch	8	6 victories, wounded in action over Wervicq by 2/Lt C Gordon Davis & Capt RM Knowles, No 20 Sqn, RFC.
Uffz Heinz Leiendecker	9	Wounded in action S of Tahure.

4 February 1917

Vfw P Bona	1	FE2b	Courcelette	1255	3	a
Ltn E Böhme	B	Sopwith	Le Transloy	1505	10	b.
Ltn E Böhme	B	BE2e	NW Puisieux	1530	11	c.
Ltn E König	B	BE2e	NW Neuville	1530	4	d.
Ltn W Voss	B	BE2d	Givenchy	1540	5	e.

a.   7023, No 11 Sqn, RFC, 2/Lts AB Coupal, INJ, & HL Villiers, KIA, departed at 1103, came down in no-man's-land near Hebuterne.
b.   A2536, No 32 Sqn, RFC, Capt WGS Curphey MC, WIA.
c.   7105, No 15 Sqn, RFC, Sgt JF Shaw & 2/Lt GWB Bradford, departed at 1350, MIAs.
d.   2768, No 16 Sqn, RFC Lt JW Boyd & 2/Lt AH Steele, came down N of Berthonval Farm, WIA/DOWs 5 February 1917.
e.   5797, No 16 Sqn, RFC, 2/Lts H Martin-Massey, WIA, & Noel M H Vernham, KIA, fell in flames.
Losses:

Ltn Christian v Scheele	B	Killed at 1500 near Le Mesnil.

5 February 1917

Vfw S Festner	11	BE	N Arras	1700	1	
Ltn O Könnecke	25	Farman	NW Mogila		1	

Losses:

Vfw Thiel	B	Wounded in action.
Vfw Alfred Ulmer	8	3 victories, severely wounded in action over Dranoutre, at 1645, by Capts G Boumphrey and F Findlay.

6 February 1917

Vfw P Bona	1	FE2b	NE Flers	1310	4	a.
Obltn R Frhr v Esebeck	8	FE2d	SE Gheluvelt	1630	1	b.
Ltn A Träger	8	FE2d	E Moorslede	1630	2	c.
Ltn A Schulte	12	Nieuport	Grande Rang-Ferme		2	
Ltn J v Carlowitz	1	Rumpf DD	Acheux		–	
Ltn O Könnecke	25	Farman	Monastir		2	

a.   4971, No 22 Sqn, RFC, Lt WN McDonald, WIA, & 2/Lt Galley, OK, forced to land near Eaucourt l'Abbaye.
b.   A38, No 20 Sqn, RFC, 2/Lt ME Woods, POW, & Lt EB Maule, KIA, departed at 1505, last seen over Moorslede.
c.   A31, No 20 Sqn, RFC, Lt TC Lucas & 2/Lt JT Gibbon, departed at 1511, last seen over Moorslede, KIAs.
Losses:

Ltn Georg Ferner	24	Severely wounded over Pompey.

7 February 1917

Ltn W v Bülow	18	Sopwith 2	Linselles	1325	8	a.
Vzflgmstr J Wirtz	MFJI	Sopwith 2	Jabbeke		1	b.

a.   7789, No 45 Sqn, RFC, 2/Lt EE Erlebach & 2/AM FJ Ridgway, KIAs.
b.   N5102, 5 Wing, RNAS, F/Lt CR Blagrove & 2/AM Milne, KIAs.
Losses – Nil

8 February 1917

VfW Rieger		17	DD	Pont-à-Mousson		zlg

Losses:
Ltn Alfred Träger   8   2 victories; severely wounded in combat.
Vfw Konrad Hess   1   Killed during a test flight, Golancourt.

9 February 1917

Ltn J Jacobs	22	EA	Cerny	1635	3
Vfw J Wolff	17	Voisin	E Martincourt		1

Losses:
Vfw Adolf Wellhausen   17   Severely wounded in combat, died of wounds 11 February 1917.

10 February 1917

Ltn E Böhme	B	FE2b	W Gommecourt	1220	12	
Ltn W Voss	B	DH2	SW Serre	1225	6	a.

a.   A2548, No 32 Sqn, RFC, Capt LP Aizelwood, MC, WIA.
Losses:
Obltn Walter Zietlow   9   Killed at 1030 between Hauviné and Leffincourt.
Vfw Heinrich Tuczek   21   Shot down in flames at 1600 over Berru, in combat with a Caudron.

11 February 1917

Ltn O Brauneck	25	AWFK8	S Hudova	1200	6	
OfStv Hüttner	14	Nieuport	Gerden	1530	1	a.
Ltn E König	B	BE2c	N St Laurent	1530	5	b.
Vfw K Holler	6	Caudron	SW Péronne	1630	zlg	
Ltn H Bussing	5	BE2			–	

a.   Brig Lambert, Détachement N 506, flying a Nieuport XVIIbis, shot down in enemy lines near Lagarde, POW.
b.   2498, No 13 Sqn, RFC, Capt J Thorburn & 2/Lt JK Howard, KIAs.
Losses:
Ltn Erwin Böhme   B   12 victories; wounded in action.

12 February 1917

Ltn W Gros		17	Nieuport	Landremont	1

Losses – Nil

13 February 1917

OfStv A Behling	1	Morane	Le Transloy	1635	1	a.

a.   A266, No 3 Sqn, RFC, Lt TS Green & 2/Lt WK Karse, departed at 1510, shot down at about 1530, KIAs.
Losses:
Ltn Jürgen v Carlowitz 1   Flying Albatros DIII 1990/16 (G.10) when killed in
                                combat over Fregicourt, by 2/Lt Stroud and Lt Burcher, No 9 Sqn, RFC.

14 February 1917

Ltn H Gutermuth	5	Morane	Gueudecourt	1100	2	a.
Ltn M v Richthofen	11	BE2d	E Loos	1200	20	b.
Ltn G Schlenker	3	Pup	Eterpigny	1245	2	c.
Ltn L Rehm	23	Balloon	Gironville	1545	1	d.

Ltn M v Richthofen	11	BE	Lens-Hulluch	1645	21	e.
Uffz Flemming	18	FE2d	Houthulsterwald	1700	1	g.
Ltn P Strähle	18	FE2d	Zuidschoote	1700	1	g.
Vfw F Manschott	7	Farman	Esnes	1710	6	f.
Vfw J Buckler	17	Caudron	W Facq-Wald		2	
Vfw R Eck	3	BE	NW Péronne-Clery		zlg	

a.   A6652, No 3 Sqn, RFC, 2/Lts FC Young & AGS de Ross, departed at 0910, brought down about 0925, KIAs.
b.   6231, No 2 Sqn, RFC, 2/Lts CD Bennett, WIA/POW, & HA Croft, KIA, departed at 0945, last seen over Cite St Auguste.
c.   A642, No 54 Sqn, RFC, 2/Lt J Fairbairn, departed at 1115, last seen over Cambrai, WIA/POW.
d.   French 85 Compagnie d'Aérostières, the observer, Adj JM Durand, WIA.
e.   2543, No 2 Sqn, RFC, Capt GC Bailey, DSO, WIA, & 2/Lt GWB Hampton.
f.   French Escadrille F 221, Adj Prisset, KIA, & Damien, WIA, shot down in flames in the Souilly Sector.
g.   No 20 Sqn, RFC, A1960, Capt HE Hartney & 2/Lt WT Jourdan, WIAs, and A15, 2/Lts FJ Taylor, injured, & FM Myers, killed, in a landing accident after combat.

Losses – Nil

---

15 February 1917

Vfw H Bussing	5	DH2	Miraumont	1045	1	a.
Ltn R Theiller	5	DH2	Miraumont	1045	8	b.
Vfw P Glasmacher	8	Nieuport	S Bixschoote	1330	2	c.
Ltn E v Stenglin	1	Pup	Lapignies-Douchy	1430	1	d.
Ltn H Baldamus	8	Nieuport	S Somme-Py	1645	12	e.
Ltn H v Keudell	27	Nieuport	Boesinghe	1740	12	f.
Vfw J Buckler	17	Caudron	Pont-à-Mousson		3	
Ltn G Schlenker	3	RE8	Rancourt-Combles		3	g.
Ltn P Strähle	18	BE2e	Ypern		–	

a.   2932, No 32 Sqn, RFC, Lt CH March, last seen over the Bois de Loupart, WIA/POW.
b.   A2335, No 32 Sqn, RFC, Capt HWG Jones, WIA.
c.   A6622, No 1 Sqn, RFC, Capt JME Shepherd, departed at 1152, seen going down over Gheluvelt Wood at 1226, KIA.
d.   No 54 Sqn, RFC, lost two aircraft: A654, Capt CLM Scott, departed at 1140; A645, 2/Lt EH Hamilton, both KIA – one to 1 Armee flak.
e.   Escadrille N 48, Sgt J Raty (1v) killed near St Marie-à-Py, flying a Nieuport XVII.
f.   Probably A229, No 46 Sqn, RFC, 2/Lt SH Pratt & 2/Lt G Bryers, OK.
g.   A87, No 52 Sqn, RFC, Lt HC Mulock & Pvt T Booth, departed at 1150, KIAs.

Losses:

Ltn Hans Keudell	27	12 victories; killed in combat flying Albatros DIII 2017/16 (G.11) 1640 near Vlammertinghe, by Lts SH Pratt and G Byers of No 46 Sqn, RFC, and 2/Lt VH Collins, No 1 Sqn, RFC.
Uffz Heinrich Schiener	27	Flying Halberstadt DV 1108/16, shot down by AA fire near Ploegsteert, and taken prisoner.
Ltn Hermann Klein	29	Injured in an accident during a test flight.
Gefr Heinrich Schneider	30	Flying Halberstadt DIII 234/16, hit by AA fire and forced to land near Ploegsteert, being taken prisoner.

---

16 February 1917

Vfw S Festner	11	FE2b	Lievin-Grenay	1210	2	a.
Ltn K Allmenröder	11	BE2c	Roeux, E Arras	1300	1	b.
Ltn H Baldamus	9	Nieuport	S Aure	1500	–	c.
Patrol	9	Nieuport	Perthes		–	

a.   7635, No 40 Sqn, RFC.
b.   4179, No 16 Sqn, RFC, 2/Lts EW Lindley & LV Munn, departed at 1150, MIAs.
c.   2409, Nieuport XVII of N 31, Brig Girard, MIA.

Losses:

Ltn Hans Gutermuth	5	2 victories; flying an Albatros DIII (G.13) killed in combat between Gommecourt and Hebuterne, by Sgt HG Smith and Lt JA Aldred, No 5 Sqn, RFC.			

17 February 1917

Vfw F Manschott	7	Caudron	Vaux-Teich	1715	7

Losses – Nil

18 February 1917

Obltn B v Lyncker	25	Nieuport	S Gjevgjeli		2

Losses:

Obltn Bodo v Lyncker	25	2 victories; killed in a mid-air collision with a Nieuport over Gjevgjeli.

19 February 1917

No Claims – No Losses

20 February 1917

Ltn E Udet	15	Nieuport	Aspach	1200	4	a.

a.   Escadrille N 81.

Losses:

Ltn Ewald Siempelkamp	15	Injured in an accident.

23 February 1917

No Claims – No Losses

24 February 1917

No Claims

Losses:

Uffz Weber	25	Severely injured in an accident.

25 February 1917

Ltn J Janzen	23	Farman	E St Mihiel	1135	1	
Ltn E König	B	DH2	St Catherine	1425	6	a.
Ltn W Voss	B	DH2	Arras-St Sauveur	1455	7	b.
Ltn W Voss	B	DH2	Arras	1500	8	c.
OfStv G Vothknecht	24	Sopwith 2	Saargemünd		1	d.
Ltn F Weitz	26	Nieuport	W Mühlhausen		2	e.

a.   No 29 Sqn, RFC.
b.   A2557, No 29 Sqn, RFC, Lt RJS Lund, shot down near Arras, WIA.
c.   7849, No 29 Sqn, RFC, Capt HJ Payn, aircraft shot up, he was not harmed.
d.   9739, 3 Wing, RNAS.
e.   2409, Nieuport XVII of Escadrille N 81, Brig Rivière, MIA.

Losses:

Ltn Werner Junge	9	Severely wounded at 1640, died next night in the hospital at Grand-pré.

26 February 1917

Ltn W Voss	B	BE2c	Ecurie	1650	9	a.

a.   2535, No 16 Sqn, RFC, Lt HE Bagot, WIA, & 2/Lt RLM Jack, WIA/DOW, departed at 1415 hours.

Losses – Nil

27 February 1917

| Ltn W Voss | B | BE2c | Blaireville | 1045 | 10 | a. |
| Ltn W Voss | B | BE2c | W Arras | 1648 | 11 | b. |

a.   2530, No 8 Sqn, RFC, 2/Lts EA Pope & HA Johnson, shot down at 0945, KIAs.
b.   7197, No 12 Sqn, RFC, Capt J McArthur & Pvt J Whiteford, departed at 1455, shot down in flames near Arras, KIAs.
Losses – Nil

28 February 1917

No Claims – No Losses

JASTA ARMEE ASSIGNMENTS AS OF 1 MARCH 1917

Western Front

1 Armee 1,2,5,21,22,36	6 Armee 4,11,12,30
2 Armee 3,6,20	7 Armee 9,17
3 Armee 10,29,31	Det 'A' 19,24,32
4 Armee 8,18,27,28	Det 'B' 15,16,26
5 Armee 7,13,14	Det 'C' 23,34

Other Fronts

11 Armee 25   Macedonia

1 March 1917

| Ltn R Theiller | 5 | Balloon | W Frise | 1810 | 9 | a. |

a.   British balloon 14-4-4, flamed at 1715, the observer, Lt GK Simpson suffered severe burns and died 7 March 1917.
Losses – Nil

2 March 1917

| Vfw F Manschott | 7 | Farman | Höhe 304 | 1525 | 8 | a. |

a.   Possibly from Escadrille F 25, Adj Caulier (P) WIA/DOW 3 Mar 17 & Adj Planche (B) KIA.
Losses – Nil

3 March 1917

| Vfw F Altemeier | 24 | Nieuport | Bois Moral | | 1 | |

Losses – Nil

4 March 1917

Ltn W Voss	B	BE2d	S Berneville	1130	12	a.
Ltn K Schäfer	11	Sopwith 2	SW Haisnes	1150	2	b.
Ltn M v Richthofen	11	BE2d	NE Loos	1245	22	c.
Ltn H Schröder	1	Pup	Inchy	1350	1	d.
Obltn H Kummetz	1	Pup	Vis-en-Artois	1405	1	e.
Ltn M v Richthofen	11	Sopwith	Acheville	1620	23	f.
Ltn R Theiller	5	RE8	N Monchy	1630	10	g.
Vfw F Manschott	7	Balloon	S Belleville	1645	10	
Ltn R Theiller	5	FE2b	Bouchavesnes	1715	11	h.
Ltn J Flink	18	Nieuport 2	Elverdinghe	1720	1	
Vfw H Büssing	5	BE2	Gueudecourt	1720	–	

Ltn G Schlenker	3	Pup	St Quentin		4	i.
Vfw F Manschott	7	Caudron	NW Fort Michel		9	
Ltn K Schäfer	11	DH2/FE8	Lens		–	
Ltn K Schäfer	11	DH2/FE8	Béthune		–	

a. 6252, No 8 Sqn, RFC, F/Sgt RJ Moody & 2/Lt EE Horn, shot down in flames at 1010, KIAs.
b. A1109, No 11 Sqn, RFC, 2/Lts PL Wood & AH Fenton, last seen over Lens at 1055, MIAs.
c. 5785, No 2 Sqn, RFC, Lt JEB Crosbee & F/Sgt JE Prance.
d. N6170, No 3 Sqn, RNAS, F/Lt HR Wambolt, departed at 1115, MIA.
e. N6165, No 3 Sqn, RNAS, F/S/Lt JP White, departed at 1115, MIA.
f. A1108, No 43 Sqn, RFC, 2/Lts HJ Green & AW Reid, shot down about 1515, S of Vimy. KIAs.
g. A4163, No 59 Sqn, RFC, 2/Lts BW Hill & W Harms, departed at 1444, shot down NW of Monchy, KIAs.
h. A5441, No 22 Sqn, RFC, 2/Lt LW Beale & 2 A/M A Davin, OK.
i. A633, No 54 Sqn, RFC, Capt A Lees, departed at 1033, last seen over St Quentin, WIA/POW.

Losses:

Obltn Ernst Frhr v Althaus	4	8 victories; wounded in combat.
Ltn Max Böhme	5	Flying Albatros DII 910/16 when shot down and taken prisoner by Lt Pearson, No 29 Sqn, RFC, & Lt Graham & Lt J A V Boddy, No 11 Sqn, RFC.

5 March 1917

No Claims – No Losses

6 March 1917

Obltn H Kummetz	1	Nieuport	Achiet-le-Grand	1130	2	a.
Ltn K Schäfer	11	Sopwith 2	Lens	1145	3	b.
Ltn K Schäfer	11	Sopwith 2	W Lens	1155	4	
Ltn K Wolff	11	BE2d	Givenchy	1230	1	c.
Ltn H Gontermann	5	FE2d	Mory-Ervillers	1315	2	d.
Ltn A Schulte	12	FE2d	Ervillers-Bory	1320	3	e.
Obltn H Kummetz	1	DH2	Eaucourt l'Abbaye	1335	3	f.
OfStv E Nathanael	5	Morane	N Gueudecourt	1345	1	
OfStv W Cymera	1	Nieuport	Bailly-Agny	1350	2	
Obltn A v Tutschek	B	DH2	Beugny-Beugnatre	1630	1	g.
Ltn W Voss	B	DH2	Favreuil	1635	13	h.
Ltn Kralewski	4	FE2b	Ransart	1645	1	
Ltn M v Richthofen	11	BE2e	Souchez	1700	24	i.
Vfw F Manschott	7	Caudron	Côte de Poivre		–	
Obltn B Loerzer	26	Nieuport	Dammerkirch		3	
Vfw H Büssing	5	FE2d	Arras		–	

a. A208, No 60 Sqn, RFC, 2/Lt PS Joyce, departed at 0915, last seen over Bapaume, MIA.
b. A978, No 43 Sqn, RFC, Lt SJ Pepler & Capt TD Stuart, departed at 0900, last seen in flames near Lens. KIAs.
c. 5856, No 16 Sqn, RFC, 2/Lts GM Underwood & AE Watts, departed at 1015, seen under attack at 1135 near Givenchy, KIAs.
d. A1948, No 57 Sqn, RFC, 2/Lts FE Hills & AG Ryall, departed at 1100, seen to go down near Adinfer Woods, POWs.
e. A1953, No 57 Sqn, RFC, Capt WSR Bloomfield & 2/Lt VO Lonsdale, departed at 1100, last seen in combat E of Bapaume.
f. A268, No 3 Sqn, RFC, Lt CW Short, MC, WIA/DOW & Lt S McK Fraser, WIA.
g. 7882., No 32 Sqn, 2/Lt M JJG Mare-Montembault, MC, 6 victories, POW.
h. 7941, No 32 Sqn, RFC, Lt HG Southon, WIA/POW.
i. A2785, No 16 Sqn, RFC, 2/Lt CMG Bibby & Lt GO Brichta, KIAs.

Losses:

Ltn Hans-Georg Lübbert	11	Wounded in action at 1200 hours over Lens.

7 March 1917

| Vfw A Schorisch | 12 | FE | Brancourt | | 1 | |

Losses – Nil

8 March 1917

No Claims – No Losses

9 March 1917

Ltn K Allmenröder	11	FE8	W Hulluch	1030	2	a.
Ltn K Wolff	11	FE8	S Annay	1120	2	b.
Ltn K Schäfer	11	FE8	Faschoda	1120	5	c.
Ltn K Schäfer	11	FE8	Pont-à-Vendin	1122	6	d
Ltn M v Richthofen	11	DH2	SW Bailleul	1155	25	e.
OfStv A Dierle	24	Nieuport	N Parroy Wald	1220	1	
OfStv G Vothknecht	24	G100	Bathelmont	1330	2	
Vfw F Manschott	7	Balloon	S Belrupt	1515	11	f.
Ltn W Albert	31	Balloon	Somme-Suippes		1	g.
Obltn K Rummelsbacher	10	Nieuport			–	

a.   6399, No 40 Sqn, RFC, 2/Lt RE Nave, departed at 0845, shot down severely wounded at 0939.
b.   6456, No 40 Sqn, RFC, 2/Lt T Shepard, departed at 0845, POW.
c.   6397, No 40 Sqn, RFC, 2/Lt WB Hills, departed at 0845, POW.
d.   4874, No 40 Sqn, RFC, 2/Lt GF Heseler, departed at 0845, POW.
e.   A2571, No 29 Sqn, RFC, 2/Lt AJ Pearson, MC, departed at 0920, last seen in flames, KIA.
f.   French 48 Compagnie d'Aérostières, the observer, S/Lt Guillotin, made a safe descent.
g.   French 40 Compagnie d'Aérostières, the observer, S/Lt Billardon, made a safe descent.

Losses – Nil

10 March 1917

Obltn B Loerzer	26	Spad	Altkirch	1630	4	a.
Ltn R Dycke	16	Balloon	Retzweiler		1	b.
Obflgmt K Schönfelder	7	EA	Sivry-le-Perche		–	

a.   Capt M Mandinaud (1v) CO N 81, flying a Spad VII when killed near Belfort.
b.   French 74 Compagnie d'Aérostières.

Losses – Nil

11 March 1917

Ltn W Voss	B	FE2b	Rancourt	1000	14	a.
Ltn F Weitz	26	Nieuport	S Ammerzweiler	1020	3	b.
Ltn A Schulte	12	FE	Gueudecourt-Ligny	1105	4	
Ltn C Krefft	11	FE8	Givenchy-Vimy	1120	1	
Ltn K Schäfer	11	BE2c	Loosbogen	1120	7	
Vfw Schendel	7	Balloon	Belrupt	1140	1	
Ltn M v Richthofen	11	BE2d	S La Folie Wald	1150	26	e.
Ltn H Baldamus	9	Voisin	Rouvroy	1200	13	c.
Ltn P Strähle	18	Sopwith 2	Zillebeke	1215	2	d.
Ltn J Flink	18	Sopwith 2	Ypern	1217	2	
Ltn H Pfeiffer	9	Caudron	Berzieux	1240	9	
Ltn H Gontermann	5	FE2b	S Bapaume	1245	3	f.
OfStv E Nathanael	5	FE2b	N Beugny	1245	2	g.
OfStv W Cymera	1	FE2b	Noreuil	1250	3	h.
Ltn W v Bülow	18	Balloon	N Armentières	1430	9	i.
Ltn W Voss	B	Nieuport	Bailleul	1430	15	j.
Vfw Kammandel	18	BE2d	NW Armentières	1435	1	

Vfw Grigo	12	DH2	Gréviller Wald	1	
Ltn Erkenbrecht	12	DH2	S Grévillers	1	
Vfw Rieger	17	Nieuport	Cormicy	1	
Vfw Ruckdeschel	13	Caudron	Moulin Vendresse	1	
Ltn E v Stenglin	1	Vikkers	Le Sars	2	k.
Ltn A Niederhoff	20	Sopwith 2	Roye	1	l.
Obflgmt K Schönfelder	7	Balloon	Sibry-le-Perche	–	
Vfw P Hoppe	5	DH2	Bapaume	1	
Vfw Strey	25	Caudron	Bitoly-Kanali	1	

a.   7685, No 22 Sqn, RFC, Lt LW Beal, OK, 2 A/M FG Davin, WIA, shot up and forced to land near Combles.
b.   Ltn Maus, N 49, flying Nieuport XVII No.2341 when killed over Bernweiler.
c.   Probably Capt Rochard, CO Escadrille F 71, (P) & S/Lt Litaud, Escadrille C 219, (O) flying a Farman F.40, shot down near the Bois de Ville.
d.   A1082, No 45 Sqn, RFC, Capt EFP Lubbock, MC, & Lt J Thompson, KIAs.
e.   6232, No 2 Sqn, RFC, 2/Lts J Smyth & E Byrne, departed at 1030, brought down over Givenchy at 1045, KIAs.
f.   A5475, No 18 Sqn, RFC, Sgt HS Burgess & 2/Lt HM Headly, departed at 0945, seen going down in flames near Bapaume, KIAs.
g.   7713, No 23 Sqn, RFC, Capt CAR Shum & 2/Lt FC Coops, departed at 0908, seen going down E of Bapaume, POWs.
h.   No 11 Sqn, RFC.
i.   British balloon 9-6-2 (BMS 18) Lts TG Bolitho & RP Sewell were not hit during the attack.
j.   A279, No 60 Sqn, RFC, Lt AD Whitehead, departed at 1300, seen going down in flames at 1340 near Bailleul.
k.   A5025, No 32 Sqn, RFC, 2/Lt JH Cross, injured, shot up and forced to land near Bapaume.
l.   Probably a Sopwith two-seater from Escadrille F 54, Adj Robin (P) & Lt Barbot (O), shot down near Crapeaumesnil, MIAs.
Losses:

OfStv Alfred Behling	1	1 victory; killed between Biefvillers and Bihucourt.
Ltn Erkenbrecht	12	1 victory; wounded in action.
Ltn Friedrich Weitz	26	3 victories; wounded in action, died of wounds on 12 March 1917.

12 March 1917

No Claims – No Losses

13 March 1917

No Claims
Losses:

Flgmt Franz Wangemann	MFJI	Wounded in action.

14 March 1917

No Claims
Losses:

Uffz Hans Rody	30	Killed in a mid-air collision over Phalempin airfield.

15 March 1917

Ltn K Küppers	6	FE2b	Péronne	1730	1	a.
Ltn G Flecken	20	Caudron	NE Lassigny		1	

a.   A780, No 25 Sqn, RFC, 2/Lt WD Matheson & Sgt G Goodburn, WIAs.
Losses – Nil

16 March 1917

Ltn W Allmenröder	29	Balloon	Moiremont	0930	2	a.

Obltn F v Bronsart und						
Schellendorf	7	Balloon	Belleville	0930	1	b.
Vfw F Manschott	7	Balloon	S Ft Vaux	1115	12	b.
Ltn H Kämmel	23	Sopwith	S Pagny	1255	1	c.
Vfw F Loerzer	26	Caudron	Oberaspach	1630	2	d.
FwLt F Schubert	6	Balloon	SW Roye	1645	1	
Obltn K Student	9	Nieuport			4	e.
Ltn A Dossenbach	36	Caudron			–	

a.　French 36 Compagnie d'Aérostières, Adj A Bry, the observer, descended safely.
b.　The French lost two balloons in the Souilly Sector: the French 78 Compagnie d'Aérostières, MdL Bes KIA; and the French 58 Compagnie d'Aérostières, MdL Berger made a safe descent.
c.　N5134, Escadrille Sop 29, Sgt L Pivette, POW.
d.　French Escadrille N 81.
e.　Possibly S/Lt R Havet (3v), N 77, MIA, flying a Nieuport XVII.

Losses:

Vfw Friedrich Manschott	7	12 victories; killed in combat with Caudrons.
Ltn Lothar v Hausen	32	Shot down wounded at 1025 N Hoeville by Capt Georges Guynemer, Escadrille N 3, 33rd victory; taken prisoner – died of wounds on 15 July 1917.
Obltn Heinrich v Schwandner	32	Shot down in flames at 1030 over Athienville, by Lt Albert Deullin, Escadrille N 3, his 12th victory.

17 March 1917

Ltn P Strähle	18	Nieuport	Wervicq	1120	3	a.
Obltn M v Richthofen	11	FE2b	Oppy	1140	27	b.
Ltn K Wolff	11	Sopwith 2	Le point de Jour	1140	3	c.
Ltn K Allmenröder	11	Sopwith 2	Athics-Oppy	1145	3	d.
Obltn K Döring	4	EA	Hendecourt	1145	–	
Vfw E Clausnitzer	4	EA	Hendecourt	1145	–	
Ltn H Baldamus	9	Nieuport	Tahure	1200	14	e.
Ltn H Baldamus	9	Nieuport	Tahure	1200	15	
Ltn W Voss	B	FE2b	NE Barlencourt	1215	16	f.
Ltn W Voss	B	DH2	NE Barlencourt	1225	17	g.
Obltn K v Grieffenhagen	18	BE2d	Gheluvelt	1300	2	h.
Ltn H Gontermann	5	FE2b	St Pierre Waast	1430	4	i.
Ltn K Schneider	5	FE2b	St Pierre Waast	1430	1	
Vfw O Gerbig	14	Caudron	N Paissy	1510	1	
Obltn M v Richthofen	11	BE2c	W Vimy	1700	28	j.
Ltn F Mallinckrodt	29	Voisin	W Roye		3	
Ltn L Hanstein	16	Nieuport	Steinbach		2	
Vfw A Schorisch	12	FE2b	Vraucourt		1	
Vfw K Möwe	29	Caudron	Mourmelon		1	k.
Vfw W Glinkermann	15	Nieuport	NW Reims		1	
Uffz Flemming	18	BE2d	E Ypres		–	
Ltn R Theiller	5	FE2b			–	

a.　A6617, No 1 Sqn, RFC, 2/Lt AJ Gilson, departed at 0931, KIA.
b.　A5439, No 25 Sqn, RFC, Lt AE Boultbee & 2/AM F King, departed at 0900, KIAs.
c.　A1097, No 43 Sqn, RFC, 2/Lts AL Constable & CD Knox, departed at 0910, KIAs.
d.　A1111, No 43 Sqn, RFC, 2/Lts JC Rimer & RH Lownds, departed at 0910, KIAs.
e.　French Détachement N 502, Brig Lautier, flying a Nieuport XVII when killed.
f.　7695, No 11 Sqn, RFC, 2/Lt RW Cross & Lt CF Lodge, departed at 0850, POWs.
g.　A2583, No 32 Sqn, RFC, Lt TA Cooch, WIA.
h.　6241, No 6 Sqn, RFC, 2/Lt A Appleton & Cpl A Cooper, departed at 1115, attacked at 1205, shot down in flames, KIAs.
i.　4900, No 22 Sqn, RFC, 2/Lt FR Hudson & 2 AM W Richman, WIAs, shot up and forced to land.
j.　2814, No 16 Sqn, RFC, 2/Lt GM Watt & Sgt EA Howlett, KIAs.

k.   Escadrille C 47, Sgts Raux & Lethon, KIAs.
Losses – Nil

18 March 1917

Ltn W Voss		B	BE2d	Neuville	1840	18	a.
Ltn W Voss		B	BE2d	Boyelles	1850	19	b.
Ltn F Mallinckrodt	20		Caudron	S Roye		4	
Ltn de Payrebrune	13		Caudron	Cerny-Beaurieux		1	
Ltn Seve	13		Caudron	Cerny-Beaurieux		1	
Vfw Strey	25		Caudron	Monastir		3	

a.   5784, No 8 Sqn, RFC, 2/Lts CR Dougall, POW, & S Harryman, WIA/POW/DOW, departed at 1710.
b.   5770, No 13 Sqn, RFC, Capt GS Thorne & 2/Lt PEH Van Baerle, departed at 1725, last seen in vicinity of Fampoux, POWs.

Losses:

Vfw Karl Schöne	23	Killed in an accident at Chambley.
Ltn Paul Retsch	32	Wounded in action while flying a Roland DII.

19 March 1917

Ltn A Mohr	3	G100	S Péronne-Brie	0910	5	a.
Ltn O Bernert	B	RE8	SE Arras	0925	8	b.
Ltn W Voss	B	RE8	St Leger	0930	20	c.
HPtm P v Osterroht	12	G100	Roisel-Templeux	0940	1	a.
Ltn G Schlenker	3	G100	E Péronne-Roisel	0945	5	a.
Ltn K Schneider	5	Spad	Homblières	1010	2	d.
Ltn A Mohr	3	BE2e	S Péronne-Brie	1210	6	e.
Ltn H Kämmerer	20	Nieuport	Flavy-le-Martel		1	f.

a.   No 27 Sqn, RFC, lost two Martinsydes this date on a bombing mission to Aulnoye: 7503, 2/Lt JG Fair, KIA; 7508, 2/Lt TW Jay, POW.
b.   No 59 Sqn, RFC, A4168, Capt CP Bertie, KIA, & 2/Lt FH Wilson, POW, came down SW of Ecoust St Mein.
c.   A4165, Capt EW Bowyer-Bower & 2/Lt E Elgey, KIAs.
d.   A6633, No 19 Sqn, RFC, 2/Lt SSB Purves, departed at 0810, last seen in combat at 0900 near Le Catelet. POW.
e.   No 8 Sqn, RFC.
f.   Sgt J McConnell, N 124, flying Nieuport #2055, killed in combat near this location.
Losses – Nil

20 March 1917

No Claims – No Losses

21 March 1917

Ltn K Allmenröder	11	BE2d	Loosbogen	1540	4	a.
Obltn M v Richthofen	11	BE2e	N Neuville	1740	29	b.

a.   A2390, No 43 Sqn, RFC, Lt HWL Poole, WIA, & 2/AM AJ Ball, WIA/DOW 22 March 1917, departed at 1345, came down near Mazingarbe, at 1445.
b.   A3154, No 16 Sqn, RFC, F/Sgt SH Quick & 2/Lt WJ Lidsey, shot down at about 1630, KIAs.

Losses:

Obltn Erich Marx	Kest 1a	Died of wounds following combat over Mannheim.

22 March 1917

Ltn R Theiller	5	BE2c	Nurlu	0930	12
Ltn F Mallinckrodt	20	Caudron	E Ham	1745	5

Losses:

Vfw Georg Hentze	34	Shot down and taken prisoner.

23 March 1917

| Ltn R Theiller | 5 | BE2e | Nurlu | 0930 | 12 | a. |
| Ltn G Weiner | 20 | Nieuport | N La Fère | | 1 | b. |

a.   3149, No 52 Sqn, RFC, 2/Lts CM White, WIA, & DM McLeay, KIA, during aerial combat near Nurlu.
b.   Probably Cpl MJ Doat, Escadrille N 79, flying a Nieuport XVII No.2283, failed to return from a photo mission in the vicinity of Noyon.

Losses – Nil

24 March 1917

Ltn H Gontermann	5	Sopwith 2	Oisy-le-Berger	0855	5	a.
OfStv E Nathanael	5	Sopwith 2	Ecoust St Mein	0900	3	a.
Lt A Schulte	12	FE2b	SW Handecourt	1030	5	
Vfw Grigo	12	FE2b	Croiselles	1030	zlg	b.
Uffz R Jörke	12	FE2b	Croiselles	1030	1	c.
Vfw L Patermann	4	FE	Hendecourt	1040	–	
Ltn K Schäfer	11	Sopwith	Anzin-Arras	1100	8	
Obltn M v Richthofen	11	Spad	Givenchy	1155	30	d.
Obltn E Dostler	34	Caudron	Les Mesnil	1230	3	e.
Ltn H Adam	34	Caudron	Rupt-en-Woevre	1230	1	e.
Obltn E Dostler	34	Caudron	Dupay-Ancemont	1240	4	e.
Ltn W Voss	B	FE2b	Vaulx-Morchies	1610	21	f.
Ltn O Bernert	B	BE2e	Pronville	1630	9	g.
Ltn W Voss	B	BE2d	Boileux-Boiry	1645	22	h.
Obltn R Berthold	14	Farman	Aizy-Vailly		9	i.
Hptm G Stenzel	8	Nieuport	NW Dixmuiden		3	
Ltn R Matthaei	21	Balloon			1	
Ltn E Löwenhardt	10	Balloon	Recicourt		1	j.

a.   No 70 Sqn, RFC, lost two aircraft that departed at 0635 engaged in combat between Douai and Cambrai: A957, Capt AM Lowrey & Lt GWW Swann, KIAs; A1907, Capt W H Costello & Lt H F Whiteside, POWs.
b.   A5471, No 11 Sqn, RFC, Capt CN Lowe & 2/Lt G Masters, departed at 0758, shot down in combat near Croiselles, crash-landed.
c.   A803, No 11 Sqn, RFC, Lt JR Middleton & 2/AM HV Gosney, departed at 0745, DOW/KIA.
d.   A6706, No 19 Sqn, RFC, 2/Lt RP Baker, last seen SE of Lens, WIA/POW.
e.   French Escadrille C 18, lost only ONE Caudron G.4 this date, Brig Marquisat (P) & Sgt Delachartre (O), were killed in combat.
f.   A5485, No 23 Sqn, RFC, Sgt EP Critchley, WIA & 1/AM F Russell, KIA.
g.   6254, No 15 Sqn, RFC, Lt EJ Hars, WIA, & Sgt JF Ridgway, KIA, departed at 1415.
h.   5769, No 8 Sqn, RFC, Lt H Norton & 2/Lt RAW Tillett, departed at 1415, shot down near Boyelles, KIAs.
i.   French Escadrille F 7, Cpl Peinaud (P) & Lt Vernes (O), KIAs.
j.   French 58 Compagnie d'Aérostières.

Losses:

| Ltn Renatus Theiller | 5 | 12 victories; killed in combat at 0900 near Arras. |

25 March 1917

Obltn M v Richthofen	11	Nieuport	Tilloy	0820	31	a.
Ltn E Nathanael	5	Sopwith 2	Velu	0920	4	b.
Vfw P Hoppe	5	Sopwith 2	W Beugny	0920	2	b.
Ltn E Nathanael	5	Sopwith 2	E Beugny	0925	5	b.
Ltn H Gontermann	5	Sopwith 2	Haplincourt	0925	6	b.
Vfw A Schramm	7	Nieuport	S Consenvoye	1550	3	
Vfw Ulrich	7	Nieuport	SE Avocourt	1610	1	
Vfw F Sauerwein	7	Spad	Fort Marre	1615	1	
Ltn F Mallinckrodt	20	Pup	Giffecourt		6	c.
Ltn K Deilmann	6	Sopwith 2	Pouchaux		3	
Vfw Häusler	6	Sopwith 2	Sablonière		1	

Ltn A Niederhoff	20	Sopwith 2	Le Catelet		2	b.
Uffz A Barth	10	Nieuport	E Esnes		–	
Vfw P Aue	10	Nieuport	Champ-Verdun		4	d.
Ltn Neumann	17	Nieuport	Coincy-Pauillon		1	

a.   A6689, No 29 Sqn, RFC, 2/Lt CG Gilbert, departed at 0705, POW.

b.   No 70 Sqn, RFC, lost five aircraft that departed at 0710, last seen over Cambrai: A954, 2/Lts JS Cooper & AW Macqueen, KIAs; Lts CS Ward-Price & HA Chuter, KIAs; 7763, Lt CS Vane-Tempest & 2/Lt F Allison, KIAs; Capt E J Henderson & 2/Lt JM Sim, KIAs; A884, Lt H Butler & 2/Lt LA Norris, KIAs.

c.   A630, No 54 Sqn, RFC, 2/Lt NA Phillips, departed at 0840, last seen going down W of St Quentin at 0915, KIA.

d.   3418, Nieuport XXIII of Escadrille N 57, Caporal J Trincot MIA.

Losses:

| Ltn Friedrich Mallinckrodt | 20 | 6 victories; wounded in action. |
| Gefr Berkling | 22 | Wounded in action. |

26 – 27 March 1917

No Claims – No Losses

28 March 1917

Vfw Ulrich	7	Balloon	Belleville	0910	2	a.
Obltn H Bethge	30	Nieuport	Roubaix	1024	4	b.
Vfw F Sauerwein	7	Nieuport	NW Douaumont	1035	2	
Ltn L v Richthofen	11	FE2b	E Vimy	1720	1	c.
Ltn E Löwenhardt	10	Balloon	Recicourt-Verdun	–		a.

a.   The French lost two balloons in the Verdun Sector; the 58 and 38 Compagnies d'Aérostières, both Observers, Lt Straehle & MdL Collin made safe descents. It appears that Löwenhardt was cheated out of a confirmed victory.

b.   A6615, No 1 Sqn, RFC, 2/Lt H Welch, departed at 0930, last seen at 1045 SE of Lille, KIA.

c.   7715, No 25 Sqn, RFC, 2/Lts NL Knight, POW, & AG Severs, KIA, departed at 1430, came down in no-man's-land.

Losses – Nil

29 March 1917

No Claims – No Losses

30 March 1917

| Ltn K Wolff | 11 | Nieuport | Fresnoy-Arras | 1145 | 4 | a. |
| Ltn K Allmenröder | 11 | Nieuport | Bailleul-Arras | 1415 | 5 | b. |

a.   A273, No 60 Sqn, RFC, Lt WP Garnett, departed at 1055, last seen over Fampoux, KIA.

b.   6780, No 40 Sqn, RFC, Lt DMF Sinclair, departed at 1306, POW.

Losses:

| Ltn Hans-Georg Lübbert | 11 | Killed in combat at 1415 between Bailleul and Thelus, |
| | | probably by Capt R Gregory, No 40 Sqn, RFC. |

31 March 1917

Ltn K Wolff	11	FE2b	Gavrelle	0750	5	a.
Obltn A v Tutschek	B	Nieuport	Loos	0900	2	b.
Ltn O Brauneck	25	Balloon	Cernabogen-Monastir		7	

a.   7691, No 11 Sqn, RFC, 2/Lts LAT Strange, POW, & WGT Clifton, KIA, departed at 0602, brought down near Vitry-en-Artois.

b.   Possibly A6769, No 60 Sqn, RFC, Lt WA Bishop, OK.

Losses – Nil

Jasta Armee Assignments as of 1 April 1917

Western Front

1 Armee 21,22,36
2 Armee 2,5,20
3 Armee 10,29,31
4 Armee 6,8,18,27
5 Armee 7,13,14

6 Armee 3,4,11,12,28,30,37
7 Armee 1,9,15,17,32
Det 'A' 19,24,33
Det 'B' 16,26,35
Det 'C' 23

Other Fronts

11 Armee 25   Macedonia

1 April 1917

| Ltn O Bernert | B | Balloon | Villers-au-Flers | 1050 | 10 | a. |
| Ltn W Voss | B | BE2c | E St Leger | 1145 | 23 | b. |

a.   British balloon 4-13-5 (FM 19) Lt Cochrane & 2/Lt Hadley, observers.
b.   2561, No 15 Sqn, RFC, Capt AM Wynne, WIA, & Lt AS Mackenzie, KIA, departed at 0925.
Losses:
Ltn Alfred Mohr   3   In Albatros DIII 2012/16 (G.18) shot down and killed by Lts D Gordon & HD Baker, No 12 Sqn, RFC, at 1150 near Arras.

2 April 1917

Ltn O Bernert	B	Nieuport	Queant	0830	11	a.
OfStv E Nathanael	5	FE2b	NE Gouzeaucourt	0830	6	b.
Obltn M v Richthofen	11	BE2d	Farbus	0835	32	c.
Ltn K Allmenröder	11	BE	Angres	0930	6	d.
Vfw S Festner	11	FE2d	SE Auby	1000	3	e.
Ltn K Krefft	11	FE2d	Oignies	1000	1	f.
Obltn M v Richthofen	11	Sopwith 2	Givenchy	1120	33	g.

a.   A6763, No 60 Sqn, RFC, 2/Lt F Williams, departed at 0715, seen going down in flames at Fontaine les Croiselles.
b.   6953, No 22 Sqn, RFC, 2/Lt PA Russell & Lt H Loveland, KIAs, departed at 0635.
c.   5841, No 43 Sqn, RFC, Lt PJG Powell & 1/AM P Bonner, departed at 0747, KIAs.
d   2510, No 13 Sqn, RFC, 2/Lt CF Fox & 2 A/M JH Bolton, OK.
e.   A1944, No 57 Sqn, RFC, Lt HP Sworder & 2/Lt AH Margoliouth, departed at 0800, last seen E of Arras, at 0945, KIAs.
f.   A5151, No 57 Sqn, RFC, Capt H Tomlinson, MC, KIA, & Lt NC Denison, WIA/POW, departed at 0800, last seen at 0945 E of Arras, in combat.
g.   A2401, No 13 Sqn, RFC, 2/Lt AP Warren, POW, & Sgt R Dunn, KIA, last seen at 1110 E of Vimy.
Losses:
Ltn Erich König   B   Shot down and killed by 2/Lts EE Pope & AW Naismith, No 57 Sqn, RFC at 0945.

Ltn Hans Wortmann   B   KIA at 0950 over Vitry-en-Artois.
Vfw Rudolf Nebel   35   Shot down flying Albatros DIII No.2107/16 near Grand Belchen, and taken prisoner; escaped to Switzerland on 5 May 1917.

3 April 1917

Ltn G Nernst	30	Nieuport	Esquerchin	1450	3	a.
Uffz L Weber	3	BE2c	NE Brébières	1450	1	
Obltn M v Richthofen	11	FE2b	Cite St Pierre	1615	34	b.
Ltn K Schäfer	11	FE2d	La Coulette	1620	9	c.
OfStv E Nathanael	5	DH2	N Boursies	1635	7	d.
Vfw E Eisenhuth	3	FE2b	Hendecourt	1655	2	
Vfw S Festner	11	FE	Lens	1717	–	

Ltn A Schulte	12	FE2b	NE St Leger	1719	6	e.
Vfw S Festner	11	FE	Hendecourt	1720	–	
Hptm P v Osterroht	12	BE2e	N Bullecourt	1720	2	f.
Ltn O Bernert	B	Balloon	Ervillers	1910	12	g.
Ltn O Bernert	B	Balloon	N Bapaume	1912	13	h.
Ltn A Schulte	12	DH2			–	

a.   A6674, No 40 Sqn, RFC, 2/Lt SA Sharpe, departed 1353, POW.
b.   A6382, No 25 Sqn, RFC, 2/Lt DP McDonald, POW, & 2/Lt John I M O'Bierne, KIA, departed at 1512, shot down near Lens.
c.   A6371, No 25 Sqn, RFC, Lt L Dodson & 2/Lt HS Richards, departed at 1530, shot down near Lens, POWs.
d.   A2536, No 32 Sqn, RFC, Lt EL Hayworth, shot down E of Lagnicourt, WIA/POW.
e.   4897, No 23 Sqn, RFC, Sgt JA Cunniffe, OK, & 2 A/M J Mackie, WIA, aircraft shot up during combat.
f.   7236, No 15 Sqn, RFC, 2/Lts JH Sayer, KIA, & VC Morris, WIA/POW, departed at 1625, shot down about 1730 near Croiselles.
g.   British balloon 13-7-5 (FM 26), Major Geddes & Lt F Mears, observers, made safe descents.
h.   British balloon 18-17-5 (FM 25) Lts D Kershaw & J Morgan, observers, made safe descents.
Losses- Nil

---

4 April 1917

Ltn H Klein	4	BE2e	SE Arras	0900	1	a.
Ltn H Malchow	4	FE	SW Arras	0930	1	b.
Ltn E Löwenhardt	10	Balloon			–	

a.   2563, No 12 Sqn, RFC, 2/Lts KC Horner & AE Emmerson, departed at 0810;
        both crewmen died of their wounds.
b.   A832, No 11 Sqn, RFC, Lt W Baillie (P) seriously wounded and forced to land, departed at 0725.
Losses – Nil

---

5 April 1917

Vfw S Festner	11	Nieuport	SW Bailleul	1100	4	a.
Ltn F Roth	12	FE2b	Gouzeaucourt	1105	2	
Ltn A Schulte	12	FE2b	Lepave	1105	–	
Obltn M v Richthofen	11	BF2a	Lewarde	1108	35	b.
Ltn O Splitgerber	12	FE2b	Honnecourt	1110	2	
Ltn G Simon	11	BF2a	N Monchecourt	1120	1	c.
Obltn M v Richthofen	11	BF2a	Quincy	1128	36	d.
Ltn E Weissner	18	FE2d	S Ypern	1145	–	
Ltn G Schlenker	3	FE2b	SW Moeuvres	1200	6	e.
Ltn G Nernst	30	Sopwith 2	W Rouvroy	1205	2	f.
Ltn H Auer	26	Nieuport	Sennheim	1806	1	g.
Vfw S Festner	11	BF2a	Aniche	1830	5	h.
Vfw K Menckhoff	3	Nieuport	W Athies	1950	1	i.
Ltn E Voss	20	Nieuport	Omissy			
Ltn A Dossenbach	36	Caudron	Sillery		10	j.

a.   A6693, No 60 Sqn, RFC, Lt EJD Townesend, departed at 1215, KIA.
b.   A3343, No 48 Sqn, RFC, Lt AT Adams & 2/Lt DJ Stewart, POWs.
c.   A3320, No 48 Sqn, RFC, Lt HA Cooper & 2/Lt A Boldison, POWs.
d.   A3340, No 48 Sqn, RFC, 2/Lt AN Leckler, WIA/POW, & 2/Lt Herbert DK George, WIA/DOW.
e.   A805, No 23 Sqn, RFC, Lt L Elsley, KIA, & Lt F Higginbottom, WIA/DOW.
f.   A1073, No 43 Sqn, RFC, 2/Lts CP Thornton, POW, & HD Blackburn, KIA, departed at 1015.
g.   Caporal Herubel, N 78, KIA flying a Spad VII near Jonchère.
h.   A3337, No 48 Sqn, RFC, Capt WL Robinson & 2/Lt ED Warburton, POWs.
i.   A6791, No 29 Sqn, RFC, Lt N A Birks, departed at 1810, WIA/POW.
j.   G.4 of Escadrille C 39, Lt d'Hericourt (P) & Sgt Mathieu (O), KIAs.

Losses:

Ltn Josef Flink   18   Flying Albatros DIII 1942/16, POW by Lt
HG White & Pvt T Allum, No 20 Sqn, RFC.

6 April 1917

Ltn W Frankl	4	FE2b	Quiery-la-Motte	0730	16	
Ltn J v Bertrab	30	G100	Ath	0815	1	a.
Ltn H Gontermann	5	FE2d	Neuville	0815	7	b.
OfStv E Nathanael	5	FE2d	Douchy	0820	8	b.
Ltn O Splitgerber	12	FE2d	Thiaut	0825	3	c.
Hptm P v Osterroht	12	FE2d	Lagnicourt	0830	3	b.
Obltn A v Tutschek	B	FE2d	Anneux	0830	3	b.
Ltn J v Bertrab	30	G100	SE Leuze	0830	2	c.
Ltn A Schulte	12	FE2b	Anneux	0830	–	b.
Ltn W Frankl	4	FE2b	Fauchy	0850	17	
Ltn W Frankl	4	FE2b	Arras	0855	18	d.
Ltn W Voss	B	BE2e	S Lagnicourt	0945	24	e.
Ltn W Frankl	4	BE2e	NE Boiry	0955	19	
Ltn O Bernert	B	RE8	Roeux	1015	14	f.
Vfw K Menckhoff	3	RE8	Fampoux	1015	2	f.
Ltn K Wolff	11	RE8	Bois Bernard	1015	6	f.
Ltn K Schäfer	11	BE2d	Givenchy	1020	10	
OfStv W Göttsch	8	FE2d	NE Polygonwald	1030	7	g.
Ltn K Schäfer	11	BE2c	SW Vimy	1037	11	h.
Ltn J v Bertrab	30	Sopwith 2	N Becq	1048	3	i.
Obltn H Bethge	30	Sopwith 2	NE Templeuve	1048	5	j.
Ltn J v Bertrab	30	Sopwith 2	NE Becq	1050	4	k.
Hptm P v Osterroht	12	Triplane	Hénin-Lietard	1215	4	l.
Obltn R Berthold	14	Caudron	Malval-Ferme	1315	10	m.
Ltn H Baldamus	9	Spad	NW Fresnes	1810	16	
Ltn J Jacobs	22	Balloon	Blanzy-Vailly	1930	–	n.
Ltn Kreuzner	13	Caudron	S Vailly		1	m.
Vfw G Strasser	17	Caudron	N Pontavert		2	m.
Ltn W Böning	19	Caudron	S Berry-au-Bac		1	m.
Ltn E Kreuzer	36	Caudron	Berry-au-Bac		2	m.
Ltn D Collin	22	Farman	Terny-Sorny		zlg	
Ltn H Bongartz	36	Spad	Witry-les-Reims		1	
Ltn W Albert	31	Spad	Mars-sous-Bourg		2	
Ltn Brauneck	25	Balloon			–	

a.   No 27 Sqn, RFC, lost two aircraft this date shot down near Ath: 7478, Lt JHB Wedderspoon, KIA, and 7465, 2/Lt JRS Proud, KIA.

b.   No 57 Sqn, RFC, lost four FE2ds this date, all were last seen at 0930 engaged in combat over Marquion: A 21, 2/Lt DC Birch & Lt JK Bousfield, MC, POWs; A22, Lt RTB Schreiber & 2/Lt M Lewis, POWs; A1959 Lt TF Burrill & 2/AM F Smith, POWs: and A6388, 2/Lt HD Hamilton & Pvt E Snelling, WIA/POWs.

c.   7714, No 100 Sqn, RFC, 2/Lt ARM Tickards & 2/AM EW Barnes, POWs.

d.   3819, No 11 Sqn, RFC, Sgt FE Evans, POW, & 2/AM E Wood, KIA.

e.   Probably A3157, No 15 Sqn, RFC, 2/Lt AH Vinson & 2/Lt ELC Gwilt, OK, shot up and crash-landed near Lagnicourt.

f.   No 59 Sqn, RFC, lost three aircraft that departed at 0935: A3206, Lt CF Bailey, KIA, & 2/AM VM Barrie, MIA; A3421, 2/Lt AC Pepper, POW, & Lt WL Day, KIA; A112, 2/Lts RWM Davies & JCD Wordsworth, KIAs.

g.   A6358 'A5', No 20 Sqn, RFC, 2/Lt R Smith & Lt R Hume,KIAs.

h.   Probably 6823, No 16 Sqn, RFC, Lt OR Knight & 2/Lt UH Seguin, KIAs.

i.   A2381, No 45 Sqn, RFC, 2/Lt CStG Campbell & Capt DW Edwards, MC, KIAs.

j.   7806, No 45 Sqn, RFC, 2/Lt JE Blake & Capt WS Brayshay, KIAs.

k.   A1093, No 45 Sqn, RFC, 2/Lts JA Marshall, KIA, & FG Truscott, WIA/DOW.

l.   N5447, No 1 Sqn, RNAS, F/S/Lt NDM Hewitt, POW.

m.   There were four French Caudrons lost this date: 1559, Escadrille F 35, S/Lt Desbordes (P), Lt Borgoltz (O) & Sol Lebleu (AG), MIAs; Escadrille R 210 Sgt Gauron (P) WIA, S/Lt Cazier (O) KIA & Sol Brasseur (AG) KIA; Escadrille C 227, Sgt Lafaille (P) WIA & S/Lt Vrolyck (O) KIA; Escadrille C 224, Sgt Sommier (P) & S/Lt Jouvenot (O), KIAs. Which claim is not valid is unknown at this time.

n.   French 21 Compagnie d'Aérostières,

Losses:

Uffz Ludwig Weber	3	Flying Albatros DII 510/16, WIA.
Obltn H Berr	5	KIA with No 57 Sqn, RFC near Noyelles – (Alb DIII 2256/17). Collided in mid-air with Vfw Paul Hoppe, killing both.
Vfw Paul Hoppe	5	Flying Albatros DIII 2241/16 (see above).
Ltn Otto Splitberger	12	Wounded in combat over Thiaut at 0805.
Vfw Reinhold Wurzmann	20	Shot down in flames and killed near Maray.

7 April 1917

Ltn H Klein	4	Balloon	W Arras	1700	2	a.
Vfw L Patermann	4	Nieuport	NW Biache	1710	1	b.
Ltn O Bernert	B	Nieuport	S Roeux	1710	15	c.
Obltn M v Richthofen	11	Nieuport	NE Mercatel	1745	37	d.
Ltn K Wolff	11	Nieuport	NE Mercatel	1745	7	e.
Ltn K Schäfer	11	Nieuport	NE Mercatel	1745	12	e.
Ltn W v Bülow	18	FE2d	S Ploegsteertwald	1815	10	f.
OfStv M Müller	28	FE2d	Ploegsteert	1820	6	f.
Ltn W Frankl	4	Nieuport	SE Fampoux	1910	20	g.
Vfw S Festner	11	Sopwith 2	NW Moreuil	1910	6	
Hptm H v Hünerbein	8	Nieuport	Becelaere		1	h.

a.   British balloon ?-9-3 (FM 32) Capt G Sansom & 2/Lt W Dreschfield, observers, made safe descents.

b.   A6692, No 29 Sqn, RFC, Capt AJ Jennings, departed at 1640, KIA.

c.   A6775, No 29 Sqn, RFC, 2/Lt JH Muir, departed at 1640, KIA.

d.   A6645, No 60 Sqn, RFC, 2/Lt GO Smart, departed at 1640, KIA.

e.   A6766, No 60 Sqn, RFC, 2/Lt CD Hall, departed at 1640, KIA.

f.   No 20 Sqn, RFC lost two aircraft this day, A6400, Lt J Lawson, OK, & 2/Lt HN Hampson, WIA/DOW, departed at 1712, shot up and forced to land S of Ploegsteert Wood; A1961, Capt GJ Mahoney-Jones & 2/Lt WB Moyes, KIAs, departed at 1713, shot down in flames.

g.   A6773, No 60 Sqn, RFC, Capt MB Knowles, departed at 1805, POW.

h.   A6605, No 1 Sqn, RFC, Lt RJ Bevington, departed at 0842, POW.

Losses – Nil

8 April 1917

Ltn H Klein	4	FE2b	SE Douai	0440	3	a.
Vfw S Festner	11	Nieuport	E Vimy	0930	7	b.
Rittm M v Richthofen	11	Sopwith 2	Farbus	1140	38	c.
Ltn W Frankl	4	EA	Arras	1330	20	
Ltn K Wolff	11	DH4	NE Blécourt	1430	8	d.
Ltn K Schäfer	11	DH4	Epinoy	1440	13	e.
Ltn O Bernert	B	BF2a	SE Eterpigny	1510	16	f.
Ltn O Bernert	B	RE8	N Bailleul	1510	17	g.
Rittm M v Richthofen	11	BE2g	W Vimy	1640	39	h.
Ltn G Schlenker	3	Nieuport	NE Croiselles	1910	7	i.
Ltn H Gontermann	5	Balloon	W St Quentin		8	j.
OfStv W Göttsch	8	BE2d	E Dixmuide		8	k.
Ltn W v Bülow	18	Nieuport	E Ypern		11	l.
Obltn E Hahn	19	Caudron	Loivre		2	m.

a.   7669, No 100 Sqn, RFC, 2/Lt L Butler & 2/AM R Robb, missing from 0300, POWs.

b.   A6764, No 60 Sqn, RFC, Maj JAA Milot, KIA.

c.   A2406, No 43 Sqn, RFC, Lt JS Heagerty, POW, & Lt L Heath-Cantle, KIA.

d.   A2141, No 55 Sqn, RFC, Lt B Evans & 2/Lt BW White, KIAs.

e.   A2140, No 55 Sqn, RFC, Lt RA Logan & Lt FR Henry, KIAs.

f.   A3330, No 48 Sqn, RFC, 2/Lts OW Berry & FB Goodison, KIAs.

g.   A4178, No 59 Sqn, RFC, 2/Lt KB Cooksey & 2/AM RH Jones, KIAs.

h.   A2815, No 16 Sqn, RFC, 2/Lt KI MacKenzie & 2/Lt G Everingham, KIAs.

i.   A6765, No 29 Sqn, RFC, 2/Lt TJ Owen, departed at 1935, KIA.

j.   French 41 Compagnie d'Aérostières, Adj Duramel, the observer, was injured in the attack.

k.   BE2 of Belgian Escadrille 6me, Lt JF Callant & Adj A Gilbert, KIAs.

l.   A156, No 46 Sqn, RFC, 2/Lt JE De Watteville & Lt RA Manby, departed at 1545, WIAs.

m.   Possibly an R4 of Escadrille C 46, MdL Theron (P) KIA, S/Lt Wilmes (O) KIA, Adj de Cuyper (AG) WIA.

Losses:

Ltn Wilhelm Frankl	4	Albatros DIII 2158/16, killed in combat with No 48 Sqn, RFC, near Vitry-Sailly.
Ltn Roland Nauck	6	Albatros DIII 2234/16 (G.21), KIA by Lt de Laage de Meux of Escadrille N 124.
Ltn Alfred Träger	8	Wounded in action.

9 April 1917   The Arras – Vimy Ridge British Offensive began.

Ltn K Schäfer	11	BE2d	Aix-Noulette	1900	14	a.

a.   5742, No 4 Sqn, RFC, Lt JHE Brink, WIA/DOW & Lt RC Heath, WIA.

Losses – Nil

10 April 1917

No Claims – No Losses

11 April 1917

Ltn F Roth	12	BE2c	NE Abancourt	0845	1	a.
Ltn A Schulte	12	BE2d	Tilloy	0855	7	b.
Ltn H Frommherz	B	Spad	Cuvillers	0900	1	c.
Vfw S Festner	11	BE	N Monchy	0900	8	
Ltn A Schulte	12	Pup	W Neuvireuil	0900	8	d.
Ltn K Schäfer	11	BF2a	SW Fresnes	0910	15	e.
Ltn K Wolff	11	BF2a	N Fresnes	0910	9	f.
Ltn L v Richthofen	11	BF2a	N Fresnes	0915	2	g.
Rittm M v Richthofen	11	BE2d	Willerval	0925	40	h.
Ltn H Klein	4	BE	Biache	1020	4	
Ltn H Klein	4	BE	Feuchy	1100	5	
Obltn R Berthold	14	Spad	S Corbeny	1145	11	i.
OfStv Hüttner	14	Spad	Berry-au-Bac	1145	2	i.
Ltn O Bernert	B	Spad	Arras	1230	18	
Ltn L v Richthofen	11	BE2e	NE Fampoux	1235	3	j.
Ltn O Bernert	B	Morane	NW Lagnicourt	1240	19	k.
Ltn K Schäfer	11	BE2c	E Arras	1250	16	
Ltn G Salzwedel	24	Nieuport	Xures		1	l.
Ltn A Dossenbach	36	Farman	Berry-au-Bac		11	m.

a.   2769, No 4 Sqn, RFC, 2/Lt F Matthews, departed at 0708, WIA/POW.

b.   5849, No 4 Sqn, RFC, Lt FL Kitchin, departed at 0709, KIA.

c.   A6690, No 23 Sqn, RFC, 2/Lt S Roche, departed at 0755, POW.

d.   5185, No 3 Sqn, RNAS, F/S/Lt Hayne, came down S of Evis Halarcq.

e.   A3318, No 48 Sqn, RFC, 2/Lts RE Adeney & LG Lovell, KIAs.

f.   A3338, No 48 Sqn, RFC, Capt DM Tidmarsh & 2/Lt CB Holland, POWs.

g.   A3323, No 48 Sqn, RFC, 2/Lts GN Brookhurst, POW, & CB Boughton, KIA.

h.   2501, No 13 Sqn, RFC, Lt Edward CE Derwin & Gunner H Pierson, WIAs.

i.   Escadrille N 73, lost two pilots this day, Adj A Barioz, who took off at 1045 flying Spad VII #370, was missing and Sgt ML Paris (1v), also flying a Spad VII was wounded in combat.

j.   A4190, No 59 Sqn, RFC, Lts GT Morris & JM Souter, KIAs.

k. A6760, No 3 Sqn, RFC, Lts LF Beynon & AC Lutyens, MC, departed at 1725, WIAs.
l. Escadrille N 68, Nieuport XVII #1955, flown by MdL Preher, MIA.
m. Escadrille F 215, Sgt Perseyger (P) & Asp Nardon (O), downed N of Berry- au-Bac.
Losses:

Vfw Karl Möwe	29	Killed between St Souplet and Aubérive, probably by Lt Armand Pinsard, Escadrille N 78 for his 6th victory.
Ltn Heinrich Karbe	22	Slightly wounded in the head over Cerny-le-Laonnois c1200, but remained with unit. (Possibly by Adjudant Jeronnez of N 26.)

12 April 1917

Hptm P v Osterroht	12	Pup	NW Bourlon	1035	5	a.
Vfw A Schorisch	12	FE2b	SE Eterpigny	1035	2	b.
Ltn A Schulte	12	FE2b	N Baralle	1040	9	c.
Uffz E Horn	21	Sopwith 2	S Nauroy	1100	1	d.
Ltn H Baldamus	9	Spad	N Pont Faverger	1900	17	e.
Ltn K Schneider	5	BE2c	Herbecourt		3	
Obltn E Hahn	19	Caudron	Orainville		3	f.

a. N6172, No 3 Sqn, RNAS, F/Lt RG Mack, WIA/POW.
b. 4984, No 18 Sqn, RFC, Ltns OD Maxted, POW, & A Todd, MC, DOW, took off 0850.
c. 4995, No 18 Sqn, RFC, Lt OT Walton & 2/AM JC Walker, departed at 0910, KIAs.
d. Escadrille N 38, MdL Richard (P) & Lt Hallier (O), MIAs.
e. Spad VII #2507 of Escadrille N 112, Adj-Chef G Chemet, POW.
f. A Salmson-Moineau of Escadrille SM 106, Lt de Montfort (P), Sol Portolieu (O) & Brig Robillard (G), MIAs.
Losses:

Ltn Adolf Schulte	12	Albatros DIII 1996/16, killed in a mid-air collision with FE2d 4995 of No 18 Sqn, RFC, Lt OT Walton & 2/AM JC Walker.

13 April 1917

Vfw S Festner	11	RE8	N Dury	0854	9	a.
Ltn L v Richthofen	11	RE8	NE Biache	0855	4	b.
Ltn H Klein	4	RE8	SW Biache	0856	6	
Ltn K Wolff	11	RE8	N Vitry	0856	10	
Rittm M v Richthofen	11	RE8	E Vitry	0856	41	c.
Ltn L v Richthofen	11	RE8	Pelves	0856	5	d.
Ltn K Schneider	5	FE2d	S Gavrelle	0900	4	
Ltn K Schneider	5	FE2d	Gavrelle	0900	5	
Ltn H Gontermann	5	FE2d	S Gavrelle	0905	9	e.
Ltn K Wolff	11	FE2b	S Bailleul	1235	11	
Rittm M v Richthofen	11	FE2b	W Monchy	1245	42	f.
Ltn A Dossenbach	36	Spad	Sapingeul	1400	12	g.
Ltn K Wolff	11	Nieuport	S Monchy	1630	12	
Ltn H Bongartz	36	Caudron	Cormicy	1700	2	h.
Ltn K Schäfer	11	FE2b	SW Monchy	1830	17	
Ltn E Dostler	34	Balloon	Genicourt	1830	–	i.
Ltn K Wolff	11	G100	Rouvroy	1852	13	j.
Ltn H Klein	4	FE2d	Vimy	1910	7	
Ltn E Bauer	3	FE2b	La Bassée	1915	1	
Vfw S Festner	11	FE2b	E Harnes	1930	10	k.
Rittm M v Richthofen	11	FE2b	Noyelle-Godault	1935	43	l.
Ltn J Jacobs	22	Farman	Barisis	1935	4	
OfStv E Nathanael	5	Balloon	W St Quentin	1935	9	m.
Ltn H Gontermann	5	Balloon	S St Quentin	1940	10	n.

Uffz S Ruckser	37	Balloon		1	
Ltn Stobel	3	BE2g	SW Oppy	1	
Ltn G Bassenge	5	EA	W St Quentin	–	

a.   A3199, No 59 Sqn, RFC, 2/Lts A Watson & ER Law, WIA/POWs.

b.   A3126, No 59 Sqn, RFC, Capt GB Hodgson & Lt CH Morris, KIAs.

c.   A3190, No 59 Sqn, RFC, Capt JM Stewart & Lt MH Wood, KIAs.

d.   A4191, No 59 Sqn, RFC, 2/Lt HMcM Horne & Lt WJ Chalk, KIAs.

e.   A5150, No 57 Sqn, RFC, Capt LS Platt & 2/Lt T Margerison, departed at 0700, KIAs.

f.   A831, No 11 Sqn, RFC, Sgt JA Cunnliffe & 2/AM WJ Batten, WIAs.

g.   French Spad VII #1057, Escadrille N 12, MdL Marcel Nogues (2v), POW.

h.   French Salmson-Moineau, Escadrille F 72, S/Lt Fequand (P), Lt Locquin (O), & Sol Hutreau (G), KIAs.

i.   French 89 Compagnie d'Aérostières, Lt Cante, the observer, made a safe descent. Dostler was cheated out of a victory as his claim was not confirmed.

j.   A784, No 25 Sqn, RFC, Sgt J Dempsey & Lt W H Green, departed at 1840, POWs.

k.   A1564, No 27 Sqn, 2/Lt M Topham, departed at 1805, KIA.

l.   4997, No 25 Sqn, RFC, 2/Lt AH Bates & Sgt WA Barnes, (3 victories), KIAs.

m.   British balloon 34-20-4.

n.   French 55 Compagnie d'Aérostières, MdL Colonna de Giovellina made a safe descent.

Losses:

Uffz Simon Ruckser	37	Wounded in action.	

14 April 1917

Ltn H Schell	30	Sopwith 2	Douai	0810	–
Rittm M v Richthofen	11	Nieuport	S Bois Bernard	0915	44 a.
Ltn K Wolff	11	Nieuport	SE Drocourt	0920	14 b.
Ltn L v Richthofen	11	Nieuport	W Fouquières	0920	6 c.
Vfw S Festner	11	Nieuport	Gavrelle	0923	11
Ltn H Frommherz	B	BE2c	Ribecourt	0930	2 d.
Vfw K Menckhoff	3	FE2b	Ecoust St Mein	0934	–
Obltn K v Döring	4	Nieuport	SE Fresnoy	0934	1
Ltn F Pütter	9	Balloon	E Suippes	1140	1 e.
Ltn H Baldamus	9	Nieuport	St Marie-à-Py	1140	18 f.
Uffz H Kramer	14	Caudron	Juvigny	1200	1
Obltn R Berthold	14	Spad	Bois de Marais	1200	12
Ltn J Veltjens	14	Spad	Craonne	1200	1
Ltn K Schäfer	11	FE2b	SW Lievin	1705	18
Ltn K Schäfer	11	BE	La Coulette	1720	19
Ltn L v Richthofen	11	Spad VII	SE Vimy	1823	7 g.
Ltn K Wolff	11	Spad	E Bailleul	1829	15
Ltn H Adam	34	Balloon	W St Mihiel		2 h.
Ltn H Gontermann	5	BE2e	Metz-en-Couture		11
Vfw O Gerbig	14	Caudron	Craonelle		2
Obltn E Dostler	34	Nieuport	SW St Mihiel		5
Vfw G Schindler	35	Sopwith 2	Schlettstadt		1 i.
Vfw R Rath	35	Sopwith 2	Scherweiler		1 j.

a.   A6796, No 60 Sqn, RFC, Lt WO Russell, POW.

b.   B1511, No 60 Sqn, RFC, Lt JH Cook, departed at 0830, KIA.

c.   A6772, No 60 Sqn, RFC, Capt A Binnie, MC, 3 victories, WIA/POW.

d.   2562, No 9 Sqn, RFC, Lt W Harle (WIA/POW) & 2/Lt WB Cramb, KIA, took off 0915.

e.   French 48 Compagnie d'Aérostières, S/Lt Guillotin, observer.

f.   French Nieuport XVII #2539, Escadrille N 37, Cpl Simon, MIA.

g.   A683, No 19 Sqn, RFC, Lt JW Baker, WIA, aircraft badly shot up but he managed to crash-land at Le Hameau airfield.

h.   French 57 Compagnie d'Aérostières, S/Lt MA Sapin, observer, was wounded in the attack, died of wounds 17 April 1917.

i.   N5171, No 3 Wing, RNAS, W/Cdr CEH Rathbone, POW, & Gunner Turner, KIA.

j.   N5117, No 3 Wing, RNAS, F/S/Lt H Edwards POW & Gunner Coghlan KIA.

Losses:

Ltn Hartmuth Baldamus	9	Killed in mid-air collision with Caporal Simon of N 37 flying Nieuport XVII No.2539, over St Marie-à-Py.
Ltn Otto Weigel	14	Killed at 1215 near Craonelle.
Ltn Friedrich Grünzweig	16	Killed after a balloon attack at Ellbach, by MdL Robert Harpedanne de Belleville of Escadrille N 49.
Ltn Fritz G Anders	35	Wounded in combat.
Ltn Margraf	35	Wounded in combat.
Obltn Herbert Theurich	35	Flying Albatros DIII 2097/16 shot down in flames and killed over Neubreisach.
Uffz Hermann Jopp	37	Shot down in flames by AA fire during a balloon attack near Mont Toulon.

The Arras – Vimy Ridge Offensive ended.

15 April 1917

Uffz M Zachmann	21	Spad	Sery	1030	1	a.
Vfw J Buckler	17	Spad	Prouvais		4	b.
Ltn Dotzel	19	Nieuport	La Neuvilette		1	c.
Ltn W Albert	31	Spad	Nauroy		3	d.
Ltn A Dossenbach	36	Nieuport	Bétheny		13	e
Ltn A Dossenbach	36	Spad	St Ferguex-Rethel		14	f.
Vfw H Mitzkeit	36	Spad	Thurgny-Rethel		2	g.
Ltn R Matthaei	21	Spad	Nauroy- Moronvillers		–	

a.   French Spad VII #1059, Escadrille Spa 15, Lt Bergeron, POW.
b.   French Spad VII #117, Escadrille N 3, Sgt A Papeil (2 victories), POW.
c.   French Nieuport XXIII #2937, Détachment N 519, Adj Siriez, MIA.
d.   French Spad VII #1056, Escadrille N 102, Cpl Quaissard, MIA.
e.   French Nieuport XXIII, Escadrille N 83, S/Lt R Senechal, N 83, WIA.
f.   French Spad VII #1234, Escadrille N 15, Adj D Epitalon, POW.
g.   French Spad VII #373, Escadrille N 15, Sgt Buisson, POW.

Losses – Nil

16 April 1917 The Nivelle Offensive began between Reims and Soissons.

Ltn L v Richthofen	11	Nieuport	E Roeux	1030	8	a.
Ltn K Wolff	11	Nieuport	NE Roeux	1030	16	a.
Vfw S Festner	11	Nieuport	NE Biache	1030	12	a.
Ltn R Oertelt	19	Caudron	Laneuville	1030	zlg	
Ltn Glinkermann	15	Farman	Juvincourt	1040	zlg	
Vfw G Strasser	17	Caudron	S Cormicy	1130	3	
Ltn E Thuy	21	Caudron	N Berry-au-Bac	1505	2	b.
Vfw J Buckler	17	Nieuport	Berry-au-Bac	1640	5	
Ltn H Gontermann	5	Balloon	Manancourt	1650	12	c.
Ltn H Gontermann	5	Balloon	Manancourt	1700	13	d.
Rittm M v Richthofen	11	BE2e	NW Gavrelle	1730	45	e.
Ltn H Wendel	15	Nieuport	Prouvais		1	
Ltn J Jacobs	22	Balloon	Laffaux		5	
Ltn H-O Esser	15	Nieuport	Laon		1	
Ltn Parlow	22	Caudron	S Cernay		1	
Ltn G Rose	22	Caudron	S Cernay		2	

a.   No 60 Sqn, RFC, lost four aircraft that departed at 0805, for a patrol over Vitry: B1501, 2/Lt DN Robertson, KIA; A6769, 2/Lt RE Kimbell, KIA; B1509, Lt JMcC Elliott, KIA; B1507, Lt T Langwill, KIA.

b.   Caudron G.4 of Escadrille C 228, Sgt Pissavi (P) & S/Lt Bekkers (O), KIAs.
c.   British balloon 6-15-4.
d.   British balloon 14-14-4.
e.   3156, No 13 Sqn, RFC, 2/Lt A Pascoe, WIA, & 2/Lt FS Andrews, WIA/DOW.
Losses:

Ltn Hans-Olaf Esser	15	Killed in combat over Winterberg.				
Vfw Rieger	17	Severely injured in a crash-landing.				

17 April 1917

No Claims – No Losses

18 April 1917

Ltn H Jöns	31	Voisin	Aubérive	0800	1

Losses – Nil

19 April 1917

Ltn W Marwitz	9	Spad	SW Aubérive	1000	1	
Ltn A Frey	9	Farman	S Moronvillers	1145	2	
Ltn R Wenzl	31	Spad	S Moronvillers		1	
Ltn W Daugs	36	Morane	Prosnes		1	a.

a.   Morane Parasol of Escadrille N 38, Capt Fevre (P) & Lt de Broglie-Revel (O), KIAs.
Losses:

Ltn Paul Herrmann	31	Killed in combat over the Bois de Malval.

The Nivelle Offensive ends.

20 April 1917

Vfw A Schorisch	12	BE2e	Ecoust St Mein	0940	3	a.
Ltn Schürz	13	Farman	Landricourt		1	b.

a.   2553, No 16 Sqn, RFC, Sgt J Dangerfield & 2/AM ED Harvey, POWs.
b.   Farman 42, Escadrille F 1, Adj Bondaire (P) KIA, & Lt Blanchi (O), WIA/DOW.
Losses:

Ltn Viktor Hebben	10	Wounded in action.

21 April 1917

Ltn L v Richthofen	11	BE2g	SE Vimy	1728	9	a.
Ltn K Wolff	11	BE2g	N Willerval	1730	17	
Ltn K Wolff	11	Nieuport	E Fresnes	1745	18	b.
Ltn K Schäfer	11	Nieuport	Fresnes	1745	20	b.
Obflgmstr K Meyer	SFS1	Airship	E North Foreland		7	c.

a.   2766, No 16 Sqn, RFC, Capt EJD Routh (P) attacked at 1620, wounded and forced to land near Vimy.
b.   No 29 Sqn, RFC, lost two aircraft that departed at 1630 this date: A6797, 2/Lt F Sadler, KIA, and A6755, 2/Lt CVdeB Rogers, KIA.
c.   British Airship C 17.
Losses:

Ltn Günther v d Hyde	9	Shot down in flames and killed at 2000 over Nauroy, probably by Lt A Pinsard of N 78.
Ltn Friedrich Wichard	24	Albatros DIII 2096/16, "Vera",shot down at 1830 and taken POW, probably by S/Lt Henri Languedoc of N 12, his 7th victory.
Ltn Gustav Nernst	30	KIA, Albatros DIII 2147/16 (G.22).

22 April 1917

Ltn A Hanko	28	Nieuport	Wavrin	0810	1	a.
Ltn H Gontermann	5	Balloon	Arras	0935	14	b.
Ltn H Gontermann	5	Balloon			–	
Ltn K Schneider	5	Balloon	Epehy	1130	6	b.
Ltn K Schneider	5	Balloon	Essigny-le-Grand	1145	7	b.
OfStv E Nathanael	5	Balloon	Bus	1430	10	b.
Ltn K Wolff	11	FE2b	Hendecourt	1710	19	c.
Rittm M v Richthofen	11	FE2b	Lagnicourt	1710	46	d.
Uffz F Gille	12	BE	Croiselles	1830	–	
OfStv E Nathanael	5	Spad	Ribecourt	2005	11	e.
Ltn K Wolff	11	Morane	Havrincourt	2005	20	
Hptm P v Osterroht	12	Spad	S Marcoing	2005	6	
Ltn F Roth	12	EA	Marcoing	2005	2	
Vfw R Jörke	12	Spad	W Havrincourt	2010	2	e.
Ltn K Schäfer	11	FE2b	W Monchy	2020	21	f.
Lt Gerlt	19	Caudron	St Etienne		1	g.

a.   A313, No 1 Sqn, RFC, Lt AW Wood, departed at 0544, WIA/POW.
b.   Four Allied balloons were lost this date, two near Arras, those of the British balloon
33-11-3 (FM 33), 2/Lt Baxter made a safe descent, and British balloon 3-13-5 (FM
27), 2/Lt Riches who also made a safe descent, the other British balloon 14-14-4,
was at Hervilly, and the French 55 Compagnie d'Aérostières, MdL Colonna de Giovellina, observer.
c.   A5501, No 11 Sqn, RFC, Sgt JK Hollis, WIA/POW & Lt BJ Tolhurst, KIA.
d.   7020, No 11 Sqn, RFC, Lts W Franklin & WF Fletcher, WIAs.
e.   No 23 Sqn, RFC, lost two aircraft that departed at 1727, and last seen E of Cambrai: A6682, 2/Lt FC
Craig, POW, and A6695, 2/Lt KR Furniss, WIA/POW/DOW.
f.   A820, No 11 Sqn, RFC, Lt CA Parker, OK, & 2/Lt J EB Hesketh, WIA/DOW.
g.   Caudron G.4 of Escadrille C 42, MdL LeClerc (P) & Lt Mercier (O), MIAs.
Losses – Nil

---

23 April 1917

Ltn K Schneider	5	FE2b	Bellenglise	0815	8	
Uffz F Gille	12	Sopwith	Javrincourt	0830	–	
Vfw A Schorisch	12	Sopwith	Wancourt	1200	4	
Hptm P v Osterroht	12	Sopwith	Fontaine	1200	7	
Rittm M v Richthofen	11	BE2f	Mericourt	1205	47	a.
Ltn K Schöck	12	Sopwith	Damville	1205	1	
Vfw Grigo	12	Sopwith	Neuville	1205	2	
Ltn L v Richthofen	11	BE2g	N Vimy	1210	10	b.
Ltn W Schunke	20	Morane	SW St Quentin	1400	1	c.
Vfw Franz	33	Sopwith 2	Boisleux	1700	–	
Vfw L v Raffay	34	Balloon	Belrupt	1715	1	d.
Ltn H Göring	26	FE2b	NE Arras	1720	4	
OfStv R Weckbrodt	26	DH4	SW Itancourt	1800	2	
Ltn K Schneider	5	FE2b	Bellenglise	1900	9	
Ltn K Schneider	5	DH2	Bellenglise	1900	10	
Ltn H Gontermann	5	RE8	SE Arras	1925	15	
Vfw Grigo	12	EA	St Martin	2000	–	
Uffz R Jörke	12	EA	Neuville	2000	–	
Ltn Rohr	22	Farman	Leuilly		2	

a.   A3168, No 4 Sqn, RFC, 2/Lt EA Welch & Sgt AG Tollervey, KIAs.
b.   A2876, No 16 Sqn, RFC, 2/Lts Charles M Crow, KIA, & ET Turner, WIA, departed at 0945.
c.   Morane Parasol #1112, Escadrille N 124, Sgt R Hoskier, an American, & Sol Dressy, KIAs.
d.   A823, No 18 Sqn, RFC, 2/Lt EL Zink WIA & 2/Lt GB Bate (O) OK.

Losses:

Vfw Arno Schramm	7	KIA between Linselles and Montfaucon.
Hptm Paul v Osterroht	12	KIA at 1800 near Cambrai in combat with No 3 Sqn, RNAS.
Uffz Nauczak	33	Severely wounded in combat.

24 April 1917

Obltn H Lorenz	33	Pup	Bourlon	0805	2	a.
Ltn O Bernert	B	Sopwith 2	S Vaucelles	0830	20	b.
Ltn O Bernert	B	BE2e	N Joncourt	0840	21	c.
Ltn O Bernert	B	BE2e	N Levergies	0842	22	c.
Ltn O Bernert	B	BE2e	S Bellecourt	0845	23	c.
Ltn O Bernert	B	DH4	W Bony	0850	24	
Ltn K Krefft	11	EA	Arras	0850	–	
Ltn H Gontermann	5	Triplane	Bailleul	0900	16	d.
Ltn W Junck	8	FE2b	Ypern	0910	1	
OfStv W Göttsch	8	FE2b	E Ypern	0910	9	
Ltn W v Bülow	18	FE2d	Ypern	0940	12	
Vfw P Felsmann	24	Spad	Prunay-Fichtelberg	1012	2	
Vfw A Haussmann	23	Nieuport	Beaurieux	1605	2	
Ltn E Udet	15	Nieuport	Chavignon	1930	5	
Ltn W Kypke	14	Spad	Berry-au-Bac		zlg	
Obltn E Dostler	34	Caudron	Ablonville		6	
Vzflgmt Wirtz	MFJ1	FE2d	Polygonwald		2	
Vzflgmt Wirtz	MFJ1	FE2d	Becelaere		3	

a. A6175, No 66 Sqn, RFC, 2/Lt RS Capon, shot down near Cambrai, POW.
b. A1002, No 70 Sqn, RFC, 2/Lt LC Halse & 2/AM W Bond, departed at 0535, shot down in flames, SE of Cambrai.
c. No 9 Sqn, RFC, lost three aircraft that departed at 0540 this day: 7195, Lt GE Hicks, POW; A2937, 2/Lt FA Matthews, KIA; A2941, Lt CL Graves, KIA. It is possible that the latter two were hit by AA fire.
d. N5467, No 8 Sqn, RNAS, F/S/Lt EJB Walter, KIA.

Losses:

Obltn Rudolf Berthold	14	Wounded in action.
Ltn Fritz Kleindienst	18	Shot down in flames and killed at 0920 near Korentje, N of Comines.
Rittm Karl v Grieffenhagen	18	Severely wounded in action.
Vfw Rudolf Rath	35	Flying Albatros DIII 2120/16, killed at 0722 near Hagenbach.
Vzflgmt Wirtz	MFJ1	Flying Albatros DIII No.2281/16, killed in a collision with an FE at 0815 over Becelaere.

25 April 1917

Ltn K Allmenröder	11	BE2e	Guémappe	1030	7	a.
Ltn K Schäfer	11	FE2b	N Bailleul	1040	22	b.
Ltn K Schäfer	11	BF2a	Bahnhof Roeux	2030	23	c.
Ltn Weltz	25	BE2e	Paljorka		1	d.

a. 7191, No 12 Sqn, RFC, Ltn T Thomson & 2/Lt AM Turnbull, KIA.
b. A837, No 25 Sqn, RFC, 2/Lt CV Darnell & 2/AM G Pawley, shot down at 0935 between Willerval and Bailleul, KIAs.
c. A3352, No 48 Sqn, RFC, 2/Lts WJ Clifford & HL Tomkies, KIAs.
d. 6810, No 17 Sqn, RFC, Lt GA Radcliffe, KIA.

Losses:

Vfw Sebastian Festner	11	Albatros DIII 2251/16, killed at 0810 near Oppy.

26 April 1917

Vfw J Buckler	17	Balloon	Bois de Génicourt	0920	7	a.
Ltn H Gontermann	5	Balloon	Arras	1150	17	b.
Ltn K Schneider	5	Balloon	Seraucourt	1600	11	
Ltn K Wolff	11	BE2g	E Gavrelle	1635	21	c.
Ltn P Erbguth	30	BE2e	SE Haisnes	1818	1	d.
Ltn L v Richthofen	11	BE2g	SE Vimy Ridge	1840	11	e.
Ltn K Allmenröder	11	BE2g	Vimy Ridge	1840	8	e.
OfStv A Strum	5	FE2b	Brandcourt	2000	1	f.
Ltn R Nebel	5	FE2b	Joncourt	2005	1	f.
Obltn E Hahn	19	Spad	N Brimont		4	g.
Ltn W Albert	31	Spad	Nauroy		4	h.

a.   French 36 Compagnie d'Aérostières, the observer, Sgt SC Saudet, was killed in the attack.
b.   British balloon 8-1-1 (BMS 22).
c.   2806, No 5 Sqn, RFC, Lts BT Hope, KIA, & LE Allen, KIA, departed at 1300 to operate in area of Gavrelle.
d.   5870, No 10 Sqn, RFC, 2/Lts F Roux & HJ Price, last seen at 1725 between Wingles and Hulloch, MIAs.
e.   No 16 Sqn RFC, lost two aircraft that were shot down at 1830 near Vimy on this date: 2859, 2/Lt WK Mercer, WIA, Pte Pea, OK; 2826, 2/Lt WS Spence & Lt WA Campbell, KIAs.
f.   No 22 Sqn, RFC, lost two aircraft that departed at 1745 and were last seen over Brancourt, this date: 4883, Capt HR Hawkins & 2/Lt GO McEntee, POWs; A1825, 2/Lts GM Hopkins & JDM Stewart, POWs.
g.   Spad VII #1447, Capt R Doumer (7 victories), CO N 76, KIA.
h.   Escadrille N 78, Cpl Egret, MIA.

Losses:

Vfw Emil Eisenhuth	3	Albatros DIII 2207/16, down in flames near Haynecourt.
Obltn Max Reinhold	15	Killed at 1930 over Lierval.
OfStv Rudolf Weckbrodt	26	Wounded in combat with FE2bs.

27 April 1917

Ltn L v Richthofen	11	FE2b	Fresnes	2015	12	a.
Ltn K Wolff	11	FE2b	S Gavrelle	2020	22	a.
Ltn K Allmenröder	11	BE2	W Fampoux	2025	9	
Ltn A Dossenbach	36	Balloon			–	
Ltn H Bongartz	36	Balloon	Berry-au-Bac		3	
Ltn H Bongartz	36	Balloon	SE Thillois		4	

a.   No 11 Sqn, RFC, lost two aircraft this date that departed at 1720: 4850, 2/Lt John A Cairns & 2/AM EG Perry, POWs; 7698, 2/Lt P Robinson & 2/AM R Tilley, came down at 2000, WIAs.

Losses:

Uffz Hans Eissfeldt	10	Severely wounded in combat.
Ltn Friedrich Vonschott	14	Severely wounded in combat over Montchâlons, DOW 14 May 1917.

28 April 1917

Ltn J Wolff	17	Caudron	Brimont	0830	2	
Rittm M v Richthofen	11	BE2e	SE Pelves	0930	48	a.
Ltn K Wolff	11	BE2g	Oppy	1120	23	b.
OfStv E Nathanael	5	Pup	La Vacquerie	1315	12	
Ltn K Wolff	11	BE2f	W Gavrelle	1745	23	
Ltn J Schmidt	3	Balloon	S Mareouil	1815	2	
Ltn H Göring	26	Nieuport	Harly	1830	5	c.
Vfw Langer	26	EA	St Quentin	1830	–	

a.   7221, No 13 Sqn, RFC, Ltn RW Follit, WIA/POW/DOW, & 2/Lt F J Kirkham, WIA/POW.
b.   A2745, No 16 Sqn, RFC, 2/Lts JV Wischer & AA Baerlein, departed at 0940, POWs.

c.   N3192, No 6 Sqn, RNAS, F/S/Lt AHV Fletcher, WIA/POW.
Losses – Nil

29 April 1917

Vfw A Bauhofer	25	Nieuport	Tepavci	0820	1	
Obltn F Burckhardt	25	Caudron	W Suhodol-Raja	1030	2	
Uffz F Gille	12	FE2d	Baralle	1055	1	
Ltn K Schneider	5	Pup	Elincourt	1130	12	
Rittm M v Richthofen	11	Spad	E Lecluse	1205	49	a.
Ltn K Wolff	11	Spad VII	Sailly	1210	24	b.
Ltn L v Richthofen	11	Spad VII	Izel	1215	13	c.
Ltn H Geigl	34	Caudron	S Pont-à-Mousson	1415	1	
Rittm M v Richthofen	11	FE2b	SW Inchy	1655	50	d.
Ltn K Wolff	11	FE2b	S Pronville	1700	25	
Ltn K Wolff	11	BE2f	W Gavrelle	1745	26	e.
Ltn E Weissner	18	FE2d	Courtrai	1850	1	
Ltn G Nolte	18	FE2b	Hooge	1900	1	
Rittm M v Richthofen	11	BE2c	S Roeux	1925	51	f.
Ltn L v Richthofen	11	BE2e	NE Monchy	1925	14	g.
Obltn B Loerzer	26	FE2b	Bellenglise	1930	–	
Rittm M v Richthofen	11	Triplane	N Hénin-Lietard	1940	52	h.
Ltn H Göring	26	Nieuport	Remicourt	1945	6	i.
Ltn H Stutz	20	FE2b	Douai	2045	1	
OfStv E Nathanael	5	Pup	Beaumont	2100	13	j.
Ltn P Strähle	18	FE2d	N Courtrai		4	
Ltn W Böning	19	Caudron	Brimont		2	k.
Ltn R Ernert	34	Balloon	Génicourt		1	l.
Vfw T Himmer	34	Farman	Génicourt		1	
Fldw M Jakobowitz	25	Nieuport	E Cernabogen		1	

a.   B1573, No 19 Sqn, RFC, Lt R Applin, KIA.
b.   A6681, No 19 Sqn, RFC, Maj HD Harvey-Kelly, DSO, KIA.
c.   A6753, No 19 Sqn, RFC, Lt WN Hamilton, POW.
d.   4898, No 18 Sqn, RFC, Sgt G Stead & Cpl A Beebee, KIAs.
e.   No 12 Sqn, RFC.
f.   2738, No 12 Sqn, RFC, Ltn DE Davies & Lt GH Rathbone, KIAs.
g.   7092, No 12 Sqn, RFC, 2/Lt CJ Pile & 2/Lt JH Westlake, KIAs.
h.   N5463, No 8 Sqn, RNAS, F/S/Lt AE Cuzner, KIA.
i.   B3192, No 6 Sqn, RNAS, F/S/Lt AHV Fletcher, KIA.
j.   A6745, No 40 Sqn, RFC, Capt FL Barwell, KIA.
k.   Letord of Escadrille C 46, Lt Campion (P), MdL Lamy (G) & Cpl Bousque (G), MIAs. Shot down in flames near Brimont.
l.   French 87 Compagnie d'Aérostières, Adj L Guerin killed.

Losses:

Ltn Peckmann	15	Wounded in action.
Ltn Ludwig Dornheim	29	Killed in combat at 1500 over Beine.

30 April 1917

OfStv M Müller	28	Sopwith 2	E Armentières	0700	7	
Ltn L v Richthofen	11	BE2g	SE Vimy	071	1	a.
Ltn Friedrich Kempf	B	BE2c	SW La Pave	0745	1	b.
Ltn L v Richthofen	11	FE2d	Izel	0755	16	c.
Obltn A v Tutschek	12	FE2d	Izel	0755	4	c.
Ltn F Gille	12	EA	Recourt	0820	–	
Ltn H Geiseler	33	FE2d	Oppy	0845	zlg	
Ltn F v Hartmann	9	Spad	N Nauroy	0925	1	

OfStv E Nathanael	5	SE5	S Fresnes	1005	14	d.
Ltn H Pfeiffer	9	Spad	Moronvillers	1030	10	
Ltn O v Breiten-Landenberg	9	Nieuport	St Hilaire-le-Petit	1100	1	e.
Ltn A Frey	9	Spad	Moronvillers	1115	3	
Ltn H Klein	4	BE2e	Ribecourt	1200	8	f.
Vfw W Wagener	21	Sopwith 2	Prosnes	1200	2	
Vfw A Franz	33	EA	Monchy	1320	–	
Ltn R Matthaei	21	Balloon	Montbré	1440	2	
Ltn K Wolff	11	BE2e	W Fresnes	1735	27	g.
Ltn P Billik	12	Pup	Romaucourt	1810	1	h.
Vfw K Menckhoff	3	Nieuport	Cantin	1850	3	
Obltn B Loerzer	26	Pup	Bourlon	1930	5	
Ltn W Böning	19	Balloon	Guyencourt		3	i.
Obltn E Hahn	19	Balloon	Guyencourt		5	
Obltn E Hahn	19	Balloon	Guyencourt		6	i.
Vfw A Rahn	19	Balloon	Reims		1	i.
Vfw A Rahn	19	Balloon	Reims		2	i.
Ltn K Deilmann	6	Sopwith	Roupy		zlg	
Ltn zS T Osterkamp	MFJ1	Nieuport	Oostkerke		1	j.

a.   A2942, No 16 Sqn, RFC, 2/Lts NA Lawrence & GRY Stout, MC, shot down in flames at 0810, near Vimy, KIAs.
b.   A2949, 9 Sqn, RFC, 2/Lt D McTavish, W/POW & Capt AS Allen MC, KIA.
c.   No 57 Sqn, RFC, lost two aircraft that departed at 0600 and were last seen near Douai: A6402, Lt PT Bowers & S/Lt ST Wills, POWs; A6352, 2/Lts ED Jennings & JR Lingard, POWs.
d.   A4866, 56 Sqn, RFC, Lt MA Kay, KIA.
e.   Nieuport XVII of Escadrille N 38, Cpl Leroy, MIA.
f.   2916, No 9 Sqn, RFC, 2/Lts PPC Freemantle & P Sherman, departed at 1000, KIAs.
g.   2910, No 30 Sqn, RFC, 2/Lts WK Trollope, WIA/DOW, A Bonner, KIA, departed at 1508.
h.   N6175, No 3 Sqn, RNAS, F/S/Lt JJ Malone, 10 victories, KIA.
i.   Four French balloons were lost this date: those of the 19, 58, 62 and 91 Compagnies d'Aérostières. Two others were attacked and forced down but not flamed, the 77 and 80 Compagnies.
j.   Belgian Escadrille 5me, Adj Sirautt, FTL, OK.
Losses:

Ltn Adolf Frey	9	Killed in combat with a Caudron over Nauroy.
Ltn Werner Marwitz	9	KIA, Nauroy, probably by S/Lt Beraud-Villars, of N 102, for his 2nd victory.
Ltn Friedrich Mallinckrodt	20	Severely wounded in combat.

JASTA ARMEE ASSIGNMENTS AS OF 1 MAY 1917

Western Front

1 Armee 17,21,22,24,29,36
2 Armee 2,5,20
3 Armee 31
4 Armee 6,8,18,27
5 Armee 7,14

6 Armee 3,4,10,11,12,26,28,30,33,37
7 Armee 1,9,13,15,23,32
Det 'A' 19,
Det 'B' 16,35
Det 'C' 34

Other Fronts

11 Armee 25   Macedonia

1 May 1917

Vfw E Ey	6	Pup	Francilly	0815	–

Obltn K v Döring	4	Triplane	NW Arleux	1020	2	a.
Ltn K Wolff	11	Triplane	S Seclin	1050	28	b.
Obltn A v Tutschek	12	Pup	Rumaucourt	1140	5	c.
Ltn K Schäfer	28	Farman	Dixmuiden	1240	24	i.
Vfw P Bona	1	Balloon	Vailly	1300	5	d.
Vfw W Dittrich	1	Balloon	Revillon	1300	1	d.
Obltn H Kummetz	1	Balloon	Condé	1300	4	d.
Ltn Zilcher	1	Balloon	Vailly	1300	1	d.
OfStv W Cymera	1	Balloon	NE Condé	1300	4	d.
Ltn K Schäfer	28	Nieuport	E Poperinghe	1300	25	e.
Ltn K Wolff	27	FE2b	S Bois Bernard	1855	29	f.
Ltn L v Richthofen	11	FE2b	W Acheville	1900	17	g.
Ltn H Kroll	9	Spad	W Moronvillers	1935	1	
Ltn L Hanstein	16	Nieuport	SW Hirzbach		3	h.
Vfw H Stöber	16	Sopwith 2	Altkirch		3	
Ltn z S G Sachsenberg	MFJ1	Farman	Dixmuiden		1	i.
Ltn z S G Sachsenberg	MFJ1	Sopwith 2	Oudekapelle		2	
Flgmt B Heinrich	MFJ1	Sopwith 2	W Dixmuiden		1	

a. N5434, No 8 Sqn, RNAS, F/S/Lt DM Shields, survived crash, WIA.
b. N5474, No 8 Sqn, RNAS, F/S/Lt ED Roach, KIA.
c. N6186, No 3 Sqn, RNAS, F/S/Lt AS Mather, departed at 1130, POW.
d. Two French balloons lost in this sector this date: 42and 49 Compagnies d'Aérostières. The balloons of the 20 and 31 Ciés were attacked but not flamed. Ens Rengard, 31 and Lt Cremière, 49 Ciés were killed.
e. A6678, No 1 Sqn, RFC, Capt ED Atkinson, WIA.
f. A815, No 25 Sqn, RFC, Lts GS French & GP Harding, MC, seen going down in flames at 1800 near Rouvroy, POWs.
g. A782, No 25 Sqn, RFC, 2/Lt B King, OK, Sgt HG Taylor, WIA.
h. Sgt G Segond, N 88, flying Nieuport XXIII #2675 when shot down in flames and killed over Hirzbach.
i. A Farman 40 of Belgian 4me Escadrille was lost over Dixmuiden, shot down by either Schäfer or Sachsenberg; Sgt Pauli & Lt de Bersaques, both KIA.

Losses:

Ltn Hermann Frommherz	B	Injured in an accident.
Ltn Gerhard Strehl	12	Shot down in flames and killed near Epinoy.
Ltn Alexander Kutscher	28	Flying Albatros DIII 771/17 (G.30), shot down near Elverdinghe, and taken prisoner, by 2/Lt EST Cole & Lt F Sharpe, of No 1 Sqn, RFC.

2 May 1917

Ltn O Bernert	6	Nieuport	S St Quentin	0830	25	
OfStv M Müller	28	BE2g	Ploegsteertwald	1615	8	a.
Ltn W Güttler	24	Nieuport	S Beine	1815	1	
Ltn W Zech	1	Balloon	Vauxtin	1900	1	b.
Vfw A Haussmann	23	Caudron	Pontavert	1900	3	
OfStv A Heldmann	10	Triplane	Souchez	1915	—	
Ltn G Meyer	22	Caudron	Braye		zlg	
Vfw E Meyer	25	Caudron	Cernabogen		1	
Vfw J Schroth	35	Nieuport	W Delle		1	
Ltn H Bongartz	36	Caudron	Bétheny-Reims		5	

a. 6281, No 12 Sqn, RFC, Lts JF Turner & PS Laughton, shot up and crash- landed, safely.
b. French balloon of the 66 Compagnie d'Aérostières, which was hit 28 times but not flamed.

Losses:

| Obltn Kurt Student | 9 | Wounded in action. |
| OfStv Franz Hilger | 27 | Injured in Roland DII 2851/16,following an accident near Bersée. |

| Ltn Albert Dossenbach | 36 | Wounded by shrapnel from an air raid on his airfield at Le Châtelet. |
| Vfw Richard Piez | K3 | Killed in combat over Gerolen. |

3 May 1917

OfStv W Göttsch	8	FE8	Draaibank		10	a.
Ltn H Dannenberg	13	Caudron	Septmonts		1	
Ltn E Weissner	18	FE8	Houthulsterwald		2	b.
Ltn z S K Mettlich	8	FE2d	W Houthulsterwald		–	

a. A4873, No 41 Sqn, RFC, Capt SF Browning, departed at 1603, last seen over Houthulst Wood, KIA.
b. 7622, No 41 Sqn, RFC, 2/Lt A Fraser, departed at 1607, last seen near Houthulst Wood, POW.

Losses:

Ltn Kleemann	5	Wounded in action.
Gefr Alfred Lemke	10	Flying Albatros DII 473/16 (G.32), he ran out of fuel and force-landed near Abbeville-Fampoux at 1600 – POW.
Ltn Fritz Mönnich	23	Wounded in action over Coucy-le-Château.
Ltn Gottlieb Görne	31	Shot down in flames between Aure and Marvaux.
Ltn Albrecht v Kobilinski	36	Injured when a munitions wagon exploded on his airfield.

4 May 1917

Ltn P Billik	12	FE2b	Croiselles	0840	zlg	
OfStv W Göttsch	8	Sopwith 2	N Lille	1317	11	a.
Ltn O Bernert	6	Balloon	Hervilly-Nauroy	1840	26	b.
Obltn A v Tutschek	12	Pup	SE Fresnes	2030	6	c.
Ltn J Veltjens	14	Farman	N Vailly		2	d.
Ltn H Gontermann	15	Spad	SE Craonne		18	e.
Ltn F Brandt	19	Spad	N Reims		1	e.

a. A1001, No 70 Sqn, RFC, 2/Lts VH Adams & IL Pinson, departed at 1025, last seen heading for Tournai, KIAs.
b. British balloon 14-14-4, Lt Sharp, the observer, was not harmed.
c. N6207, No 3 Sqn, RNAS, F/S/Lt HS Murton, POW.
d. Farman of Escadrille F 55, Sgt Bonnomet (P) & Lt Gilles (O), KIAs.
e. One of these was probably S/Lt R Rollet, N 12, shot down in flames landing between the lines, returned safely to his unit unharmed.

Losses:

Hptm Hans v Hünerbein	5	SSW DI 3761/16, killed in an accident during a test flight.
Ltn Gerlt	19	Severely wounded in action.
Vfw Hans Brinkmann	21	Killed in combat between Berru and Witry-les- Reims.
Vfw Eduard Horn	21	Killed in the same area as Brinkmann.
Vfw Albert Franz	33	Albatros DIII 2067/16, severely wounded in combat between Erchin and Sailly; died three days later.

5 May 1917

Ltn W Böning	19	Farman	Pontavert	1040	zlg	
Ltn J Veltjens	14	Spad	Vailly	1050	3	
Ltn W Zech	1	Nieuport	Aizy	1105	2	
Obltn F-K Burckhardt	25	Balloon	Ribarci	1140	3	
Ltn K Schöck	12	Spad	E Chérisy	1205	2	
Ltn P Bona	1	Morane	Courtecon	1730	6	a.
OfStv W Cymera	1	Morane	Courtecon	1730	–	
Ltn E Udet	15	Spad	Bois de Ville	1930	6	

Ltn W Göttsch	8	FE2d	Schaep-Baillie	12	b.
OfStv Hüttner	14	Balloon	Craonne	3	
Patrol	14	Balloon	Vailly	–	
Ltn E Weissner	18	FE2d	W St Eloi	3	c.
Vfw Flemming	18	FE2d	Zillebeke See	1	c.
Vfw A Rahn	19	Caudron	Cormicy	3	

a.   Morane of Escadrille C 225, Sgt Victorin (P) & Lt de Mornac (O), MIAs.
b.   A1942, No 20 Sqn, RFC, 2/Lt LG Bacon, WIA/POW, 2/AM G Worthing, KIA.
c.   A5147, No 20 Sqn, RFC, 2/Lts GC Heseltine & FJ Kydd, OKs, one of these claims apparently is not valid.

Losses:

Vfw Peter Glasmacher	8	Killed in action.
OfStv Anton Dierle	24	Killed in combat over Rotenberg.
Ltn Philip Wieland	27	Wounded in action.

6 May 1917

Ltn L v Richthofen	11	AWFK8	SE Givenchy	1050	18	a.
Ltn H Klein	4	AW	SE Lens	1630	9	b.
OfStv E Nathanael	5	Nieuport	NE Bourlon	1840	15	c.
OfStv K Stiller	1	Spad	Aizy	1845	1	
Ltn K Schneider	5	Nieuport	Ecourt-St Quentin	1845	13	d.
Vfw E Dahlmann	5	Sopwith	Cambrai		–	
Vfw J Buckler	17	Spad	Pontavert		zlg	

a.   A4596, No 16 Sqn, RFC, 2/Lt AC Sanderson, WIA, & Lt HK Lytton, crash-landed near Farbus after combat, aircraft shelled.
b.   A9999, No 16 Sqn, RFC, 2/Lts G Wood & CG Copeland, KIAs.
c.   B1514, No 60 Sqn, RFC, 2/Lt CW McKissock, departed 1650, POW.
d.   B1597, No 60 Sqn, RFC, Lt GD Hunter, departed at 1650, POW.

Losses:

Vfw Jäger	20	Injured in a landing accident.

7 May 1917

Ltn H Kroll	9	Spad	E Aubérive	1125	2	
Ltn Neisen	5	BE2b	Inchy-en-Artois	1140	1	
Ltn W v Bülow	18	FE2d	Halluin	1200	13	a.
Ltn G Flecken	20	Nieuport	Vendeuil	120	zlg	
Ltn A Hanko	28	Nieuport	E Ypern	1200	2	
OfStv M Müller	28	FE2d	Boesinghe	1215	9	
Ltn K Allmenröder	11	BE2c	Fresnoy	1245	10	b.
Ltn H Kroll	9	Spad	St Hilaire-le-Grand	1420	3	
Vfw K Menckhoff	3	RE8	Tilloy	1500	4	
Ltn O Bernert	6	BE2e	Pontreut	1540	27	
Ltn W Zech	1	Spad	Martigny	1600	3	c.
Ltn O Maashoff	11	RE8	W Fresnes	1830	1	
Ltn L v Richthofen	11	Nieuport	W Biache	1830	19	d.
Ltn W Voss	B	SE5	Etaing-Lecluse	1925	25	e.
Ltn L v Richthofen	11	SE5	Annoeullin	2030	20	f.
OfStv W Cymera	1	Spad	SW Vendeuil		5	
Ltn J Jacobs	22	Spad	Braye		–	

a.   A5149, No 20 Sqn, RFC, Lt AW Martin & Pvt WG Blakes, POWs.
b.   4595, No 13 Sqn, RFC, 2/Lt R Owen & 2/AM R Hockling, departed at 1040, KIAs.
c.   Adj Violleau, Escadrille N 75, flying a Spad VII, MIA NE of Pontavert.
d.   A6609, No 29 Sqn, RFC, 2/Lt CS Gaskain, KIA.
e.   A4867, No 56 Sqn, RFC, 2/Lt RM Chaworth-Musters, left at 1730, KIA.
f.   A4580, No 56 Sqn, RFC, Capt A Ball, DSO, MC, killed but although 56 and Jasta 11 were in action, Ball crashed after he become disorientated in cloud.

Losses:

OfStv Wilhelm Dietrich	1	Killed in combat over St Fergeux.
Ltn Wolfgang Plüschow	11	Wounded in action.

8 May 1917

No Claims – No Losses

9 May 1917

Vfw K Menckhoff	3	Triplane	SW Farbus	0850	5	a.
Ltn W Voss	B	BE2e	Havrincourt	1400	26	b.
Vfw Dilcher	5	Sopwith 2	St Hilaire	1500	1	
Ltn W Voss	B	Pup	Lesdain	1645	27	c.
Ltn W Voss	B	FE2b	Le Bosquet	1650	28	d.
Ltn L v Richthofen	11	BF2b	NE Fampoux	1830	21	e.
Ltn K Schäfer	28	Sopwith 2	Warneton	1900	26	f.
Vfw K Wittekind	28	Sopwith	Wytschaetebogen	1900	–	
Vfw Münnichow	1	Spad	Courtecon	1910	1	
Ltn H Tammann	23	Nieuport	Cerny	1945	1	
Vfw R Treptow	25	Balloon	Opticar		1	

a.   N5458, No 8 Sqn, RNAS, F/S/Lt Lee & EB Wimbush, DOW.
b.   7209, No 52 Sqn, RFC, Lt Roland H Coles & 2/Lt John CS Day, KIAs.
c.   A6174, No 54 Sqn, RFC, 2/Lt George CT Hadrill, departed at 1423, came down near Lesdain, POW.
d.   4991, No 22 Sqn, RFC, 2/Lts CAM Furlonger & CW Lane, departed at 1400, forced to land SW of Lesdain, POWs.
e.   A7110, No 48 Sqn, RFC, 2/Lt WT Price & Lt CG Claye, WIAs.
f.   7803, No 45 Sqn, RFC, Lt WL Mills, KIA, & 2/AM JW Laughlin, WIA, departed 1530.

Losses:

OfStv Wilhelm Cymera	1	Killed in combat over Chamouille.
OfStv Karl Stiller	1	Killed in combat at 1800 over Barisis-au-Bois.
Ltn Hans Klein	4	Wounded in action.
Vfw Friedrich Sauerwein	7	Flying Roland DII 822/16, wounded in action.
Vfw Kairis	13	Injured in a forced landing.

10 May 1917

Ltn K Allmenröder	11	Pup	Vitry	0740	11	a.
Ltn L v Richthofen	11	Pup	S Vitry	0750	22	b.
Ltn A Heldmann	10	Triplane	Fromelles	0920	zlg	
Ltn H Gontermann	15	Spad	NE Berry-su-Bac	1230	19	c
Obltn A v Tutschek	12	Sopwith	Monchy	1320	zlg	
Vfw F Krebs	6	DH4	S Solesmes	1500	1	d.
Ltn H Göring	26	DH4	NE La Pavé	1505	7	d.
Ltn W Blume	26	DH4	NE Gouzeaucourt	1510	1	d.
Vfw W Reiss	3	RE8	Bailleul	1820	1	
Ltn H Gontermann	15	Caudron	Berry-au-Bac	1820	20	e.
Ltn K Schneider	5	DH2	Villers Guislain		zlg	f.
Uffz Ruppert	19	Spad	S Berry-au-Bac		1	
Vfw M Wackwitz	24	Spad	S Moronvillers		1	

a.   A6178, No 66 Sqn, RFC, Lt TH Wickett, WIA/POW.
b.   A7303, No 66 Sqn, RFC, 2/Lt DJ Sheehan, KIA.
c.   Adj C Sanglier (2 victories), N 3, flying a Spad VII, MIA, departed at 1040 hours.
d.   A7416, No 55 Sqn, RFC, 2/Lts BW Pitt & JS Holroyde, seen to go down in flames and crash at Le Cateau, KIAs. A7419, No 55 Sqn, RFC, 2/Lt T Webb & 1/AM W Bond, departed at 1255, also said to have been hit by AA fire. A7413, No 55 Sqn, RFC, Capt N Senior, KIA, & Cpl PH Holland, WIA, shot down near Gouzeacourt.
e.   Escadrille C 46, Capt D Lecour-Grandmaison (P) (5v) KIA, Cpl Crozet, (G) KIA & Sgt Boye (G), WIA.

f.   A2581, No 24 Sqn, RFC, Lt HC Cuttler, departed at 1330, came down E of Ephey, KIA.
Losses:
Ltn Werner Albert   31   Killed in combat over Vaudesincourt.

11 May 1917

Vfw F Krebs	6	Pup	S Lesdain	0935	2	a.
Ltn H Gontermann	15	Spad	Berry-au-Bac	1030	21	
Ltn O Maashoff	11	BE	Willerval	1225	2	
Uffz O Rosenfeld	12	FE	Tilloy	1330	1	
Vfw R Riessinger	12	Pup	SE Haynecourt	1535	1	
Obltn A v Tutschek	12	Pup	Croiselles	1540	7	b.
Ltn L v Richthofen	11	BF2b	Izel	1710	23	c.
Ltn W Allmenröder	11	BF2b	Beaumont	1715	2	c.
Ltn K Küppers	6	Nieuport	NE Hargicourt	2040	2	d.
Vfw W Hoffmann	36	Caudron	Aubérive		–	

a.   A7308, No 54 Sqn, RFC, 2/Lt HC Duxbury, departed at 0700, shot down in flames, KIA.
b.   N6464, No 3 Sqn, RNAS, F/S/Lt JB Daniell, departed at 1515, POW.
c.   No 48 Sqn, RFC, lost two BFs that departed at 1500 this date: A7101, Capt AT Cull, KIA, & 1/AM A Trusson, KIA, last seen in flames over Fresnes; A7111, Lt WOB Winkler & 2/Lt ES Moore, shot down at Gavrelle and taken prisoner.
d.   N3189, No 6 Sqn, RNAS, F/S/Lt OJ Gagnier, injured in a forced landing.
Losses:
OfStv Edmund Nathanael   5   Shot down in flames and killed at 2015 over Bourlon Wood, by
                                         Capt WJCK Cochrane-Patrick of No 19 Sqn, RFC, his 9th victory.

12 May 1917

Ltn J Schmidt	3	EA	Bailleul	0745	–	
Uffz F Gille	12	Nieuport	Inchy	0800	2	a.
Uffz R Jörke	12	EA	Lagnicourt	0825	–	
Obltn A v Tutschek	12	Pup	W Baralle	1050	8	b.
Obflgmt K Schönfelder	7	Pup	SW Moeuvres	1150	zlg	
OfStv M Müller	28	RE8	S Ypern	1525	10	c.
Vfw J Buckler	17	Nieuport	La Malmaison	1840	7	d.
Ltn P Billik	12	Spad	E Fresnoy	2020	2	e.
Ltn W Leusch	19	Spad	Berry-au-Bac		1	
Ltn T Osterkamp	MFJ1	Sopwith	Ostende		2	
Flgmt B Heinrich	MFJ1	Sopwith	NW Zeebrugge		2	
Ltn zS G Sachsenberg	MFJ1	Sopwith	Zeebrugge		3	f.
OfStv W Kühne	29	Spad	Primay-Aubérive		–	

a.   B1544, No 29 Sqn, RFC, 2/Lt CR Sloan, departed at 0600 hours.
b.   A664, No 66 Sqn, RFC, Lt JH Robertson, KIA.
c.   A3243, No 53 Sqn, RFC, 2/Lts F Adams & OR Kelly, departed at 1345, also said to have been hit by AA fire, KIAs.
d.   Adj Joussaud, Escadrille N 75, flying a Nieuport XXIII, MIA, departed at 1700 hours.
e.   B1560, No 19 Sqn, RFC, Capt WGB Williams, MC, departed at 1823, KIA.
f.   No 3 Sqn, RNAS.
Losses:
Ltn Kreutzer   19   Wounded in action.
Vfw Max Wimmer   28   Severely wounded over Ypres.

13 May 1917

Ltn Ermecke	33	Spad	SW Baralle	0945	1	
Ltn L v Richthofen	11	BE2e	W Fresnoy	1135	24	a.
Ltn K Allmenröder	11	RE8	SE Arleux	1145	12	b.
Ltn K Wolff	29	Spad	Beine	1155	30	c.

Ltn H-G v d Marwitz	30	Balloon	W Dixmuiden	1440	2	d.
Ltn K Allmenröder	11	Nieuport	Ostricourt	2115	13	e.
Ltn H Hintsch	11	Nieuport	E Fresnes	2120	2	f.
Ltn P Strähle	18	FE2d	Polygonwald		5	g.

a.   7130, No 13 Sqn, RFC, 2/Lt F Thompson & Lt ACC Rawlins, OKs.
b.   A4245, No 16 Sqn, RFC, 2/Lts VF Stewart & JG Troup, departed at 1000, shot down at 1040, KIAs.
c.   French Spad, N 37, Adj F Garrigou, flying Spad VII N1377, MIA.
d.   A Belgian balloon.
e.   B1567, No 29 Sqn, RFC, 2/Lt AM Sutherland, POW.
f.   A6665, No 29 Sqn, RFC, Sgt WH Dunn, departed at 1905, POW.
g.   A6445, No 20 Sqn, RFC, 2/Lt GC Heseltine (P) WIA, forced to land near Brandhoek.

Losses:

| Ltn Lothar V Richthofen | 11 | Wounded in action near Arleux. |
| Ltn Oskar Lang | K1 | Killed in action near Karlsruhe. |

14 May 1917

Ltn H Pfeiffer	9	Salmson	Bois de Ville	0900	11	
Hptm F Walz	B	DH2	Vis-en-Artois	1115	7	a.
Ltn K Allmenröder	11	BE2e	E Guemappe	1130	14	b.
Obltn H Lorenz	33	Pup	S Estrées	1235	3	c.
Ltn W Kirchbach	35	Farman	Lusse-Wissenbach		zlg	

a.   A2622, No 32 Sqn, RFC, Capt WGS Curphy, MC, 6 victories, on balloon attack mission, KIA.
b.   2555, No 8 Sqn, RFC, Ltn JW Brown & EJ McCormick, departed at 0840, KIAs.
c.   N6158, No 3 Sqn, RNAS, F/S/Lt WR Walker, departed at 1300, last seen over Ecourt St Quentin.

Losses – Nil

15 May 1917

| Ltn J v Bertrab | 30 | FE2d | SE Quesnoy | 0830 | 5 | a. |
| Ltn K Pokrantz | 29 | Spad | S Pont Faverger | | 2 | |

a.   A6446, No 20 Sqn, RFC, S/Lt EJ Grout, RNVR, & 2/AM A Tyrrell, departed at 0554, POWs.

Losses:

| Ltn Karl Pockrantz | 29 | Killed in a mid-air collision with Lt Pollet, of N 102, S of Pont Faverger, who was also killed in Spad N1199. |

16 – 17 May 1917

No Claims – No Losses

18 May 1917

| Ltn K Allmenröder | 11 | BE2e | E Fontaine | 2005 | 15 | a. |
| Vfw R Jörke | 12 | Morane | Vraucourt | 2020 | – | |

a.   7074, No 12 Sqn, RFC, Lts B Strachan & AG Mackay, KIAs.

Losses:

| Vfw Edward Ey | 6 | Killed in an accident flying a SSW DI. |
| OfStv Ernst Kleimenhagen | K8 | Killed in an accident. |

19 May 1917

Obltn A v Tutschek	12	Triplane	E Eterpigny	0905	9	a.
Ltn K Allmenröder	11	Sopwith	Cuinchy	0910	16	b.
Ltn J Schmidt	3	Spad	N Sailly	1110	3	c.
Vfw K Holler	6	FE2b	Villers Guislain	1720	1	
Ltn O Bernert	6	FE2b	Villers Guislain	1720	zlg	d.
Ltn G-W Groos	4	Triplane	NW Izel	2055	1	e.
Ltn H Pfeiffer	9	Spad	S Moronvillers		–	

a.   N5461, No 1 Sqn, RNAS, F/S/Lt GG Bowman, crashed at Eterpigny, KIA.

b.   7074, No 12 Sqn, RFC.

c.   A6711, No 23 Sqn, RFC, Sgt CJ Abrahams, departed at 0935, KIA.

d.   A5457, No 22 Sqn, RFC, 2/Lts MS Goodban & PHB Ward, shot down in flames at about 1615 hours over Gouzeaucourt, KIAs.

e.   N5488, No 1 Sqn, RNAS, F/S/Lt Oliver OB Ellis, last seen over Hénin-Lietard, KIA.

Losses:

Ltn Georg Noth	B	Flying Albatros DIII 796/17, shot down wounded and taken prisoner by Capt WM Fry, No 60 Sqn, RFC. Died of wounds.
Ltn Karl Baur	3	Flying Albatros DIII 2139/16, killed over Guisnain airfield at 2000 hours.
Ltn Stobel	3	Killed in action.
Ltn Eberhard Fügner	4	Flying Albatros DIII 1969/16, killed at 2057 over Izel.
Ltn Karl Schöck	12	Killed by AA fire at 0740 between Dury and St Quentin.

20 May 1917

Uffz O Rosenfeld	12	FE	E Bullecourt	0807	2	
Obltn A v Tutschek	12	Spad	Riencourt	1110	10	a.
Ltn K Schäfer	28	FE2d	Hollebeke	1110	27	b.
Ltn H Kroll	9	Spad	St Hilaire-le-Petit	1850	4	
Ltn F Anslinger	35	Spad	Hochstadt		3	c.
Ltn H Bongartz	36	Balloon	Bouvancourt		6	
Ltn H Bongartz	36	Balloon	Villers-Marmery		7	

a.   B1587, No 23 Sqn, RFC, 2/Lt HT Garrett, departed at 0950, KIA.

b.   A6457, No 20 Sqn, RFC, Lt AC Lee & 2/AM C Beminster, POWs.

c.   MdL J Insard, Escadrille N 82, flying Spad VII No 1325, WIA/POW.

Losses:

Ltn Albert Münz	B	Killed in action N of Ecourt St Quentin.
Ltn Kurt Francke	B	Severely wounded in combat over Ecourt St Quentin, died of wounds 1 June 1917.
Ltn Hermann Pfeiffer	9	Killed in a flying accident.
Ltn Eberhard Voss	20	Killed in a flying accident.

21 May 1917

Ltn E Mohnicke	11	FE2d	Hulluch	1740	2	a.
Hptm P Backhaus	23	Spad	Aizy	1900	1	
Ltn W v Bülow	36	Balloon	Bouvancourt		14	b.
Ltn W v Bülow	36	Balloon	Bouvancourt		15	b.
Ltn T Quandt	36	Balloon	Bouvancourt		1	b.
Ltn T Quandt	36	Balloon	Bouvancourt		2	b.
Ltn H Bongartz	36	Balloon	Bouvancourt		5	b.
Ltn H Bongartz	36	Balloon	Villers Marmery		8	b.

a.   No 25 Sqn, RFC, 2/Lts JH Blackall & BC Moody, departed at 1435, seen going down E of Vermelles, WIA/POWs.

b.   Two French balloons were lost in this vicinity, those of the 59 and the 77 Compagnies d'Aérostières.

Losses:

Fw Paul Markwirth	7	Killed in an accident flying Roland DII 883/16.
Ltn Wolfgang Günther	17	Injured in an accident.
Ltn Hans v Schell	30	Injured in an accident at Phalempin flying Albatros DV 414/17.

22 May 1917

Vfw W Glinkermann	15	Spad	Beaurieux	2
Ltn H Bongartz	36	Spad	Prosnes	zlg

Losses:

Vfw Johann Schroth	35	Injured in an accident.

23 May 1917

Ltn W Voss	5	FE2b	N Havrincourt	1425	29	a.
Ltn K Schäfer	28	FE2d	Warneton	1615	28	b.
OfStv M Müller	28	FE2d	SW Houthem	1615	11	b.
Ltn K Schäfer	28	Pup	Wytschaetebogen	1845	29	c.
OfStv P Aue	10	Triplane	Carvin	2115	–	
Ltn H Hintsch	11	Triplane	Carvin	2115	3	d.
Ltn D Collin	22	Nieuport	SW Laffaux		3	
Ltn G Salzwedel	24	Spad	SW Fresnes		2	
Ltn H Bongartz	36	Balloon	W Prunay		8	
Uffz Tolischuss	K 3	Balloon	Croismare		–	

a.   A5502, No 18 Sqn, RFC, 2/Lt WF Macdonald & Lt FC Shackill, KIAs.
b.   A6467, No 20 Sqn, RFC, Lt RG Masson & 2/Lt FW Evans, KIAs.
c.   A665, No 46 Sqn, RFC, 2/Lt JP Stephen, KIA.
d.   N5481, No 8 Sqn, RNAS, F/S/Lt HA Pailthorpe, KIA.

Losses:

Obltn Rudolf Berthold	14	Injured in an accident.
Ltn Ernst Ritter und Edler von Lössl	18	Severely wounded in combat, died of wounds 24 May 1917.
Uffz Tolischuss	K3	Shot down, taken POW after a balloon attack.

24 May 1917

Ltn K Allmenröder	11	FE2b	Boiry	0850	17	a.
Ltn O Maashoff	11	Triplane	N Douai	0902	3	b.
Ltn K Allmenröder	11	Sopwith 2	Izel-Fe	0915	18	c.
Ltn v Beaulieu	7	Triplane	Monchy	0915	–	
Ltn J Schmidt	3	Pup	Monchy	0940	4	d.
Obltn R Greim	34	Spad	S Mamey	1050	zlg	
Obflgmt K Schönfelder	7	Sopwith	Hénin-Lietard	2020	–	
Ltn W Güttler	24	Spad	Prunay	2030	2	
OfStv M Müller	28	Nieuport	S St Eloi	2050	12	
Obltn E Dostler	34	Nieuport	Dieulouard		7	
Ltn F Anslinger	35	Spad	E Obertraubach		2	e.
Ltn J Kirchbach	35	Nieuport	S Neideraspach		1	f.

a.   A5517, No 11 Sqn, RFC, Lt WGD Turner, KIA & 2/Lt L Holman, WIA/POW.
b.   N5450, No 8 Sqn, RNAS, F/S/Lt HL Smith.
c.   A973, No 43 Sqn, RFC, Lt GM Goode & 2/Lt J Gagne, KIAs.
d.   A6194, No 66 Sqn, RFC, Capt LA Smith, POW.
e.   Cpl A Rondot, Escadrille N 92, flying a Spad VII, POW.
f.   Lt P Rigoulet, Escadrille N 92, flying a Nieuport, killed in combat over Traubach.

Losses:

Ltn Ernst Bauer	3	Flying Albatros DIII 2216/16, killed in combat over Villers-les-Cagnicourt.
Ltn Hans Hintsch	11	Albatros DIII 2016/16, KIA at 0930 over Izel, probably by F/Cdr CD Booker, No 8 Sqn, RNAS, his 24th victory.
Ltn Wilhelm Allmenröder	11	Flying Albatros DIII 776/17, was severely wounded in combat over Fonciers.
Ltn Willi Schunke	20	Killed over Le Catelet.
Ltn Karl Sonntag	37	Severely injured in an accident.

25 May 1917

Ltn P Strähle	18	Nieuport	Tenbrielen	0845	6	a.
Ltn A Hanko	28	FE2d	W Messines	0907	3	b.
Ltn K Allmenröder	11	Nieuport	Bois de Vert	1035	19	c.
Uffz F Gille	12	Spad	NE Monchy	1140	3	
Vfw K Bärenfänger	28	Sopwith 2	Langemarck	1205	1	d.
Obltn R Greim	34	Caudron	SE Rambucourt	1215	2	
Obltn H Lorenz	33	DH4	Ecourt St Quentin	1340	4	e.
Ltn J Hesselink	33	Spad	Guemappe	1400	–	
Ltn J Schmidt	3	FE2b	Gavrelle	1430	5	
Vfw K Schmelcher	4	BE	Arras	1850	–	
Ltn O v Breiten-Landenberg	9	Spad	W Moronvillers	2005	2	
Ltn H Kroll	9	Spad	Ft de la Pompelle	2015	5	f.
Ltn K Allmenröder	11	DH4	Monchy	2045	20	
Ltn R Matthaei	21	Nieuport	St Hilaire-le-Petit	2045	3	g.
Obltn E Schleich	21	Spad	Moronvillers	2100	1	
Ltn J Schmidt	3	Sopwith	Monchy-le-Preux		5	
Ltn R Wenzl	31	Caudron	Malmy		zlg	
Ltn sZ Rohe	MFJ1	FE2d	W Ypern		2	
Flgmt B Heinrich	MFJ1	Short 184	Westende		3	h.

a.   A6678, No 1 Sqn, RFC, 2/Lt JR Anthony, departed at 0657, KIA.
b.   A6366, No 20 Sqn, RFC, 2/Lt JH Baring-Gould, WIA, & Lt C A Coy, injured, shot down and forced to crash-land.
c.   A6776, No 60 Sqn, RFC, 2/Lt W Gilchrist, WIA/POW.
d.   A963, No 45 Sqn, RFC, 2/Lts J Johnstone & TS Millar, departed at 0910, POWs.
e.   A7409, No 55 Sqn, RFC, 2/Lts RE Jeffrey & PR Palmer, departed at 1155, seen to go down near Noyelles, KIAs.
f.   S/Lt R Dorme, 23 victories, Escadrille N 3, flying a Spad VII, KIA, departed at 1840 hours – KIA.
g.   Sgt Gross, Escadrille N 94, flying a Nieuport XVII, MIA.
h.   Possibly 9060, Dunkirk Seaplane Station, POWs, rescued by a U-boat.

Losses:

Vfw Heinrich Müller	15	Killed in an accident at Mortiers.
Ltn Alfons Paulus	21	Shot down in flames and killed at 1715 near Dontrien, probably by anti-aircraft fire.

26 May 1917

Ltn P Strähle	18	Nieuport	Mourveaux	0700	7	a.
Ltn F Hochstetter	12	Pup	Cagnicourt	0810	1	
Vfw K Schmelcher	4	BE	Oppy	1030	–	
Ltn W Voss	5	Pup	SW Gouzeaucourt	1545	30	b.
Vfw Dilcher	5	FE2b	Villers Plouich	1545	2	
Vfw R Jörke	12	Pup	Etaing	2015	3	
Uffz O Rosenfeld	12	SE5	S Etaing	2050	3	c.
Obltn H Bethge	30	Nieuport	Esquerchin	2055	6	d.
Ltn O Kissenberth	16	Spad	Somme-Py		4	e.
Ltn Strang	SFS2	Fr FBA			1	f.
Ltn Strang	SFS2	Fr FBA			2	f.
Vzflgmstr Müller	SFS2	Fr FBA			3	f.
Flgmt Burgstaller	SFS2	Fr FBA			2	f.

a.   B1685, No 1 Sqn, RFC, 2/Lt RR Macintosh, departed at 0550, POW.
b.   A6168, No 54 Sqn, RFC, 2/Lt MBGW Cole, WIA.
c.   A8902, No 56 Sqn, RFC, 2/Lt J Toogood, departed at 1830, last seen in combat over Gouz-sous-Bellone, WIA/POW.
d.   B1626, No 29 Sqn, RFC, 2/Lt GM Robertson, departed at 1915, POW.
e.   S/Lt A Cabaud (1v), N 37, flying a Spad VII, KIA.

f.   French Navy seaplanes from Dunkirk.

Losses:

OfStv Grigo	12	Wounded in action.
Ltn Eberhard Hänisch	15	Killed in combat over Chermizy, near Laon.
Uffz Erich Leyh	29	Killed in action over Caurel.

27 May 1917

Ltn J Hesselink	33	Pup	SE Hamblain	0730	1	a.
Vfw M Altemaier	33	SE5	NE Corbehem	0735	1	b.
Uffz Oppel	10	Sopwith	Fampoux	0745	–	
OfStv P Aue	10	SE5		0810	–	
Ltn K Schneider	5	FE2b	Quéant	0830	14	c.
OfStv M Müller	28	Sopwith 2	NE Ypern	1215	13	d.
Vfw A Haussmann	23	Balloon	SE Condé	1910	4	e.
Uffz E Barheine	35	Caudron	SW Wattweiler	2000	1	
Vfw Maier	36	Balloon	S Nauroy		1	f.

a.   A7340, No 66 Sqn, RFC, Lt SS Hume, POW.
b.   A8905, No 56 Sqn, RFC, 2/Lt EA Lloyd, POW.
c.   A5474, No 18 Sqn, RFC, 2/Lt E West-White & Sgt JR Cumberland, OKs.
d.   A8226, No 45 Sqn, RFC, Capt LW MacArthur, MC, & 2/Lt AS Carey, KIAs.
e.   French 42 Compagnie d'Aérostières, the observer, Asp Bouley, was not injured.
f.   French 64 Compagnie d'Aérostières, Sgt Icard OK, balloon not flamed.

Losses:

Ltn Jansen	K8	Injured in an accident.

28 May 1917

Ltn K Allmenröder	11	SE5	SW Feuchy	0830	21	a.
Ltn K Schuhmann	5	Nieuport	NE Lens	1310	1	b.
Ltn W Blume	26	Pup	Malincourt	1330	2	c.
Vfw O Könnecke	5	FE2d	Beaumont	1350	3	d.
Ltn W Voss	5	FE2d	SE Douai	1400	31	e.
Ltn K Schneider	5	SE5	Montigny	1400	15	
Ltn W Herwarth	22	Nieuport	Malmaison		1	
Ltn J Jacobs	22	Nieuport		–		

a.   B1575, No 60 Sqn, RFC, Maj AJL Scott, MC, OK.
b.   B1624, No 60 Sqn, RFC, 2/Lt RU Phalen, departed at 1100, KIA.
c.   B1715, No 66 Sqn, RFC, Lt RM Roberts, POW.
d.   A6410, No 25 Sqn, RFC, Lts TM Southorn & V Smith, departed at 1110, POWs.
e.   A6378, No 25 Sqn, RFC, Capt A de Selincourt & Lt H Cotton, POWs.

Losses:

Vfw Johannes Walter	36	Wounded in action.

29 May 1917

Ltn K Allmenröder	11	RE8	N Gavrelle	1750	22	a.
Vfw H Bowski	14	Spad	Filain		1	b.

a.   A4221, No 5 Sqn, RFC, 2/Lt JL Murray & Lt GM Dick, departed at 1500, seen to go down in flames, KIAs.
b.   Cpl E Perot, N 3, departed at 1825 flying a Spad VII, MIA.

Losses:

Vfw Willy Glinkermann	15	Killed in combat over Orgeval.

30 May 1917

Vfw C Holler	6	Pup	E Beaurevoir	0810	2	a.
Ltn J Wolff	17	Balloon	Berry-au-Bac	1415	3	

Ltn A Crüsemann	17	Balloon	Bouvancourt		1	
OfStv K Gregor	29	Balloon	Montbré		–	b.
Ltn H Kroll	24	Spad	S Moronvillers		–	

a.   B1721, No 54 Sqn, RFC, Lt PW Cantell, departed at 0545, came down E of Hesbecourt, POW.
b.   French 59 Compagnie d'Aérostières.

Losses:
Ltn Julius Völker   31   Severely injured in a landing accident.

31 May 1917

Obltn F-K Burckhardt	25	Nieuport	Caniste	0820	4	a.
Gefr J Funk	30	Balloon	Nieppe	1008	1	b.
Ltn J Veltjens	14	Spad	Oulches		4	

a   Serbian Escadrille N 524, Lt YE Allain-Launay & Sgt R Marc, KIAs.
b.   British balloon 9-6-2, the observers, 2/Lts H Cresswell and Jolly, made safe descents.

Losses:
Uffz Christoph Hertel   10   Injured in an accident.

Jasta Armee Assignments as of 1 June 1917

Western Front

1 Armee 16,17,21,24,29,36
2 Armee 2,5
3 Armee 31
4 Armee 4,6,8,10,18,20,27,28,36
5 Armee 14,22

6 Armee 3,7,11,12,26,30,31,33,37
7 Armee 1,9,13,15,23,32
Det 'A' 19
Det 'B' 35
Det 'C' 34

Other Fronts

11 Armee 25   Macedonia

1 June 1917

Obltn H Lorenz	33	Nieuport	S Hamblain	0620	5	a.
Ltn O Brauneck	11	RE8	Mericourt	1158	8	b.
Ltn J Veltjens	14	Spad	Moulins		5	c.
Ltn T Dahlmann	29	Balloon	Prosnes		1	d.
Obltn H Bethge	30	FE8	W Houthem	2130	7	e.

a.   B1583, No 29 Sqn, RFC, Lt EA Stewardson, departed at 0430, POW.
b.   A3265, No 16 Sqn, RFC, Lt WE McKissock & 2/Lt A W L Nixon, departed at 0925, KIAs.
c.   Probably Sgt C Durand, N 75, KIA in a Spad VII.
d.   British balloon 9-6-2 (BMS 4), 2/Lts S Jolley & H Cresswell, OK.
e.   A4887, No 41 Sqn, RFC, 2/Lt PCS O'Langan, departed at 1856, KIA.

Losses:
Vfw Ernst Dahlmann   5   Killed in combat between Cambrai and
    Gouzeaucourt.

2 June 1917

Ltn G Nolte	18	Pup	Coxyde	1000	3	a.
Ltn G Nolte	18	Nieuport	Thourout	1030	2	b.
Ltn E Wiessner	18	FE8	Zillebeke See	1100	4	
Ltn E Wenig	28	Pup	NE Ypern	1900	1	a.
Vfw O Gerbig	14	Caudron	Berry-au-Bac		3	

a.   No 46 Sqn, RFC.
b.   B1691, No 1 Sqn, RFC, 2/Lt RE Waters, departed 0750, POW.

Losses:

Ltn Paul Jänicke	22	KIA over Vecgny, near Soissons, in combat with N 65.	

3 June 1917

Ltn K Allmenröder	11	RE8	Monchy	0730	23	
Uffz M Meinberg	8	Sopwith 2	Menin	1645	1	a.
Vfw R Francke	8	Sopwith 2	Pembrouck	1645	1	a.
Vfw R Jörke	12	FE2b	Epéhy	1750	4	
Vfw O Gerbig	14	Sopwith 2	Corbeny	1850	4	
OfStv J Klein	27	Sopwith	Bousbecque	1850	2	b.
OfStv M Müller	28	Sopwith 2	Quesnoy	1900	14	
Obltn E Dostler	34	Spad	SE Belrupt		8	
Ltn H Adam	34	Caudron	W Belrupt		3	
Flgmt B Heinrich	MFJ1	Nieuport	N Ypern		4	
Fltmt Künstler	MFJ1	Nieuport	N Ypern		1	

a.　No 70 Sqn, RFC, lost two Sopwith two-seaters that departed at 1430 and last seen in the vicinity of Menin: A1012, 2/Lt RM Neill & Lt FW Harley, KIAs, and A981, Lt AS Bourinot, POW & Cpl A Giles, KIA.
b.　N6297, No 10 Sqn, RNAS, F/S/Lt PG McNeil, KIA.
Losses – Nil

4 June 1917

Ltn W Voss	5	Pup	Aubenscheul-aux-Bois	0710	32	a.
Vfw O Könnecke	5	FE2b	S Vendheuille	0720	4	b.
Vfw K Wittekind	28	SE5	NE Ypern	0840	1	c.
OfStv M Altemaier	33	Triplane	St Leger	0910	–	
Flgomt F Kühn	MFJ1	Sopwith	W Zonnebeke	1010	1	
Flgmstr O Haggemüller	MFJ1	Sopwith 2	N Frezenberg	1010	1	
Ltn Rohe	MFJ1	Sopwith 2	Polygonwald	1015	2	
Ltn K Schäfer	28	DH4	Moorslede	1410	30	d.
Ltn z S K Crüger	MFJ1	G100	Aeltre	1450	1	e.
Ltn K Allmenröder	11	RE8	SE Arras	1925	24	
Ltn K Allemnröder	11	RE8	Monchy	2215	25	

a.　B2151, No 54 Sqn, RFC, Capt RGH Pixley, MC, departed at 0500, POW.
b.　No 22 Sqn, RFC.
c.　A8920, No 56 Sqn, RFC, Lt TM Dickinson, departed at 0630, last seen west of Moorslede, WIA/POW.
d.　A7420, No 55 Sqn, RFC, 2/Lt DJ Honer & Pvt G Cluncy, departed at 1210, last seen SW of Ingelmünster, KIAs.
e.　A1566, No 27 Sqn, RFC, 2/Lt DT Steeves, departed 1215, POW.
Losses:

Ltn Georg Simon	11	Albatros DIII 2015/16 (G.42), shot down at 1925 between Fontaine & Heniel, and taken POW, by Capt CMB Chapman, No 29 Sqn, RFC.
Vfw Wilhelm Eichenauer	15	Killed in combat over Filain after a balloon attack, probably by Adj L Jailler, N 15, who claimed his 11th victory E of Filain.
OfStv Matthais Dennecke	18	Killed in combat over Houthem, possibly by Lt TF Hazell No 1 Sqn, RFC.

5 June 1917

Ltn F Kempf	B	Pup	Masnières	0840	1	a.
Ltn W Voss	5	FE2b	N Vaucelles	0930	33	b.
Ltn K Allmenröder	11	Sopwith 2	Terhand	1120	26	c.
Ltn O Brauneck	11	Sopwith 2	Terhand	1120	9	c.
Ltn A Niederhoff	11	Sopwith 2	S Ypern	1130	3	c.

Ltn R Runge	18	Sopwith 2	Dadizeele	1130	2	c.
Obltn H Bethge	30	Spad	W Frélinghein	1245	8	d.
Vfw W Reiss	3	Nieuport	N Lambres	2135	2	e.
Ltn W Kirchbach	35	Spad	Gewenheim		2	
Ltn T Osterkamp	MFJ1	Triplane	Nieuport		3	

a.   B1729, No 54 Sqn, RFC, 2/Lt BG Chambers, departed at 0625, POW.
b.   A857, No 22 Sqn, RFC, Capt FP Don & 2/Lt H Harris, last seen SW of Lesdains, WIA/POWs.
c.   No 45 Sqn, RFC, lost three Sopwith two-seaters that departed at 0900 this date: A 8280, 2/Lt B Smith & 2/AM S Thompson, departed at 0900, WIA/POWs; A1925, S/Lt RS Binnie & Lt TA Metheral, KIAs; 8268, Sgt EA Cook & 2/AM HV Shaw, MIAs.
d.   A6747, No 19 Sqn, RFC, 2/Lt CD Grierson, departed 1001, POW.
e.   B1548, No 40 Sqn, RFC, Capt ATL Allcock, departed at 1922, KIA.

Losses:

Ltn Oskar v Schickfuss und Neudorff	3	Flying an Albatros DIII (G 43), shot down and killed at 0938 over Monchy, by Major AJ Scott, CO No 60 Sqn, RFC.
Ltn Kurt Schneider	5	Wounded in action by Capt CM Clement & 2/Lt LG Davies, No 22 Sqn, RFC, DOW 14 July 1917.
Vfw Heinrich Küllmer	6	Wounded in action.
Ltn Karl Emil Schäfer	28	Killed at 1605, by Lts HL Satchell and TAMS Lewis, No.20 Sqn, RFC.

6 June 1917

Vfw R Francke	8	SE5	NE Hooglede	1030	2	a.
Ltn W Voss	5	Nieuport	W Graincourt	1310	34	b.
Vfw R Riessinger	12	Pup	SE Inchy	1310	2	
Vfw O Rosenfeld	12	Nieuport	Moeuvres	1310	4	
Ltn O Hunzinger	B	Pup	N Inchy	1315	–	
Ltn Strobel	5	Pup	NW Moeuvres	1315	–	
Ltn H Becker	12	Pup	SW Sains	1320	1	c.
Vfw F Krebs	6	AW	SE Le Catelet	1355	3	d.

a.   A8899, Lt H Hamer, last seen N of Roulers, KIA.
b.   N3204, No 6 Sqn, RNAS, F/Lt FP Reeves, departed at 1030, KIA.
c.   B1730, No 54 Sqn, RFC, Maj CE Sutcliffe, KIA.
d.   A2693, No 35 Sqn, RFC, Lts GW Devenish & HCK Cotterill, departed at 1030, seen in flames near Fremont, KIAs.

Losses:

Vfw Paul Bona	1	Killed in combat over Allemont at 1205.
Ltn Werner Voss	5	Wounded in action by 6 Naval Sqn.

7 June 1917   The First Battle of Messines begins.

Uffz H Brettel	10	Spad	S Rumbeke	0720	1	a.
Yffz J Heiligers	30	FE2d	Koelberg	0800	1	b.
OfStv P Aue	10	Spad	Coucou	0815	5	c.
OfStv M Müller	28	Spad	Comines	0815	15	d.
OfStv M Müller	28	Pup	S Roulers	1145	16	e.
Vfw H Oberländer	30	Pup	Roulers	1145	2	f.
Flgmstr O Haggenmüller	MFJ1	Nieuport	Bixschoote	1205	2	g.
Hptm G Stenzel	8	Nieuport	Polygonwald	1445	4	
Ltn E Wiessner	18	RE8	Hollebeke	1710	5	h.
Ltn zS G Sachsenberg	MFJ1	Pup	Potyze		5	i.
Ltn zS G Sachsenberg	MFJ1	FE2d	St Eloi		4	j.
Ltn zS G Sachsenberg	MFJ1	Sopwith	Gheluvelt		–	
Flgmt Künstler	MFJ1	Nieuport	Gheluvelt		2	

a.   3460, No 23 Sqn, RFC, 2/Lt Count LBT de Balme, departed at 0422, POW.

b.　A1957, No 25 Sqn, RFC, 2/Lt GH Pollard (WIA/POW) & Lt FS Ferriman, KIA, departed at 0610.

c.　B1524, No 23 Sqn, RFC, 2/Lt FW Illingsworth, departed at 0635, POW.

d.　B1527, No 23 Sqn, RFC, 2/Lt GC Stead, departed at 0630, POW.

e.　A6157, No 46 Sqn, RFC, Lt AP Mitchell, departed at 0910, WIA/POW.

f.　A7314, No 66 Sqn, RFC, 2/Lt RM Marsh, POW.

g.　B1674, No 40 Sqn, RFC, Lt JW Shaw, departed at 0950, POW.

h.　4210, No 6 Sqn, RFC, Lt A JE Phillipo KIA & 2/Lt F V Durkin POW, departed at 1530, seen to crash E of Hollebeke.

i.　No 3 Sqn, RNAS.

j.　A6403, No 20 Sqn, RFC, 2/Lt BS Marshall, MC, & Pvt C Lloyd, departed at 1517, KIAs.

Losses:

Ltn P Lohmann	14	Wounded in action.
Ltn Ernst Wiessner	18	Killed in action at 1750 near Wambeke, N Warneton, probably by Capts FH Thayre & FR Cubbon, of No 20 Sqn, RFC.
Vfw Franz Eberlein	33	Wounded in action, remained with jasta.
Flgomt Fritz Kühn	MFJ1	Shot down and taken prisoner, later died of wounds at Staden.

8 June 1917

Ltn H Göring	27	Nieuport	Moorslede	0730	8	a.
Vzflgmstr Bottler	MFJ1	Triplane	N Warneton	1125	1	b.
Obltn B v Voigt	8	Nieuport	W Dadizeele	1415	1	c.
Obltn K Mettlich	8	Pup	Moorslede	1420	1	d.
Obltn K Mettlich	8	Pup	Moorslede	1420	2	e.
OfStv Max Müller	28	Triplane	Quesnoy	1910	17	f.

a.　B1656, No 1 Sqn, RFC, 2/Lt FD Slee, departed at 0525, last seen over Becelaere, POW.

b.　N5491, No 1 Sqn, RNAS, F/Lt TG Culling, DSC, KIA.

c.　B1644, No 1 Sqn, RFC, 2/Lt RSL Boote, departed at 1135, last seen over Becelaere, POW.

d.　A6207, No 66 Sqn, RFC, 2/Lt AG Robertson, KIA.

e.　B1745, No 66 Sqn, RFC, 2/Lt AV Shirley, KIA.

f.　N6295, No 1 Sqn, RNAS, F/S/Lt TR Swinburne, KIA.

Losses:

Vfw Grigo	12	Wounded in action.
Vfw Franz Bucher	30	Killed in action over Wervicq.

9 June 1917

Vfw R Francke	8	Nieuport	Menin	0940	3	a.
Obltn K v Döring	4	Nieuport	Zandvoorde	1525	3	b.
Ltn A Hübner	4	Spad	Zillebeke	1555	zlg	

a.　B1550, 29 Sqn, RFC, 2/Lt WJ Mussared, left at 0735, last seen E of Gheluwe, POW.

b.　B3481, 1 Sqn, RFC, Lt F Sharp departed at 1327, last seen near Gheluwe, POW.

Losses – Nil

10–11 June 1917

No Claims – No Losses

12 June 1917

Vfw K Wittekind	28	RE8	Wytschaete	1100	2	a.

a.　A4207, No 53 Sqn, RFC, 2/Lt W Turnbull & Lt WB Protheroe, KIAs.

Losses:

Vfw Otto Rosenfeld	12	Wounded in action.
Hptm Eberhardt v Seel	17	Shot down in flames during combat with a Spad near Montigny.
OfStv Martin Altmaier	33	Flying Albatros DIII 2146/16, killed at 1210, N of Monchy-le-Preux.

13 June 1917

| Uffz F Gille | 12 | Triplane | St Laurent | 2105 | 4 | |

Losses:
Ltn Phillip Wieland   8   Wounded in action.

14 June 1917

| Vfw F Krebs | 6 | Triplane | W Poezelhoek | 0830 | 4 | a. |
| Ltn K Küppers | 6 | SE5 | NW Dadizeele | 2030 | 3 | b. |

a.   N5470, No 10 Sqn, RNAS, F/S/Lt LH Parker, last seen at 0720 near Zonnebeke, KIA.
b.   A8919, No 56 Sqn, RFC, Lt H Rogerson, departed at 1800, POW.

Losses:
Vzflgmstr Kurt Lichtherz   MFJ1   Killed in combat over Middlekerke, 0930.
Vzflgmstr Bottler   MFJ1   Wounded in action at 0930 near Ghistelles.

The First Battle of Messines ends.

15 June 1917

Vfw H Bowski	14	Nieuport	SE Ailles	0730	2	a.
Vfw R Riessinger	12	RE8	Quéant	1415	3	b.
Ltn P Billik	12	Morane	S Bullecourt	1545	zlg	c.
Vfw K Wüsthoff	4	Spad	Voormzeele	2130	1	
Ltn G Schuster	17	Caudron	Berry-au-Bac		2	

a.   Possibly Cpl P Rey, N 80, flying a Nieuport XXIVbis, shot down in flames at 0625 hours near Heurtebise, only French Nieuport lost this date.
b.   A4310, No 15 Sqn, RFC, 2/Lts J De Conway & AH Powell, departed at 1235, KIAs.
c.   No 3 Sqn, RFC, 2/Lt AMcN Denavon, WIA, and his aircraft was shot up.

Losses:
Gefr Paul Laukandt   13   Killed in combat over Foucaucourt.
Obltn Heinrich Lorenz   6   Wounded in action

16 June 1917

Ltn H Klein	4	RE8	Messines	1200	10	a.
Vfw L v Raffay	6	FE2d	NE Ypern	1835	2	
Obltn E Dostler	6	FE2d	W Ypern	1850	9	
Obltn E Dostler	6	Sopwith 2	Korentje	1905	10	b.
FwLt F Schubert	6	Sopwith 2	NE Messines	1906	zlg	c.
Vfw R Riessinger	12	Nieuport	Buissy	2130	4	d.

a.   A6572, No 20 Sqn, RFC, 2/Lt PJ Gardiner, WIA, & Pvt J MacLeod, OK, aircraft shot up during combat.
b.   A381, No 45 Sqn, RFC, 2/Lt TStG Caulfield & Pvt G Edwards, departed at 1700, KIAs.
c.   A1021, No 45 Sqn, RFC, 2/Lts WA Wright & DC Eglington, MC, OKs, their aircraft badly damaged in combat.
d.   B1610, No 60 Sqn, RFC, Lt DRC Lloyd, departed at 1935, last seen over Marquion, KIA.

Losses:
Vfw Leopold v Raffay   6   Wounded in action.
Ltn Friedrich v Hartmann   9   Killed in a mid-air collision with Vfw G Stemmler during combat practice.

Vfw Gottfried Stemmler   9   See above – injured.
Vfw Robert Riessinger   12   Killed in a collision with Nieuport B1610, Lt DRC Lloyd of No 60 Sqn, RFC, S of Buissy.

Ltn Hermann Becker   12   Wounded in action.
Vfw Eugen Weiss   29   Wounded in action.

17 June 1917

| Ltn M Pollandt | 6 | SE5 | Beaucamps | 0955 | 1 | a. |

Vfw F Krebs	6	SE5	Beaucamps	1002	5	a.
Ltn J Schmidt	3	Spad	Liévin	2040	zlg	b.
Obltn E Schleich	21	Sopwith 2	Thuizy	2045	2	
Obltn E Dostler	6	FE2d	St Eloi	2120	11	c.
Vfw K Jentsch	1	Spad	Berry-au-Bac	–		

a. No 56 Sqn, RFC, lost two SE5s that departed at 0800, and last seen over Hanbourin, this date: A8922, Lt WT Coles, POW and A4862, 2/Lt HG Spearpoint, POW.
b. No 23 Sqn, RFC, Capt AB Wright, WIA.
c. A6469, No 20 Sqn, RFC, Lts N Boucher & W Birkett, shot down in flames, but both were only wounded.
Losses:

Obltn Georg Zeumer	B	Killed in combat at 1000 during combat with an RE8 SE of Honnecourt.
Uffz Fritz Pohlmann	31	Killed in an accident during a test flight.

18 June 1917

Ltn K Allmenröder	11	Nieuport	Verlorenhoek	0950	27	a.
Rittm M v Richthofen	JGI	RE8	NE Ypern	1315	53	b.
Ltn H Klein	4	RE8	Messines	1530	10	
Ltn L Hanstein	16	Balloon	Verdun		4	c.

a. B1638, No 1 Sqn, RFC, 2/Lt RS Lloyd, departed at 0805, KIA.
b. A4290, No 9 Sqn, RFC, Lt RW Ellis & Lt HC Barlow, departed at 1100, both KIAs.
c. French 58 Compagnie d'Aérostières, the observer Adj Moulard made a safe descent.
Losses:

Vfw Walter Dittrich	1	Wounded in action.
Ltn Walter Bordfeld	11	Killed in combat over Zandvoorde.
Vfw Gustav Schindler	35	Wounded in combat over Galsingen, in combat with two-seaters.

19 June 1917

Ltn O Kissenberth	16	Balloon	Aubreville		5	a.
Ltn K Odebrett	16	Nieuport	Chattancourt		2	
Vzflgmt Bieber	SSFII	Sopwith			1	
Ltn Bachmann	SSFII	Sopwith			1	
Vzflgmt W Dyck	SSFII	Sopwith			1	

a. French 38 Compagnie d'Aérostières, Adj Pierrot made a safe descent.
Losses – Nil

20 June 1917

Ltn G Rose	25	Nieuport	Rastani	0730	1	
Vfw R Treptow	25	Nieuport	Monastir	0730	2	a.
Obltn E Dostler	6	Balloon	W Nieppe	1800	12	b.
Ltn E Reiher	6	Balloon	W Nieppe	1800	1	c.
OfStv M Müller	28	RE8	Armentières	1900	18	

a. Serbian Escadrille N 503.
b. British balloon 9-6-2 (BM 98), Lt H Olivier & 2/Lt H Cresswell, OK.
c. British balloon 32-6-2 (BM 99/D), Capt P G Bateman & 2/Lt W F M Forrest, OK.
Losses – Nil

21 June 1917

Ltn O Fuchs	30	BF2b	SE Izel	0800	1	a.
Hptm O Hartmann	28	Pup	Rollenberghe	1055	3	b.
Obltn E Schleich	21	Caudron	W Aubérive	1115	3	
Ltn K Wewer	26	Nieuport	Becelaere	1145	1	c.

Uffz J Heiligers	30	Nieuport	Beaumont	1940	–

a.   A7139, No 11 Sqn, RFC, 2/Lt DCH MacBrayne (P) KIA & Sgt W Mollison (G) POW, last seen at 0645 going east between Bailleul and Oppy.

b.   B1707, No 46 Sqn, RFC, 2/Lt HAC Tonks, last seen at 1030, MIA.

c.   B3495, No 1 Sqn, RFC, 2/Lt TM McFerran, departed at 0913, last seen in combat over Polygon Wood, POW.

Losses:

Obltn Eduard Dostler	6	12 victories; injured in an accident.
Ltn Otto Maashoff	11	3 victories; wounded in action.
Ltn Heinrich Russel	28	Killed in combat over Gheluwe.

22 June 1917

Obflgmstr K Meyer	MFJ1	DH4	SW Dixmuide	2145	8	a.

a.   A7443, No 57 Sqn, RFC, Lt PH Bigwood, KIA.

Losses:

Uffz Fritz Wistermann	1	Wounded in action.

23 June 1917

Ltn H Klein	4	Balloon	S Ypern	1443	11	a.
Vfw K Wüsthoff	4	Balloon	S Ypern	1443	2	b.
Vfw E Clausnitzer	4	Balloon	S Ypern	1443	2	c.
Uffz K Jentsch	1	Spad	NW La Fère	2110	4	
Vfw Bussmann	1	Spad	N La Fère	2115	1	
Rittm M v Richthofen	JGI	Spad	N Ypern	2115	54	d.

a.   British balloon 38-7-2 (BMS 116/D), Lt A Rowbottom, OK.

b.   British balloon 2-5-2 (FM 68), 2/Lt O L Vetter, OK.

c.   British balloon 32-6-2 (BM 107), 2/Lts W F M Forrest & H Browne, OK.

d.   B1530 23 Sqn RFC, Lt R W Farquhar unhurt.

Losses – Nil

24 June 1917

Ltn K Allmenröder	11	Triplane	Polygonwald	0920	28	a.
Ltn G-W Groos	11	Triplane	Keibergmolen	0920	2	b.
Rittm M v Richthofen	JGI	DH4	Becelaere	0930	55	c.
Ltn H Klein	4	Balloon	N Armentières	1240	12	d.
Ltn H Gontermann	15	Balloon	Pontavert	1515	22	e.
Uffz J Heiligers	30	Nieuport	SW Beaumont	1940	2	f.
Ltn K Müller	9	Balloon	Chaude Fontaine	2020	1	g.
Ltn H Dannenberg	13	Nieuport	Versigny		2	h.
Obltn E Schleich	21	Balloon	Guyencourt		4	
OfStv Fahlke	37	Spad	SE Kemmel		1	i.
Uffz Ruckser	37	Spad			–	
Ltn Skarupke	37	Caudron			–	

a.   N6303, No 10 Sqn, RNAS, F/S/Lt AB Holcroft, KIA.

b.   N5358, No 10 Sqn, RNAS, F/S/Lt RS Saunders, KIA.

c.   A7473, No 57 Sqn, RFC, Capt NG McNaughton, MC, & Lt AH Mearns last seen over Becelaere at 0830, KIAs.

d.   British balloon 32-6-2 (BM131/D), 2/Lt B P Fletcher & Lt W J E Griffiths, OK .

e.   French 65 Compagnie d'Aérostières.

f.   B1607, No 29 Sqn, RFC, Capt WP Holt, KIA.

g.   French 90 Compagnie d'Aérostières.

h.   Nieuport XVII #2523, N 67, Cpl R Hegy, departed at 0615, POW.

i.   Possibly B1531, No 23 Sqn, RFC, 2/Lt DP Collins, injured in crash-landing after being shot up during combat.

Losses:

Ltn Erich Reiher	6	Shot down and killed in his Albatros DIII (G 49) during a balloon attack on the 12th Balloon Section.		
Ltn Georg Weiner	20	Injured in an accident.		

25 June 1917

OfStv K Lang	1	Spad	Chaillevois	1130	1	a.
Rittm M v Richthofen	JGI	RE8	Le Bizet	1720	56	b.
Ltn K Allmenröder	11	Triplane	W Quesnoy	1845	29	c.
Ltn O Schmidt	7	Balloon	Elsendamen		3	

a.   Spad VII #5128, Sgt Michel, N 84, departed at 0930 and was shot down near Laon.
b.   A3847, No 53 Sqn, RFC, Lt LS Bowman & 2/Lt JE Power-Clutterbuck, KIAs.
c.   N5376, No 10 Sqn, RNAS, F/S/Lt GE Nash, 6 victories, POW.
Losses – Nil

26 June 1917

Vfw K Schattauer	23	Spad	NE Ostel	1900	1	
Ltn K Allmenröder	11	Nieuport	N Hollebeke	2200	30	a.
Vfw H Bowski	14	Spad	Cerny		3	
Ltn E Thuy	21	Spad	Cauroy		3	
Ltn J Jacobs	7	Spad	Pontavert		–	

a.   B1649, No 1 Sqn, RFC, Lt C Street, departed at 0756, last seen in combat over Becelaere, KIA.
Losses – Nil

27 June 1917

Ltn H Gontermann	15	Balloon	SE Reims	1200	23	a.
Ltn A Dossenbach	10	Balloon	Ypern	1610	15	b.
Ltn O Schmidt	7	Balloon	Welsvlederen	1830	4	b.
Vfw F Schmitt	7	Balloon	Elverdinghe	1830	1	b.
Obltn B v Voigt	8	Spad	N Bixschoote	2000	2	c.
Ltn O v Nostitz	12	Nieuport	S Haucourt	2000	2	
Ltn B Knake	12	Nieuport	Croiselles	2000	1	d.
Ltn K Wolff	29	Nieuport	SW Noyelles	2030	31	e.
Ltn J Jacobs	7	Spad	Cerny		–	

a.   51 Compagnie d'Aérostières, the observer, Sgt Leclerc made a safe descent.
b.   Only two British balloons lost this date: 15-7-2 (BMS129/D) and 39-8-5 (BMS60).
c.   B1663, No 19 Sqn, RFC, Lt M Lawe, departed at 1756, last seen over Houthulst Forest, KIA.
d.   B1572, No 29 Sqn, RFC, 2/Lt D Bird, departed at 1800, KIA.
e.   A6718, No 60 Sqn, RFC, Lt DCG Murray, departed at 1900, POW.
Losses:

Ltn Karl Allmenröder	11	Killed by AA fire at 0945 over Zillebeke.
Vfw Moritz Förster	32	Killed at 1000 hours over St Hilaire-le-Petit.

28 June 1917

Vfw Bock	25	Spad	Wischnew		2	

Losses – Nil

29 June 1917

Ltn P Billik	12	Nieuport	Plouvain	0910	3	a.
Ltn O Kunst	22	Nieuport	SW Vailly	1530	1	
OfStv K Gregor	29	Nieuport	SW Fresnoy	1910	1	

a.   B1677, No 29 Sqn, RFC, Lt VA Noryill, departed at 0650, WIA/POW.

Losses:

Ltn Alfred Ulmer	8	Flying an Albatros DV when shot down in in flames,1415 over Hollebeke, by Lt HW Joslyn and Pvt EA Potter of No 20 Sqn, RFC.

30 June 1917

No Claims – No Losses

Jasta Armee Assignments as of 1 July 1917

Western Front

1 Armee 19,21	6 Armee 2,12,29,30,31,33,37
2 Armee 2,5	7 Armee 1,9,13,15,22,23
3 Armee –	Det 'A' –
4 Armee 4,6,7,8,10,11,17,18,20,24,26,27,28,36	Det 'B' 35
5 Armee 14,16,32	Det 'C' 34

Other Fronts

11 Armee 25   Macedonia
 1 Armee 38   Bulgarian Armee
Kuk 2 Armee OberOst Russia

1 July 1917

No Claims – No Losses

2 July 1917

Rittm M v Richthofen	JGI	RE8	Deulemont	1020	57	a.
Ltn G Groos	11	RE8	Messines	1025	3	b.
Ltn G Pastor	29	Rumpf DD	Vimy	1050	–	
Uffz K Rahier	31	BE	Chérisy	1730	–	
Vfw R Treptow	25	Nieuport	Cerna-Sumpfe		3	
Ltn G Rose	25	Farman	Puturos		2	

a.   A3538, No 53 Sqn, RFC, Sgt HA Whatley (P) & 2/Lt FGB Pascoe (O), KIA.
b.   A3249, No 53 Sqn, RFC, Capt WP Harsley, MC, KIA, & 2/Lt AG Knight, WIA.

Losses

Ltn Horst Hellinger	5	Flying an Albatros DV (G.50), killed by AA fire of KBS 12 during a balloon attack near Hendecourt.
Ltn Hans Forstmann	30	Killed in action at 1130 near Dourges canal by Capt AE Godfrey, No 40 Sqn, RFC.

3 July 1917

Obltn A v Tutschek	12	Sopwith 2	N Vaulx	1030	11	
Ltn P Billik	12	Nieuport	SW Villers	1920	4	a.

a.   Cpl de la Torre, N 77, flying a Nieuport XXIV, missing in action. Only French Nieuport lost this date.

Losses

Ltn Albert Dossenbach	10	Killed in action during combat with DH4s of 57 Sqn RFC over Frezenberg.
Lt z S Kurt Krüger	MFJ1	Wounded in action.

4 July 1917

Obltn O Schmidt		32	Farman	S Pohlberg		zlg

Losses:

Ltn Walter Kirchbach	35	Killed in action at 1850 near Hartwald, in Albatros DIII 2085/16.

5 July 1917

Obltn E Dostler	6	Balloon	N Ypern	1820	13	a.
Obltn F-K Burckhardt	25	Farman	NE Monastir		5	b.
Ltn R Otto	ObOst	Farman	E Pomorzany		zlg	

a.   British Balloon 4-13-5 (BMS 106D).
b.   Escadrille MF 503.
Losses – Nil

6 July 1917

Vfw F Rumey	5	Balloon	Ytres	1000	1	a.
Ltn K Wissemann	3	BF2b	N Cambrai	1020	1	b.
Vfw F Jacobsen	31	BF2b	Sailly	1050	1	b.
Obltn O Schmidt	32	Spad	Guyencourt	1150	5	c.
Ltn W v Bülow	36	Spad	St Julien	1245	16	d.
Ltn H Rolfes	32	Farman	Moronvillers	1320	1	
Vfw K Starck	32	Farman	Keilberg	1330	1	
Ltn H Klein	4	Sopwith 2	S Ypern	1515	13	
Ltn G Pastor	29	AWFK8	W Lens	1545	1	
FlgMt B Heinrich	MFJ1	Triplane	Reckem	1650	5	e.
Ltn K Wolff	11	RE8	Zillebeke	2120	32	f.
Vfw Klüpfel	ObOst	Farman	Mlynowcze		1	
Vfw Klüpfel	ObOst	Balloon	S Zborow		2	
Ltn J Jacobs	22	Spad			–	

a.   British Balloon 41-15-4.
b.   No 48 Sqn, RFC, lost two BFs this date both departed at 0750 and were seen to go down near Cambrai: A7137, 2/Lt H Smither (P) & 2/Lt HC Clarke, and A7109, Lt HC Farnes (P) & Cpl JT Park (G). Only two BFs claimed and only two lost this date.
c.   Possibly Sgt R Lecomte, N 103, FTL at 1040 hours after a combat.
d.   B3475, 2/Lt WH Clark, No 23 Sqn, RFC, last seen over Houthulst Wood at 1140.
e.   N5435, No 1 Sqn, RNAS, F/S/Lt EC Hillaby, KIA.
f.   A 4313 4 Sqn RFC 2/Lt JY Taylor & Lt G Mutch DSO. KIAs.
Losses

Rittm Manfred von Richthofen	JGI	Wounded in action by Capt DC Cunnell & 2/Lt AE Woodbridge, No 20 Sqn, RFC.
Vfw Hermann Denkhaus	7	KIA, probably by Capt CW Warman, No. 23 Sqn, RFC.
Vfw Manfred Stimmel	32	Shot down and taken POW at 1150 between Courcy and Thil near Reims, by Capitaine Georges Matton and Lt Armand de Turenne, N 48, for their 9th and 4th victories.

7 July 1917

Ltn K Wolff	11	Triplane	Comines	1100	33	a.
Ltn R Krüger	4	Triplane	W Wervicq	1105	1	b.
Vfw F Altemeier	24	Triplane	Bousbecque	1105	2	c.
Ltn A Niederhoff	11	Triplane	Bousbecque	1110	4	c.
Vfw F Krebs	6	RE8	S Zillebeke	1135	6	
Vfw M Krauss	27	RE8	NW Ypern	1145	1	
Obltn E Dostler	6	DH4	SW Warneton	1200	14	d.
Vfw E Clausnitzer	4	Nieuport	Zillebeke	1430	3	
Ltn H Klein	4	Sopwith 2	Comines	1807	14	
Vfw J Lautenschlager	11	Sopwith 2	W Comines	1810	1	

Ltn F Anders	4	Sopwith	Hollebeke	1820	1	e.
Ltn W v Bülow	36	FE2d	Hooge	1940	17	f.
Ltn H Bongartz	36	FE2d	Ypern	1945	9	g.

a.   N 6309, No 1 Sqn, RNAS, F/S/Lt HK Millward.
b.   N 5480, No 1 Sqn, RNAS, F/S/Lt DW Ramsey,.
c.   N 6291, No 1 Sqn, RNAS, F/Cdr CA Eyre, Niederhoff is probably the victor as it was a JG I combat with Naval 1, also possible that Altemeier got him.
d.   A7493, No 55 Sqn, RFC, Lt PW Battersby & Capt WW Fitzherbert, departed at 0850, last seen over Lille, KIAs.
e.   N6462, No 9 Sqn, RNAS, F/S/Lt JC Tanner.
f.   A6494, No 20 Sqn, RFC.
g.   A6498, No 20 Sqn, RFC, Lt T Crafter, MC, POW/DOW & Sgt WDA Backhouse, KIA.
Losses
Ltn Reinhold Oertelt   19   KIA at 1110 near Cauroy, by Capt Georges Guynemer of Spa 3, for his 47th victory.

---

8 July 1917

Ltn F Vossen	33	Balloon	SE Arras	2105	2	a.
Ltn F Kuke	33	Rumpf DD	Inchy	2130	–	
Ltn M Schön	ObOst	Balloon	Jezierna		1	
Vfw Klüpfel	ObOst	Nieuport	Batkow		zlg	

a.   British balloon 24-21-1 – not flamed.
Losses – Nil

---

9 July 1917

No Claims – No Losses

---

10 July 1917

Vfw G Strasser	17	Sopwith	S Nieuport	2100	4	a.

a.   MdL C Gauthier and Soldat A Denis, N 31, shot down and taken prisoner flying Morane-Saulnier No.937. Only French combat loss this date; no RFC losses.
Losses – Nil

---

11 July 1917

Vfw J Buckler	17	Triplane	SE Zillebeke	0850	8	
Ltn H Bongartz	36	Triplane	S Tenbrielen	0900	10	
Ltn R Runge	18	Nieuport	Becelaere	0940	3	
Ltn H Klein	4	Balloon	S Ypern	1510	15	
Ltn H Klein	4	Balloon	S Ypern	1510	16	
Vfw K Wüsthoff	4	Balloon	S Ypern	1510	3	
Obltn A v Tutschek	12	RE8	Thelus	1815	12	
Obltn A v Tutschek	12	FE2d	Monchy	1845	13	
Ltn O Creutzmann	20	DH4	Ledeghem	1945	1	a.
Ltn W Blume	26	Triplane	Comines	2100	3	b.
Ltn E Mohnicke	11	Triplane	W Comines	2115	3	b.
Vfw L Patermann	4	Sopwith	W Houthem	2140	2	
Ltn sZ T Osterkamp	MFJ1	Sopwith 2	N Furnes	2145	4	

a.   A7484, No 57 Sqn, RFC, 2/Lt R Trattles (P) & 2/Lt AJ Savory (O), departed at 1700, last seen over Roulers, POWs. Only DH4 claimed and lost this date.
b.   Naval 10 lost one aircraft during a fight at 2045 hours over Polygon Wood: N5357 'K' F/S/Lt R Kent taken prisoner.
Losses
Ltn Kurt Wolff   11   Wounded in action at 1020.
Vfw Rotzczinka   7   Wounded in action.

12 July 1917

Ltn W Güttler	24	Triplane	Klein Zillebeke	0850	3	a.
Uffz P Bäumer	5	Balloon	Nurlu	1000	1	
Ltn F Vossen	33	Sopwith 2	W St Quentin	1050	1	
Obltn E Dostler	6	Nieuport	Houthem	1150	15	b.
Ltn K Deilmann	6	Nieuport	Hollebeke	1150	4	b.
Ltn F Götte	20	Camel	Slype	1155	1	c.
Obltn W Jahns	18	Spad	Quesnoy	1515	1	d.
Obltn A v Tutschek	12	Balloon	NW Lens	1800	14	e.
Obltn E Schleich	21	AR2	SW Bethélainville	1805	5	
Ltn H Adam	6	Sopwith	E Dickebusch	1835	4	f.
Ltn K Küppers	6	Sopwith	Wtyschaete	1940	4	
Vfw F Altemeier	24	Spad	Zillebeke See	2000	3	
Ltn zS T Osterkamp	MFJ1	Sopwith	Zandvoorde	2100	5	
Vfw O Marquardt	4	SE5	Zandvoorde	2105	1	
Ltn A Hübner	4	Triplane	Zuidschote	2120	1	
Vfw J Heiligers	30	G100	Annequin	2125	zlg	
Ltn H Bongartz	36	Sopwith	SE Zillebeke	2135	11	
Obltn E Dostler	6	Sopwith	Zillebeke	2145	16	
Ltn A Kuen	14	Caudron	E Cernay		2	g.
Ltn L Hanstein	16	AR2	Vauquois		5	h.
Vfw K Starck	32	Sopwith 2	SW Reims		2	
Vfw K Petzinna	32	Spad	Reims		zlg	
Ltn E Hess	28	RE8	Wytschaete		–	

a.   N 5368, F/S/Lt CR Pegler, No 10 Sqn, RNAS, last seen over Polygon Wood.
b.   No 29 Sqn, RFC, lost two Nieuports that departed at 0955: A 6782, 2/Lt HH Whytehead and B1658, 2/Lt JW Fleming both KIA.
c.   N6350, S/L/Lt EK Kendall, No 6 Sqn, RNAS, down in flames over Slype at 1050.
d.   A6663, Lt DW Weld, No 19 Sqn, RFC, left at 1320, last seen N Lille.
e.   British balloon 36-16-1 (FM80).
f.   A1025, No 43 Sqn, RFC, Capt KL Gospil & 2/Lt A Buschmann, WIAs.
g.   Escadrille C 4, Sgt Poncet and S/Lt Avril who were killed near Cernay this date.
h.   Escadrille F 8, S/Lts St Genest & Libkind, KIAs.

Losses

Vfw Linus Patermann	4	Killed in action at 1100 over Gheluvelt.
Ltn Günther Pastor	29	Wounded in action at 2004 during combat with a Sopwith two-seater; forced to land SE of Annay.
Vfw Maier	36	Wounded in action.
Ltn Rabe	27	Injured in an accident.

13 July 1917

Obltn A v Tutschek	12	G100	Noeux-les-Mines	0800	15	
Ltn H Geigl	34	Sopwith 2	Mandres	1025	2	a.
Ltn K Deilmann	6	Nieuport	Zandvoorde	1120	5	b.
Ltn H Adam	6	Nieuport	E Ypern	1130	5	b.
Vfw F Krebs	6	Sopwith 2	NW Zonnebeke	1130	7	
Obltn E Dostler	6	Sopwith 2	S Becelaere	1135	17	c.
Obltn E Dostler	6	Nieuport	N Zonnebeke	1140	18	b.
Vfw F Krebs	6	Sopwith 2	NE Zonnebeke	1140	8	
Vfw J Buckler	17	FE2d	Stuivekenskerke	1320	9	
Ltn E Hess	28	DH4	Dycke-Audenaarde	1630	3	d.
Uffz P Bäumer	5	Balloon	Marteville	1700	2	e.
Obltn E Schleich	21	AR2	W Cuisy	1810	6	
Vfw W Dahm	26	Nieuport	NE Langemarck	2005	1	

Ltn E Thuy	21	Spad	S Avocourt	2015	4	
Ltn G Flecken	20	Pup	De Haan	2030	2	

a.   A8786, No 70 Sqn, RFC, Lts CG Mathew & ED Sliter, departed at 0900, POWs.

b.   No 29 Sqn, RFC, lost two Nieuports that departed at 0950 this date: B 1577, Lt FW Winterbotham, POW, and B1506, Lt AWB Miller, last seen over Gheluvelt, KIA.

c.   A8335, 2/Lt MO Baumann & E Fletcher No 70 Sqn, RFC, departed at 0900 last seen going down in flames near Becelaere, KIAs.

d.   A7421, No 55 Sqn, RFC, Lt AP Matheson & 2/Lt FL Oliver, departed at 1330, last seen W of Audenarde, KIAs.

e.   French 41 Compagnie d'Aérostières, Lt Ancely WIA.

Losses

Ltn Hans Klein	4	Wounded at 1130 near Ghistelles.
Ltn Heinrich Bongartz	36	Wounded during combat with DH4s.

14 July 1917

Ltn E Böhme	29	Nieuport	W Bersée	0720	13	a.
Ltn J Schmidt	3	G100	E Lens	0745	6	b.
Ltn J Schmidt	3	FE2b	Hénin-Lietard	0750	7	
Uffz J Heiligers	30	G100	W Leforêt	0800	3	b.
Obltn R Greim	34	Spad	S Nomeny	0850	3	
Vfw G Oefele	12	FE8	N Boursies	1650	1	c.
Vfw J Buckler	17	G100	Leffinghe	1750	10	d.
Ltn L Hanstein	16	AR2	Esnes		6	

a.   A6783, No 40 Sqn, RFC, 2/Lt G Davis, departed at 0525 to bomb La Brayelle, unwounded POW.

b.   No 27 Sqn, RFC lost two Martinsydes that had departed at 0500:7124, 2/Lt TE Smith, KIA, and A1572, 2/Lt GH Palmer, POW.

c.   A4885, 2/Lt WG Thompson, No 41 Sqn, RFC, last seen at 1535 NE of Bapaume, KIA.

d.   A6266, 2/Lt CM De Rochie, No 27 Sqn, RFC, departed at 1500 to bomb Zarren. KIA.

Losses – Nil

15 July 1917

Ltn K Jabob	33	DH4	NW Fressain	1820	1	a.
Uffz P Bäumer	5	Balloon	Trefcon	1840	3	b.
Ltn Schäfer	7	Farman	Essen	1840	1	
Obltn A v Tutschek	12	Nieuport	S Douai	2025	16	c.
Obltn H Bethge	30	Camel	Loison	2110	9	d.

a.   A7490, No 18 Sqn, RFC, 2/Lts VC Coombs & HM Tayler, departed at 1605, WIA/POWs.

b.   French 45 Compagnie d'Aérostières.

c.   B1575, No 60 Sqn, RFC, 2/Lt GAH Parkes, shot down W of Douai during a fight at 1930. WIA/POW.

d.   B3758, No 8 Sqn, RNAS, F/S/Lt F Bray, departed at 1900, KIA.

Losses

Ltn Erich Schlegelmilch	29	Slightly wounded, remained with unit.

16 July 1917

Ltn H Göring	27	SE5	E Ypern	0805	9	a.
Vfw M Krauss	27	Sopwith	NE Ypern	0810	2	
Ltn O Kissenberth	16	Spad VII	Mort Homme	1235	6	b.
Ltn H Gontermann	15	Balloon	S Reims	1400	24	c.
Obltn O Schmidt	32	Balloon	Mourmelon	1445	6	
Ltn F Kieckhäfer	32	Balloon	Villers Mamery	1447	1	
Vfw K Petzinna	32	Balloon	.... le-Petit	1450	1	
Vfw K Wüsthoff	4	Balloon	Kemmel	1815	4	d.
Vfw F Tabaka	32	Farman	Cornilette-Höhe	194	1	
Ltn H Adam	6	Sopwith	NE Ypern	2005	6	

a.   A8931, No 56 Sqn, RFC, 2/Lt RG Jardine, shot up and forced to land inside Allied lines near Dranoutre.
b.   Spad #1286, MdL P Roux, N 85, shot down in flames and taken prisoner. Only Spad lost this date.
c.   French 53 Compagnie d'Aérostières, not flamed.
d.   British Balloon 38-7-2.

Losses

Vfw Ernst Clausnitzer	4	Shot down and taken prisoner SE of Poperinghe after a balloon attack.
Vfw Fritz Krebs	6	Killed in action at 1945 NE of Zonnebeke.
Ltn Heinrich Geist	9	Killed in an accident S of Vouziers.
Ltn H Göring	27	Shot up and forced to land by Jardine of 56 Sqn RFC (see victory list above).

17 July 1917

Vfw J Buckler	17	Camel	S Keyem	0730	11	a.
Vfw A Werner	17	BF2b	Middlekerke	0930	1	b.
Ltn W Göttsch	8	Nieuport	SW St Jean	1250	13	c.
Vfw G Beerendonk	20	Camel	Nieuport	1930	1	
Ltn R Tüxen	6	Pup	Comines	2105	1	
Vfw R Francke	8	Camel	Waterdamhoek	2120	4	d.
Ltn A Niederhoff	11	Nieuport	Nordschoote	2125	5	

a.   B1713, Sopwith Scout, 2/Lt GT Felton, No 54 Sqn, RFC, shot down at 0630, taken prisoner.
b.   A7166, Lt RB Hay, MC, (P) & Lt OJ Partington (O), No 48 Sqn, RFC, departed at 0705, landed on a beach NE of Nieuport, pilot killed, observer taken prisoner. Only BF claim and loss this date.
c.   N3453, 2/Lt PE Palmer, No 29 Sqn, RFC, shot down at 1215, KIA.
d.   N6332, No 70 Sqn, RFC, Lt WE Grosset, departed at 1930, POW.

Losses

Ltn Richard Krüger	4	Wounded in action at 1315, DOW in a field hospital at 2105 hours.
Ltn Karl Meyer	11	Wounded at 2055 near Ypern, probably by Captain NWW Webb, No 70 Sqn, RFC, for his 7th victory.
Vfw Julius Buckler	17	Wounded in action, remained with Jasta.
Ltn Hans Böhning	36	Injured in an accident, remained with Jasta.
Vfw Debus	36	Wounded in action.

18 July 1917

No Claims

Losses

Vfw Kunze	ObOst	Shot down and taken prisoner.

19 July 1917

Vfw Klüpfel	ObOst	Balloon	Zukowze		3	

Losses – Nil

20 July 1917

Ltn H Adam	6	FE2d	SW Ypern	0740	7	a.
Ltn W Stock	6	RE8	Armentières	0840	1	
Ltn H Jöns	20	Camel	NW Wilskerke	2010	2	b
OflgMt K Schönfelder	7	SE5	Passchendaele	2025	1	c.
Ltn O v Bönigk	4	Sopwith	NW Tenbrielen	2100	1	b.
Ltn H Kroll	24	SE5	N Zandvoorde	2100	6	c.
Ltn A Niederhoff	11	Sopwith	Zonnebeke	2110	6	b.
Vfw K Wüsthoff	4	Sopwith	SW Becelaere	2120	5	b.
Obltn H Bethge	30	Camel	Mericourt	2130	10	

a.   No 20 Sqn, RFC.
b.   Two Sopwith Camels lost this date. N6360, No 6 Sqn, RNAS, F/Cdr G McLennan, or B3806, No 4 Sqn, RNAS, F/S/Lt FW Akers, KIA, both downed in the same area.
c.   No 56 Sqn, RFC, lost two SE5s, A8945, Capt ED Messervy, KIA (Kroll) and A8931, 2/Lt RG Jardine, (Schönfelder) KIA.
Losses – Nil

21 July 1917

Uffz G Schneidewind	17	Sopwith	Nordschoote	1530	1	
FwLtn F Schubert	6	Spad	W Roubaix	2020	2	a.
Obltn A v Tutschek	12	Nieuport	S Moeuvres	2130	17	
Ltn H Geigl	34	Spad	Fort Troyon		zlg	

a.   Capitaine J Lamon, N 73, flying a Spad departed at 1815 hours and was shot down and taken prisoner.
b.   B 1694 40 Sqn RFC, 2/Lt FW Rook, KIA.

Losses

Obltn Fritz von Bronsart und Schellendorf	7	Shot down in flames and killed near the Praet-Bosch – Wynendaele-Beerst Road.

22 July 1917

Ltn E Lamprecht	28	RE8	Ploegsteertwald	0925	zlg	
Vfw A Heldmann	10	RE8	Deulemont	1020	1	a.
Obltn E v Döring	4	Spad	NE Bixschoote	1040	4	b.
Hptm O Hartmann	28	Sopwith 2	S Ypern	1045	4	
Ltn A Niederhoff	11	Sopwith 2	SE Zonnebeke	1120	7	
Ltn O Brauneck	11	Triplane	Becelaere	1125	10	c.
Obltn W Reinhard	11	Sopwith	W Comines	1130	1	
OfStv K Lang	1	Caudron	La Fère	1200	zlg	
Ltn B Knake	12	Camel	W Hulluch	2040	2	
Obltn E v Döring	4	Nieuport	Oostaverne	2050	5	d.
Ltn H Geigl	34	Sopwith 2	Sanzey		3	
Vfw W Kempe	34	Caudron	E Sanzey		1	

a.   A3446, No 42 Sqn, RFC, Lt BH Smith & Pvt A McLaughlin, departed at 0820, shot down near Frelinghem, MIAs.
b.   Spad #1543, Lt L Pandevan, N 73, departed 0800, MIA, only Spad lost this date in this sector.
c.   N5478, No 10 Sqn, RNAS, F/S/Lt JA Page, MIA.
d.   B3481, No 1 Sqn, RFC, Ltn F Sharp, POW .

Losses

Vfw Georg Oefele	12	KIA at 0925 over Oppy, during combat with Camels, by F/Cdr PA Johnstone, 8 Naval.
Uffz Heinrichs	18	Wounded in action.
Vfw Willi Kempe	34	Shot down by ground fire and taken POW.

23 July 1917

Ltn H Geigl	34	Spad	Flugplatz Toul	0920	4	a.
Obltn A v Tutschek	12	Balloon	Neuville	1755	18	
Ltn B Knake	12	Balloon	S Neuville	1800	3	
Vfw H Bowski	14	Caudron	Ft Malmaison		zlg	

a.   Adj J Fabre, N 68, flying a Spad when killed in action. Only Spad lost in combat this date.
Losses – Nil

24 July 1917

Ltn H Gontermann	15	Spad	SE Aisne-Staubecken	0945	25	
Ltn H Göring	27	Camel	S Passchendaele	1045	10	a.
Ltn H Dilthey	27	Triplane	SE Passchendaele	2015	1	b.

| Obltn E v Althaus | | 10 | Camel | SE Moorslede | 2035 | 9 | c. |

a. B3792, No 70 Sqn, RFC, Lt G Budden, WIA, shot up and forced to land mear Bailleul.
b. N5364, F/S/Lt TC May, No 10 Sqn, RNAS, KIA.
c. B3825, Lt HD Trapp, No 70 Sqn, RFC, last seen going down at 1930, KIA.

Losses

| Ltn Oskar Dänkert | 9 | Killed in action near Pont-à-Chin. |
| Ltn Bernard Knake | 12 | Killed in an accident at Epinoy. |

25 July 1917

| Vfw J Oehler | | 24 | Sopwith | Potyze | 0800 | 2 | a. |
| Ltn H Adam | | 6 | Spad | Nordhofwyk | 1820 | 10 | b. |

a. A1020, 2/Lt HN Curtis (P) & Sgt WJ Wickham, No 45 Sqn RFC, departed at 0515, both killed.
b. No 19 Sqn, RFC.

Losses

| Uffz Walter Reichenbach | 5 | Landing accident near Busigny – died of injuries later in the day. |

26 July 1917

Ltn F Götte		20	Sopwith	Dixmuiden	1900	zlg	a.
Vfw A Muth		27	Sopwith	S Becelaere	2040	1	b.
Flgmt B Heinrich		MFJ1	Camel	W Dunkerque	–		

a. Probably B3814, 2/Lt JC Smith, No 70 Sqn, RFC, badly shot up, pilot OK.
b. Probably B3756, Capt NWW Webb, No 70 Sqn, RFC, OK, shot up and forced to land.

Losses

| Ltn Otto Brauneck | 11 | KIA at 2045 S Zonnebeke, by Capt NNW Webb, No 70 Sqn, RFC, for his 9th victory. |
| Ltn Hans Helmigk | 27 | Injured in an accident. |

27 July 1917

Ltn M Ziegler gen Stege	26	G100	SW Langemarck	0800	1	
Ltn A Ziegler gen Stege	26	SE5a	W Moorslede	0805	2	a.
Ltn Wolff	5	BF2b	Esquerchin	0900	2	b.
Vfw J Werner	17	EA (Br)	S Dixmuiden	1515	2	
Ltn J Wolff	17	Sopwith	SW Dixumiden	1635	4	
Ltn E Hess	28	RE8	NW Messines	1640	4	c.
FlgMt B Heinrich	MFJ1	Pup	W Nieuport	1810	6	d.
Ltn A Thurm	24	Sopwith	Ostrand Ypern	1940	1	
Ltn K-A v Schönebeck	11	Triplane	Beythem	2040	1	e.
Ltn K Wewer	26	Camel	Zonnebeke	2040	2	
Ltn K Wüsthoff	11	Sopwith	Dadizeele	2040	–	

a. A8911, 2/Lt TW White, No 56 Sqn, RFC, MIA.
b. A 7134, 2/Lt J Chapman (P) & Lt WB MacKay (O), N 11 Sqn, RFC, last seen going down over Vis-en-Artois, at 0750, POWs.
c. A4303, No 53 Sqn, RFC, 2/Lts PJ Rodocanachi, KIA, & NL Watt, WIA.
d. N6174, No 4 Sqn, RNAS, F/S/Lt EJK Buckley.
e. N5492, F/S/Lt G Roach, No 10 Sqn, RNAS, last seen over Moorslede, KIA.

Losses

Ltn Jakob Wolff	17	Wounded in action.
Ltn Erich Limpert	21	Shot down in flames and killed over Cheppy Wood.
OfStv Karl Gregor	29	Wounded in action.
Ltn Werner Kathol	29	Wounded in action, remained on unit.
Ltn Fritz Vossen	33	Killed in action at 0900 over Moorslede, probably by Capitaine Georges Guynemer, Spa 3, for his 50th victory.

| Vfw Wilhelm Weise | 35 | Wounded in action during combat with a Sopwith two-seater. | | | |
| VzFlgMstr Otto Brandt | MFJ1 | Killed in action at 1820 hours between Middlekerke and Westende. | | | |

28 July 1917

Ltn G Meyer	22	Spad	Craonne	0705	–	
Ltn J Jacobs	22	Spad	Craonne	0705	–	
Obltn A v Tutschek	12	Triplane	Mericourt	0730	19	
Vfw M Krauss	27	G100	Staden	0745	–	
Uffz E Schäpe	33	Pup	NW Mangelaere	0945	2	a.
Obltn A v Tutschek	12	Nieuport	NW Lens	1040	20	
Ltn E Hess	28	Sopwith 2	Westhoek	1110	5	
Vfw C Menckhoff	3	Camel	Gravenstafel	1120	6	
Vfw H Küllmer	6	Nieuport	N Terhand	1150	1	
Ltn J Jacobs	22	Spad	Soissons	1200	–	
Ltn J Schmidt	3	Nieuport	Becelaere	1210	8	
Ltn J Schmidt	3	BE	Wilsbeke	1210	9	
Ltn H Adam	6	Sopwith	E Becelaere	1210	8	
Ltn W Bockelmann	11	Caudron	Merckem	1720	zlg	
Vfw F Matthies	20	Sopwith	Coxyde	1725	1	
OfStv M Müller	28	Sopwith 2	NE Ploegsteert	1810	19	
Obltn R Greim	34	Nieuport	Bannoncourt	1840	4	
Obltn Dostler	6	DH4	NE Courtrai	1850	19	
Ltn J Czermak	6	DH4	SW Thielt	1850	1	
Ltn H Adam	6	DH4	Oostroosebeke	1855	9	
Ltn R Tüxen	6	DH4	E Ingelmünster	1855	2	
Obltn E v Dostler	6	DH4	Oostroosebeke	1900	20	
Ltn W Stock	6	DH4	Bahnhof Kruis	1900	2	
Ltn E Hess	28	RE8	W Deulemont	1950	6	
Ltn E Monicke	11	BE	Gheluvelt	2045	4	
Obltn E Weigand	10	Sopwith	Beythem	2100	1	b.
Ltn O v Bönigk	4	Pup	Moorslede	2105	2	c.
Ltn H Auer	26	Camel	Gulleghem	2120	2	b.
Vfw R Francke	8	Spad	Bixschoote		zlg	d.
Vfw A Schrader	31	Nieuport	Jeperen		1	e.

a.   A6216, No 66 Sqn, RFC, 2/Lt JB Hine, POW.
b.   No 70 Sqn, RFC, lost two Camels near Roulers that departed at 1900 this date: N3874, 2/Lt JC Smith, KIA, and B3823, 2/Lt RC Hume, POW.
c.   N5479, No 6 Sqn, RNAS, F/S/Lt JH Forman, WIA.
d.   Capitaine A Auger, CO Spa 3, flying a Spad, killed in action between Woesten and Zuidschoote. Only French Spad lost this date in this Sector.
e.   A6783, No 40 Sqn, RFC, Lt D Godfrey, POW.

Losses:

Hptm Gustav Stenzel	8	Killed in action near Rumbeke.
Ltn Alfred Niederhoff	11	Killed in action at 1200 W of Terhand.
Ltn Albrecht Crüsemann	17	Killed in action, 1935 NW of Nieuport Mole.
Ltn Gustav Nolte	18	Killed in action probably by Lt RTC Hoidge, No 56 Sqn, RFC.
Uffz Friedrich Thässler	35	KIA at 2000 between Oostneiuwkerke and Westroosebeke, probably by 66 Sqn, RFC.

29 July 1917

| Ltn zS Mattheus | MFJ1 | RE8 | Nieuport | 0640 | 2 |
| Ltn Weingarten | 1 | AR2 | La Ferté Bois | 0750 | 1 |

Vfw A Heldmann	10	Spad	Hooge-Westhoek	0755	2	
Obltn A v Tutschek	19	SE5	Hénin-Lietard	0805	21	a.
Ltn H Schröder	1	Spad	Cerny	0845	2	
Vfw Misch	29	Spad	Poelkapelle	1000	1	b.
Ltn R Wendelmuth	8	Camel	Wallenmolen	1025	2	c.
Uffz M Kahlow	34	Nieuport	Mailly	1320	2	d.
Obltn H Kummetz	1	Nieuport	Festieux		5	e.

a.   A8937, 2/Lt WH Gunner, MC, No 60 Sqn, RFC, left at 0615, last seen over Douai, KIA.
b.   B3531, Lt FB Best, No 19 Sqn, RFC, last seen at 0930 E of Ypres.
c.   B3780, Lt HO McDonald, No 70 Sqn, RFC, departed at 0815, POW.
d.   MdL O de Ginestet, N 77, flying a Nieuport XXIII, POW.
e.   Sgt S Nazare-Aga, N 82, flying a Nieuport XXIIIbis, No.3714, KIA.
Losses –Nil

30 July 1917

No Claims – No Loss

31 July 1917   The First Battle of Passchendaele began.

Ltn A Hübner	4	RE8	S Zillebeke See	1250	2	
Ltn K Meyer	11	RE8	Deimlingseck	1300	1	
Ltn K-A v Schönebeck	11	RE8	Frezenberg	1310	2	
Ltn W Göttsch	8	FE2d	NE Becelaere	1340	14	a.
Obltn E Dostler	6	Nieuport	W Bellewaarde	1405	21	
Ltn K Wüsthoff	4	FE2d	S Zillebeke See	1445	6	
Uffz K Reinhold	24	Triplane	Bailleul	1630	1	

a.   A 1956, No 20 Sqn, RFC, Lt CH Beldam & 2/Lt WH Watt, departed at 1432, POWs.
Losses – Nil

JASTA ARMEE ASSIGNMENTS AS OF 1 AUGUST 1917

Western Front

1 Armee 19
2 Armee 2,5
3 Armee –
4 Armee 3,4,6,7,8,10,11,17,18,20,24,27,28,29,31,35b,36,37
5 Armee 13,14,21,23b

6 Armee 12,30
7 Armee 1,9,13,15,22
Det 'A' –
Det 'B' 41
Det 'C' 40

Other Fronts

11 Armee 25   Macedonia
 1 Armee 38   Bulgarian Armee
Kuk 2 Armee OberOs   Russia

1–3 August 1917

No Claims – No Losses

4 August 1917

| Ltn A Hübner | 4 | Caudron | Reninghe | 2055 | 3 |

Losses – Nil

5 August 1917

| Ltn K Wüsthoff | 4 | Nieuport | W Ypern | 1500 | 7 |

Obltn O v Boenigk	4	Camel	W Staden	1515	–	
Ltn K Wissemann	3	Camel	Terrest	1530	2	a.
Ltn H Gontermann	15	Nieuport	Staubecken	1940	26	
Ltn H Göring	27	Sopwith	NE Ypern	2015	11	b.

a.   B2304, 2/Lt HJ Ellam, No 70 Sqn, RFC, departed at 1250, last seen over Werkem, WIA/POW.
b.   B3792, Lt G Budden, WIA, No 70 Sqn, RFC, shot up and forced to land.

Losses:
| Ltn Burkhardt Lehmann | 12 | Killed in action at 2040 near Hendecourt-les-Cagnicourt. |

6–7 August 1917

No Claims – No Losses

8 August 1917

| Ltn H Stutz | 20 | Camel | N Nieuport | 1215 | zlg |

Losses – Nil

9 August 1917

Vfw J Buckler	17	Camel	SE Nieuport	0745	12	a.
Ltn E Hess	28	Sopwith 2	Neuve Elgise	0750	zlg	
Ltn W Güttler	24	Sopwith 2	N Essen	0910	4	b.
Ltn M Müller	28	Sopwith 2	N Ypern	0930	zlg	
Ltn E Hess	28	Spad	Passchendaele	1035	7	c.
Ltn zS G Sachsenberg	MFJ1	Spad	NE Lampernisse	1840	6	
Obltn E Dostler	6	Nieuport	NE Poelkapelle	1855	22	d.
Ltn F Berkemeyer	35	DH4	S Stadenberg	2005	1	
Ltn V Schobinger	12	SE5	Feuchy	2100	1	
Ltn H Gontermann	15	Balloon	Forêt de Hesse		27	e.
Ltn H Gontermann	15	Balloon	Forêt de Hesse		28	f.
Ltn E Hess	28	Rumpf DD	Neuve Eglise		zlg	

a.   3870, No 10 Sqn, RNAS, F/S/Lt MG Woodhouse, down in flames SE of Nieuport, KIA.
b.   Sgt Janny & S/Lt Lauvergne, C 226, flying a Sopwith, missing in action in the Flanders Sector.
c.   B3519, No 23 Sqn, RFC, Lt W H Howes, POW.
d.   No 29 Sqn, RFC, 2/Lt HB Billings, POW/DOW.
e.   French 46 Compagnie d'Aérostières, S/Lt Barrière.
f.   French 51 Compagnie d'Aérostières.

Losses – Nil

10 August 1917

Ltn M Müller	28	Spad	Wervicq	1010	20	a.
Ltn M Müller	28	DH4	Ingelmünster	1020	21	
Ltn J von Busse	3	RE8	Vierlawenhoek	1425	1	
Uffz K Steudel	3	RE8	Poelkapelle	1437	2	
Ltn W Stock	6	SE5	Dadizeele	1530	2	b.
Ltn K Wissemann	3	Nieuport	N Ste Marquerite	1540	3	
Uffz H Brettel	10	Spad	SW Clerkem	1625	2	c.
Ltn W Voss	10	Spad	S Dixmuiden	1625	35	c.
Vfw Weber	8	Pup	Slypshoek	1630	1	
Vfw O Könnecke	5	DH5	Malassise-Ferme	1940	5	
Ltn H Auer	26	DH5	E Passchendaele	2045	3	
Ltn E Hess	28	RE8	Messines	2120	8	
Ltn T Rumpel	16	Balloon	Belleville		1	d.
Ltn M Müller	28	Sopwith	N Ypern	am	zlg	
Ltn H-G Geigl	34	Spad	Koeur		5	

Ltn E Thuy	21	Balloon	Montzéville	5	e.
Ltn M Müller	28	Sopwith 2	N Ypres	–	

a. 2/Lt DP Collis, No 23 Sqn, RFC, shot down near Zillebeke at 0930 hours, POW.
b. A8923, Capt WA Fleming, No 56 Sqn, RFC, departed at 1250, last seen near Roulers-Menin road, KIA.
c. MdL E Camus (1victory) and Capitaine H Rousseau, N 31, both flying Spads were reported as missing this date in this sector.
d. French 80 Compagnie d'Aérostières, one claim invalid.
e. French 34 Compagnie d'Aérostières, not flamed.

Losses:

Ltn Oskar Rousselle	4	Wounded at 2000 over Artishoek.
Vfw Hugo Stöber	16	Wounded in action.
Ltn Erwin Böhme	29	Wounded in action.

11 August 1917

Obltn A v Tutsckek	12	BF2b	E Biache	0910	22	a.
Vfw J Buckler	17	RE8	W Spermalie	1415	13	b.
Obltn A v Tutschek	12	BF2b	W Courcelles	1830	23	c.
Ltn J Schmidt	3	RE8	Ypern	1920	10	
Ltn F Wendland	35	Nieuport	Couckelaere	1930	3	d.
Ltn T Quandt	36	RE8	W Zonnebeke	2010	3	e.
Ltn V Schobinger	12	Triplane	Farbus	2040	2	

a. A7169, No 2 Sqn, RFC, Capt PW Chambers, KIA, & 2/AM Richman, POW, departed at 0655, last seen over Arleux.
b. 4645, No 52 Sqn, RFC, Lt DB Davies & Lt RH Sawlor, departed at 1240, brought down in flames, KIAs.
c. A7179, No 22 Sqn, RFC, Lt EAH Ward & Lt KW Holmes, departed at 1715, last seen NE of Douai, KIAs.
d. B1518, No 29 Sqn, RFC, Lt CG Guy, last seen at 1940 over Houlthust Forest in a spin with three EA following, WIA/POW/DOW.
e. A3863, No 21 Sqn, RFC, 2/Lt C E Holaway & 2/Lt PG Harris, departed at 1825, KIAs.

Losses:

Obltn Adolf v Tutschek	12	Severely wounded by F/Cdr CD Booker, No. 8 Sqn, RNAS.
Uffz Wilhelm Thuir	35	Killed in an accident, 1910 near Ichteghem, flying Albatros DV 2240/17.

12 August 1917

Vfw W Hoffmann	36	Rumpf DD	Boesinghe	0850	1	
Ltn E Stapenhorst	11	Sopwith	NW Bixschoote	0900	1	
Ltn H Kroll	24	Triplane	N Ypern	0900	7	
Vfw H Fritzsche	29	Spad	Poelkapelle	1000	1	
Vfw Misch	29	Nieuport	SW Stadenberg	1020	2	
Vfw O Sowa	7	Camel	Pervyse	1150	1	
Vfw W Kampe	27	Nieuport	Moorslede	1345	1	a.
Ltn H Dilthey	27	Nieuport	Brodsiende	1352	2	a.
Hptm O Hartmann	28	G100	SW Wervicq	1410	5	b.
Obltn E Dostler	6	Spad	W Gheluwe	1555	23	c.
Ltn J Schmidt	3	DH5	N Poelkapelle	1710	11	d.
Obltn zS K Mettlich	8	Balloon	NW Vlamertinghe	1730	3	e.
Ltn X Dannhuber	26	Balloon	NW Vlamertinghe	1730	1	e.
Obltn zS K Mettlich	8	Sopwith 2	N Ypern	1731	4	
Ltn O Kissenberth	23	Spad VII	Avocourt Wald	1810	7	f.
Uffz J Heiligers	30	Nieuport	SE Courrières	2030	4	g.
Ltn H Adam	6	DH4	Poperinghe	2110	11	
Vfw Schönfeldt	K2	Sopwith	Saargemünd		1	

a. No 1 Sqn, RFC, lost two Nieuports near Menin this date, both departed at 1120: B1648, 2/Lt FM McLaren, KIA, and B3481, 2/Lt L Read, POW.

b.   A1573, No 27 Sqn, RFC, 2/Lt SC Sillem, brought down in flames, KIA.
c.   B3491, No 23 Sqn, RFC, 2/Lt CW Elliott, last seen E of Langemarck at 1610, KIA.
d.   A9398, No 32 Sqn, RFC, Capt RM Williams, last seen at 1720 w of Houthulst, KIA.
e.   British balloon 23-8-5 (BMS 151/D) only loss this date, one claim is invalid.
f.   Adj G Baillou, N 86, flying a Spad missing in action.
g.   A6771, No 40 Sqn, RFC, Lt WO Cullen.

Losses:

Vfw Julius Buckler	17	Wounded in action.
Uffz Friedrich Wassermann	27	KIA, Ypres, flying an Albatros DIII (G.61) by Lts FM Green and RMD Fairweather, No 7 Sqn, RFC.
Ltn Erich Schlegelmilch	29	KIA, 1055 between Staden and Houthulst.
Ltn Joachim von Bertrab	30	Albatros DV 2191/17, shot down during a balloon attack and POW by Lt E Mannock, No.40 Sqn, RFC, for his 6th victory.

13 August 1917

Ltn H Brügmann	30	Sopwith	Annay	0825	1	
Ltn W Bockelmann	11	DH4	E Gent	0920	2	
Ltn F Berkemeyer	35	RE8	Ramskapelle	0930	2	
Vfw G Strasser	17	2 seater	SE Oostdunkerke	0925	5	
Ltn H Arntzen	15	Caudron	Monampteuil	0945	5	a.
Ltn F Loerzer	26	Spad	Frezenberg	1004	3	b.
Uffz A Ulbricht	9	Balloon	Chaude Fontaine	1020	1	
Obltn W Reinhard	11	Sopwith	N Polygonwald	1045	2	
Ltn H v Budde	15	Caudron	Hubértise-Ferme	1115	1	
Vfw A Haussmann	15	Balloon	Braisne	1155	5	c.
Ltn J Czermak	6	Sopwith	W Langemarck		zlg	
Ltn A Hübner	4	Sopwith	S St Jean	2000	4	
Ltn K Mendel	15	Balloon	Pontavert		1	c.
Vfw A Haussmann	15	Nieuport	Braisne		6	

a.   Sgt Lefevre and S/Lt Outhenin-Chalandre, C 4, flying a Caudron G.4 fell in flames after combat with two Albatros Scouts N of Bevelle.
b.   B1698, No 23 Sqn, RFC, 2/Lt HG Tinney, departed at 0900, last seen over Langemarck.
c.   Two French balloons were lost this date, the 43 and 71 Compagnies d'Aérostières, in the operating area of Jasta 15. The observers MdL Couillard and Adj Ducasse made safe descents.

Losses:

Uffz Arno Ulbricht	9	Severely wounded at 1015 S of Medeah Ferme; died of wounds on 17 August.

14 August 1917

Vfw W Seitz	8	RE8	N Bixschoote	0850	3	
Ltn E Löwenhardt	10	RE8	Zillebeke See	1015	2	
Obltn W Reinhard	11	RE8	Boesinghe	1040	3	
Obltn E Weigand	10	Sopwith	Nieuwekapelle	1045	2	
Obltn W Reinhard	11	Spad	Boesinghe	1050	4	a.
Uffz K Reinhold	24	RE8	S Kemmel	1635	2	b.
Ltn L Luer	27	Balloon	W Ypern	1637	1	
Vfw M Krauss	27	Balloon	NW Ypern	1642	3	
Uffz K Steudel	3	Triplane	Langemarck	1720	3	c.
Ltn F Müller	11	Sopwith	Bixschoote	1735	1	
Ltn W Blume	26	DH4	Hollebeke	1740	4	
Ltn E Hess	28	DH5	Oostaverne	1840	zlg	
Ltn G Meyer	7	Balloon	SE Furnes	1850	2	
Ltn O Fitzner	17	Sopwith	W Slype	1850	1	d.

Ltn H Adam	6	SE5	Scaepe Baillie	1930	12	e.
Obltn E v Dostler	6	SE5	NE St Julien	1930	24	e.
Ltn E Udet	37	DH4	Pont-à-Vendin	2025	7	
Uffz H Horst	7	Balloon	NE Poperinghe		1	

a.   Cpl O Chadwick (an American), N 73, KIA at 0945 hours, only Spad lost.
b.   A3828, No 55 Sqn, RFC, 2/Lt JE Goodman & 2/Lt FE Kebbelwhite, KIAs, departed at 1415.
c.   N5367, No 10 Sqn, RNAS, F/S/Lt SH Lloyd, last seen at 1700 over Polygon Wood, KIA.
d.   B3280, No 9 Sqn, RNAS, F/S/Lt M N Baron, KIA.
e.   No 56 Sqn, RFC, lost two SE5s which departed at 1700, last seen near Houthulst: B509, 2/Lt DA Page, POW/DOW, and A8943, Lt JG Young, POW.

Losses:

Ltn Alfred Hübner	4	KIA, flying an Albatros DV at 2035 over Moorslede.
Ltn Hans Joachim Wolff	11	WIA at 0920 over Zillebeke See.
Vfw Haass	29	Wounded in action.

15 August 1917

Vfw O Sowa	7	Sopwith 2	NW Leke	0920	2	
Ltn E Udet	37	Sopwith 2	NE Loison	1000	8	
Ltn H Kroll	24	FE2d	N Ypern	1855	8	
Ltn W Voss	10	FE2d	Zillebeke See	1910	36	a.
Obltn H Bethge	30	Nieuport	W Annay	2045	11	b.

a.   A5152, No 20 Sqn RFC, 2/Lt CH Cameron, OK, & Pvt SE Pilbrow, MM, KIA, aircraft shot up and crash-landed.
b.   B1662, No 40 Sqn, RFC, Capt WG Pender, MC, departed at 1850, last seen E of La Bassée, KIA.

Losses:

Uffz Hermann Brettel	10	WIA at 1900 near Moorslede.
Ltn Heinrich Brügmann	30	WIA with Nieuports over Douvrin; died of wounds at 1400 in an ambulance.

16 August 1917

Ltn A Träger	8	RE8	St Julien	0725	3	
Ltn R Wendelmuth	8	RE8	SE Langemarck	0725	3	
Rittm M v Richthofen	JGI	Nieuport	SW Houthulst	0755	58	a.
Obltn B Loerzer	26	Spad	Langemarck	0935	6	b.
Obflgmstr K Schönfelder	7	Spad	NE Ypern	1045	2	b.
Ltn G-W Groos	11	Triplane	Hollebeke	1120	4	c.
OfStv J Klein	18	Spad	Passchendaele	1120	1	d.
Ltn W Mohnicke	11	G100	N Linselles	1220	5	e.
Ltn F Wendland	35	RE8	Langemarck	1805	4	
Ltn W Voss	10	Camel	St Julien	2100	37	f.
Obltn R Greim	34	Sopwith	Ornes		5	

a.   A6611, No 29 Sqn, RFC, 2/Lt WHT Williams, last seen at 1850 S of Houthulst Forest, WIA/POW/DOW.
b.   S/Lt H Rabatel (2victories) Spa 3, taken prisoner, and Cpl J Cornet,also of Spa 3, failed to return from a patrol. The only two French Spads lost in this sector.
c.   N6304, No 1 Sqn, RNAS, F/S/Lt AT Gray, WIA/POW/DOW.
d.   A6634, No 19 Sqn, RFC, Lt AT Shipwright, departed at 1156, POW.
e.   6261, No 27 Sqn, RFC, 2/Lt AR Baker, departed 1040, last seen between Menin and Courtrai, KIA.
f.   B3756, No 70 Sqn, RFC, Capt NWW Webb, MC & Bar, 14 victories, KIA.

Losses:

Ltn Ehlers	17	Wounded in action.
Vfw Anton Schrader	31	Killed in action over Ypres.
Vfw Walter Hoffmann	36	KIA, possibly by Capt DU McGregor, No 23 Sqn, RFC.

17 August 1917

Ltn M Müller	28	SE5	Quesnoy	0705	22	a.
Ltn G-W Groos	11	SE5	Passchendaele	0725	5	a.
Obltn Dostler	6	G100	N Menin	0810	25	
Ltn J Wintrath	B	Camel	Spermelie	0815	1	
Ltn J Ohlrau	10	Sopwith	Becelaere	1015	1	
Vfw R Eck	3	Spad	Ypern	1030	1	
Ltn K Deilmann	6	FE2d	St Julien	1110	6	
Ltn H Drekmann	26	FE2d	NW Menin	1110	1	
Vfw F Kosmahl	26	FE2d	Zonnebeke	1110	6	
Ltn H Böhning	19	Caudron	S Cornillet	1132	4	
Ltn E Thuy	21	Spad	S Höhe 304	1200	6	
Ltn H Gontermann	15	Balloon	Aisne	1205	29	b.
Ltn H Gontermann	15	Balloon	.... Staubecken	1205	30	c.
Vfw G Beerendonk	20	Camel	N Dixmuiden	1215	2	
Ltn F Büchner	9	Nieuport	SE Cheppy	1230	1	d.
Obltn R Greim	34	Sopwith 2	Ornes	1900	5	
Obltn H Bethge	30	Camel	SW Wingles	1905	2	e.
Obltn H Bethge	30	Camel	SW Wingles	1905	13	e.
Vfw F Altemeier	24	RE8	N Zillebeke See	2010	4	f.
Ltn H-G von der Osten	11	BF2b	Staden	2015	1	g.
Ltn W Becker	17	Sopwith	NE Cortemarck	2125	1	
Vfw F Altemeier	24	Spad	S Zillebeke See	2040	5	
Ltn X Dannhuber	26	BF2b	Staden	2050	3	g.
Obltn H Kummetz	1	Caudron	SW Laval		6	
Ltn G Meyer	7	Camel	Nieuport		3	
Ltn O Kissenberth	23	Nieuport	Avocourt		8	d.
Ltn X Dannhuber	26	FE2d	St Julien		2	h.
Ltn K Bohny	K7	Balloon	Ft Rozelier		1	i.
Ltn K Bohny	K7	Balloon	SE Verdun		2	j.
Vfw L Hilz	K4	Sopwith	Hirzfelden		1	k.

a. No 56 Sqn, RFC lost two SE5s that departed at 0540 this date, both last seen E of Polygon Woods: B514, Lt RT Leighton, WIA/POW, and A8903, Lt DS Wilkinson, WIA/POW/DOW 26 August 1917.
b. French 28 Compagnie d'Aérostières.
c. French 39 Compagnie d'Aérostières.
d. MdL L Laurent (1 victory), N 92, and MdL R Lonet, N 92, both flying Nieuport XXIVs were reported as missing in action in this sector.
e. No 8 Sqn, RNAS, lost two Camels that departed at 1800 and collided in mid-air during combat: B3877, F/S/Lt EA Bennetts & B3757, F/Cdr PA Johnstone, 6 victories, KIAs.
f. A4363, No 7 Sqn, RFC, 2/Lts HL Saver & JG Tobin-Willis, KIAs.
g. A7201, No 22 Sqn, RFC, S/Lt RS Phelan, POW, & Lt JL MacFarlane, KIA, last seen at 2000 hours.
h. B1891, No 20 Sqn, RFC, Lt WH Joslyn, 7 victories, & 2/Lt A Urquhart, departed at 0812, KIAs. (Deilmann and Kosmahl also claimed FEs during actions with 20 Sqn.)
i. French 23 Compagnie d'Aérostières.
j. French 59 Compagnie d'Aérostières.
k. Adj Maneval (P) & Cpl Gaillard (G) Escadrille Sop 123, MIAs.

Losses:

Ltn Franz Götte	20	Killed in action at 1215 over Slype.
Ltn Otto Rath	MFJ1	Killed, 2030 over Mannekeusvere, after a balloon attack near Furnes.

18 August 1917

Ltn R Matthaei	5	BF2b	NW Biache	0725	5	a.
Ltn R Schuhmann	5	BF2b	S Brebières	0727	2	a.
Ltn V Schobinger	12	BF2b	S Lallaing	0800	3	b.

Ltn K Bolle	28	DH4	Kachtem	0803	1	b.
Ltn P Billik	7	Camel	Vladsloo	1010	5	c.
Hptm O Hartmann	28	Sopwith	W St Eloi	1025	6	
Vfw O Könnecke	5	DH5	Ribécourt	1050	6	
Vfw H Kramer	9	AR2	S Avocourt	1200	2	
Ltn W Schulze	4	RE8	Boesinghe	1205	1	
Ltn F Pütter	9	Balloon	S Vauquois	1535	2	d.
Obltn E Dostler	6	DH4	S Roulers	2015	26	e.
Vfw W Reiss	3	BE	Becelaere	2034	3	
Vfw Dilcher	5	DH5	Villers Plouich		3	
Ltn W Schulz	16	Spad	Dun-sur-Meuse		1	f.
Vfw K Rahier	31	Spad	Bixschoote		1	g.
Vfw F Jacobsen	31	Camel	Linselles		2	

a.   No 11 Sqn, RFC, lost three BFs: A7126, 2/Lt TW Abbott & 2/Lt M Nicholson KIAs; A7147, 2/Lt GA Rose & Cpl HG Bassenger, POWs; and A7191, 2/Lt LO Harel, KIA, & Capt WH Walker, POW. All last seen at 0615 over Douai.

b.   A7454, No 57 Sqn, RFC, Sgt CJ Comerford & 2/Lt N Bell, departed 0545, last seen NW of Roulers, KIAs.

c.   B3938, No 4 Sqn, RNAS, F/S/L CRW Hodges, KIA.

d.   French 48 Compagnie d'Aérostières, the observer, S/Lt J Mathieu, made a safe descent.

e.   7510, No 57 Sqn, RFC, Lt J Hood & 2/Lt JR MacDaniel, last seen in combat at 1915 SW of Roulers, KIAs.

f.   Spad #1615, Sgt H Willis, N 124, POW.

g.   Cpl CJ Biddle, N 73, flying a Spad, OK.

Losses:

Obltn Fritz Bernert	B	Wounded in action.
Ltn Albrecht Weinschenk	18	Wounded in action.
Vfw Otto Gerbig	18	Mortally wounded in combat at 2045 hrs near Passchendaele.
Ltn Edwin Kreuzer	36	Wounded in accidental firing of machine-guns.

19 August 1917

Ltn W Brachwitz	17	BF2b	Oudenberghe	0750	1	a.
Ltn M Müller	28	Spad	Ypern	0815	23	
Vfw F Rumey	5	RE8	Epéhy	0820	2	
Ltn H Gontermann	15	Spad	SW Jouy	1040	31	
Ltn E Thuy	21	Spad	Chattancourt	1100	7	
Ltn H Pütter	9	Balloon	Vraincourt	1500	3	b.
Obltn B v Voigt	8	RE8	Passchendaele	1715	3	
Ltn O Kissenberth	23	Nieuport	Mort Homme	1735	9	c.
Ltn J Wintrath	B	Camel	Oostdunkerke	1745	zlg	
Ltn E Hess	28	FE2d	E Wervicq	1800	9	d.
Ltn M Müller	28	Nieuport	Menin	1805	24	e.
Ltn H Gontermann	15	Balloon	S Aisne-Tal	1923	32	f.
Ltn H Gontermann	15	Balloon	S Aisne-Tal	1924	33	f.
Ltn H Gontermann	15	Balloon	S Aisne-Tal	1925	34	f.
Ltn H Gontermann	15	Balloon	S Aisne-Tal	1926	35	f.
Ltn K Odebrett	16	Spad	Mort Homme		3	g.

a.   A7171, No 48 Sqn, RFC, 2/Lt R Dutton KIA, & 2/Lt HR Hart-Davies, WIA/POW, left at 0545, last seen over Ostende.

b.   French 48 Compagnie d'Aérostières, the observer, Adj Guy Benoist made a safe descent.

c.   MdL J Wetzel, N 86, flying a Nieuport XXIV missing in action.

d.   B1890, No 20 Sqn, RFC, 2/Lt CR Richards, MC, 12 victories, & 2/Lt SF Thompson, WIA/POWs, departed at 1351, last seen over Oostaverne Wood.

e.   B1683, No 1 Sqn, RFC, 2/Lt HEA Waring, departed at 1600, last seen over Menin, WIA/POW.

f.   French Résumés for this date show that three balloons were destroyed in this sector, but the numbers of the balloon companies were not given.

g.   Sgt A Thevenin, N 15, flying a Spad, KIA.

Losses:
Uffz Paul Felix   15   Killed in action near Boncourt.

20 August 1917

Ltn M Raspe	21	Nieuport	Avocourt	0600	1	
Vfw R Heibert	33	Triplane	NE Dixmuiden	0855	1	
OfStv J Mai	5	Camel	SE Rumaucourt	0905	1	a.
Vfw R Jörke	12	Sopwith 2	SE Fresnes	0915	5	b.
Ltn R Matthaei	21	DH4	Tortequesnes	0915	5	
Ltn O Kissenberth	23	Spad	Mort Homme	1015	10	c.
Vfw W Kampe	27	DH4	W Becelaere	1220	2	d.
Vfw A Muth	27	DH4	W Becelaere	1220	2	
Ltn J Jacobs	7	Camel	Ramskapelle	1735	6	
Ltn P Billik	7	Camel	Pilckem	1845	zlg	
Vfw A Lochner	23	Spad	Samogneux	1947	1	
Ltn O Kissenberth	23	Spad	Haumont	1950	11	
Ltn A Dietlen	23	Spad	Haumont	1952	2	
Uffz P Hiob	13	Spad	Esnes		1	
Ltn Schröder	13	Spad	SE Malancourt		1	
Ltn L Hanstein	16	Spad	Mort Homme		7	
Ltn K Odebrett	16	Caudron	Côte de Talou		4	
Ltn K Odebrett	16	Caudron	Louvemont		5	
Ltn K Odebrett	16	Sopwith 2	NE Douaumont		6	
Ltn H Geigl	16	Caudron	Louvemont		6	
Vfw J Neumaier	16	Spad	Louvemont		1	
Vfw G Fieseler	25	Nieuport	S Prilip		1	

a.   B3876, No 70 Sqn, RFC, 2/Lt HD Turner, KIA.
b.   A8336, No 43 Sqn, RFC, 2/Lt FE Winser & 2/Lt HF Young, departed at 0645, last seen over Vitry, KIAs.
c.   S/Lt P Barthes, N 93, KIA at 0900 hours east of Mort Homme.
d.   A7567, No 57 Sqn, RFC, 2/Lt AB Cook, OK, 2/Lt R N Bullock, WIA, crash-landed after combat.

Losses:

Ltn Reinhold Schuhmann	5	Killed in action probably by Lt HD Layfield, 70 Sqn, RFC.
Ltn Heinrich Geigl	16	Wounded in action by ground fire.
Ltn Albert Dietlen	23	Wounded in action.
Vfw Josef Oehler	24	Killed in action during fight with triplanes at 1945 hrs, flying Albatros DIII 756/17.
Flgmstr Grosch	MFJ1	Wounded in action.

21 August 1917

Ltn J Fichter	22	Nieuport	Morancourt-Fé	0800	2	
Obltn H Bethge	30	G100	SW Fretin	0805	14	a.
Ltn K Bolle	28	G100	N Seclin	0810	2	a.
Obltn R Berthold	18	G100	Dixmuiden	0817	13	a.
Ltn M Müller	28	G100	S Douvrin	0820	25	a.
Ltn E Udet	37	DH4	Ascq	0845	9	
Ltn E Hess	28	Sopwith	SW Frezenberg	0950	10	
Ltn E Hess	28	RE8	Verlorenhoek	1025	11	
Ltn S v Lieres und Wilkau	29	RE8	Langemarck	1030	1	
Ltn E Thuy	21	AR2	SW Avocourt	1200	8	
Vfw O Könnecke	5	RE8	La Pavé	1605	7	b.
Ltn E Hess	28	Triplane	Ypres	1840	–	
Ltn M Müller	28	DH4	Ledeghem	1925	26	
Ltn A Hanko	28	DH4	Hooge	1930	4	

Ltn E Welss	28	Sopwith	E Ypern	1930	1	
Hptm O Hartmann	28	Triplane	E Becelaere	1935	7	c.
Vfw R Francke	8	Sopwith	Passchendaele	2015	5	d.
Ltn R Wendelmuth	8	SE5	Passchendaele	2015	4	
Ltn F Loerzer	26	Nieuport	Westroosebeke	2015	4	e.
Ltn X Dannhuber	26	Nieuport	Poelkapelle	2020	4	
Obltn E Dostler	6	RE8	Zonnebeke		–	
Vfw H Bowski	14	Sopwith 2	Fosseswald		4	
Ltn F Brandt	19	Balloon	Mourmelon		2	f.
Ltn J Schmidt	3	Triplane			–	

a.   No 27 Sqn, RFC, lost three Martinsydes this date in the vicinity of Lille: 7276, 2/Lt S Thompson, POW: A3992, 2/Lt DP Cox, KIA, and A6259, Capt GK Smith, MC, KIA.
b.   A3535, No 59 Sqn, RFC, Capt FD Pemberton, KIA, and Lt JA Manners-Smith, WIA, departed at 1215.
c.   N5425, No 10 Sqn, RNAS, F/S/Lt C Lowther, last seen over Menin at 1840, KIA.
d.   B2177, No 66 Sqn, RFC, 2/Lt PH Raney, last seen NW of Roulers, KIA.
e.   B1613, No 1 Sqn, RFC, 2/Lt CA Moody, left 1820, last seen over Houthulst, KIA.
f.   French 87 Compagnie d'Aérostières.

Losses:

Obltn Eduard Dostler	6	Killed in action by Ltn N Staples and 2/Lt MA O'Callaghan, No 7 Sqn, RFC.
Ltn Alfred Träger	8	Wounded in action.
Vfw Willi Spudich	21	Killed in a mid-air collision with Vfw Zachmann over Vauquois, who landed safely.
Ltn Hugo Geiger	34	Killed in action N of Verdun, probably by S/Lt Robert de Bonnefoy, N 84.
Ltn Max Wirth	34	Killed in action NW of Etain.

22 August 1917

Gefr J Funk	30	Nieuport	N Meurchin	0950	2	
Ltn O Kissenberth	23	AR2	Höhe 304	1216	12	
Obltn K Student	9	Nieuport	Höhe 304	1540	5	
Ltn R Wendelmuth	8	Nieuport	E Ypern	1835	5	
Uffz H Horst	7	Pup	Houthulst Forest	1945	2	
Ltn J Schmidt	3	Camel	Ypern	2035	12	
Obltn E Schleich	21	Caudron	Bourruswald		7	
Vfw K Thom	21	AR2	S Avocourt		1	
Ltn H Büssing	K4	Sopwith	Kaysersberg		2	a.
Ltn H Hoyer	36	Sopwith	Houthulst Forest		–	

a.   Lt du Plessis & Lt Sainte Claire-Deville, C 227, flying a Sopwith, fell in flames during combat.

Losses:

Ltn Egon Könemann	B	KIA over Lombardzyde, probably F/S/Lt G B Anderson, No 3 Sqn, RNAS.
Ltn Wilhelm Gros	17	Killed in action at 1105 over Vlisseghem.
Vfw Jahnke	21	Wounded in action.
Flgobmt Luitjen Luitjens	MFJ1	Killed in action between St Pierre Capelle and Spermalie at 1030 hours.

23 August 1917

Ltn H Auer	32	Spad	Esnes	0705	4	
Ltn G-W Groos	11	Camel	Houthulst Forest	0750	6	
Ltn H Hoyer	36	BF2b	NE Zillebeke	0835	1	a.
Ltn H Böhning	36	BF2b	Vinke	0840	1	a.
Obltn O v Boenigk	4	Triplane	Boesinghe	0905	3	
Ltn W Voss	10	Spad	SW Dixmuiden	1000	38	b.
Ltn H Kroll	24	RE8	Ypern	1010	zlg	

Vfw H Bowski	14	Balloon			5	
Vfw P Rothe	14	Balloon			1	
Ltn Scheller	19	Caudron	SW Loivre		1	

a.   No 22 Sqn, RFC, lost two BFs this date which were last seen in combat at 0730: A7204, 2/Lt HG Tambling & F/Sgt W Organ, POWs; and B1101, Sgt CL Randall & 1/AM JV Hurley KIAs.
b.   B3528, No 19 Sqn, RFC, Capt AL Gordon-Kidd, DSO, WIA, but managed to bring his aircraft back to base; died of wounds on 27 August.
Losses:
Vfw Konrad Poralla   32   Wounded in action over Dannevoux.

24 August 1917

Vfw Gillardoni	ObOst	Balloon	Kekkau		1

Losses – Nil

25 August 1917

OfStv J Mai	5	DH5	Salvigny	0725	2	a.
Ltn H-G von der Osten	11	Triplane	Langemarck	0805	2	b.
Ltn H Göring	27	Sopwith	SW Ypern	0845	12	c.

a.   A9212, No 41 Sqn, RFC, Capt JSdeL Bush, departed at 0525, last seen over Sorel-le-Grand, KIA.
b.   N5367, No 10 Sqn, RNAS, F/S/Lt ADM Lewis, last seen over Roulers at 0730, POW.
c.   B3918, No 70 Sqn, RFC, 2/Lt OC Bridgeman, WIA, his Camel badly damaged during combat.
Losses:
Vfw Fritz Rumey   5   Wounded in action.

26 August 1917

Vfw K Menckhoff	3	Spad	Zonnebeke	0645	7	
Ltn K Wissemann	3	Spad	S Becelaere	0655	4	
Rittm M v Richthofen	JGI	Spad	Poelkapelle	0730	59	a.
Vfw K Menckhoff	3	RE8	Langemarck	1005	8	
Obltn W Reinhard	11	RE8	Bixschoote	1005	5	
Obltn O Schmidt	29	Balloon	S Loos	1430	7	b.
Vfw K Petzinna	29	Balloon	N Elverdinghe	1440	2	b.
Ltn L Hanstein	16	Balloon	Belrupt		8	c.
Obltn E v Schleich	21	Spad	S Esnes		8	
Ltn W v Bülow	36	Spad			zlg	

a.   B3492, No 19 Sqn, RFC, 2/Lt CP Williams, last seen in combat at 0600 over Courtrai, KIA.
b.   It is not known which pilot flamed which balloon but both the French 49 and 93 Compagnies d'Aérostières balloons were destroyed this date in this Sector. The observers, S/Lt Caron and Adj M Beaufiest, made safe descents.
c.   French 59 Compagnie d'Aérostières, the observer, Adj Glaize, made a safe descent.
Losses:
Uffz Carl Conradt   17   KIA 2040 between Slype and Vlisseghem.

27 August 1917

Vfw D Averes	ObOst	Balloon	NE Uextull		1

Losses – Nil

28 – 30 August 1917

No Claims – No Losses

31 August 1917

Ltn K Hammes	35	Spad	W Dixmuiden	1910	1	
Ltn H Adam	6	SE5	NW Zandvoorde	1950	13	a.

a.   B1794, No 66 Sqn, RFC, 2/Lt ES Bacon, last seen over Houlthust Wood, KIA.
Losses:
Vfw Wilhelm Reiss   3   KIA, probably by Lt GM Wilkinson,
                                  56 Sqn, RFC.

JASTA ARMEE ASSIGNMENTS AS OF 1 SEPTEMBER 1917

Western Front

1 Armee 19   6 Armee 12,30,37
2 Armee 5   7 Armee 1,9,13,15,22
3 Armee –   Det 'A' 40s
4 Armee 2,3,4,6,7,8,10,11,17,18,20,24,26,27,28,29,33,35b,36   Det 'B' 39,41
5 Armee 14,16b,21,23b,32b,34b   Det 'C' –

Other Fronts

11 Armee 25   Macedonia
 1 Armee 38   Bulgarian Armee
Kuk 2 Armee OberOst   Russia

1 September 1917

Rittm M v Richthofen	JGI	RE8	Zonnebeke	0750	60	a.
Ltn K Hammes	35	Spad	Wervicq	0810	2	b.
Obltn W Reinhard	11	Camel	W Frezenberg	0815	6	

a.   B782, No 6 Sqn, RFC, Lt JBC Madge WIA/POW & 2/Lt Walter Kember KIA, last seen at 0640 over Polygon Wood.
b.   B 3569, No 19 Sqn, RFC, 2/Lt E M Sant, departed at 0633, last seen over Houthulst Wood, POW.
Losses – Nil

2 September 1917

Ltn H Dilthey	27	Spad	W Roubaix	0850	3	a.

a.   A312, No 19 Sqn, RFC, 2/Lt WAL Spencer, last seen north of Menin at 0740, WIA/POW.
Losses – Nil

3 September 1917

Ltn E Mohnicke	11	Pup	SE Tenbrielen	0730	6	a.
Rittm M v Richthofen	JGI	Pup	S Bousbecque	0735	61	a.
Ltn E Thun	.7	Spad	Pervyse	0825	zlg	
Ltn P Billik	7	Camel	Eesen-Zarren	0825	6	
Ltn G Meyer	7	Camel	Dixmuiden	0825	4	
Ltn C Degelow	7	Camel	W Dixmuiden	0830	zlg	
Ltn K Wüsthoff	4	Sopwith	Tenbrielen	0830	8	
Ltn W v Bülow	36	Sopwith	Tenbrielen	0830	18	
Ltn W Voss	10	Camel	N Houthem	0955	39	b.
Ltn K Hammes	32	Triplane	SE Essen	0955	3	
Ltn A v Schönebeck	11	Triplane	E Hollebeke	1005	3	
Ltn E Stapenhorst	11	Triplane	Wytschaete	1030	2	
Ltn H Hoyer	36	RE8	W Tenbrielen	1040	2	
Ltn T Quandt	36	Rumpf DD	Bellewaarder	1100	4	c.
Vfw O Fruhner	26	Pup	S Wervicq	1130	1	d.
Obltn K v Döring	4	RE8	NW Houthem	1210	6	
Vfw O Fruhner	26	Camel	Zillebeke See	1600	2	
Ltn K Wüsthoff	4	RE8	E Zillebeke	1710	9	

Vfw K Thom	21	Caudron	Forêt de Hesse	1730	2
Obltn E Schleich	21	AR2	Forêt de Hesse	1730	9
Obltn E Schleich	21	Spad	S Forêt de Hesse	1735	10
Ltn H Adam	6	Nieuport	Koelenberg	1950	14 e.
Obltn H Göring	27	Spad XI	N Lampernisse	1955	13
Obltn O v Boenigk	4	Camel	Houthem	2000	4
OBltn O v Boenigk	4	Pup	Brielen	2015	–
Uffz M Mallman	19	Balloon	Pontavert		1 f.
Uffz A Tybelsky	19	Balloon	Pontavert		1 f.
Ltn W Kypke	41	Salmson	Rodern		2

a. No 46 Sqn, RFC, lost two Sopwith Scouts this date, both departed at 0545 and were last seen at 0645 over Menin; B1754, Lt KW McDonald, WIA/POW; & B1795, Lt AF Bird, POW.
b. B3917, No 45 Sqn, RFC, Lt AT Heywood, last seen at 1100 over Comines, KIA.
c. Voisin, Escadrille VB 109, S/Lt Navarin & Sgt Delaunay.
d. A7333, No 46 Sqn, RFC, Lt S Williams, last seen over Linselles at 1030, POW.
e. B1582, No 1 Sqn, RFC, 2/Lt C Pickstone, departed at 1810, last seen north-east of Gheluvelt, KIA.
f. There were two French balloons flamed at 1535 in Soissons Sector, those of the 66 and 70 Compagnies d'Aérostières. The respective observers, Adj Legude and S/Lt Cabanet made safe parachute jumps.

Losses:

Ltn Wilhelm Brockelmann	11	Wounded in action at 1430 near Bousbecque, probably by a No 1 Sqn, RNAS, patrol.
Vfw Hans Bowski	14	Wounded in action.
OfStv Hans Malz	20	Killed during a bombing attack on his airfield.
Vfw Freidrich Matthies	20	Severely wounded during bombing attack on Varsenaere airfield; DOW 4 September.
Vfw Gustav Beerendonk	20	Wounded during attack on Varsenaere.
Hptm Otto Hartmann	28	Killed in action at 0815 N of Dixmuiden by Lts RE Dodds and TCS Tuffield, 48 Sq, RFC.
Vfw Kurt Petzinna	29	Killed in an accident during take-off near Torhut Revinse.
Uffz Walter König	31	Killed in action over Tidietelhof.
Ltn Heinrich Vollertsen	36	Killed in action near Tenbrielen by AA fire.
Ltn Josef Klever	39	Killed in action near Wattweiler.
Obltn Maximillian Ziegler gen. Stege	41	Killed in an accident at the Ensisheim airfield.
FlgMt Brenner	MFJ1	Wounded in action.

4 September 1917

Ltn K Wüsthoff	4	Nieuport	NW Polygonwald	0805	10	a.
Uffz A Techow	7	Camel	E Pervyse	0815	zlg	
Obltn R Berthold	18	RE8	N Ypern	0825	14	b.
Ltn E Mohnicke	11	Camel	Becelaere	0830	7	
Ltn E Stapenhorst	11	Camel	S Becelaere	0840	3	
Ltn R Matthaei	5	G100	Le Catelet	0915	6	
Ltn K Wüsthoff	4	Camel	S Ypern	1045	11	
Ltn V Schobinger	12	RE8	Monchy	1120	4	
Vfw J Pütz	23	AR2	Esneswald	1213	zlg	
Obltn O Schmidt	29	Balloon	Loo	1450	–	
Ltn J Schmidt	3	RE8	Poelkapelle	1630	13	
Obltn R Berthold	18	RE8	St Jean	1700	15	
Obltn H Bethge	30	BF2b	Auchy	1945	15	
Obltn H Bethge	30	BF2b	.... La Bassée	1950	16	
Ltn R Wendelmuth	8	SE5	Ypern	2030	6	
Ltn L Hanstein	16	Spad	Forêt de Hesse		9	
Ltn K Odebrett	16	Caudron	Recicourt		7	c.
Ltn G Flecken	20	Camel	SW Nieuport		3	
Obltn E Schleich	21	AR2	S Vauquois		11	

a.   B6679, No 29 Sqn, RFC, 2/Lt JH Binns, last seen at 0650 over Zonnebeke, KIA.
b.   A3778, No 9 Sqn, RFC, Lt BKB Barber, & Pvt AW Brimell, departed at 1330, KIAs.
c.   Letord, Escadrille R 214, S/Lt Lasnier (P), Lt Garret-Flandy (O) & Sgt Paolaggi (G), shot down in flames in this sector.

Losses:

Obltn Wilhelm Reinhard	11	Wounded 0915 over Houthulst Forest.
Obltn Erich Hahn	19	Killed in action at 1935 over Beine, by S/Lt Georges Madon, N 38, 16th victory.
Ltn Lutz	28	Wounded in action by AA fire.
Ltn Gebhard Emberger	29	Shot down in flames and killed at 2006 hrs over Poelkapelle.
Ltn Siegfried v Lieres und Wilkau	29	Wounded at 2000 between Poelkapelle and Houthulst Forest.
Vfw Heinrich Mertens	35	Wounded and forced to land nr Hazewind.

5 September 1917

Uffz K Steudel	3	Camel	S Armentières	0906	4	
OfStv J Klein	18	Camel	Amerika	0955	2	
Ltn K Wüsthoff	4	Camel	SE Zillebeke	1000	12	
Obltn R Berthold	18	DH4	Thielt		16	a.
Ltn J v Busse	3	Camel	Houthulsterwald	1530	2	b.
Ltn W Voss	10	Pup	St Julien	1550	40	c.
Ltn E Löwenhardt	10	Pup	St Julien	1550	3	c.
Ltn W Voss	10	Caudron	Bixschoote	1630	41	d.
Ltn D Collin	22	Spad	Froide Terre	1900	4	
Vfw R Jörke	12	Sopwith	W Lens	1945	6	
Ltn R Rumpel	16	Morane	Fort Belleville		2	e.
Ltn L Hanstein	16	Balloon	Belleville		10	f.
Obltn E Schleich	21	Spad	Höhe 304		12	
Ltn E Thuy	21	Spad	Bethélainville		9	
Uffz Krause	K3	Caudron	Remoncourt		1	d.

a.   A7530, No 55 Sqn, RFC, Lt JW Neill & 2/Lt TM Webster, departed at 1204, MIAs.
b.   B3777, No 70 Sqn, RFC, 2/Lt JC Huggard, departed at 1300, POW.
c.   B1842, No 46 Sqn, RFC, 2/Lt CW Odell, badly shot up but landed without incident.
d.   Caudron G.6 of Escadrille C 53, MdL Thabaud-Desthouilières & Lt Mulard fell in flames in this sector, KIAs.
e.   MS P of Escadrille F 215, Sgt Maurice Leroux & Lt Goutier, KIAs.
f.   47 Compagnie d'Aérostières, Lieutenant Gadel, the observer, unharmed.

Losses:

Ltn Franz Pernet	B	Killed in action near Westende testing AEG DI 4400/17, probably by 2/Lt KR Park & 1/AM H Lindfeld, No 48 Sqn, RFC.
Vfw Alfred Muth	27	Killed in action near Moorslede, 1945 hrs.

6 September 1917

Ltn Armbrecht	1	EA	Mont St Martin	0715	1	
Ltn W Göttsch	8	Sopwith	Elverdinghe	0910	15	
Ltn O Kissenberth	23	Spad	Beaumont	1402	13	a.
Vfw O Pelz	23	Spad	Ornes	1403	1	a.
Ltn W Lehmann	5	Sopwith 2	Mont St Martin	1405	1	b.
Ltn A Scheck	5	Sopwith 2	Montbrehain	1407	1	
Ltn H Auer	32	Spad	Bourruswald	1555	zlg	
Ltn W Voss	10	FE2d	SE Boesinghe	1635	42	c.
Ltn P Billik	7	Spad	Schaep Baillie		7	d.
Obltn Schleich	21	Nieuport 2	S Vacquois		13	
Ltn D Collin	22	Nieuport	E Charny-Bras		5	

a.   Two Spad VIIs lost in this area; Cpl ET Buckley,(an American), N 65 & Sgt H Callinet N 86.
b.   Escadrille Sop 128, MdL Barbe & Soldat Bartaire.
c.   B1895, No 20 Sqn, RFC, Lt JO Pilkington & 2/AM HF Matthews, KIAs.
d.   B3488, No 23 Sqn, RFC, 2/Lt EGC Quilter, last seen at 0800, WIA/POW.

Losses:

Ltn Diether Collin	22	Wounded in action.

7 September 1917

Ltn E Thuy	21	Spad	S Höhe 304	1040	10
Ltn M Raspe	21	Spad	S Malancourt	1040	zlg

Losses:

Ltn Karl Odebrett	16	Wounded in action by AA fire.
Ltn Walter Entz	38	Injured in a landing accident at Kainkowa, died the next day.

8 September 1917

No Claims

Losses:

Ltn Wilhelm Neumann	40	Killed in an accident during a test flight at Montey, near Montingen-Metz.

9 September 1917

Ltn E Stapenhorst	11	Spad	SW Zonnebeke	1247	4	a.
Ltn L Luer	27	Sopwith	Frezenberg	1300	2	
Obltn zS K Mettlich	8	BF2b	N Zillebeke See	1445	zlg	
Ltn R Wendelmuth	8	BF2b	SW Langemarck	1500	7	
Ltn J Schmidt	3	Nieuport	Comines	1520	14	
Uffz P Bäumer	B	RE8	Manekensevere	1525	4	b.
Ltn E Hess	28	BF2b	Frelinghein	1640	12	c.
Ltn H Kroll	24	Triplane	NE Zillebeke	1835	9	d.
Vfw F Altemeier	24	Spad	Ypern 1843		6	
Vfw F Kosmahl	26	Camel	Westroosebeke	1900	7	e.
Obltn O v Boenigk	4	Sopwith	E Langemarck	1905	5	e.
Ltn K Hammes	35	Camel	SW Stadenberg	1910	4	e.
Ltn M Müller	28	Camel	Houthulsterwald	1930	27	
Ltn E Löwenhardt	10	Balloon	Alveringhem	2055	4	f.
Vfw G Fieseler	25	Nieuport	Progradec		zlg	

a.   A6713, No 23 Sqn, RFC, 2/Lt KR Sayers, last seen 1145 east of Poelkapelle, MIA.
b.   3597, No 52 Sqn, RFC, 2/Lts AG Davidson & BB Bishop, departed at 1340, shot down in flames, KIAs.
c.   A7202, No 22 Sqn, RFC, Sgt JH Hamer & Sgt GE Lambeth, departed at 1425, seen to fall in flames near Wambrechies, KIAs.
d.   N5477, No 1 Sqn, RNAS, F/S/Lt LE Adlam, last seen E of Ypres, KIA.
e.   B3928, No 70 Sqn, RFC, Lt NC Saward, POW, last seen 1800 over Houthulst, all three claims in this vicinity.
f.   93 Compagnie d'Aérostières, S/Lt Berthon, the observer, was not harmed.

Losses:

Ltn Karl Hammes	35	WIA, Albatros DV 2336/17, probably by Capt CF Collett, No 70 Sqn, RFC.

10 September 1917

Ltn E Hess	28	Camel	SE Nieuwekapelle	1615	13	
Ltn W Voss	10	Camel	Langemarck	1750	43	a.
Ltn W Voss	10	Camel	SW Poelkapelle	1755	44	b.
Ltn W Göttsch	8	Spad	Frezenburg	1810	16	

Ltn W Voss	10	Spad	S Langemarck	1815	45	c.
Ltn J Jacobs	7	Spad	Keyem	1905	7	d.
Ltn F Ray	28	Camel	NW Houthulst	1930	2	

a.   B3927, No 70 Sqn, RFC, 2/Lt AJS Sisley, MIA.
b.   B3787, No 70 Sqn, RFC, 2/Lt OC Pearson, last seen between Roulers and Staden, at 1720, KIA.
c.   Spad VII, Escadrille Spa 37, Adj P Tiberghein, MIA.
d.   Spad VII, Capitaine G Matton (9 victories), CO N 48, KIA.
Losses – Nil

11 September 1917

Ltn J Jacobs	7	Camel	SE Koekuit	0830	8	
Ltn H Kroll	24	Triplane	Bellewaarde	0945	–	
Vfw K Menckhoff	3	Camel	Moorslede	0950	9	
Vfw M Wackwitz	24	Camel	Wallenmolen	1005	2	
Ltn K Wüsthoff	4	Camel	Langemarck	1020	13	
Obltn E Weigand	10	Spad	Bixschoote	1020	–	
Ltn W Voss	10	Camel	Langemarck	1030	46	
Ltn K Wissemann	3	Spad	Poelkapelle	1030	5	a.
Ltn H Böhning	36	Sopwith	Houthulsterwald	1101	2	
Ltn F v Götz	MFJ1	BF2b	Wynedaele	1210	1	
Ltn J Schmidt	3	Spad	Ypern	1235	15	
Ltn W Dingel	18	DH4	Moorslede	1335	2	
Ltn M Müller	28	Camel	SW Dixmuiden	1335	zlg	
Ltn O Schober	18	DH4	S Terhand	1338	1	
Ltn W Voss	10	Camel	E St Julien	1625	47	b.
Ltn W Göttsch	8	Spad	Frezenberg	1810	15	
Flgmt B Heinrich	MFJ1	Camel	Schoore	1910	7	
FlgMt Künstler	MFJ1	Camel	SW Schoore	1910	3	
Obltn O Schmidt	29	Nieuport	NE Bixschoote	1930	8	c.
Vfw K Thom	21	Nieuport 2	Verdun		3	
Obltn E Schleich	21	AR2	S Verdun		14	
Ltn E Thuy	21	Spad	Forgeswald		11	d.
Ltn W v Bülow	36	Camel	Merkem		zlg	

a.   Capitaine G Guynemer (53 victories), CO Spa 3, KIA.
b.   B6136, No 45 Sq, RFC, Lt OL McMaking (6 victories), KIA.
c.   B3635, No 1 Sqn, RFC, Captain LF Jenkin, MC, (22 victories), KIA.
d.   S/Lt R de Bruce (3 victories), Spa 75, flying a Spad XIII, missing over Consenvoye, on the edge of the Bois de Forges.
Losses:

Uffz Ernst Schaetzle	19	Killed in action, hit by AA fire over St Loup.
Ltn Werner Richard	OberOst	Killed in an accident during a test flight.
Ltn Friedrich v Götz	MFJ1	Killed in action at 1900 near Schoore.

12 September 1917

| Ltn K Wüsthoff | 4 | Camel | SW Deulemont | 0800 | 14 | |
| Ltn H Kroll | 24 | Spad | SW Linselles | 1315 | 10 | a. |

a.   B3506, No 23 Sqn, RFC, 2/Lt SW Dronsfield, last seen at 1215 over Menin, POW.
Losses – Nil

13 September 1917

Ltn W v Bülow	36	Camel	Becelaere	0810	19	a.
Ltn K Wüsthoff	4	Triplane	S Wervicq	0830	15	b.
Vfw K Menckhoff	3	Spad	Zillebeke	1520	10	

a.   B3933, No 10 Sqn, RNAS, F/S/Lt ED Abbott, last seen at 0710 west of Roulers, WIA/POW.
b.   N5429, No 1 Sqn, RNAS, F/S/Lt John R Wilford, WIA/POW.
Losses:
Ltn Wilhelm Finhold   34   Killed in action over Bonvillers.

14 September 1917

Vfw G Schneidewind	17	Sopwith	Menin	0850	2	a.
Ltn J Schmidt	3	SE5	de Ruiter	1900	–	
Vfw K Menckhoff	3	SE5	de Ruiter	1905	11	b.

a.   B2333, No 70 Sqn, RFC, 2/Lt ESC Sen, last seen 0730 west of Roulers, POW.
b.   B516, N 56 Sqn, RFC, 2/Lt NH Crow, departed at 1700, last seen in combat near Menin, KIA.
Losses:

Ltn Maximillian v Chelius	B	Shot down in flames and killed near Dixmuiden, flying an Albatros DVa (G 70) by 2/Lts KR Park and H Owen, 48 Sqn, RFC.
Obltn Ernst Weigand	10	WIA, by Captain JTB McCudden, 56 Sqn.
Ltn Gisbert-Wilhelm Groos	11	Wounded in action.

15 September 1917

Ltn H Gontermann	15	Caudron	Cerny	0720	36	
Obltn E Schleich	21	Caudron	Parois	0805	15	
Ltn Hans-Georg von der Osten	11	Sopwith 2	Frezenberg	1245	3	
Obltn R Berthold	18	Sopwith	Zillebeke See	1410	17	
Obltn B Loerzer	26	Nieuport	Bousbecque	1625	7	a.
Vfw F Gille	12	RE8	Guémappe	1810	5	
Ltn Hans Adam	6	Sopwith	N Ypern	1900	17	b.
Ltn F Berkemeyer	27	Sopwith	NW Wervicq	1938	3	b.

a.   B1672, No 1 Sqn, RFC, 2/Lt ED Tyzak, departed at 1340, last seen NW of Ypres, KIA.
b.   No 70 Sqn, RFC, lost two Camels that departed at 1700 this date: B2343, 2/Lt H Ibbotson, POW, and 6250, 2/Lt JBH Wyman, WIA/POW.
Losses:

Obltn Kurt Wolff	11	KIA flying Fokker Dr I No. F1 102/17, by FSL NM McGregor of No 10 Sqn, RNAS.
Ltn Adolf Wiehle	20	KIA over Nieuport, his plane exploding in the air.

16 September 1917

Ltn K Wüsthoff	4	Camel	W Staden	1245	16	a.
Obltn K v Döring	4	Camel	W Staden	1245	7	a.
Ltn F Ray	28	Camel	Dixmuiden	1300	3	a.
Vfw R Jörke	12	Pup	Monchy	1400	7	
Ltn V Schobinger	12	Pup	SW Lecluse	1410	5	
Ltn H Auer	32	AR2	Marre	1650	5	
Obltn R Berthold	18	RE8	W Becelaere	1800	18	b.
Ltn E Hess	28	Camel	Passchendaele	1800	14	
Ltn A Hanko	28	G100	Sleyhage	1800	5	c.
Obltn R Berthold	18	RE8	Zonnebeke	1825	19	d.
Ltn J Veltjens	18	RE8	NW Boesinghe	1830	6	
Obltn E Schleich	21	Caudron	Hessenwald	1845	16	
Obltn E Schleich	21	Spad	Hessenwald	1850	17	
Ltn O Fitzner	17	SE5	Gheluwe	1845	2	e.
Ltn W Göttsch	8	Sopwith	SW Houthulst		17	
Vfw R Francke	8	Sopwith	SW Houthulst		6	
Obltn H Auffarth	18	Sopwith	Vierlewenhoek		1	

Obltn E Turck	18	DH4	SW Houthulst	1	
Obltn O Schmidt	29	Balloon	NW Loos	9	f.
Ltn H Weiss	41	Sopwith 2	Colmar	1	g.
Ltn W Kypke	41	Sopwith 2	Colmar	3	g.
Ltn R Klimke	27	Sopwith	Ypres	-	
Vfw G Nestler	K4a	Sopwith 2	Bitsche	1	g.

a.   No 70 Sqn, RFC, lost two Camels that were last seen over Houthulst Forest at 1130: B3753, Lt GB McMichael, POW, and B3836, 2/Lt LF Wheeler, WIA/POW.
b.   A4693, No 6 Sqn, RFC, 2/Lt H Haslam & L/Cpl AJ Lindy, KIA s.
c.   6287, No 27 Sqn, RFC, 2/Lt NW Goodwin, departed at 1455, last seen in combat over Staden, KIA.
d.   No 4 Sqn, RFC, 2/Lt HW Weller, WIA, & 2/AM F Farmer,DOW.
e.   8909, No 60 Sqn, RFC, 2/Lt JJA Hawtrey, last seen over Tenbrielen at 1830, WIA/POW/DOW.
f.   49 Compagnie d'Aérostières, S/Lt Perrissin-Pirasset, the observer was not harmed.
g.   Two Sopwith two-seaters from Escadrille Sop 131 were lost this date in this sector; Brig Marquis & S/Lt Lavigne, MIAs, and Brig Grandry & Adj- Chef J Simon KIAs. Also one was lost from Sop 123 MdL Canivet & S/Lt Blehaut, KIAs.

Losses

Ltn Alfred Bauer	17	KIA in Albatros DIII (G.71) by Lt Robert Chidlaw-Roberts, No 60 Sqn, RFC, for his 2nd victory.

17 September 1917

Vfw R Jörke	12	Pup	Feuchy	0700	8
Vfw F Bachmann	6	Camel	S Zillebeke See	0720	1
Ltn E Udet	37	DH5	S Izel-Quiéry	0800	10
Uffz E Liebert	30	DH5	SW Izel	0810	1
Ltn K Hertz	4	Nieuport	N Houthulst	0840	–
Vfw K Thom	21	AR2	Mort Homme		4

Losses – Nil

18 September 1917

Ltn V Schobinger	12	RE8	SE Mory	0840	6
Vfw Dilcher	5	DH5	Villers-Plouich	1035	–
Obltn H Bethge	30	DH5	Fontaine	1035	17
Obltn E Schleich	21	Caudron	Verdun	1040	8
Vfw K Thom	21	Spad	W Verdun	1050	5
Ltn W Ewers	12	DH5	Wambaix	110	1	a.
Vfw R Jörke	12	DH5	SW Moeuvres	1105	9	a.
Ltn E Thuy	21	Spad	Chattancourt	1430	12
Ltn R Windisch	32	AR2	Fleury	1547	2
Vfw O Stadter	32	Spad	NW Douaumont	1607	1
Vfw K Thom	21	AR2	Hessenwald	1655	6
Vfw K Thom	21	Caudron	NE Cumières	1720	7
Vfw J Neumaier	16	Balloon	Fort Belleville		2
Ltn E Thuy	21	Caudron	Mort Homme		13

a.   No 41 Sqn, RFC, lost two DH5s this date: A9208, 2/Lt AJ Chapman, last seen at 1120 near Cambrai, KIA; and A9426, Lt HF McArdle, last seen at 1050 over the Scarpe Valley, KIA.

Losses – Nil

19 September 1917

Obltn H Waldhausen	37	Sopwith 2	Fresnes	0730	1
Vfw F Gille	12	BF2b	SW Sailly	0850	6	a.
Ltn H Adam	6	RE8	W Ypres	1000	18	b.
Obltn R Berthold	18	RE8	Becelaere	1000	20

Ltn H Adam	6	Sopwith	Houthulst	1005	16	c.
Ltn C Galetschky	6	Sopwith	Houthulst	1005	1	
Ltn E Böhme	B	RE8	Boesinghe	1047	14	d.
Obltn R Flashar	5	Morane 2	Elincourt	1203	2	e.
Ltn R Matthaei	5	Morane 2	SW Caudry	1217	7	e.
Obltn H Auffarth	18	Spad	Verbrandenmolen	1520	2	
Ltn O Kissenberth	23	Spad	S Mort Homme	1640	14	f.
Ltn T Rumpel	23	Spad	Montzéville	1640	3	f.
Vfw F Kosmahl	26	Triplane	Passchendaele	1755	8	g.
Obltn E Schleich	21	Caudron	NE Verdun	1835	19	
Ltn J Werner	14	Spad	Damloup		2	
Uffz M Mallmann	19	Caudron	Villers		2	h.
Vfw K Thom	21	AR2	N Verdun		8	
Vfw K Thom	21	AR2	E Verdun		9	
Vfw H Fritzsche	29	Sopwith	Langemarck		2	
Obltn H Waldhausen	37	RE8	Souchez		zlg	
Vfw J Schwendemann	41	AR2	W Lusse		1	

a.   A7130, No 11 Sqn, RFC, 2/Lt HT Taylor & Lt GW Mumford, last seen over Bullecourt at 0845, WIA/POWs.

b.   B 3427, No 4 Sqn, RFC, 2/Lt JS Walthew & Lt MC Hartnett, KIAs.

c.   N6374, No 10 Sqn, RNAS, F/S/Lt EGV Grace, shot down in flames over Houthulst Forest at about 1000 hours, MIA.

d.   B5012, No 9 Sqn, RFC, Lt HL Devlin & 2/Lt FA Wright, departed at 0945, shot down near Langemarck, KIAs.

e.   No 3 Sqn, RFC, lost two Moranes that departed at 1045, last seen E of Estourmel: A6655, 2/Lts CA Sutcliffe & T Humble, POWs, and A234, Lt E Golding, KIA, and Cpl L Goss, WIA/POW/DOW.

f.   One of these may have been Cpl Marcel Vassel of N 80, in a Spad VII, MIA.

g.   N5490, No 1 Sqn, RNAS, F/S/Lt RE McMillan, POW.

h.   Probably Escadrille C 64, Cpl Abraham & Sol Mauvillier, MIAs, in a G 4.

Losses:

Ltn Alhard Scheck	5	Killed in action between Nauroy and Le Cateau.
OfStv Paul Aue	10	Wounded at 1000 over Roulers.
Gefr Becker	20	Shot down and taken prisoner.

20 September 1917

Ltn H Adam	6	Sopwith	W Bellewaarde	0940	19	a.
Ltn H Adam	6	Sopwith	Becelaere	0950	20	b.
Ltn R Wendelmuth	8	Triplane	N Passchendaele	0950	8	c.
Ltn K Stock	6	Triplane	Kemmel	0950	1	
Ltn H Kroll	24	Spad	W Zonnebeke	1104	11	
Vfw F Altemeier	24	Spad	W Zonnebeke	1105	7	d.
Obltn R Berthold	18	Spad	E Zillebeke See	1130	21	
Vfw F Kosmahl	26	Camel	Passchendaele	1150	9	
Obltn B Loerzer	26	Camel	Gravenstafel	1150	8	
Ltn W Lange	B	Camel	SW Stade	1210	1	
Ltn K Wüsthoff	4	Spad	Amerika	1215	17	
Ltn R Runge	18	Nieuport	Zillebeke See	1320	4	
Vfw F Bachmann	6	Balloon	Kemmel	1400	2	
Ltn K Wüsthoff	4	Spad	W Langemarck	1430	18	
Uffz P Bäumer	B	Camel	Ramskapelle	1510	5	e.
Obltn E Schleich	21	Nieuport 2	NE Verdun	1850	20	
Ltn F Ray	28	RE8	Zillebeke See		4	
Vfw F Schmitt	29	Nieuport	Blankaartsee		3	
Ltn J Veltjens	18	2 seater	W Hooge		zlg	

a.   A9179, No 32 Sqn, RFC, 2/Lt WO Cornish, last seen at 0900, WIA/POW/DOW.

b.   A8931, No 60 Sqn, RFC, Sgt JW Bancroft, POW.
c.   N6292, No 1 Sqn, RNAS, F/S/Lt J H Winn, KIA.
d.   B3493, No 23 Sqn, RFC, Lt F Bullock-Webster, WIA/DOW.
e.   B3906, No 9 Sqn, RNAS, F/S/Lt R Sykes, shot down and FTL in no-man's- land, WIA.

Losses:

Ltn E Löwenhardt	10	Wounded in action over Roulers at 1110, but remained with the unit.	

21 September 1917

Vfw W Jumpelt	27	DH4	Becelaere	0700	1	
Ltn W Rosenstein	27	DH4	Zonnebeke	0715	1	
Vfw G Schneidewind	17	Sopwith	E Ypres	0821	3	a.
Ltn W Böhme	B	RE8	Comines	0852	15	b.
Obltn H Göring	27	BF2b	Sleyhage	0905	14	c.
Gefr U Neckel	12	Pup	SW Boiry	0915	1	d.
Obltn H Auffarth	18	Spad	N Menin	0940	3	e.
Ltn R Runge	18	Spad	Amerika	0950	5	e.
Obltn R Berthold	18	Spad	W Menin	0950	28	e.
Ltn P Erbguth	30	Camel	S Wewelghem	1150	2	
Ltn G Bellen	10	Balloon	Elverdinghe	1445	1	f.
OfStv R Weckbrodt	26	2 seater	Wervicq	1745	3	
Uffz P Bäumer	B	Camel	Boesinghe	1750	6	
Obltn E Schleich	21	Caudron	W Verdun	1835	21	
Obltn E Schleich	21	AR2	Verdun	1845	22	
Ltn E Löwenhardt	10	Balloon	Vlamertinghe	1925	5	f.
Vfw K Bohnenkamp	22	AR2	Höhe 344		1	
Ltn F Kieckhäfer	29	BF2b	Hooglede		2	g.

a.   A4857, No 56 Sqn, RFC, Lt WJ Potts, KIA.
b.   3617, No 53 Sqn, RFC, Capt RNF Mills & Lt WA Browne, departed at 0635, shot down near Warneton, KIAs.
c.   A7224, No 48 Sqn, RFC, 2/Lts RL Curtis, 15 victories, WIA/POW/DOW, & DP Fitzgerald-Uniacke, 13 victories, WIA/POW departed at 0800 last seen over Roulers.
d.   A7321, No 46 Sqn, RFC, 2/Lt RS Asher, KIA.
e.   No 19 Sqn, RFC, lost three Spads that departed at 0916 and were last seen engaged in combat over Dadizeele: B 3533, 2/Lt FW Kirby, B3642, 2/Lt WG McRae, B3557, 2/Lt RA Inglis, all KIA.
f.   British Balloon 47-11-2 (BMS 167/D) lost this date in the vicinity of Ypres, one of these two pilot's claim is not confirmed.
g.   A7234, No 20 Sqn, RFC, Lt CHC Woods & 2/Lt TW McLean, departed at 1636 last seen between Menin and Wervicq, KIAs.

Losses:

Ltn Richard Plange	B	Wounded in action.
Ltn Friedrich Weber	21	Killed in action at 1830 over Louvemont.
Vfw Heinrich Schott	25	Injured in a landing accident

22 September 1917

Obltn R Berthold	18	Camel	Zillebeke See	0900	23	a.
Ltn J Fichter	22	Spad	NW Douaumont	1000	3	
Obltn B Loerzer	26	Camel	Stadenreef	1030	9	
Vfw K Thom	21	AR2	Verdun	1115	10	
Vfw K Thom	21	AR2	Bourrus	1122	11	
Uffz Becker	21	Caudron	Bethélainville	1140	1	
Ltn K Wüsthoff	4	Camel	Langemarck	1410	19	
Ltn O Kissenberth	23	Spad	Vaux	1430	15	
Ltn O Förster	15	Balloon	W le Fère	1820	1	b.
Ltn E Thuy	21	Spad	Höhe 304		14	

a.   A7205, No 22 Sqn, RFC, 2/Lts EA Bell & RE Nowell, departed at 0800, seen to fall in flames near Hollebeke, KIAs.
b.   26 Compagnie d'Aérostières.
Losses:

Vfw Fritz Kosmahl	26	Wounded in action S of Poelkapelle; DOW, 26 September.				

23 September 1917

Ltn O Kissenberth	23	Spad VII	E Vauquois	0815	16	
Ltn W Voss	10	DH4	S Roulers	0930	48	a.
Ltn O Kissenberth	23	Sopwith	Höhe 304	0950	17	
Ltn H Adam	6	RE8	N Ypres	1045	20	
Ltn F Ray	28	Camel	N Nieuport	1055	5	
Obltn K v Döring	4	Camel	Langemarck	1130	8	
Ltn R Wendelmuth	8	Sopwith	Kruisstraat	1230	9	
Obltn zS K Mettlich	8	Sopwith	S Kruisstraat	1230	5	
Vfw W Seitz	8	Nieuport	St Jean	1230	4	
Ltn H Becker	12	Nieuport	SW Oppy	1655	2	
Ltn R Wendelmuth	8	Sopwith	W Frezenberg	1830	10	
Ltn W Böning	19	Nieuport	Merlet-Mühle		5	b.
Ltn W Böning	19	Nieuport	W Orainville		6	c.
Ltn O Kissenberth	23	Caudron	Fort Marre		zlg	
Ltn W v Bülow	36	Nieuport	N Warneton		20	

a.   A7643, No 57 Sqn, RFC, S/Lt Samuel LJ Bramley & 2/Lt JM DeLacey, KIAs.
b.   Probably Nieuport XXIVbis of Escadrille N 96, MdL J Petre MIA.
c.   Probably Nieuport XXIVbis of Escadrille N 96, Cpl A Mulon (2 victories), MIA.
Losses:

Ltn Werner Voss	10	In Fokker FI 103/17, (G.72) killed in action at 1935 N of Frezenberg, by Lt APF Rhys Davids of No 56 Sqn, RFC, his 19th victory.				
Ltn Hugo Jöns	20	Killed in action over Dixmuiden.				

24 September 1917

Obltn E Schleich	21	AR2	W Verdun	0720	23	
Obltn E Schleich	21	Rumpf DD	SW Verdun	0735	24	
Ltn O Kissenberth	23	Spad	Hessenwald	0815	16	
Ltn E Udet	37	Camel	E Loos	1230	11	
Obltn B Loerzer	26	Camel	Pervyse	1300	10	
Obltn H Waldhausen	37	G100	SW Cagnicourt	1445	2	a.
Ltn E Udet	37	EA	Beugny	1450	11	
Ltn F Ray	28	Camel	Ramskapelle	1530	6	
Ltn K Wüsthoff	4	Camel	Moorslede	1650	20	
Ltn E Thuy	21	Spad	N Höhe 304		15	
Ltn zS T Osterkamp	MFJ1	Spad	W Westroosebeke		6	b.

a.   A3976, No 27 Sqn, RFC, 2/Lt W English, last seen at 1450 near Souchy Lestrées, WIA/POW.
b.   Capt d'Aymery, Escadrille Spa 31, MIA.
Losses:

Ltn Julius Schmidt	3	Wounded, fight with No 70 Sqn, RFC.				
Vfw Fritz Rumey	5	Wounded in action.				
Obltn Werner Jahns	28	Killed in action at 1530 SE of Slype.				

25 September 1917

Vfw K Menckhoff	3	Spad	Nordschoote	1525	12	
Obltn R Berthold	18	Spad	Gheluvelt	1630	24	a.

Vfw Bärwald	37	DH5	Monchy	1830	1
Obltn K Waldhausen	37	Balloon	Bethune	1835	3	b.
Ltn R Matthaei	5	Pup	Boursies	1845	8
Uffz Tönjes	3	DH4	Oekene		1
Uffz Goretzki	13	AR2	Douaumont		1
Ltn Breuer	14	Rumpf DD			1
Ltn L Hanstein	16	Morane	SW Douaumont		11	c.
Lth H Kroll	24	Sopwith	SW Langemarck		12
Vfw F Altemeier	24	Spad	SW Langemarck		9
Ltn K Meierdirks	40	Breguet	Nancy		1

a. B3520, No 19 Sqn, RFC, Lt BA Powers, departed at 1608, KIA.
b. British balloon 46-4-1 (BMS 157/D), Lt WY Walls and Sgt Moncrieff, the observers were not harmed.
c. MSP of Escadrille F 41, Capitaine Lafont (P) and Lt de Nonancourt (O), shot down in flames and killed.

Losses:

Ltn Johannes Wintrath	B	Shot down in flames and killed at 1230 near Westende-Bad.
Ltn Walter Göttsch	8	Wounded in combat with No 20 Sqn, RFC.
Obltn Ernst Weigand	10	Shot down in flames and killed at 1740 near Nachtegaal, by pilots of No 56 Sqn, RFC.
Uffz August Werkmeister	10	Shot down in flames and killed, 1742 over Houthulst Forest, probably by 56 Sqn, RFC.
Vfw Ludwig Hilz	40	Wounded in combat with a Caudron.

26 September 1917

Ltn K Stock	6	Spad	NW Dadizeele	0720	1
Ltn K Wüsthoff	4	Spad	E Bellevaarder	1040	21
Obltn B Loerzer	26	RE8	Gravenstafel	1100	11	a.
Ltn Joschkowitz	4	Spad	Becelaere	1040	1
Ltn R Runge	18	Camel	E Becelaere	1115	6
Ltn W Rosenstein	27	Sopwith	Blankaart See	1145	2
Obltn R Berthold	18	Camel	Becelaere	1200	25	b.
Vfw O Stadter	32	Spad	Esnes	1700	2	c.
Vfw A Hurrle	13	Spad	Pinon		2
Vfw K Thom	21	Caudron	Hessenwald		12
Vfw M Wackwitz	24	Triplane	SE Linselles		3
Vfw F Altemeier	24	Triplane	W Comines		8	d.
Ltn R Klimke	27	Sopwith	S Houthulst		3
Ltn R Klimke	27	Sopwith	S Pierkenhoek		4
Ltn W v Bülow	36	RE8	Polygonwald		21	e.
Ltn H Böhning	36	Nieuport	Gheluvelt		3	f.
Ltn H Bongartz	36	Sopwith	Houthulst		12
Ltn T Quandt	36	Triplane	Paschendaele		5
Ltn A Raben	39	Caproni	Lom		1
Ltn A Raben	39	Caproni	Lom		2

a. A4216, No 6 Sqn, RFC, 2/Lt J Worstenholm, KIA, & Lt FL McCreary, WIA, departed at 0845, pilot killed during combat, observer brought aircraft back but crashed trying to land.
b. B2358, No 70 Sqn, RFC, Lt WHR Gould, departed at 1105, last seen over Passchendaele at 1215, KIA.
c. Probably Adj E Ronserail of N 75, Spad VII, POW.
d. N5388/F15, French Naval Escadrille.
e. A4615, No 21 Sqn, RFC, 2/Lt AL Sutcliffe, WIA/POW.
f. B3649, No 29 Sqn, RFC, 2/Lt HV Thompson, last seen at 0730 over Houthulst Forest, KIA.

Losses – Nil

27 September 1917

Ltn R Windisch	32	Spad	Belleville	1028	3

Vfw L Weber	3	Camel	Benkenberg	1600	2	
Obltn K Waldhausen	37	Balloon	Neuville	1705	4	a.
Obltn K Waldhausen	37	RE8	Farbuswald	1710	5	b.
Obltn K Waldhausen	37	Balloon	SW Aix Noulette	1815	6	a.
Ltn X Dannhuber	26	BF2b	Dixmuiden	1840	5	c.

a. Two British balloons lost 20-1-1 (BMS 74) and 37-3-1 (FM 79).
b. B3441, No 9 Sqn RFC, 2/Lt CB Andrews WIA & Spr AG White, KIA.
c. A7150, No 48 Sqn, RFC, Sgt H Clark KIA, AM EA Nash WIA/DOW, shot down in flames at 1855 near Ostende.

Losses:

| Obltn Kurt Waldhausen | 37 | Flying Albatros DV 2284/17 (G.74) shot down and taken POW by Lt JH Tudhope,40 Sqn, RFC and F/Cdr CD Booker, No 8 Sqn, RNAS. |

28 September 1917

Obltn O Schmidt	29	Pup	SE Bixschoote	0815	10	
Obltn H Auffarth	18	BF2b	S Wervicq	1230	4	a.
Ltn J Veltjens	18	BF2b	E Hollebeke	1230	7	a.
Obltn R Berthold	18	G100	s Zillebeke See	1230	26	
Ltn E Udet	37	Camel	W Wingles	1805	12	
Ltn E Udet	37	Camel	Vermelles	1810	13	
Uffz U Neckel	12	DH5	Biache	1810	2	
FlgMt M Brenner	MFJ1	RE8	Wenduyne		1	
Vfw F Jacobsen	31	Nieuport	S Lucia		–	

a. No 20 Sqn, RFC, lost two BF2bs this date: A7241, 2/Lts HF Tomlin, & HT Noble, departed at 1140, KIAs; and A7210, Capt J S Campbell, & Dvr G Tester, departed at 1140, last seen in combat between Wervicq and Menin, KIAs.

Losses:

Ltn Kurt Wissemann	3	Killed in action by No 56 Sqn, RFC.
Ltn Herbert Pastor	29	Killed in action, 0800 W of Veldhoek, by Captain JTB McCudden, 56 Sqn, RFC.
Ltn zS Tinschert	MFJ1	Wounded in action during combat over Schoorbacke.

29 September 1917

Obltn E Schleich	21	Spad	Bethélainville	1630	25	
Vfw J Buckler	17	BF2b	Fleurbaix	1805	14	
Ltn M Müller	28	Sopwith 2	W Houthulst		–	

Losses:

| Ltn Ewald Gläser | 31 | Killed in an accident during a test flight. |

30 September 1917

Obltn B Loerzer	26	SE5	Koekuit	1120	12	
Vfw F Schmidt	32	Spad	Höhe 304	1130	1	
Ltn H Gontermann	15	Spad	Staubecken	1145	37	
Obltn R Berthold	18	Pup	Deulemont	1150	27	a.
Ltn R Runge	18	Pup	St Marguerite	1150	7	a.
Obltn H Auffarth	18	Pup	Wambeke	1155	5	a.
Ltn J Veltjens	18	Pup	Ploegsteertwald	1155	8	a.
Vfw J Buckler	17	Sopwith	SW Lens	1155	15	
Vfw E Hamster	37	RE8	E Tilloy	1155	1	b.
Ltn O Förster	15	Spad	Staubecken	1200	2	
Vfw E Hamster	37	RE8	SW Fresner	1205	2	c.
Ltn H Gontermann	15	Caudron	NE La Fère	1250	38	d.

a.   No 66 Sqn, RFC, lost two Pups that were last seen over Gheluwe this date: B2185, 2/Lt JG Warter, KIA; and B1768, Lt JW Boumphrey, POW; also Capt TPH Bayetto, was injured in a crash-landing in B2168 after returning from a patrol.
b.   3731, No 13 Sqn, RFC, Sgt A Stanley & 1/AM A Wardlaw, departed at 1055, shot down in flames, KIAs.
c.   A3736, No 5 Sqn, RFC, Lt EH Pember & 2/AM A Morley, brought down in combat at 1205, KIAs.
d.   Letord of Escadrille C 46, MdL François de Villeneuve (P), Sgt Durand (G) and Cpl Deschamps (G) MIAs.
Losses:

Vfw Gottfried Stumpf	6	Injured in a landing accident.
Uffz Bolkenius	K7	Injured in an accident.

JASTA ARMEE ASSIGNMENTS AS OF 1 OCTOBER 1917

Western Front

1 Armee 19	6 Armee 12,30,37
2 Armee 5	7 Armee 9,15
3 Armee –	Det 'A' –
4 Armee 2,3,4,6,7,8,10,11,17,18,20,24,26,27,28,29,33,35b,36	Det 'B' 41
5 Armee 13,14,16b,21,22,23b,32b,34b	Det 'C' 40s

Other Fronts

11 Armee 25	Macedonia
14 Armee 1,31,39	Italy
1 Armee 38	Bulgarian Armee
8 Armee OberOst	Russia

1 October 1917

Ltn X Dannhuber	26	SE5	Westroosebeke	1750	6	a.

a   A8928, No 56 Sqn, RFC, 2/Lt RH Sloley, departed at 1630, KIA.
Losses:

Ltn Ernst Wendler	17	Wounded in action.
Ltn Friedrich Cleiss	33	Flying an Albatros DV (G.78), killed over Hooge, probably by Capt WA Wright of 45 Sqn, RFC, and Lt Reeder & Cpl Holmes of No 53 Sqn, RFC.
Ltn Theodor Siebold	38	Killed near Matnica, Macedonia.

2 October 1917

Ltn H Klein	10	DH4	Meulebeke	1040	17	a.
Obltn R Berthold	18	DH4	Roulers	1330	28	b.
Ltn R Runge	18	DH4	Roulers	1330	8	b.
Ltn W Kleffel	18	DH4	Roulers	1330	1	b.
Ltn H Gontermann	15	Spad	Laon	1335	39	c.
Vfw W Hippert	39	SavPom	Modrejce	1510	2	d.
Vfw H Oberländer	30	BF2b	SW Marquette	1810	3	e.
Ltn O Kissenberth	23	Sopwith	Avocourt		18	f.

a.   A7642, No 55 Sqn, RFC, 2/Lt WR Bishop & Lt G Mathews, departed at 0859, last seen near Ypres, KIAs.
b.   No 57 Sqn, RFC, lost three DH4s that departed at 1145, last seen over Roulers: 7451, 2/Lt CRB Halley & 1/AM J Barlow; 7581, 2/Lts CGO MacAndrew & LP Sidney, all KIA; and 7583,2/Lts CG Crane, POW, & NL Inglis, KIA.
c.   Spad VII #1633 of Escadrille Spa 62, S/Lt R de Francq, MIA.
d.   Italian 40a Sqn.
e.   A7138, No 11 Sqn, RFC, 2/Lt S Sutcliffe & Lt J M McKenna, last seen in combat at 1800 between Douai and Cambrai, KIAs.

f.   French Sopwith of Escadrille C 28, Adj Poisard and S/Lt Henry, KIAs.

Losses:

Uffz Karl Steudel	3	Shot down in flames and killed over Houthulst Forest.
Ltn Max Roemer	10	Shot down in flames and killed at 1030 over Westroosebeke.
Ltn Walter Kleffel	18	Wounded in combat with a DH4.

3 October 1917

Ltn H Schröder	1	Hanriot	Tolmein	1150	3

Losses – Nil

4 October 1917

No Claims – No Losses

5 October 1917

Ltn Wilde	4	Triplane	Dadizeele	0750	1	a.
Ltn E Böhme	B	BF2b	N Dadizeele	0815	16	b.
Obltn B Loerzer	26	SE5	E Menin	0820	13	c.
Vfw E Patzer	36	DH5	Westroosebeke	1625	1	

a.   N5377, No 1 Sqn, RNAS, F/S/Lt Malcolm J Watson, POW .
b.   B1133, No 20 Sqn, RFC, Capt DD Walrend-Skinner & Pte FT Jones, departed at 0739, last seen over Roulers, POWs.
c.   B524, No 56 Sqn, RFC, Lt CH Jeffs, departed at 0700, last seen over Roulers-Menin Road, POW.
Losses: Nil

6 October 1917

Gefr J Funk	30	Spad	SE Seclin	1030	3

Losses: Nil

7 October 1917

Ltn C Galetschki	6	RE8	E Ypres	0810	1	
Ltn H v Haebler	36	BF2b	Menin	0840	1	a.

a.   A7280, No 22 Sqn, RFC, Lt JC Rush, MC, & Lt W W Chapman, last seen at 0730 over Kruiseik, KIAs.
Losses:
Ltn Paul Billik   7   Wounded in action.

8 October 1917

Vfw W Reichenbach	B	RE8	SW Terhand	0940	–	a.

a.   A4315, No 7 Sqn, RFC, 2/Lt CB Wattson & Lt J Diamond, MC, departed at 0830, KIAs.
Losses:
Vfw Walter Reichenbach   B   Badly injured in an accident at Rumbeke.

9 October1917

Obltn B Loerzer	26	RE8	NW Langemarck	1010	14	a.
Ltn H Dilthey	27	Sopwith	Poelkapelle	1115	4	
Ltn F Müller	11	Nieuport	Gheluwe	1430	2	b.
Ltn X Dannhuber	26	Spad	Zonnebeke	1620	7	
Ltn K Gallwitz	B	Triplane	N Zevekote	1815	2	

a.   A3663, No 9 Sqn, RFC, 2/Lts IU MacMurchy & F T Brasington, departed at 0740, KIAs.
b.   B3577, No 1 Sqn, RFC, 2/Lt MA Peacock, last seen over Menin at 1330, POW.

Losses:

Ltn Richard Wagner	26	Shot down in flames and killed at 1615, SE Zonnebeke, during combat with a RE8.				

10 October 1917

Ltn E Böhme	B	SE5	N Zillebeke	0725	17	a.
Ltn H Bongartz	36	DH4	Westroosebeke	1700	13	b.
Ltn W Ewers	12	DH5	Hendecourt	1705	2	c.
Ltn X Dannhuber	26	Camel	S Becelaere	1800	8	

a.   B23, No 56 Sqn, RFC, 2/Lt GM Wilkinson, departed at 1340, last seen E of Ypres, KIA.
b.   A 2138, No 57 Sqn, RFC, Sgt FV Legge & 1/AM J S Clarke, departed at 1500, MIAs.
c.   B360, No 41 Sqn, RFC, 2/Lt AW Edwards, departed at 1455, last seen going down over Hendecourt, KIA.

Losses:

Obltn Rudolf Berthold	18	Wounded in action.
Vfw Ruppert	19	Wounded in action.
Ltn Johann Raithel	34	Wounded in action S of Bezonvaux.

11 October 1917

Ltn H Hoyer	36	SE5	Koelberg	0830	3	a.
Vfw J Buckler	17	RE8	Roclincourt	0945	16	b.
Ltn H Viebig	20	BF2b	Bovekerke	1115	1	c.
Ltn X Dannhuber	26	SE5	NW Eesen	1605	9	
Vfw J Buckler	17	Sopwith	Armentières	1725	17	d.
Ltn W Ewers	12	Pup	E Sains	1745	3	e.

a.   B542, No 56 Sqn, RFC, 2/Lt RJ Preston-Cobb, left at 0615, last seen E of Ypres, KIA.
b.   A4330, No 5 Sqn, RFC, Lt FCE Clarke & Lt P Mighell, WIA/DOWs.
c.   A7181, No 22 Sqn, RFC, Lt RIV Hill & 2/Lt RS Gilbert, departed at 0825, POWs.
d.   B6314, No 28 Sqn, RFC, 2/Lt WH Winter, MIA.
e.   A2160, No 46 Sqn, RFC, 2/Lt AA Allen, departed at 1525, last seen over Marquion, KIA.

Losses:

Ltn Gustav Bellen	10	Severely wounded in combat while flying Pfalz DIII 8169/17.
Gefr Zimmermann	35	Injured in an accident.

12 October 1917

Vfw K Menckhoff	3	Triplane	Zonnebeke	1020	13	
Vfw K Menckhoff	3	HP	Broodseinde	1025	14	
Ltn H v Bülow	36	DH4	Roulers	1155	1	a.
Obltn B Loerzer	26	DH4	SE Thielt	1215	15	a.
Uffz H Stumpert	35	Camel	NW Courtrai	1215	1	b.
Ltn H v Häbler	36	Pup	NW Moorslede	1215	2	c.
Ltn T Quandt	36	Pup	Rollemolenhoek	1215	6	c.
Ltn H Hoyer	36	Pup	Westroosebeke	1215	4	c.
Uffz J Kaiser	35	Camel	SW Courtrai	1220	1	b.
Ltn H Klein	10	Camel	Lauwe	1220	18	b.
Vfw F Eberlein	33	Spad	Westroosebeke	1245	1	
Ltn F Kieckhäfer	29	DH4	SW Rumbeke	1340	3	a.
Ltn H Staats	12	DH5	Quéant		1	

a.   Three DH4s were lost this date: A7426, No 25 Sqn, RFC, Sgt AL Clear & 2/Lt FW Talbot, departed at 1035, POWs. No 57 Sqn, RFC, lost two DH4s: A2135, 2/Lts GW Armstrong & H Pughe-Evans, departed at 1145, POWs; A7515, Lt SH Allen and 2/Lt GCE Smithett, departed at 1007 hours, KIAs.
b.   No 45 Sqn, RFC, lost two Camels that departed at 1045 and last seen over Houthulst this date: B2375, Capt HB Coomber, and B2386, 2/Lt KH Willard, KIAs.
c.   No 66 Sqn, RFC, lost three Pups near Ypres this date: B1830, 2/Lt RWB Matthewson, POW; B1836, Lt AW Nasmyth, KIA; A635, 2/Lt M Newcomb, POW.

Losses – Nil

13 October 1917

Ltn E Böhme	B	Pup	SW Couckelaere	0850	18	a.
Ltn H Klein	10	Pup	Praet Bosch	0855	19	a.
Vfw H Körner	8	Pup	Bovekerke	0900	3	a.
Ltn A Heldmann	10	Pup	N Dixmuiden	0900	–	
Vfw R Francke	8	Pup	Vladsloo	0905	7	a.
Ltn H Staats	12	DH5	Quéant	1100	1	b.
Ltn E Hess	19	AR2	Bourgogne	1730	15	

a.   No 54 Sqn, RFC, lost four Sopwith Scouts this date that departed at 0645 last seen over Zarren: B 5918, 2/Lt WW Vick, POW; A7344, 2/Lt PC Norton, POW; B1800, 2/Lt FW Gibbes, KIA; B2161, 2/ Lt JHR Salter, KIA.
b.   A9277, No 68 Sqn, RFC, Lt DG Morrison, WIA, shot down and crash-landed, his aircraft destroyed by artillery.
Losses – Nil

14 October 1917

Ltn K Gallwitz	B	RE8	S Wieltje	0742	3	a.
Ltn E Böhme	B	Camel	Wieltje	0742	19	b.
Ltn R Wendelmuth	8	Sopwith	N Zillebeke See	1225	11	
Ltn H Bongartz	36	RE8	Zonnebeke	1620	14	c.
Ltn Hebler	15	Balloon	Staubecken	1645	1	d.
Ltn X Dannhuber	26	Spad	SE Dixmuiden	1735	10	
Ltn F Ray	28	Spad	S Schoorbacke	1740	7	
Ltn E Löwenhardt	10	Balloon	NE Ypres	1830	6	e.

a.   B3652, No 6 Sqn, RFC, Ltn C Smythe, MC, & 2/Lt A Ward, POWs.
b.   B6778, No 29 Sqn, RFC, 2/Lt HD MacPherson, departed at 0545, KIA.
c.   A4444 , No 21 Sqn, RFC, 2/Lts BF Braithwaite & JC Garratt, departed at 1455, WIA/POWs.
d.   French 27 Compagnie d'Aérostières, Lt Bacquet, the observer, made a safe descent.
e.   British Balloon 34-20-5 (FMD 106).
Losses:

Ltn Martin Schoen	OberOst	Killed in action at Zyazcuncy, near Huskatin, Russia.
OfStv Rudolf Weckbrodt	26	Flying Albatros DV 636/17 (G.79) killed at 1715 while attacking an RE8, by Lt WR Jones No 32 Sqn, RFC & a 22 Sqn BF2b.

15 October 1917

Ltn H Arntzen	15	Balloon	E Crouy	1300	6	a.
Obltn B Loerzer	26	BF2b	Aarseele	1400	16	b.
Ltn H Hoyer	36	DH4	Becelaere	1510	5	
Ltn F Büchner	13	Spad	Margival		2	

a.   French 82 Compagnie d'Aérostières, Asp Prouvost and Sgt Topart, the observers,were not harmed.
b.   A7244, No 22 Sqn, RFC, 2/Lt HS Wellby & 2/AM W Nicol, last seen at 1315 over Maldegem, emitting smoke, POWs.
Losses – Nil

16 October 1917

Ltn E Böhme	B	Nieuport	Magermairie	0925	20	a.
Ltn W Kypke	41	Salmson	E Obertraubach	1130	4	
Vfw R Treptow	25	Nieuport	Krusevica	1200	4	
Ltn E Hess	19	AR2	Asfeld le Ville	1210	16	b.
Ltn E Hess	19	Caudron	Hochberg	1215	–	
Obltn R Greim	34	Nieuport	Bras	1245	6	
Obltn R Greim	34	Spad	Bethélainville	1345	7	

Vfw M Taucher	34	Spad	Bethélainville	1350	1	
Ltn W Kypke	41	AR2	Courtelevent	1635	5	c.
Ltn G Schlenker	41	AR2	Lepuix	1635	8	c.
Vfw A Bauhofer	25	AR2	Caniste		2	

a.   B3598, No 29 Sqn, RFC, 2/Lt FJ Ortweiler, last seen over St Julien at 0825, POW.
b.   AR from Escadrille F 72, MdL Houdusse (P) & Soldat Rouille (G) KIAs.
c.   Two French ARs were lost in the Belfort Sector: One from Escadrille F 14, Capt. Garcin (P) & Soldat Millet (G), KIAs; one from Escadrille F 58, Adj Raoul Chasneau (P) & Sgt Boitel (G), KIAs.

Losses:

Vfw Max Taucher	34	Shot down over the Forêt de Hesse and taken prisoner. Possibly the victim of MdL Delore of N 78. However, four other pilots, Adj de Cazenove de Pradines, Adj Simon and S/Lt Defourneaux of N 81 assisted by Sgt Guerin of N 78, sent a scout down near Verdun, not far from this location.

17 October 1917

Ltn H Bongartz	36	DH4	Houthulsterwald	0930	15	
Ltn T Quandt	36	DH4	Poelkapelle	0930	7	
Vfw Bärwald	37	Camel	Tolhoek	0930	2	
Vfw J Buckler	17	BF2b	E Roucourt	1120	18	a.
Ltn K v Bülow	14	Nieuport	Douaumont	1140	1	
Ltn H Kütt	23	Spad	Verdun	1500	1	
Obltn B Loerzer	26	Camel	SW Nieuport	1620	17	
Ltn K Wever	26	Camel	SW Nieuport	1630	3	
Vfw O Könnecke	5	Sopwith 2	Origny		8	
Vfw K Bey	5	BF2b	SW Cambrai		1	b.
Ltn R Dycke	16	Spad	Montfaucon		2	c.

a.   A7271, No 20 Sqn, RFC, 2/Lt AGV Taylor & Sgt WJ Benger, last seen at 0825 over St Julien, WIA/POW/DOW.
b.   No 11 Sqn, RFC, lost two BFs this date: A7231, 2/Lts E Scholtz & HC Wookey, last seen at 1045 over Cambrai, POWs; A7209, 2/Lts SE Stanley, WIA/POW/DOW & EL Fosse, POW, departed at 0850, last seen in combat N of Cambrai.
c.   Sgt M Montagne (1 victory), N 112, flying a Spad VII, KIA.

Losses:

Ltn Johann Wiedenmann	K8	KIA between Ostende and Zevecote.

18 October 1917

Ltn P Lotz	7	Camel	Ramskapelle	0910	1	
Ltn H Dilthey	27	Scout	E Klerken	0940	5	
Ltn H Kunz	7	Camel	SW Thourout	0945	3	
Obflgmt K Schönfelder	7	BF2b	Ingelmünster	0945	3	a.
Ltn J Jacobs	7	DH4	Zillebeke See	0950	9	
Ltn E Löwenhardt	10	BF2b	Ardooje	0950	7	a.
Vfw W Kampe	27	Sopwith	Ypres	0950	3	
Ltn H Klein	10	BF2b	Staden	0955	20	a.
Vfw Rudolf Eck	3	DH5	Wildermann	0955	2	b.
Vfw W Kampe	27	Sopwith	W Passchendaele	0955	4	
Ltn E Udet	37	Camel	Deulemont	1035	14	
Ltn W v Bülow	36	Spad	E Passchendaele	1045	22	c.
Ltn H Contag	29	Balloon	Oostvlederen	1402	1	d.
Ltn H Bongartz	36	RE8	Molenhoek	1505	16	
Uffz U Neckel	12	DH5	Boursies	1640	3	
Vfw L Reimann	41	Spad	Altmunsterol		1	

| Ltn H Hoyer | 36 | BF2b | Moorslede | | – |

a.   No 22 Sqn, RFC, lost three BFs that all departed at 0730 this date and last seen in combat over Ardoye: A7125, 2/Lts BB Perry & CH Bartlett, MIAs; A7247, 2/Lts CE Ferguson & AD Lennox, KIAs; A7264, Capt H Patch & Pte R Spensley, MIAs.
b.   A9494, No 24 Sqn, RFC, 2/Lt GW Forbes, last seen over Nieuport at 0830, POW.
c   Probably Spad VII #1118 of MdL P Jolivet of Escadrille Spa 73, KIA.
d.   French 81 Compagnie d'Aérostières.

Losses:

| Ltn Xavier Dannhuber | 26 | Wounded in action. |
| Obltn Otto Schmidt | 29 | Wounded in action at 1400 hours. |

19 October 1917

No Claims

Losses:

| Ltn Franz Josef Karg | 23 | KIA at 1530 over Jametz Airfield. |

20 October 1917

Ltn G Bassenge	B	Camel	E Passchendaele	1220	1	a.
Ltn F Kempf	B	Camel	Gravenstafel	1220	3	a.
Ltn L Hanstein	35	Camel	SW Moorslede	1230	12	b.
Ltn J v Busse	3	RE8	W Houthulst	1415	3	
Vfw M Kämmerer	35	Camel	Oostnieuwkerke	1430	1	
Ltn F Kieckhäfer	29	Camel	Houthulsterwald	1450	4	
Vfw G Schindler	35	Camel	Westhoek	1500	2	

a.   No 70 Sqn, RFC lost two Camels this date: B2370, 2/Lt FB Farquharson, last seen in combat over the Menin-Columines Road, POW; and B6532, Capt JR Wilson, KIA, both departed at 1030 hours.
b.   Probably B3887, No 28 Sqn, RFC, Lt HE Singh-Malik, shot down and crash-landed, not harmed.

Losses:

Ltn Walter Lange	B	Killed at 1220 near Passchendaele during combat with Sopwith Camels.
Uffz Hardel	10	WIA at 1310 near Potteriburg.
Ltn Alfred Gerstenberg	11	WIA at 1200 near Wasenmolen.
Uffz Emil Barnheine	35	WIA NW of Roulers.

21 October 1917

Flgmt B Heinrich	MFJ1	Spad	S Nieuport	0810	8	
Flgmt B Heinrich	MFJ1	Spad	W Ramskapelle	0810	9	
Flgmt M Brenner	MFJ1	Spad	SW Ramskapelle	0810	3	
Obltn B Loerzer	26	Camel	W Wynendaele	1130	18	a.
Ltn H Contag	29	DH4	NW Middlekerke	1240	2	b.
Ltn F Kuke	33	Camel	NE Ypres	1415	2	
Ltn V Schobinger	12	RE8	SW Lecluse	1540	7	
Obltn H Göring	27	Sopwith	Linselles	1545	15	c.
Ltn F Berkemeyer	27	Sopwith	S Rumbeke	1555	4	c.
Obltn K v Döring	4	SE5	Vierlawenhoek	1610	9	
Ltn O Förster	15	Balloon	S Aisne	1830	3	d.
Gefr J v Stein	35	Camel	W Roselaere		1	
Vfw H Mittermayer	K2	DH4	W St Avold		1	

a.   B3937, No 4 Sqn, RNAS, F/S/Lt EGA Eyre, shot down near Ichteghem, KIA.
b.   7503, No 25 Sqn, RFC, 2/Lts D McLauren & OM Hills, MC, departed at 1130, MIAs.
c.   No 84 Sqn, RFC, lost three aircraft that were last seen over Roulers at 1515; B547, 2/Lt AE Hempel; B560, 2/Lt FL Yeoman, both POW, and B551, 2/Lt RB Steele POW/DOW.
d.   French 31 Compagnie d'Aérostières, not flamed.

Losses:

| Vfw Fritz Bachmann | 6 | Killed in combat at 1120 E of Ypres. |

22 October 1917

Ltn M Müller	28	Pup	W Beerst	1625	28	a.
Ltn M Müller	28	Pup	W Beerst	1625	29	a.
Ltn W Jannsen	28	Pup	W Beerst	1630	1	

a. 54 Sqn RFC.
Losses:
Vfw Adolf Techow 7 Killed near Dixmuiden in combat with Camels. Possibly by Belgian pilots Adj G Lallemand and Lt H Cornelius at 1410 hrs.

23 October 1917

Vfw H Fritzsche	29	RE8	W Dixmuiden	1730	3	
Ltn F Kieckhäfer	29	RE8	SW Dixmuiden	1740	5	a.
Ltn K Mendel	15	Spad XI	Staubecken		2	

a. 6me Belgian Escadrille, S/Lt HW Van Geel & Sgt EL Herman both KIA.
Losses – Nil

24 October 1917

Ltn R Klimke	27	Sopwith	SE Becelaere	0950	5	
Ltn W v Bülow	36	Spad	Linselles	0950	23	a.
Ltn W v Bülow	36	Spad	S Lille	1005	24	b.
Obltn H Karbe	22	Spad	Malmaison	1010	1	
Ltn L Luer	27	Sopwith	NE Zonnebeke	1010	3	
Ltn S Büttner	22	Spad	Maison Rouge	1020	1	
Ltn W Blume	26	Triplane	Tenbrielen	1250	5	c.
Ltn H Hoyer	36	Spad	S Westroosebeke	1457	6	d.
Vfw J Buckler	17	RE8	S Mericourt	1620	19	e.
Ltn F Kieckhäfer	29	BF2b	Houthulst	1720	6	f.

a. A6709, No 19 Sqn, RFC, 2/Lt KL Golding, KIA.
b. A6627, No 19 Sqn, RFC, 2/Lt JD Laing, KIA.
c. N5476, No 1 Sqn, RNAS, F/S/Lt JEC Hough, MIA.
d. B3571, No 23 Sqn, RFC, 2/Lt WFG March, last seen between Zillebeke and Ypres, POW/DOW.
e. B5896, No 16 Sqn, RFC, Lts AO Balaam & DSP Prince-Smith, KIAs.
f. B1117, No 48 Sqn, RFC, Capt JL Milne, MC, & Lt S Wright, MC, brought down at 1625 near Merckem, KIAs.
Losses:
Ltn Heinrich Breidt 13 Killed in combat over Chevregny.
Vfw Otto Rössler 23 KIA by AA fire between Eix & Abancourt.

25 October 1917 Battle of Caporetto, Italy

Ltn F v Kerssenbrock	39	Voisin	Volarje	0825	3
Uffz B Ultsch	39	Caproni	San Leonardo	1420	4
Vfw L Gaim	39	Caproni	San Leonardo	1420	1
Ltn F v Kerssenbrock	39	Farman	Tersimonte	1520	4
Vfw W Hippert	39	Hanriot	W Dolje	1520	3
Ltn H Schröder	1	Spad	W Tolmein		4
Vfw Münnichow	1	Spad	Woltschach		2
Ltn E Härtl	1	Caproni	E Canale		1
Ltn A Thurm	31	Farman	S Tolmein		2
Ltn Kosslick	31	SAML	Roncina		1
Ltn Busch	39	Voisin	W Ste Lucia		1
Ltn R Bertelsmeier	39	Voisin	Kolovrat		2
Uffz K Ueberschär	39	Voisin	Roechin		1

Uffz K Ueberschär	39	Voisin	Roechin			zlg

Losses – Nil

26 October 1917

Ltn J v Busse	3	Camel	Kruisstraet	0950	4	a.
Uffz B Ultsch	39	Caproni	Srednje	1035	5	
Vfw W Schmidt	39	Caproni	NE Tolmein	1035	1	
Ltn W Wagener	39	Caproni	Chiapovano	1035	3	
Vfw A Rüsche	39	Caproni	Olizza	1035	1	
Vfw L Gaim	39	Caproni	Bordez-Canale	1035	2	
Uffz B Ultsch	39	Caproni	Olizza	1035	6	
Ltn W Wagener	39	Caproni	Cauce	1055	2	
Ltn H Schröder	1	SAML	Wocheiner	1102	5	
Vfw F Jacobsen	31	SAML	Feistritz	1102	–	
Vfw K Rahier	31	Caproni	Vividale	1445	2	
Vfw K Rahier	31	Caproni	Olizza	1500	3	
Vfw A Hurrle	13	Spad	Pinon		2	b.
Ltn K Bieler	14	Sopwith 2	Vendresse		1	c.
Ltn Addix	31	Caproni	E Grudenka		1	
Vfw E Oppermann	31	Caproni	N Logarce		1	

a.   B5152, No 45 Sqn, RFC, 2/Lt EALF Smith, departed at 0815, POW.
b.   Probably Spa VII #1825, S/Lt E Decazes (3 victories), N 88, KIA.
c.   A Sopwith of Escadrille F 208, Adj Danglard & S/Lt Levy, KIAs.

Losses:

Ltn Otto Schober	18	Killed in combat at 2020 over Sleyhage.
Ltn Addix	31	Wounded in action.
Ltn Fritz Jacobsen	31	Slightly wounded in fight with a Caproni, remained with Jasta.

27 October 1917

Ltn A Seifert	24	Spad	N Wervicq	0830	1	a.
Ltn K Wüsthoff	4	Triplane	Hooge	0930	22	b.
Ltn O Fuchs	30	Camel	Harnes	1047	2	
Ltn F Kuke	33	Camel	Ypres	1125	1	c.
Ltn W Brackwitz	17	Camel	W Acheville	1235	2	
Vfw F Hemer	6	RE8	N Gheluvelt	1420	1	
Vfw K Knocke	35	Camel	NW Dixmuiden	1430	1	c.
Ltn H Bongartz	36	Camel	Kaphoek	1500	17	c.
Ltn H v Häbler	36	Camel	Houthulsterwald	1510	3	c.
Ltn K Menckhoff	3	SE5	Bellewaarde	1550	15	d.
Ltn H Böhning	36	Camel	Winkler-St Eloi	1640	4	e.
Obltn B Loerzer	26	Camel	W Dixmuiden	1650	19	c.
Ltn K Gallwitz	B	SE5a	Polterrjeberg		4	f.
Vfw H Kramer	13	Spad	S Fresnes		3	
Ltn K Bieler	14	Caudron	Pargny		2	g.
Vfw K Bohnenkamp	22	Spad	Chevregny		2	

a.   6776, No 19 Sqn, RFC, 2/Lt SL Whitehouse, last seen over Zillebeke See heading west, WIA/POW.
b.   N5455, No 1 Sqn, RNAS, F/S/Lt WM Clapperton, seriously wounded with his left arm shattered, he managed to make it back to his airfield at Bailleul.
c.   Five Camels were lost this date in this sector: B6374, No 43 Sqn, RFC, 2/Lt GP Bradley, shot down in flames over Sallaumines, KIA; B2382, No 45 Sqn, RFC, 2/Lt CI Phillips, last seen E of Moorslede, KIA; B5178, No 28 Sqn, RFC, 2/Lt RA Cartledge,last seen W of Dixmuiden, POW; B2349, No 70 Sqn, RFC, 2/Lt CW Primeau, last seen E of Roulers, KIA; B2361, No 70 Sqn, RFC, 2/Lt RJEP Goode, last seen E of Roulers,POW. Also B2463, No 70 Sqn, RFC, Capt CN Jones, WIA over Houthulst Forest.
d.   B534, No 60 Sqn, RFC, Lt WB Sherwood, seen to go down in flames, KIA.

e.   N6371, No 10 Sqn, RNAS, F/S/Lt GH Morang, seen to go down in flames NE of Dixmuiden, KIA.
f.   B31, No 56 Sqn, RFC, 2/Lt APF Rhys Davids DSO MC, 25 victories, last seen SW of Roulers, KIA.
g.   Letord from Escadrille F 8, MdL Bertin, Capt de Lagerie & S/Lt Chambron, KIAs.

Losses:

Ltn Franz Müller	11	Killed in an accident during a test flight at 0830 at Kortryk.	

28 October 1917

Ltn R Wendelmuth	20	Camel	S Ramskapelle	1325	12	
Vfw J Buckler	17	RE8	N Mont Sr Eloi	1705	20	a.

a.   A4426, No 16 Sqn, RFC, 2/Lt EH Kier & Capt CWC Wasey, departed at 1510, KIAs.

Losses – Nil

29 October 1917

Vfw J Buckler	17	Balloon	Neuville	0914	21	a.
Ltn O Fuchs	30	Camel	S Gavrelle	1105	3	
Vfw K Thom	21	Spad	Fleury	1110	13	
Vfw J Buckler	17	Nieuport	S Houthem	1210	22	b.
Ltn R Heydacker	38	BE12	Hodz-Obasi		2	
Vfw E Dürre	38	AWFK8	E Carniste		1	
Vfw Lage	38	BE12	Dojran-See		zlg	

a.   British Balloon 20-1-1 (FM 118/D), Lt J M O'Connell and Capt J L Fry, OK.
b   B3630, No 1 Sqn, RFC, 2/Lt AW MacLaughlin, last seen over Houthem, KIA.

Losses:

Vfw Josef Lautenschlager	11	In Fokker Dr.I 113/17 killed in error by a German two-seater at 10 45 over Houthulst Forest.	
Ltn Fritz Berkemeyer	27	Shot down in flames and killed over Zandvoorde.	

30 October 1917

Obltn B Loerzer	26	Nieuport	Westroosebeke	0945	20	a.
Ltn E Hess	19	Letord	S Moronvillers	1235	17	
Ltn W Güttler	13	Spad	Pargnan		5	
Ltn L Zencominierski	32	AR2	Oulches		zlg	
Ltn A King	40	Nieuport	Buxières		2	b.

a.   B3627, No 1 Sqn, RFC, 2/Lt ED Scott, seen to crash near Westroosebeke, KIA.
b.   Probably a Nieuport XXIVbis of N 92, Cpl H Fabre, shot down in flames, MIA.

Losses:

Ltn Heinrich Gontermann	17	Severely injured in an accident at 1614 at La Neuville airfield testing Fokker Dr.I 115/17; died at 2205 at a hospital in Marle.	
Ltn Anton Warmuth	34	Killed in combat over Filain.	
Ltn Hermann Scholl	34	Shot down in flames and killed in combat with a French two-seater, probably by Sgt Lignereux and Lt Mangematin of Sop 24.	

31 October 1917

Ltn H Bongartz	36	RE8	S Poelkapelle	0820	18	a.
Ltn H Bongartz	36	Spad	Haullin	0840	19	b.
Ltn H v Bülow	36	Spad	S Becelaere	0845	2	b.
Ltn H Becker	12	Camel	S Boiry	1115	3	
Vfw J Buckler	17	AW	La Bassée	1130	23	c.
Ltn K Wüsthoff	4	SE5	N Bellewaarde	1230	23	d.
Obltn H Bethge	30	RE8	NE Plouvain	1310	18	a.

Ltn H Bongartz	36	SE5	S Roulers	1610	20	
Ltn H Hoyer	36	Spad	Ketzelberg	1610	7	
Vfw J Buckler	17	Balloon	Laventie	1620	24	e.
Ltn V Schobinger	12	BF2b	S Sains	1710	8	f.
Ltn E Böhme	B	SE5a	E Zillebeke See	1715	21	d.

a.   Two RE8s lost this date: 4214, No 53 Sqn, RFC, Capt WAL Poundall, MC, & 2/Lt ER Ripley, seen going down SE of Gheluvelt, KIAs; and 3827, No 13 Sqn, RFC, Lt WLO Parker, & 1/AM HL Postons, seen going down over Biache-St Vaast, KIAs.

b.   No 23 Sqn, RFC, lost two Spads this date: 1565, 2/Lt NH Kemp last seen over Ypres, POW; and B3551, 2/Lt RM Smith, last seen over Roulers, POW.

c.   B319, No 10 Sqn, RFC, 2/Lt W Davidson, & Lt W Crowther, shot down in flames N of La Bassée at 1040, KIAs.

d.   No 84 Sqn, RFC, lost two SE5s this date near Menin: B544, 2/Lt GR Gray, DOW; and B4874, 2/Lt EW Powell, KIA.

e.   British Balloon 42-4-1 (FM 91/D).

f.   B1109, No 11 Sqn, RFC, 2/Lts SW Randall KIA, & WdeC Dodd, POW/DOW, departed at 1434, last seen near Fressies.

Losses:

Ltn Günther Pastor	11	Flying Fokker DrI 121/17 when killed at 1520 hours N Moorslede.
Uffz Kurt Reinhold	24	Wounded in action, remained with Jasta.
Obltn Erwin Wenig	28	Wounded in action.

JASTA ARMEE ASSIGNMENTS AS OF 1 NOVEMBER 1917

Western Front

1 Armee 19	6 Armee 12,30
2 Armee 5,15	7 Armee 9,16b,32b,34b
3 Armee –	Det 'A' –
4 Armee 2,3,4,6,7,8,10,11,17,18,20,24s,26,27,28,29,33,35,36,37	Det 'B' 41
5 Armee 13,14,21,22,23	Det 'C' 40

Other Fronts

11 Armee 25	Macedonia
14 Armee 1,31,39	Italy
1 Armee 38	Bulgarian Armee
Sudarmee 81	Russia

1 November 1917

Ltn F Pütter	9	Balloon	St Jean	1225	4	b.
Ltn F Pütter	9	Balloon	Hans	1225	5	a.
Ltn G Schlenker	41	Sopwith 2	Colmar	1520	9	c.
Obltn K Student	9	Nieuport	E Ripont	1540	6	d.
Ltn O v Breiten-Landenberg	9	Nieuport	S Navarin Ferme	1540	3	d.
Ltn R Windisch	32	Spad	Braye		4	e.
Vfw K Ueberschär	39	Sav Pom	Montegliano	1645	2	

a.   French 65 Compagnie d'Aérostières.

b.   French 67 Compagnie d'Aérostières, S/Lt FPA Cons & Asp E Lenglet, the observers were both killed.

c.   French Sopwith of Escadrille Spa 132, Lt Le Gorju (P) & S/Lt Chauvin (O), MIAs.

d.   French Nieuport XXIV, Cpl J Wilmart, Escadrille N 155, shot down in flames over Souain.

e.   Probably French Spad, Escadrille N 112, MdL Vernaudon, MIA.

Losses – Nil

2 November 1917

OfStv B Ultsch	39	Balloon	W San Giovanni	1010	7
Vfw L Gaim	39	Hanriot	SW Arzene	1515	3
Vfw F Schröder	39	Hanriot	SW San Vito	1600	1
Vfw F Zogmann	39	Hanriot	W San Giovanni	1608	1

Losses – Nil

3 November 1917

No Claims

Losses:
Vfw Gillardoni   81   Shot down and taken prisoner.

4 November 1917

Ltn F Kieckhäfer	29	Camel	N Alveringhe	1045	7
Ltn H Contag	29	SE5	Pervyse	1455	3

Losses:
Ltn Fritz Kieckhäfer   29   WIA at 1520, remained with Jasta.
Flg A Huchler   39   Killed over Cividale, Italy.
Vfw Fleischmann   81   Killed in an accident.

5 November 1917

Vfw P Bäumer	B	Camel	S St Julien	1250	7
Ltn K Wüsthoff	4	Camel	Poelkapelle	1245	24
Ltn K Wüsthoff	4	Camel	S Staden	1300	25
Ltn W Blume	26	RE8	N Zillebeke See	1437	6
Ltn L Luer	27	Camel	W Dixmuiden		4

Losses – Nil

6 November 1917

Vfw P Bäumer	B	Spad	E Zonnebeke	0825	8	
Ltn R Plange	B	SE5a	Passchendaele	0845	1	
Vfw G Stumpf	6	Nieuport	Zonnebeke	0845	1	a.
Ltn H Adam	6	Sopwith	W Passchendaele	0850	21	b.
Ltn E Böhme	B	Camel	Scherminksmolen	1150	22	b.
Vfw P Bäumer	B	Camel	Vierlawenhoek	1150	9	b.
Ltn G Bassenge	B	Camel	Staden	1150	2	b.
Vfw Weimar	41	Salmson	SW Eglingen		1	

a.   B6779, No 29 Sqn, RFC, 2/Lt HG Downing, departed at 0715, KIA.
b.   No. 65 Sqn RFC lost three Camels, Ypres area; B2408, Lt WL Harrison, POW; B2414, 2/Lt EH Cutbill, POW; B2441, Lt EGS Gordon, POW – 1050 hrs.
Losses:
Ltn Gerhard Bassenge   B   Wounded in action with 65 Sqn RFC.

First Battle of Passchendaele ends

7 November 1917

Ltn P Bäumer	B	RE8	SW Moorslede	0810	10	a.
Ltn E Härtl	1	Savoia-P	NE Cordenus	0900	2	
Obltn H Göring	27	DH5	NW Poelkapelle	0915	16	
Ltn M Müller	B	Spad	SW St Julien	0930	30	
Ltn Bussmann	1	Nieuport	San Pietro	1045	zlg	

Vfw Amschl	31	Savoia-P	NW Sacile		1	
Ltn R Windisch	32	Spad	SW Brancourt		5	
Vfw L Gaim	39	Savoia-P	NE Cordenone		4	
Vfw E Hannemann	39	Caproni	Pordenone		1	
Ltn F v Kerssenbrock	39	EA	Sacile		zlg	
Ltn W Kypke	K5	Nieuport	Hagenbach		6	
Vfw F Ehmann	K5	AR2	Dammerkirch		zlg	

a.   A3746, No 4 Sqn, RFC, 2/Lts A Gross, DOW & BCR Grimwood, MC, KIA; left at 0625.

Losses:

| Flg Karl Jäger | 31 | Killed in action over Cividale, Italy. |

---

8 November 1917

Ltn W v Bülow	36	Spad	Houthem	0950	25	a.
Ltn H v Häbler	36	SE5	Tenbrielen	1010	4	b.
Ltn F Loerzer	26	SE5	W Roulers	1010	5	c.
Vfw J Walter	36	SE5	Houthem	1010	1	
Vfw H Oberländer	30	DH4	Monchecourt	1300	4	d.
Ltn W Dahm	26	BF2b	SW Moorslede	1500	2	e.
Ltn H Bongartz	36	BF2b	Ledeghem	1500	21	f.
Ltn H Hoyer	36	SE5	W Roulers	1510	8	g.
Ltn T Quandt	36	SE5	Roulers	1510	8	h.
Ltn F Ray	28	RE8	W Keyem	1610	8	
Vfw P Bäumer	B	Camel	N Zonnebeke	1645	11	
Vfw P Bäumer	B	Camel	N Zonnebeke	1645	12	

a.   B6777, No 19 Sqn, RFC, Lt GA Cockburn, departed at 0807, KIA.
b.   B4883, No 56 Sqn, RFC, Capt PC Cowan, KIA.
c.   B630, No 56 Sqn, RFC, Lt FRC Cobbold, departed at 0825, last seen over Moorslede, WIA/POW.
d.   A7517, No 18 Sqn, RFC, 2/Lt WC Pruden & 2/AM J Conlin, departed at 1005, last seen between Vitry-en-Artois and Henin-Liétard at 1200, POWs.
e.   A7283, No 22 Sqn, RFC, 2/Lt HG Robinson & Lt FBJ Hammersley, POWs.
f.   B1123, No 22 Sqn, RFC, Lt WG Meffitt, MC, WIA/POW.
g.   B4877, No 84 Sqn, RFC, 2/Lt WR Kingsland, POW.
h.   B4869, No 84 Sqn, RFC, Lt JH Deans, KIA.

Losses:

| Flg Hellmuth Riensberg | 10 | WIA, remained with Jasta. |
| Ltn zS Ritter | SFS2 | Shot down W of Dunkerque, not harmed. |

---

9 November 1917

Ltn K Wüsthoff	4	RE8	N Bellewaarder	1030	26	
Ltn L v Richthofen	11	BF2b	Zonnebeke	1030	25	
Vfw R Francke	8	Sopwith	SE Dixmuiden	1040	8	a.
Ltn F Loerzer	26	Camel	S St Julien	1040	6	b.
Ltn R Wendelmuth	20	RE8	E Oostkerke	1200	13	
Ltn W Schwartz	20	RE8	S Pervyse	1200	1	
Ltn J Jacobs	7	Spad	Woumen	1530	10	c.

a.   B1757, No 54 Sqn, RFC, 2/Lt A Thompson, left 0830, last seen E of Dixmuiden, POW.
b.   6290, No 8 Sqn, RNAS, F/Lt WS Margrath, last seen W of Lens at 1030, POW.
c.   Probably French Spad of Escadrille N 102, S/Lt P Constantini, MIA.

Losses – Nil

---

10 November 1917

| Ltn K Kuke | 33 | RE8 | NW Boesinghe | | zlg | |

Losses – Nil

11 November 1917

Ltn M Müller	B	SE5a	E St Julien	1220	31
Ltn G Schlenker	41	Nieuport	Balschweiler		10
Vfw O Rosenfeld	41	Nieuport	Hagenbach		5

Losses:
Vfw Gustav Schindler   35   Injured in an accident.

12 November 1917

Ltn L Hanstein	35	Camel	SW Houthulst	0925	13	
Vfw F Hemer	6	RE8	N Ypres	1035	2	
Ltn H Bongartz	36	RE8	E Merckem	1135	22	a.
Ltn H Kroll	24	Camel	NE Armentières	1305	13	b.
Vfw Gondermann	35	Camel	NW Houthulst	1405	1	b.
Vfw J Buckler	17	RE8	Oostkerke	1545	25	

a.   B5086, No 5 Sqn, RFC, 2/Lt JA Higham & 1/AM S Hookway, WIAs.
b.   Two Camels were lost during this time period: B2405, No 65 Sqn, RFC, Lt K S Morrison, who departed at 1045, WIA/POW; and B6342, No 10 Sqn, RNAS, F/Lt G L Trapp, whose Camel was seen to break up between Forthen and Dixmuiden, KIA.
Losses – Nil

13 November 1917

Ltn H Kroll	24	Camel	N Zillebeke See	1435	14
Obltn H Auffarth	29	Sopwith	Blankaartsee	1510	6
Ltn Clauss	29	RE8	W Blankaartsee	1515	1
Obltn B Justinus	35	Camel	Boesinghe	1655	1

Losses:

Ltn Hans Sakowski	14	Flying Albatros DVa 5253/17 (G.90) shot down by AA fire over La Gorgue, at 1203, and taken prisoner.
Uffz Theodor Seffzig	34	Shot down and taken prisoner during combat with two Spads. Probably by MdL Marcel Henriot and MdL Georges Lienhard of N 65 (2nd and 1st victories).
Maat Friedrich Heinze	MFJ2	Flying an Albatros DIII (G.89), shot down and taken prisoner near Schoorbakke, by Capt BPG Beanlands, No 24 Sqn, RFC.

14 November 1917

Ltn O Splitgerber	38	Avro 2	N Majadag		4
Ltn R Heydacker	38	BE2e	Ardzan-See		1
Ltn Bussmann	1	Sopwith	Il Montello		zlg

Losses – Nil

15 November 1917

Vfw J Buckler	17	RE8	NE Ypres	0845	26	a.
Ltn J Veltjens	18	SE5	Langemarck	0950	9	
Vfw O Esswein	26	Camel	St Marquerite	1055	1	b.
Ltn H Bongartz	36	Sopwith	NE Zillebeke See	1115	23	
Uffz K Reinhold	24	Camel	E Zillebeke See	1325	1	c.
Ltn Kosslick	31	Balloon	NE Treviso		1	
Ltn A Thurm	31	Balloon	Roncade		3	
Ltn H Hoyer	36	Spad	Zandvoorde		-	

a.   A4652, No 21 Sqn, RFC, 2/Lts WA Barnett & GJ Bakewell, departed at 0650, KIAs.

b.   B2458, No 65 Sqn, RFC, 2/Lt TP Morgan, departed at 0845, last seen over Comines in combat, POW.

c.   B2444, No 70 Sqn, RFC, Lt R Mayberry, departed at 1150, last seen in combat over Tenbrielen, KIA.

Losses:

Ltn Hans Adam	6	Flying Albatros DV 5222/17 KIA by Lt KB Montgomery, 45 Sqn, RFC, his 7th victory.
Ltn Victor Schobinger	12	Wounded in action.
Ltn Ehlers	17	Wounded in action.
Ltn Richard Runge	18	Flying an Albatros DV, shot down in flames and killed.
Ltn Hans Hoyer	36	Killed in combat NE of Tenbrielen, probably by Capt PF Fullard, 1 Sqn, RFC,(39th victory).
Ltn Siebel	SFS2	Flying a Pfalz DIII shot down, but unharmed.

16 November 1917

Ltn Armbrecht	1	Balloon	NE Treviso		2
Vfw R Treptow	25	Avro	Dedebal	1215	5

Losses –Nil

17 November 1917

No Claims

Losses:

Ltn August Raben	39	Wounded in action by AA fire.

18 November 1917

Vfw J Buckler	17	Balloon	Ypres	0910	27	a.
Vfw P Bäumer	B	RE8	NE Zillebeke See	0920	13	
Vfw Wawzin	10	Spad	N Ypres	0925	1	b.
Vfw J Buckler	17	Balloon	Dickebusch	0925	28	
Ltn W Papenmeyer	B	Spad	NE Langemarck	1100	1	c.
Ltn R Wendelmuth	20	BF2b	Lampernisse	1310	14	d.
Vfw J Buckler	17	RE8	Bixschoote	1415	29	e.
Ltn zS G Sachsenberg	MFJ1	Sopwith	Nieuport		7	
Ltn R Windisch	32	Spad	Laval		6	

a.   British Balloon 36-17-2 (FM 124/D), Lt Dalrymple, the observer not harmed.

b.   B6817, No 19 Sqn, RFC, 2/Lt A Reid-Walker, shot down but OK.

c.   3575, No 23 Sqn, RFC, 2/Lt GA Crashwick, departed at 0928, last seen flying NE from Passchendaele, KIA.

d.   A7282, No 48 Sqn, RFC, 2/Lts WS McLaren, WIA/DOW, & DW Hardie, KIA.

e.   Possibly A3669, No 9 Sqn, RFC, 2/Lts W J H Courtis & E T Taylor, shot down near Langemarck, both unharmed.

Losses:

Ltn Fritz Kuke	33	Killed in an accident on a test flight at Wyngene airfield.
Ltn Günther Lüdecke	36	Injured in an accident.

19 November 1917

Vfw P Bäumer	B	RE8	NW Dixmuiden	1600	14	
Ltn R Windisch	32	Spad	Laval		6	a.

a.   A French Spad of Spa 65, Capt O de Montiero-Torres,(a Portuguese pilot), MIA.

Losses:

Obltn Otto Deindl	1	Wounded in action over Treviso.
Vfw Kasper Rahier	31	Killed near Vidor-Piave.

20 November 1917   The British Offensive against Cambrai starts

OfStv J Mai	5	Camel	E Estourmel	0840	3	
Ltn E Böhme	B	Nieuport	Oostkerke	1030	23	a.
Ltn O Splitgerber	38	AR2	Mojina		5	
Ltn Kirscht	38	Nieuport	W Gjevgjeli		1	
Ltn R Bertelsmeier	39	SAML	Il Montello		3	

a.   No.1 Belgian Escadrille, Sgt R Cicelet, KIA.
Losses:
Vfw Josef Heiligers   30   Flying Albatros DV No 2196/17, killed in
                                            combat over Ostricourt, at 1347.

21 November 1917

No Claims – No Losses

22 November 1917

Vfw O Könnecke	5	DH5	Anneux	0840	9	a.
OfStv J Mai	5	BF2b	Cantaing	0840	4	
Vfw F Rumey	5	Camel	Marcoing	0910	3	b.
Obltn H Auffarth	29	Camel	S Houthulst	1115	7	b.
Ltn R Matthaei	5	Camel	SE Fontaine	1130	9	b.
Ltn R Bertelsmeier	39	Hanriot	De Ros	1530	4	
Ltn W Wagener	39	Balloon	Crespano	1630	4	
Vfw F Piechulek	K5	Nieuport	Dammerkirch		1	
Vfw H v Puttkammer	K5	Paul Schmitt	Dammerkirch		1	
Vfw Rausch	40	Balloon	Haudainville		1	

a.   Probably a No 68 Sqn, RFC, (Australian) aircraft.
b.   No 43 Sqn, RFC, lost two Sopwith Camels that departed at 0755 this date: B6267, Capt GB Crole MC, WIA/POW; B 2366, 2/Lt EP Marchand, POW. No 46 Sqn, RFC, lost one Camel that departed at 0840, B1747, 2/Lt TL Atkinson, POW.
Losses – Nil

23 November 1917

Ltn H Bongartz	36	Camel	Becelaere	1150	–	a.
Ltn H Bongartz	36	Camel	Becelaere	1150	24	a.
Vfw F Rumey	5	Camel	Bourlonwald	1200	4	b.
Vfw E Hamster	37	Camel	E Voormzeele	1210	3	a.
Vfw F Rumey	5	AWFK8	SW Marcoing	1300	5	c.
Vfw O Könnecke	5	Camel	Fontaine	1320	10	b.
Rittm M v Richthofen	JGI	DH5	SE Bourlonwald	1400	62	d.
Ltn L v Richthofen	11	BF2b	W Seranvillers	1400	26	e.
Ltn K Küppers	6	Sopwith	N Cambrai	1500	5	
Ltn W v Bülow	36	Sopwith	Passchendaele	1630	26	
Vfw B Ultsch	39	Balloon	S Monte Grappa		8	

a.   No 65 Sqn, RFC, lost three Sopwith Camels that departed at 1045, last seen between Becelaere and Dadizeele. Two of them are believed to have collided during combat, B2409, 2/Lt A Rosenthal, KIA, and B5222, Lt CF Keller, POW, the third B2415, 2/Lt L Marshall, KIA.
b.   Probably from No 46 Sqn, RFC, which had six Camels shot up this date, one N2396, Lt SR Hanafy, WIA/POW/DOW.
c.   A2170, No 25 Sqn, RFC, 2/Lt R Main & 1/AM GP Leach, departed at 1015, POWs
d.   A9299, No 64 Sqn, RFC, Lt JAV Boddy, WIA, rescued by a fellow pilot – lost a leg.
e.   B1116, No 11 Sqn, RFC, 2/Lts ED Perney & EJ Blackledge, departed at 1235, last seen over Cambrai, both KIA.
Losses:
Vfw Karl Bey   5   KIA over Anneux, near Cambrai.

Ltn Hans-Joachim Wolff	11	Wounded in action.
Vfw Karl Ueberschär	39	KIA, 1500, over the Paive River, N Italy.
Uffz Eduard Feig	76	Killed in an accident at Habsheim.

24 November 1917

Vfw W Horn	37	RE8	SE St Jean	0920	1
Ltn O Splitgerber	38	Balloon	Majadag	1630	6
Ltn R Bertelsmeyer	39	Hanriot	W Montebelluna		zlg

Losses – Nil

25 November 1917

Obltn O v Boenigk	21	2 seater	Pfefferrucken	1640	6

Losses:

Ltn Werner Wagener	39	Wounded in combat.

26 November 1917

No Claims – No Losses

27 November 1917

No Claims

Losses:

Vfw Otto Esswein	26	Wounded in action.
Ltn Erwin Härtl	1	WIA at 1230 near Treviso, Italy.

28 November 1917

Ltn K Menckhoff	3	BF2b	Pilckem	1140	16	
Ltn F Ray	28	BF2b	SW Dixmuiden	1310	9	
Ltn E Udet	37	DH5	NW Passchendaele	1340	15	a.
Vfw P Bäumer	B	RE8	N Gheluwe	1400	15	b.
Vfw E Dürre	38	BE2e	Smol		2	
Vfw Lage	38	Nieuport	S Stojakovo		1	
Ltn sS H Rolshoven	SFS2	DH5	Brugge		1	a.

a.   Possibly from No 32 Sqn, RFC, 2/Lt D Francis, WIA.
b.   A4458, No 7 Sqn, RFC, 2/Lts WG Mann & RA Forsyth, departed at 1145, KIAs.

Losses:

Vfw Ernst Oppermann	31	Seriously wounded in combat over Udine; died 28 December.

British Offensive against Cambrai ends

29 November 1917

FwLtn F Schubert	6	SE5	Wambaix	0945	3	
Ltn H Klein	10	Camel	Crevecoeur	1000	21	
Ltn A Heldmann	10	Camel	Crevecoeur	1000	3	
Vfw J Buckler	17	Balloon	Bapaume	1205	30	a.
Ltn E Böhme	B	Camel	Zonnebeke	1255	24	
Ltn H v Bülow	36	BF2b	NE Moorslede	1300	3	b.
Ltn M Müller	B	DH4	S Schaep Baillie	1610	32	
Ltn W v Bülow	36	Spad	Passchendaele	1635	27	c.
Vfw Cremer	5	DH4	Cauroir		1	

a.   British Balloon 31-18-3 (BMS 89/D), the observers, Lts Weeks and Goodwin, were not harmed.
b.   A7253, No 20 Sqn, RFC, 2/Lts EV Clark & G Noon, last seen N of Westroosebeke, KIAs.

c.   B6758, No 19 Sqn, RFC, 2/Lt AH Rice, departed at 1430, KIA.
Losses:

Ltn Erwin Böhme	B	Killed during an attack on an AWFK of No 10 Sqn, RFC, over Zonnebeke.
Ltn Karl Wewer	26	Wounded in action.
Ltn Walter Blume	26	Wounded in action.

30 November 1917   The German Counter-Offensive at Cambrai starts

Vfw W Hippert	39	SAML	Rogare	1200	4	a.
Ltn H Klein	10	Balloon	W Ribecourt	1230	22	b.
Ltn E Thuy	28	Camel	E Ypres	1240	16	
Ltn H Bongartz	36	BF2b	Moorslede	1255	25	
Ltn H-G von der Osten	11	DH5	S Bourlonwald	1345	4	c.
Rittm M v Richthofen	JGI	SE5	Moeuvres	1430	63	d.
Ltn S Gussmann	11	DH5	W Bourlonwald	1445	2	c.
Ltn F Gräpel	28	RE8	S Pervyse	1510	1	
Ltn J Janzen	6	Sopwith	SW Marcoing	1545	2	e.
Ltn E Löwenhardt	10	Sopwith	S Moeuvres	1545	8	e.
OfStv J Mai	5	SE5a	NE La Pave	1548	5	f.

a.   Italian 1a Squadron.
b.   British Balloon 41-15-3 (FM 94/D).
c.   A9509, No 24 Sqn, RFC, 2/Lt ID Campbell, left at 1215, last seen in combat over Bourlon Wood at 1300, KIA.
d.   B644, No 41 Sqn, RFC, Lt DADI MacGregor, departed at 1300, shot down in flames near Cambrai, KIA.
e.   No 3 Sqn, RFC, lost two Camels that departed at 1225: B2496, 2/Lt LW Timmis, and B6336, Capt DB King, POWs.
f.   B40, No 56 Sqn, RFC, Capt RT Townsend, left at 1415, seen going down in flames near Cambrai, KIA.
Losses:

Ltn Wilhelm Schultze	4	Flying a Pfalz DIII collided in mid- air with Ltn R Wendelmuth of Jasta 20 between Fontaine and Notre Dame, W of Cambrai, killing both.
Ltn Rudolf Wendelmuth	20	see above.
Ltn Walter Göttsch	8	Wounded in action.
Ltn Heinrich Richter	9	Injured in a landing accident.
Ltn Friedrich Demandt	10	Flying Pfalz DIII 4116/17 (G.93), killed in combat at 1600 over Flesquières, by Lt GE Thomson, No 46 Sqn, RFC, his 3rd victory.
Ltn Johann v Senger und Etterlin	12	Killed at 1700 between Moeuvres and Bourlon Wood. Possibly collided with 2/Lt RE Dusgate, No 46 Sqn, RFC.
Ltn Julius Buckler	17	Wounded in combat.
Ltn Hans Hofacker	33	WIA over Havrincourt, DOW on 1 December.
Ltn Otto Napp	MFJ1	Albatros DV 4680/17, killed in an accident.

JASTA ARMEE ASSIGNMENTS AS OF 1 DECEMBER 1917

Western Front

1 Armee 19,22s	6 Armee 12,18,20,24s
2 Armee 4,5,6,8,10,11,15,17,29,30,35b	7 Armee 9,13,14,23b,32b
3 Armee –	Det 'A' –
4 Armee 2,3,7,26,27,28w,33,36,37	Det 'B' 41
5 Armee 16b,21s,34b	Dec 'C' 40

Other Fronts

11 Armee 25	Macedonia	
14 Armee 1,31,39	Italy	
1 Armee 38	Bulgarian Armee	
Sudarmee 81	Russia	

1 December 1917

Vfw K Thom	21	Caudron	Samogneux	1145	14	a.
Ltn F Höhn	21	Letord	S Chattancourt	1200	1	
Vfw G Schniedewind	17	RE8	Noble Ville	1350	4	
Vfw K Thom	21	Spad	S Forgeswald		zlg	
Ltn H Böhning	76	Sopwith 2	Hagenbach		5	

a.   Probably a G.6 from C 10, Brig Reingeissen & Asp Goguet, MIAs.

Losses:
Ltn Walter Brachwitz   17   WIA, died of wounds, 23 December.

2 December 1917

Ltn M Müller	B	DH4	Menin	0945	33	a.
Ltn W v Bülow	36	BF2b	Becelaere	1135	28	b.
Ltn H Bongartz	36	DH4	NE Moorslede	1205	26	c.
Ltn W Güttler	13	AWFK8	Villeret	1310	6	d.

a.   4432, No 57 Sqn, RFC, 2/Lts D Miller, WIA/POW, & AHC Hoyles KIA, departed at 0800.
b.   A7292, No 20 Sqn, RFC, Capts HGE Luchford, KIA, & JE Johnstone, POW, last seen at 1030 SE of Passchendaele.
c.   7661, No 57 Sqn, RFC, 2/Lts JT Orrell & JG Glendinning, departed at 1010, KIAs.
d.   B3903, No 8 Sqn, RFC, Lt TR Hepple, WIA, & 1/AM F Rothwell, KIA, brought down in flames over Villeret.

Losses – Nil

3 December 1917

Ltn H Leptien	21	Caudron R4	Damloup-Aix	1630	1

Losses:
Vfw Otto Pelz	32b	KIA N of Verneuil, probably by Lt Pierre Jailler of Spa 75, his 2nd victory.
Ltn Franz v Kerssenbrock	39	Killed in combat over Conegliano, Italy.
FlgMt Karl Meyer	SFS2	Shot down but unharmed.

4 December 1917

Ltn H Kroll	24	SE5	E Cantaing	1600	15
Vfw O Rosenfeld	41	Letord	Hagenbach		6

Losses:
Vfw Max Kämmerer   35   Injured in an accident.
Vfw Walter Horn   37   Killed over Wynghene.

5 December 1917

Ltn K Menckhoff	3	SE5	Passchendaele	1015	17	
Ltn O Löffler	B	Nieuport	E Houthulst	1030	1	a.
Ltn F Oppenhorst	5	BF2b	Abancourt	1100	1	
Vfw A Barth	10	BF2b	N Cambrai	1120	1	
Vfw M Wackwitz	24	RE8	NW Fampoux	1130	4	
Vfw W Kampe	27	Spad	NE Warneton	1150	5	b.
Ltn E Koepsch	4	Camel	Graincourt	1230	1	c.
Ltn F Loerzer	26	BF2b	S Houthulst	1400	7	d.

Ltn E Udet	37	SE5a	E Poelkapelle	1430	16
Ltn M Müller	B	SE5a	SW Poelkapelle	1440	34
Ltn O Könnecke	5	Camel	Seranvillers		11
Fdlw H Seidel	26	BF2b	Westroosebeke		1

a.   B6753, No 1 Sqn, RFC, 2/Lt CE Ogden, last seen over Moorslede at 0915, POW.
b.   A6642, No 23 Sqn, RFC, 2/Lt S Kendall, last seen over Ypres at 1040, WIA/POW.
c.   B6234, No 3 Sqn, RFC, 2/Lt LG Nixon, departed at 1045, POW.
d.   A7250, No 20 Sqn, RFC, Sgt F Hopper (P), WIA.

Losses:

Fw Hermann Seidel	26	Killed over Passchendaele.
Ltn Leo Strauch	31	Wounded in action.
Vfw Alfred Rüsche	38	Killed in an accident at Aviano, Italy.
Flgmstr Ottomar Haggenmüller	MFJ2	Killed N of Dixmuiden.

6 December 1917

Ltn J Jacobs	7	Spad	Passchendaele	1035	11	a.
Vfw W Kampe	27	Spad	N Becelaere	1035	6	
Ltn L Luer	27	BF2b	Zandvoorde	1400	zlg	
Vfw Iversen	41	Nieuport	N Fontaine		1	
Ltn F Schleiff	41	AR2	Butweiler		3	

a.   B1623, No 23 Sqn, RFC, 2/Lt W Whittaker, KIA.

Losses – Nil

The German Counter-Offensive against Cambrai ends

7 December 1917

Uffz K Reinhold	24	G100	Mercatel	1130	4	
Ltn M Müller	B	Spad	Moorslede	1155	35	a.
Vfw P Bäumer	B	Spad	Zonnebeke	1155	16	a.
Ltn H Weiss	41	Balloon	Lepuix	1410	2	b.
Uffz Walther	76	Caudron	Gewenheim	1550	1	
Vfw M Mallmann	19	Caudron	Berry-au-Bac		3	

a.   Two Spads lost this date: 3559, No 19 Sqn, RFC, 2/Lt HA Yeo, last seen at 1030 E of Moorslede, POW; B3552, No 23 Sqn, RFC, 2/Lt MG Gunn, last seen 1010 in a spin over Passchendaele, KIA.
b.   French 51 Compagnie d'Aérostières, S/Lt Gilbert & Asp Grandjean, both killed in the attack.

Losses:

Vfw Max Wackwitz	24	Albatros DV 4545/17 (G 97), shot down by ground fire and taken prisoner.
Ltn Prasse	26	Injured in an accident.

8 December 1917

Ltn J Jacobs	7	Camel	Passchendaele	1355	zlg	
Ltn C Degelow	7	Camel	Passchendaele	1400	zlg	
Ltn E v Stenglin	1	Sopwith	Montello		3	
Obltn H Kummetz	1	Camel	Villamata		7	a.
Vfw W Hippert	39	Camel	Pezzar		5	

a.   B4604, No 66 Sqn, RFC, 2/Lt JA Robertson, departed at 1310, last seen going down with three EA on his tail, MIA.

Losses:

Ltn Erich Daube	B	Killed in combat near Moorslede.
Ltn Rudolf Bertelsmeyer	39	Flying an Albatros, shot down and taken prisoner at 1500 near Valstagna.

9 December 1917

| Ltn W Böning | 76 | Spad | Massmünster | 1615 | 9 | a. |
| Ltn M Langer | 40 | 2 seater | Nancy | | 1 | |

a.   Possibly Adj P de Cazenove de Pradines (5 victories), Spa 81, WIA, in a Spad XIII.

Losses:

| Ltn Bernard Kilian | 21 | Killed in an accident on Pauvres airfield. |
| Vfw Fritz Schröder | 39 | KIA at 1330 nr San Michele, Italy. |

10 December 1917

Ltn H Schlömer	5	RE8	Hendecourt	1045	1	
Ltn F Janzen	6	SE5	SE Gonnelieu	1320	3	
Ltn O Hohmuth	23	Caudron	S Bras	1500	3	a.
Vfw G Strasser	17	Balloon	Jussy	1545	6	b.
Ltn F Poesch	16	Spad	Champneuville		1	
Vfw J Neumaier	16	Caudron	Vacherauville		3	a.
Vfw R Lander	7	Sopwith	Ghent		1	

a.   Probably a G.6 from C 56, Adj Malancon & S/Lt Ballureau, KIAs.
b.   French 92 Compagnie d'Aérostières, Sgt Contal descended safely.

Losses:

Ltn Herbert Wallner	3	Killed in action over Wynghene.
Ltn Paul Wigand	3	Killed during a test flight near Waterdammhoek.
Vfw Gustav Beerendonk	20	Killed in a collision with Uffz Friedrich Becker, who also died, over Guesnain a/f.
Uffz Friedrich Becker	20	See above.
Uffz Kurt Reinhold	24	Killed in an accident during a test flight at Emerchicourt.

11 December 1917

| Ltn M Langer | 40 | DH4 | Mamey | | 2 | |

Losses:

| Vfw Walter Starck | 32 | Injured in an accident. |

12 December 1917

Ltn E Just	11	Balloon	Hermies	1320	1	a.
Ltn T Rumpel	23	Spad	Cumières	1330	4	
Ltn O v Breiten-Landenberg	9	Spad	St Souplet	1402	4	b.
Vfw G Strasser	17	Balloon	Villers Faucon	1550	7	c.
Vfw H Horst	7	Spad	S Houthulst	1615	zlg	
Ltn P Billik	7	Camel	Keyem	1630	8	d.
Ltn sZ K-H Voss	MFJ1	Camel	Leke		1	

a.   British balloon 31-18-2 (SB 211).
b.   Spad VII No.6024, Cpl B Walcott (1v), N 84, MIA.
c.   British balloon 29-14-3 (FM 134), 2/Lt B Thomas, WIA.
d.   N6330, No 10 Sqn, RNAS, F/S/Lt JG Clark, POW.

Losses:

Uffz Oswald Rottmann	14	Killed in action near Asch.
Ltn Walter Börner	27	Flying Albatros DV (G 98), KIA over Boesinghe, by Lt V Wigg, 65 Sqn RFC.
Uffz Kählert	27	Shot down and taken prisoner.
Ltn Wilhelm Kolb	76	Albatros DV 5294/17, KIA 1630 over Habsheim.

13 December 1917

Vfw K Schattauer	16	Balloon	Belleville	1135	2	a.
Vfw J Neumaier	16	Caudron	Belleville		4	
Vfw Amschl	31	Camel	N Crespano		2	
Ltn A Thurm	31	Balloon	Asolo	1700	4	

a.　　　French 61 Compagnie d'Aérostières, S/Lt Lebegue and Adj Depoux made safe descents.
Losses:
Ltn Paul Erichson　　　　K7　　wounded in action.

14 December 1917

No Claims – No Losses

15 December 1917

Uffz F Neubauer	26	RE8	SW Zillebeke See	0947	1	
Ltn H-G v d Osten	11	SE5	Havrincourt	1025	5	
Vfw M Mallmann	19	AR2	Craonne		zlg	a.
Ltn Scheller	19	Spad	Brimont		2	b.
Vfw P Färber	22	AR2	N Craonne-Cerny		zlg	

a.　　　Possibly an AR2 from F 54, Cpl Beynet & Sol Bayen, both injured in a crash landing. Only AR lost this date.
b.　　　S/Lt H Astor, Spa 80, in a Spad VII, POW 1015 hrs between Chevregny & Juvincourt.
Losses:
Uffz Bockstegers　　10　　Injured in an accident during a test flight;
　　　　　　　　　　　　　　died on 18 December 1917.

16 December 1917

Ltn M Müller	B	Camel	W Passchendaele	1410	36
Vfw P Bäumer	B	RE8	N Boesinghe	1410	17

Losses – Nil

17 December 1917

Vfw E Weiss	29	Nieuport	Armentières	1600	1	
Vfw E Weiss	29	RE8	Hazebrouck	1610	2	a.

a.　　　A3816, No 69 Sqn, AFC, Lt JL Sandy & Sgt HF Hugues, crashed near the Bruay-St Pol Road at 1500, KIAs.
Losses:
Ltn Clauss　　　　　　29　　　Flying Albatros DV 5390/17 (G 101), shot
　　　　　　　　　　　　　　　down in combat with an RE8, Lt JLM Sandy
　　　　　　　　　　　　　　　& Sgt HF Hughes of No 3 Sqn, AFC.
Ltn Karl-Heinrich Voss　　MFJ1　　Flying Albatros DV 2356/17 (G 100), shot
　　　　　　　　　　　　　　　down in flames and killed over Houthulst
　　　　　　　　　　　　　　　Forest, by 2/Lt Kelsey of No 1 Sqn, RFC.

18 December 1917

Ltn H v Häbler	36	RE8	Zonnebeke	1140	5	a.
Uffz H Werner	26	Camel	N Zillebeke See	1245	1	
Ltn H Bongartz	36	Camel	Kaphoek	1525	27	b.
Ltn K Bolle	28	Camel	NW Staden	1530	3	b.
Ltn H v Häbler	36	Camel	Kaphoek	1530	6	b.
Ltn J Jacobs	7	Camel	Dixmuiden	1545	12	b.
Ltn P Lotz	7	Camel	S Dixmuiden	1545	2	b.
Vfw P Bäumer	B	Camel	W Becelaere	1600	18	b.
Ltn zS G Sachsenberg	MFJ1	Sopwith 2	NW Keyem		8	

FlgMt A Buhl		SFS2	2 seater	-		

a.   B5899, No 21 Sqn, RFC, 2/Lts FG Flower & CW Cameron, departed at 0910 and was seen to go down in flames, KIAs.

b.   No 65 Sqn, RFC, lost three Camels that departed at 1350 and last seen over Roulers at 1410 this date: B2388, 2/Lt RH Cowan, POW; B6271, 2/Lt I D Cameron, POW; B2410, 2/Lt DM Sage, KIA.

Losses:

Ltn Stanislaus Zentzytzky	17	Killed in an accident at Bohain airfield.

19 December 1917

Obflgmstr A Buhl	SFS	HP	Ostende	1335	1	
Obflgmstr A Buhl	SFS	DH4	Blankenbergh	1347	2	a.
Vfw A Weber	5	SE5a	Havrincourt Wald	1430	1	
Vfw P Färber	22	Balloon	Terny-Sorny	1610	1	
Vfw J Hohly	29	Sopwith	N Ypres		–	

a.   N6008, No 5 Sqn, RNAS, F/S/Lt SS Richardson & AC/1 RA Furby, MIAs.

Losses:

Ltn Walter Braun	20	Severely wounded at 1405 over Faumont; died at Dourges 20 December.

20 – 21 December 1917

No Claims – No Losses

22 December 1917

Ltn A Wunsch	22	Sopwith 2	Vivaise	1530	–	a.
Uffz H Boy	14	Bréguet	St Loup	1630	1	b.

a.   Possibly from Escadrille Sop 216, Capt Bloch & Sol Frieur, MIAs.

b.   Possibly a Bréguet assigned to Escadrille Sop 108, Sgts Mespleine & Baslignac; MIAs.

Losses:

Ltn Massmann	14	Wounded in action.
Ltn Hans Villinger	18	Killed at 1530 nr Le Mesnil-en-Vespres.
Uffz Wilhelm Föge	30	Severely wounded over Armentières; died later in Field Hospital Nr.12.

23 Deecmber 1917

Vfw J Landin	32	AR2	S Vailly		1

Losses:

Ltn Ernest Hess		19	Flying Albatros DV 5347/17, shot down and killed at 1310 near Fresnes, by Adj Joseph de Kergolay of N 96, his 1st victory.
OfStv Karl Thom		21	Wounded during a balloon attack.
Ltn Otto Frhr von Türchkeim zu Altdorf		K4b	Killed in action over Waldkirch.

24 December 1917

Vfw O Rosenfeld	41	AR2	Vauthiermont		7

Losses – Nil

25 – 26 December 1917

No Claims – No Losses

27 December 1917

No Claims

Losses:

Vfw Hecht	10	Flying Pfalz DIII 1370/17 (G 110), shot down and taken prisoner at Estrées-en-Chaussée, by 2/Lts AG Hanna and RA Burnand, No 35 Sqn, RFC.
Ltn Traugott v Schweinitz	11	Flying Albatros DVa 5313/17, killed in combat at 1435 near Avesnes-le-Sec.

28 December 1917

Ltn E Thuy	28	DH4	Gheluvelt	1330	17

Losses:

Vfw Max Brandenberg	29	Flying Pfalz DIII 4020/17 (G 116), shot down POW, by AA fire over Le Transloy.
ObFlgMstr Karl Meyer	SFS	Severely wounded in action, died of injuries at Leipzig, on 31 December.
Ltn Wilhelm Mattheus	MFJ1	Severely wounded in combat with three Sopwiths near Clerkem; died of wounds.

29 December 1917

Ltn K Menckhoff	3	Spad	Draaibank	1120	18	a.
Ltn K v Bülow	14	Spad XI	Reims		–	
Ltn Golz	13	Caudron	Cernay		1	
Vfw O Rosenfeld	41	Balloon	Lepuix		8	b.

a.   B6780, No 19 Sqn, RFC, 2/Lt HE Galer, departed at 0950, POW.
b.   French 51 Compagnie d'Aérostières, Sgt Prieur made a safe descent.

Losses:

Vfw Otto Rosenfeld	41	POW after balloon attack. He escaped in April 1918, and rejoined his unit.

30 December 1917

Vfw L Gaim	39	Spad	W Susegana	1515	5
Vfw K Bohnenkamp	22	Spad	SE Pinon	1555	3
Ltn A Thurm	31	Balloon	S Asolo		5
Vfw E Hannemann	39	Caproni	Susegana		2
Ltn E v Stenglin	1	Camel	W Conegliano		4
Ltn E v Stenglin	1	Spad	S Susegana		5

Losses:

Vfw Ludwig Gaim	39	Wounded in combat at 1515 hours.
Vfw Karl Eisele	43	Killed during a test flight of an Albatros DIII at Metz.

31 December 1917

No Claims

Ltn A Thurm	31	Balloon	Asolo	1050	–

Losses:

Ltn Alwin Thurm	31	Flying Albatros DIII No 4879/17, killed in a balloon attack by Ltns RJ Brownell and HM Moody of 45 Sqn, RFC, Paderno, Italy.

WWI Jasta Pilot Victories & Casualties
1918

JASTA ARMEE ASSIGNMENTS AS OF 1 JANUARY 1918

Western Front

1 Armee 19,21s,22s
2 Armee 4,5,6,10,11,15,35b
3 Armee 9,44s
4 Armee B,3,7,26,27,28w,36,37,47w,51,MFJI,MFJII
5 Armee 16b,34b,45
6 Armee 12,18,20,29,30,46

7 Armee 13,14,23b,32b
18 Armee 8,17,24s
Det 'A' 33,43,K3
Det 'B' 41,76b,77b
Det 'C' 40s,42,78b

Other Fronts

11 Armee 25	Macedonia
14 Armee 1,31,39	Italy
1 Armee 38	Bulgarian Armee
Südarmee 81	Russian Front

1 January 1918

Obltn H Kummetz	1	Camel	Vittorio, Italy	1105	1	a.
Ltn E Frhr v Stenglin	1	Camel	S Vittorio, Italy	1109	6	a.
Vfw Teigeler	22	Spad	Terny-Sorny	1220	1	
Vfw O Könnecke	5	BF2b	Bullecourt	1420	zlg	
Vfw H Küllmer	23	Spad	W Masschleifs		2	
Vfw M Kahlow	34	Spad	Varennes		3	
Ltn G Kröhl	34	Spad	Bois de Cheppy		1	
Vfw J Pütz	34	Spad	Varennes		1	

a.   Only loss B6414, 66 Sqn RFC, Capt. R Erskine, DOW.

Losses

OfStv Karl Lang	1	Killed in action 1110 Vittorio, Italy.
Uffz Albert Meinhardt	21	Killed in action Bétheny near Reims, by Sgt J N Hall of N 124, E of Fort Brimont.

2 January 1918

No Claims

Losses

Ltn Günther Auffarth	29	Killed in action 1210 St Auguste near Lens.

3 January 1918

Vfw J Pütz	34	AR2	Mort Homme	1205	2	
Ltn L Hanstein	35	SE5	by Guillemont	1210	14	a.
Vfw O Fruhner	26	Camel	S Armentières	1235	3	
Obltn B Loerzer	26	BF2b	SW Gheluvelt	1310	19	b.
Vfw E Thomas	9	Balloon	Somme-Suippes	1330	1	c.
Uffz E Liebert	30	Camel	Mourchin	1450	2	d.
Vfw H Oberländer	30	Camel	Billy, Provin	1450	5	e.
Ltn E Kämpfe	13	Spad	S Pargnan		1	
Ltn E Kämpfe	13	Balloon	NW Pargnan		2	
Uffz O Stadter	32	Spad	Pontavert		3	f.
Vfw J Kettel	32	P Schmitt	Pontavert		1	

| Ltn R Windisch | 32 | Balloon | Villers | | 7 | |
| Vfw Gnädig | 38 | BE | NW Doiran See | | 1 | |

a.   C1753, 56 Sqn RFC, 2/Lt RJG Stewart, WIA, POW.
b.   DH4, A7687, 57 Sqn RFC, Capt AFE Pitman,KIA & Lt CW Pearson,KIA.
c.   French 67 Compagnie Aérostières.
d.   B5658, Naval 10, F/S/Lt F Booth, KIA.
e.   N6351, Naval 10, F/S/Lt AG Beattie, POW.
f.   Probably 2018, Adj G Bourdet, KIA.

Losses

| Ltn Wigan | 12 | Taken prisoner of war. |
| Uffz Emil Liebert | 30 | Killed in action Lens. |

4 January 1918

OfStv W Kampe	27	Camel	Rolleghem-Kappelle	1140	7	a.
Vfw K Schulz	37	Camel	Passchendaele	1140	1	b.
Obltn W Reinhard	6	BF2b	S Cambrai	1220	7	c.
Ltn W Papenmeyer	B	SE5	Gheluvelt	1245	2	d.
Vfw O Fruhner	26	DH4	Neuville	1350	4	e.
Ltn H Weiss	41	Balloon	Ellbach	1458	3	f.
Ltn R Windisch	32	Spad	S Staubecken		8	
FlgMt Müller	SFSII	Caudron	Coxyde		1	

a.   B2413, 65 Sqn RFC, 2/Lt RE Robb, KIA.
b.   65 Sqn RFC, ?
c.   DH4 B2074, 27 Sqn RFC, 2/Lt KP Ewart,KIA & Lt AN Westlake,MC,KIA.
d.   C5334, 60 Sqn RFC, Capt FHB Selous,MC KIA.
e.   A7424, 57 Sqn RFC, Capt EEE Pope,POW & Lt AF Wynee,POW.
f.   French 79 Compagnie Aérostières.

Losses

| Ltn Friedrich Graepel | 28 | Killed in action 1130 Becelaere. |

5 January 1918

Ltn E Löwenhardt	10	Balloon	Attilly	1605	9	a.
Vfw P Hiob	13	P Schmitt	Aisne-Staubecken		2	
Patrol	20	Balloon			26	
Vfw F Piechulek	41	Balloon	S St Die		2	b.
Ltn W Ewers	77	P Schmitt	Liggert		4	
Ltn W Ewers	77	Spad	SW Retzweiler		5	c.

a.   French 82 Compagnie Aérostières.
b.   French 64 Compagnie Aérostières.
c.   Escadrille N 157, Brig Jouve, WIA/DOW (flying a Nieuport), this was the only French scout loss this date.

Losses – Nil

6 January 1918

Ltn G Schlenker	41	Sopwith 2	SW Mühlhausen	1510	11	a.
Ltn E Udet	37	Nieuport	Bixschoote	1615	17	
Vfw J Landin	32	Nieuport	Paissy		2	
Ltn F Ehmann	33	P Schmitt	Gottestal		1	
Vfw Gnädig	38	DD	NW Doiran See		2	

a.   Escadrille Sop 123.

Losses

| Ltn Walter von Bülow-Bothkamp | B | Killed in action St Julien, Albatros DV 2080/17. |

7 – 8 January 1918

No Claims – No Losses

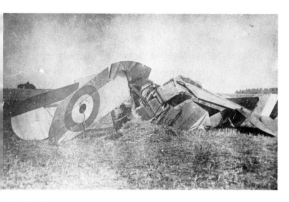

Top left: A British BE2d (No.5873) of 12 Squadron, shot down in combat 17 September 1916.

Top right: Martinsyde G100 of 27 Squadron in German markings following capture on 24 September 1916. 27 Squadron lost two G100s the previous day to Jasta 2.

Middle: No. 12 Squadron RFC lost this BE2c (2546) to Stefan Kirmaier of Jasta 2 on 21 October 1916, the German's 5th victory.

Bottom: Nieuport XVII N1831 of N77, flown by Lt Santa Maria who died of wounds, the first victory of Ltn Hermann Kunz of Jasta 7 on 23 October 1917. It was also the Jasta's first victory.

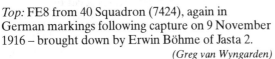

Top: FE8 from 40 Squadron (7424), again in German markings following capture on 9 November 1916 – brought down by Erwin Böhme of Jasta 2.
(Greg van Wyngarden)

Middle left: Sopwith Pup (N5190), 8 Naval Squadron RNAS, shot down by Franz Ray of Jasta 18, 23 November 1916.

Middle right: BE2c 4498, 5 Squadron, brought down by Hans Bethge, Jasta 1, 26 December 1916.
(P Baillie via Bruce/Leslie)

Bottom left: Sopwith Pup A626 of 8 Naval Squadron, lost 4 January 1917, the same date Manfred von Richthofen of Jasta 11 shot down another Pup from this unit for his 16th victory.

Bottom right: AWFK3 of 47 Squadron shot down by Oblt Burkhardt of Jasta 25 near Lake Dorian, Greece, 15 January 1917. Photo dropped by the Germans showing the fate of the unfortunate crew with the serial number of their aeroplane.

Top: Pup N6161, 3 Naval Squadron (1 Wing), captured after a combat with Obfm Karl Meyer of Seefrontstaffel 1, 1 February 1917.

Above: Nieuport XVII (2405) of N 506, shot down by Ofstv Hüttner of Jasta 14, 11 February 1917.

Left: Sopwith 1½ Strutter N5102 from 5 Naval Wing, shot down by Vfm J Wirtz of MFJ1, 7 February 1917.

Top left: FE8, 40 Squadron, shot down by Jasta 11 on 9 March 1917.

Top right: The remains of a Nieuport XVII from 1 Squadron, claimed by Paul Strähle of Jasta 18, 17 March 1917.

Middle: Spad VII 19 Squadron, shot down by Manfred von Richthofen, 24 March 1917.

Bottom: Bristol F2a of 48 Squadron, A3343, another of von Richthofen's victims, 5 April 1917.

Top left: Richthofen's second 48 Bristol (A3340) was burnt totally this same date.

Top right: Spad VII from Spa 31, shot down by Heinrich Bongartz of Jasta 36, 6 April 1917, flown by Lt Mistarlet. Just aft of the cockpit the Germans have written – 'Abgerschossen von der Jagdstaffel 36' and the date.

(van Wyngarden)

Above: Sopwith Pup from 3 Naval Squadron shot down by Paul von Osterroht, leader of Jasta 12, 12 April 1917 (N6172 'Black Tulip').

Left: The same Pup, repaired and with the German markings now completed. *(van Wyngarden)*

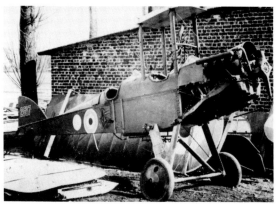

Top left: Spad VII A6682 of 23 Squadron, another victory for von Osterroht, 23 April 1917. *(van Wyngarden)*

Top right: RE8 from 10 Squadron (2567), shot down by Hermann Frommherz of Jasta 2, 14 April 1917. Pilot was on a bombing sortie (no observer); note bomb racks and that three of the propeller blades have been sawn off.

Above: Another RE8 lost on 14 April was this 34 Squadron machine (A78) brought down by Karl Schäfer of Jasta 11.

Right: Nieuport XVII (A313) from 1 Squadron, shot down 22 April, by August Hanko of Jasta 28. Note the number '5' on the fuselage and at an odd angle on top of the fuselage.

Top: Manfred von Richthofen shot down this 16 Squadron BE2e on 23 April (A3168), seen here as it came out of the factory in England.

Middle: 'Big Ack' (AWFK8) A2709 of 35 Squadron, destined to be shot down by Jasta 12, 23 April 1917. Coming down in Allied lines no credit was given, but Jasta 12 had two 'Sopwith' claims at midday which tie up with this loss.

Left: Sopwith Pup A6175 of 66 Squadron. Heinrich Lorenz of Jasta 33 claimed this on 24 April 1917.

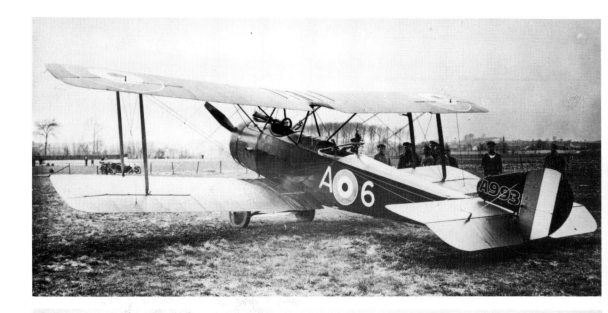

Top: Jasta 5's Edmund Nathanael shot down this Sopwith 'Strutter' of 43 Squadron, on 28 April 1917.

Middle: Another victim of Edmund Nathanael was this 60 Squadron Nieuport XXIII (B1514), on 6 May 1917.

Bottom left: FE2d A5149 from 20 Squadron, shot down 7 May 1917, brought down on Jasta 18's aerodrome by Walter von Bülow-Bothkamp.

Bottom right: Werner Voss made this 54 Squadron Pup (A6174) his 27th victory on 9 May 1917; it had CANADA written across the centre section of the top wing.

Top left: This Pup (A6185) of 4 Naval Squadron was coded 'A' for 'Anzac', brought down on 10 May 1917 near Zeebrugge.

Top right: Sopwith Pup of 3 Naval Squadron N6464, shot down by Vfw Robert Riessinger of Jasta 12, his first of four victories, 11 May 1917.

Middle left: Another view of N6464, with its wings taken off, languishing in a German scrap yard.

Note the prop blades had been sawn through.

Middle right: Another 3 Naval Pup, this one shot down by Lorenz of Jasta 33 on 14 May 1917 (A6158), putting FSL WR Walker in a prison camp.

Bottom: Nieuport XVII A6678 of 1 Squadron, downed by Paul Strähle of Jasta 18, 25 May 1917. Lt J R Anthony died of wounds.

Top left: Jasta 28's Kurt Wittikind brought down this 56 Squadron SE5 – A8920 – on 4 June 1917 for his first victory.

Top right: Nieuport XVII N3204 from 6 Naval Squadron, which broke up in a fight with Jasta 5 on 6 June 1917 – possibly in action with Werner Voss.

Middle left: Sopwith Triplane N5358, 10 Naval Squadron, shot down on 24 June 1917 in a fight

with Jasta 11, probably by Karl Allmenröder.

Middle right: Morane-Saulnier P, of Escadrille MS31, forced down 10 July 1917 – cause unknown.

(van Wyngarden)

Bottom: Erwin Böhme of Jasta 29 shot down this 40 Squadron Nieuport XVII (A6783) on 14 July 1917. Lt G Davis was made PoW.

(van Wyngarden)

Top: Martinsyde 'Elephant' from 27 Squadron, downed by Ernst Hess of Jasta 28, 9 August 1917 but he lost his claim to M.Flakzug 61.

Above and left: Two views of a Spad VII of the *Lafayette Escadrille* (N 124), shot down by Willi Schulz of Jasta 16 over Dun-sur-Meuse, 18 August 1917 – his first victory.

(*van Wyngarden*)

Top left: Martinsyde G100 of 27 Squadron, shot down by Max Müller of Jasta 28, 21 August 1917.

Top right: Pup B1795 'Z' from 46 Squadron, shot down by Manfred von Richthofen, 3 September 1917. To ensure its destruction, the British pilot ran it into a tree after force landing behind the enemy lines.

Above: DH4 bomber of 57 Squadron, A7439, downed by Otto Schober of Jasta 18, 11 September 1917 – his only victory.

Right: RE8 A3535, 59 Squadron, downed by Vfw Otto Könnecke of Jasta 5, 21 August 1917.

Two views of Triplane N5429 of No.1 Naval Squadron, shot down by Kurt Wüsthoff of Jasta 4,
13 September 1917. Note Albatros in the background with Jasta 4's well-known spiral marking.

(van Wyngarden)

Top left: Sopwith Pup A 673, from 46 Squadron, claimed by Viktor Schobinger of Jasta 12, 16 September 1917.

Top right: SE5 B507, 60 Squadron, shot down and force landed on Jasta 18's airfield on 5 October 1917. This machine had been flown by Captain R Chidlaw-Roberts in the Voss fight of 23 September 1917.

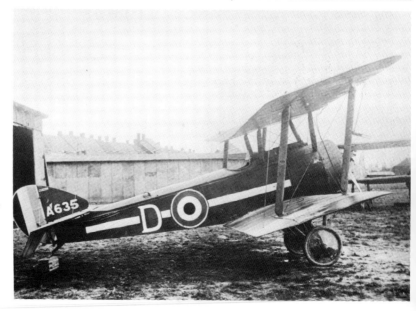

Above: Pup B1800, 54 Squadron, shot down by Erwin Böhme, Jasta 2, 13 October 1917.

Right: Pup A635 of 66 Squadron, Theodor Quandt's (Jasta 36) victory of 12 October 1917.

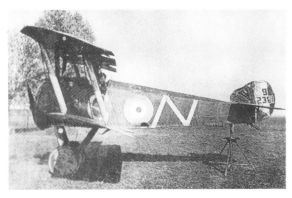

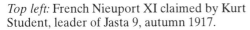

Top left: French Nieuport XI claimed by Kurt Student, leader of Jasta 9, autumn 1917.

Top right: SE5a B4876, 84 Squadron, downed on 20 October 1917. 2/Lt W E Watts became a PoW.
(van Wyngarden)

Middle: Ltn Victor Schobinger of Jasta 12 forced down this 59 Squadron RE8 (A3859) on 21 October 1917.

Bottom left: Sopwith Camel of 70 Squadron – B2361 – shot down by Ltn Josef Jacobs of Jasta 7, 27 October 1917.

Bottom right: Nieuport XXVII of 1 Squadron (B6827) shot down by Jasta 6, 6 November 1917.

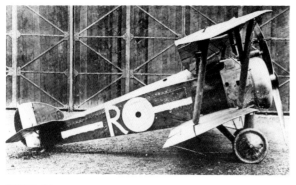

Top left: Camel B2458, 65 Squadron, Otto Esswein, Jasta 26, 15 November 1917.

Top right: An 11 Squadron BF2b, A7130, shot down by Friedrich Gille, Jasta 12, 19 November 1917.

Middle left: SE5a B4890, 56 Squadron, shot down by Fritz Schubertof Jasta 6, 29 November 1917 for his third and final victory.

Middle right and bottom: Otto Könnecke of Jasta 5 brought down this 3 Squadron Camel (B6234) on 5 December 1917.

Top: Jasta 10 pilots and 'guests', 5 December 1917. They were the crew of BF2b A7143 from 11 Squadron, brought down by Adam Barth.
(van Wyngarden)

Bottom left: Victor and victims; Barth with Sgt M H Everix and Lt H Whitworth, 11 Squadron.
(van Wyngarden)

Middle right: While it is difficult to tie up some French losses, most of the following aircraft would have been brought down by Jasta pilots, including this Spad VII of Spa 15. *(van Wyngarden)*

Bottom right: Captured Spad VII of Spa 37.
(van Wyngarden)

Top: Captured Spad VII from Spa 3, still in its VB103 markings.

Bottom: Captured Nieuport XVII of N 48, being used here by the Jastaschule at Valenciennes. Note another captured Nieuport in the background.

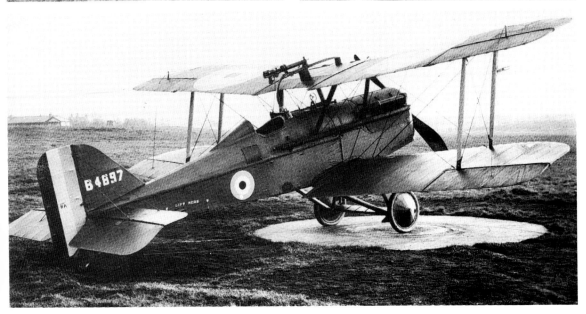

Top: Captured Spad XIII from Spa 159.

Middle left: Captured Nieuport Scout of N 48.

(van Wyngarden)

Middle right: The same or another N 48 Nieuport, with Eduard Ritter von Schleich of Jasta 21, seated in the cockpit.

Bottom: SE5 of 60 Squadron lost in a collision with the Albatros flown by Ltn Mobius of Jasta 7 over Becelaere on 24 January 1918. He and Lt A W Morey were both killed.

Top left: Spad B6732 of 23 Squadron, forced down by Adolf von Tutschek of JGII, 26 February 1918.
(van Wyngarden)

Top right: Von Tutschek inspecting Lt Doyle's 23 Squadron Spad. *(van Wyngarden)*

Middle left and bottom: Von Tutschek again, this time with the SE5a of 24 Squadron (C1057) he shot down on 5 March 1918. *(van Wyngarden)*

Top left: Spad XIII of Spa 93, 6 March 1918.

Top right: Camel B7230 'T' of 3 Naval Squadron, shot down in combat 10 March 1918.

(van Wyngarden)

Middle: B7230 with wings taken off, ready to be transported to the rear.　　*(via G H Williams)*

Bottom left: A 3 Naval Squadron Camel now in German markings, showing the Flight 'eagle'

marking. This was used by Otto Kissenberth of Jasta 23 and in which he was badly injured in a crash in May 1918. (Sometimes said to be B7230, it is clearly another Camel as B7230 does not have the Flight marking on its starboard side. Probably B7184, brought down by Ltn Carl Degelow of Jasta 40 on 23 January 1918.)

Bottom right: Camel C1576 of 54 Squadron, forced down by Vfw Edgar Scholtz of Jasta 11 on March 1918.

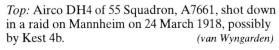

Top: Airco DH4 of 55 Squadron, A7661, shot down in a raid on Mannheim on 24 March 1918, possibly by Kest 4b. *(van Wyngarden)*

Middle left: BF2b C4630 of 62 Squadron, shot down by August Delling of Jasta 34 on 19 May 1918, but awarded to a flak unit.

Middle right: SE5a, shot down 12 June 1918, probably C6497 of 74 Squadron (there was a letter 'G' on the cowling). Note the Germans had

marked it as a French aeroplane! Possible victory of Johann Schäfer of Jasta 16b.

Bottom left: DH4, A8073, 55 Squadron, IAF, shot down by Willi Rosenstein flying with Kest 1b, 26 June 1918, during a raid on Karlsruhe.

Bottom right: DH9 D1679 from 99 Squadron IAF, shot down on 20 July 1918 by Ltn Heinrich Drekmann of Jasta 4.

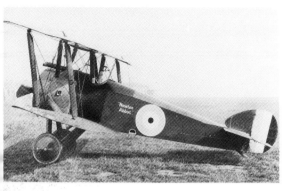

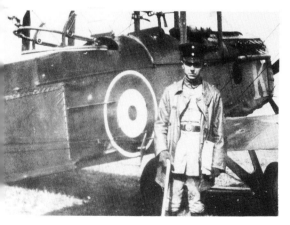

Top left: A 65 Squadron Camel, E1548, claimed by Wilhelm Neunhofen of Jasta 27, 9 August 1918.

Top right: DH9 D3084 of 104 Squadron, IAF, brought down in combat during a raid on Hagenau, by aircraft of Jasta 18, 12 August 1918.

Middle: DH9 of 104 Squadron, IAF, brought down in combat during a raid on Mannheim on 22 August 1918.

Bottom left: August Raben, leader of Jasta 18 with DH4 No. A7708 of 55 Squadron, brought down on 30 August 1918 during a raid on Thionville by the IAF.

Bottom right: Camel of 73 Squadron, D1922, shot down 1 September 1918, possibly by Robert Ritter von Greim of Jasta 34b.

Top left: SE5a E5939 of 32 Squadron (Lt J O Donaldson PoW), brought down by Ltn Theodor Quandt of Jasta 36 on 1 September 1918.

Top right: DH4 of the American 20th Aero Squadron, shot down by Jasta 12's Alfred Greven on 26 September 1918. *(van Wyngarden)*

Middle: Jasta 12's ground personnel gather around the 20th Aero DH4 at Giraumont airfield where the stricken bomber force landed.

Left: The captured crew being entertained by Jasta 12 at Giraumont airfield. *(van Wyngarden)*

9 January 1918

Ltn H Müller	15	P Schmitt	Staubecken	1200	1

Losses

Ltn Max Ritter v Müller	B	Killed in action 1250 Moorslede Albatros DVa 5405/17.
Ltn Hans Kiessling	34	Wounded in action Verdun Pfalz DIII 4031/17.
Ltn zS P Achilles	SFSII	Shot down 1235 between Brugge and Coxyde.

10 January 1918

No Claims – No Losses

11 January 1918

Obltn J Loeser	39	Camel	Szomigo, Italy		1	a.
Vfw W Hippert	39	Camel	Cimadolmo, Italy		6	b.

a.   B2494, 45 Sqn RFC, Lt HT Thompson, WIA.
b.   B2436, 45 Sqn RFC, 2/Lt DW Ross, KIA.

Losses

Ltn Hans Kummetz	1	Killed in action Conegliano, Italy.

12 January 1918

Ltn F Pütter	9	Balloon	Mourmelon le Petit	1205	7	a.
Vfw E Thomas	9	Balloon	Hans	1205	2	b.
Ltn L Hanstein	35	AWFK8	SW Bellicourt	1250	15	c.
Ltn H Stutz	20	Camel	Beaumont	1630	2	d.
Ltn F Pütter	9	Spad	Binarsville		6	e.

a.   French 53 Compagnie Aérostières.
b.   French 65 Compagnie Aérostières.
c.   B283, 35 Sqn RFC, 2/Lt TA Urwin,POW/DOW & 2/Lt JH Young,POW/DOW.
d.   B2354, 43 Sqn RFC, Lt J Boyd, POW.
e.   Possibly 4267, Escadrille Spa 65, Sgt J Le Bouscher, POW.

Losses – Nil

13 January 1918

Ltn H Kroll	24	Spad	Flesquières	1107	16	
OfStv J Mai	5	BF2b	Gonnelieu	1158	6	a.
Vfw F Rumey	5	BF2b	Beaumont	1230	6	a.
Vfw M Krauss	27	Spad	SW Gheluvelt	1240	4	
Ltn G Schuster	29	Camel	Ennecourt	1230	3	b.
Ltn H Schlömer	5	BF2b	Gonnelieu	1328	2	c.
Ltn W Steinhäuser	11	Balloon	Hendecourt	1637	2	d.

a.   11 Sqn RFC had one loss, A7174, 2/Lt HV Biddington,POW & 2/Lt JH Corbet,KIA.
b.   B5602, 71 Sqn AFC, 2/Lt FB Willmott, POW.
c.   Possibly AWFK8 B5826, 8 Sqn RFC, Lt FH Hall,WIA & Lt AS Balfour,KIA.
d.   British Balloon 41-15-5 (FM 137/D).

Losses

Ltn Eberhardt Stapenhörst	11	Taken prisoner of war, Fokker DrI 144/17.

14 January 1918

Vfw H Reisch	41	Sopwith 2	Gebweiler	1540	1	a.
Vfw J Schwendemann	41	Sopwith 2	Orschweiler	1540	2	a.
Ltn F Pütter	9	Balloon	Vraincourt	1630	8	b.

a.   Two French Sopwiths lost this date in this sector; Escadrille Sop 123, Sgt Silbermann, MIA & Sgt Liauzu,MIA, and Escadrille Sop 129, Brig Piel, MIA & MdL Ruse,MIA.
b.   French 36 Compagnie Aérostières.

Losses
Ltn Theodor Wrege   39   Killed in action Conegliano, Bocca, Italy.

15 January 1918
No Claims – No Losses

16 January 1918

Uffz Eggebrecht		25	Balloon	Opticar	1

Losses
Vfw Otto Klüpfel   77   Injured in a crash.

17 January 1918
No Claims – No Losses

18 January 1918

Ltn O v B-Landenberg	6	Sopwith	Hagricourt	1020	5	
Ltn E Löwenhardt	10	BF2b	Le Catelet	1023	10	
Ltn K Gallwitz	B	Camel	N Passchendaele	1120	5	a.
Vfw U Neckel	12	AWFK8	Lens-Loos	1125	14	b.

a.   B4629, 65 Sqn RFC, 2/Lt AE Wylie, KIA.
b.   B273, 2 Sqn RFC, 2/Lt WK Fenn-Smith,KIA & 2/Lt NL Cornforth,KIA.

Losses
Flg Hellmuth Riensberg   10   Killed in action 1030 Beaurevoir Pfalz DIII 4059/17.

19 January 1918

No.68, 69, and 71 Australian Sqns were redesignated No. 2, 3, and 4, Sqns AFC

Lth H J v Hippel	5	Camel	W Vendhuille	1000	1	a.
Ltn Koch	12	Camel	Biache	1145	1	b.
Obltn B Loerzer	26	FB2b	N Houthulst Wood	1235	20	c.
Ltn K Gallwitz	B	SE5	S Houthulst Wood	1445	6	d
Ltn O Homuth	16	Balloon	Belleville	1520	4	e.
Ltn F Pütter	9	Nieuport	E Tahure	1610	9	f.
Ltn A Dietlen	41	Spad	NE Thann		3	

a.   B5423.6, 54 Sqn RFC, 2/Lt FM Ohrt, POW.
b.   B6208, 43 Sqn RFC, 2/Lt CN Madeley, KIA.
c.   A7193, 20 Sqn RFC, 2/Lt B Starfield,KIA & Lt A Hutchinson,KIA.
d.   Camel B2468, 65 Sqn RFC, 2/Lt ET Baker, KIA.
e.   French 24 Compagnie Aérostières.
f.   Escadrille N 156, Adj H Variot, KIA.

Losses
Vfw Martin Mallmann   19   Killed in action Vandetre.
Ltn Schmidt   24   Severely injured in a crash at Guise airfield.
Vfw Max Krauss   27   Killed in action 1430 Blankaart See,
                                     combat with 2-Seater.
Uffz Richard Kade   50   Killed in a crash at La Neuville.

20 January 1918

Ltn H J Rolfes		45	Nieuport	Chattancourt	1510	2	a.

a.   Escadrille N 98, Cpl H F Johnson, an American, WIA.

Losses

Ltn Fritz Schönberger	16	Wounded in action near Verdun.
Uffz Johannes Diekhaus	19	Killed in a collision at Ecly.
Gefr Christian Schiller	19	Killed in a collision at Ecly.
Vfw Gustav Schindler	35	Killed in a crash at Premont airfield Albatros DVa 5625/17.
FlgMt Müller	SFSII	Severely injured in a crash Albatros DVa 6588/17.

21 January 1918

No Claims

Losses

Gefr Josef Mayer	32	Killed in action 1150 Mars-sous-Bourcq.
Ltn Umberto Mario Antonio Rosa	38	Severely injured in a crash Hudova airfield.
Ltn Günther Gellenthin	40	Killed in action at Longuyon.

22 January 1918

Ltn R Plange	B	Camel	Langemarck	1140	2	a.
Ltn K Gallwitz	B	BF2b	Oostnieuwkerke	1205	7	b.
Ltn T Cammann	B	BF2b	St Julien	1205	1	b.
Ltn K Menckhoff	3	RE8	S Draaibank	1305	19	c.
Ltn O Fruhner	26	Camel	Coucou, Bousbecque	1355	5	d.
Ltn F Ehmann	33	Balloon	Lepuix		–	

a.   N6370, 9 Naval Sqn, F/S/Lt JE Beveridge, WIA.
b.   One BF2b lost, C4825, 20 Sqn RFC, 2/Lt AR Paul, POW/DOW & 2/AM A Mann, POW.
c.   AWFK8 B3313, 35 Sqn RFC, 2/Lt R Buchanan, WIA & Lt TG Mather, OK.
d.   B6426, 70 Sqn RFC, 2/Lt FW Dogherty, POW.

Losses

Ltn Guenter   8   Severely injured in a crash.

23 January 1918

Ltn G Wandelt	36	Camel	Staden	1545	1	a.
Ltn G Wandelt	36	Camel	Staden, Zarrenlinde	1550	2	b.
Ltn F Brandt	27	Camel	Frenzenberg	1650	3	

a.   B7184, 3 Naval Sqn, F/S/Lt JE Youens, POW.
b.   B5663, 10 Naval Sqn, F/S/Lt RA Blyth, KIA.

Losses

Ltn Gustav Wandelt   36   Killed in action E Staden collision.

24 January 1918

Uffz F Jacob	12	Camel	Izel	1235	zlg	
Ltn W Schulz	41	AR2	Obersept	1335	2	a.
Ltn M Möbius	7	SE5	Becelaere	1350	1	b.
Ltn P Lotz	7	DH4	N Kortryk	1420	3	c.

a.   Escadrille AR 58, Sgt Joubert, MIA & S/Lt Dechery, MIA.
b.   B4897, 60 Sqn RFC, Lt AW Morey, KIA in collision.
c.   A7912, 57 Sqn RFC, Lt JO Beattie, KIA & 1/AM WJ Belchamber, POW.

Losses

Ltn Martin Möbius	7	Killed in a collision with the 60 Sqn SE5, 1350 hrs at Becelaere.
Ltn Hans Karl v Linsingen	11	Wounded in action 1535 Iwuy Pfalz DIII 4223/17.
Uffz Fritz Jacob	12	Killed in action 1240 Izel.
Uffz Heinrich Naegele	38	Killed in action Cerniste, Hudova, Macedonia.

25 January 1918

Ltn H Arntzen	50	Balloon	Pontavert	1045	7	a.
Ltn G Michaelis	41	AR2	S Ammerzweiler	1235	1	b.
Ltn O Kissenberth	23	Spad	Hill 304, Verdun	1250	18	c.
Ltn F Röth	23	Balloon	Recourt, SW Verdun	1300	1	d.
Ltn F Röth	23	Balloon	Bethélainville	1304	2	e.
Ltn F Röth	23	Balloon	Frommerville	1308	3	f.
Ltn C Degelow	7	BF2b	Kortemarck	1315	2	g.
Ltn H Kroll	24	BF2b	N St Quentin	1735	17	h.
Uffz J Santjer	26	BF2b	Stadenberge		1	i.
Vfw Amschl	31	Camel	Zenson, Italy		3	

a. French 43 Compagnie Aérostières.
b. Two AR's were lost this date; Escadrille AR 1, S/Lt Jacob, & Adj Jacob, and Escadrille AR 32, MdL Mendanais, & Lt Ressec, all MIA.
c. Escadrille Spa 67, Cpl P Benney, an American, POW.
d. French 55 Compagnie Aérostières.
e. French 59 Compagnie Aérostières.
f. French 80 Compagnie Aérostières.
g. B883, 20 Sqn RFC, Sgt HO Smith,WIA/POW & 2/Lt HS Clemons,WIA/POW.
h. 22 Sqn RFC ?
i. DH4 B2085, 27 Sqn RFC, 2/Lt DTC Rundle-Woolcock,OK & 2/Lt JH Holland,OK.

Losses

Ltn Ernst Paland	20	Wounded in action.
Vfw Herbert Werner	26	Killed in action Staden.
Vfw Hermann Reisch	41	Killed in action Amerzweiler.

26 January 1918

No Claims – No Losses

27 January 1918

Ltn H Weiss	41	Balloon	La Croix	1700	4	a.
Ltn F Pütter	9	Nieuport	Dontrien	1730	10	b.

a. French 28 Compagnie Aérostières.
b. Escadrille N 151, Lt Belloc, FTL, POW.

Losses

Uffz Eugen Foertig	16	Killed in crash Mercy le Haut airfield Pfalz DIII 4034/17.
Uffz Karl Preuss	31	Killed in action 1340 Roverodo, Italy.

28 January 1918

OfStv J Mai	5	BF2b	Bourlon Wood	1210	7	a.
Vfw F Rumey	5	BF2b	Graincourt	1210	7	b.
Vfw O Könnecke	5	SE5	Tilloy	1450	12	c.
Ltn R Klimke	27	DH4	Zonnebeke	1515	–	
Ltn J Huth	14	Balloon	Sept-Saulx, Baconnes	1520	1	d.
Ltn E Udet	37	Camel	Bixschoote	1655	18	
Vfw H Kramer	13	Caudron	Vendeuil		4	
FlgMt H Groth	MFJII	Spad	Westende-Bad		1	

a. B1189, 11 Sqn RFC, 2/Lt JL Milne-Henderson,KIA & 2/Lt E Cunningham,KIA.
b. A7288, 11 Sqn RFC, 2/Lt S Reay,KIA & 2/AM A Patterson,KIA.
c. B610, 56 Sqn RFC, Lt LJ Williams, POW.
d. French 57 Compagnie Aérostières.

Losses

Uffz Maier	8	Wounded in action.

Ltn Reinhold Maier	30	Wounded in action.
FlgMt Arnim Undiener	MFJII	Killed in action at Saeskerke.
VfFlgMstr Hirth	MFJII	Severely injured in a crash.

29 January 1918

Ltn W Güttler	13	Camel	Essigny le Grand	1135	7	
Ltn H Kroll	24	Camel	S St Quentin	1135	18	
Ltn E Udet	37	BF2b	Zillebeke	1200	19	
Vfw F Rumey	5	BF2b	St Quentin	1215	8	a.
Ltn R Klimke	27	Eng 2	Houthulsterwald	1235	–	
Ltn H Arntzen	50	RE8	La Fère, Travecy	1305	8	b.
Ltn H Bongartz	36	Sopwith	Poelkapelle	1350	28	
Ltn H Müller	15	P Schmitt	S Staubecken	1515	2	
Ltn H Müller	15	P Schmitt	S Staubecken	1515	zlg	
Ltn H v Freden	1	Balloon	Spresiano, Italy	1530	1	c.
Ltn K Bolle	28	Camel	E Poelkapelle	1610	4	d.
Ltn E Thuy	28	Camel	E Poelkapelle	1615	18	
Ltn P Hoffmann	12	Camel	Méricourt	1630	–	
Vfw C Brunnengräber	13	Balloon	Saucy		1	e.
Vfw A Hurrle	13	Caudron	Remigny		3	
Ltn zS Tinschert	MFJ1	DH4	Leffinghe		1	

a.   DH4 A7600, 25 Sqn RFC, Capt AG Whitehead & Lt WJ Borthistle,KIAs.
b.   16 Sqn RFC.
c.   British 34th Balloon Section.
d.   B3890, 70 Sqn RFC, Lt KM Rodger, WIA/POW.
e.   French 45 Compagnie Aérostières.

Losses

Vfw Christian Brunnengräber	13	Killed in action Saucy, Spa 12 pilots Capt AJGJM De Turenne & Adj de la Fregoelière in flames, after balloon attack noted above.
Gefr Hellmann	27	Severely injured in a crash.
Ltn Kurt Brecht	36	Killed in action Passchendaele.
Vfw Josef Kettel	50	Killed in action La Fère Albatros DIII 2370/17.

30 January 1918

Vfw Mikat	14	Spad	La Ville au Bois	1230	1	a.
Obltn H Auffarth	29	BF2b	Neuve Chapelle	1245	8	b.
Ltn K Bolle	28	DH4	E Wilskerke	1420	5	c.
Ltn H Kroll	24	BF2b	by Hesbécourt	1425	19	b.
Vfw G Feiseler	25	Nieuport	S Moglia		2	
Obltn W Plüschow	39	Camel	E Spresiano, Italy		1	

a.   Escadrille Spa 57, Adj R Vanier, WIA.
b.   Only BF2b lost C4832, 22 Sqn RFC, 2/Lt GG Johnstone,KIA & 2/AM RA Duff,DOW.
c.   N5982, Naval 5, F/S/Lt FP Williams & G/L CA Leitch,KIAs.

Losses

Vfw Adam Barth	10	Killed in action Anneux Albatros DV 4565/17.
Vfw Albert Hurrle	13	Killed in action Lavergnie Ferme.
Obltn Bruno Justinus	35	Killed in action 1200 m W Forenville and 800 m N Serainvillers at 1420, in Albatros DV 4630/17.

31 January 1918

| Ltn H v Freden | 1 | Balloon | Volpago, Italy | 1600 | 2 | a. |

a.   British 33rd Balloon Section.

Losses – Nil

Jasta Armee Assignments as of 1 February 1918

Western Fronts

1 Armee 19,22s,62
2 Armee 4,5,6,10,11,15,35b,54s,56
3 Armee 9,44s,53,79b
4 Armee B,3,7,26,27,28w,36,37,47w,51,MFJI,MFJII
5 Armee 16b,34b,45
6 Armee 12,18,29,30,46,49,52,57

7 Armee 13,14,21s,23b,50,60,61
17 Armee 20,32b,58,59
18 Armee 8,17,24s,48,63
Det 'A' 33,43,78b,K3
Det 'B' 41,76b,77b
Det 'C' 40s,42

Other Fronts

11 Armee 25	Macedonia
14 Armee 1,31,39	Italy
1 Armee 38	Bulgarian Armee
Südarmee 81	Russian Front

1 February 1918

No Claims – No Losses

2 February 1918

OfStv O Esswein	26	Camel	St Julien	1335	2	
Ltn M Kühn	10	SE5	Bouchain	1540	3	a.
Ltn W Steinhäuser	11	RE8	Havrincourt Wood	1720	3	
Vfw E Thomas	9	Balloon	Mourmelon	1750	3	b.
Ltn K Bieler	14	Breguet	Avacan		3	c.
Ltn G Keitsch	39	Camel	W St Veto, Italy		1	d.

a.   B8273, 41 Sqn RFC, Maj FJ Powell,MC, WIA.
b.   French 57 Compagnie Aérostières.
c.   Escadrille Br 66, Adj Ragez,MIA & MdL Duffrène,MIA.
d.   B2607, 66 Sqn RFC, Lt FDC Gore, POW.

Losses

Ltn Albert Krönig	3	Killed in action 1750 Thielt.
Ltn Askan Frhr von und zu der Tann	24	Killed in action 1130 Bellenglise Alb DV 4757/17.
Ltn Emil Thuy	28	Injured in a crash.

3 February 1918

Ltn O Löffler	B	DH4	Gent-Mariakerke	1040	2	a.
Vfw O Fruhner	26	Camel	Poelcappelle	1145	7	
Vfw O Könnecke	5	DH4	Villers Gueslain	1230	–	
Ltn S Büttner	22	Balloon	Terny-Sorny	1245	2	b.
Ltn P Schröder	B	Camel	E Moorslede	1510	1	
Ltn H Vallendor	B	SE5	E Moorslede	1510	1	
OfStv O Esswein	26	Camel	E Langemarck	1600	3	c.
OfStv O Esswein	16	Camel	Poelkapelle	1610	4	c.
OfStv O Fruhner	26	Camel	Sleyhage	1615	8	c.
OfStv O Esswein	26	Camel	SE Westroosebeke	1615	5	c.
Vfw H Boy	14	Spad XIII	Aguilcourt		2	
Ltn K v Bülow	19	Sopwith 2	Berru		2	d.

a.   A7873, 25 Sqn RFC, Lt EG Green,MC, & Lt PC Campbell-Martin, both POW.
b.   French 46 Compagnie Aérostières, S/Lt Joussaume OK & Cpl Boucher OK.
c.   Only two losses this date: B6430, 9 Naval Sqn, A/F/Cdr RR Winter, KIA and B6370, 10 Naval, F/S/Lt WH Wilmot, KIA.

d.   Escadrille Sop 260, MdL Mettivier,MIA & S/Lt Picard-Destelan,MIA.
Losses
Ltn Erwin Klumpp   B   Killed in a crash Thielt.
Ltn Max Kersting   48   Killed in action Aubenchel.
Ltn Karl Stock   48   Killed in action Villers Outreaux.

4 February 1918

Obltn J Loeser	39	Camel	Barbisano, Italy	1130	1	a.
Uffz Dierenfeld	39	Camel	Susegana, Italy	1130	1	a.
Ltn F Schröder	39	Camel	Susegana, Italy	1130	1	a.
Ltn K Menckhoff	3	BF2b	Poelkapelle	1220	20	b.
Ltn U Fischer	22	Sopwith 2	Sinceny	1550	1	
Ltn K Bieler	14	Camel	Pontavert		3	
Ltn W Böning	76	Spad	Füllern-Lorgitzen		8	

a.   45 Sqn RFC lost B2494, Lt DG McLean,KIA.
b.   20 Sqn RFC, 2/Lt FD Miller, KIA.
Losses
Ltn Bruno Langer   3   Killed in action Westroosebeke.
Ltn Konrad Bieler   14   Severely wounded in action Pontavert.
Uffz Dierenfeld   39   Wounded in action 1130 Susegana, Italy.
Obltn Josef Loeser   39   Wounded in action 1130 Barbisano, Italy.
Vfw Rudolf Wiesner   39   Killed in action 1300 Vittorio, Italy.
Vfw Paul Wagner   76   Killed in action 1046 Colmar-Nord.

5 February 1918

OfStv O Esswein	26	BF2b	Moorslede	1221	6	a.
OfStv O Esswein	26	SE5	Staden, Hooglede	1230	7	b.
Ltn G Schuster	29	Camel	NW Annay	1345	4	c.
Ltn H Dilthey	27	Sopwith 1	Hooglede	1435	6	d.
Ltn F Brandt	27	Spad 1	Houthulsterwald	1505	–	
Ltn H Bongartz	36	DH4	Kanegaun, Thielt	1540	29	e.
Ltn H Bongartz	36	DH4	Oudenbourg	1543	30	f.
Ltn H v Freden	1	Balloon	E Treviso	1710	3	

a   A7255, 20 Sqn RFC, Lt DG Campbell,OK & 2/Lt WH Nash,OK, FTL.
b.   B533, 60 Sqn RFC, 2/Lt AC Ball, POW.
c.   N6379, Naval 8, F/S/Lt H Day,DSC, KIA.
d.   B2394, 65 Sqn RFC, 2/Lt HVC Luyt, WIA.
e.   A7680, 25 Sqn RFC, 2/Lt EO Cudmore,POW & 1/AM LJW Bain,POW.
f.   A7865, 25 Sqn RFC, 2/Lt RP Pohlmann,KIA & 2/AM R Ireland,KIA.
Losses
Vfw Ernst Höfer   42   Wounded in action.
Ltn Vetter   Kest3 Wounded in action forced to land at
                               Landorf.

6 February 1918

Ltn H Becker	12	Camel	Rémy	4	a.
OfStv Dobberahn	12	Camel	Lécluse	1	b.

a.   C1552, 3 Sqn RFC, 2/Lt PF Kent, KIA.
b.   C6706, 3 Sqn RFC, 2/Lt AGD Alderson, POW.
Losses – Nil

7 February 1918

No Claims – No Losses

8 February 1918

No Claims

Losses

Ltn Georg Michaelis	41	Killed in action Füllern, Sundgau. Claimed by Sgt F H Chavannes of Spa 112 – only claim this date in this Belfort Sector.

9 February 1918

No Claims

Losses

Vfw Schille	47	Severely injured in crash testing Pfalz DIIIa 5904/17.

10 February 1918

No Claims

Losses

Ltn Robert Denkhardt	35	Killed in a crash 1500 Premont airfield Pfalz DIII 4163/17.
Ltn Georg Ferner	61	Killed in crash Voyenne airfield Pfalz DIIIa.

11 February 1918

Ltn Niebecker	43	Balloon	Minorville	1010	2	a.
Obltn R v Greim	34	Spad	Chattencourt	1620	zlg	
Ltn W Böning	76	P Schmitt	Füllern	1650	9	
Uffz Walther	76	P Schmitt	Carsbach	1650	2	
Ltn E Raabe	41	Balloon	Ellbach	1710	1	b.
Ltn H Weiss	41	Balloon	Willern, Mansbach	1715	5	c.
Ltn A King	40	Spad	Pont-à-Mousson		3	
Ltn W Schulz	41	Sopwith 2			3	d.

a. French 82 Compagnie Aérostières, S/Lt HT Parizy, KIA.
b. French 26 Compagnie Aérostières, 1Lt JB Wallace, USBS, OK.
c. French 27 Compagnie Aérostières.
d. Probably 3504, Escadrille Sop 60, Adj Desbaux, MIA & S/Lt Turinaz, MIA, only French Sopwith lost this date.

Losses

Ltn Xaver Dannhuber	79	Severely injured in crash at Thugny airfield, in a Pfalx DIII.

12 February 1918

Ltn H Weiss	41	Spad	Staden Airfield	1420	6	
Ltn H Arntzen	50	Balloon	La Ville aux Bois	1515	9	a.

a. French 45 Compagnie Aérostières, Lt P Bacalou, OK & 2Lt Doherty, USBS, OK.

Losses – Nil

13 February 1918

No Claims – No Losses

14 February 1918

Ltn H Leptien	21	P Schmitt	Silléry	1115	2

Losses

Ltn Max Raspe	44	Severely injured in a crash.

15 February 1918

Ltn S Büttner	22	Balloon	Nanteuil	1600	3	a.

a.   French Balloon (not destroyed), 2/Lt Allport, OK and S/Lt Allegrie, OK.

Losses

Uffz Paul Proske	7	Severely wounded in action.
Vfw Paul Hüttenrauch	7	Lightly injured in a crash.

16 February 1918

Vfw R Heibert	46	RE8	W Meurchin	1215	2	a.
Obltn H Auffarth	29	RE8	Wingles	1220	9	b.
Vfw G Wagner	29	RE8	N Pont-à-Vendin	1230	2	c.
Vfw R Heibert	46	RE8	La Valée, Carvin	1230	3	d.
Obltn W Reinhard	6	BF2b	Fayet, St Quentin	1345	8	e.
Ltn H Bongartz	36	DH4	Becelaere		–	f.

a.   A4423, 5 Sqn RFC, 2/Lt FC Gilbert, POW.
b.   A7724, 18 Sqn RFC, Lt Hudson,OK & Lt T Nicholson,WIA.
c.   A4756, 16 Sqn RFC, Capt FS Thomas, KIA.
d.   A4455, 5 Sqn RFC, 2/Lt R MacDonald, POW.
e.   A7229, 48 Sqn RFC, Sgt ET Hardeman,& 2/Lt GW Croft, KIAs.
f.   18 Sqn RFC ?

Losses

Ltn Bastgen	30	Taken prisoner SE Bailleul Alb DV 4422/17.

17 February 1918

Uffz Freter	42	Spad	Toul, Flirey	1325	1	
Obltn H Auffarth	29	DH4	Ham	1330	10	a.
Uffz Schweppe	35	SE5	N Beaumetz	1340	1	b
Oblt A Thomas	13	Balloon	NE La Fère	1450	2	c.
Ltn G Schulte	50	Balloon	Roucy	1515	1	
Ltn Wendland	53	RE8	Boursies		–	d.

a.   B2077, 27 Sqn RFC, 2/Lt AW Greene, & Sgt A Hughesden,KIAs.
b.   B8231, 24 Sqn RFC, 2/Lt DN Ross,DCM,MM, KIA.
c.   British Balloon 3-13-5 (FM 141/D), Lt Medlin & AM Braham, OK.
d.   B6549, 59 Sqn RFC, 2/Lt RH Williams, WIA & 1/AM SW Egan, WIA.

Losses

Ltn Friedrich-Wilhelm Lübbert	11	Wounded in action 1230 Rumilly.
Ltn Friedrich Poesch	78	Killed in a crash 0930 Burscheid airfield Albatros DIII (OAW) 5120/17.

18 February 1918

Ltn E Udet	37	Camel	Zandvoorde	1050	20	a.
Ltn H Kroll	24	Camel	Vendeuil-Remigny	1220	20	
Ltn J Veltjens	18	Camel	Violaines	1230	10	
Obltn B Loerzer	JGIII	Camel	Nachtegaal	1255	21	b.
Ltn M Gossner	23	AWFK8	Armentières	1315	1	c.
Ltn T Rumpel	23	Camel	Givenchy	1320	5	d.
Vfw H Küllmer	23	Camel	Bailleul		3	e.
Ltn F Röth	23	BF2b			zlg	
Ltn K Odebrett	42	Spad 2	Bernecourt		8	f.
Ltn W Böning	76	AR2	W Altkirch		zlg	

a.   N6347, 10 Naval Sqn F/S/Lt RE Burr, WIA, DOW 20 Feb18.
b.   B2499, 70 Sqn RFC, 2/Lt CJW McKeown, POW.
c.   B211, 2 Sqn RFC, Lt AJ Homersham, KIA & Capt S Broadbent,KIA.
d.   B7188, 8 Naval Sqn, F/S/Lt CR Walworth, KIA.
e.   B7204, 8 Naval Sqn, F/Cdr GW Price,DSC, KIA.
f.   Escadrille Spa 20, S/Lt Finat,WIA & Sgt Roux, WIA.

Losses

Vfw Martin Klein	5	Killed in action 1205 Beaurevoir.
Ltn Heinrich Kutt	23	Wounded in action.
Ltn Willy Etzold	26	Killed in action 1240 Houthulst Wood.
Uffz Joachim v Stein	35	Wounded in action Douai.
Uffz Justus Kaiser	35	Killed in action S Izel, W Douai Albatros DV 4448/17.

19 February 1918

Ltn F Schleiff	56	AWFK8	SE Epéhy	0810	4	a.
OfStv F Altemeier	24	Sopwith	Wald von St Gobin	1125	10	
Obltn H J Buddecke	30	Camel	La Bassée	1400	13	b.
Obltn H Bethge	30	Camel	N Lorgies	1405	19	c.
Ltn H-G v d Marwitz	30	Camel	Marquillies	1405	3	d.
Uffz F Classen	26	Balloon	Jeperen	1512	2	e.
OfStv O Esswein	26	BF2b	Potyze	1515	8	f.
Ltn U Fischer	22	Inf a/c	Jouy	1605	2	
Ltn A Dietlen	41	Balloon	Ellbach	1630	4	g.
Obltn R v Greim	34	Spad	Mort Homme	1640	8	
Ltn H Leptien	21	P Schmitt	Sapigneuil	1730	3	
Ltn W Güttler	13	Bréguet	Guise		8	h.
Obltn H Karbe	22	Spad	Bruyères		2	
Flgmstr M Brenner	MFJI	Bf2b	N Ypres		3	

a.   B3305, 35 Sqn RFC, 2/Lt HH Wilson, & Capt JS Gregory, KIAs.
b.   B9185, 80 Sqn RFC, 2/Lt SR Pinder, KIA.
c.   B9171, 80 Sqn RFC, 2/Lt E Westmoreland, KIA.
d.   80 Sqn RFC, Lt SLH Potter, WIA.
e.   British Balloon 19-44-4, Lt D Gordon-Campbell, KIA & Lt TH Stream, KIA.
f.   C4837, 20 Sqn RFC, Lt DG Campbell, & Lt JH Stream, KIAs.
g.   French 27 Compagnie Aérostières.
h.   Escadrille PS 126, Cpl Perry, & Lt Huguet, MIAs.

Losses

Ltn Hans v Puttkammer	3	Taken prisoner 1130 Hollebeke Albatros DVa 4495/17.
Vfw Erich Windmüller	9	Killed in action 1115 Tahure.
Ltn Hans Klein	10	Wounded in action 1300 Pfalz DIII 4283/17.
Obltn Hans Karl Frhr von Wolfskeel-Reichenberg	34	Killed in action Mort Homme.

20 February 1918

Ltn C Degelow	7	BF2b			—	
Ltn Wittenhagen	31	Camel	Marco, Italy		1	a.
Ltn Niebecker	43	Nieuport	Château-Salins		3	b.

a.   B5193, 28 Sqn RFC, Lt DC Wright, POW, DOW 22Feb18.
b.   Nieuport 24 N3305, Escadrille N 159, Cpl Six, WIA/POW.

Losses

Ltn Wolfgang Güttler	13	Killed in a crash 2 km SE Reneuil Ferme.
Vfw Paul Hiob	13	Killed in a crash 2 km SE Reneuil Ferme.
Vfw Harling	31	Wounded in action 1000 hours.

21 February 1918

Obltn H Göring	27	SE5	Ledeghem	1000	17	a.
Ltn R Klimke	27	SE5	Rolleghem-Kapelle	1000	7	b.
Ltn R Matthaei	46	Camel	SW Wavrin, Lille	1200	10	c.
Ltn H Pippart	13	Balloon	NW La Fère	1635	7	d.
Ltn F Schleiff	56	RE8	Havrincourt Wood	1715	5	e.
Vfw U Neckel	12	SE5	Pinon-Vauxillon		—	f.

| Vfw R Joerke | 13 | SE5 | Reneuil Ferme | | 10 | g. |

a.   C5325, 60 Sqn RFC, 2/Lt GB Craig, POW/DOW 22 Feb18.
b.   B4860, 60 Sqn RFC, 2/Lt WM Kent, KIA.
c.   B5552, 4 Sqn AFC, 2/Lt A Couston, POW.
d.   British Balloon 3-13-5 (FM 143/D), 2/Lts Fairbairn & Ratcliffe, OK.
e.   16 Sqn RFC, Lt WJ Blitch, WIA.
f.   B535, 2 Sqn AFC, 2/Lt R Lang, MM, WIA.
g.   B619, 2 Sqn AFC, 2/Lt GC Logan, POW.

Losses

Uffz Rudolf Lingenfelder	16	Killed in crash Aetrycke airfield.
Vfw Artur Weber	46	Killed in action 1140 Ascq by Carvin, Camel.
FlgObMt Hermann Hildemann	MFJ1	Severely injured in crash Coolkerke, in Albatros DV 2076/17,DOI, 21 February,, Brussels.

22 February 1918

No Claims – No Losses

23 February 1918

Ltn F Danker	32	RE8	Bailleul	1530	2	
OfStv J Landin	32	RE8	Willerval	1535	3	
Ltn W Ewers	77	Spad	Oberburnhaupt	1630	6	a.
Ltn H Weiss	41	RE8	Oberspach		7	

a.   Escadrille Spa 49, S/Lt H Schneider, WIA, DOW, 24 February.

Losses – Nil

24 February 1918

OfStv F Altemeier	24	RE8	by Marcy	1415	11	a.
Ltn W Papenmeyer	B	RE8	St Julien	1545	3	b.
Ltn H Weiss	41	Breguet	Heinsbrunn	1610	8	c.
Ltn G Schlenker	41	Breguet	Schweighausen	1615	12	c.
Ltn A Dietlen	41	Breguet	Niedersulzbach	1620	5	c.

a.   B2293, 52 Sqn RFC, 2/Lt GRT Marsh, POW & 2/Lt IM Dempser, KIA.
b.   B5071, 4 Sqn RFC, 2/Lt RD White, KIA & 2/Lt WA Keeler, KIA.
c.   Two Breguets lost from Escadrille Br 29,1346, S/Lt Arnault, & Cpl Robanet, and1354, Adj Levy, & Cpl Albrecht, all MIA.

Losses

| Uffz Weber | 25 | Severely injured in a crash landing. |

25 February 1918

| Ltn E Kreuzer | 39 | Balloon | Ponzano, Italy | | 2 | a. |

a.   Italian Balloon 1a Sezione.

Losses – Nil

26 February 1918

Ltn R Plange	B	Spad VII	Warneton	1110	3	a.
Hptm A v Tutschek	JGII	Spad VII	Athies, NE Laon	1120	24	b.
ObFlgMstr Kurt Schönfelder	7	DH4	Kortryk	1125	4	c.
Ltn F Röth	23	RE8	Méricourt, Arleux	1250	4	d.
Ltn E Weiss	33	Nieuport	NE Blamont	1250	1	e.
Ltn G Schulte	50	Balloon	Bouvancourt	1540	2	f.
Vfw F Rumey	5	DH4	N Busigny	1600	9	g.
Vfw P Rothe	14	AR2	Nauroy	1700	2	
Gefr R Kassner	65	Balloon	Bethélainville	1700	1	h.
Gefr R Kassner	65	Balloon	Bethélainville	1700	2	

Vfw U Neckel	12	SE5	Vauxillon	5	i.
Ltn K Schwartz	22	Balloon	Pont St Mard	1	j.
Vfw P Färber	22	Balloon		2	k.
Uffz Diem	76	AR2		zlg	

a.   B6871, 19 Sqn RFC, 2/Lt JL McLintock, KIA.
b.   B6732, 23 Sqn RFC, 2/Lt DC Doyle, POW.
c.   A7804, 57 Sqn RFC, 2/Lt JM Allen, POW & Capt FR Sutcliffe, POW.
d.   A3531, 16 Sqn RFC, 2/Lt WG Duthie, WIA & 2/Lt RWStG Cartwright, KIA.
e.   Escadrille N 87.
f.   French 90 Compagnie Aérostières.
g.   A7697, 25 Sqn RFC, Lt GM Shaw,WIA,POW & Lt CHS Ackers,POW.
h.   French 33 Compagnie Aérostières.
i.   B548, 24 Sqn RFC, 2/Lt CH Crosbee, POW.
j.   French 55 Compagnie Aérostières.
k.   French 59 Compagnie Aérostières.

Losses

Ltn Egon Koepsch	4	Slightly wounded in action.
Ltn Max Hillmann	7	Severely injured in a crash.
Vfw Hegeler	15	Taken prisoner 0900 near Bonneuil Pfalz DIII 4184/17, claimed by 24 Sqn RFC (G141).
Uffz Paul Hess	42	Killed in action Pannes.

27 February 1918

Oblt P Blumenbach	12	Spad	Essigny le Grand	1	a.

a.   Possibly GDE, Cpl Janet, only French aircraft lost this date.

Losses

OfStv Jakob Landin	32	Killed in crash 1730 Guesnain airfield.
Ltn Bernhard Benninghoff	54	Killed in crash Neuvilly airfield.

28 February 1918

Ltn Koch	12	SE5	St Gobain Wood	2	a.
Vfw U Neckel	12	SE5	St Gobain Wood	6	a.
Ltn H Becker	12	SE5	St Gobain Wood	5	a.
Vfw A Bauhofer	25	2 Seater		zlg	

a.   84 Sqn RFC lost C5379, 2/Lt EO Krohn, KIA.

Losses – Nil

JASTA ARMEE ASSIGNMENTS AS OF 1 MARCH 1918

Western Front

1 Armee 22s,62
2 Armee 4,5,6,10,11,54s,56
3 Armee 9,44s,53,72s,79b
4 Armee B,3,7,16b,26,27,28w,36,37,47w,51,MFJI,MFJII
5 Armee 34b,45,64w,65,67
6 Armee 18,29,30,46,49,52,57
7 Armee 12,13,14,15,19,21s,50,60,61,66

17 Armee 20,23b,32b,35b,58,59
18 Armee 8,17,24s,48,63,68, 69
19 Armee 43,80b
Det 'A' 33,70,78b,K3
Det 'B' 41,71,75,76b,77b
Det 'C' 40s,42

Other Fronts

11 Armee 25	Macedonia
14 Armee 1,31,39	Italy
1 Armee 38	Bulgarian Armee
Südarmee 81	Russian Front

1 March 1918

Hptm A v Tutschek	JGII	Balloon	Terny	0845	25	a.
Uffz H Krätzschmer	48	Spad	W St Quentin		–	
Ltn C Galetschky	48	Spad	Francilly		–	

a.   French ? Compagnie Aérostières, Lt Bacalon, OK & 2Lt F M Morgan, USBS, OK.

Losses

Ltn Eberhardt Mohnicke	11	Wounded in action Fokker Dr.I 155/17.
Ltn Erich Just	11	Lightly wounded in action, Fokker Dr.I 110/17, remained with unit.
Flg Gustav Koriath	19	Killed in a crash St Loup airfield.

2 March 1918

No Claims – No Losses

3 March 1918

No Claims – No Losses

4 March 1918

Ltn H Weiss	41	Farman	Ballersdorf	1310	–

Losses – Nil

5 March 1918

Ltn H Contag	65	Balloon	Bethélainville	1040	4	a.
OfStv A Schreder	17	SE5	SE Vendhuille	1500	1	b.
Vfw F Piechulek	56	DH4	SE Havrincourt	1650	3	
Ltn F Schleiff	56	RE8	S Havrincourt Wood	1655	6	c.
Ltn H Schmidt	13	Caudron	Verneuil-Gouy		zlg	
Uffz G Sandleitner	77	AR2	Butweiler		1	
Gefr R Mossbacher	77	AR2	Gildweiler		zlg	
Vfw B Ultsch	77	AR2	Gildweiler		zlg	

a.   French 80 Compagnie Aérostières, Brig J Duteurtre, WIA.
b.   B145, 24 Sqn RFC, 2/Lt WF Poulter, WIA/POW, DOW 6 March 1918.
c.   A4748, 4 Sqn RFC, 2/Lt WH Boston,WIA & Lt JEG Mosby, OK.

Losses

Uffz Hellmuth Krätzschmer	48	Lightly injured in a crash.
Vfw Kurt Jentsch	61	Shot down by Breguets near Chavignon, OK but Pfalz DIIIa destroyed.
Gefr Lothmann	65	Taken prisoner 1445 SE Bras.

6 March 1918

Ltn E Thomas	9	Balloon	Somme-Suippes	0900	4	a.
Ltn P Jäger	9	Balloon	Mourmelon le Grand	0900	1	b.
Ltn H Pippart	13	SE5	Fort Mayot	1040	8	
Vfw K Brendle	45	P Schmitt	Fort Marre	1135	1	c.
Vfw G Dobberke	45	Spad	Fort Marre	1140	1	d.
Ltn H Rolle	9	Nieuport	Machault	1245	1	
Ltn A Dietlen	41	Nieuport	Dammerkirch	1315	6	e.
Ltn H Weiss	41	Caudron	Füllern	1315	–	
Ltn H Weiss	41	Nieuport	Füllern	1315	9	f.
Ltn W Böning	76	Spad	Rodern, Belfort	1340	10	g.
Ltn W Böning	76	Spad	Rodern	1340	11	h.
Hptm A v Tutschek	JGII	SE5	Bertaucourt	1440	26	i.
Ltn H Becker	12	SE5	Bertaucourt	1445	6	j.

Obfm K Schönfelder	7	Nieuport	W Rumbeke	zlg	
Ltn R Rienau	19	SE5	St Quentin	1	k.
Ltn K Küppers	48	AWFK8	SW Itancourt	6	l.
Ltn G Weiner	K3	Spad	Eschen	2	

a. French 80 Compagnie Aérostières, Brig Duteurtre, WIA.
b. French 56 Compagnie Aérostières.
c. Escadrille AR 253, Sgt Cheredanne & Cpl Nguyen-Xuan-Nha, KIAs.
d. Escadrille Spa 93, Brig J Lafay, MIA.
e. Escadrille Spa 152, Cpl F Deltour, KIA.
f. Spad VII 1765, Escadrille Spa 87, Sgt T Hitchcock, an American, WIA/POW.
g. Escadrille Spa 150, S/Lt H Dorizon, KIA.
h. Escadrille Spa 150, Cpl P Brun, KIA.
i. C1057, 24 Sqn RFC, 2/Lt APC Wigan, POW.
j. C9535, 24 Sqn RFC, 2/Lt DM Clementz, KIA.
k. A8946, 84 Sqn RFC, Lt RE Duke, POW.
l. B5838, 82 Sqn RFC, 2/Lt DL Sisley,KIA & Lt AC Glimour, KIA.

Losses

Ltn Erich Bahr	11	Killed in action at 1040, Nauroy & Atricourt, in Fokker Dr.I 106/17.
Ltn Hans Staats	12	Killed in action 1445 Rony, collision with 2/Lt DM Clementz, 24 Sqn.(G145).
Ltn Otto Hohmuth	23	Taken prisoner S Feuchy, Arras, Albatros DV 2359/17, by 13 Sqn RE8 crew (G144).
Obltn Rudolf Schonger	23	Wounded in action over Arras.
Gefr WaltherConderert	52	Killed in action NW Lens at 1525 in Pfalz DIII 4236/17, by 40 Sqn RFC (G146).
Ltn Hellmuth Contag	65	Killed in action Beaufort near Stenay 1730.

7 March 1918

No Claims

Losses

Ltn Niebecker	43	Injured in a crash.
Vfw Krause	80	Injured in a crash.

8 March 1918

OfStv J Mai	5	DH4	S Montbrehain	1110	8	
Ltn W-M v Manteuffel-Szöge	35	SE5	Bourlon Wood	1140	1	a.
OfStv W Kampe	27	DH4	Gheluvelt	1208	8	b.
Ltn O Fitzner	17	Breguet	Tilloy Ferme	1215	3	
Ltn J Keller	21	Morane	E Nauroy	1215	1	c.
Ltn A Heldmann	10	Breguet	Fresnoy le Grand	1220	4	
Ltn A Heldmann	10	Breguet	Fresnoy le Grand	1230	–	
Ltn H v Haebler	36	Camel	Roulers-Menin	1430	7	d.
Ltn A Hellwig	77	Breguet	Oberaspach	1630	1	
Vfw A Triebswetter	16	Balloon	N Ypres	1710	1	e.

a. B8264, 64 Sqn RFC, 2/Lt RH Topliss, WIA/POW.
b. B2094, 27 Sqn RFC, 2/Lt JFRI Perkins & Lt RG Foley, MC,KIAs.
c. Escadrille Spa 156, Cpl WC Winter, an American, KIA.
d. B3905, 12 Naval Sqn, F/S/Lt HR Casgrain, POW.
e. British Balloon 38-7-2 (FM 92/D).

Losses

Ltn Skauradzun	4	Wounded in action, Pfalz DIII 4042/17.
OfStv Willi Kampe	27	Killed in action Gheluvelt 1208, with DH4s.
Vfw Heinrich Gockel	33	Wounded in action.
Flg Langenheim	49	Injured in a crash Bruille airfield.

| Ltn Heinrich Minder | 51 | Killed in action Rumbeke. |
| Uffz Wilhelm Rincke | 54 | Killed in action Fontaine Notre Dame. |

9 March 1918

Ltn E Udet	37	Camel	Houthem	1040	zlg	
Vfw P Bäumer	B	Camel	N Zonnebeke	1110	19	
Ltn F Schleiff	56	DH4	NW Havrincourt	1210	7	
Ltn K Odebrett	42	Sopwith 2	Anably	1400	9	a.
Ltn zS H Wessels	MFJ1	DH4	Nieuport-Sylpe	1510	1	
Ltn K Odebrett	42	Spad	Apremont	1520	10	
Ltn P Billik	52	SE5	Malmaison, E Dourges	1704	9	b.
Ltn P Billik	52	SE5	Noyelles sous Lens	1710	10	c.
Ltn J Janzen	6	Sopwith	W Le Catelet	–		
Ltn R Hildebrandt	13	Spad VII	SW Laon		1	d.
Uffz E Buder	26	SE5	Zillebeke	–		e.
FlgMt Mayer	MFJ1	Camel	nr Boistschoeke		1	
FlgMt Kulbe	MFJ2	Camel	Boistschoeke		2	
FlgMt Kulbe	MFJ2	Camel	Boistschoeke		zlg	

a.   Escadrille C 47, Sgt Curtet & S/Lt Posse, MIAs.
b.   C5348, 40 Sqn RFC, Lt P LaT Foster, POW.
c.   C9538, 40 Sqn RFC, Major LA Tilney, MC, KIA.
d.   3144, 95th Aero, Capt JE Miller, KIA.
e.   B587, 40 Sqn RFC, Capt RJ Tipton, WIA.

Losses

Ltn Max Naujock	36	Killed in action Moorslede-Rumbeke.
Uffz Fritz Liese	50	Killed in action Montigny.
Ltn Joachim Nissen	52	Killed in action Evin-Malmaison.
VzFlgMstr Hans Bossler	MFJ2	Wounded in action.

10 March 1918

Ltn K Hertz	59	Camel	Sains-les-Marquion	0730	1	a.
Oblt H Bethge	30	DH4	Allennes	1210	20	b.
Ltn F Schleiff	56	DH4	NW Havrincourt	1210	zlg	
Ltn K Wüsthoff	4	Camel	La Bassée-Bethune	1305	27	c.
Vfw F Hemer	6	Camel	Montbrehain	1420	3	d.
Hptm A v Tutschek	JGII	Spad	Chavignon	1745	27	e.
Gefr Zell	42	AR2	Les Paroches		1	

a.   B9147, 3 Sqn RFC, 2/Lt EPP Edmonds, WIA/POW.
b.   A7719, 18 Sqn RFC, 2/Lt JNB McKim & Lt CRH Ffolliott, KIAs.
c.   3 Sqn RFC, Lt BA Cooke, WIA.
d.   C6719, 80 Sqn RFC, 2/Lt CH Flere, POW.
e.   Escadrille Spa 86, Adj E Vallod, MIA.

Losses

Ltn Wilhelm Gürke	5	Killed in action Honnecourt.
Uffz Beschow	4	Wounded in action.
Obltn Hans Joachim Buddecke	8	Killed in action W Harnes 1310, combat with 3 Naval Sqn RNAS.
Uffz Paul Noeckel	28	Wounded in action.

11 March 1918

Ltn L v Richthofen	11	BF2b	NE Fresnoy	1310	27	a.
Vfw E Scholtz	11	SE5	Holnon Wood	1310	2	b.
Ltn H Viebig	57	RE8	Arleux	1615	2	c.
Gefr Sielemann	57	RE8	Rouvrey	1620	1	d.
Vfw F Ehmann	47	Camel	Nr. Zonnebeke	1705	1	e.

| VfFlgMstr B Heinrich | MFJ1 | DH4 | in Sea off La Panne | | 10 | f. |

a.   A7227, 48 Sqn RFC, 2/Lt WL Thomas,OK & Cpl J Bowles, OK.
b.   B54, 56 Sqn RFC, 2/Lt D Woodman, KIA.
c.   B835, 5 Sqn RFC, Lt JA Convery & Lt JLP Haynes, KIAs.
d.   C5096, 5 Sqn, Major EJ Tyson,DSO,MC,DOW & 2/Lt B Bidmead, WIA.
e.   1 Naval Sqn.
f.   N5965, 2 Naval Sqn, F/S/Lt CG MacDonald & 1/AM PJ Clapp, KIAs.

Losses

| Vfw Otto Rückert | 48 | Wounded in action. |
| Uffz Josef Henn | 53 | Killed in a crash on take-off Menil 1230. |

12 March 1918

Ltn W v Dazur	20	SE5	Quéant & Riencourt	0710	1	
Vfw R Heibert	46	SE5	Dixmuiden	1045	4	
Ltn F Schleiff	56	RE8	Gouzeaucourt	1045	8	
Vfw H Steinbrecher	46	SE5	W Houthulst	1050	1	a.
Uffz E Gürgenz	46	SE5	Merckem	1050	1	
Ltn W Steinhäuser	11	BF2b	Beauvais	1100	4	b.
Ltn L v Richthofen	11	BF2b	Maretz, Betry	1100	28	c.
Ltn L v Richthofen	11	BF2b	Clary	1100	29	d.
Rittm M v Richthofen	JGI	BF2b	S Nauroy	1115	64	e.
OfStv F Altemeier	24	BF2b	Villeret	1140	12	f.
Ltn K Wüsthoff	4	SE5	Souchez	1640	–	
Ltn E Löwenhardt	10	Balloon	W La Bassée	1945	11	g.
Ltn F Bohlein	10	Balloon	W La Bassée	1945	1	h.
Obltn K Mettlich	8	Camel	Villeveque		6	i.
Vfw W Seitz	8	a/c	Cambrai, Le Cateau		–	
Ltn W Ewers	77	Spad	Belfort		7	
Vfw B Ultsch	77	Spad	Belfort		8	
Gefr R Mossbacher	77	Spad	Belfort		1	

a.   B4889, 1 Sqn RFC, Lt AH Fitzmaurice, KIA.
b.   C4824, 62 Sqn RFC, Lt JAA Ferguson & Sgt LSD Long,both WIA/POW.
c.   B1247, 62 Sqn RFC, Capt DS Kennedy, KIA & Lt HG Gill, KIA.
d.   B1250, 62 Sqn RFC, 2/Lt CB Fenton & Lt HBP Boyce, both POW.
e.   B1251, 62 Sqn RFC, 2/Lt LCF Clutterbuck & 2/Lt HJ Sparks, both WIA/POW.
f.   A7290, 48 Sqn RFC, 2/Lt CH Hore,OK & Cpl J Cruickshank, KIA.
g.   British Balloon 37-3-1 (SB 209).
h.   British Balloon 46-4-1 (BM 114/D).
i.   C6400, 24 Sqn RFC, 2/Lt PJ Nolan, OK.

Losses

| Ltn Karl Peveling | 46 | Wounded in action by SE5. |
| Flg Georg Boit | 51 | Killed in action Zandvoorde. |

13 March 1918

Ltn J Fichter	67	Spad	Tahure	1015	4	
Ltn R Heins	56	BF2b	Marcoing	1016	1	a.
Ltn F Schleiff	56	BF2b	La Terrière	1020	9	b.
Vfw F Piechulek	56	SE5	NE Gonnelieu	1030	4	c.
Rittm M v Richthofen	JGI	Camel	Gonnelieu	1035	65	d.
Vfw F Hemer	6	SE5	S Cambrai	1040	4	
Ltn L Beckmann	56	RE8	Gouzeaucourt	1050	1	
Obltn H Auffarth	29	DH4	Brielen	1215	11	
Flg K Pech	29	DH4	Vlamertinghe	1215	1	
Ltn H Weiss	41	Balloon	St Liggert	1437	10	e.
Vfw E Scholtz	11	Camel	Vaucelles	1440	3	f.

Uffz E Meyer	45	Balloon	Belleville	1523	1	g.
Ltn W Schulz	41	DH4	Heiteren	1610	4	h.
Ltn G Schlenker	41	DH4	Rüstenhart	1650	13	i.
Ltn E Thomas	9	Balloon	Ham		5	j.
Ltn E Raabe	41	AR2	Dammerkirch		2	
Vfw Iversen	56	SE5	Marcoing		–	
Ltn A Benzler	65	Spad	Esnes		2	
Vfw Weber	K4b	DH4	nr Freiburg		3	k.

a. B1207, 62 Sqn RFC, 2/Lt C Allen, KIA & Lt NT Watson, WIA/POW.
b. B1268, 62 Sqn RFC, 2/Lt NB Wells, POW & Lt GR Crammond, POW.
c. C1070, 24 Sqn RFC, 2/Lt EA Whitehead, KIA.
d. B2523, 73 Sqn RFC, Lt EE Heath, WIA, POW.
e. French 26 Compagnie Aérostières, Lt Tiau, OK.
f. 73 Sqn RFC.
g. French 61 Compagnie Aérostières, S/Lt Depoux, OK.
h. A7579, 55 Sqn RFC, 2/Lt TS Wilson, WIA/POW & 2/Lt L Cann, KIA.
i. A7489, 55 Sqn RFC, 2/Lt RB Brookes, KIA & Sgt H Gostling, KIA.
j. French 53 Compagnie Aérostières.
k. B3966, 55 Sqn RFC, 2/Lt A Gavaghan, KIA & Sgt A Brockbank, KIA.

Losses

Obltn Konrad Mettlich	8	Killed in action Remaucourt.
Vfw Adolf Besenmüller	8	WIA Remaucourt, DOW 14 March, Lesdins.
Ltn Lothar Freiherr von Richthofen	11	Wounded in action Awoingt 1030, BF2bs and Camels.
Ltn Heinrich Kämmerer	20	Killed in action La Bassée.
Ltn Otto Splitgerber	38	Killed in action Hudova, Macedonia.
Ltn Walter Bowien	56	Killed in action Grevecoeur 1015, by BF2b.
Ltn Werner Haffner	57	Killed in action Auchy La Bassée 1330.

14 March 1918

Uffz E Birkenstein	51	Ballooon	Jeperen nr Ypres	1630	1	
Ltn E Thomas	9	Balloon	Ham	1805	6	a.
Vfw J Schwendemann	41	Spad	Gommersdorf		3	
Ltn F Hengst	64	Bréguet	Bras		zlg	

a. French 85 Compagnie Aérostières, Adj Guggenheim, WIA.

Losses – Nil

15 March 1918

FlgMstr A Nitzsche	MFJ2	DH4	in Sea off Nieuport	1315	1	
Ltn E Löwenhardt	10	Balloon	Villers Francon	1905	12	a.
Ltn R Windisch	66	Spad	Vitry-Reims		9	
Uffz Hapf	76	Spad	Alt-Thann		1	
Ltn W Böning	76	Sopwith 2	Lautenbach		12	b.
Ltn W Böning	76	Sopwith 2	Lautenbach		13	

a. British Balloon 19-14-5 (FM 132/D).
b. 3476, Escadrille Sop 252, Sgt Gacon & S/Lt Malot, MIAs.

Losses

Hptm Adolf Ritter von Tutschek	JGII	Killed in action Brancourt 1113, flying Fokker Dr.I 404/17, in combat with 24 Sqn RFC.
Vfw August Wagner	58	Killed in action Ecourt.

16 March 1918

Ltn B Hobein	20	Camel	by Neuville	0715	2	a.
Vfw G Wagner	29	Camel	SE Sainghin	1000	3	b.
Uffz K Heidelberg	48	DH4	Escaufort	1050	–	

OfStv J Mai	5	DH4	St Benin	1110	9	c.
Ltn R Heins	56	DH4	Villeret	1130	2	d.
Ltn E Thomas	9	Balloon	Somme-Suippes	1207	7	e.
Ltn E Thomas	9	Balloon	S Suippes	1210	8	f.
Ltn H J Rolfes	45	Balloon	Fort Marre	1255	3	g.
Gefr R Kassner	65	Balloon	Sivry-la-Perche	1305	3	
Ltn H v d Marwitz	30	AWFK8	Richebourg	1420	4	
Obltn H Auffarth	29	DH4	Fournes nr Amiens	1555	12	h.
Ltn zS T Osterkamp	MFJ2	Camel	3 km S Pervyse	1555	7	
Ltn Bleibtrau	45	Spad	Maasbogen	1730	1	i.
Vfw Gondermann	42	AR2			2	
Ltn A Benzler	65	Spad XIII	Bethélainville		3	j.
Ltn zS Tinschert	MFJ1	Breguet	Wielsie		2	

a. B5442, 46 Sqn RFC, 2/Lt ALT Taylor, POW.
b. B5208, 4 Sqn AFC, 2/Lt WH Nicholls, POW.
c. A7908, 5 Naval Sqn, F/Cdr LW Ormerod, DSC & F/S/Lt WLH Pattisson, DSC, KIAs.
d. N6005, 5 Naval Sqn, F/S/Lt Cartmell, WIA & A/G/L RB Wilcox, WIA.
e. French 41 Compagnie Aérostières.
f. French 44 Compagnie Aérostières.
g. French 36 Compagnie Aérostières.
h. A8043, 18 Sqn RFC, 2/Lt RA Mayne, WIA/POW & Lt VW Scott, MC, KIA.
i. 6084, Escadrille Spa 62, Cpl d'Argence & Cpl Ledg, MIAs (Spad XI).
j. 2167, Escadrille Spa 23, S/Lt F de Rochechouart de Mortemart, MIA.

Losses

| Ltn Paul Jäger | 9 | Killed in action Berru near Reims 1755, claimed by Adj H Garaud, Spa 86. |
| Ltn Franz Bohlein | 10 | Killed in action Marcq 1100. |

17 March 1918

Ltn H J Rolfes	45	Spad	Malancourt, Verdun	0710	4	
Vfw K Brendle	45	AR2	Avocourt	0715	2	
OfStv G Dörr	45	Sopwith	Montzéville	0720	1	
Uffz E Meyer	45	Balloon	Brabant	0735	2	a.
Uffz E Meyer	45	Spad	Brabant, Verdun	0740	3	
Vfw F Rumey	5	SE5	Marcoing	1025	10	b.
Ltn Matzke	54	Camel	Lesdain	1025	1	
Ltn G Bürck	54	Camel	NE Bantonzelle	1030	1	
Vfw Weimar	56	SE5	Holnon Wood	1030	2	c.
Uffz R Schwarz	77	Spad	Hagenbach	1035	1	
Ltn H Kroll	24	Camel	Attily, St Quentin	1100	21	d.
Vfw F Ehmann	47	Camel	Moorslede	1225	2	e.
Gefr Gebhardt	47	Camel	SW Staden	1230	1	
Vfw O Könnecke	5	DH4	Graincourt	1320	12	
Vfw F Piechulek	56	BF2b	Dernpise, Le Catelet	1620	5	f.
Ltn F Schleiff	56	BF2b	Bruy, Bony	1625	10	f.
Ltn K Odebrett	42	Spad		1630	11	g.
Vfw R Francke	8	a/c	S Cambrai	–		
Ltn W Frickart	38	SE5			6	
Ltn J Strauch	41	Sopwith	Lusse, W Rossberg		1	
Ltn R Windisch	66	Spad	Vitry-Reims		10	
Uffz K Straube	66	Balloon	Nanteuil		1	
Ltn zS G Saschenberg	MFJ1	Breguet	Pervyse		9	

a. French 59 Compagnie Aérostières, MdL Houard, OK.
b. B673, 64 Sqn RFC, 2/Lt JFT Barrett, OK.
c. B684, 64 Sqn RFC, 2/Lt Ps Burge, OK.

d.   80 Sqn RFC.
e.   B6420, 1 Naval Sqn, A/F/Cdr RP Minifie, DSC, POW .
f.   Only one BF2b B1231,FTL, 48 Sqn RFC, 2/Lt N Roberts, OK & Cpl T Ramsden, OK.
g.   B6843, 23 Sqn RFC, 2/Lt TG Shaw, KIA.

Losses

Ltn Gotthilf Pleiss	9	Taken prisoner Fôret de Hesse 0830.
Ltn Werner Steinhäuser	11	Wounded in action and FTL Briastre.
OfStv Adolf Schreder	17	Killed in action Busigny near Bohain 1150.
Vfw Hans Kehr	20	Killed in action Quéant.
Vfw Otto Schulz	20	Killed in a crash Douai.
Ltn Waldemar Janssen	28	Killed in action Roulers near Moorslede 1230.
Obltn Hans Bethge	30	Killed in action Passchendaele 1130 Pfalz DIIIa 5888/17, in combat with DH4 of 57 Sqn RFC.
Vfw Jedweil	46	Wounded in action by BF2b.
Ltn Otto Wachhorst de Wente	46	Killed in action S Cambrai.
Ltn Knape	47	Shot down in Pfalz DIIIa 5919/17, OK but a/c destroyed.
Ltn Gerhard Laack	61	Killed in a crash Vivaise airfield.

18 March 1918

Ltn S Gussmann	11	BF2b/DH4	Joncourt	1100	3	
Gefr A Schwind	54	Camel	Honnechy	1100	1	
Hptm W Reinhard	6	DH4	St Souplet	1105	9	a.
Ltn H Kirschstein	6	Camel	Vaux-Audigny	1105	1	b.
Ltn E Löwenhardt	10	Breguet	Awoingt	1110	13	
Vfw K Bohnenkamp	22	Camel	St Martin	1110	4	c.
Vfw R Heibert	46	Camel	Honnechy	1110	5	d.
Rittm M v Richthofen	JGI	Camel	Molain-Vaux-Audigny	1115	66	e.
Oblt H Kohze	3	Camel	NW Montbréhain	1115	1	
Ltn H Wolff	11	SE5	Escaufort	1115	1	f.
Ltn H Geigl	16	BF2b	Joncourt	1115	7	g.
Ltn F Oppenhorst	5	Camel	S Awoigt	1120	2	
Vfw E Scholtz	11	Camel	La Valle Mulotre	1120	4	h.
Vfw B Jehle	16	Camel	Busigny	1120	1	
Ltn H v Haebler	36	Camel	Gondecourt, Carvin	1120	8	i.
Ltn F Friedrichs	10	Camel	Awoigt	1125	–	
Vfw E Pabst	51	Nieuport	Den Asp	1155	1	
Vfw J Hohly	65	P Schmitt	St Mihiel	1200	1	
Vfw F Ehmann	47	Nieuport	Hooglede	1205	3	j.
Ltn E Thuy	28	Camel	Zvervessve	1250	19	k.
Vfw A Bauhofer	25	Balloon	Opticar	1400	3	
Ltn W Ewers	77	P Schmitt	Ballersdorf	1620	8	
Vfw M Holtzem	16	SE5	S Le Cateau		–	
Vfw J Schwendemann	41	Breguet	Altkirch		4	l.
Ltn A Dietlen	41	Nieuport	Füllern		7	m.
Vfw O Wandelt	43	Balloon	Champernoux Wald		1	n.
Ltn Seewald	54	SE5	Le Cateau		1	
Uffz Hess	60	Spad			1	
Ltn F Pütter	68	DH4	Beaurevoir		11	o.

a.   A7663, 5 Naval Sqn, FS/Lt RB Ransford, KIA & A/G/L G Smith, KIA.
b.   C6720, 54 Sqn RFC, Capt FL Luxmoore, POW.
c.   C1566, 54 Sqn RFC, 2/Lt G Russell, POW, DOW.
d.   B5421, 54 Sqn RFC, Lt N Clark, KIA.
e.   B5243, 54 Sqn RFC, 2/Lt WG Ivamy, POW.
f.   B172, 84 Sqn RFC, 2/Lt JA McCudden, MC, KIA.
g.   C4844, 11 Sqn, Capt AP McLean, POW/DOW & Lt FH Cantlon, MC, KIA.

h.   C1576, 54 Sqn RFC, 2/Lt EB Lee, POW.
i.   B7217, 3 Naval Sqn, F/S/Lt JL Allison, KIA.
j.   B6823, 29 Sqn RFC, 2/Lt RE Neale, KIA.
k.   B3781, 10 Naval Sqn, F/S/Lt GT Steeves, POW.
l.   1479, Escadrille Br 131, Capt Lavidalie,MIA & S/Lt Le Bouter, MIA.
m.   Escadrille N 315, MdL Adenot, WIA.
n.   French 73 Compagnie Aérostières.
o.   Probably 5 Naval Sqn, FTL.

Losses

Flg Rudolf Ihde	10	Killed in action Audigny 1120.
Ltn Franz Riedle	16	Killed in action Moslain by Camel.
Uffz Brinkmann	44	POW, S St Quentin, in Albatros DVa (OAW) 6691/17 by Spads of 23 Sqn RFC (G151).
Uffz Gustav Ecke	54	Killed in action Busigny.
Uffz Kurt Straube	66	Killed in action Aguilcourt by 1Lt G deF Larner, Spa 86.
Vfw Karl Arnold	72	Injured in a crash.

19 March 1918

No Claims – No Losses

20 March 1918

No Claims

Losses

Ltn August Raben	18	Injured in crash landing at Bruille airfield.

21 March 1918

'Der Tag' – The German Offensive in Picardy (Operation Michael)

Ltn W-M v Manteuffel-Szöge	35	Camel	N Bapaume	0900	2	a.
Ltn F Röth	23	Balloon	N Beugny	1130	5	b.
Ltn F Röth	23	Balloon	Marcoing-Ervillers	1135	6	c.
Ltn E Löwenhardt	10	Balloon	Fins	1310	14	d.
Ltn F Friedrichs	10	Balloon	Royaulcourt	1355	1	*
Oblt R Greim	34	Camel	S Vermand	1425	9	e.
Ltn F Pütter	68	SE5	Holnon Wood	1430	12	f.
Ltn W-M v Manteuffel-Szöge	35	Camel	Bertincourt	1620	3	g.
Ltn E Thomas	22	Balloon	Guiscard	1630	9	h.
Ltn L Hanstein	35	Camel	Noreuil, Bapaume	1745	16	i.
Ltn L Hanstein	35	Camel	Bertincourt	1750	–	
Ltn H Arntzen	50	Balloon	Nanteuil	1805	10	
Ltn F Höhn	21	Balloon	Brimont		–	
Ltn F Höhn	21	Balloon	Brimont		–	
Vfw M Kahlow	34	SE5	S Vermand		4	j.
Ltn L Schmid	34	Camel	S Vermand		–	
Uffz H Krätzschmer	48	AWFK8	NW Seraucourt		1	k.
Ltn E Schulze	48	SE5	Dury		1	

a.   3 Sqn RFC.
b.   British Balloon 44-19-3 (BMS 127/D), 2/Lt AH Burton, OK.
c.   British Balloon 1-18-3 (BMS 155/D).
d.   British Balloon 31-18-3 (FM 138/D).
e.   B2456, 80 Sqn RFC, 2/Lt CSL Coulson, FTL, OK.
f.   24 Sqn RFC.
g.   3 Sqn RFC.
h.   British Balloon 41-15-5 (FM 140/D).
i.   3 Sqn RFC.
j.   24 or 29 Sqn RFC.

k. 8 Sqn RFC.
* Possibly 11 Section, 3 Wing (FM133/D).

Losses

Ltn Herbert Kohl	34	Taken prisoner S Bellicourt.
Ltn Ludwig Hanstein	35	Killed in action Vaulx-Noreuil 1800 Alb DVa 5285/17,understood while in combat with 11 Sqn RFC.
Flg Franz Matuszewsky	73	Killed in action Nauroy, by S/Lt Lutzius of Spa 153.
Oblt Erich Marx	K1a	Killed in action Mannheim.

22 March 1918

OfStv F Altemeier	24	RE8	Essigny le Grand	1440	13	a.
Ltn F Schleiff	56	Camel	Verinaux	1440	11	
Ltn F Schleiff	56	DH4	Templeux	1455	12	
Ltn H Kroll	24	RE8	Wald von Genlis	1500	22	b.
Ltn F Loerzer	26	Camel	Graincourt-Flesquières	1555	8	c.
OfStv O Esswein	26	Camel	Havrincourt	1555	9	c.
Ltn M Hänichen	53	BF2b	Croix	1600	1	d.
Uffz K Waldherr	53	BF2b	Croix	1600	1	d.
Vfw J Walter	53	BF2b	Croix	1600	2	d.
Ltn E Thomas	22	Camel	Jugny	1615	10	
Ltn H v Haebler	36	Camel	Metz-en-Couture		–	
Ltn L Beckmann	56	RE8	FTL British Lines		–	
Vfw H Behrends	61	Spad	Roye		zlg	
Vfw Dettmering	68	Camel	St Quentin		1	e.
Flg E Tresenreuter	68	Camel	St Quentin		1	e.
Ltn H Böhning	79	SE5	Vermand		6	f.
Ltn W Buchstett	79	SE5	Vermand		1	

a. 53 Sqn RFC.
b. 53 Sqn RFC.
c. 70 Sqn RFC.
d. 48 Sqn RFC.
e. B7216, 3 Naval Sqn, F/S/Lt LA Sands, KIA, collision with B7219.
e. B7219, 3 Naval Sqn, F/S/Lt WA Moyle, KIA, collision with B7216.
f. D212, 2 Sqn AFC, Capt RW Howard, DOW.

Losses

Ltn Fritz Theide	24	FLT W La Fère AA fire, OK.
Ltn Hans Gottfried v Haebler	6	WIA and POW at Bapaume in Fokker DrI 509/17. Died of wounds 23 March (G152).
Gefr Ernst Diehl	53	Taken prisoner.
Flg August Schulze	53	Taken prisoner.
Ltn Hermann Manger	56	Killed in action Bichecourt, NW Marteville.
Ltn Zwiters	62	POW, NW Ham Albatros DVa (G153).
Vfw Dettmering II	68	Taken prisoner W Ham Albatros DVa.
Flg Erwin Tresenreuter	68	Downed by Camels, no-man's-land in
	68	Albatros DVa, OK.
VzFlgMstr Bertram Heinrich	MFJ1	Lightly wounded in action Vlissighem.

23 March 1918

Ltn R Klimke	27	SE5	Hendecourt	0935	8	
Vfw O Könnecke	5	BF2b	Hervilly	1125	13	a.
Uffz J Fritzsche	69	BF2b	W Nesle	1145	1	a.
Vfw Scheuren	69	BF2b	Roye	1157	1	a.
Ltn W Schwartz	69	2 Seater	Ham	1230	zlg	

Ltn H Bongartz	36	Camel	Lagnicourt	1300	31	b.
Ltn L Schmid	34	DH4	E Péronne	1315	1	
Vfw F Rumey	5	Dolphin	Cartigny	1320	11	c.
Vfw J Pütz	34	Dolphin	Cartigny	1325	3	c.
Ltn R Stark	34	DH4	S Barleux	1327	1	
Vfw P Bäumer	B	Camel	S St Léger	1330	20	b.
Obltn B Loerzer	JGIII	Camel	Chérisy	1440	23	
Vfw P Bäumer	B	RE8	N Tilloy	1545	1	d.
Ltn W Schwartz	69	BF2b	Beaulieu	1550	zlg	
Vfw P Bäumer	B	RE8	N Beugnâtre	1615	22	e.
Vfw U Neckel	12	Camel	Ham		7	f.
Ltn J Werner	14	BF2b			3	
Ltn F Loerzer	26	Camel	Bussigny, S Chérisy		9	
Vfw F Beckhardt	26	SE5	Chérisy		–	
Vfw J Pütz	34	DH4	Cartigny		–	
Vfw R Heibert	46	Spad			6	
Oblt H-H v Boddien	59	DH4	Morchies		1	
Ltn R Windisch	66	Sopwith 2	Le Buin Ferme		11	
Vfw W Schäfer	66	Spad	Verneuil		2	g.

a.   22 Sqn RFC.
b.   46 Sqn RFC.
c.   Only loss, C3905, 79 Sqn RFC, 2/Lt AFG Clarke, POW.
d.   C4574, 5 Sqn RFC, 2/Lt PW Woodhouse, OK & Lt CH Brown, OK.
e.   59 Sqn RFC ?
f.   C8244, 70 Sqn RFC, 2/Lt CH Clarke, POW.
g.   Escadrille Spa 215, MdL Maillet & S/Lt Tomberlain, MIAs, Spad XI.

Losses

Vfw Dobberahn	12	Wounded in action.
Ltn Joachim Friedrich Huth	14	Severely wounded in action.
Ltn Erich Thomas	22	Taken POW, Bohain area Spas 57 and 100.
Ltn Hans Unger	22	Taken prisoner Bohain area Spa 57.
Uffz Max Rentsch	69	Killed in a crash Mont Origny airfield 1120.

24 March 1918

Ltn F Schleiff	56	SE5	Villers-Carbonnel	1040	13	
Gefr A Schwind	54	SE5	Péronne	1045	2	
FlgMt C Kairies	SFS	Camel	Nieuport	1130	1	a.
Uffz Freter	42	Spad	St Mihiel	1135	2	
Ltn R Stark	34	Camel	W Barleux	1310	2	
Ltn F Ehmann	33	DH4	Bartenach	1315	3	b.
Ltn L Schmid	34	SE5	Brie-Eterpigny	1315	2	c.
Obltn R v Greim	34	SE5	Brie-Eterpigny	1317	10	c.
Ltn R Kommoss	50	BE	Cressy	1425	2	
Sgt Pfänder	69	BF2b	SW Noyon	1430	1	
Rittm M v Richthofen	JGI	SE5	Combles	1445	67	d.
OfStv F Altemeier	24	Sopwith	NE Chauny	1545	14	e.
Ltn F Pütter	68	DH4	S Péronne	1700	13	f.
Uffz W Borlinghaus	43	Caudron	Champernoux Wald	1745	1	
Vfw F Rumey	5	RE8			12	g.
Vfw O Könnecke	5	RE8			14	g.
Vfw W Seitz	8	SE5	S Epenancourt		5	h.
Vfw A Jühe	8	BF2b	Happlincourt		–	
Obltn L Cordes	16	Camel	Ablaincourt		1	
Ltn A Handl	16	DH4	Flaucourt		1	b.
Vfw F Schwarz	33	DH4	Monhofen		1	b.

Ltn W Frickart	38	SE5	Humkos		zlg	
Ltn O Creutzmann	43	DH4	Anslinger		–	b.
Uffz K Heidelberg	48	Breguet	NW Hambleux		1	
Vfw P Müller	48	Breguet	NE Remansart		1	
Ltn P Billik	52	SE5	Phalempin		–	
Vfw Weimar	56	Camel	Barteux		3	
Uffz W Zorn	60	Camel			1	
Uffz J Santjer	63	BF2b	SE Ham		2	
Ltn R Windisch	66	Spad 2	Chauny-Ablecourt		12	
Ltn R Windisch	66	Spad	Manicamp, Tergnier		13	
Ltn R Windisch	66	Spad	Noyon-Bretigny		14	
Uffz W Sonneck	66	Spad	Tergnier		–	

a.   B3774, 13 Naval, F/S/Lt LC Messiter, shot down, rescued.
b.   55 Sqn RFC.
c.   56 Sqn RFC.
d.   C1054, 41 Sqn RFC, 2/Lt JP McCone, American, KIA.
e.   C1554, 46 Sqn RFC, Lt JD Currie, POW.
f.   Camel, 73 Sqn RFC.
g.   53 Sqn RFC.
h.   41 Sqn RFC ?

Losses

Ltn Keseling	10	POW in Fokker Dr.I 147/17, to ground fire (G158).
Obltn Ludwig Cordes	16	Killed in action Fresnes.
Ltn Theodor Rumpel	23	Wounded in action Bapaume.
Gefr Linus Luger	79	Wounded in action.
FlgMt Christian Kairies	SFS	Wounded, Middlekerke 13 Naval Camel.

25 March 1918

Uffz J Fritzsche	69	Inf a/c	SW Noyon	1455	2	
Rittm M v Richthofen	JGI	Camel	Contalmaison	1555	68	a.
Ltn H Becker	12	Camel	St Christ		7	b.
OfStv W Kühne	18	Camel	S Bapaume		1	c.
Vfw Mäurer	18	Camel	S Bapaume		–	
OfStv Münnichow	59	RE8	Bapaume		3	d.
Uffz W Zorn	60	Sopwith			2	
Ltn F Hengst	64	AR2			zlg	

a.   C1562, 3 Sqn RFC, 2/Lt D Cameron, KIA.
b.   C8216, 43 Sqn RFC, 2/Lt HV Highton, KIA.
c.   C6724, 80 Sqn RFC, 2/Lt G Miller, POW/DOW.
d.   B5860, 16 Sqn RFC, 2/Lt GG Newbury & Lt EM Chant, POWs.

Losses

Vfw Karl Behringer	80	Severely wounded in action Embercourt 1710. Died of wounds 18 May.
Ltn Karl Romeis	80	Lightly wounded in action Parroy 1710.

26 March 1918

Rittm M v Richthofen	JGI	Camel	S Contalmaison	1645	69	a.
Rittm M v Richthofen	JGI	RE8	NE Albert	1700	70	b.
Ltn S Gussmann	11	Camel	N Albert	1700	4	
Ltn F Riemer	26	SE5	Arras, Bihucourt	1700	1	c.
Ltn R Plange	B	G100	Grévillers Wood	1715	4	d.
Vfw O Fruhner	26	SE5	Albert	1720	9	c.
Ltn H Lange	26	SE5	Graundeuvert	1730	1	d.
OfStv O Esswein	26	SE5	Mortefontaine	1745	10	d.
Uffz E Buder	26	RE8	Bapaume-Le Sars		1	e.

Ltn zS T Osterkamp	MFJ2	Camel	Avekapelle		8
FlgMt E Blaas	MFJ2	Camel	NW Dixmuiden		1

a.   SE5 B511, 1 Sqn RFC, 2/Lt AMcN Denovan, KIA.
b.   B742, 15 Sqn RFC, 2/Lt V Reading, KIA & 2/Lt M Leggat, KIA.
c.   1 Sqn RFC.
d.   Dolphins, 19 Sqn RFC.
e.   52 Sqn RFC.

Losses

FlgObMt Hans Groth	MFJ2	POW/DOW, flying Pfalz DIIIa 5923/17 nr Vlaabach, Combat with Belgian Hanriots of 9me Escadrille, 1700.

27 March 1918

Obltn H Auffarth	29	SE5	Bray-sur-Somme	0715	13	a.
Uffz K Pech	29	Camel	Bray-sur-Somme	0715	2	b.
Ltn H Vallendor	B	SE5	NW Albert	0725	2	c.
Vfw F Hemer	6	BF2b/DH4	SE Albert	0750	5	d.
Ltn E Löwenhardt	10	DH4	W Miraumont	0750	15	e.
Ltn H Bongartz	36	BF2b	Albert	0755	32	e.
Ltn H Bongartz	36	Camel	S Albert, Aveluy	0800	33	
Rittm M v Richthofen	JGI	Camel	Ancre, NE Aveluy	0900	71	f.
Ltn J Janzen	6	RE8	S Bois d'Aveluy	0920	4	g.
Ltn F Friedrichs	10	SE5	N Pozières	1030	2	h.
Ltn F Ray	49	RE8	Albert	1055	10	i.
Ltn K Gallwitz	B	BF2b	S Albert	1100	8	j.
Ltn H Habich	49	DH4	Bapaume	1100	1	k.
Hptm W Reinhard	6	RE8	S Morcourt	1150	10	l.
Ltn E Udet	11	RE8	S Morcourt, Albert	1150	21	
Vfw E Scholtz	11	BF2b	S Albert	1205	5	m.
Ltn H Kirschstein	6	AWFK8	SW Albert	1520	2	n.
Patrol	6	RE8	E Albert	1525	103	
Ltn H Kirschstein	6	Camel	NE Albert	1525	3	o.
Rittm M v Richthofen	JGI	BF2b	Foucaucourt	1630	72	p.
Rittm M v Richthofen	JGI	BF2b	NE Chuignolles	1635	73	q.
Ltn R Plange	B	RE8	SW Albert		5	
Ltn R Plange	B	SE5	SW Albert		6	
Ltn H Müller	18	RE8	no-man's-land		3	r.
Vfw A Hübner	36	BF2b	Aveluy Forest		1	s.

a.   Camel 3 Sqn RFC.
b.   3 Sqn RFC.
c.   56 Sqn RFC.
d.   Dolphin 79 Sqn RFC.
e.   25 Sqn RFC.
f.   C6733, 73 Sqn RFC, Capt TS Sharpe, DFC, WIA/POW.
g.   B7722, 59 Sqn RFC, 2/Lt WL Christian, OK & Lt JE Hanning, OK.
h.   D3507, 40 Sqn RFC, 2/Lt FCB Wedgewood, WIA/POW.
i.   52 Sqn RFC.
j.   B1156, 20 Sqn RFC, Capt RK Kirkman & Capt JH Hedley, POWs.
k.   A7767, 18 Sqn RFC, 2/Lt RB Smith & 1/AM H Sinclair, POWs.
l.   B6528, 42 Sqn RFC, 2/Lt JVR Brown, WIA & Lt CF Warren, WIA.
m.   11 Sqn RFC ?
n.   B5773, 2 Sqn RFC, 2/Lt AA McLeod, DOW & Lt AW Hammond, MC,WIA.
o.   73 Sqn RFC.
p.   AWFK B288, 2 Sqn RFC, 2/Lt ET Smart & 2/Lt KP Barford, KIAs.
q.   Dolphin C4016, 79 Sqn RFC, 2/Lt GH Harding, American, KIA.
r.   59 Sqn RFC ?

s. DH4 25 Sqn RFC.

Losses

Ltn Franz Schleiff	56	Severely wounded, left hand amputated.
Gefr Sielemann	57	POW, Meault, W Bapaume Pfalz DIIIa 8178/17.
OfStv Schüschke	64	Taken prisoner in the French lines in a Pfalz
		DIIIa 8078/17 (G157), by Sgt Prevost, Spa 68 at Fleville.

28 March 1918

Vfw F Rumey	5	Camel	Dernacourt	0910	13	a.
Ltn E Udet	11	Camel	Thiépval-Courcelette	0910	22	b.
Uffz Kaleta	56	SE5	Chaulnes	0915	2	
Ltn R Heins	56	Camel	Morcourt	0925	3	c.
Ltn V v Pressentin						
gen v Rautter	4	Camel	Suzanne, Somme	0930	1	d.
Ltn P Billik	52	Spad/Camel	Fampaux-Arras	0945	11	e.
Ltn J Werner	14	Camel	Bailleul	0955	4	f.
Ltn P Billik	52	Camel	Etaing, Sailly	1000	12	g.
Ltn E Koch	32	Sopwith	Mercatel	1010	1	h.
Ltn H Weiss	10	BF2b	Sailly	1115	11	i.
Ltn H Grabe	14	SE5	Gavrelle	1210	1	j.
Rittm M v Richthofen	JGI	AWFK8	E Mancourt	1230	74	k.
Ltn H Schäfer	15	RE8	Foucaucourt	1235	1	l.
Ltn K Bohny	17	AR2	Marquevillers	1425	3	m.
Ltn A Rahn	15	Breguet	SE Amiens	1730	4	
Ltn W Papenmeyer	B	RE8	Arleux		4	
Vfw A Jühe	8	Breguet	Voyennes		1	
Vfw Weber	8	Breguet			2	
Ltn H Schmidt	13	BF2b	Proyart		1	
Ltn R Hildebrandt	13	Spad	Montdidier, Poudry		2	n.
Obltn R Greim	34	DH4	Villers Bretonneux		11	o.
Vfw J Hohly	65	P Schmitt	Verdun		2	

a. C8267, 43 Sqn RFC, 2/Lt HT Adams, KIA.
b. C8224, 43 Sqn RFC, 2/Lt CR Maasdorp, POW, DOW.
c. D6404, 43 Sqn RFC, 2/Lt WJ Prier, POW.
d. C8259, 43 Sqn RFC, 2/Lt RJ Owen, POW.
e. B2395, 4 Sqn AFC, Lt CM Feez, POW.
f. D1777, 43 Sqn RFC, 2/Lt CF King, WIA.
g. C8270, 43 Sqn RFC, Capt JL Trollope, MC, WIA, POW.
h. A8913, 2 Sqn AFC, 2/Lt T Hosking, KIA.
i. B1273, 48 Sqn RFC, 2/Lt ER Stock, OK & 2/Lt WD Davidson, OK, FTL.
j. B102, 2 Sqn AFC, 2/Lt OT Flight, POW.
k. C8444, 82 Sqn RFC, 2/Lt JB Taylor, KIA & 2/Lt E Betley, KIA.
l. B6571, 52 Sqn RFC, 2/Lt AD Pope, POW & Lt HS Redpath, POW.
m. AWFK8 C8456, 82 Sqn RFC, 2/Lt T Watson, KIA & 2/Lt T Taylor, KIA.
n. Four French Spad VIIs lost, three from Spa 96, S/Lt Coulin, Brig Gay and MdL Zoeffel; Spad 3072, Spa 57, Lt J Pozzo di Borgo, all MIA.
o. A7976, 5 Naval Sqn, F/S/Lt JG Carroll & Gnr GE Daffey, KIAs.

Losses

Ltn Wilhelm Papenmeyer	B	Killed in action Acheville-Oppy Fokker Dr 1409/17.
Ltn Hans-Georg v d Osten	4	Wounded in action Albatros DV 4566/17.
Uffz Otto Stadter	32	Severely injured, broke left arm starting prop.
Vfw Walter Schäfer	66	Killed in action La Fère Charles.

29 March 1918

Ltn D Collin	22	Spad VII		1645	6	a.
Ltn W Balzer	44	2 Seater	Noyon	1750	1	

| Vfw F Schattauer | 16 | Camel | NW Abancourt | | 3 | b. |
| Vfw K Schulz | 37 | AWFK8 | | | 2 | c. |

a.   Escadrille Spa 89, Lt L Servais, MIA.
b.   B9267, 54 Sqn RFC, 2/Lt ACR Hawley, WIA.
c.   C3661, 8 Sqn RFC, Capt EW Monk & Lt CB Wilkinson,both KIA.
Losses – Nil

30 March 1918

Ltn F Riemer	26	SE5	Zillebeke See	0700	2	a.
OfStv Klein	15	Breguet	Montdidier	0850	5	e.
OfStv Behncke	54	RE8	Villers Bretonneux	0945	1	e.
Ltn F Pütter	68	Balloon	Assainvillers	0950	14	b.
Ltn A Freytag	44	RE8	Chauny	1030	1	e.
Vfw Becker	44	RE8	S Chauny	1035	2	e.
Ltn R Stark	34	Dolphin	Hamelet, E Vaire	1230	3	c.
Vfw A Triebswetter	16	BF2b	Pronville		2	
Ltn H Geigl	16	BF2b	Villers Bretonneux		8	
Vfw F Neubauer	63	Spad VII			2	d.
Vfw F Neubauer	63	2 Seater			3	e.

a.   B72, 1 Sqn RFC, 2/Lt AE Sweeting, WIA.
b.   French 64 Compagnie Aérostières.
c.   C3791, 79 Sqn RFC, 2/Lt HW Browne, POW.
d.   3216, Escadrille Spad 86, MdL E Guillory, POW.
e.   Five French two-seaters lost this date: Sal 50, Cpl Sigaud, & S/Lt du Peuty, KIAs; Breguet Escadrille Br 66, Adj Caravel & Sgt Baudier, MIAs, Breguet. Br 127, MdL Audinot & Asp Hellouin de Genival, MIAs; Breguet Br 127, Sgt Landragui & Lt Le Courtaulx, MIAs and a Sopwith 2, Sop 279, Brig Voirin & Asp Breuil, KIAs.
Losses

Uffz Max Marczinke	30	Taken prisoner Ploegsteert Wood at 1053 in Pfalz DIIIa 8278/17.
Ltn Heinrich Bongartz	36	Lightly wounded in action, remained with unit.
Uffz Hellmuth Krätzschmer	48	Taken prisoner Blérancourt 1115.

31 March 1918

Ltn H Schäfer	15	Spad	W Montdidier	1130	2	
OfStv J Klein	15	Spad	W Montdidier	1130	4	
Ltn F Pütter	68	Breguet	Guerbigny	1410	15	c.
Ltn H Becker	12	Spad	W Montdidier		8	
Vfw U Neckel	12	Spad XIII	W Montdidier		8	
Ltn H Geigl	16	BF2b	Beugnatre		9	a.
Vfw F Schattauer	16	Camel/SE5	Abancourt		4	
Ltn W Jumpelt	19	Breguet	Guerbigny		2	c.
Ltn H Körner	19	Spad	E Montdidier		3	c.
Ltn W Göttsch	19	AR2	E Montdidier		18	c.
Vfw Gerdes	19	Breguet	E Montdidier		1	c.
Ltn Tönjes	62	SE5	Montdidier		1	
Ltn H Leptien	63	Sopwith 1			4	b.
Uffz R Merkle	63	Sopwith 1			zlg	b.
Ltn M Johns	63	Sopwith 1			1	b.
Ltn H Böhning	79	AR2	Varennes		7	

a.   DH4 A2161, 57 Sqn RFC, 2/Lt ESC Pearce, KIA & 2/Lt CB Coleman, WIA/POW.
b.   Two French Spads lost this date: Spad VII, Escadrille Spa 93, S/Lt P Vieljeux, POW, NE Montdidier and Spad VII, Escadrille Spa 100, Cpl Amblard, MIA.
c.   Four French two-seaters lost this date: Escadrille Br 111, Sgt Jouneau & Sgt Bisch, MIAs; Breguet. Br 117, Sgt Kerwoo & Sgt Biot, MIAs; Br 127, Adj Ballard & Cpl Folonceau, MIAs, and a Sopwith, from Sop 141, Cpl Villatte & S/Lt Balvet, MIAs.

Losses

Uffz Rupert Merkle	63	Killed in action Hainvillers with Spads.
Uffz Jon Santjer	63	Killed in action Hainvillers with Spads. Both claimed by Spa 84 – Triplanes over Orvillers – Sgt Delcuze & S/Lt P Wertheimer.
Vfw Friedrich Neubauer	63	Killed in action over Rollot with Spads of Spa 37.

JASTA ARMEE ASSIGNMENTS AS OF 1 APRIL 1918

Western Front

1 Armee 31,39,74
2 Armee 3,4,5,6,10,11,16b,34b,37,46,54s,56,76b,77b
3 Armee 1,73
4 Armee 7,28w,51,MFJI,MFJII
5 Armee 65,67
6 Armee 29,30,33,41,43,47w,52,57
7 Armee 9,21s,42,45,50,60,61,66,81
17Armee B,14,18,20,23b,26,27,32b,35b,36,40s,49,58,59
18 Armee 8,12,13,15,17,19,22s,24s,44s,48,53,62,63,68,69,72s,79b
19 Armee 80b
Det 'A' 70,78b,K3
Det 'B' 71,75
Det 'C' 64w

Other Fronts

11 Armee 25	Macedonia
1 Bulgarian Armee 38	Macedonia
55	Turkey

1 April 1918   The RAF was formed by combining the RFC and RNAS

Ltn E Siempelkamp	4	Camel	SE Fouilly	0800	1	a.
Vfw F Hemer	6	BF2b	Achiet le Petit	0800	6	b.
Ltn H Kroll	24	Spad	NW Noyon	0815	23	
Ltn W Becker	17	AR2	Mesnil	0840	2	
Ltn H Wolff	11	DH4	Grévillers	0900	2	c.
Ltn H Böhning	79	Balloon	Boulogne le Grosse	1000	–	
Ltn H Schäfer	15	SE5	Moreuil-Ailly	1045	3	d.
OfStv E Bergmann	22	Sopwith 2	Domfort	1145	1	
Vfw A Lux	27	SE5	NE Lens	1230	1	e.
Vfw O Könnecke	5	SE5	Albert	1245	15	f.
Hptm W Reinhard	6	SE5	Martinpuich	1305	11	g.
Vfw G Wagner	29	Balloon	Grenay	1515	4	h.
Sgt Pfänder	69	AR2	W Ville	1640	2	
Ltn H Wolff	11	SE5	NE Moreuil	1700	3	i.
Ltn F Röth	23	Balloon	Cambrun, N Arras	1730	7	j.
Ltn F Röth	23	Balloon	Hulluch, N Arras	1734	8	j.
Ltn F Röth	23	Balloon	Loos, N Arras	1736	9	j.
Ltn F Röth	23	Balloon	S Loos, N Arras	1738	10	j.
OfStv J Klein	15	Spad	SE Montdidier	1810	7	k.
Ltn H Pippart	13	Balloon	W Montdidier	1820	9	l.
Vfw R Francke	8	Spad	Piennes		9	
Vfw W Seitz	8	Spad	Piennes		6	

Ltn H Geigl	16	BF2b	SW Aubercourt	10	m.
Ltn H Geigl	16	BF2b	SW Aubercourt	11	m.
Vfw A Triebswetter	16	BF2b	S Villers Bretonneux	3	
Ltn W Göttsch	19	Breguet	Montdidier	19	
Ltn A Rahn	19	Breguet	Montdidier	5	
Gefr A Schwind	54	BF2b	Villers Bretonneux	3	
Ltn K Menckhoff	72	Breguet	Mesnil	21	
Ltn W Buchstett	79	Spad		2	

a. D1811, 65 Sqn RAF, 2/Lt PR Cann, WIA, DOW 2 April 1918.
b. DH4 A7401, 57 Sqn RAF, 2/Lt E Whitfield, KIA & Lt WCF Nicol-Hart, KIA.
c. A7872, 57 Sqn RAF, 2/Lt DP Trollip, KIA & Lt JD Moses, KIA.
d. D265, 32 Sqn RAF, 2/Lt HF Proctor, WIA.
e. C6413, 32 Sqn RAF, Capt DM Faure, OK.
f. C5433, 56 Sqn RAF, Lt F Beaumont, POW.
g. C6351, 56 Sqn RAF, 2/Lt B McPherson, POW.
h. British Balloon 37-3-1 (FM 119/D).
j. British Balloons 10-2-1 (SR 12), 8-1-1 (BMS 146/D), 20-1-1 (FM 128/D) & 24-2-1 (BMS 161/D).
k. Cpl Houston Woodward, Spa 94, an American,killed in combat S Montdidier, flying Spad VII No.1419.
l. French 89 Compagnie Aérostières.
m. AWFK8s of 35 Sqn RAF, B3380, 2/Lt BL Norton & Lt RW Briggs and C3642, 2/Lt A McGregor & 2/Lt M Balston,all OK.

Losses

Ltn Paul Hoffmann	12	Severely wounded in action, died 2 April.
Ltn Richard Grüter	17	Killed in action over Montdidier.
Flg Hans Weigeld	49	Killed in action over Aniche.
Ltn Rudolf Kommoss	50	Killed near Bouvancourt during a balloon attack.
Vfw Weimar	56	Parachuted from his burning aircraft over Gontelles and taken POW, flying Albatros DVa 5734/17 (G159), by 60 Sqn RAF.
Uffz Müller	79	Downed, wounded in action and taken POW.

2 April 1918

Vfw J Wieland	68	Sopwith 2	Braches	0720	1	
Vfw F Piechulek	56	BF2b	Bois de Vaire	0940	6	a.
Rttm M v Richthofen	JGI	RE8	NE Moreuil	1235	75	b.
Ltn H Wolff	11	BF2b	SE Morcourt	1650	4	c.
Ltn H Weiss	11	BF2b	Harbonnières	1700	14	c.
Ltn P Wenzel	6	BF2b	NE Bray	1805	1	d.
Vfw J Pütz	34	SE5	Villers Bretonneux	1815	4	e.
Ltn H Kirschstein	6	SE5	W Harbonnières	1820	4	e.
Ltn W Schwartz	69	2 Seater	Ourscamp	1850	2	
Ltn J Jacobs	7	RE8	Zonnebeke		zlg	
Uffz Dannemann	56	AWFK8	Warfusée		1	

a. AWFK8 C8524, 82 Sqn RAF, Capt GI Paterson, KIA & Lt TI Findly, WIA.
b. A3868, 52 Sqn RAF, 2/Lt ED Jones & 2/Lt RF Newton, KIAs.
c. A7286, 22 Sqn RAF, 2/Lt F Williams & 2/Lt R Critchley, KIAs.
d. C4862, 11 Sqn RAF, 2/Lt AR Knowles & Lt EA Matthews, KIAs.
e. B8236, 60 Sqn RAF, 2/Lt EW Christie, KIA.
e. C5388, 60 Sqn RAF, 2/Lt KP Campbell, OK.

Losses

Uffz Peter Wenn	57	Killed in action at 1130 over Quesnoy.
Uffz Georg Sandleitner	77	Killed in a crash at Wasquehal airfield.

3 April 1918

Ltn V v Pressentin gen v Rautter	4	AWFK8	Blangy-Tronville	1005	2	a.

Sgt Pfänder	69	Balloon	Ribécourt	1145	3	b.
Ltn K Schwartz	22	Camel	Mézières	1218	2	c.
Ltn K Schwartz	22	Camel	La Neuville	1230	3	c.
Ltn A Lenz	22	Camel	Cachy	1236	2	c.
Ltn K Bolle	B	DH4	Ypres, Frenzenberg	1410	6	d.
Ltn H Geigl	16	SE5	Villers Bretonneux		12	
Vfw K Schattauer	16	Camel	S Villers Bretonneux		5	c.
Ltn M Johns	63	Camel			2	
Ltn F Pütter	68	Spad XIII	Hargicourt		16	e.
Ltn W Böning	76	Camel			14	f.
Obltn T Cammann	74	Spad XIII	Mourmelon, Reims		3	

a. C3682, 35 Sqn RAF, Lt RMC MacFarlane & 2/Lt AE Lancashire, WIAs.
b. French 69 Compagnie Aérostières.
c. 54 and 65 Sqns RAF.
d. AWFK8 C8457, 35 Sqn RAF, 2/Lt Phillips,OK & 2/Lt M Balston,OK, FTL.
e. Probably Sgt P Devaulx, Spa 26, Spad VII, MIA near Montdidier.
f. D1797, 54 Sqn RAF, 2/Lt RT Cuffie, OK.

Losses

Vfw Hurrle	45	Taken prisoner at 0850 near Bailly.
Uffz Kurt Reismann	55	Killed in an accident at Rajak.
Ltn Ernst Hensel	62	Severely wounded in action over Courtemanche, nr Ham. DOW on 8 April.
Ltn Paul Quast	63	Killed in action over Montdidier. (Last two possibly by Spa 26 who claimed two probable victories over Fignières.)

4 April 1918

Obltn R v Greim	34	Camel	Villers Bretonneux	1515	12	a.
Ltn H Geigl	16	Camel	Warfusée		13	b.
Ltn R Stark	34	DH4	S Hamelet, Estrées		4	
Ltn R Stark	34	RE8	Fouilly		5	
Ltn G Kröhl	34	AWFK8	Bois de Hamel		2	c.

a. 210 Sqn RAF.
b. D6552, 65 Sqn RAF, 2/Lt JG Kennedy, KIA.
c. 35 Sqn RAF, 2/Lt ED Stevens, WIA.

Losses

| Ltn Heinrich Geigl | 16 | Killed in action at Warfusée, collided with Camel D6552, 2/Lt JG Kennedy. |
| Uffz Erich Gürgenz | 46 | Killed in action at Marcelcave in Albatros DVa 7161/17, 'STROPP'. Only one French claim, by Adj PA Petit, Spa 154. |

5 April 1918

Vfw G Fieseler	25	Nieuport	Caniste	0815	3	a.
Uffz R Kassner	65	DH4	Mars-la-Tour	1300	–	
Uffz W Zorn	60	Caudron			3	

a. 4047, Escadrille N 508.

Losses

| Vfw Konrad Brendle | 45 | Injured in an accident. |

6 April 1918

Ltn H Böhning	79	RE8	S Noyon	1000	9	
Ltn E Udet	11	Camel	S Hamel	1415	23	a.
Ltn Stickforth	24	AR2	E Elincourt	1420	1	
Ltn H Wolff	11	BF2b	NE Vauvillers	1500	5	b.

Ltn H Kirschstein	6	Camel	NE Warfusée	1525	5	c.
Rttm M v Richthofen	JGI	Camel	Villers Bretonneux	1545	76	d.
Ltn H Wolff	11	Camel	E Lamotte	1555	6	e.
Ltn H Weiss	11	Camel	S Marcelcave	1600	15	f.
Vfw E Scholz	11	Camel	Cérisy	1605	6	f.
Ltn E Just	11	Camel	Mericourt	1610	2	f.
Vfw F Hemer	6	SE5	S Demuin Hill	1715	7	g.
Ltn H Weiss	11	Camel	NE Sailly-le-Sec	1750	16	f.
Ltn A Delling	34	Camel	S Morcourt	1800	1	h.
Ltn P Erbguth	54	Camel			–	
Ltn K Hertz	59	Camel	Lens		2	
OfStv O Sporbert	62	Spad	Montdidier		1	i.
Ltn F Pütter	68	Spad	Moreuil		17	j.
Ltn K Menckhoff	72	Caudron			22	

a.   C8247, 43 Sqn RAF, Lt HS Lewis, KIA.
b.   C4864, 48 Sqn RAF, 2/Lt BGA Bell & 2/Lt GG Bartlett, KIAs.
c.   C1577, 3 Sqn RAF, 2/Lt DG Gold, POW.
d.   D6491, 46 Sqn RAF, Capt SP Smith, KIA.
e.   C8252, 70 Sqn RAF, 2/Lt DV Gillespie, KIA.
f.   43 Sqn.
g.   Dolphin C3939, 79 Sqn RAF, 2/Lt HG Dugan, American, POW.
h.   B6419, 201 Sqn RAF, F/S/Lt MH Findlay, OK.
i.   Escadrille Spa 77, Cpl H Whitmore, an American, Spad VII POW near Montdidier.
j.   Escadrille Spa 154, Adj PA Petit, FTL.

Losses

Ltn Hans Lutteroth	7	Killed in a crash at Meulebeke.
Vfw Willi Hampel	55	Taken prisoner at Mulibis.
Sgt Pfänder	69	Wounded in action attacking a Caudron R9.
Uffz Georg Erdmann	73	Killed in action between Somme-Py and Marie-à-Py at 1930 hours. Possibly by 1/Lt P Baer, 103rd Aero.
Uffz Robert Schwarz	77	Killed in action at Fouilly at 1130 hours.

7 April 1918

Ltn P Billik	52	Camel	Steinwäldchen	1110	13	a.
Rttm M v Richthofen	JGI	SE5	Hangard	1130	77	b.
Ltn H Kirschstein	6	Camel	Proyart	1145	6	c.
Ltn H Wolff	11	SE5	N Dommart	1150	zlg	
Rttm M v Richthofen	JGI	Camel	Villers Bretonneux	1205	78	c.
Obltn H Göring	27	RE8	Merville-Hazebrouck	1250	18	d.
Ltn F Brandt	27	Camel	SE Merville	1251	4	
Ltn F Pütter	68	Caudron	Moreuil-	1540	18	e.
Ltn F Pütter	68	SE5	N Montdidier	1545	19	f.
Ltn W Müller	60	Engl 2-seater			1	
Ltn K Menckhoff	72	Spad	Montdidier		23	

a.   B6417, 208 Sqn RAF, F/S/Lt DC Hopewell, POW.
b.   D6550, 73 Sqn RAF, 2/Lt AV Gallie, OK.
c.   D6554, 73 Sqn RAF, Lt RGH Adams, POW.
d.   B876, 42 Sqn RAF, 2/Lt HW Collier, OK & Lt EC Musson, WIA.
e.   Escadrille C 74, S/Lt Mouy & S/Lt Laroche, MIAs; Caudron G6.
f.   B63, 24 Sqn RAF, 2/Lt PJ Nolan, KIA.

Losses

| Ltn Siegfried Gussmann | 11 | Lightly wounded in action. |

8 April 1918

No Claims – No Losses

9 April 1918   The Battle of the Lys (Operation St George)

No Claims – No Losses

10 April 1918

Ltn S Büttner	22	Balloon	Lamortier Wood	0800	4	a.
Ltn J Veltjens	15	AWFK8	Rouvrel	0930	11	b.
Ltn W Göttsch	19	RE8	Amiens		20	c.

a.   British Balloon 6-28-3.
b.   C8528, 35 Sqn RAF, 2/Lt JE Phillips,OK & 2/Lt HW White, OK.
c.   B6441, 52 Sqn RAF, 2/Lt HL Taylor & 2/Lt WIE Lane,both WIA.

Losses
Ltn Walter Göttsch	19	Killed in action at Gentelles Fokker Dr.I 419/17.(G163), by 52 Sqn RAF crew.

11 April 1918

Ltn F Höhn	21	Balloon	Merval	1145	2	a.
Ltn Spille	58	Camel	Sailly-sur-Lys	1450	1	
Ltn A Dietlen	58	Camel	NE Steenwerck	1455	8	b.
Ltn K Menckhoff	72	Nieuport	Belle Assise	1535	24	
Vfw O Könnecke	5	SE5	Bucquoy, Bapaume	1715	16	c.
Vfw F Beckhardt	26	RE8	Bethune, N Arras	1750	1	
Ltn J Jacobs	7	RE8	E Ostende	1805	13	d.
Uffz Diem	76	RE8	Henancourt	1815	zlg	
Ltn W Böning	76	SE5	NE Albert	1825	15	
Vfw R Francke	8	Spad	SE Courtemanche	1835	10	e.
Ltn H Viebig	57	SE5	Le Leuthe	1900	3	
Ltn F Pütter	68	Camel	Villers-aux-Erables	1925	20	f.
OfStv Dörr	45	Spad	Tracy le Mont		2	
Ltn Hinneberg	59	RE8	Lens		1	
Gefr E Bielefeld	60	Sopwith			1	
Ltn R Windisch	66	Breguet	S Noyon		15	

a.   French 33 Cie Aérostières.
b.   B5750, 210 Sqn RAF, F/S/Lt MT McKelvey, WIA/POW.
c.   C5445, 60 Sqn RAF, Capt K Crawford, KIA.
d.   B6522, 16 Sqn RAF, Capt TB Jones & Lt V King,KIAs.
e.   Escadrille Spa 80, S/Lt J Milliat, Spad VII, POW.
f.   D1827, 73 Sqn RAF, 2/Lt RG Lawson, POW.

Losses
Uffz Georg Storr	60	Killed in action at Mortiers, Laon.
Ltn Ernst Braasch	68	Killed in action at Auberville.
Vfw Johann Wieland	68	Killed during a bomb raid on Balâtre.
Ltn Richard Emmerich	76	Killed at Millencourt near Albert at 1820 in Albatros DVa 5726/17 (G/3/1), by RE8 crew of 15 Sqn RAF.
Uffz Gottfried Stemmler	76	Killed in action at Albert at 1825 in Albatros DVa 7249/17.
Ltn Wilhelm Buchstett	79	Shot down and taken prisoner of war, by S/Lt Herisson of Spa 75 near Marqueglise.

12 April 1918

Ltn Hans-G v d Marwitz	30	Camel	Wambrechies	0830	5	a.
Ltn F Höhn	21	Balloon	SE Staubecken	0915	3	b.
Vfw F Ehmann	47	Camel	Frélinghem	1030	4	c.
Ltn Haevernik	47	Camel	Le Petit Mortier	1030	1	d.
Ltn A Dietlen	58	RE8	Le Pont Mortier	1035	9	

Ltn H v d Marwitz	30	Camel	Aubers	1125	6	e.
Ltn E Löwenhardt	10	Camel	NW Péronne	1225	16	f.
Hptm W Reinhard	6	Spad	N Roye	1330	12	g.
Ltn F Hübner	4	Spad	Bayonvillers	1400	1	h.
Ltn V v Pressentin gen v Rautter	4	Spad	Bayonvillers	1400	3	i.
OfStv J Klein	15	Spad	Orvillers	1525	8	
Vfw U Neckel	12	Spad	Villers Bretonneux	1530	9	
Ltn O Creutzmann	43	BF2b	Calonne	1650	2	j.
Ltn P Lotz	7	AWFK8	N Bailleul	1700	4	k.
Ltn H Arntzen	50	Breguet	Laffaux	1700	–	
Ltn F Pütter	68	SE5	Villers-aux-	1810	21	l.
Uffz W Stör	68	SE5	Erables	1815	1	l.
Ltn F Höhn	21	Spad	S Selens	1815	4	
Ltn R Hepp	24	Sopwith 2	Thourotte	1845	1	
Vfw O Könnecke	5	SE5	N Albert	1850	17	
Vfw F Rumey	5	Dolphin	N Albert	1900	14	
Ltn W Kypke	47	RE8	Merris, Bailleul	1930	7	
Ltn H Becker	12	Spad	Balâtre		9	
Ltn A Benzler	45	Balloon	Epagny		4	m.
Vfw Stein	45	Balloon	Epagny		1	n.
OfStv A Kopka	61	Spad	Juvigny		2	
Sgt Brüner	75	Sopwith 2	Gottesthal		zlg	
Ltn H Böhning	79	RE8	Boulogne le Gross		9	

a. B524, 54 Sqn RAF, 1Lt JR Sanford, USAS, KIA.
b. French 23 Compagnie Aérostières, Lt Herbert,OK & S/Lt Reb, OK.
c. C1559, 54 Sqn RAF, Lt I MacNair, KIA.
d. 54 Sqn RAF.
e. D1850, 73 Sqn RAF, 2/Lt MF Korslund, KIA.
f. 43 Sqn RAF ?
g. Escadrille Spa 96, Cpl S Lee, an American, Spad VII, MIA.
h. Escadrille Spa 155, MdL G Paumier, Spad VII, MIA.
i. Escadrille Spa 155, Brig Joubert, Spad VII, MIA.
j. B1257, 20 Sqn RAF, Lt AL Pemberton, POW & Cpl F Archer, POW.
k. B271, 10 Sqn RAF, Capt AM Maclean & 2/Lt FB Wright, KIAs.
l. C1094, 84 Sqn RAF, Lt CM McCann, POW.
m. French 45 Compagnie Aérostières, Adj Renard, OK.
n. French 46 Compagnie Aérostières, MdL Reynard, OK.

Losses

Ltn Wolff	6	Lightly wounded, remained with unit.
Uffz Robert Eiserbeck	11	Killed in action at Meault, 1510.
Vfw Gilbert Wagner	29	Killed in action over Armentières.
Ltn Hoevelhaus	33	Lightly wounded in action.
Ltn Karl Lupp	46	Killed in action at Ovillers la Boiselle.
Ltn Albert Dietlen	58	Killed in action at Le Bizet near Le Petit Mortier 1035, believed to have collided with RE8 or shot down.
Ltn Erich Ziffer	69	Taken prisoner at Péronne-Chauny (XG14). Two pilots of Spa 75 claimed a Pfalz DIII north of Gury – PoW.
Flg Friedrich Schlötzer	76	Killed in action at Cappy.

13 April 1918

No Claims

Losses

Ltn Daemrich	29	Lightly injured in a crash landing.

14 April 1918

No Claims

Losses

Uffz Heinrich Simon	64	POW at Toul 0951, by 94th Aero.
Vfw Anton Wroniecki	64	WIA and POW at Toul 0952, by 94th Aero.

15 April 1918

No Claims – No Losses

16 April 1918

Ltn J Buckler	17	Breguet	Vaux, Belgium	1635	31	a.

a.   Only French two-seater. Escadrille Sal 224, Cpl Ricard & S/Lt Pruvot, MIAs, Salmson 2A2.

17 April 1918

Ltn K Legel	52	Camel	Merville	0720	1	
Ltn E Koch	32	RE8	Farbus	1125	2	a.
Ltn Haevernik	47	RE8	S Estaires	1200	2	
Ltn G Schlenker	41	RE8	Haute Maison	1310	4	b.
Ltn A v Brandenstein	49	Camel	Fletre	1340	1	
Vfw H Juhnke	52	Camel	Caestre	1340	zlg	
Ltn P Strähle	57	RE8	NW Nieppe	1500	8	c.
Ltn J Jensen	57	DH4	Petit-sec-Bois	1500	1	
Ltn P Strähle	57	Camel	N Bleu	1500	9	d.
Uffz Meyer	57	Camel	Hazebrouck	1505	1	
Uffz O Wieprich	57	DH4	Hazebrouck	1510	2	

a.   C2274, 5 Sqn RAF, 2/Lt AGE Edwards, WIA & Lt N Sworder, WIA/DOW.
b.   B5048, 7 Sqn RAF, Lt SS Wright, DCM, KIA.
c.   B830, 4 Sqn RAF, 2/Lt ML James & 2/Lt OA Broomhall, both WIA.
d.   D1837, 54 Sqn RAF, Lt CC Lloyd, KIA.

Losses

Ltn Fritz Danker	32	Severely wounded in action at 1820, DOW on 23 April, at Guesnain.
Ltn Rudolf Matthaei	46	Killed in a crash at Liéramont airfield.

18 April 1918

No Claims – No Losses

19 April 1918

No Claims

Losses

Ltn Wolff	6	Severely wounded in action.

20 April 1918

Ltn H Weiss	11	Camel	SW Bois de Hamel	0640	17	a.
Rittm M v Richthofen	JGI	Camel	SW Bois de Hamel	0640	79	b.
Rittm M v Richthofen	JGI	Camel	NE Villers Bret.	0643	80	c.
OfStv O Sporbert	62	SE5	NW Thennes	1100	2	
Ltn F Höhn	21	Balloon	S Noyon	1405	5	d.
Ltn H Pippart	19	Spad	W Chauny	1500	10	e.
Gefr Gebhardt	47	SE5	W Vieux Berquin	1820	2	
Ltn F Höhn	21	Balloon	S Chemin des Dames	1900	6	f.
Uffz W Zorn	60	DH4	Ribécourt		5	

| Ltn G Keitsch | 74 | Nieuport | Prunay | | 2 |
| Ltn H Wessels | MFJ1 | Sopwith | Leke | | 2 |

a. D6475, 3 Sqn RAF, 2/Lt GR Riley, WIA.
b. D6439, 3 Sqn RAF, Maj R Raymond-Barker, MC, KIA.
c. B7393, 3 Sqn RAF, 2/Lt DG Lewis, POW.
d. French 75 Compagnie Aérostières, Adj Renard, OK.
e. Ecadrille Spa 100, Lt C Boudoux d'Hautefeuille, MIA, Spad XIII.
f. French 45 Compagnie Aérostières, Adj Breyer, OK & Cpl Guyot, OK.

Losses

Ltn Rudolf Eck	16	Wounded in action.
Ltn Fritz Höhn	21	Severely wounded in action.
Ltn John Färber	22	Killed in action at Bries.

21 April 1918

Vfw G Wandelt	43	RE8	N Neuve Eglise	0840	2	a.
Ltn C Degelow	7	Camel	by Bailleul	1110	3	
Ltn J Jacobs	7	Camel	by Bailleul	1115	14	
Ltn F Thiede	24	Spad	Tricot	1140	1	
Ltn U Neckel	12	Breguet	St Quentin	1145	10	b.
Ltn H Wolff	11	Camel	S Hamelet	1150	7	c.
Ltn J Buckler	17	Breguet	Moreuil	1230	32	b.
Ltn R Abt	69	Spad	SW Anézy	1230	1	
Ltn K Gallwitz	B	Camel	W Bailleul	1350	9	d.
Uffz Glatz	18	Spad	Foyelles	1530	1	
Vfw F Ehmann	47	SE5	SE Hazebrouck	1625	5	e.
Ltn W Blume	9	Spad	W Chiry	1720	7	f.
Ltn H Rolle	9	Spad	l'Ecouvillon by...	1725	2	f.
Ltn Bitsch	9	Spad	Chiry	1725	1	f.
Ltn K Legel	52	SE5	Bailleul	1925	2	
Ltn P Lotz	7	Camel	by Bailleul	zlg		g.
Gefr A Schwind	52	DH4		—		
Uffz Hess	60	SE5	SW Noyon		2	
Uffz W Zorn	60	Sopwith 2	by Carlepont		6	h.
Uffz W Zorn	60	SE5	SW Noyon		7	
Ltn R Windisch	66	Spad	Chauny-La Fère,..		16	
Ltn R Windisch	66	Spad	by Guy		17	
Uffz E Sonneck	66	Spad	Chauny-La Fère...		1	
Ltn P Turck	66	Spad	by Dives		1	

a. C5037, 53 Sqn RAF, Lt EHN Stroud & Capt CG White, MC, KIAs.
b. Only one Breguet 14 missing, MdL D de Conflans & Asp Millardet.
c. B7245, 209 Sqn RAF, Lt W Mackenzie, WIA.
d. D6959, 54 Sqn RAF, Lt CJ Mason, KIA
e. D269, 74 Sqn RAF, Lt CEL Skeddon, OK.
f. Spa 12 lost Cpl Donald E Stone, an American, and Sgt Marie, both killed in a collision; Sgt Renaud-Bernard de la Frégolière, WIA.
g. B6319, 203 Sqn RAF, F/Cdr RA Little, FTL, OK.
h. Probably Escadrille Sop 269, Cpl Lafarge & S/Lt Ponsard, KIAs.

Losses

Ltn Erich Schmidt	8	Killed in a crash at Champien-Roiglise.
Rittm Manfred Frhr von Richthofen	JGI	Killed in action 1145 hours near Vaux sur Somme, in Fokker Dr.I 425/17, (G/5/2).
Vfw Mäurer	18	Severely wounded in action.
Ltn Adolf Thörmälen	22	POW, at Sains-en-Amienois, Alb DVa.
Uffz Fritsche	41	Wounded in action.
Uffz Müller	43	POW, Hazebrouck, Albatros DVa (G/2/4).
Ltn Waldemar Christensen	46	Killed in action at Le Forêt.

Vfw Hans Erich Kauffmann	47		Severely wounded 1415 at le Petit Martier Estaires. Died of wounds the next day.			
Uffz Karl Heidelberg	48		Killed in action over Reims.			
Ltn Alois Frhr von Brandenstein	49		Lightly injured in an accident, stayed on unit			
Ltn Rudolf Abt	69		Taken prisoner near Collezy.			
Ltn Alfred Schubert	81		Killed in a crash at Liesse.			

22 April 1918

Ltn H Weiss	11	Camel	N Moreuil	1158	16	a.
Ltn H Wolff	11	Camel	N Moreuil	1200	8	b.
Uffz K Pech	29	Spad	NW Armentières	1250	3	c.
Vfw H Kiep	43	AWFK8	Nieppe	1330	1	
Ltn K Menckhoff	72	Spad	Montdidier	1840	25	
Uffz P Knopf	72	Breguet	S Montdidier	1840	1	
Ltn L Luer	62	Spad	Mézières	2020	5	
OfStv O Sporbert	62	Spad	Mézières	2020	3	
Ltn J Jacobs	7	RE8	N Hazebrouck		zlg	
Ltn W Frickart	38	SE5	Humkos		zlg	

a.   B6428, 201 Sqn RAF, Capt GA Magor, KIA.
b.   N6377, 201 Sqn RAF, 2/Lt WH Easty, KIA.
c.   Camel, 70 Sqn RAF.

Losses

| Ltn August Handl | 16 | Wounded in action and taken prisoner. |

23 April 1918

Ltn E Löwenhardt	10	BF2b	W Morisel	0830	17	
FlgMstr M Brenner	MFJ1	Sopwith	Sea off Middlekerke	1430	4	
Ltn E Koepsch	4	SE5	N Sailly-Laurette	1855	2	a.
Ltn H Arntzen	50	Breguet	Thiescourt		11	b.
Uffz W Zorn	60	Breguet	Noyon		8	b.
Uffz Hess	60	Breguet	Noyon		3	b.
Ltn zS T Osterkamp	MFJ2	Camel	N Ostende		9	
FlgMt H Goerth	MFJ2	DH4	at Sea		1	

a.   C1086, 56 Sqn RAF, Capt KW Junor, KIA.
b.   Three French two-seaters lost this date: Escadrille AR 272, Sgt Hebert & S/Lt Bajard,KIAs; AR 272, MdL Cazaux & Lt Gaudy,WIAs, and Br 127, Lt Abadie & Lt Mativon,MIAs, Breguet XIV.

Losses

Ltn Paul Lotz	7		Lightly wounded in action.
Uffz Emil Dassenies	13		Killed in action at Moreuil. Possibly by Br 127.
Uffz Wilhelm Zorn	60		Shot down and taken prisoner after combat with Breguets. Probably shot down by Cpl Tilloy & Lt Boisse of AR 272, an Albatros DIII – PoW.
FlgMt Jannsen	MFJ1		Injured in a crash.
FlgMt Fammen	MFJ1		Injured in a crash.

24 April 1918

No Claims – No Losses

25 April 1918   The Battle for Kemmel Ridge

Vfw O Wandelt	43	RE8	Fletre	0940	3	a.
Vfw F Schattauer	16	RE8	E Reninghelst	1050	6	b.
Vfw H Schorn	16	RE8	Dickebusch Lake	1115	1	c.
Ltn K Bolle	B	Camel	Niewkerke-Wulverghem	1425	7	d.

Ltn A King	40	DH9	Dickebusch	1500	4	
Vfw A Jühe	8	Camel	S Marcelcave	1745	2	
OfStv J Mai	5	Camel	Dommart	1825	10	e.
Ltn H-R v Decker	20	Camel	Dickebusch	1930	1	
Vfw K Kressner	5	BF2b	Marcelcave		1	f.
Vfw H Schott	25	Balloon	Opticar, Macedonia		1	
Ltn K Meierdirks	55	RE8	Nablus		2	
Ltn zS G Sachsenberg	MFJ1	Sopwith 2	Avekapelle		10	
Ltn zS T Osterkamp	MFJ2	Spad	Avekapelle, Pervyse		10	
FlgMt Strucke	MFJ2	Camel	Steenkerke		1	

a.   B7827, 53 Sqn RAF, 2/Lt GWT Glasson,OK & 2/Lt WW Porter, OK.
b.   B6615, 53 Sqn RAF, Capt HM Gibbs & Lt A Lomax, WIAs.
c.   53 Sqn RAF, 2/Lt GJ Hutcheson, WIA.
d.   D1776, 73 Sqn RAF, Lt AN Baker, KIA.
e.   D1801, 65 Sqn RAF, 2/Lt MA Newnham, OK.
f.   B1126, 48 Sqn RAF, Capt T Colvill-Jones, POW/DOW & 1/AM F Finney, POW.

Losses

Ltn Karl A Seifert	24	Killed in a crash at Ercheu airfield, Albatros DVa 7253/17.
Vfw Heinrich Schott	25	Killed in action, Opticar, Macedonia, attacking a balloon.
Uffz August Meyer	34	Killed in action 1810 at Marcelcave.
Obltn Arthur Dieterle	34	Wounded in action between Wiencourt and Marcelcave.
Flg Andreas Köhler	35	Taken prisoner at Vimy-Combles, Pfalz DIII 8282/17,(G/3/4).
Ltn Heinrich Bongartz	36	Lightly wounded, remained with unit.
Ltn Max Fuhrmann	36	Lightly wounded, remained with unit.
Vfw Alfred Hübner	36	Lightly wounded, remained with unit.
Ltn Alfred King	40	Wounded 1500 at Dickebusch by DH9s.
FlgObMt Bruno Fietzmann	MFJ2	Killed in action at Coxysde.

26 April 1918

No Claims

Losses

| Flg Franz Dürrwächter | 23 | Killed in a crash 1830 Epinoy airfield. |
| Sgt Fritz Demandt | 52 | Killed in action at Chémy. |

27 April 1918

| FlgMt A Bühl | SFSII | Camel | Middlekerke | 1605 | – | |
| Ltn zS H Rolshoven | SFSII | Camel | | | 2 | |

Losses

| Ltn Kurt Legel | 52 | Killed in a crash at Faumont. |

28 April 1918

No Claims

Losses

| Vfw Kurt Kressner | 5 | Injured in an accident. |
| Ltn Fritz Bötzow | 55 | Killed in action at Nablus. |

29 April 1918

Vfw E Pabst	51	DH4	W Sailly	1840	2	
Vfw F Schattauer	16	Balloon	SW Poperinghe	1935	7	a.
Ltn R Plange	B	Spad	Westoutre	2015	7	
Ltn W Lehmann	5	DH4	N Cauchy		2	b.

a.   British Balloon 23-8-2 (BMS 127/D).
b.   98 Sqn RAF ?
Losses
Ltn Ludwig Vortmann	B	Killed in action NW Kemmelberg by SE5s.
Ltn Heinrich Bongartz	36	Severely wounded in action 1300 over Ploegsteert by SE5, flying Fokker Dr.I 575/17.
Gefr August Schwind	54	Severely injured in a crash.

30 April 1918

No Claims – No Losses

Jasta Armee Assignments as of 1 May 1918

Western Front

1 Armee 31,39,74
2 Armee 4,5,6,10,11,16b,34b,37,46,76b,77b
3 Armee 1,73
4 Armee B,3,7,20,26,27,28w,33,36,40s,49,51,54s,56,57,58,MFJI,MFJII
5 Armee 65,67
6 Armee 14,18,29,30,41,43,47w,52
7 Armee 9,21s,45,50,60,66,81
17 Armee 23b,32b,35b,59
18 Armee 8,12,13,15,17,19,22s,24s,42,44s,48,53,61,62,63,68,69,72s,79b
19 Armee 80b
Det 'A' 70,78b,K3
Det 'B' 71,75
Det 'C' 64w

Other Fronts

11 Armee	25	Macedonia
11 Armee	38	Macedonia
	55	Turkey

1 May 1918

No Claims – No Losses

2 May 1918

Ltn E Löwenhardt	10	SE5	N Montauban	1230	18	a.
Ltn H Pippart	19	Breguet	E Noyon, Roye	1315	11	
OfStv J Mai	5	Camel	Morcourt	1415	11	b.
Fldw K Schmückle	21	2 Seater	SW Staubecken	1750	1	
Vfw H Juhnke	52	Camel	E Locon	1845	1	c.
Vfw F Rumey	5	Camel	W Villers Bret'x		15	b.
Ltn K Hertz	59	Camel	Chérisy		3	d.
Obltn H Schlieter	70	Spad	W Badonvillers		1	
Vfw F Megerle	70	AR2	Manonvillers		1	e.

a.   C1796, 56 Sqn RAF, Maj R Balcombe-Brown, KIA.
b.   65 Sqn RAF.
c.   C1685, 46 Sqn RAF, 2/Lt LC Hickey, KIA.
d.   43 Sqn RAF ?
e.   Probably from Escadrille AR 259, Capt Bourgungnon & Cpl Gasnier, FTL, OK.

Losses

Ltn Erich Schmidt	8	Killed on a test flight at Roye.
Ltn Stoy	10	Lightly wounded in action 2 km W of Péronne, remained with unit.
Ltn Hans Weiss	11	Killed in action 1750 hours Méricourt by Cappy, Fokker Dr.I 545/17, in combat with 209 Sqn RAF.
Ltn Edgar Scholz	11	Killed in action 1750 hours Cappy, Fokker Dr.I 591/17, in combat with 209 Sqn RAF.
Uffz Ernst Messtorff	26	Killed in action Armentières.
Ltn Josef Determeyer	47	Shot down, severely injured, 1505 hours.
Vfw Friedrich Megerle	70	Wounded in action by an AR2.
Ltn Moritz Weig	76	Taken prisoner of war.
Ltn Fritz Edler von Braun	79	Lightly wounded in action Montdidier.
Vfw Philipp Jopp	79	Killed in action 2000 hours Montdidier.
Vfw Konrad Porella	81	Injured in a crash.

3 May 1918

Ltn F Pütter	68	Spad	SE Mailly	1025	22	
Ltn F Hübner	4	AWFK8	Buire-Morlancourt	1100	2	
Obltn E Wenig	80	Spad	Remoncourt	1205	2	a.
OfStv P Aue	10	BF2b	Proyart	1215	6	b.
Vfw H Behrends	61	Spad	E Beaucourt	1215	1	
Ltn M-W B-Bodemer	6	Spad	Cayeux-Caix	1220	1	
Vfw Rebbe	33	BF2b	W Beauchamps	1220	1	
Ltn H Kirschstein	6	Spad	W Rosières	1250	7	
Ltn K Bolle	B	Camel	Nieppe-Bailleul	1345	8	c.
Ltn C Galetschky	48	Spad	NE Plessier	1350	3	
Ltn P Billik	52	Camel	W Estaires	1400	zlg	d.
Ltn K Mendel	18	DH4	NE Steenwerck	1530	3.	
Ltn V v Pressentin gen v Rautter	4	Breguet	Chuignes	1750	4	e.
Ltn P Billik	52	Camel	Neuve Chapelle	1800	14	
Ltn P Billik	52	Dolphin	N La Bassée	1830	15	f.
Ltn F Friedrichs	10	DH9	Fontaine les Cappy	1850	3	
Uffz K Pech	29	DH9	Vieux Berquin	1930	4	g.
Vfw E Pabst	51	DH4	N Estaires	1930	3	h.
Uffz R Kassner	65	Spad	Toter Mann	2000	4	
Ltn J v Winterfeld	4	AWFK8	Blangy-Tronville	2005	1	
Ltn J Buckler	17	Balloon	Montdidier, Tricot	2100	33	i.
Ltn H Becker	12	Spad	Morisel-Hailles		–	
Ltn R Windisch	66	Balloon	by Juvigny		18	j.

a. Nieuport 28 N6138 'Ø', 94th Aero, 2Lt CW Chapman, DSC, KIA.
b. C814, 48 Sqn RAF, 2/Lt ACG Brown, POW/DOW & Cpl AW Sainsbury, WIA/POW.
c. D6480, 73 Sqn RAF, Lt AF Dawes, POW.
d. C6101, 98 Sqn RAF, Lt RA Holiday & Lt CB Whyte, KIAs.
e. Escadrille Br 218, MdL-Chef Rochas & Cpl l'Heritier, KIAs, or Br 44, MdL Moreau & Adj Noel, KIAs,
f. C3828, 19 Sqn RAF, Capt G Chadwick, WIA/POW.
g. C2157, 206 Sqn RAF, Lt AE Steel & 2/Lt AE Slinger, KIAs.
h. D1663, 206 Sqn RAF, Lt T Roberts, OK & Sgt J Chapman, OK.
i. French 67 Compagnie Aérostières, Lt Weiss, OK & Asp Tricot, OK.
j. French 88 Compagnie Aérostières, Lt Leriche, OK.

Losses

Ltn Erich Just	11	Wounded in action Proyart.
Ltn Bigalk	14	Severely injured in a crash.
Ltn Ewald König	23	POW, N Gonnelieu, Pfalz DIIIa 8151/17 (G/1/2) – believed due to engine trouble.

Uffz Paul Noeckel	28	Killed in action Lille.				
OfStv Karl Angermayer	SFS2	Killed in a crash at Neumünster.				

4 May 1918

Ltn M-W B-Bodemer	6	Breguet	S Champien	1750	2	
Ltn R Hildebrandt	13	Breguet	Ham-Aubigny	1800	3	
Ltn H Schultz	18	Camel	Vieux Berquin	1850	1	
Ltn H Müller	18	Camel	Nieppe Wald	1850	4	a.
Ltn K Mendel	18	Camel	Grand sec Bois	1855	4	
Ltn R Spies	SFS2	Camel	5 km off Westende	1910	1	b.
FlgMt G Hubrich	SFS2	Camel	8 km off Nieuport	1910	1	b.
Ltn zS R Poss	SFS2	Camel	5 km off Westende	1910	1	b.
Ltn zS R Spies	SFS2	Camel	5 km off Westende	1915	2	b.
Ltn zS R Poss	SFS2	Camel	10 km off Nieuport	1915	2	b.
Ltn K Odebrett	42	Spad	Montdidier	1935	12	
Ltn A Heldmann	10	SE5	Mametz	1950	5	c.
Ltn J Janzen	6	Spad	S Etinehem	1955	5	
Ltn H Pippart	19	Spad	SE Montdidier	2000	12	d.
Ltn A Rahn	19	Spad	SE Piennes	2000	6	e.
Ltn Stickforth	24	Spad	Thiescourt Wald	2010	2	
Ltn F Kieckhäfer	29	BF2b/DH4	Festubert	2045	8	f.
Vfw A Bauhofer	25	AR2	Sudohol-Rajah		4	g.
Ltn R Windisch	66	Spad	by Carlepont		19	

a.   B5629, 4 Sqn AFC, Lt BW Wright, KIA.
b.   Two were DH4s of 202 Sqn RAF, N5985, Lt JP Everitt, WIA & Lt WR Stennett, KIA & N5989, Capt GW Biles,OK & Lt EE Gowing, WIA.
c.   C1793, 24 Sqn RAF, 2/Lt RA Slipper, WIA, POW.
d.   3411, Escadrille Spa 77, Cpl TG Buffum, POW.
e.   Escadrille Spa 77, Cpl Laraud, KIA.
f.   204 Sqn RAF.
g.   Serbian Escadrille 508, 2/Sgt RJ Roland & Lt J Nuaje, KIAs.

Losses

Ltn Fritz Kieckhäfer	29	Severely wounded in action with an RE8 at 2045 hours. Died 7 June, Gondecourt.
Ltn Karl Meierdirks	55	Killed in action Jericho.
Ltn Richard Schmidt	77	Injured in a crash.
Uffz Hans Wagner	80	Killed in action 2015 hrs Juvencourt in combat with Spads.

5 May 1918

Vfw A Nagler	74	Spad	Baconnes, N Mourmelon		zlg	

Losses

Uffz Meyer	57	Injured in a crash Halluin airfield.
OfStv Bernhardt Ultsch	77	Injured in a crash.

6 May 1918

Ltn V v Pressentin gen v Rautter	4	RE8	S Méricourt	0815	5	a.
Fldw K Schmückle	21	Balloon	SW Noyon	1515	2	b.
Uffz E Meyer	45	Spad	Blérancourt	1650	4	
Ltn H-J Rolfes	45	Breguet	Pimprez	1700	5	c.
Ltn W Schwartz	13	Breguet	Frière	1710	3	c.
Ltn R Hildebrandt	13	Breguet	La Fère, Nesle	1710	4	c.
Vfw H Stock	42	AR2	NW Ricquebourg	1810	1	

Vfw G Kowallik	42	AR2	SE Lassigny	1810	1	
OfStv W Beyer	42	Sopwith 2	Domfront	1815	1	
Ltn Grosse	72	Spad	Grivesnes	1940	1	
Uffz P Knopf	72	Spad	N Coullemelle	1945	2	
Obltn R v Greim	34	Camel	N Hamel	2000	13	
Ltn H Pippart	19	Spad	NE Montdidier	2030	13	d.
Ltn H Becker	12	Spad	N Montdidier		10	e.
Vfw Weiner	55	Balloon			1	

a.   A4404, 3 Sqn AFC, Capt HDE Ralfe & Lt WAJ Buckland, KIAs.
b.   French 93 Compagnie Aérostières.
c.   Br 131 lost three aircraft this date.
d.   Escadrille Spa 96, Lt M Barthe.
e.   Escadrille Spa 57, Lt J Chaput, WIA/DOW.

Losses

Ltn Hans Joachim Rogalla Frhr von Bieberstein	3	Killed in a crash 1735 hours Rumbeke.
Ltn Julius Buckler	17	Severely wounded in action Tricot.
Flg Heinrich Görzel	19	Taken prisoner of war.
Ltn Günther Derlin	20	Killed in action Ploegsteert Wood.
Vfw Otto G Wandelt	43	Killed in action 1115 hrs N Bethune.
Ltn zS Hans Rolshoven	SFS2	Killed in a crash 1830 hrs Zeebrugge.

7 May 1918

Ltn F Hengst	64	Nieuport	Vieville en Haye	0950	1	a.
Vfw W Borlinghaus	43	SE5	E St Jean	1705	–	
Vfw E Meyer	25	Nieuport	Poliste		2	
Obltn T Cammann	74	Spad 2	5 km S Cornillet		4	

a.   Nieuport '17' 6153, 94th Aero, Capt JN Hall, Inj/POW.

Losses

OfStv Waldemar von der Weppen	27	KIA, Ypres in a Fokker Dr.I by SE5s.
Ltn. Werner Scheerer	64	KIA, Vieville en Haye.

8 May 1918

Ltn K Bolle	B	SE5	S St Eloi	0820	9	a.
Ltn H v Bülow-Bothkamp	36	SE5	Kemmel	0835	4	b.
Vfw E Buder	26	SE5	W Becelaere	0937	2	c.
Ltn F Loerzer	26	SE5	Zillebeker See	0940	10	c.
Vfw F Classen	26	SE5	Zillebeker See	0940	3	c.
Ltn H Lange	26	SE5	Zillebeker See	0945	2	c.
Vfw O Rosenfeld	41	SE5	Strazeele	1150	9	
OfStv J Trotzky	43	Camel	S Auchy	1230	2	d.
Obltn E v Schleich	23	SE5	Auchenvillers	1230	26	
Obltn E v Schleich	23	SE5	Auchenvillers	1232	27	
Obltn E v Schleich	23	SE5	Auchenvillers	1235	28	
Vfw Drexler	43	Spad	Merris	1412	–	
Ltn K Bolle	B	Camel	W Steenwerk	1420	10	e.
Ltn F Kempf	B	Camel	Steenwerk	1420	4	e.
Ltn E Thuy	28	DH9	Zillebeker See	2015	20	
Ltn G Flecken	43	DH9	Richebourg	2030	4	
Ltn H Kunz	55	Balloon			4	f.
Vfw G Schniedewind	55	Balloon			5	
FlgMt A Bühl	SFS2	DH4	Sea off Nieuport		3	
Ltn zS R Weinert	MFJ2	DH4	Oostkerke		1	
Ltn zS G Brockhoff	MFJ2	Sopwith	Pervyse		1	
Ltn zS T Osterkamp	MFJ2	Spad	Sea off Nieuport		–	g.

a.   C6408, 1 Sqn RAF, Lt JC Wood, WIA/POW.
b.   B8410, 1 Sqn RAF, Capt CC Clark, WIA, POW.
c.   74 Sqn RAF, 2 losses; B8373, Lt RE Bright & Lt PJ Stuart-Smith, both KIA.
d.   D1852, 208 Sqn RAF, Capt CR McDonald, KIA.
e.   43 Sqn RAF, only loss was C8298, Lt TM O'Neill, KIA.
f.   British Balloon, 50th KBS, Lt WH Hargreaves, KIA.
g.   Spa 80, Sgt A Ferat. KIA, Spad SVII, lost off Bray Dunes.

Losses

Ltn Heinz Müller	27	Killed in action Ypres.
Uffz Johann P Meyer	32	Killed in action Roeux.
Ltn Wolf Fr v Manteuffel-Szöge	35	Killed in action 1 km E Biaches between Douai and Cambrai with Sopwith fighter.
Vfw Wilhelm Borlinghaus	43	Killed in action Ypres.
Vfw Karl Käppeler	55	Killed in action Djenin.

9 May 1918

Ltn G Schuster	29	SE5	SW Laventie	1005	5	a.
Ltn M Paulin	23	SE5	Monchy	1150	1	b.
Vfw F Hemer	6	RE8	E Cachy	1230	8	c.
Ltn P Billik	52	AWFK8	Neuve Chapelle	1255	16	d.
Ltn V v Pressentin gen v Rautter	4	DH9	Wiencourt	1315	6	e.
Ltn K v Schönebeck	59	Camel	Warlencourt	1420	4	
Uffz K Pech	29	Camel	Lacouture	1615	5	f.
Ltn D Collin	56	BF2b	Houthulst Wood	1840	8	g.
Ltn D Collin	56	Camel	Ypres	1850	9	
Ltn L Beckmann	56	Camel	Dickebusch	1900	2	
Ltn zS T Lodemann	SFS2	Camel	Sea off Ostende	1905	1	
Ltn E Löwenhardt	10	SE5	Hamel	1950	19	
Hptm W Reinhard	JGI	Camel	W Morlancourt	2000	13	h.
Vfw F Rumey	5	Breguet	N Villequier		16	i.
Ltn H Becker	12	Spad	SW Faverolles		11	
Obltn H Auffarth	29	DH4	Locon		–	
Vfw R Heibert	46	BF2b	Corbie		7	j.
Vfw G Schniedewind	55	Balloon			6	

a.   D5966, 29 Sqn RAF, Lt LE Bickel, OK.
b.   D3566, 29 Sqn RAF, Lt T Ratcliffe, POW.
c.   3 Sqn AFC, Capt JR Duigan,MC & Lt AS Paterson, WIAs.
d.   B5792, 2 Sqn RAF, Lt RL Johnson & Lt AJ Melanson, KIAs.
e.   C6094, 49 Sqn RAF, Lt GA Leckie & Lt GR Cuttle, MA, KIAs.
f.   D1790, 43 Sqn RAF, Lt S Birch, POW.
g.   C4851, 20 Sqn RAF.
h.   D1821, 43 Sqn RAF, Lt A Whitford-Hawkey, KIA.
i.   Escadrille Br 107, MdL Genot & S/Lt Jardin, KIAs – Breguet XIV.
j.   C4750, 48 Sqn RAF, Capt CGD Napier,OK & Sgt W Beales, OK.

Losses

Ltn Seeländer	37	Injured in a forced landing.
Uffz Höhne	37	Injured in a forced landing.
Uffz Otto Kutter	48	Killed in action Montdidier.
Ltn Ernst Schulze	48	Killed in action Montdidier.
Ltn Erich Wolff	55	Killed in action Djenin.
Ltn Karl Hertz	59	Killed in action 1415 hours Thilloy.
ObMt Franz Hasler	MFJI	Killed in a crash Jabbeke.

10 May 1918

Ltn J Veltjens	15	Spad	Braches	1500	12	a.

Ltn V v Pressentin gen v Rautter	4	BF2b	Chuignes	1640	7	b.
Ltn P Wenzel	6	Camel	SW Caiz	1950	2	c.
Ltn H Kirschstein	6	Camel	Chipilly	1950	8	d.
Vfw F Hemer	6	Camel	Chérisy	1950	9	e.
Ltn P Wenzel	6	DH9	Vrell-Chaulnes	2000	3	f.
Ltn V v Pressentin gen v Rautter	4	DH4	Rosières	2030	8	g.
Ltn J v Winterfeld	4	Camel	N Hamel	2030	2	
Ltn E Löwenhardt	10	DH9	Chaulnes	2030	20	h.
Vfw F Rumey	5	SE5	E Hamel		17	
Obltn E v Wedel	11	Camel	Chipilly, Chérisy		1	c.
Ltn W Steinhäuser	11	Camel	Chipilly, Chérisy		5	c.
Ltn H Wolff	11	Camel	S Sailly-Laurette		9	c.
Uffz Zell	42	AR2			1	
Uffz H v Goessel	71	AR2	Glocker Wald		1	

a. Escadrille Spa 94, Adj H Chan, POW, Spad XIII.
b. B1299, 48 Sqn RAF, Lt NG Stransom & Pvt CV Taylor, KIAs.
c. 80 Sqn RAF.
d. D6419, 80 Sqn RAF, 2/Lt GA Wateley, KIA.
e. B2463, 80 Sqn RAF, Lt AW Rowdon, KIA.
f. B2087, 27 Sqn RAF, Lt AH Hill & 1/AM GS Richmond, KIAs.
g. A7514, 27 Sqn, Capt GBS McBain, DSC & 2/Lt W Spencer, KIAs.
h. B2081, 27 Sqn RAF, Lt LE Dunnett & Lt HD Prosser, KIAs.

Losses

Uffz Fritz Zopf	80	Killed in a crash Morsberg.
Ltn Heinrich Büssing	K4b	Killed in action Rücken am Feldberg.

11 May 1918

Ltn H Stutz	71	AR2	S Frömmingen	1145	3	
Ltn zS T Osterkamp	MFJ2	Camel	Sea off Breedene	1702	11	a.
OfStv R Schleichhardt	18	SE5	Dranoutre	1821	1	
Ltn K Mendel	18	SE5	NW Bailleul	1825	5	b.
Ltn K Monnington	18	SE5	Bailleul	1825	1	c.
Vfw F Ehmann	47	SE5	Messines	1835	6	b.
Ltn R v Barnekow	20	SE5	Dickebusch	1910	1	
Uffz K Pech	29	Camel	Armentières	2035	6	d.

a. B7192, 213 Sqn RAF, Lt J Reid, KIA.
b. 1 Sqn RAF.
c. D3442, 41 Sqn RAF, Lt RH Stacey, WIA.
d. B7480, 4 Sqn AFC, Lt OC Barry, KIA.

Losses

Ltn Otto Aeckerle	47	KIA 1835 hours, Deulemont à Lys.
Ltn Obermeier	76	Wounded in action.

12 May 1918

No Claims – No Losses

13 May 1918

No Claims

Losses

Ltn Wilhelm Oberstadt	56	Injured in a crash, remained with unit.

14 May 1918

Gefr Deberitz	18	a/c	La Bassée	1145	–

Ltn R Schneider	79	AR2	Courcesses	1530	1	
Ltn J Jacobs	7	Balloon	N Ypres	1640	15	a.
Ltn J Jacobs	7	Balloon	N Ypres	1647	16	b.
Uffz M Mertens	7	Balloon	NW Ypres	1647	1	c.
Ltn E Thuy	28	Camel	Kemmel	1915	21	
Ltn K Christ	28	Sopwith	Erkinghem, Sailly	1930	1	d.
Ltn D Collin	56	Camel	Kemmel	2120	9	
Vfw Meissner	38	AR2	S Huma		2	
Vfw O Hennrich	46	Balloon	W Albert		1	e.
Obltn T Cammann	74	AR2	5 km S Brimont		5	

a. French 27 Compagnie Aérostières.
b. French 50 Compagnie Aérostières.
c. British Balloon 15-7-2 (badly damaged but not destroyed).
d. D1818, 4 Sqn AFC, Lt LR Sinclair, American, WIA/POW.
e. British Balloon 1-18-3 (SB 224/S).

Losses

Vfw Paul Hüttenrauch	7	Wounded in action.
Ltn Erich Weiss	33	Killed in action Poperingen-Waten, Dickebusch flying an Albatros DVa (G/2/8), combat with 20 Sqn RAF.
Uffz Friedrich-Karl Florian	51	Taken prisoner Menin area Alb DV 5161/17 (G/2/9), combat with 20 Sqn RAF.

15 May 1918

Ltn F Friedrichs	10	Camel	NW Albert	0815	4	a.
Ltn K Müller	24	Spad		0930	2	
Uffz R Mossbacher	77	Camel	Villers Bretonneux	0930	2	
Ltn P Wenzel	6	DH4	Aveluy	1030	4	b.
Ltn H v Gluczewski	4	Breguet	N Harbonnières	1115	1	
Ltn H Böhning	79	Spad	Montdidier	1120	10	
Ltn H Kirschstein	6	Camel	E Demuin	1205	9	c.
Sgt O Schmutzler	4	Camel	Lacouture	1210	1	
Ltn V v Pressentin gen v Rautter	4	Camel	S Aubercourt	1215	9	d.
Ltn J Janzen	6	BF2b	N Hamel	1250	6	e.
Ltn E Löwenhardt	10	DH9	Mametz	1325	21	f.
Ltn H Wolff	11	BF2b	W Guillaucourt	1510	10	g.
Ltn H Kirschstein	6	BF2b	SE Caix	1515	10	g.
Obltn E v Wedel	11	BF2b	SE Guillaucourt	1515	2	g.
Ltn C Degelow	7	DH4	Dixmuiden	1655	zlg	
Ltn V v Pressentin gen v Rautter	4	Breguet	Harbonnières	1805	10	
OfStv J Mai	5	BF2b	Orvillers	1815	12	h.
Ltn H Kirschstein	6	BF2b	Contalmaison	1820	11	i.
Ltn R Ruckle	33	DH9	Beerst	2045	1	
Ltn Feuereissen	51	BF2b	W Langemarck	2010	1	
Ltn W Schwartz	13	Breguet	Quesnoy		4	
Ltn H Kunz	55	RE8			6	
Obltn M Edler v Daniels	61	Spad			1	
Ltn R Windisch	66	Spad 2	by Trosly-Loire		20	j.
FlgMstr C Kuring	MFJ2	Pup	NW Oostkerke		1	

a. D6438, 70 Sqn RAF, 2/Lt JW Williamson, KIA.
b. C6177, 49 Sqn RAF, Capt WG Chambers & Lt RJ Burky, USAS, KIAs.
c. B6257, 209 Sqn RAF, Lt G Wilson, KIA.
d. B5666, 209 Sqn RAF, 2/Lt OG Brittorous, KIA.

e.   DH4 A7645, 57 Sqn RAF, Lt FL Mond & Lt EM Martyn, KIAs.
f.   A7725, 57 Sqn RAF, LT EH Piper & 2/Lt HLB Crabbe, KIAs.
g.   48 Sqn RAF had two losses: B1337, Capt CGD Napier, MC & Sgt P Murphy, KIAs, & C855, 2/Lt CL Glover & 2/Lt JC Fitton, KIAs, along with two other crewmen wounded.
h.   C845, 11 Sqn RAF, Lt HW Sellars, KIA & Lt CC Robson, MC, POW.
i.   C4882, 11 Sqn RAF, Capt JV Aspinall & Lt PV de la Cour, KIAs.
j.   Probably Spad two-seater from Spa 265, Lt Chotard & Asp Fropo – KIA/DOW.

Losses

Flg Rudolf Reissmann	24	Killed in action 0930 hours.
Vfw Rudolf Warschen	51	Killed in action Zillebeker See.
OfStv Josef Wolski	51	Killed in action Zillebeker See.
Ltn Walter Lütjohann	63	Killed over Amiens in fight with Camels.
Uffz Erwin Tresenreuter	68	Wounded in action Hangest (by a DrI).
Obltn Walter Ewers	77	Killed in action Villers Bretonneux 0930, in Albatros DVa 7220/17 fighting Camels.

16 May 1918

Ltn H v d Marwitz	30	Camel	Lorgies	0840	7	a.
Ltn M Gossner	23	SE5	Hamblain	1050	2	
Ltn L Luer	62	Spad	Montdidier	1050	6	b.
Ltn O Kissenberth	23	SE5	Tilly-Neuvill	1055	19	c.
Ltn M Näther	62	Spad	Trignières	1100	1	
Ltn Hospelt	9	Breguet	SE Guny	1125	1	
Ltn C Degelow	7	RE8	Dixmuiden	1220	4	
Ltn H Kirschstein	6	BF2b	Sailly-le-Sec	1440	12	d.
Ltn J Jacobs	7	Camel	Middlekerke	1500	–	
Ltn E Löwenhardt	10	Spad	Cappy, Graincourt	1545	22	
Obltn H v Wedel	75	Balloon	Mansbach	1615	2	e.
Vfw F Rumey	5	SE5	Beugny-Bapaume	1645	18	f.
Ltn W Blume	9	Spad	SE Elincourt	1800	8	
FlgMt Stucke	MFJ2	Spad	Sea off Middlekerke	1840	2	
Ltn R Wenzl	6	SE5	S Bois de Vaire	1930	2	g.
Vfw T Boelcke	67	AR2	Avocourt	1945	1	
ObFlgM Kurt Schönfelder	7	Camel	Middlekerke	2027	5	
Ltn H Kirschstein	6	SE5	Contalmaison	2110	13	h.
Ltn R Windisch	66	Spad	Thiescourt		21	
Vfw R Rübe	67	AR2			1	
Vfw A Auersbach	67	AR2			1	

a.   D9540, 208 Sqn RAF, Lt WE Cowan, POW.
b.   Possibly S/Lt C Albanal, Spa 3, took off 0800, Spad XIII.
c.   C1859, 64 Sqn RAF, Lt SB Reece, OK.
d.   C4859, 62 Sqn RAF, Lt CH Arnison, WIA & Lt CD Wells, MC, KIA.
e.   French 84 Compagnie Aérostières.
f.   D3912, 60 Sqn RAF, Lt HNJ Proctor, KIA.
g.   C1847, 84 Sqn RAF, Capt HP Smith, WIA.
h.   B183, 56 Sqn RAF, Capt T Durrant, KIA.

Losses

Ltn Feodor Hübner	4	Taken prisoner of war 1615 hours Corbie in Fokker Dr.I 546/17 (G/5/8).
Sgt Otto Schmutzler	4	Killed in action 2000 hours Rosières.
Ltn Hans Joachim Wolff	11	KIA 0820 hours N Lamotte Ferme.
Ltn Heinrich Küllmer	23	Killed in action Sailly.
Ltn Hans Nissen	54	Killed in action Passchendaele.
Ltn Karl Hubertus von Plessen	59	Killed in action over Thilloy.
ObMt Heinrich Hahn	MFJ1	Wounded in action over Ghistelles.
FlgMt Illig	MFJ2	Wounded in action.

17 May 1918

Ltn H Schlömer	5	SE5	SW Achiet-le-Grand	0715	3	a.
Ltn O Creutzmann	43	SE5	SW Lorgies	0915	3	b.
Gefr M Schumm	52	SE5	Le Parc	1045	1	c.
Ltn H Kirschstein	6	Breguet	Cappy-sur-Somme	1110	14	d.
Ltn J Janzen	6	Breguet	E Cachy	1115	7	d.
Ltn W Balzar	44	Spad	Montdidier	1150	–	
Ltn W Saint-Mont	52	SE5	La Gorgue	1147	1	
Obltn E Wenig	80	AR2	NW Parroy Wald	1210	3	
Uffz K Pech	29	SE5	Morbecque	1220	7	
Obltn H Auffarth	29	Camel	Vierhoek	1225	14	e.
Ltn H Drekmann	4	Spad	Framerville	1230	2	
Ltn J Werner	14	SE5	Floris	1230	5	
Ltn V v Pressentin gen v Rautter	4	SE5	E Foucaucourt	1705	11	f.
Vfw A Triebswetter	16	DH4	Zillebeker See	1825	4	
Vfw F Schattauer	16	Balloon	NW Ypres	1940	8	g.
Vfw R Lander	52	BF2b	Sailly	1945	2	
Vfw F Rumey	5	SE5	Puzieux		19	
Ltn F Imme	42	Spad			1	
Vfw K Koller	76	DH4	Henancourt		1	

a.　32 Sqn RAF ?
b.　D3535, 40 Sqn RAF, Lt L Seymour, POW.
c.　C6404, 74 Sqn RAF, Lt LM Nixon, KIA.
d.　Only two Breguets lost this date – from Br 120 – S/Lt Tanner & MdL Attal, and Adj Michelaut and Lt du Sapin – all MIA.
e.　B6408, 203 Sqn RAF, 2/Lt ER Prideaux, KIA.
f.　C1105, 24 Sqn RAF, Lt E Harrison, KIA.
g.　Belgium Balloon Number 4.

Losses

OfStv Julius Trotzky	43	Killed in action 1945 hrs Carvin, Albatros DVa 7450/17.
Vfw Alfred Philipp	57	Killed in action Somme Valley.
Ltn Heinrich Zürn	62	KIA, Avre, Gratibus by Montdidier.
Gefr Albert Wendt	63	Killed in action Villers Bretonneux during combat with 65 Sqn RAF.

18 May 1918

Ltn H Kirschstein	6	Breguet	E Caix	0700	15	
Ltn F Friedrichs	10	Balloon	Ransart	0730	5	a.
Ltn E Löwenhardt	10	Camel	Beaucourt	0745	23	
Ltn R Eck	16	BF2b	Poelkapelle	0825	3	b.
OfStv Behncke	54	BF2b	E Ypres	0840	2	b.
Ltn G Weiner	K3	Spad	SW Armaucourt	0940	3	c.
Ltn v Borries	22	Spad	SW Mailly	1105	1	
Ltn H Hager	32	Camel	Vitry	1110	1	
Vfw Wiest	32	DH4	Boiry	1115	1	
Uffz K Pech	29	Camel	NW Lestrem	1150	8	d.
Uffz K Pech	29	Camel	NW Lestrem	1155	9	d.
Ltn V v Pressentin gen v Rautter	4	DH9	Aubercourt	1240	12	e.
Ltn H Eggers	30	RE8	Brielen	1240	–	
Ltn J Veltjens	15	Breguet	Caucy	1255	13	
Vfw F Rumey	5	Spad	Moreuil		20	
Ltn v Borries	22	Spad			zlg	

OfStv W Beyer	42	Spad	Pierrepont	2	
Vfw R Heibert	46	Camel	S Morlancourt	8	f.
Uffz Richter	46	Camel	Bayonvillers	zlg	
Vfw O Hennrich	46	Camel	SE Albert	2	f.
Uffz W Stör	68	BF2b	Le Quesnil	2	

a.   British Balloon 35-12-3 (BMS 201/D).
b.   88 Sqn RAF lost 2 BF2bs this date: C780, Lt RJ Cullen FTL, OK and C783, 2/Lt LGS Gadpaille & 2/Lt S Griffin, KIAs.
c.   Escadrille Spa 90, S/Lt J Bordes, OK.
d.   210 Sqn RAF lost 2 Camels this date: D3390, Lt J Hollick, KIA & D3391, Lt MF Sutton, WIA/POW.
e.   D8401, 205 Sqn RAF, 2/Lt HCR Conron & 2/Lt JM Finnigan, KIAs.
f.   65 Sqn RAF lost two Camels this date: B7178, Lt KP Hunt and C8256, Lt WF Scott-Kerr, POWs.

Losses

Sgt Fritz Brodereck	42	Killed in action Pierrepont by a Spad.
Ltn Feuereissen	51	Lightly wounded in action.
Ltn Reinhold Klimsch	51	Killed in a crash Ste Marguerite.

19 May 1918

Ltn K Bolle	B	BF2b	Zonnebeke	0820	11	a.
Obltn R v Greim	34	BF2b	Guillaucourt	1010	14	b.
Vfw M Kahlow	34	BF2b	Proyart	1015	5	b.
Vfw O Könnecke	5	BF2b	Villers Bretonneux	1030	18	b.
Ltn F Pütter	68	SE5	Contoine	1040	23	c.
Ltn A Delling	34	BF2b	Bois de Hangard	1045	–	d.
Ltn P Billik	52	Dolphin	Wingles	1110	17	d.
Ltn W Steinhäuser	11	BF2b	Hamel	1130	6	e.
FlgMt K Engelfried	SFS2	DH4	Blankenberge	1330	1	f.
Vfw F Schattauer	16	Balloon	S Furnes	1830	9	g.
Uffz E Binge	16	Balloon	S Furnes	1830	1	h.
Uffz E Binge	16	SE5	S Furnes	1835	2	
Ltn K Menckhoff	72	Spad		1840	26	
Vfw F Hemer	6	Spad	Harbonnières	1940	10	
Oblt E v Wedel	11	Spad	E Harbonnières	2000	3	
Vfw W Gabriel	11	DH9	NE Marcelcave	2010	2	i.
Ltn W Steinhäuser	11	DH9	Villers Bretonneux	2010	7	
Ltn F Bacher	3	DH9	Klein-Zillebeke	2025	1	
Vfw O Wieprich	57	SE5	Moorslede	2030	3	
Ltn P Strähle	57	DH9	Dadizeele	2030	10	j.
Vfw R Heibert	46	Camel	Chuignolles		9	k.
Ltn F Pütter	68	BF2b	Bois de Hangard		–	
Obltn A Rostock	77	Camel	W Marcelcave		1	

a.   DH9 C6159, 206 Sqn RAF, Lt BF Dunford & 2/Lt FF Collins, KIAs.
b.   62 Sqn RAF lost four BF2bs this date: B1336, Lt DA Savage, MC, OK & Lt EW Collis, OK; C796, Lt HC Hunter, WIA/POW & Sgt J Lake, KIA; C4630, Lt HA Clarke & Capt H Claye,POWs, and C4751, 2/Lt F Atkinson, POW/DOW & Sgt CC Brammer, POW.
c.   C6449, 84 Sqn RAF, 1/Lt EM Hammer, USAS, KIA.
d.   C4017, 19 Sqn RAF, Maj AD Carter, DSO, POW.
e.   D1002, 49 Sqn RAF, Lt FD Nevin, KIA & Sgt H Barfoot, KIA.
f.   D2784, 211 Sqn RAF, Lt NA Taylerson,KIA & 2/Lt CL Bray, KIA.
g.   Belgium Balloon No 6.
h.   Belgium Balloon No 3.
i.   C6181, 49 Sqn RAF, Lt CG Capel, WIA & 1/AM J Knight, WIA.
j.   C6161, 206 Sqn RAF, Lt H Mitchell, POW & A/G CF Costen, POW.
k.   D6433, 3 Sqn RAF, Lt FJ Brotheridge, KIA.

Losses

| Vfw Andreas Triebswetter | 16 | Killed in action S Furnes. |

Vfw Karl Pech	29	Killed in action 1203 hours Lestrem collided with an SE5 of 29 Sqn, whose pilot survived.
Ltn Karl Bauernfeind	34	Wounded, Proyart, in Pfalz DIII 8023/17.
Ltn. Richard Plange	36	Killed in action Ypres Fokker Dr.I 453/17 (G/2/10) during combat with 10 Sqn RAF.
Ltn Alois Weber	46	Taken prisoner of war Villers Bretonneux.
Oblt Hans Witt	46	Killed in action Villers Bretonneux Albatros DV, in combat with 84 Sqn RAF.

20 May 1918

Ltn E Löwenhardt	10	Balloon	Ransart, SW Arras	0730	24	a.
Ltn K Schwartz	22	Spad	Beauvraignes	0830	4	
Ltn K Christ	28	DH4	W Merville	0915	–	
Ltn J Janzen	6	Camel	Hamel	0930	8	b.
Ltn M-W B-Bodemer	6	SE5	Harbonnières	0930	3	
Ltn H Oberländer	30	SE5	Ville Chapelle	1100	6	c.
Ltn v Pressentin gen v Rautter	4	BF2b/DH4	Warfusée	1125	13	
Vfw F Rumey	5	Camel	Morlancourt	1905	21	d.
OfStv J Mai	5	Camel	Morlancourt	1905	13	d.
Ltn H Schlömer	5	DH4	Meault		zlg	
OfStv J Mai	5	Camel	Dernaucourt			
OfStv J Mai	5	Camel	Lahoussoye		–	
Vfw O Könnecke	5	Camel	Hailles		–	
OfStv W Kühne	18	Spad	Merville		–	
Vfw E Schütze	25	AR2	N Monastir		1	
Ltn R Heydacker	25	AR2	N Monastir		3	

a.   British Balloon 41-15-5 (BMS 158/D).
b.   Dolphin C3807, 23 Sqn RAF, Lt CA Crysler, KIA.
c.   D3438, 40 Sqn RAF, Lt G Watson, KIA.
d.   65 Sqn RAF, only loss D1876, Capt LE Whitehead, KIA.

Losses
Ltn Vivigenz v Wedel   1   Killed in a crash at Blaise near Vouziers.

21 May 1918

Ltn zS T Lodemann	SFS2	BF2b	In Sea off	0823	2	a.
Ltn zS R Poss	SFS2	BF2b	Mariakerke	0825	3	a.
Vfw Ehrhardt	32	SE5	Bullecourt	0910	1	
Ltn H Holthusen	30	SE5	Calonne	1100	1	
FlgMt Held	MFJ2	Camel	Ramskapelle	1300	1	
Ltn J Gildemeister	20	Camel	Armentières	2025	1	b.
Ltn W Lehmann	5	Camel			3	
Ltn H Viebig	57	Camel	Steenwerk		4	c.
Ltn R Windisch	66	Spad	by Thiescourt		–	
Ltn K Menckhoff	72	Breguet			27	
Vfw K Arnold	72	Breguet			1	
FlgMt Wagner	MFJ1	DH4	Uitkerke		1	d.
Ltn zS Tinschert	MFJ1	BF2b	at Sea		3	a.
Ltn zS G Saschenberg	MFJ1	DH9	Sea off Mariakerke		11	d.

a.   88 Sqn RAF lost two BF2bs this date: B1341, Lt CG Scobie & 2/Lt FJD Hudson,KIAs and C839, Lt KO Millar & 2/Lt S Davidson, KIAs.
b.   D6604, 73 Sqn RAF, Lt JL Brewster, KIA.
c.   D9539, 73 Sqn RAF, Lt TG Drew-Brook, WIA/POW.
d.   211 Sqn RAF lost two DH9s this date: B7604, Lt RFC Metcalfe, OK & 2/Lt DR Bradley, OK, & B7661, 2/Lt HE Tansley & 2/Lt NB Harris, POWs.

Losses

Vfw Hans Schorn	16	Killed in action Wytschaete.
Flg Klaus Sakowski	29	Killed in action 1203 hours La Gorgue.
OfStv Emil Richter	50	Taken prisoner.
Vfw Friedrich Goethe	52	Killed in a crash 1545 hours Laventhin.

22 May 1918

Ltn F Köhler	25	AR2	W Prespa-See	0900	1	
Vfw E Meyer	25	Nieuport	S Tomaros	0900	3	
Ltn H Müller	18	Spad XIII	Estaires	1053	5	a.
Gefr Deberitz	18	Spad XIII	Fleurbaix	1105	1	b.
Vfw H Boy	14	SE5	Armentières	1220	3	c.
Vfw P Stenzel	14	SE5	Neuf Berquin	1225	1	c.
Vfw P Rothe	14	SE5	SE La Gorgue	1230	3	c.
Ltn F Thiede	24	Caudron	NE Ercheu	2325	2	
Ltn F Thiede	24	Voisin	Avricourt	2345	3	d.
Ltn F Thiede	24	Caudron	SE Ercheu	2404	zlg	
OfStv W Kühne	18	SE5	Deubaix	–		
Ltn H Schmidt	69	Spad	Noyon		2	e.

a.   Spad XIII No.2282, 103rd Aero, 1Lt EA Giroux, KIA.
b.   Spad VII No.3173, 103rd Aero, 1Lt PF Baer, POW.
c.   B132, 64 Sqn RAF, 2/Lt GA Rainer, POW
d.   2736, Escadrille V 116, S/Lt Desgardes, KIA & Cpl Lacout, MIA.
e.   Escadrille Spa 12, Cpl Gibier, MIA, Spad VII.

Losses

Ltn Breuer	47	Wounded in action.
Uffz Mathias Schmid	80	Injured in a crash at Mörchingen airfield.

23 May 1918

Ltn J Jacobs	7	SE5	Ploegsteert	0940	17	
Ltn D Collin	56	BF2b	Maria-Alter	0930	10	a.
Ltn H Seywald	23	BF2b	La Bassée	1110	1	b.
Ltn R Schneider	79	BF2b	Tricot	1150	2	

a.   DH9 D5616, 27 Sqn RAF, 2/Lt GE Ffrench & Cpl FY McLauchlan, KIAs.
b.   AWFK8 C8526, 2 Sqn RAF, Lt TH Crossman,OK & Lt LC Spence MC, DOW.

Losses

Ltn Hauffe	9	Severely injured in a crash.
Ltn Hans Oberländer	30	WIA with DH9s and to Hospital Nr.74.
Ltn Erich Kayl	32	Severely wounded in action 1145 hours near Douai in Albatros DVa 7372/1; DOW 27 May, at Vis-en-Artois.
Vfw Gustav Schniedewind	55	Wounded by BF2bs of 1 AFC Sqn.
Uffz Richard Jentzsch	71	Killed in action Habsheim.
Ltn Walter Angermund	76	Wounded, 0950, combat with SE5s.

24 May 1918

FlgMt Bieler	SFS2	DH4			1
FlgMt Bieler	SFS2	DH4			2

25 May 1918

OfStv R Schleichhardt	18	SE5	W Lens	1245	zlg
Ltn W Kypke	47	RE8	Beythem	1430	8
Ltn R Stark	77	RE8	W Gentelles		zlg

Losses

Vfw Karl Koller	76	Taken prisoner of war 2000 hours Albatros DV 7221/17 (G/3/7), combat with 65 Sqn RAF.

26 May 1918

Vfw F Schwarz	33	Spad	E Dranoutre	1600	2

Losses

Obltn Hubertus v Rudno-Rudzinski	60	Taken prisoner of war.	

27 May 1918 The German Offensive on the Aisne (Operation Blücher)

Ltn J Jacobs	7	SE5	Ypres	0610	zlg	
Uffz Staudacher	1	Spad	Somme-Suippes	1030	zlg	
Ltn O Fitzner	65	Spad	Apremont	1100	4	a.
OfStv Tiedje	65	Spad	Mont Sec	1115	1	
Vfw H Krüger	70	DH4	Erlingen	1320	1	
Vfw K Kallmünzer	78	Spad	Parroy Wald	1515	1	
Ltn V v Pressentin gen v Rautter	4	Breguet	Pont Arcy	1815	14	b.
Ltn F Ray	49	RE8	Meteren	2030	11	c.
Ltn R Windisch	66	Spad	Lesges-Couvrelles		22	
Ltn A Laumann	66	Spad	,, ,,		1	
Ltn P Turck	66	Spad	,, ,,		2	
Vfw W Peters	66	Spad	,, ,,		1	
Ltn P Turck	66	AR2	,, ,,		3	
Sgt Dittberner	66	Spad	,, ,,		1	
Obltn T Cammann	74	AR2	Trigny		6	
Ltn R Otto	74	Sopwith 2	Prouilly		1	
Vfw A Nagler	81	Spad	Trigny		1	
Ltn R Schultze	MFJ1	DH4	Ostdunkerke-Bad		1	

a.   Nieuport 28 N6142, 94th Aero, 1Lt WD Hill, WIA.
b.   Escadrille Br 126, Sgt Des Salles, MIA & Sgt Linguelia, MIA.
c.   B4100, 4 Sqn RAF, Lt AH Maltby, OK & 2/Lt JBP Simms, OK.

Losses

Vfw Fritz Schattauer	16	Severely wounded in action SE Ypres.
Hptm Rudolf Frhr von Esebeck	17	Killed in action 1930 hours Chiry-Ourscamp in combat with Breguets of Br 127.
Ltn Franz Hausner	23	Killed in a collision W Bourlon nr Cambrai.
Ltn Otto Hornfischer	23	Killed in a collision W Bourlon nr Cambrai.
Vfw Artur Schiebler	30	Killed in action 0910 hours Douvrin with SE5s.
Ltn Johannes Lieberz	35	Injured in a crash Guesnain, remained.
Ltn Heinrich Arntzen	50	Severely wounded by Flak, Villosnes.
Ltn Walter Fritzsche	65	Killed, Mont Sec, in combat with Spads.
Ltn Rudolf Windisch	66	POW, Couvrelles and died in captivity.
Oblt Amandus Rostock	77	Wounded in action.
Flg Haitsch	79	Wounded in action.

28 May 1918

FlgMt Bieber	SFS2	DH4	Jehkooke	0620	3	a.
Flg Kuhlmey	28	SE5	S Dickebusche See	0845	1	
Ltn P Billik	52	SE5	Locon	0850	18	b.
Vfw O Sowa	52	SE5	Neuf Berquin	0900	3	
ObFlgMstr Kurt Schönfelder	7	Camel	Hazebrouck	0945	6	
Hptm R Berthold	JGII	Breguet	Crouy	1115	29	
Ltn O von B-Marconnay	15	AR2	S Soissons	1115	1	
Ltn K Baier	18	BF2b	La Gorgue	1120	1	
Ltn W Kypke	47	SE5	Neuf Berquin	1120	–	
Vfw E Pabst	51	DH4	E Neuf Berquin	1120	4	
Ltn F Loerzer	26	Spad	Bruys	1230	11	

Ltn E Koch	32	SE5	Eterpigny	1245	3	c.
Flg Marchner	32	SE5	NE Pelves	1245	1	
OfStv G Dörr	45	AR2	Vendeuil	1500	3	
Ltn F Friedrichs	10	Balloon	S Chavigny	1730	6	
Vfw F Ehmann	47	SE5	Vlamertinghe	2020	7	
Uffz Diem	76	SE5	Hangard		zlg	
Ltn R Stark	77	RE8	SW Gentelles		zlg	

a.　　A8065, 217 Sqn RAF, Lt/Col PFM Fellowes, WIA/POW & Sgt FN Pritchard, POW.
b.　　C6455, 64 Sqn RAF, Lt WP Southall, KIA.
c.　　B8394, 41 Sqn RAF, Lt RS Milani, WIA/POW.

Losses

Obltn Richard Flashar	5	Wounded in action.
Uffz Peisker	7	Wounded in action.
Uffz Sicho	7	Wounded in action.
Ltn Bitsch	9	Severely wounded in action.
Oblt. Harald Auffarth	29	Lightly wounded in action.
Ltn Johannes v Etzdorff	SFS2	Killed in action 0615 hours Wenduyne in combat with DH9s.

29 May 1918

Ltn F Röth	16	Balloon	Dixmuide-Ypres	1600	11	a.
Ltn F Röth	16	Balloon	Dixmuide-Ypres	1604	12	a.
Ltn F Röth	16	Balloon	Dixmuide-Ypres	1609	13	a.
Ltn F Röth	16	Balloon	Ypres-Hazebrouck	1612	14	a.
Ltn F Röth	16	Balloon	Ypres-Hazebrouck	1615	15	
Hptm R Berthold	JGII	Spad XIII	S Soissons	1820	30	
Ltn J Veltjens	15	Spad	S Soissons	1830	14	
Ltn G v Hantelmann	15	Spad	S Soissons	1830	zlg	
Hptm R Berthold	JGII	Breguet	S Soissons	1840	31	
OfStv W Kühne	18	Balloon	Thiennes	2050	2	b.
Ltn R v Barnekow	20	SE5	N Bailleul	2100	2	
Ltn K Bolle	B	Spad	Soissons		12	
Vfw O Hennrich	46	Balloon	NW Albert		3	
Vfw O Hennrich	46	Balloon	NW Albert		–	
Obltn J Loeser	46	Camel			zlg	
Ltn G Schulte	50	Spad	E Marchais		3	
Ltn G Keitsch	74	Sopwith 2	Bétheny nr Reims		3	
Ltn zS G Saschenberg	MFJ2	DH4	SW Nieuwekapelle		12	

a.　　Belgium Balloons Numbers 1 and 4 and British Balloons 25-5-2 (BMS 1) and 39-8-2 (SR 22).
b.　　British Balloon 40-11-1 (BMS 204).

Losses

Ltn Paul Bäumer	B	Injured in a crash 2230, Vivaise airfield.
Uffz Reuss	7	Wounded in action 2045 hours.
Ltn Otto Kissenberth	23	Severely injured in a crash 2130 hours in captured Camel believed to be B7184.
Ltn Wilhelm Pannes	46	Killed in action Meault-Albert.
Ltn Günther Keitsch	74	Killed in action nr Reims, shot down by 1 Sqn RAF; wreckage of Albatros DVa became G/2/12.

30 May 1918

OfStv Tiedje	65	Nieuport	S Euvezin	0900	2	
Ltn J Janzen	6	Spad	by Beauvardes	1030	9	a.
Ltn F Pütter	68	BF2b	Castel	1120	24	b.
Ltn H Kiessling	34	AWFK8	N Corbie	1200	1	

Ltn E Koch	32	SE5	Hébuterne	1230	4	
Ltn F Pütter	68	Spad	Lassigny, S Roye	1305	25	c.
Ltn F Ray	49	Dolphin	Nieppe Wald	1545	12	
Obltn H-E Gandert	51	SE5	Nieppe Wald	2035	3	d.
Ltn Seewald	54	SE5	N Ypres	2050	2	
Vfw O Könnecke	5	DH4	Dernaucourt		19	e.
Vfw O Könnecke	5	Camel	Ribemont		zlg	
Ltn H Schlömer	5	Camel	Heilly		4	
Vfw O Könnecke	5	Camel	Hamel		20	f.
Ltn W Blume	9	Spad			9	
Ltn W Schwartz	13	Balloon	N Vic		5	
Ltn H Pippart	19	Breguet	Cuts-Carlepont		14	
Obltn B Loerzer	JGIII	Spad			24	
Vfw F Classen	26	Breguet	Souvy-Montgobert		4	
Vfw F J Jacobsen	73	AR2	Aubérive near Bligny		3	
Ltn W Böning	76	Camel	Contalmaison		16	g.
Ltn W Böning	76	Camel	Bray-sur-Somme		17	h.
Vfw G Markert	76	Camel	Albert		1	

a. Escadrille Spa 154, MdL M Fuchs, MIA, Spad VII.
b. C871, 48 Sqn RAF, 2/Lt WB Yuille & 2/Lt WD Davidson, KIAs.
c. Escadrille Spa 37, MdL Lostalot, MIA.
d. C1862, 85 Sqn RAF, Capt EL Benbow,MC, KIA.
e. 49 Sqn RAF ?
f. 70 Sqn RAF ?
g. D1793, 43 Sqn RAF, 2/Lt PT Bruce, KIA.
h. D6483, 3 Sqn RAF, Lt CP Macklin, KIA.

Losses

Ltn Karl Köhler	9	Killed in a crash Chambry.
Vfw Hillerbrand	32	Wounded in action 0830 hours Arras.
Ltn Willibald Dehner	32	Severely wounded in action 0830 hours Arras, Albatros DVa 6511/17. DOW 2 Jun in Hospital Nr.51 at Beaulencourt.
Ltn Emanuel Riezler	34	Wounded in action SW Albert.
Gefr Theodor Bauer	34	Killed in action SE Albert.
Ltn Bieck	36	Taken prisoner of war Morcourt.
Vfw Jacob Pollinger	77	Taken POW – fuel problem – came down near Bourney – Pfalz DIIIa 8284/17 (G5/13).

31 May 1918

Uffz M Hutterer	23	SE5	S Arras	1150	zlg	
Ltn V v Pressentin gen v Rautter	4	Breguet	SW Soissons	1255	15	
Ltn E Udet	4	Breguet	SW Soissons	1300	24	
FlgMt Mayer	MFJ2	DH9	Aertyke	1433	2	a.
Ltn H Kirschstein	6	Breguet	by Grand Rozoy	1435	16	
Ltn H Helten	20	SE5	Laventie	1640	1	
Ltn H Lange	26	Spad	S Longpont	1705	3	
OfStv O Esswein	26	Spad	Mortefontaine	1705	11	
Vfw C Mesch	26	Spad	Compiègne Wald	1706	1	
OfStv O Esswein	26	Spad	Mortefontaine	1710	12	
Obltn M v Förster	27	Spad	W Soissons	1810	1	
Uffz A Eigenbrodt	7	Camel	Nieppe Wald	1830	1	
Ltn H Kroll	24	Breguet	Compiègne	1830	24	
ObFlgMstr Kurt Schönfelder	7	SE5	Nieppe Wald	1840	7	
Ltn M Skowronski	6	Breguet	by Marizy St Mard	1940	1	
Hptm W Reinhard	JGI	Spad	by Bonneserle	1945	14	

Ltn E Bormann	B	Breguet	Taille-Fontaine	zlg	
Ltn A Lindenberger	B	Breguet	Villers Cotterêts	4	
Vfw O Könnecke	5	Dolphin	Morlancourt	zlg	
Obltn E v Wedel	11	Spad	Bois de Barbillon	4	
Vfw Steinbrecher	46	Camel	S Albert	2	b.
Vfw Dettmering	68	Breguet	Thennes	2	
Ltn K Menckhoff	72	Camel	Soissons	28	
Ltn H v Dechend	72	Camel	Blangy-Tronville	1	
Uffz Diem	76	Breguet	Hangard	1	
Vfw A Nagler	81	Spad	Romigny	2	
Ltn H Knappe	81	Spad	Romigny	2	
Ltn P Blunk	K1b	DH4	Dax-Landen,Karlsruhe	1	c.

a.   D7657, 98 Sqn RAF, Capt GD Horton & 2/Lt HJ McConnell, KIAs.
b.   C8217, 70 Sqn RAF, 2/Lt WE Taylor, American, KIA.
c.   A7825, 55 Sqn RAF, Lt JKL Anderson, POW/DOW & Sgt H Nelle, KIA.

Losses

Uffz Wilhelm Kutschera	3	Killed in action Rumbeke, combat with Breguets.
Ltn V v Pressentin gen v Rautter	4	Killed in action 1300 hours Soissons, in combat with Breguets.
Ltn Hans Schlömer	5	Killed in action 1050 hours Morlancourt.
Ltn Edouard Stratmann	9	WIA/POW, 10 km SW Villers Cotterêts.
Ltn Rademacher	10	Taken prisoner of war, in Albatros DV, (G/2/13).
Ltn Hans Grabe	14	Severely wounded in action. DOW 6 June at Phalempin.
Ltn Ulrich Buchholz	20	Wounded in action with SE5s.
Ltn Erich Kaus	30	Wounded in action.
Uffz Heinrich Koch	36	Killed in action Reims, SW Soissons, during combat with a two-seater.
Vfw Flatow	45	Wounded in action.
Uffz Schille	47	Lightly wounded in action, remained with unit.
Ltn Gerhard Schulte	50	Taken prisoner of war.
Ltn Walter Böning	76	Wounded in action 1815 hours, collision with Vfw Markert, then shot down by a Camel.
Vfw Georg Markert	76	Killed in action 1815 hours Fricourt – collision.

Jasta Armee Assignments as of 1 June 1918

Western Front

1 Armee 31,39,73,74
2 Armee 5,34b,37,46,76b,77b
3 Armee 1
4 Armee 3,7,16b,20,28w,33,40s,49,51,54s,56,57,58,MFJI,MFJII
5 Armee 67
6 Armee 14,18,29,30,41,43,47w,52
7 Armee B,4,6,9,10,11,21s,22s,26,27,36,45,50,60,66,81
17 Armee 23b,32b,35b,59
18 Armee 8,12,13,15,17,19,24s,42,44s,48,53,61,62,63,68,69,72s,79b
19 Armee 80b
Det 'A' 70,78b,K3
Det 'B' 71,75
Det 'C' 64w,65

Other Fronts

11 Armee 25   Macedonia

11 Armee	38	Macedonia
	55	Turkey

1 June 1918

Ltn G Weiner	K3	DH4	Antullen, NW Metz	0650	4	a.
Ltn J Jacobs	7	BF2b	NW Dickebusch	0735	18	b.
Obltn O v Boenigk	21	Breguet	Priez	0815	7	
Ltn L Laveuve	77	DH4	Longneau	1100	1	
Ltn H Kroll	24	Balloon	Carlepont	1150	–	c.
Ltn J Werner	14	SE5	Liévin	1235	6	d.
Vzflgmstr C Kuring	MFJ2	DH9	Ruidenberg	1530	2	e.
Obfm K Schönfelder	7	Camel	Laventie	1610	8	f.
Ltn K Mendel	18	Camel	Laventie	1610	6	g.
Vfw W Gabriel	11	Spad	by Fleury	1710	3	
Ltn P Billik	52	SE5	E Merville	1740	19	h.
Ltn G Bürck	54	RE8	N Teil von Ypres	2020	2	
Ltn A Lindenberger	B	Breguet	Priez		5	
Obltn A v Brackel	21	Breguet	by Priez		1	
Ltn H Roer	27	Fr DD	by Château Thierry		1	
Vfw G Schalk	34	SE5	Bray-sur-Somme		1	i.
Ltn G Meyer	37	SE5	Albert		5	i.
Ltn A Hets	37	BF2b	S Albert		1	
Uffz E Meyer	45	Spad			5	
OfStv G Dörr	45	RE8	La Ferté Milon		zlg	j.
Ltn M Näther	62	Balloon	Cuvilly		2	
Ltn P Turck	66	Balloon	Villers Cotterêts		4	
Ltn K Menckhoff	72	Breguet			29	
Ltn H v Dechend	72	Breguet	Soissons		2	
Vfw K Arnold	72	Breguet			2	
Uffz P Knopf	72	Breguet	Soissons		3	
Vfw F Jacobsen	73	Spad	Silléry near Reims		4	
OfStv W Schluckebier	73	Spad	Silléry		1	k.
Obltn T Cammann	74	AR2	Villers Marmery		7	
Ltn R Stark	77	SE5	Foucaucourt		–	

a.   A7482, 55 Sqn RAF, 2/Lt LdeG Godet & 2/Lt A Haley, KIAs.
b.   C4749, 20 Sqn RAF, Lt TC Traill, OK & 2/Lt PG Jones, OK.
c.   A loose German balloon.
d.   D3530, 40 Sqn RAF, Maj RS Dallas, KIA.
e.   C6271, 98 Sqn RAF, 2Lt LIA Peers, USAS & Pte Wentworth, POWs.
f.   C8231, 4 Sqn AFC, 2/Lt A Rintoyl, POW.
g.   4 Sqn AFC ?
h.   C6443, 74 Sqn RAF, Capt WJ Cairnes, KIA.
i.   2 Sqn AFC ?
j.   B7738, 52 Sqn RAF, 2/Lt A Nugent & 2/Lt GAB Ross, KIAs.
k.   5837, Escadrille Spa 124, Cpl L Charton, an American, severely WIA.

Losses

Uffz Kroeger	7	Wounded in action.
Vfw Wilhelm Stein	27	Killed in action Soissons.
Uffz Graf	31	Wounded in action Laon.
Ltn Wilhelm Rupprecht	31	Killed in action Laon.
Vfw Friedrich Neumann	37	KIA between Etinheim & Péronne.
Ltn Paul Billik	52	Lightly wounded in action 2110 Estaries, remained with unit.
Ltn Wilhelm Saint Mont	52	Killed in action 2110 Neurillon by Lille.
Vfw Sokolowski	60	Taken prisoner.
Flg Andreas Herold	77	KIA Foucaucourt 2030 Allied side.
Gefr Alfred Dölger	80	Wounded in action.

2 June 1918

Ltn A v Brandenstein	49	BF2b	W Grand Sec Bois	0710	2	a.
Ltn E Udet	4	Breguet	NW Neuilly	1150	25	g.
Vfw M Kiep	43	SE5	W Merville	1325	2	
Ltn J Veltjens	5	RE8	W Soissons	1330	15	
Ltn F Hengst	64	Nieuport	E St Mihiel	1615	2	b.
Oblt H-E Gandert	51	SE5	SW Bailleul	1630	4	c.
Ltn J Janzen	6	Spad	W Ploisy	1720	10	
Ltn H Kirschstein	6	Spad	by Cagny	1735	17	
Ltn E Löwenhardt	10	Spad	Croix	1745	25	
Ltn W Steinhäuser	11	Spad	S Troesnes	1745	8	
Hptm W Reinhard	JGI	Spad	S Bonnes	1745	15	
Ltn H Maushake	4	Breguet	Montigny-Labier	1820	zlg	g.
Vfw F Rumey	5	Camel	Hangard	1910	22	d.
OfStv J Mai	5	Camel	S Hangard	1911	14	d.
OfStv W Kühne	18	RE8	Haverskerque	1930	zlg	
Hptm W Reinhard	JGI	Spad	by La Ferté Milon	2030	16	
Obfm K Schönfelder	7	Camel	Oudekapelle	2055	9	e.
Ltn H Kirschstein	6	Breguet	by Troesnes	2100	18	g.
Hptm W Reinhard	JGI	Spad	Buisson de Borny	2100	17	
Uffz G Staudacher	1	Spad	Villers Maranery		zlg	
Ltn J Heemsoth	B	Breguet	Chezy-Chevillon		1	g.
Fldw Schmückle	21	Brequet			–	g.
Vfw A Hübner	36	Spad	Beaumetz		2	f.
Ltn A Benzler	60	Inf a/c	Coulommes		5	
Uffz E Bielefeld	60	Spad	by Le Ferté		2	
Ltn K Menckhoff	72	Spad			30	
Ltn K Menckhoff	72	Camel	Fôret de Laigne		31	
Ltn H v Dechend	72	Camel	Fôret de Laigne		.3	
Ltn zS G Saschenberg	MFJI	Spad	Sea off Ostende		13	
Vzflgmstr B Heinrich	MFJI	Spad	Oudekapelle		11	

a.   DH4 A7882, 25 Sqn RAF, Lt JR Zieman & 2/Lt H Tannenbaum, POWs.
b.   Nieuport 6193 '2', 94th Aero, 2Lt PW Davis, KIA.
c.   C1113, 1 Sqn RAF, Capt KS Henderson, KIA.
d.   65 Sqn RAF.
e.   D6621, 54 Sqn RAF, Lt WA Hunter, WIA.
f.   Escadrille Spa 62, Capt M Rebreget, KIA.
g.   Four Breguets were lost: Escadrille Br 108, Sgt Commandeur & Sgt Hedman, MIAs; Br 129, S.Lt Istria & Cpl Charvet, KIAs; Br 131, MdL Liger-Belair & Sgt Lehmann, MIAs; and Br 226, Cpl Poulhes & Sold Audoybaud, MIAs, plus one crew wounded, Escadrille Br 132, MdL Rivoire & Sgt Bougeard.

Losses

Gefr Adolf Schneider	1	Killed in action Reims, Allied side. Either by Sgt Putnam or Lt Madon of Spa 38.
Ltn Heidenreich	6	Taken prisoner.
Ltn Gerhard Schreiber	37	Killed in action Hesbécourt.
Ltn Johann Dunkelberg	58	Killed in action Bailleul.
Flgmt Horst Sawatzki	MFJI	Wounded Middlekerke & Nieuport at 2100 hrs in Albatros DV 4635/17.

3 June 1918

Ltn K Monnington	18	DH4	La Bassée	0925	zlg	
Ltn O Fitzner	65	Spad	S Heudicourt	1030	5	a.
Ltn M Skowronski	6	Spad	SE Neuilly	1250	2	
Obfm K Schönfelder	7	Balloon	Wattines	1630	10	b.
Ltn E Löwenhardt	10	Spad	by Dammard	1830	26	

OfStv F Kublum	26	Breguet	Armentières	1920	1	
Ltn H Kirschstein	6	Breguet	Fère en Tardenois	1930	19	c.
Ltn M-W B-Bodemer	6	Breguet	by Epaux-Bezu	1930	4	c.
Ltn H Kirschstein	6	Breguet	by Epaux-Bezu	1935	20	c.
Ltn K Bolle	B	Spad	Faubourg		13	
Ltn H Frommherz	B	Spad VII	Ancienville		3	
OfStv W Beyer	42	AR2			3	
Flgmt C Kairies	SFSII	DH4	Zuidschoote		2	d.

a.   Escadrille Spa 23, Sgt Burello, POW.
b.   French 78 Compagnie Aérostières, Lt Payen, WIA.
c.   Two Breguets were lost by Escadrille Br 127: S/Lt Xambo & Cpl Guilain, MIAs and Lt de Lille de Loture & Sgt Grisval, also MIAs.
d.   C6274, 98 Sqn RAF, Lt BA Bird, WIA/POW & Lt AR Cowan, POW.

Losses

Gefr Max Bauer	23	Wounded, in hospital until 20 June.
Obltn Josef Loeser	46	KIA N Hamel, with RE8 3 Sqn AFC.
Ltn Baum	79	Prisoner Montdidier.
Flg Sturmkeit	81	Injured in a crash.

4 June 1918

Obltn O v Boenigk	21	Balloon	Château Thierry	0830	8	a.
Ltn K Mendel	18	RE8	Canveseure	1520	7	
Ltn H Rolfes	45	Spad	Coulomb	1640	6	
OfStv W Kühne	18	Balloon	Steenbecque	1715	3	b.
Vfw R Schleichhardt	18	AWFK8	Neuf Berquin	1720	–	
Hptm W Reinhard	JGI	Spad	by Dammard	1725	18	
Ltn W v Richthofen	11	Spad 2	by Dammard	1725	1	e.
Uffz E Bielefeld	60	Inf a/c	St Imoges	1830	3	
Ltn A Benzler	60	Spad	St Imoges	1830	6	
Uffz E Bielefeld	60	Spad	St Imoges	1835	4	c.
Ltn H Drekmann	4	Spad	Longpont	1845	3	d.
Vfw E Hannenmann	39	Breguet	S Prosnes	2030	3	e.
Obltn E v Wedel	11	Spad 2	by Faverolles	2050	5	e.
Ltn K Bolle	B	Breguet	Fresnes		14	e.
Ltn Langen	39	Spad	Jonquerie		1	
Uffz E Sonneck	66	Breguet	by Château Thierry		2	e.
Ltn W Schulz	66	Spad	by Château Thierry		5	
Ltn W Preuss	66	Spad	by Château Thierry		1	

a.   French 88 Compagnie Aérostières.
b.   British Balloon 40-11-1 (SR 7).
c.   147th Aero, 2Lt EA Lawrence, KIA (also AA fire).
d.   Escadrille Spa 124, Adj Vaclav Pilat, WIA.
e.   There was only one Breguet lost this date, but there were two Sopwiths, and two Salmsons, a total of 5 French two-seaters: Escadrille Br 108, S/Lt de la Chapelle & S/Lt de Masin, MIA; Sop 279, Cpl Fenious & Cpl Barbarin, MIAs; Sop 279, Lt Vogelin & Asp Wesbecher, MIAs; Sal 106, Sgt Champagnole & S/Lt Lasvignes, KIAs, and Escadrille Sal 205, Sgt Letellier & S/Lt Nicodeua, MIAs.

Losses

Ltn Emmerich Honig	14	Killed in a crash at Phalempin airfield.
Ltn Bohnert	43	Wounded in action.

5 June 1918

Ltn J Grassmann	10	Balloon	Château Thierry	0745	1
Obltn O v Boenigk	21	Balloon	by Château Thierry	0905	9
Vfw F Nüsch	22	DH4		0905	1
Obltn H Göring	27	AR2	Villers Cotterêts	1000	19

Ltn J Jacobs	7	Camel	W Bailleul	1115	19	a.
Obfm K Schönfelder	7	Camel	by Bailleul	1115	–	
Ltn C Degelow	7	Camel	W Bailleul	1115	–	
Ltn F Friedrichs	10	Balloon	W V-Cotterêts	1120	7	
Ltn H Kirschstein	6	Spad	by Villemont	1135	21	b.
Ltn J Janzen	6	Spad	by Viercy	1140	11	
Obltn A Rostock	77	BF2b	Plainville	1145	2	
Ltn E Udet	4	Spad	S Buczany	1200	26	
OfStv W Kühne	18	SE5a	La Bassée	1210	4	c.
Ltn K Monnington	18	BF2b	N Violaines	1210	2	d.
Vfw H Juhnke	52	SE5	Vieux Berquin	1300	2	e.
Ltn M Näther	62	Balloon	Cuvilly	1445	3	
Ltn W Schulz	66	Balloon	Château Thierry	1510	6	
Ltn H Kirschstein	6	Breguet	by Ambleny	1735	22	f.
Ltn R Wenzl	6	Breguet	by Soissons	1735	3	
Ltn M Skowronski	6	Breguet	Montigny l'Engrain	1735	3	
Flgmt A Zenses	MFJ2	Camel	Pervyse	1832	1	
Vfw P Reimann	52	BF2b	E Aubers	1835	1	g.
Vfw H Juhnke	52	BF2b	Nieppe Wald	1840	3	g.
Ltn E Löwenhardt	10	Spad	by Château Thierry	1845	27	
Ltn A Heldmann	10	Spad	by Château Thierry	1845	6	
Ltn F Friedrichs	10	Balloon	W V-Cotterêts	2010	8	
Ltn H Kirschstein	6	Spad	by Chezy en Ormois	2025	23	
Ltn J Janzen	6	Spad	by La Ferté	2025	12	
Ltn Hebler	18	BF2b	Givenchy	2025	zlg	
Ltn H Dilthey	40	Balloon	Poperinghe	2050	7	h.
Ltn H Gilly	40	Balloon	Poperinghe	2055	1	i.
Hptm R Berthold	JGII	DH9	N St Juste		32	j.
Sgt M Kuhn	21	Breguet	by Nogentel		zlg	
Vfw Steinsträter	50	Spad	Celles		1	
Ltn K Menckhoff	72	Breguet	St Leger		32	
Ltn zS T Osterkamp	MFJ2	Spad	Pervyse		–	

a.   B7220, 203 Sqn RAF, FSL AN Webster, KIA.
b.   Escadrille Spa 163, Cpl Girardeau, MIA, Spad VII.
c.   C6416, 1 Sqn RAF, 2/Lt AF Scroggs, WIA.
d.   A7243, 22 Sqn RAF, Lt JE Gurdon, OK & Sgt Hall, WIA.
e.   D337, 1 Sqn RAF, Lt HS Hennessey, KIA.
f.   Escadrille Br 227, Cpl Blumenthal & Lt de Coopermann, KIAs.
g.   20 Sqn RAF lost two BF2bs this date: B1114, Lt JEW Sudgen & Sgt W O'Neill, and C817, Lt EA Magee & 2/Lt RJ Gregory, all POWs.
h.   British Balloon 2-5-2 (SR33).
i.   British Balloon 25-5-2 (SR32).
j.   D9256, 205 Sqn RAF, Lt WV Theron, OK & Sgt HF Monday, OK, FTL.

Losses

Uffz Karl Schneider	23	Wounded in action Haynecourt.
Ltn Friedrich Holthaus	48	Killed in action Moyencourt.
Vfw Paul Reimann	52	Killed in action Aubers 1850, collision with a BF2b of 20 Sqn RAF.
Ltn Fritz Ree	68	Killed in action Méry 1330 in Albatros DVa.

---

6 June 1918

The IAF was formed consisting of 55, 99, 104 (day) and 100, 216 (night) Squadrons

Ltn F Friedrichs	10	Balloon	La Fontaine-Crois	0725	9	
Ltn H Otto	10	Balloon	Villers Cotterêts	0750	1	a.
Ltn O v B-Marconnay	15	DH4	Assainvillers	1102	2	b.

Ltn E Udet	4	Spad	S Faverolles	1140	27	c.
Ltn G v Hantelmann	15	DH4	Ferrières	1140	1	b.
Ltn J v Ziegesar	15	DH4	Maguelay	1140	1	b.
Ltn E Spindler	18	SE5		1855	–	
Ltn Hebler	18	SE5		1855	–	
Ltn O v B-Marconnay	15	SE5	SW Montdidier	1950	3	d.
Ltn J Veltjens	15	SE5	SW Montdidier	1950	16	d.
OfStv J Klein	15	SE5	SW Montdidier	1950	9	d.
OfStv J Mai	5	SE5	Hébuterne		–	

a.   French 43 Compagnie Aérostières, Adj Etienbied, OK.
b.   Two Spads lost this date: Escadrille Spa 69, Sgt J Bouilliant, MIA, Spad VII, and Spa 92, Sgt L Durin, MIA, Spad XIII.
c.   27 Sqn RAF.
d.   32 Sqn RAF.

Losses

Ltn Heinrich Otto	10	Severely wounded in balloon attack 0750 at Villers Cotterêts.
Ltn Karl A Mendel	18	Killed in action Estaires 1140, SE5s.
Ltn Hans Schultz	18	Taken prisoner N Hazebrouck 1850 in Fokker DVII 2455/18, combat with SE5s.
Ltn Fritz Kieckhäfner	29	Died of wounds received on 4 May Gondecourt, near Lille.
Vfw Otto Heller	40	Killed in action Warneton 0845 with SE5s.
Ltn Karl Becker	61	Killed in action Fretoy with Spads.

7 June 1918

Ltn J Janzen	6	Spad	E V-Cotterêts	0705	13	
Ltn H Kirschstein	6	Spad	by Montgobert	0710	24	
Ltn H Kroll	24	Spad	Fôret de Laigne	0825	25	
Vfw Ehrhardt	32	DH4	Abscon	1120	2	a.
Uffz T Weischer	15	2 Seater	N Compiègne	1200	–	
Ltn J Veltjens	15	DH9	S Noyon	1200	17	b.
Ltn O v B-Marconnay	15	DH4	S Noyon	1200	4	b.
Ltn zS T Osterkamp	MFJ2	Camel	Ramskapelle	1310	12	
Oblt O v Boenigk	21	Balloon	Château Thierry	1435	10	e.
Ltn H Böhning	79	Balloon	Machemont	1830	11	e.
Ltn E Udet	4	Spad	E V-Cotterêts	1900	28	
Vfw K Schmelcher	71	Balloon	Struth-St Ulrich	1900	2	c.
Vfw F Rumey	5	SE5	N Rosières		23	d.
Ltn A Rahn	19	SE5	Rosières		–	
Ltn U Fischer	22	Spad	Estrées, St Denis		3	
Ltn A Lenz	22	DH	Méry		3	b.
Ltn E Raabe	41	Balloon	Villers Cotterêts		3	e.
Ltn H Brüning	50	Balloon	Château Thierry		1	e.
Ltn M Näther	62	Balloon	Montigny		4	e.
Vfw F Jacobsen	73	Breguet	Beine		5	
Oblt T Cammann	74	Breguet	Prosner		8	
Ltn R Otto	74	Breguet	Villers Marmery		2	
OfStv W Hippert	74	AR2	Beaumont sur Vesle		7	
Ltn M Schick	76	Spad	Millencourt		1	
Ltn H Knappe	81	Balloon	Fleury la Rivière		3	e.

a.   D9266, 25 Sqn RAF, Lt LA Hacklett & Sgt WC Elliott, POWs.
b.   49 Sqn RAF.
c.   French 84 Compagnie Aérostièrs, Lt Ternynck, OK.
d.   B611, 24 Sqn RAF, 2/Lt JJ Dawe, KIA.

e.   There were four other French balloons lost on the Asine Front.

Losses

Vfw Maschinsky	19	Taken prisoner.
Ltn Heinrich Kütt	23	Severely wounded in action Douai, died of wounds 9 June, at Phalempin.
Ltn Hans Friedrich	34	Injured in a crash Foucaucourt airfield.
Flg Wilhelm Schade	41	Taken prisoner. Possibly by S/Lt Leroy de Boiseamarie of Spa 78 in collaboration with ground fire.
Oblt Maximilian Edler von Daniels	61	KIA, Avricourt, Mesnil St Georges.
Ltn Josef Weckerle	79	Taken prisoner N Bois de Cossu.

8 June 1918

Ltn F Friedrichs	10	Balloon	Villers Cotterêts	0710	10	a.
Ltn Feuereissen	51	DH4	W Kruisstraat	1830	2	b.
Vfw O Rosenfeld	41	Spad			10	

a.   French 73 Compagnie Aérostières, Lt Andrieux, OK.
b.   25 Sqn RAF, 2/Lt WH Dixon WIA?

Losses

Uffz Friedrich Heckel	16	Wounded in action Houthulst Forest.
Gefr Leonhard Horn	16	Wounded in action Houthulst Forest.
Ltn Wilhelm Erlewein	47	KIA, Suzanne, Bray sur Somme.
Ltn Rüdiger Frhr vonKünsberg	55	Killed in action 0800, Tulkern.

9 June 1918   Battle of the Matz Begins (code name unknown)

Vfw F Poeschke	53	BF2b	Orval	0750	1	
Ltn H v Freden	1	Spad	Cernay-Reims	0815	4	
Ltn H Helten	20	Camel	S Ploegsteert	0835	2	
Obltn H Göring	27	Spad	Bois de Faverolles	0845	20	a.
Ltn W Steinhäuser	11	Spad	by Cravancon	0900	9	
Obltn E v Wedel	11	Spad	by Longpont	0900	6	b.
Hptm W Reinhard	JGI	Spad	by Dormiers	0900	19	
Ltn H v d Marwitz	30	Camel	Vieux Berquin	0911	8	c.
Ltn K Katzenstein	30	Camel	La Gorgue	0920	1	d.
Ltn H Kroll	24	Spad	Moreuil by	1015	26	e.
Ltn H Kroll	24	Spad	.... by Ellincourt	1025	27	f.
Ltn J Veltjens	15	AR2	S Méry	1215	18	
Ltn W Steinhäuser	11	Spad	by St Baudry	1220	10	
Ltn W v Richthofen	11	Spad	by Tartures	1220	2	
Oblt W Pritsch	17	Salmson	Montigny	1320	1	
Ltn F Friedrichs	10	Breguet	by Allemont	1630	11	g.
Ltn A Delling	34	Camel	Marguéglise	2100	2	h.
Ltn K Bolle	B	Spad	Dampleux		15	
Ltn H Frommerz	B	Spad	Vauzbin		4	
Ltn E Udet	4	Spad	Compiègne		–	
Vfw R Francke	8	DH9			11	i.
Ltn E Henke	13	SE5	Magnelay-.....		1	
Uffz H Piel	13	Spad	... Thiescourt		1	
Ltn W Niethammer	13	Breguet	Ribécourt		1	g.
Vfw A Haussmann	13	Spad	Dreslincourt		7	
Ltn A Lenz	22	Camel			4	j.
Vfw W Neuenhofen	27	Spad			1	
Ltn H Knappe	81	AR2	Ville Dommange		4	

a.   Escadrille Spa 94, Brig P Chan, POW.
b.   Escadrille Spa 159, S/Lt du Tremblay, WIA, Spad XIII.
c.   B7163, 210 Sqn RAF, 2/Lt C Marsden, POW.

d.   D3348, 210 Sqn RAF, 2/Lt W Breckenridge, WIA/POW.
e.   Escadrille Spa 88, Sgt B Savot, MIA.
f.   Escadrille Spa 88, Sgt J Poullain, MIA.
g.   There were three Breguets lost this date: No.2085, Escadrille Br 45, Col Jenn & S/Lt Tisnes, POWs; Br 120, MdL Ropartz & Lt Menaud, MIAs, and Br 120, MdL Boulanger & Sgt Millioud, MIAs.
h.   B5244, 73 Sqn RAF, 2/Lt RA Baring, KIA.
i.   C6155, 103 Sqn RAF, Lt Chrispin,OK & Lt Wadsworth, OK.
j.   D1844, 43 Sqn RAF, Lt JH Johnson, POW/DOW.

Losses

Ltn Johann Janzen	6	Taken prisoner, shot off own propeller in combat with Spads,in Fokker DrI 517/17.
Gefr Preiss	14	Taken prisoner 0645 Dickebusch.
Ltn Heinrich Küffberger	23	Killed in action Phalempin.
Ltn zS Heinrich Sattler	MFJ2	Killed in action Langenhoek-Wadsland, in Albatros DVa 7265/17.
Ltn zS Weinert	MFJ2	Wounded in action.

10 June 1918

Vfw H Gockel	33	Camel	Gournay	0745	1	a.
Ltn J Jacobs	7	Camel	S Poperinghe	0845	20	b.
Vfw W Gabriel	11	Balloon		1635	4	
Ltn W Balzer	44	Spad	Ressons-sur Matz	1725	2	c.
Uffz W Kretzschmar	44	Spad	....	1730	1	c.
Ltn G v Hantelmann	15	Spad	Plessing-Brion	2010	2	c.
Ltn F Büchner	13	Spad	S Vauxaillon		3	c.
Gefr W Laabs	13	SE5	Sorel Château		1	d.

a.   D8117, 73 Sqn RAF, Lt J Balfour, OK.
b.   D1963, 73 Sqn RAF, 1/Lt BW deB Leyson USAS, POW.
c.   Three French Spads were lost this date: No.5553, Escadrille Spa 69, S/Lt Pequin, MIA; Spa 87, Adj R Legrand, WIA, Spad VII, and Spa 151, Sgt A Ambrosio, MIA, Spad VII.
d.   C9626, 32 Sqn RAF, 1Lt P Hooper USAS, KIA.

Losses

Ltn Walter Balzer	44	KIA, Ressons-sur-Matz, body not found until 2 weeks later in his smashed machine.

11 June 1918

OfStv K Thom	21	Breguet	S Crépy	0810	15	
Ltn O v B-Marconnay	15	Camel	Méry	1420	5	a.
Ltn J Veltjens	15	DH9	W Courcelles	1525	19	b.
Ltn J Veltjens	15	DH9	W Tricot	1550	20	b.
Ltn H Jeschonneck	40	RE8	Vlamertinge	1550	1	
Flg E Mix	54	AR2	Tricot	1940	1	
Ltn F Backer	3	SE5			–	
Ltn R Hildebrand	12	Camel	Montdidier		5	
Ltn F Büchner	13	Spad			4	c.
Uffz W Hertzsch	13	SE5			1	
Ltn K Hetze	13	Spad	Montener-Metz		1	d.
Uffz H Piel	13	Spad			2	c.
Hptm R Berthold	JGII	Fr Inf a/c			33	
Obltn E v Schleich	23	DH 9	Englebelmer		29	e.
Obltn E v Schleich	23	BF2b	Englebelmer		30	
Gefr W Schmelter	42	AR2	Méry		1	
Ltn K Menckhoff	72	Camel	Faverolles		33	f.
Ltn Schmid z Nedden	72	Camel	Faverolles		1	

a.   D1962, 73 Sqn RAF, Lt CWH Douglas, KIA.

b.   49 Sqn RAF.
c.   Two other French Spad VIIs were lost this date: Escadrille Spa 159, S/Lt Cramoisy, KIA, and Spa 87, Sgt
E Mieille, WIA.
d.   Escadrille Spa 94, Lt G de la Rochefordière, Spad XIII.
e.   103 Sqn RAF.
f.   B2351, 73 Sqn RAF, Lt JI Carpenter, KIA.

Losses

Gefr Kleineberg	20	Taken prisoner.
Ltn Fritz Imme	42	Killed in action Méry.
Flgmt Wilhelm Grabowski	MFJI	Lightly wounded in action.

12 June 1918

Sgt M Kuhn	21	Breguet	S Crépy	0810	zlg	
Ltn zS T Osterkamp	MFJ2	DH4	SW Pervyse	1150	13	a.
Ltn J v Ziegesar	15	Camel	Compiègne	1300	–	
Ltn R v Barnekow	20	Camel	W Meteren	1300	3	b.
Ltn J Veltjens	15	Camel	NE Compiègne	1315	21	c.
Ltn O v B-Marconnay	15	Camel	NE Compiègne	1315	6	c.
Ltn G v Hantelmann	15	Camel	NE Compiègne	1315	3	c.
Vfw H Klose	54	AR2	Antheuil	1840	1	
Ltn G v Hantelmann	15	Breguet	Méry	1900	–	
Ltn H Schäfer	15	Breguet	Méry	1900	4	
Ltn J Schäfer	16	SE5	S Bailleul	2120	1	
Ltn F Theide	24	Spad	Mechemont	2130	4	
Hptm W Reinhard	JGI	Spad 2			20	d.
Hptm R Berthold	JGII	Spad 2			34	d.
Ltn H Pippart	19	SE5	Lagny		15	e.
Ltn A Delling	34	Breguet	Cuvilly		3	
OfStv G Dörr	45	Spad VII	Haramont		4	
Ltn zS G Saschenberg	MFJI	DH4	Sea off Ostende		14	f.
Ltn zS T Osterkamp	MFJ2	Sopwith	La Pannes		zlg	
Ltn zS G Brockhoff	MFJ2	DH4	Ostdunkerke-Bad		2	

a.   98 Sqn RAF ?
b.   B5646, 4 Sqn AFC, Lt WS Martin, KIA.
c.   43 Sqn RAF.
d.   Escadrille Spa 266, Lt Charette, WIA/DOW & S/Lt Weismann, KIA.
e.   D3960, 2 Sqn AFC, Lt TJ Hammond, KIA.
f.   C6321, 218 Sqn RAF, Lt CLW Brading,OK & Sgt RS Joysey, OK.

Losses

Ltn Hugo Schulz	12	KIA, Fôret de Laigne, Plesses-Brion.
Ltn Hubert Helten	20	Killed in action Bailleul.
Ltn Fritz Loerzer	26	POW, Cutry, 7 miles SW Soissons.
Obltn Kurt Grasshoff	38	Killed in action Predejce, Macedonia.
Ltn Arond Erich	63	Killed in action Tricot 0845 Allied side.
Ltn Rudolf Croissant	68	KIA, Méry 1930, Fokker DVII 2062/18.
Ltn Ernst	69	POW near Courcelles, SE Montdidier.
Vfw Ernst Sperling	69	Killed in action Noyon.
Uffz Fritz Kühn	79	Wounded in action.
Ltn Gerhard Schulze	MFJI	Killed in action off Nieuport Mole 1840 Albatros DVa 7337/17.

13 June 1918

Ltn M-W B-Bodemer	6	Spad	Château Thierry	0630	5	
Ltn O Creutzmann	43	SE5	SW Aubers	0950	4	a.
Flg Bünning	K3	Nieuport	S Goin	1030	1	b.
Ltn H Zempel	65	DH9	Uckingen	1245	1	c.

Vfw W Gabriel	11	Spad		1605	5	d.
Ltn E Udet	4	Spad	NE Faverolles	1745	29	d.
Ltn H Drekmann	4	Spad	NE Noroy	1745	4	d.
Obltn B Loerzer	JGIII	Spad	Dommiers	1920	25	d.
Vfw C Mesch	26	Spad	Villers Cotterêts	1930	2	d.
Ltn W Lehmann	5	SE5	Bouzincourt		4	e.
Ltn W Blume	9	Breguet	St Pierre Aigle		10	f.
Vfw F Classen	26	Spad	Dommiers		–	d.
Ltn K Jacob	36	Spad	N Chavigny		2	d.
Ltn K Jacob	36	Balloon	Retheuil		3	
Vfw J Schwendemann	41	Spad	Neuve-Maison Ferme		5	d.
Vfw K Handrock	K2	DH4	Ruhr Valley, Trier		2	g.

a.   B8508, 1 Sqn RAF, Lt ETS Kelly, KIA.
b.   Nieuport 6218, 27th Aero, 2Lt WH Plyler, POW.
c.   DH4 A7466, 55 Sqn IAF, 2/Lt W Legge & 2/Lt A McKenzie, KIAs.
d.   Seven French Spads were lost this date: Spa 37, MdL Delannoy, MIA, Spa XIII; Spa 75, Cpl H Lacombe, MIA, Spad XIII; Spa 98, Sgt CF Chamberlain, an American, KIA, Spad VII; Spa 98, Cpl Chapel, MIA, Spad VII; Spa 98, Brig Aleppe, MIA, Spa VII; 3332, Spad 100, Brig M Ouizille, MIA, Spad VII and Escadre 2, Lt Friedel, MIA, Spad VII.
e.   56 Sqn RAF ?
f.   Escadrille Br 35, S/Lt Masson & S/Lt Ruf, MIAs.
g.   104 Sqn IAF, C6267, FTL – 2/Lt WJ Rivett-Carnac, WIA, & 2/AM WE Flexman, DOW.

Losses

Uffz Dannemann	56	Injured in a crash on take-off.
Uffz Rudolf Kassner	65	KIA, Amanweiler, combat with DH4.
Ltn Kurt von Seelen	K3	Slightly wounded in action.

14 June 1918

OfStv K Thom	21	Spad	N Villers Cotterêts	0845	16	a.
Ltn H Kirschstein	6	Balloon	Villers Cotterêts	0900	25	
Ltn H Kirschstein	6	Spad	Villers Cotterêts	0915	26	
Obltn O v Boenigk	21	Spad	N Villers Cotterêts	1755	11	
Ltn B v Alvensleben	21	Balloon	Crépy-en-Valois	1800	1	b.
Ltn E Udet	4	Spad	N St Pierre Aigle	2000	30	
Ltn W Schwartz	13	Camel	Dreslincourt	2000	6	c.
Ltn U Neckel	13	Camel	Dreslincourt	2010	11	c.
Ltn U Neckel	13	Camel	Dreslincourt	2015	12	c.
Ltn K Bolle	B	Breguet	Laversine		16	
Sgt K Schlegel	45	Balloon	Villers Cotterêts		1	
Ltn F Anders	73	Spad	Tinqueux		2	

a.   Escadrille Spa 163, S/Lt M Majon de la Debuterie, POW, Spad XIII.
b.   French 29 Compagnie Aérostières, S/Lt R Carré, OK.
c.   80 Sqn RAF lost two Camels this date: D6420, 2/Lt AR Melbourne, KIA and D6597, Lt PR Beare, WIA.

Losses

Vfw Josef Degen	6	Taken prisoner; left AFP Valenciennes at 1100 and lost his way.
Ltn Busso von Alvensleben	21	Wounded in action in balloon attack and taken prisoner at Crépy-en-Valois; DOW 15 June at Villers Cotterêts.

15 June 1918

Ltn R v Barnekow	20	SE5	E Ypres	0910	4	
Ltn K Menckhoff	72	Spad	Rethondes	1800	34	a.
Ltn F Thiede	24	Spad	by le Fretoy	2130	5	
Vfw W Neuenhofen	27	Spad			2	

a.   Escadrille Spa 94, Cpl JM Martre, MIA, Spad VII.

Losses

Ltn Wilhelm Schwartz	13	Severely wounded in action during balloon attack.

16 June 1918

OfStv P Aue	10	Balloon	Villers Cotterêts	0645	7	a.
Ltn F Friedrichs	10	Balloon	Vendresse	0700	12	
Ltn H Viebig	57	BF2b	Popincourt	0900	5	b.
Ltn M Dehmisch	58	Balloon	Houdencourt	0900	1	
Ltn Seewald	54	SE5	Villers Bretonneux	0905	1	
Ltn M Näther	62	Balloon	Amienois	0953	3	
Vfw W Gabriel	11	Balloon		1000	6	
Ltn H Schäfer	15	DH9	Breches	1150	5	c.
Uffz T Weischer	15	DH4	Grivesnes	1150	1	c.
Ltn J Veltjens	15	DH4	Erches	1200	22	c.
OfStv J Klein	15	DH9	Grivesnes	1200	10	c.
Ltn O v B-Marconnay	15	DH9	Roye	1200	7	c.
Ltn U Neckel	13	Camel		1955	13	d.
Vfw G Schalk	34	Camel	Proyart	2100	2	e.
Uffz H Preiss	54	DH4	Villers Bretonneux	2105	1	
Ltn J Heemsoth	B	DH9	S Roye		2	f.
Ltn W Suer	B	DH9	S Roye		1	f.
Ltn K Bolle	B	DH9	by Bus		17	f.
Obfm K Schönfelder	7	Balloon	NW Bethuen		11	g.
Ltn W Nebgen	7	SE5	Brielen-Ypres Rd		–	
Obfm K Schönfelder	7	SE5	Ypres		–	
Vfw O Rosenfeld	41	Caudron			11	h.
Ltn Vogt	54	SE5	Römerstrasse		1	
Uffz E Sonneck	66	Balloon	Villers Cotterêts		3	i.
Vfw W Peters	66	Balloon	Villers Cotterêts		2	i.

a.   French 83 Compagnie Aérostières.
b.   C788, 62 Sqn RAF, Lt JM Goller & 2/Lt M Ross-Jenkins,KIAs.
c.   25 Sqn and 103 Sqn RAF.
d.   B2524, 80 Sqn RAF, 2/Lt GH Glasspoole, POW.
e.   B7347, 65 Sqn RAF, Lt JA Sykes, KIA.
f.   27 Sqn RAF.
g.   British Balloon 47-11-1 (SB 264).
h.   Possibly Escadrille C 227, S/Lt Allaert, S/Lt Laurier, & MdL Buisson, this R11 was listed as being involved in an accident, crew killed. It could have been caused by combat damage – only Caudron lost.
i.   One of these was French 76 Compagnie Aérostières.

Losses

Ltn Johannes Lieberg	35	Lightly injured in crash, remained with unit.
Vfw Willy Peters	66	Taken prisoner SW Taissy after combat with Capt Lahoulle & S/Lt Henot of Spa 154.
Ltn Hansjorg v Dechend	72	Killed in action Moulin-sous-Touvent 1100.
Ltn Langenbach	81	Taken prisoner Mont St Quentin.
Gefr Flach	81	Taken prisoner.
Ltn Herbert Knappe	81	Forced to land inside own lines, OK.

17 June 1918

Ltn M Hillmann	7	Camel	Dickebusch Lake	0800	1	a.
Uffz A Eigenbrodt	7	Camel	Dickebusch Lake	0800	2	a.
Obltn H Göring	27	Spad	Longpont, Ambleny	0830	21	b.
Ltn R Klimke	27	Spad	Longpont, Ambleny	0830	9	c.

Ltn F Brandt	26	Spad	Longpont	0830	5	d.
Uffz M Mertens	7	Dolphin	S Dickebusch Lake	1015	–	e.
Ltn J Werner	14	Dolphin	Loos	1015	7	e.
Flg A Rüdiger	59	DH9	Quéant	1025	1	f.
Obltn F Krafft	59	DH4	Bapaume	1030	1	f.
Ltn A Delling	34	SE5	SE Villers Bret.	1100	4	g.
Vfw E Schäpe	33	Balloon	Maignelay	1130	3	h.
Ltn G Meyer	37	Balloon	Allonville	1500	6	i.
Ltn zS P Achilles	SFS2	DH4	Walchern	1630	1	j.
Ltn U Neckel	13	Spad			14	
Ltn W Leusch	19	Spad	W Roye		2	k.
Ltn R Rienau	19	Spad	W Roye		2	
Vfw J Schwendemann	41	Spad			6	

a.   210 Sqn RAF.
b.   Spa 93, Adj B Breton, POW, Spad VII, escaped in Oct 1918.
c.   Spa 93, MdL G Franceschi, POW, Spad VII, escaped in Oct 1918.
d.   Escadrille Spa 162, MdL L Dol, MIA, Spad XIII.
e.   19 Sqn RAF.
f.   B9332 98 Sqn RAF, 2/Lt WJT Atkins,POW & Sgt JH Read, WIA/POW.
f.   D1694, 98 Sqn, Lt DA Macartney, KIA & 2/Lt JR Jackmann, POW/DOW.
g.   D3955, 41 Sqn RAF, Lt JS Turnbull, KIA.
h.   MdL Grisset, OK.
i.   British Balloon 29-13-5 (SR 9).
j.   A7935, 217 Sqn RAF, Lt GB Coward & Lt JF Reid, both Interned.
k.   Escadrille Spa 3, Sgt FL Baylies, MM,CdeG; KIA.

Losses

Ltn Kurt Wüsthoff	JGII	Severely wounded and taken prisoner Cachy in action with 24 Sqn, in Gontermann's Fokker DVII 2469/18.
Ltn Hugo Schäfer	15	Shot down by SE5s, OK.
Uffz Kurt Meinel	22	Collision over Thiesecourt and killed.
Flg Fritz Moser	22	Collision over Thiesecourt and killed.
Obltn Maximilian von Förster	27	Killed in a crash at Mont de Soissons Ferme airfield, in a two-seater.
Vfw Wilhelm Schäffer	27	Also killed in the above crash.
Ltn Hans Georg von der Marwitz	30	Wounded in action.
Gefr Jakob Tischner	35	Landing a Roland DVIb, crashed into Pfalz DIIIa 8132/17and smashed both a/c, OK.
Sgt Johann Braun	69	Killed in a collision with Gefr Stehling Assainvillers. Stehling was unhurt.

18 June 1918

Obfm K Schönfelder	7	Camel	Ypres-Comines	0845	12	
Ltn R Heins	56	Camel	Dickebusch Lake	0915	4	
Uffz M Mertens	7	Camel	S Dickebusch Lake	0920	2	
Ltn C Degelow	40	SE5	Vieux Berquin	0930	5	a.
Ltn W Nebgen	7	Camel	Ypres-Lys	1000	1	
Ltn B Lauscher	31	AR2	Hochberg	1020	1	
OfStv K Thom	21	Spad	Villers Cotterêts	1045	17	b.
Obltn R v Greim	34	AWFK8	E Vaux-sur-Somme	1100	15	
Vfw J Pütz	34	SE5	Hamelet, Hamel	1105	5	c.
Ltn G v Hantelmann	15	Spad	S Ressons-s-Matz	1135	5	d.
Hptm R Berthold	JGII	SE5	SE Abancourt	1150	35	e.
Hptm R Berthold	JGII	SE5	SE Abancourt	1155	36	e.
Ltn O v B-Marconnay	15	SE5	SE Abancourt	1155	8	e.
Ltn M Dehmisch	58	Balloon	Chevières	1450	2	f.

Obltn H Kohze	3	BF2b	Bray sur Somme	–	g.
Ltn M Dehmisch	58	Balloon	Rethondes	3	

a.   C8870, 29 Sqn RAF, Lt RG Pierce, OK.
b.   Escadrille Spa 100, Sgt Mallet, KIA, Spad VII.
c.   C1883, 85 Sqn RAF, 1/Lt John M Grider, KIA.
d.   Escadrille Spa 100, MdL Rouxel, MIA, Spad XIII.
e.   84 Sqn RAF.
f.   French 56 Compagnie Aérostières, Sgt-Major Boom, OK.
g.   22 Sqn RAF ?

Losses

Ltn Max Hillmann	7	Killed in crash Ste Marguerite a/f 0845.
Gefr Gustav Reuter	20	Killed in a crash Menin airfield.
Vfw Erich Dürre	38	Killed in action Stojakowo, Macedonia.
Ltn Rudolf Heins	56	Severely wounded in action.
Uffz Köhler	56	Severely wounded in action.
Obltn Erwin Wenig	80	Slightly wounded, remained with unit.

19 June 1918

Uffz M Mertens	7	Balloon	Poperinghe	1900	3	
Uffz M Mertens	7	Balloon	Bailleul	1905	–	
Ltn J Jacobs	7	DH4	E Zwartelen	2025	21	a.

a.   RE8 21 Sqn RAF.

Losses

Uffz Max Mertens	7	Killed in action Bailleul, Nieppe Forest, during a balloon attack.

20 June 1918

Ltn E Thuy	28	Camel	W Cérisy	1850	22	a.
Ltn K Christ	28	Sopwith	Ablaincourt	1900	2	a.
Ltn P Wenzel	6	Breguet	N La Ferté Milon	1910	5	
Ltn H Böhning	79	AR2	Autheuil	1915	12	
Vfw G Fieseler	25	Spad	NE Orahovo		4	b.
Ltn G Rose	25	Spad	Kanista, S Trojaci		3	c.
Vfw G Fieseler	25	Spad	Dunse		–	
Vfw R Treptow	25	Spad	Makova		–	
Ltn H Rolfes	45	Salmson	Chezy-sur-Marne		7	

a.   209 Sqn RAF.
b.   Serbian Escadrille 503.
c.   5790, Serbian Escadrille 503, 2/Lt B Sauné, KIA.

Losses

Obltn Bruno Loerzer	JG3	Lightly wounded, remained with unit.
Ltn Paul Piepiorka	71	Killed in action Sierenz.
Vfw Ludwig Bergmann	79	Killed in action Autheuil 1912 by an AR2, but more likely to have been by Asp Bos & Cpl Digeon of Sop 270; only French claim this date.

21 June 1918

Obfm K Schönfelder	7	Camel	Menin	1445	13	a.
Ltn R Maier	30	Balloon	Aix Noulette	1630	1	b.
Obltn H-E Gandert	51	Camel	Gapaard	1815	5	c.

a.   B7227, 210 Sqn RAF, 2/Lt RG Carr, POW, escaped 1 July 1918.
b.   British Balloon 21-31-1 (SR 226s).
c.   B6326, 54 Sqn RAF, Lt WK Wilson, POW.

Losses

Ltn Otto Maashoff	K2	Wounded in action.

22 June 1918

Ltn E Löwenhardt	10	Breguet	Beauvardes	2045	28	a.
Vfw A Auersbach	67	Balloon	Montzéville		2	

a.   Escadrille Br 11, Adj Vaillat & S/Lt Lemoine, MIAs.
Losses – Nil

23 June 1918

Ltn A Benzler	60	Spad	Champ Fleury	0845	7	
Ltn A Heldmann	10	Spad	Epaux	0945	7	a.
Vfw F Schumacher	10	Spad	Fossoy	0945	1	a.
Ltn F Friedrichs	10	Spad	W Fossoy	0945	13	a.
Ltn E Udet	4	Breguet	La Ferté Milon	1210	31	b.
Ltn A Delling	34	DH9	Nr Morlancourt	1830	5	c.
Ltn E Udet	4	Breguet	Crouy	2015	32	
Ltn B Linke-Schluckbier	9	Spad			1	
Ltn W Müller	60	Spad	Courmont		2	

a.   One of these was No.7231, Escadrille Spa 62, Sgt A Voisin, MIA.
b.   Escadrille Br 216, Lt Tournade & Soldat Pic, KIAs.
c.   A7742, 57 Sqn RAF, Lt CW Peckham, POW & 2/Lt AJ Cobbin, DOW.
Losses

Uffz Ernst Bielefeld	60	Killed in action Reims French side of lines. *
Ltn Max Schick	76	Taken prisoner 2015 Albatros DVa 5765/17.

* If the date is correct he was probably claimed by Adj Gasser of Spa 87, a Fokker DVII SW of Reims, BUT on the 24th it seems Bielefeld was a passenger in a Rumpler shot down by Spa 57. It is confirmed the passenger was from Jasta 60 although his name is not recorded.

24 June 1918

Ltn P Strähle	57	DH9	E Montdidier	0730	11	a.
Ltn P Billik	52	BF2b	S Merignies	0820	20	b.
Ltn K Jacob	36	Spad	S Château Thierry	0925	4	
Ltn H Kirschstein	6	Breguet	Oulchy le Château	0945	27	c.
Ltn E Udet	4	Breguet	SE Montigny	1000	33	c.
Ltn W Oberstadt	56	Camel	Poperinghe	1030	1	d.
Ltn K Bolle	B	Breguet	Saponay		18	

a.   D1012, 206 Sqn RAF, Lt WC Cutmore & 2/Lt WG Duncan, KIAs.
b.   D8028, 62 Sqn RAF, Lt F Williams, KIA & 2/Lt E Dumville, KIA.
c.   Two Breguets were lost this date: Escadrille Br 107, S/Lt Triollet & Sgt Boyreau, MIAs and Br 128, Sgt Cachard, MIA & Sgt Morle, WIA.
d.   D3367, 210 Sqn RAF, Lt GA Learn, KIA.
Losses – Nil

25 June 1918

Flgmstr Wagner	MFJ1	DH4	Sea off Ostende	1215	2	a.
Ltn zS R Schultze	MFJ2	Spad	Sea off Wenanger	1215	2	
Ltn U Neckel	13	BF2b	S Albert	1240	15	b.
Ltn K Hetze	13	BF2b	S Albert	1250	2	b.
Uffz W Hertzsch	13	BF2b	S Albert	1250	–	b.
Gefr J Diebold	71	Balloon	St Ulrich	1620	1	c.
Vfw K Beinecke	51	Balloon	NW Poperinghe	1650	1	
Ltn P Billik	52	SE5	Vieux-Berquin	1826	21	d.
Ltn E Udet	4	Spad	NE Longpont	1845	34	e.
Ltn E Udet	4	Spad	Chavigny-Ferme	1845	35	f.
Ltn J Veltjens	15	Breguet	Roye	1850	23	g.

Ltn G v Hantelmann	15	Breguet	Roye	1855	5	g.
Ltn H Borck	15	Breguet	Rony le Grand	1900	1	g.
Ltn U Neckel	13	Camel	S Albert	2000	16	h.
Ltn C Degelow	40	Camel	Zandvoorde	2025	6	i.
Ltn W Oberstadt	56	Camel	Zandvoorde	2030	2	j.
Ltn F Friedrichs	10	Balloon	Roches Wald	2040	14	k.
Vfw F Rumey	5	SE5	near Roye		24	l.
Ltn K Jacob	36	Spad	S Mortefontaine		–	
Vfw G Dobberke	60	Spad			2	
Ltn A Laumann	66	Spad			2	
Ltn A Laumann	66	Spad			3	
Vfw Gondermann	66	Spad	nr Dormans		3	m.
Sgt W Rössel	K1b	DH9	Karlsruhe		1	n.
OfStv G Vothknecht	K2	DH4			3	o.
Vfw Heidfeld	K5	DH4	Offenberg		1	p.

a.   C2176, 211 Sqn RAF, 2/Lt F Daltrey, WIA/POW & A/G R Shepherd, KIA.
b.   48 Sqn RAF lost three a/c: C789, 2/Lt F Cabburn & Sgt WE Lawder, KIAs; C983, 2/Lt N Roberts, OK & 2/Lt CC Walmsley, OK, and C4719, 2/Lt NH Muirden, WIA/POW & 2/Lt E Roberts, POW.
c.   French 84 Compagnie Aérostières.
d.   C1102, 1 Sqn RAF, 1/Lt HB Bradley, KIA.
e.   Escadrille Spa 96, Sgt V Booth, an American, DOW, Spad XIII.
f.   Escadrille Spa 96, Cpl Aury, WIA, Spad VII.
g.   1655, Escadrille Br 134, Brig Adam & Asp Desages, MIAs and also Br 134 had two gunners and one observer wounded; Br 131 had one pilot and one gunner WIA; All probably involved in this combat.
h.   B7278, 201 Sqn RAF, Lt LE Nightingale, KIA.
i.   C8238, 54 Sqn RAF, Lt OJF Jones-Lloyd, POW.
j.   B7164, 54 Sqn RAF, Lt WH Stubbs, POW/DOW.
k.   French 55 Compagnie Aérostières.
l.   C1800, 24 Sqn RAF, Lt EB Wilson, WIA.
m.   2330, Escadrille Spa 57, Adj-Chef PP Galgani, WIA, Spad VII.
n.   C2170, 104 Sqn IAF, Lt SCM Pontin & 2/Lt J Arnold, POWs.
o.   B7866, 55 Sqn IAF, 2/Lt GA Sweet & 2/Lt CRF Goodyear, KIAs.
p.   D5570, 99 Sqn IAF, Lt NS Harper & 2/Lt DG Benson, KIAs.

Losses

Uffz Walter Hertzsch	13	Wounded in action S Albert 1145, crash landed Jasta 28's airfield, died next day.
Ltn Fritz Hilberger	13	Killed in action Chaulnes.
Uffz Peter Albin	14	Killed in a crash Phalempin airfield.
Ltn Alfred Rothe	27	Killed in a crash Mont de Soissons Ferme airfield during a practice flight.
Ltn Wilhelm Schulz	66	Killed in action over Dormans by Spads, probably by S/Lts Nuville & Hasdenteufeul of Spa 57.

26 June 1918

Obltn H Schlieter	70	DH4	Schirmeck	1305	2	a.
Ltn J Jacobs	7	Camel	Menin	2015	22	b.
Ltn F Rumey	5	Camel	Bouzincourt	2020	26	c.
Vfw F Schumacher	10	Balloon	S La Ferté Milon	2025	2	d.
Vfw J Schwendemann	41	Spad	La Charmel		7	e.
Ltn W Rosenstein	K1b	DH4	Kefferdingen W Hagenau		3	f.

a.   C6256, 104 Sqn IAF, 2/Lt CG Jenyns, WIA/POW & 2/Lt HC Davis, KIA.
b.   D9614, 210 Sqn RAF, 2/Lt CD Boothman, POW/DOW.
c.   D6630, 65 Sqn RAF, Lt EC Eaton, KIA.
d.   French 59 Compagnie Aérostières, MdL Wissemberger, OK.
e.   1535, Escadrille Spa 154, S/Lt H de Mirman, MIA, Spad XIII.
f.   A8073, 55 Sqn IAF, 2/Lt FFH Byran & Sgt A Boocock, POWs.

Losses

Ltn Wilhelm Lehmann	5	Killed in action Albert.
Obfm Kurt Schönfelder	7	KIA, Bousbecque, combat with Camel.
Ltn Werner Steinhäuser	11	Killed in action Neuilly 0800.
Ltn Hans-Rudolf v Decker	20	Lightly wounded, remained with unit.
Uffz Georg Zillig	79	Severely injured in a crash Ercheu, DOW 28 June.

27 June 1918

Ltn F Friedrichs	10	Spad	La Ferté Milon	0900	15	
Ltn E Löwenhardt	10	Spad	Dommières	0915	29	
Ltn H Gilly	40	Dolphin	Armentières	0930	2	a.
Vfw Rausch	40	Camel	Bailleul	0935	2	b.
Ltn C Degelow	40	SE5	La Creue, Merris	0940	7	c.
Ltn A v Brandenstein	49	BF2b/RE8	Méricourt	0950	3	d.
Ltn M Näther	62	Balloon	Ailly	0951	6	
Vfw E Busch	62	Balloon	Amienois	0953	1	
Ltn R Schwarz	52	Camel	NE Herlies	1030	1	
Gefr Kämmer	49	Salmson	Framerville	1050	1	e.
Ltn F-K Weber	29	Camel	Hantay	1110	1	
Vfw H Kiep	43	SE5	SE Bethune	1115	–	
Ltn J Raesch	43	SE5	NE Hantay	1115	1	
Ltn J Schulte	14	Camel	Rouge Croix	1120	1	
Ltn A Burhard	29	BF2b	E Pacaut Wald	1140	–	
OfStv K Thom	21	Spad	Crezancy	1202	18	f.
Ltn F Friedrichs	10	Spad	Neuilly	1300	16	
Sgt M Kuhn	21	Spad	Zussiares	1300	1	
Vfw H Juhnke	52	DH4	Vaches Wald	1405	4	g.
Vfw Stadly	62	Balloon	Montiers	1516	1	
Ltn H Müller	18	DH9	W Diedenhofen	1725	6	h.
Vfw A Haussmann	13	BF2b	Villers Bretonneux	1900	8	i.
Uffz J Fritzsche	13	BF2b	Villers Bretonneux	1900	–	i.
Ltn U Neckel	13	BF2b	Villers Bretonneux	1905	17	i.
Hptm R Berthold	JGII	BF2b	Villers Bretonneux	1905	37	i.
Ltn U Neckel	13	SE5	Villers Bretonneux	1910	18	
Uffz Haar	68	Balloon	Estrées St Denis	1915	1	
Vfw K Ungewitter	24	Balloon	St Juste	1940	3	
Ltn H Drekmann	4	Balloon	Villers Cotterêts	2000	5	j.
OfStv J Mai	5	Camel	Thiépval	2133	15	k.
Ltn F Rumey	5	Dolphin	Bray-sur-Somme	2133	26	k.
Ltn F Rumey	5	Camel	Thiépval	2133	27	k.
Uffz W Höhne	61	Balloon			1	
Flgmt Kutschke	SFS2	DH4			1	
Ltn zS T Osterkamp	MFJ2	Camel	Sea off Wenduyne		14	l.
Flgmt A Zenses	MFJ2	DH9	Sea off Zeebrugge		2	m.
Flgmt H Bossler	MFJ2	DH4	Sea off Wenduyne		2	n.
Flgmt Strucke	MFJ2	Camel	near Wenduyne		zlg	
Flgmt A Zenses	MFJ2	Camel	near Wenduyne		3	l.

a.   C3816, 79 Sqn RAF, Lt LR Lang, OK.
b.   Dolphin C3806, 79 Sqn RAF, Capt WA Forsyth, POW/DOW.
c.   C9573, 29 Sqn RAF, Lt FR Brand, KIA.
d.   RE8 A3661, 3 Sqn AFC, Lt PH Kerr, WIA & Lt AO'C Brook, KIA.
e.   Two Salmsons were lost: 270 Escadrille Sal 10, Brig Devenoux & Brig Juin, and Sal 28, S/Lt Douladoure & S/Lt Marchand, all MIA.
f.   Escadrille Spa 88, S/Lt J Vidal, KIA, Spad XIII.

g.   D1669, 99 Sqn IAF, Lt EA Chapin, KIA & 2/Lt TH Wiggins, KIA.
h.   A7670, 25 Sqn RAF, Lt J Webster, POW & 2/Lt GM Gray, POW.
i.   48 Sqn RAF lost two Bristol Fighters: C877, 1/Lt JM Goad & Sgt C Norton, and C935, Lt EA Foord &
Sgt L James, all KIA.
j.   French 83 Compagnie Aérostières.
k.   70 Sqn RAF Camels.
l.   213 Sqn RAF.
m.   D5687, 218 Sqn RAF, Lt C Briggs & 2/Lt HWH Warner, KIAs.
n.   202 Sqn RAF.

Losses

Uffz Johann Meeder	23	Wounded in action Roland DVIb.
Ltn Josef Müller	29	Killed in action Billy SE La Bassée 1135.
Gefr Eduard Hellwig	40	Badly wounded Ploegsteert, DOW 1 July.
Vfw Helmut Steinbrecher	46	Shot down in flames NW Albert 2100 during combat with Camels and SE5s, parachuted from Albatros DV, safely and returned to unit.
Vfw Otto Wieprich	57	Shot down by Camels near Albert OK.
Vfw Stadly	62	POW, Montier-Compiègne, during balloon attack.

28 June 1918

Ltn zS R Poss	SFSII	DH4	Sea off Westende	0700	4	a.
Obltn O v Boenigk	21	Spad	Missy-aux-Bois	0710	12	b.
Ltn E Löwenhardt	10	Spad	Billy	0820	30	b.
Ltn F Friedrichs	10	Spad	Longpont	0830	17	b.
Ltn E Mohnicke	11	Spad		0900	8	c.
Ltn E Mohnicke	11	Spad		0905	9	c.
Ltn E Thuy	28	Sopwith	Morcourt	0905	23	
Uffz E Engler	62	Balloon	Rocquencourt	0912	1	d.
Ltn M Näther	62	Balloon	Mesnil	0915	7	e.
Ltn H Maushake	4	Spad	E Viercy	0945	1	c.
Ltn H Drekmann	4	Spad	Puissieux	0945	6	b.
Ltn K Meyer	4	Spad	Villers Cotterêts	0950	2	b.
Ltn F Ray	49	BF2b	Albert	1015	13	
Vfw F Hemer	6	Spad 2	Sailly-la-Potterie	1230	11	
Ltn E Löwenhardt	10	Spad XI	N Dampleux	1230	31	
Ltn zS T Osterkamp	MFJ2	DH4/BF2b	S Blankartsee	2055	15	f.
Ltn F Büchner	13	SE5		2100	5	g.
Ltn K Bolle	B	Spad	Longpont		19	b.
Ltn W Blume	9	Spad			11	b.
OfStv K Thom	21	Spad	Bois de Mandry		19	b.
Vfw O Rosenfeld	41	Spad			12	b.
OfStv G Dörr	45	Spad XIII	Villers Cotterêts		5	b.
OfStv G Dörr	45	Spad VII	Villers Cotterêts		6	b.
Ltn H Brünig	50	Spad	Dommiers		2	b.
Ltn W Kohlbach	50	Spad	Longpont		1	b.
Ltn L Schütt	66	Spad			1	b.
Ltn A Laumann	66	Spad			4	b.
Ltn A Hellwig	77	BF2b			2	
Vfw A Nagler	81	Spad	Bapaume		3	b.
Vfw H Horst	81	Spad	Courmes		3	b.
Flgmt A Zenses	MFJ2	Camel/F2b	SW Blankartsee		4	

a.   A8023, 217 Sqn RAF, Lt AE Bingham & 2/Lt LJ Smith, POWs.
b.   In addition to (c.) the following French Spads were lost this date:Spa 48, Adj R Montrion, KIA during
balloon attack near Villers-Hellon, Spad VII; Spa 88, Cpl G Joblot, POW, Spad XIII; Spa 88, Capt M Doumer,
KIA, Spad XIII; Spa 162, Adj C Schlumberger, MIA, Spad XIII; Spa 82, Sgt M Ventre, WIA, Spad XIII,
remained with unit, and Spa 159, MdL F Divoy, DOW, Spad VII.

c.   Spa 159 lost three Spads; Lt M Patret, Spad VII; Sgt Lafarge, Spad XIII and Cpl Javet, Spad XIII – all MIA.
d.   French 63 Compagnie Aérostières, Adj Auclerc & S/Lt Guibillon, WIAs.
e.   French 51 Compagnie Aérostières, S/Lt Mauret, OK.
f.   C4880, 88 Sqn RAF, 2/Lt JP West & A/Gnr AJ Loton, KIAs.
g.   D6086, 56 Sqn RAF, Lt H Austin, WIA/POW.

Losses

Flg Hugo Jauch	47	Killed in a crash Epénancourt-sur-Somme.
Vfw Ernst Busch	62	KIA Montdidier during balloon attack.
Obltn Hasso von Wedel	75	Lightly wounded in action.

Note: In the VI Armee Compt-Rendu it states that a Ltn Siegfried of Jasta 37 in an Albatros DV came down in French lines and made PoW. No claim and no other record of this German pilot appears anywhere.

29 June 1918

Ltn W Oberstadt	56	SE5	Poperinghe	1045	3	
Ltn A Fleischer	17	Spad	Nr Soissons	1845	1	a.
Gefr A Wadowski	52	Camel	SE La Bassée	2010	1	
Ltn H Kroll	24	RE8	W Villers-	2125	28	b.
Ltn H Kroll	24	SE5	.... Bretonneux	2135	29	
Vfw M Kahlow	34	Camel	W Caix		6	c.
Vfw J Schwendemann	41	Spad	near Rosnay		8	d.
Vfw A Nagler	81	Spad	S Bapaume		4	d.
Flgmt C Kähler	SFS2	DH4	St Andre, Varssenaere		1	e.
Ltn zS T Lodemann	SFS2	DH4			3	
Flgmstr Wagner	MFJI	Sopwith	Leke		3	
Ltn H Wessels	MFJI	Camel	Nieuport		3	
Ltn T Osterkamp	MFJ2	BF2b	Pervyse		16	f.
Flgmt A Zenses	MFJ2	BF2b	SE Dixmuiden		5	f.
Flgmt Kulbe	MFJ2	Balloon	6 km W Oostkerke		3	

a.   Escadrille Spa 103, Cpl J Mandray, KIA, Spad VII.
b.   D4834, 53 Sqn RAF, 2/Lt JN Gatecliff & 2/Lt J Harrison, KIAs.
c.   B7829, 65 Sqn RAF, Lt RP Whyte, POW.
d.   Escadrille Spa 68, MdL J Planiol, MIA, Spad VII.
e.   217 Sqn RAF ?
f.   88 Sqn RAF lost two Bristol Fighters: C983, Capt KR Simpson,OK & Sgt C Hill, OK, FTL. and D8022, 2/Lt RJ Cullen, WIA & 2/Lt EH Ward, OK, FTL.

Losses

Uffz Heinrich Piel	13	KIA, Amiens, in combat with Spads.
Ltn Heinrich Seywald	23	Wounded in action.
Uffz Heinrich Reckendress	56	Killed in action Steenwerk 2020.
Gefr Friedrich Bär	81	Killed in action Reims

30 June 1918

Vfw W Gabriel	11	Dolphin		0930	7	a.
Ltn F Friedrichs	10	Balloon	Fleury	1040	18	b.
Ltn J Grassmann	10	Balloon	Château Thierry	1105	2	c.
Ltn F Bornträger	49	Spad	Auchin-Ferme	1105	1	d.
Vfw F Schumacher	10	Balloon	Château Thierry	1550	3	e.
Ltn F Friedrichs	10	Balloon	Château Thierry	1555	19	e.
Ltn E Udet	4	Spad	Faverolles	2000	36	d.
Ltn E Löwenhardt	10	Spad	La Ferté Milon	2000	32	d.
Flgmt A Zenses	MFJ2	DH4	Mariakerke	2040	6	f.
Flgmt H Goerth	MFJ2	DH4	Sea off Mariakerke	2040	2	f.
Uffz J Fritzsche	13	Breguet			3	
Vfw H Steinbrecher	46	Camel			3	g.

Ltn A Wunsch	67	Salmson			1	h.
Vfw H Krüger	70	DH4	Schirmeck		2	
Sgt Dörr	70	DH4	St Die		1	
Flgmt Borschert	MFJI	DH4	Blankenberghe		1	
Vzflgmstr W Thöne	MFJI	Camel	Blankenberghe		1	i.
Vzflgmstr W Thöne	MFJI	Camel	Nieuport Mole		2	j.

a.   Camel C8212, 70 Sqn RAF, 2/Lt JW Gibson, WIA.
b.   French 54 Compagnie Aérostières, S/Lt Leboue, OK.
c.   French 69 Compagnie Aérostières, S/Lt Graffe, WIA.
d.   One French Spad lost this date, Spa 87, S/Lt J Lavergne, MIA.
e.   One was French 43 Compagnie Aérostières, Adj Couillard, OK.
f.   A8013, 217 Sqn RAF, Lt CJ Moir & Pvt EE Hunnisett, KIAs.
g.   D6564, 70 Sqn RAF, Lt JE Sydie, POW.
h.   Escadrille Sal 28, Adj Pliez & S/Lt Mars, KIAs, Salmson 2A2.
i.   D3359, 204 Sqn RAF, Lt JM Wilson, KIA.
j.   D3361, 204 Sqn RAF, Lt S Harston, KIA.

Losses

Ltn Müller	5	Wounded in action, shot in the leg.
Ltn Lothar Feige	10	Killed in action Noroy.
Ltn Friedrich Hoffmann	11	Killed in action Passy 2000.
Ltn Ewald Carl	51	KIA, Kemmelberg, Wulverghem.
Flg Wilhelm Schädlich	53	Broken leg in a crash landing.
Ltn Hans Viebig	57	Severely wounded in action Harbonnières in combat with 41 and 70 Squadrons RAF, 1810 hrs – FTL.
Vfw Wunnenberg	60	Wounded in action.

JASTA ARMEE ASSIGNMENTS AS OF 1 JULY 1918

Western Front

1 Armee 31,33,73,74
2 Armee 3,5,12,13,15,19,28w,34b,37,46,47w,49,54s,58,76b,77b
3 Armee –
4 Armee 7,16b,20,40s,51,56,MFJI,MFJII,MFJIII
5 Armee 67
6 Armee 14,29,30,43,52
7 Armee 1,B,4,6,9,10,11,21s,22s,26,27,36,39,41,45,50,60,66,81
17 Armee 23b,32b,35b,59
18 Armee 8,17,24s,42,44s,48,53,57,61,61,63,68,69,72s,79b
19 Armee 18,80b
Det 'A' 70,78b,K3
Det 'B' 71,75
Det 'C' 64w,65

Other Fronts

11 Armee 25	Macedonia	
11 Armee 38	Macedonia	
55	Turkey	

1 July 1918

Ltn E Spindler	18	DH9	W Avning	0820	1	
Vfw F Piechulek	56	DH4	Ruddervoorde	0920	7	a.
Ltn R Stark	35	RE8	NE Arras	1007	6	b.

Vfw F Schumacher	10	Balloon	Cuchery	1030	4	c.
Ltn E Udet	4	Breguet	Pierrepont-Mortefontaine	1145	37	d.
Ltn F Ray	49	SE5	Villers Bretonneux	1145	14	
Vfw K Gerster	62	Dolphin	Saulchey	1230	1	e.
Uffz F Engler	62	Dolphin	Guerbigny	1240	2	e.
Ltn M Näther	62	Dolphin	Guerbigny	1250	8	e.
Vfw O Fruhner	26	Spad	Château Thierry	1645	10	
Ltn E Udet	4	Spad	E Faverolles	2055	38	
Ltn F Rumey	5	Camel			28	f.
Ltn F Büchner	13	Camel			6	
Ltn W Niethammer	13	Camel	S Albert		2	g.
Vfw E Schäpe	33	Camel			4	
Ltn W Preuss	66	Nieuport 28	Charly		2	h.
Ltn A Laumann	66	Nieuport 28			5	h.
Ltn P Turck	66	Spad 2			5	

a. A8054, 25 Sqn RAF, Lt GE Dobeson & 2/Lt JE Pilling, KIAs.
b. C5090, 13 Sqn RAF, Lt KW Murray & 2/Lt HL Wilson, KIAs.
c. French 25 Compagnie Aérostières.
d. Escadrille Br 219, Lt Dupont & S/Lt Schalbar,KIAs, Breguet 14B2.
e. 23 Sqn RAF lost two Dolphins: C3871, Capt HV Puckridge, POW and C4181, Lt CLA Sherwood, KIA.
f. C8264, 65 Sqn RAF, Lt HH Borden, KIA.
g. B6369, 209 Sqn RAF, 2/Lt LC Story, KIA.
h. 94th Aero, 1Lt HH Tittmann, severely wounded.

Losses

Vfw Georg Schalk	34	Killed in action Albert.
Ltn Walter Reher	48	Killed in a crash nr Moyencourt airfield.
Ltn Kralewski	63	Killed in crash Wancourt 2130, test flight.
Obltn Gottlieb Rassberger	80	Lightly wounded in action.

2 July 1918

Ltn E Löwenhardt	10	Nieuport 28	Bonnes	0810	33	a.
Ltn E Udet	4	Nieuport 28	Bezu-St Germain	0815	39	b.
Ltn E Löwenhardt	10	Nieuport 28	Courchamps	0815	34	a.
Ltn F Friedrichs	10	Nieuport 28	Eterpilly	0820	20	a.
Ltn C Degelow	40	SE5	Kruisstraat	0845	8	c.
Ltn R Schneider	79	Spad		0855	3	d.
Vfw F Piechulek	56	BF2b	Wervicq	0940	8	e.
Ltn J Schäfer	16	BF2b	Zandvoorde	0950	2	e.
Ltn D Collin	56	BF2b	Ypres	0955	11	e.
Ltn F Büchner	13	Dolphin	Contay	1045	7	f.
Ltn O Fitzner	65	Salmson	Fresnes	1657	6	g.
Vfw K Brendle	45	Spad	Chezy-sur-Marne		3	h.
Gefr A Wadowski	52	SE5	Caestre		2	i.
Vfw F Jacobsen	73	2 Seater			–	
Uffz Harbers	73	2 Seater			–	

a. Nieuport 6234 '9', 27th Aero, 1Lt Elliott, KIA.
b. 6347 '3', 27th Aero, 1Lt WB Wanamaker, WIA/POW.
c. B8524, 29 Sqn RAF, Lt WE Durant, KIA.
d. Escadrille Spa 159, MdL J Graillot, KIA, Spad XIII.
e. 20 Sqn RAF lost two Bristol Fighters plus one shot up: C850, Lt BT Davidson & Sgt J Helsby, KIAs; D8090, Lt HC McCreary & Sgt WJH Barter, KIAs, and, 2/Lt PG Jones (O), KIA.
f. D3671, 87 Sqn RAF, Maj JC Callaghan, MC, KIA.
g. 91st Aero, No.591, 2Lt HG Mayes, WIA/POW & 1Lt FF Schilling, KIA.
h. Escadrille Spa 163, Sgt Kernevez, KIA, Spad VII.
i. D8444, 29 Sqn RAF, Lt RG Pierce, KIA.

Losses

Ltn Wuebben	14	Lightly wounded in action.
Ltn Hellmuth Roer	27	Killed in action Chéry les Pouilly.
Obltn Robert Ritter von Greim	34	Injured in a crash, returned 31 July.
Ltn Furchtbar	52	Wounded in action.

3 July 1918

Vfw F Hemer	6	Spad	E Courtieux	0800	12	a.
Ltn H Drekmann	4	Breguet	Nouvron	0820	7	b.
Ltn E Udet	4	Spad	E Laversine	0825	40	a.
Ltn H Drekmann	4	Spad	NW Dompierre	0825	8	a.
Ltn W Nöldecke	6	Spad	Courtieux	1910	1	a.
Ltn E Bormann	B	Spad	Noray		1	c.
Ltn F Rumey	5	Camel			29	
Ltn U Neckel	13	Camel	Roye		19	
Ltn W Preuss	66	Spad			3	d.

a.   Escadrille Spa 65, Adj G Lienhard, MIA, XIII.
b.   Escadrille Br 128, Adj Gillet & Sgt Duhamel, MIAs.
c.   Escadrille N 471, Lt Compte Sanche de Gramont, KIA.
d.   8341, Escadrille Spa 65, Adj J Gerard, KIA, Spad XIII.

Losses

Flg Jacob Lux	1	Killed in action Anthenay.
(Hptm Wilhelm Reinhard	JGI	Killed in a crash Berlin-Adlershof testing a Zeppelin-Lindau D.I 2085/18.)
Vfw Hans Vietzen	12	Killed in action Corbie.

4 July 1918   The Battle for Hamel Begins

Sgt M Kuhn	21	Spad	La Ferté Milon	0900	2	
Ltn D Collin	56	Camel	Armentières	0955	12	
Ltn F Ray	49	SE5	Villers Bretonneux	1005	15	
Ltn M Dehmisch	58	RE8	S Hamel	1030	4	a.
Ltn E Thuy	28	Camel	SE Cérisy	1415	24	b.
Sgt K Schlegel	45	Balloon	Villers-Cotterêts	1845	2	c.
Ltn Vonshott	46	Dolphin	S Morlancourt	1845	–	
Ltn A v Brandenstein	49	Dolphin	Chérisy	1845	4	
Ltn L Zencominierski	45	Breguet	Villers-Cotterêts	2000	1	
Vfw R Treptow	25	Nieuport	NE Lopatnica		6	d.
Obltn H Auffarth	29	DH4	Noeux les Mines		–	
Ltn HJ Rolfes	45	Breguet	Villers-Cotterêts		8	
Ltn A Laumann	66	Spad	Villers-Cotterêts		6	
Ltn W Preuss	66	Spad	Villers-Cotterêts		4	
Ltn K Menckhoff	72	Dolphin			35	e.
Uffz R Mossbacher	77	Camel			–	

a.   C4580, 9 Sqn RAF, Lt SE Harris & 2/Lt DE Bell, KIAs.
b.   B3858, 209 Sqn RAF, 2/Lt HR Frank, KIA.
c.   French 24 Compagnie Aérostières.
d.   Serbian Escadrille 508, Art Sgt J Demdier, KIA.
e.   Camel D6494, 54 Sqn RAF, 2/Lt CH Atkinson, KIA.

Losses

Ltn Alfred Ponath	68	KIA, Davesnescourt, N Montdidier.
Ltn Theodor Lodemann	SFS2	Killed in action Ypres.
FlgMt Clements Kähler	SFS2	Crash landed at Thourout, OK.

5 July 1918

OfStv J Mai	5	BF2b	Guillemont	0920	16	a.

Ltn L Zencominierski	45	Breguet	Neuilly	1100	2	
OfStv G Dörr	45	Breguet	Burmetz	1110	7	
Ltn P Schwirzke	68	Balloon	Montigny	1330	1	b.
Ltn H Stoer	35	Balloon	Anzin, NW Arras	1725	–	
Flgmt Kulbe	MFJ2	DH4	Sea off Ostende	1920	4	
Ltn H Kroll	24	Spad	S Cournay	2145	30	
Ltn K Bolle	B	Nieuport 28	Courchamps		20	c.
Ltn H Frommherz	B	Nieuport 28	Courchamps		5	d.
Vfw G Fieseler	25	Nieuport	Trap, SE Prilep		5	e.
Ltn G Balz	47	Camel	E Vaux-sur-Somme		1	
Uffz Baumgarten	67	Caudron			1	
Ltn A Hellwig	77	RE8			–	

a.   C791, 48 Sqn RAF, 2/Lt BS Hillis & Sgt SJ Pratt, KIAs.
b.   French 67 Compagnie Aérostières, Lt Richard, OK.
c.   95th Aero, 1Lt C Rhodes, POW.
d.   95th Aero, 1Lt SP Thompson, KIA.
e.   Serbian Escadrille 506, Art 2/Sgt R Bavillon & Lt J Levook, KIAs.

Losses
| Obltn Wolfgang Plüschow | 31 | Killed in action Euba, Chemnitz. |
| Flg Stefan Meier | 79 | Killed in a crash 1545 test flight. |

6 July 1918

Ltn E Simpelkamp	29	Camel	Estaires	1250	2	a.
Sgt K Schlegel	45	Balloon	Bezu		3	b.
OfStv H Hünninghaus	66	Spad			1	

a.   D9631, 210 Sqn RAF, 2/Lt WJ Saunders, WIA/POW.
b.   2nd Balloon Co USBS, 2Lt LM Murphy & 2Lt M Sedgwick, OK.

Losses
| Ltn Werner Junck | 8 | Wounded in action. |
| Ltn Robert Schwarz | 52 | Wounded in action Lestrem. |

7 July 1918

Ltn P Billik	52	DH9	Sailly-sous-Lys	0720	22	
Ltn F Brandt	26	Nieuport 28	Soisson Ferme	1110	6	a.
Ltn F Büchner	13	Camel	Roye	1115	8	b.
Ltn U Neckel	13	Camel	Roye	1115	20	c.
Vfw E Buder	26	Nieuport 28	Soisson Ferme	1115	3	a.
Vfw O Fruhner	26	Nieuport 28	S Soisson Ferme	1128	11	a.
Ltn Sauermann	70	DH4	Kaiserslauten	1730	1	d.
Vfw J Schwendemann	41	Nieuport			9	
Ltn E Raabe	41	Balloon			4	e.
Vfw O Rosenfeld	41	Nieuport			13	
Ltn H Mittermayr	K2	DH4	Kaiserslauten		2	d.
Flgmt H Goerth	MFJ2	DH9	Sea off Nieuport		3	f.

a.   Nieuport 6181 '15', 94th Aero, 1Lt WW Chalmers, POW.
a.   Nieuport 95th Aero, 1Lt SE McKeown, POW.
b.   D3329, 209 Sqn RAF, Lt MS Taylor, KIA.
c.   C8279, 209 Sqn RAF, Lt DY Hunter, KIA.
d.   104 Sqn IAF lost two DH4s: D2868, Lt A Moore, POW & Lt FP Cobden, KIA, and D2878, Lt MJ Ducray,, POW & 2/Lt NH Wildig, KIA.
e.   French 90 Compagnie Aérostières.
f.   D1730, 206 Sqn RAF, Lt JR Harrington & 2/Lt CL Bray, KIAs.

Losses
| Vfw Otto Rosenfeld | 41 | KIA, Coincy, by American fighters. |

8 July 1918

Ltn P Billik	52	BF2b	Salome, Lorgies	0830	23	a.
Ltn P Billik	52	SE5	Annoeuillin	0850	24	b.
Ltn Becker	52	Camel	Meurchin	0850	1	c.
Vfw M Lüderitz	52	SE5	Bauvin	0900	2	d.
Obltn O v Boenigk	21	Spad	Fismes, S Louatre	1100	13	
Ltn Marcard	26	Spad	Corcy	1105	1	
Ltn F Brandt	26	2 Seater	SW Oigny	1110	7	
Vfw O Fruhner	26	Breguet	Hartennes	1130	12	e.
OfStv G Dörr	45	Breguet	Villers-Cotterêts	1130	8	e.
Ltn F Friedrichs	10	Nieuport 28	S Sarcy	1230	21	f.
Ltn J Schulte	14	Camel	Wingles	2030	2	
Ltn v Wulffen	14	Camel	Pont-à-Vendin	2030	1	
Ltn J Schulte	14	Camel	Annoeullin	2045	3	
Vfw H Boy	14	SE5	Carvin	2100	4	
Ltn H Hentzen	9	Spad			1	
Vfw R Schneider	19	Spad	Fismes		1	
Ltn J Raesch	43	Camel	Nieppe Forest		–	
Ltn Schulze	51	Camel			1	

a.   C1002, 62 Sqn RAF, Lt JA Chubb & Sgt J Borwein, POWs.
b.   C1089, 32 Sqn RAF, Capt A Claydon, KIA.
c.   B2473, 73 Sqn RAF, 2/Lt EG Reynolds, KIA.
d.   B8346, 32 Sqn RAF, Lt HW Burry, POW.
e.   Escadrille Br 224, MdL Hays & Asp Girard, MIAs, only Breguet lost.
f.   Nieuport 6264, 147th Aero, 2Lt MO Parry, KIA.

Losses

Ltn Walter Noack	29	Wounded in action.
Gefr Anton Wadowski	52	Killed in action Allennes.
Gefr Rudolf Lang	78	Wounded in action during a bombing raid on the airfield at Burscheid.

---

9 July 1918

Ltn H Henkel	37	Balloon	S Varennes	0715	1	a.
Ltn J v Busse	20	SE5	SW Dickebusch	1025	5	b.
Ltn W v Dazur	20	Camel	Millekruisse	1030	2	
Ltn K Plauth	20	Spad	E Kemmel	1030	1	
Ltn H-R v Decker	20	SE5	Dickebusch	1030	2	c.
Ltn O Könnecke	5	Dolphin	N Albert		21	d.

a.   British Balloon 44-19-3 (AR 24), Lt A Burton, OK & Lt H McKay, OK.
b.   74 Sqn RAF.
c.   C1950, 74 Sqn RAF, Lt AJ Battel, KIA.
d.   BF2b B1113, 48 Sqn RAF, 1/Lt ED Shaw & Sgt TW Smith, KIAs.

Losses

Ltn Helmuth Dilthey	40	Killed in action Annappes near Lille with DH9s of 107 Sqn RAF.
Uffz Maier	46	Wounded in action.
Ltn Hermann Munzert	59	Killed in action Willerval & Fampoux, on Allied side of lines.

---

10 July 1918

Ltn H Houlthusen	30	Camel	Kemmel	1109	2	a.
Ltn A Hets	37	Balloon	S Varennes	1355	2	b.
Ltn W Sommer	39	AR2	Thillois		1	
Ltn Guntrun	52	Camel	l'Epinette		–	a.

a.   43 or 80 Sqn RAF.

b.   British Balloon 1-19-3 (AR 4).

Losses

Gefr Paul Göhler	3	Injured on test flight Blaise a/f Pfalz DXII.
Ltn Eberhard Horn	3	Injured on test flight Blaise a/f Pfalz DXII.
Ltn August Hartmann	30	Lightly wounded in action.
Ltn Wilhelm Oberstadt	56	Wounded in action left arm.
Flgmt Eduard Schwarz	SFSI	Wounded in action Kenberge at 1125, Albatros DVa 7322/17, – DOI 14 July at Blankenberge.

11 July 1918

Ltn E Siempelkamp	29	DH9	Molembaix	0915	3	a.
Ltn H Nebelthau	29	DH9	N Marquain	0915	1	a.
Vfw G Wackwitz	29	DH9	Pecq near Tournai	0920	1	a.
Obltn A Gutknecht	43	DH9	W La Bassée	2035	2	b.

a.   107 Sqn RAF lost three DH9s: C2182, 2/Lt JD Cook & 2/Lt HH Ankrett,KIAs; C2183, Lt RA Arnott & 2/Lt HR Whitehead,both WIA/POW, and D5647, 2/Lt AT Simons & Lt TF Blight,both WIA/POW.
b.   Possibly 98 Sqn RAF if claim time is wrong (ie: am, not pm), D1724, 2/Lt FC Wilton, OK & 2/Lt EV Austin, KIA, FTL.

Losses

Gefr Johann Diebold	71	Wounded near Fontaine 1710, Spads of Spa 315 – Lt Praslop & MdL Uteau.
Ltn Hansjörg v Schulz	K7	Killed in a crash Berlin-Tempelhof, Adlershof.

12 July 1918

Obltn H Schlieter	70	Spad	SW Blamont	1055	3	a.
Vfw E Prime	78	Spad	Blamont	1110	–	
Ltn G Kröhl	34	2 Seater	E Herville	1140	–	
OfStv W Hippert	74	a/c			zlg	

a.   Escadrille Spa 90, 1/Lt GN Jerome, an American, KIA.

Losses

Uffz Josef Thomas	23	Injured in a crash, machine destroyed.
Vfw Meyer	36	Wounded in action.
Uffz Karl Röttgen	39	Killed in action Vrigny on the Somme, probably by Lt P C Homo & S/Lt Guérin of Br 235, 0650 hrs.
Uffz Ludwig Artmann	79	Killed in action Juniville-Bignecourt 2100.

13 July 1918

Obltn R v Benz	78	Salmson	Manonvillers	0910	1	
Ltn C Degelow	40	SE5	Erquinghem	0940	9	a.
Ltn G Meyer	37	Balloon	Lahoussoye	0945	7	b.
Ltn A Hets	37	Balloon	Pont Noyelles	0945	4	c.
Ltn J v Busse	20	SE5	N Bailleul	0955	6	d.
Vfw K Ungewitter	24	Balloon	Nouenville	1140	–	
Flgmt E Blaas	MFJ2	DH9	Sea off Wenduyne	1805	2	e.
Ltn zS G Saschenberg	MFJI	Spad	Sea off Westende	2135	15	
Flgmt Ludewig	MFJ2	DH9	Off Middlekerke		1	f.

a.   C1818, 85 Sqn RAF, Lt WS Robertson, KIA.
b.   British Balloon 43-16-5 (AR 23).
c.   British Balloon 12-16-5 (AR 45).
d.   D6908, 74 Sqn RAF, Lt FJ Church, KIA (reported lost on 12 July).
e.   B9346, 211 Sqn RAF, 2/Lt WJ Gilman & Pvt WJ Atkinson, KIAs.
f.   211 Sqn RAF, 2/Lt CWT Colman (O), WIA.

Losses

Ltn Hans-Rudolf v Decker	20	Severely wounded in action.
Ltn Karl Plauth	20	Lightly injured in a crash, remained.

Flg Tollmann	20	Killed in action (details lacking).				
Vfw Michael Lüderitz	52	Killed in action Neuve Chapelle.				

14 July 1918

Ltn E Löwenhardt	10	Breguet	Verdilly	0815	35	a.
FlgMt Held	MFJ2	Spad	Sea off Ostende	0850	2	
Ltn W Rosenstein	40	SE5	SE Vieux Berquin	0930	4	b.
Ltn C Degelow	40	SE5	SE Vieux Berquin	0935	10	b.
Ltn H Gilly	40	SE5	nr Vieux Berquin	0940	3	b.
Ltn C Degelow	40	SE5	W Merville	0940	11	b.
Ltn E Thuy	28	Spad			25	
Ltn C Degelow	40	SE5	Bailleul, Merris		–	
Ltn H v Freden	50	Spad 2	Vaissient, Veneuil		5	
Uffz C Gräper	50	Nieuport 28	Vaissient, Chambry		1	c.

a.   Escadrille Br 233, Cpl de Elguezabel & Lt Le Gallic, MIAs.
b.   Engaged in combat with 64 and 85 Sqns RAF, Degelow brought down C6447, 64 Sqn RAF, 2/Lt BN Garrett, POW and C6490, 85 Sqn RAF, 2/Lt NH Marshall, POW.
c.   Nieuport 6177 '14', 95th Aero, 1Lt Q Roosevelt, KIA.
Losses – Nil

15 July 1918

The final German Offensive on the Marne, the Battle of Reims (Operation 'Friedenstrum' – Peace Offensive)

Obltn O v Boenigk	21	Breguet	SW Pourcy	0610	15	a.
OfStv F Thom	21	Spad 2	S Pourcy	0632	20	
Obltn P Blumenbach	31	AR2	SE Prosnes	0750	2	
Ltn E Stahl	79	Spad	Berseuil	0940	1	
Vfw E Soltau	20	SE5	NW Dadizeele	0950	2	b.
Flg J Schlimpen	45	Balloon	Dormans	0950	1	c.
Ltn P Wenzel	6	Balloon	Bois de Breuil	1045	6	
Ltn W Blume	9	Nieuport	S Mareuil	1210	12	
Vfw E Buder	26	Breguet	Boucheres	1255	4	a.
Ltn E Löwenhardt	10	Camel	N Dormans	1307	36	d.
Ltn K Bolle	B	Camel	Dormans	1400	21	e.
Ltn H v Bülow	36	Nieuport 28	Dormans, Marne	1410	5	f.
Ltn K Jacob	36	SE5	S La Capelle	1420	5	g.
Vfw G Dobberke	60	Spad 2	Champ Fleury	1445	3	
Ltn Hagen	62	Balloon	Chugny	1455	1	
Ltn M Näther	62	Spad XIII	Prosnes	1500	9	
Ltn G Meyer	37	Balloon	Lahoussoye	1538	8	h.
Ltn K Meyer	4	Spad	NE Fossoy	1640	3	
Sgt K Schlegel	45	Spad	Comblizy	1640	4	
OfStv G Dörr	45	Spad VII	Comblizy	1645	9	
Sgt K Schlegel	45	Spad	Comblizy	1650	5	
OfStv G Dörr	45	Breguet	Comblizy	1700	10	a.
Ltn K Jacob	36	Caudron	Festigny	1735	6	i.
Ltn U Könnemann	45	Breguet	Conde	2105	1	
Ltn H Frommherz	B	Nieuport 28	Château Thierry		6	j.
Ltn B Linke-Schluckbier	9	Breguet			2	a.
Ltn G Schuster	17	Balloon	Suippes		6	
Ltn H Pippart	19	Spad XIII	S Tahure		16	
Vfw C Mesch	26	Spad	Fôret de Vassy		–	
Uffz R Neumann	36	Spad	S Dormans		1	
Ltn M Johns	63	Spad			3	

Ltn M Johns	63	Spad		4
Ltn A Laumann	66	Breguet		7
Ltn K Menckhoff	72	Spad	Bony	36
Ltn K Menckhoff	72	Spad	Bony	37
Ltn G Tschentschel	72	Spad		zlg

a.   Two French Breguets lost: Escadrille Br 29, Lt Guillot & Sgt Beraud, MIAs; Br 234, Lt Delord & S/Lt Fontaine, KIAs; and also Br 222, Sgt Lassaigne,WIA & S/Lt Chastaing, DOW, and Br 222, Sgt Gros & S/Lt Mazet, both WIA.

b.   D6910, 74 Sqn RAF, 2/Lt RH Gray, POW.

c.   2nd Balloon Co USBS, 1Lt RK Patterson & 1Lt G Phelps, OK.

d.   D9401, 54 Sqn RAF, Sgt PH Williams, KIA.

e.   D1778, 43 Sqn RAF, 2/Lt TE Babbitt, KIA.

f.   147th Aero, 2Lt TJ Abernathy, OK.

g.   D1945, 54 Sqn RAF, 2/Lt MB Lewis, KIA.

h.   British Balloon 43-16-5 (SR 95), Lt Acland & Lt Davidson, OK.

i.   Possibly a Caudron R11 of Escadrille R 46, Sgt-Maj Lacassagne, WIA, & Sol W K MacKerness, an American, WIA as crewmen, – pilot ?

j.   95th Aero.

Losses

Ltn Friedrich Friedrichs	10	Killed over Arcq at 2100, Fokker DVII 309/18, his ammunition igniting which set his fighter on fire. Baled out but his parachute ripped and he fell to his death.
Vfw Alfred Hübner	36	Lightly wounded in action, remained with unit.
Ltn Lambert Schütt	66	Killed in action over the Marne.

16 July 1918

Ltn F Ray	49	Spad	Tahure	0545	16	
Ltn Stoltenhoff	27	Spad	Chaumizy	0640	1	
Vfw A Nagler	81	Spad	Höhe 96, Chaudry	0650	5	
Ltn M Näther	61	Spad XIII	Thuizy	1217	10	
Ltn W Blume	9	Nieuport		1220	13	a.
Ltn zS R Poss	SFS2	DH9	Zeebrugge	1230	7	b.
Gefr L Möller	10	Spad	Igny-le-Jard	1355	1	
Vfw R Rübe	67	Balloon		1355	2	c.
Ltn P Turck	21	Spad	Chaméry	1405	6	
Vfw O Fruhner	26	Spad	SW Igny	1410	13	
Ltn zS G Saschenberg	MFJ1	Spad	Sea off Zeebrugge	1415	16	
Ltn zS G Saschenberg	MFJ1	DH4	Uberschwemm	1420	17	b.
Ltn zS G Saschenberg	MFJ1	DH4	Middlekerke	1425	18	b.
Obltn O v Boenigk	21	Balloon	Villers-Allerand	1450	15	d.
Vfw F Piechulek	56	DH4	Pilkem	1540	9	e.
Obltn B Loerzer	JGIII	Spad/N 28	Putnay	1545	26	f.
Ltn M-W B-Bodemer	6	Spad	E Igny-le-Jard	1725	6	
Vfw F Hemer	6	Camel	S Dormans	1730	13	g.
Vfw F Hemer	6	Camel	S Dormans	1735	14	g.
Ltn E Löwenhardt	10	Spad	Igny-le-Jard	1820	37	
Flgmt H Goerth	MFJ2	DH	N Zebekote	1825	4	b.
OfStv K Thom	21	Spad	S Pourcy	2027	21	
Ltn P Turck	21	Spad	S Villers-Allerand	2029	7	
Uffz Schneck	9	Nieuport			1	h.
Ltn F Büchner	13	Breguet			9	i.
Ltn F Büchner	13	Breguet			10	i.
Ltn H Pippart	19	Spad XIII	Suippes nr Malmy		17	j.
Vfw R Schneider	19	Spad XIII	Suippes nr Virginy		2	k.
Ltn S Garsztka	31	Spad VII	Rilly-la-Montagne		1	

Vfw Schneevogel	46	Dolphin	Grandcourt		1	l.
Ltn W Kypke	47	Spad			9	
Ltn H v Freden	50	DH9	Nesle		6	
Vfw G Dobberke	60	Nieuport			4	
Vfw P Völker	60	Nieuport			1	
Ltn K Menckhoff	72	Spad	Reims		38	
Ltn zS H Wessels	MFJ1	DH4	Middlekerke		4	b.

a.   Nieuport 6210, 147th Aero, 1Lt DW Cassard, KIA.
b.   Combat with 202 Sqn RAF and 218 Sqn RAF.
c.   French 65 Compagnie Aérostières.
d.   French 49 Compagnie Aérostières.
e.   D8380, 25 Sqn RAF, Capt E Waterlow, KIA & Lt JM Mackie, KIA.
f.   27th Aero, 1Lt RF Raymond, DSC, POW.
g.   54 Sqn RAF lost two Camels: C1609, Capt RA James and D6511, Lt JH Spence, both KIA.
h.   27th Aero, 1Lt MB Gunn, KIA.
i.   Two French Breguets were lost: 4072, Escadrille Br 132, Cpl Gloaguen & Cpl Burckel, MIAs, & Br 236, Adj-Chef Castets & S/Lt Laharrague, KIAs.
j.   Escadrille Spa 153, S/Lt A Barcat, KIA, Spad XIII.
k.   Escadrille Spa 153, S/Lt G Lutzius, KIA, Spad XIII.
l.   C4225, 87 Sqn RAF, Lt EB Crickmore, POW.

Losses

Ltn Julius Bender	4	Downed by his ammunition auto-igniting, 1945 hours. Parachuted OK from Fokker DVII 2063/18, but sprained ankle on landing.
Ltn Hans Kirschstein	6	Killed in a crash of Hannover CLIII Magneux near Fismes.
Ltn Johannes Markgraf	6	Killed in the above crash as pilot of the two-seater.
Uffz Willi Laabs	13	Killed in action Semide.
Ltn Hilmar Glöcklen	21	Shot down parachuted, broke right foot landing.
OfStv Otto Esswein	26	Shot down 1750 attacking a balloon, parachuted safely.
Ltn Friedrich K Weber	29	Injured in a forced landing.
Vfw Gustav Wackwitz	29	Killed in a crash at Gondecourt airfield on a practice flight.
Vfw Gustav Nolte	36	Killed in action Treloup, Marne 1800.
Ltn Karl Wernicke	43	Killed in a crash Hallennes, ammo self-ignited.
Uffz Erich Meyer	45	Injured in a crash Beugneux 1830.
Ltn Fritz Pütter	68	Severely burned St Remy le Petit, due to ammo igniting – died of his injuries on 10 August.
Vfw Friedrich Megerle	70	Killed in action Saarburg, parachute failed.
Ltn Ludwig Schmid	76	Wounded in action.
Ltn Edmund Neu	76	Wounded in action Spad during balloon attack.
Flgmt Weigel	MFJ2	Wounded in action in combat with DH4s.

17 July 1918

Ltn A Lenz	22	Spad 2	Mourmelon-le ...	0710	5	a.
Vfw K Bohnenkamp	22	Spad	... Grand	0712	5	
Gefr Bergmann	66	Breguet	Dormans	1030	1	
Ltn W Preuss	66	Breguet	Dormans	1030	5	
Ltn P Wenzel	6	Breguet	Igny-le-Breuil	1035	7	
Ltn Matzdorf	6	Breguet	Igny-le-Breuil	1035	1	
Ltn E Rolff	6	Breguet	Monthurd	1040	1	
Ltn H Maushake	4	Breguet	Dormans	1045	2	
Ltn E Koepsch	4	Breguet	Combizy	1050	3	
Flg Oltzeschner	64	Spad	St Louie-Fé Wald	1102	1	
Ltn H Pippart	19	Breguet		1215	18	
Ltn K Jacob	36	Nieuport 28	W Troissy	1500	7	b.
Ltn O Franke	30	Dolphin	Erquinghem	1900	1	c.

Ltn J Jacobs	7	Camel	SW Nieuport	2110	23
Ltn K Bolle	B	BF2b	Soilly		22
Ltn E Bormann	B	BF2b	Soilly		2
Ltn H Frommherz	B	BF2b	Vassy, Soilly		7
Vfw Gnädig	38	Nieuport 28			3 d.
Uffz H Pfaffenritter	60	AR2	Villers Allerand		1
Uffz H Pfaffenritter	60	Spad	Villers Allerand		2
Ltn A Laumann	66	Breguet			8
Ltn K Schwartz	66	Breguet	Dormans		5

a.   Possibly Spa 140, Sgt Foin & S/Lt Borg, MIAs.
b.   147th Aero.
c.   C3792, 19 Sqn RAF, 2/Lt RE White, POW.
d.   Spad VII 7137 '9', 139th Aero, 1Lt HG McClure, POW (engine problem).

Losses

Ltn Arthur Rahn	19	Wounded in action.
Ltn Otto Franke	30	KIA Erquinghem, near Armentières, 1910 in combat with SE5s and Dolphins.
Ltn Kurt Krüger	55	Killed in action Bet-Dedschan.
Uffz Heinrich Pfaffenritter	60	Wounded in action.
Ltn Heinrich Zempel	65	Fokker in flames, slightly injured in a parachute descent.

18 July 1918

Ltn E Löwenhardt	10	Spad	Chouy	0620	38	
Vfw F Schumacher	10	Spad	Chouy	0629	5	
OfStv G Dörr	45	Spad XIII	Pernant	0650	11	
Flg J Schlimpen	45	Breguet	Montigny	0700	2	
OfStv G Dörr	45	Breguet	Montigny	0705	12	
Ltn A Heldmann	10	Spad	Chaudun	0735	8	a.
Ltn Bussmann	1	Spad	Lechelle	0810	3	
Obltn H Göring	JGI	Spad	St Bandry	0815	22	
Obltn E v Wedel	11	Spad	St Bandry	0830	7	
Ltn E Mohnicke	11	Spad	St Bandry	0830	–	
Vfw G Dobbercke	60	Spad	La Neuville	0850	5	
Ltn H Maushake	4	DH9	SW Authenay	0915	3	b.
Vfw F Hemer	6	Breguet		0915	15	
Ltn K Meyer	4	Camel	Mareuil	0930	4	
Vfw W Gabriel	11	Spad		0950	8	
Vfw W Gabriel	11	Spad		1000	9	
Vfw W Gabriel	11	Breguet	Beugneux	1022	10	
Ltn P Turck	21	Spad	S Montgobert	1120	8	
Ltn E Löwenhardt	10	Spad	Grisolles	1430	39	
Vfw W Gabriel	11	Spad		1530	11	
Vfw F Jacobsen	73	2 Seater	Dormans	1630	–	
Ltn R Schneider	79	Sopwith	Soissons	1820	4	
Uffz J Schmidt	79	Dolphin	Soissons	1820	1	
Vfw Kister	1	Caudron	Neuilly	1930	1	
Ltn G Frädrich	72	Spad VII	St Imoges	1940	1	
Ltn H Mahn	72	Spad	St Imoges	1940	1	
Ltn H v Freden	50	DH9	NE Dormans	2017	7	b.
Ltn K Bolle	B	Breguet	Ferté Henelles Fm		23	
Ltn K Bolle	B	Spad	Beuvarder		24	c.
Ltn W Blume	9	SE5			14	d.
Vfw W Neuenhofen	27	Breguet	W St Crespin		3	
Ltn F Noltenius	27	Breguet	Soissons		–	

Ltn H Brünig	50	DH9	La Magnerelle		3	b.
Ltn A Laumann	66	Spad	Billy		9	
Uffz Berner	66	Breguet			1	
Ltn A Laumann	66	Spad	Festigny		10	
Ltn A Laumann	66	Breguet	Villers Cotterêts		11	
Ltn W Preuss	66	Breguet	Villers Cotterêts		6	

a.   Possibly Escadrille Spa 80, S/Lt J Bourhis, KIA, Spad XIII.
b.   107 Sqn RAF lost two DH9s: C6252, Lt FN Mollett & 2/Lt B Rawlings, KIAs and D5684, Capt RE Dubber & Lr CB Dickie, KIAs.
c.   Escadrille Spa 159, Lt Daire, KIA.
d.   F6060, 32 Sqn RAF, 2/Lt WA Anderson, KIA.

Losses

Ltn Hermann Bolle	B	Wounded with Breguets, Grand-Rozoy.
Ltn Moritz-Waldemar-Bretschneider Bodemer	6	Killed in action Grand-Rozoy.
Gefr Ludwig Möller	10	Killed in action Chaudun.
Ltn Kurt Jacob	36	Wounded in combat with a Spad
Ltn Konrad Schwartz	66	Wounded, taken POW, DOW 24 August.

19 July 1918

Vfw Jeep	58	Balloon	W Livry, S Vesle	0720	1	a.
Obltn B Loerzer	JG3	Spad	Coeuvres	0740	27	
Vfw K Schlegel	45	Balloon	Mareuil	0850	6	
Vfw Stein	45	Balloon	Mareuil	0850	2	
Vfw K Bohnenkamp	22	Spad	Suippes	0900	6	
Ltn J Jacobs	7	SE5	Moorslede	0930	24	b.
Ltn J Schulte	14	SE5	Wattignies	0930	4	c.
Ltn Vogel	69	Sopwith	Mourmelon	1000	zlg	
Ltn E Löwenhardt	10	Spad	Courchamps	1130	40	
Vfw J Schwendemann	41	Camel	by Nanteuil	1150	10	d.
Ltn G Tschentschel	72	Spad	SE Mareuil	1220	2	
Ltn K Menckhoff	72	Spad	S Mont Voisin	1225	39	
Ltn O Könnecke	5	Camel	Bray	1316	–	
Ltn O Könnecke	5	Camel	La Neuville	1318	–	
Vfw Belz	1	Spad	S Billy	1340	1	
Ltn H Stutz	71	Breguet	Aspach	1400	4	
Uffz Huar	68	Balloon	Mourmelon le Petit	1435	2	e.
Vfw W Seitz	8	Spad	Château Thierry	1515	7	
Ltn H Maushake	4	Spad	Hartennes	1530	4	
Ltn O Könnecke	5	Camel	Etinehem	1755	22	f.
Uffz M Schumm	52	SE5	N Estaires	1845	–	g.
Ltn H Pippart	19	Spad	Dormans	1930	19	
Uffz F Engler	62	Balloon	Sauvercy	2005	3	h.
Ltn E Löwenhardt	10	Spad	Dormans	2050	41	
Ltn F Kirchfeld	73	Spad	Champillon	2125	–	
Ltn F Büchner	13	Spad			11	
Hptm R Berthold	JGII	Spad	Soissons		38	
Ltn A Laumann	66	Spad	Villers Cotterêts		12	
Ltn W Preuss	66	Spad	Villers Cotterêts		7	
Ltn H Quartier	67	Balloon			1	i.
Vfw R Rübe	67	Balloon			3	j.

a.   French 72 Compagnie Aérostières, S/Lt Chinit & S/Lt Vieban, OK.
b.   E5948, 74 Sqn RAF, Lt AM Roberts, POW.
c.   E3921, 64 Sqn RAF, 2/Lt JA van Tilburg, POW.
d.   F6150, 43 Sqn RAF, Lt VRSVT Irvine, KIA.
e.   French 57 Compagnie Aérostières, Adj Guggenheim, WIA.

f.   209 Sqn RAF lost two Camels near Cappy this date: C193, 2/Lt DB Griffith, KIA and D9629, Lt E Scadding, POW.

g.   Possibly E5940, 85 Sqn RAF, Lt DJ Trapp, KIA.

h.   French 50 Compagnie Aérostières.

i.   French 36 Compagnie Aérostières, Lt Brisset, OK.

j.   French 86 Compagnie Aérostières, Lt Desbouis & Lt Clement, OK.

Losses

Ltn Hans Stelzer	26	Killed in action Coeuvres.
Vfw Karl Schmelcher	71	Killed in action Gebweiler, possibly by Adj Bouyer & MdL Hamot of Spa 49, 0610 hrs.
Gefr Linus Luger	79	Killed in action Ercheu 1630.

20 July 1918

Vfw K Schlegel	45	Balloon	Neuilly	0750	7	a.
OfStv E Prime	78	DH9	Blaesheim	0810	1	
Ltn P Wenzel	6	Balloon	NW Longpont	0835	8	b.
Ltn G Kröhl	34	SE5	Hamel Forest	1000	3	
Ltn W v Dazur	20	Camel	S Houthulst Wood	1010	3	
Uffz P Hüttenrauch	7	Camel	Thourout	1015	1	c.
Ltn J v Busse	20	Camel	Passchendaele	1015	7	c.
Ltn T Osterkamp	MFJ2	Camel	E Nieuport	1025	17	
Flgmt A Zenses	MFJ2	Camel	Mulenhof	1025	7	
VzFlgMstr H Bottler	MFJ2	Camel	N Nieuport	1025	3	
Vfw E Buder	26	Spad	NE Chaudun	1047	5	d.
Ltn P Billik	52	BF2b	Warneton-Bersée	1100	23	
Uffz M Schumm	52	Camel	Erquinghem	1100	2	e.
OfStv J Mai	5	DH4	Achiet le Petit	1205	17	f.
Hptm R Berthold	JGII	Spad	SE Dormans	1905	39	d.
Ltn H Drekmann	4	DH9	Morsain	2025	9	g.
Ltn R Klimke	27	Nieuport 28	Fère-Hartennes	2050	10	h.
Vfw W Neuenhofen	27	Nieuport 28	Fère, Soissons	2050	4	h.
Obltn B Loerzer	JGIII	Spad			28	d.
Vfw J Schwendemann	41	Spad			11	d.
Ltn H Brünig	50	Breguet	Pargny-Tigny		4	i.
Ltn W Kohlbach	50	Spad	Droisy		2	d.
Vfw Heppner	K4b	DH4	Oberndorf		1	
OfStv Pohlmann	K4b	DH4	Oberndorf		1	

a.   French 25 Compagnie Aérostières.

b.   French 5 Compagnie Aérostières, Adj G Poirier, OK.

c.   70 Sqn RAF lost two Camels this date: B5572, 2/Lt KR Angus and D6502, 2/Lt T Conlan, both POWs.

d.   Four French Spads were lost: Spa 62, Sgt A Bosson, Spad XIII; Spa 99, Adj T Cancel, Spad XIII; Spa 151, Brig R Vignes, Spad VII – all MIA, and Spa 159, Lt G Mazimann, KIA, Spad XIII.

e.   B9273, 46 Sqn RAF, Lt AJ Cyr, POW.

f.   B7865, 57 Sqn RAF, Lt JT Kirkland, KIA & 2/Lt EJ Riley, POW.

g.   D7234, 49 Sqn RAF, Sgt SJ Oliver, POW & Sgt A Davis, POW.

h.   27th Aero lost three Nieuport 28s: 6293, 1Lt J MacArthur, DSC, KIA; 1Lt ZR Miller, POW, and 6296, 1Lt FW Norton, DSC, DOW.

i.   Escadrille Br 211, Lt Garsault & S/Lt Charasse, KIAs.

Losses:

Ltn Werner Meyer	34	WIA near Morcourt 1100, DOW 21 July.
OfStv Paul Felsmann	K4b	Killed in action over Schwarzwald.
Flgmt Carl Küring	MFJ2	Forced to land in Fokker DVII 612/18, OK.
Flgmstr Alfons	MFJ2	KIA, Leffinghe, 1020 Fokker DVII 506/18, 'Nitzche'.

21 July 1918

Ltn P Lotz	44	BF2b	Mézières	1000	5	a.
OfStv G Dörr	45	Spad 2	Neuilly	1425	13	
Vfw W Seitz	8	Spad	Jouy	1925	8	
Vfw Hoppe	8	Spad	Reimser Wald	1925	1	
Uffz R Francke	8	Spad	Courcy	1925	12	
Obltn E v Wedel	11	Camel	near Fère	2015	8	b.
Ltn W v Richthofen	11	Camel	near Fère	2015	3	b.
Ltn E Löwenhardt	10	Camel	Fère-en-Tardenois	2015	42	b.
Ltn W Blume	9	Spad			15	
Ltn H v Bülow	36	Camel	Fère-en-Tardenois		6	c.
Uffz K Klein	37	BF2b	Mézières		–	
Ltn A Laumann	66	Breguet	La Ferté Milon		13	
Ltn W Preuss	66	Spad	La Ferté Milon		8	

a.   C974, 48 Sqn RAF, 2/Lt BM Batty & 2/Lt J Gondre, POWs.
b.   54 Sqn RAF lost three Camels: B2490, 2/Lt B Fisher; F2103, Lt RT Cuffe, and F2160, Lt FW Dougall, MC, all KIA.
c.   D1918, 73 Sqn RAF, Maj RH Freeman, MC, KIA.
Losses
OfStv Otto Esswein   26   Killed in action Hartennes.

22 July 1918

Ltn E Koch	32	SE5	Avedy Wood	0640	5	a.
Vfw C Mesch	26	Spad	Party Ferme	0825	4	
Ltn G Meyer	37	BF2b	Harbonnières	0830	9	
Ltn F Jakobs	43	DH9	Cysoing	0835	1	
Obltn H Auffarth	29	RE8	S Lestrem	0930	15	b.
Ltn C Degelow	40	BF2b	Lestrem	0930	12	c.
Obltn H Auffarth	29	SE5	Loos	0940	16	d.
Vfw K Gregor	29	SE5	S Courrières	0940	2	d.
Sgt B Brunnecker	29	SE5	Carvin	0940	1	d.
Uffz Reuss	7	DH 9	Ypres	1000	1	e.
Ltn H Pippart	19	Caudron	Mourmelon	1030	20	f.
Uffz M Hutterer	23	SE5	Grenay	1030	1	
Vfw F Jacobsen	73	Breguet	NE Dormans	1030	–	
Ltn H Pippart	19	Spad XIII	Dormans	1035	21	
Obltn A Gutknecht	43	Camel	Oignies	1120	3	g.
Vfw E Wiehle	43	Camel	S La Bassée	1145	1	g.
Ltn M Näther	62	Spad	Courtagnon	1250	11	
OfStv O Sporbert	62	Spad	Marfaux	1252	4	
Ltn O Fitzner	65	Balloon	Noviant	1305	7	h.
Ltn R Neitzer	65	Balloon	Mandres	1307	1	i.
Ltn H Henkel	37	Balloon	Bray, Bussy	1445	2	j.
Ltn R Wenzl	6	Spad		1620	4	
Vfw F Hemer	6	Spad		1620	16	
Ltn K Seit	80	DH4	Celles Wood	1700	1	k.
Vfw E Prime	78	DH9	Celles Wood	1700	–	
Ltn P Billik	52	DH4	Sante & Sailly	1730	26	l.
Obltn Beerendonk	74	Spad	Champ-Fleury	1745	1	
Ltn L Beckmann	56	Camel	Coolskamp	1820	3	m.
Ltn L Beckmann	56	Camel	Koekelaere	1822	4	m.
OfStv Bansmer	44	BF2b	S Sailly	1850	1	
Ltn K Bolle	B	Camel	Quency	1910	25	n.
Ltn E Koepsch	4	DH9	S Braisne	1910	4	o.

Ltn E Löwenhardt	10	Camel	Longpont	2030	43	
Ltn R Klimke	27	Spad	Thierry-Reims		-	
Vfw K Schlegel	45	Breguet	Gland		8	
Ltn H v Freden	50	Balloon	Longpont		7	p.
Ltn H Brünig	50	Balloon	Longpont		5	p.
Uffz R Lüdecke	81	Spad	Châtillon-Fleury		2	
Ltn H Knappe	81	Spad	Fleury		5	

a.   D6183, 60 Sqn RAF, Lt JEC MacVickar, KIA.
b.   E136, 21 Sqn RAF, Lt A Lewis & 2/Lt A Summerfelt, POWs.
c.   F5810, 62 Sqn RAF, 2/Lt WE Coulson & 2/Lt WHE Labatt, POWs.
d.   Fight with 40 Sqn RAF, B180, Lt IL Roy, DFC (Indian), KIA.
e.   C1213, 103 Sqn RAF, Lt CT Houston & Lt JK Clarke, KIAs.
f.   Possibly Escadrille R 240, Sgt Vicaire, Asp Roques, & Sgt Chalye, all WIA, R11, or C 239, Sgt Pithois, WIA & Sgt-Maj Caillot, KIA, R11.
g.   D9624, 203 Sqn RAF, Lt AE Rudge, KIA.
h.   French 82 Compagnie Aérostières, MdL Bonnemaison, OK.
i.   4th Co USBS, Lt PNA Rooney & Lt LC Ferrinback, OK.
j.   British Balloon 29-13-5 (SR 6), Lt FW Smith & Lt Hogg, OK.
k.   99 Sqn IAF.
l.   A7862, 18 Sqn RAF, 2/Lt HC Tussaud & Sgt LG Vredenburg, POWs.
m.   210 Sqn RAF lost two Camels: D9626, 2/Lt EH Bullen, POW and F5914, Capt HT Mellings, DSC, KIA.
n.   D9478, 73 Sqn RAF, Lt WSG Kidder, WIA, POW.
o.   D490, 27 Sqn RAF, 2/Lt SM Feuer & 2/Lt HB Steckley, KIAs.
p.   One of these was French 69 Compagnie Aérostières.

Losses

Ltn Willi Schuster	5	Killed in a crash at Cappy on a practice flight.
Ltn Werner Nöldecke	6	Lightly wounded, remained with unit.
Vfw Emil Soltau	20	Killed in action Gheluvelt.
Uffz Paul Marczinski	30	KIA, Pont Maudit near Lens, SE5s.
Uffz Bergmann	66	Taken prisoner.
Flgmt Alexandre Zenses	MFJ2	Lightly wounded in action by Flak over Ostende-Oudenburg, remained with unit.

23 July 1918

Vfw J Pütz	34	AWFK8	Mailly-Raineville	0900	6	a.
Vfw D Averes	81	Spad	Boumigny		2	b.

a.   D5108, 8 Sqn RAF, Lt HW Walker & 2/Lt GG Ashton, KIAs.
b.   Escadrille Spa 86, Sgt D Desgouttes, KIA, Spad XIII.

Losses – Nil

24 July 1918

OfStv K Thom	21	SE5	Blesmes	0655	22	
Ltn P Turck	66	SE5	Le Charmel	0658	9	
OfStv K Thom	21	SE5	Courtemont	0700	23	
Ltn G Meyer	37	BF2b	Bray	0830	10	a.
Ltn P Lotz	44	2 Seater	Berny	0920	–	
OfStv K Thom	21	SE5	E La Ferté	1105	24	
OfStv G Dörr	45	Spad	Pernant	1130	14	b.
Uffz M Schumm	52	SE5	S Hulloch	1920	3	c.
Vfw E Schäpe	33	Breguet	NE Sept-Saulx	1950	5	
Obltn H-E Gandert	51	BF2b	Armentières	2100	6	d.
Ltn R Maier	30	Balloon	NW Grenay	2200	2	e.
Ltn H Frommherz	B	Spad	Acy		8	f.
Obltn O v Boenigk	JGII	Balloon			16	
Vfw G Fieseler	25	Nieuport	S Dobro-Polje		6	
Vfw G Fieseler	25	Nieuport	Gradesnica		7	

| Uffz Ebert | 40 | BF2b | | | zlg |

a.   D7902, 48 Sqn RAF, 2/Lt SN Waddy & Sgt WJ Shuker, KIAs.
b.   5214, Escadrille Spa 99, Cpl Bendix, POW, Spad VII.
c.   D6900, 64 Sqn RAF, Capt PS Burge, MC, KIA.
d.   C4606, 20 Sqn RAF, Sgt HD Aldridge, POW & Sgt MS Samson, KIA.
e.   British Balloon 21-31-1 (SR 15).
f.   8262, Escadrille Spa 83, MdL A Conraux, KIA, Spad XIII.

Losses

Uffz Reuss	7	Severely wounded near Menin.
Vfw Fritz Schumacher	10	Wounded and crashed into a tree.
Ltn Höfig	37	Killed in action (no details).
Ltn Friedrich Jakobs	43	Wounded, shot in the foot, Lille.
Uffz Kurt Hoffmann	51	Killed in action Pont Ronge.
Vfw Kurt Beinecke	51	Killed in action Pont Ronge.

25 July 1918

Vfw K Schlegel	45	Breguet	Missy en Bois	0700	9	
Vfw K Schlegel	45	Balloon	La Croix	0730	10	a.
OfStv K Thom	21	SE5	SW Hartennes	0810	25	b.
Ltn R Klimke	27	SE5	Vaux-Loupeigne	0820	11	c.
Ltn P Billik	52	Camel	Vieux-Givenchy	0840	27	d.
Uffz M Schumm	52	SE5	S Armentières	0850	–	e.
Ltn A Weinschenk	16	BF2b	Zonnebeke	0915	1	
Uffz M Hutterer	23	SE5	N La Bassée	0915	2	
Uffz M Schumm	52	SE5	N Lorgies	0915	4	f.
Ltn C Degelow	40	Camel	Roulers	0935	13	g.
Ltn D Collin	56	Camel	...... Wytschaete	0940	13	h.
Ltn F v Röth	16	BF2b	Gheluvelt	0950	16	i.
Ltn L Beckmann	56	Camel	Gheluvelt	0955	5	j.
OfStv G Dörr	45	Breguet	La Croix	1100	15	
Ltn P Turck	21	SE5	W Le Charmel	1115	10	
Ltn P Vogel	23	SE5	Bourlon Wood	1140	–	
Uffz F Engler	62	AR2	Villers Allerand	1145	4	
Ltn H Drekmann	4	Spad	Dulchy	1930	10	k.
Ltn G Tschentschel	72	Balloon	Verdilly	1940	3	l.
Ltn L v Richthofen	11	Camel	Fismes	1950	30	m.
Ltn E Just	11	Spad		2030	3	
Ltn zS H Wessels	MFJI	Camel	Ramskappelle	2035	5	
Ltn zS H Wessels	MFJI	Camel	Pervyse	2035	6	
Ltn G Saschenberg	MFJI	Camel	Pervyse	2035	19	
Ltn E Löwenhardt	10	Spad	Villers Helon	2050	44	
Ltn zS T Osterkamp	MFJ2	Camel	S Nieuport	2053	18	
Ltn K Bolle	B	Camel	Fère-en-Tardenois		26	n.
Ltn G Bassenge	B	Camel	Fère-en-Tardenois		3	n.
Ltn H Frommherz	B	Camel	Mareuil		9	n.
Vfw K Strünkelnberg	9	Camel			2	
Ltn W Blume	9	Camel			16	
Vfw J Schwendemann	41	Camel			12	
Ltn K Brendle	45	Breguet	Roucourt		4	
Vfw D Averes	81	Spad	Jony-Pargny		3	

a.   1572, 1 Balloon Co USBS, Lt RW Thompson, OK.
b.   C1929, 64 Sqn RAF, Lt WR Henderson, WIA, POW.
c.   E5966, 32 Sqn RAF, Lt HM Struben, POW.
d.   D9585, 203 Sqn RAF, Lt CF Brown, POW, DOW.
e.   C6475, 64 Sqn RAF, Lt ML Howard, FTL, DOW.

f.   C8734, 64 Sqn RAF, Lt AS Barrett, OK.

g.   D8199, 208 Sqn RAF, Lt WO Carveth, POW.

h.   D9636, 209 Sqn RAF, Lt JH Siddall, KIA.

i.   C976, 20 Sqn RAF, Lt FJ Shearer,KIA & Sgt D Malpas, KIA.

j.   D9621, 209 Sqn RAF, 2/Lt AGS Blake, POW.

k.   Escadrille Spa 75, S/Lt de Beauchamp, MIA, Spad XIII.

l.   French 59 Compagnie Aérostières.

m.   73 Sqn RAF lost three Camels: B7874, 2/Lt KS Laurie, POW; D1794, 2/Lt WA Armstrong, KIA and D9398, Lt RF Lewis, KIA.

n.   43 Sqn RAF lost three Camels: D1870, Lt RE Meredith, KIA; D1894, Lt FS Coghill, POW and D8197, 2/Lt N Wilson, POW/DOW.

Losses

Ltn v Dorrien	11	Wounded, shot through the left foot.
Ltn Friedrich-Franz Graf Frhr v Hehenau	11	Wounded 1945 Grugny,DOW 26 July.
Ltn Paul Vogel	23	Baled out safely over Boulon Wood,1145.
Ltn Josef Raesch	43	Shot down by an SE5, baled out, slightly burnt.
Ltn Karl Menckhoff	72	Taken prisoner near Château Thierry attacking a balloon; shot down by an American of 95th Aero – 2Lt W Avery – in his first combat.

26 July 1918

Vfw K Delang	54	Balloon	Suippes	1220	2	a.

a.   French 21 Compagnie Aérostières.

Losses – Nil

27 July 1918

No Claims – No losses

28 July 1918

Ltn E Koch	32	DH4	Croisselles	0845	6	a.
Obltn H Krauss	32	DH4	Croisselles	0845	1	
Ltn H Seywald	23	DH9	Thelus	1130	2	
Ltn E Löwenhardt	10	Spad	Fère-en-Tardenois	1510	45	
Ltn Grimm	13	Spad	Chaudun	1850	1	
Ltn J Grassmann	10	Camel	Bac-St Maur	1950	3	b.
Ltn K Bolle	B	Spad 2	Villers-sur-Fère		27	c.
Ltn H Frommherz	B	Spad 2	Sergy		10	c.
Vfw G Fieseler	25	Breguet	Kanatlarci		8	d.

a.   B2065, 18 Sqn RAF, Lt RV Irwin, POW & Sgt GH Tench, MM, POW/DOW.

b.   C8296, 73 Sqn RAF, Lt WS Stephenson, MC, POW.

c.   12th Aero lost two Salmson 2A2s: '13', 2Lt AP Baker, WIA/POW & 2Lt JC Lumsden, KIA, and 1Lt JC Miller, DOW & 1Lt SW Thompson, WIA.

d.   Serbian Escadrille 506.

Losses – Nil

29 July 1918

Ltn K Brendle	45	Breguet	Fère-en-Tardenois	1200	5	
Ltn P Wenzel	6	Breguet	Coeuvres	1210	9	
Obltn E v Wedel	11	Breguet		1215	9	
OfStv G Dörr	45	Breguet	Armentières	1700	16	
Vfw K Schlegel	45	Breguet	Armentières	1700	11	
Gefr J Schlimpen	45	Spad VII	Fère-en-Tardenois	1710	3	
Ltn F Büchner	13	Camel	Vénizel	1840	12	a.
Flgmstr Ledy	MFJ2	Camel	Ostende	1915	–	
Ltn E Löwenhardt	10	Spad	Coincy	1930	46	

Ltn W v Dazur	20	Camel	Lochean	2020	4	
Ltn F v Röth	16	RE8	Gheluvelt	2035	17	b.
Ltn A Laumann	66	Breguet	Villers Cotterêts		14	
Ltn zS T Osterkamp	MFJ2	DH4	S Oudenkapelle		19	c.
Flgmt A Zenses	MFJ2	DH4	S Oudenkapelle		zlg	

a.   D9498, 73 Sqn RAF, 2/Lt E Cotton, KIA.
b.   DH9 B7668, 206 Sqn RAF, 1/Lt G Cheston, KIA & Cpl JW Pacey, WIA/POW.
c.   D8402, 202 Sqn RAF, Lt W Chalaire & Pvt AE Humphrey,both WIA.

Losses

| Ltn Müller | 19 | Injured in take-off crash – motor quit. |
| OfStv Johann Dierle | K4b | Killed in action Schwarzwald. |

30 July 1918

Vfw K Kallmünzer	78	DH9	Rombach	0840	2	a.
Vfw F Piechulek	56	BF2b	Kemmel	0845	10	b.
Ltn H Seywald	23	RE8	Englebelmer	1130	3	
Vfw M Hutterer	23	RE8	SW Albert	1130	3	c.
Obltn J Mühlfeldt	23	RE8	W Albert	1130	1	
OfStv G Dörr	45	Spad VII	Coincy	1150	17	
Ltn L Zencominierski	45	Spad	Coincy	1150	3	
Vfw K Schlegel	45	Breguet	Grisolles	1210	12	
Ltn H v d Marwitz	30	Camel	W Merville	1230	9	
Ltn E Löwenhardt	10	Camel	Arcy	1510	47	d.
Ltn H Drekmann	4	Spad	N Grand Rozoy	1820	11	
Ltn E Löwenhardt	10	Camel	Saponay	2010	48	e.
Ltn P Lotz	44	Camel	W Corbie	2040	–	
Ltn F v Röth	16	BF2b	S Ypres	2100	18	f.
Ltn K Monnington	18	DH9	Rombach		3	g.
Vfw R Heibert	46	SE5	NW Quesnel		10	h.
Uffz Richter	46	SE5			zlg	
Vfw O Heinrich	46	RE8	NW Römerstrasse		4	i.
Ltn J Filbig	80	2 Seater	W Parry Wald		–	
Vzflgmstr H Bottler	MFJ2	2 Seater	Pervyse		–	

a.   D7233, 99 Sqn IAF, 1/Lt P Dietz & 2/Lt HW Batty, KIAs.
b.   C904, 20 Sqn RAF, 1/Lt GH Zellers & Sgt JD Cormack, KIAs.
c.   C5056, 52 Sqn RAF, Lt KV King & 2/Lt J Kelly, KIAs.
d.   D9480, 73 Sqn RAF, Lt KWA Symons, KIA.
e.   F6087, 43 Sqn RAF, Lt LH Parsons, Inj.
f.   E2471, 20 Sqn RAF, Sgt JJ Cowell, MM, & Cpl C Hill, KIAs.
g.   C6210, 99 Sqn IAF, 2/Lt G Martin,WIA & 2/Lt SG Burton, KIA.
h.   D6895, 74 Sqn RAF, Capt JIT Jones, MC, MM, FTL, OK.
i.   C2237, 52 Sqn RAF, 2/Lt STC Roberts & 2/Lt DP Ogilvy, KIAs.

Losses

Ltn Heinrich Drekmann	4	Killed in action Grand Rozoy 1835 by Spads, probably by S/Lt Bamberger of Spa 85 & Lt de la Poeze, on staff of GC14.
Leopold v Raffay	6	Accidently broke left ankle at Puisieux a/f.
Ltn Paul Vogel	23	Baled out safely in combat over Hill 475.
Uffz Wilhelm Meyer	16	Wounded in action near Ypres.
Ltn Ernst Kleinhempel	46	Killed in action Allaines, drowned.
Ltn Robert Dycke	78	Wounded in action Thannweiler in Albatros DVa 7225/17 against DH9s.
Ltn Hans Laurisch	K4b	Killed in action Freiburg in Baden.
Ltn Wieland	SFS2	Wounded in action.

31 July 1918

Vfw L Reimann	78	DH9	Ruhlingen	0915	–	f.
Vfw Gullmann	56	SE5	Armentières	1005	1	a.
Ltn J Müller	23	Camel	Estevelles	1245	1	
Ltn E Rolff	6	Nieuport 28	Fère-en-Tardenois	1840	2	b.
Uffz L Jeckert	56	Camel	Ypres	1845	1	
Gefr W Blumensaath	43	SE5	SE La Bassée	2000	1	
Vfw Rothe	61	AR2	S Carlepont	2000	1	
Ltn H Nebelthau	29	BF2b	by Doulieu	2010	2	
Ltn J Klein	15	Spad	Château Thierry	2020	11	
Ltn K Plauth	20	Camel	W Roulers	2030	2	c.
Obltn H Auffarth	29	BF2b	Vieux Berquin	2030	17	d.
Uffz P Hüttenrauch	7	Camel	Hooglede	2040	2	e.
Ltn K Bolle	B	Spad	Courtemain		28	
Ltn W Blume	9	Spad 2	Olizy		17	
Vfw K Strünkelnberg	9	Spad 2	Olizy		2	
Ltn W Peckmann	9	Spad 2	Olizy		1	
Gefr Herrmann	9	Spad 2	Olizy		1	
Ltn K Monnington	18	DH9	Grossblittersdorf		–	f.
Ltn F Brandt	26	Spad	Verbeuil		–	
OfStv Tiedje	65	DH4			–	f.
Vfw J Hohly	65	DH4			–	f.
Vfw E Sonneck	66	Spad			4	g.
Vfw E Sonneck	66	Spad			5	g.
Ltn A Laumann	66	Spad			15	g.
Uffz O Stockmann	66	Spad			1	g.
OfStv H Hünninghaus	66	Spad			2	g.
Vfw E Prime	78	DH9	Willerwald		–	f.
Flg L Wittmann	80	DH9	Willerwald		–	f.
Uffz F Salb	80	DH9	N Saargemünd		-	f.
Vzflgmstr W Thöne	MFJI	Camel			–	

a.   E1310, 40 Sqn RAF, Capt GEH McElroy, MC, DFC, KIA.
b.   Spad XIII 15067, 94th Aero, 1Lt AF Winslow, POW.
c.   B7234, 204 Sqn RAF, Lt RL Hollingsworth, POW.
d.   C859, 20 Sqn RAF, Lt WH Shell & Sgt JDC Summers, POWs.
e.   D8182, 204 Sqn RAF, Lt J Farquhar, POW/DOW.
f.   99 Sqn IAF lost seven DH9s on a raid to Saarbrücken: C6145, Lt EL Doidge & Lt HT Melville, KIAs; C6149, 2/Lt TM Ritchie, POW & 2/Lt LWD Stagg, POW/DOW; C6196, Lt WJ Garrity & 2/Lt GH Stephenson, POWs; C6278, Lt SMcB Black & 2/Lt E Singleton, POWs, D1029, 2/Lt F Smith & 2/Lt KH Ashton, POWs; D1032, 2/Lt LR Dennis & 2/Lt FW Wooley, KIAs, and D3039, Lt MTS Papenfus, DFC, WIA/POW & Lt AL Benjamin, POW.
g.   Some of these were probably in a fight with 94th and 95th Aero; only loss, except for (b) was 1Lt PH Montague, 95th Aero, POW.

Losses

Ltn Barth	7	Severely wounded, shot in the head.
Gefr Ludwig Zellner	32	KIA, Heudicourt-les-Cagnicourt, 2056 hrs.
Ltn Paul Erichson	40	Wounded in action.
Uffz Fritz Salb	80	KIA, Grossblittersdorf by Saargemünd flying an Albatros DIII against DH9s.
Flgmt Kulbe	SFS2	Taken prisoner.
Vzflgmstr Willy Thöne	MFJI	Hit in the engine and crash landed; machine destroyed but he was OK.

Jasta Armee Assignments as of 1 August 1918

Western Front

    1 Armee 8,22s,28w,31,33,57,58,62,63,68,69,72s,73,74,76b
    2 Armee 5,34b,37,46
    3 Armee 3,47w,49,54s,77b
    4 Armee 7,16b,20,40s,51,56,MFJI,MFJII,MFJIII
    5 Armee 67
    6 Armee 14,29,30,43,52
    7 Armee 1,B,4,6,9,10,11,21s,26,27,36,39,41,45,50,60,66,81
    9 Armee 12,13,15,17,19,48,53,61
   17 Armee 23b,32b,35b,59
   18 Armee 24s,42,44s,79b
   19 Armee 18,80b
   Det 'A'   70,78b,K3
   Det 'B'   71,75
   Det 'C'   64w,65

Other Fronts

   11 Armee 25   Macedonia
   11 Armee 38   Macedonia
          55   Turkey

1 August 1918

Ltn F Kirchfeld	73	AR2	Ronchères	0810	1	a.
Vfw F Hemer	6	Nieuport 28	Fère-en-Tardenois	0910	17	b.
Ltn R Wenzl	6	Nieuport 28	Fère-en-Tardenois	0915	5	c.
Ltn J Jessen	4	Nieuport 28	Cuiry Housse	0930	1	d.
Ltn E Udet	4	Nieuport 28	NE Cramaille	0930	41	e.
Ltn E Koepsch	4	Nieuport 28	S Braisne	0930	5	f.
Ltn A Fleisher	17	Nieuport 28	by Arcy	0930	2	g.
OfStv W Kühne	18	DH9	by Wingles Holz	0940	–	
Ltn K Seit	80	DH9	Loveninghem	0940	2	h.
Hptm R Berthold	JGII	AR2	Fère-en-Tardenois	0945	40	a.
Uffz E Binkenstein	51	DH9	NW Menin	0945	2	
Ltn L Beckmann	56	DH9	Ypres	0945	6	i.
Ltn HJ Rath	22	Spad	Suippes	1050	2	
OfStv G Dörr	45	Nieuport 28	Bruyères	1100	18	
Ltn E Udet	4	Breguet	N Muret-Crouttes	1215	42	
OfStv K Thom	21	Spad	NW Le Charmel	1245	26	
Obltn O Boenigk	21	Spad	Le Charmel	1245	17	j.
Ltn GW Groos	11	Spad		1305	7	
Ltn L v Richthofen	11	Spad		1310	31	
OfStv R Heibert	46	Balloon	Bussy	1752	11	k.
Vfw O Hennrich	46	Balloon	Bonnay	1755	5	l.
Vfw O Hennrich	46	Balloon	Blanchy	1758	6	m.
OfStv R Heibert	46	Balloon	Daours	1800	12	n.
Ltn L v Richthofen	11	Spad		2025	32	
Ltn E Udet	4	Spad VII	N Bagneux	2030	43	
Flgmstr C Kuring	MFJ2	1 Seater		2045	3	
OfStv J Mai	5	Camel	by Warfusée		–	
Vfw Hasenpusch	67	AR2			1	
Uffz H Marwede	67	DH4	Wiegingen		1	o.

| Gefr Hamann | 67 | DH4 | | | 1 |

a.   Possibly Salmson 2A2s of 1st Aero who lost three: 1Lt WP Erwin, OK & 1Lt EB Spencer, WIA, FTL; No.1011, 1Lt EG Wold, DOW & 1Lt JC Wooten, KIA and No.792 '18', 1Lt WP Miller, DOW & 2Lt JJ Sykes, KIA.
b.   27th Aero, 1Lt AL Whiton, POW.
c.   No.15143 '5', 27th Aero, 1Lt OT Beauchamp, KIA.
d.   27th Aero, 1Lt RC Martin, POW.
e.   Nieuport 6275, 27th Aero, 1Lt CB Sands, KIA.
f.   Nieuport 6259, 27th Aero, 1Lt JS Hunt, KIA.
g.   27th Aero, 1Lt CA McElvain, POW.
h.   99 Sqn IAF.
i.   D2855, 206 Sqn RAF, Capt JW Mathews & 2/Lt WA John, KIAs.
j.   Escadrille Spa 96, Adj-Chef J Raszewski, MIA.
k.   British Balloon 12-16-5 (SR 94).
l.   British Balloon 43-16-5 (AR 46).
m.   British Balloon 29-13-5 (AR 51).
n.   British Balloon 3-13-5 (AR 8).
o.   D2960, 104 Sqn IAF, Lt WH Goodale & 2/Lt LC Prentice, KIAs.

Losses

Ltn Paul Wenzel	6	Lightly wounded, remained with unit.
Ltn Heinrich Böving	9	Killed in 2-seater crash, 1700 Sissone.
Sgt Alexander Wittke	9	Killed in the above crash.
Ltn Walter Lehmann	10	Taken POW in a Fokker DVII Villemoyene, S of Fère-en-Tardenois probably by S/Lt A Coadou of Spa 88.
Ltn Günther Schuster	17	Wounded in action Soissons.
Ltn Joachim v Busse	20	Wounded in action.
Ltn Waldemar v Dazur	20	Lightly wounded, remained with unit.
Vfw Dralle	51	Taken prisoner in the Linselles area.
Vzflgmstr Alexandre Zenses	MFJ2	Wounded in action in Fokker DVII 610/18.

2 August 1918

| Ltn A Laumann | 66 | Spad | | 16 |

Losses – Nil

3 August 1918

Ltn L Beckmann	56	Camel	Stadenberg	0945	7	a.
Vfw Dettmering	68	AR2	Rémy, Reims	1025	3	
Feldw K Schmückle	21	Spad 2	Arcy	1720	3	
Sgt M Kuhn	21	Balloon	W Sapponay	1725	3	b.
Ltn Selzer	74	Spad	S Hourges	1930	zlg	
Ltn P Billik	52	RE8	Vimy-Douai	1940	28	c.
Vfw Kautz	46	RE8	Assevillers		1	d.
Vfw H Horst	81	Spad	Jonchéry		4	
Vfw D Averes	81	AR2	Reims		zlg	
Flgmt Held	MFJ2	Balloon	Wenduyne		–	e.

a.   E5159, 17th Aero, Lt MK Spidle, KIA.
b.   French 45 Compagnie Aérostières.
c.   C2518, 16 Sqn RAF, Lt PC West & Lt CV Todman, KIAs.
d.   D4882, 9 Sqn RAF, Lt AF Forsyth, WIA & 2/Lt ES Coombes, POWs.
e.   Loose German captive balloon.

Losses

Vfw Drexler	43	Wounded in action.
Ltn Triebner	51	Wounded in action and taken POW.
Ltn Selzer	74	Shot down by Spad, POW but escaped.

4 August 1918

| Vfw K Schlegel | 45 | Spad XI | Braisne | 0810 | 13 |

OfStv G Dörr	45	Breguet	Nampteuil	0810	19	
Ltn A Benzler	60	Spad		1415	8	
Vfw G Dobberke	60	Spad 2		1415	6	
Vfw A Korff	60	Spad		1415	1	
Obltn O v Boenigk	21	Balloon	Arcy-Ste Restuite	1930	18	
Sgt M Kuhn	21	Balloon	Hartennes-	1930	4	
Uffz H Haase	21	Balloon	Arcy	1930	2	
Obltn O v Boenigk	21	Spad 2	E Ambrief	1935	19	
OfStv K Thom	21	Spad	N Arcy	1937	27	
Ltn J Jessen	4	Spad	N Vauxtin	2005	2	
Ltn E Udet	4	Spad VII	S Braisne	2005	44	
Vfw G Fieseler	25	Nieuport	Strecke		9	a.
Ltn H Knappe	81	Spad	Chaméry		6	

a.   Serbian Escadrille 503, Lt AE Utman, KIA.
Losses
Uffz Strecker   10   Injured in a crash.

5 August 1918

Vfw G Fieseler	25	Nieuport	Gradesnica		10

Losses – Nil

6 August 1918

Vfw K Schlegel	45	Balloon	Mareuil-en-Dole	1250	14	a.
Ltn W Blume	9	Spad 2	S Bazoches		18	
Vfw G Dobberke	60	Spad 2	S Courville		7	
Uffz O Stockmann	66	Spad 2	S Braisne		2	
Ltn A Laumann	66	Spad 2	S Braisne		zlg	

a.   76, 1st Balloon Co USBS, 1Lt WS Anderson, OK.
Losses – Nil

7 August 1918

Obltn H Auffarth	29	SE5	Locon	0740	–	
Uffz E Binkenstein	51	DH9	Le Pont Mortier	0825	3	
Obltn R v Greim	34	SE5	SE Hangard	1000	16	a.
Ltn J Kithil	34	SE5	Hangard	1000	1	
Ltn P Lotz	44	SE5	SW Villers Bret.	1000	6	
Ltn F Kirchfeld	73	AR2	St Gilles	1545	–	
Ltn K Ritscherle	60	Spad	Mt Notre Dame	1630	4	
Ltn A Benzler	60	Spad	Magneux	1700	9	
Vfw A Korff	60	Spad	Magneux	1700	2	
Obltn O v Boenigk	21	Balloon	S Fismes	1720	20	b.
Sgt M Kuhn	21	Balloon	S Fismes	1720	5	c.
Gefr J Schlimpen	45	Breguet	Courville	1940	4	
Ltn A Laumann	66	Balloon			17	
Ltn H Knappe	81	AR2	Braisne		7	

a.   C1944, 84 Sqn RAF, Sgt HJN Guy, WIA/POW.
b.   2nd Balloon Co USBS, Lt G Phelps, OK & Lt HE Montgomery, OK.
c.   French 54 Compagnie Aérostières, Lt Dumas & Asp Bonnet, OK.
Losses
OfStv Walter Horing   17   Killed in a crash Vivaise airfield.
Vfw Ernst David   30   Killed in a crash Fleurbaix testing a
                               Roland DIVa.
Vfw Prinz   40   Lightly injured in a crash.

8 August 1918   The Battle of Amiens

Ltn O Könnecke	5	BF2b	by Méricourt	0900	23
OfStv J Mai	5	BF2b	by Méricourt	0900	18
Ltn A Scheicher	34	DH9	E Soyecourt	0900	1
Ltn G Meyers	37	DH9	Méricourt	0910	11
Ltn G Meyer	37	DH9	Villers Bretonneux	0915	12
Ltn H Kroll	24	RE8	W Villers Bret.	0940	–
Ltn P Lotz	44	SE5	SW Villers Bret.	1045	7
Vfw Borges	44	SE5	SE Villers Bret.	1045	1
Ltn O Könnecke	5	SE5	W Méricourt	1145	24
Uffz Löhr	44	SE5	SW Proyart	1230	–
Obltn R v Greim	34	RE8	S Morcourt	1240	17	a.
Ltn E Löwenhardt	10	Camel	Proyart	1245	49
Obltn R v Greim	34	Camel	NE Bayonvillers	1250	18
Ltn A Scheicher	34	Camel	E Méricourt	1250	2	b.
Ltn A Scheicher	34	DH9	S Morcourt	1255	3
Ltn K Baurenfeind	34	DH9	NW Proyart	1255	1
Ltn G Kröhl	34	DH9	SE Morcourt	1255	4
Obltn A Gutknecht	43	SE5	Foucaucourt	1400	4
Obltn A Gutknecht	43	DH9	SW Estrées	1405	zlg
Ltn O Creutzmann	46	SE5	Morcourt	1445	5	c.
Ltn P Billik	52	DH4	Berquin	1445	29	d.
Ltn Leppin	24	Engl 2	by Miséry	1545	1
Ltn A Hellwig	79	Camel	Lamotte	1615	3
Vfw K Gregor	29	DH9	SW Warfusée	1620	3
Ltn H Kroll	24	SE5		1625	–
Obltn H Auffarth	29	DH9	Harbonnières	1625	18
Obltn H Auffarth	29	DH9	Péronne a/f	1625	19
Ltn A Burkard	29	BF2b	Méricourt	1640	1
Uffz J Schmidt	79	BF2b	S Caix	1720	2
Ltn J Keller	43	SE5	SW Bray	1725	1
Vfw H Juhnke	52	SE5	Proyart	1725	5
Ltn E Udet	4	SE5	Fontaine/Cappy	1730	45
Ltn E Löwenhardt	10	Camel	Bray-sur-Somme	1730	50
Ltn L v Richthofen	11	Camel(DH9?)		1730	33	e.
Ltn L v Richthofen	11	SE5		1745	34	f.
Obltn A Gutknecht	43	Camel	Warfusée	1810	5
Ltn O Könnecke	5	SE5	NW Römerlager	1815	25
Ltn E Udet	4	SE5	SE Barleux	1830	46
Ltn J Grassmann	10	BF2b	Chaulnes	1830	4	g.
Ltn E Löwenhardt	10	Camel	Estrées	1850	51
Ltn L v Richthofen	11	SE5	Estrées	1850	35	h.
OfStv J Mai	5	BF2b	Ham	1855	19
Vfw F Hemer	6	DH12 (9)	Nesle	1900	18
Uffz H Reimers	6	DH9	Bethencourt	1930	1
OfStv F Altemeier	24	DH4	Haynecourt	1930	15
Ltn R Wenzl	6	DH9	Genermont	1940	6	i.
Ltn R Klimke	27	SE5	2 km S Herleville	1955	12	j.
Vfw O Fruhner	26	SE5	Estrées	2003	14	k.
Vfw C Mesch	26	BF2b	Proyart	2015	5	l.
Ltn E Udet	4	Camel	SE Foucaucourt	2040	47
Ltn A Scheicher	34	DH9	NE Cérisy	2200	4	m.
Vfw W Skorz	36	DH9			1	m.
Ltn G Meyer	37	DH9	St Christ		13	n.

Ltn G Meyer	37	Balloon	Villers Bretonneux		–
Ltn A Hets	37	RE8			4
Ltn H Henkel	37	BF2b			3
Vfw R Wirth	37	Camel	Warfusée		3
Uffz Gengelin	37	Camel			1
Ltn Schöbel	37	Camel			1
Vfw O Hennrich	46	SE5			7

Allied losses this date were too numerous to distinguish to any degree, especially with much of the fighting being over the Battle area.

The following are the most probable:

a. C2309, 3 Sqn AFC, Lt EJ Bice & 2/Lt JE Chapman, KIAs.
b. B7868, 73 Sqn RAF, Lt GW Gorman, POW.
c. C8732, 84 Sqn RAF, Capt R Manzer, DFC, POW.
d. D3078, 98 Sqn RAF, Capt FG Powell & Capt GHP Whitfield, both WIA/POW.
e. 49 Sqn.
f. B151, 60 Sqn RAF, 2/Lt JG Hall, an American, KIA.
g. D6962, 1 Sqn RAF, Capt KC Mills, KIA.
h. C786, 48 Sqn RAF, Lt JC Nuttall, POW & 2/Lt BC Pearson, WIA/POW.
i. D1719, 27 Sqn RAF, Lt LH Forest & Lt SWP Foster-Sutton, POWs.
j. B8423, 56 Sqn RAF, 1/Lt TJ Herbert, WIA.
k. E5975, 24 Sqn RAF, Lt FE Beauchamp, POW.
l. DH9 D7317, 27 Sqn RAF, 2/Lt HM Brown & 2/Lt DE Chase, POWs.
m. BF2bs of 48 Sqn RAF ?
n. 98 Sqn RAF.

Losses

Vfw Walgenbach	42	Taken prisoner.
Uffz Löhr	43	Taken POW, SW Villers Bretonneux.
Ltn Rudolf Neitzer	65	Killed in action Metz with DH4 bombers.
Ltn Hans Kiessling	79	Wounded, combat with Camels.
Uffz Johann Schmidt	79	Wounded in action, combat with Camels.

9 August 1918

Ltn A Heldmann	10	Camel	Chuignolles	0725	9	
Ltn L v Richthofen	11	DH9	Villers Carbonnel	0730	36	a.
Ltn E Just	11	Camel		0735	4	
Obltn E Löwenhardt	10	Camel	Estrées	0740	52	b.
Ltn P Wenzel	6	DH9	Vauvillers	0800	10	
Uffz H Reimers	6	DH9	Epenancourt	0800	2	
Vfw A Lux	27	DH9	Morcourt	0810	2	c.
Ltn R Klimke	27	DH9	Proyart	0810	13	d.
Ltn H Frommherz	27	DH9	Herleville	0810	11	d.
Vfw W Neuenhofen	27	Camel	E Framerville	0810	5	e.
Ltn P Billik	52	DH4	Rancourt	1105	30	f.
Ltn F Brandt	26	SE5	Rosières	1230	8	
Vfw C Mesch	26	SE5	Rosières	1230	6	g.
Ltn P Billik	52	SE5	Herville	1240	31	
Ltn H Maushake	4	DH9		1620	–	
Ltn O Könnecke	5	BF2b		1620	26	
Ltn E Udet	4	Camel	S Vauvillers	1625	48	h.
Uffz Schlemmel	9	AWFK8	Harbonnières	1725	1	
Ltn O v B-Marconnay	15	Spad	NW Tricot	1800	9	
Hptm R Berthold	JGII	Spad/Sop	Tricot	1800	41	
Ltn R Klimke	27	SE5	S Bray	1800	14	i.
Ltn O v B-Marconnay	15	Spad 2	Beaucourt	1815	10	j.
Ltn F Büchner	13	Spad 2	Lignières	1820	13	j.
Ltn J Klein	15	Camel	Beaucourt	1830	12	

Ltn J v Ziegesar	15	Camel	W Le Quesnel	1830	–	
Hptm R Berthold	JGII	Sopwith 2	Beaucourt	1830	42	
Ltn L v Richthofen	11	DH9	Foucaucourt	1840	37	k.
Obltn E Löwenhardt	10	Camel	W Cérisy	1855	53	l.
Vfw Kettelhack	63	Spad	S Mourmelon	1900	1	
Ltn Gutsche	36	Spad	Ligières	1915	1	m.
Ltn H Kroll	24	SE5	Le Quesnel	2020	–	
Ltn E Udet	4	Camel	SE Herlevillers	2120	49	n.
Ltn K Bolle	B	RE8	Rosières		29	o.
Ltn O Löffler	B	AWFK8	Maricourt		· 3	p.
Ltn O Könnecke	5	SE5			27	
Ltn O Könnecke	5	BF2b			28	
Ltn A Scheicher	34	DH9/BF2b	Ablaincourt		5	
Ltn A Hets	37	BF2b/DH4			5	
Ltn O Creutzmann	46	SE5			6	
OfStv R Heibert	46	DH9			13	
Vfw O Hennrich	46	Camel			8	
Ltn A Laumann	66	Spad	Reims		18	
Ltn A Laumann	66	Spad	S Reims		19	
Ltn A Laumann	66	Spad	S Reims		20	

a. D5666, 107 Sqn RAF, Capt WH Dore & Lt JE Wallace, KIAs.
b. F2167, 54 Sqn RAF, Lt ACR Hawley, KIA.
c. C6343, 107 Sqn RAF, Lt G Beveridge, WIA & Lt SL Dunlop, DFC, OK.
d. 107 Sqn RAF also lost: C6320, 2/Lt SJ Hill, POW & 2/AM FA Ellery ,DOW; D1722, Lt H Butterworth & Lt RO Baird, KIAs; E621, Lt JE Emtage & Lt P Willis, MM, KIA and E633, Lt SR Coward, WIA/POW & Lt LG Cooper, DOW.
e. E1548, 65 Sqn RAF, Lt CFW Illingworth, POW.
f. D8416, 57 Sqn RAF, Lt WJ Pitt-Pitts, KIA & 2/Lt HS Musgrove, DOW.
g. B8374, 32 Sqn RAF, 2/Lt PTA Reveley, WIA, POW.
h. D6520, 201 Sqn RAF, Lt R Stone, KIA.
i. E1327, 32 Sqn RAF, 1/Lt RL Paskill, KIA.
j. Two Spad XVIs lost this date: Escadrille Spa 289, Sgt Léger & Lt Flammang, KIAs and Spa 289, Sgt Pollet & S/Lt Bouvier, KIAs.
k. F6066, 107 Sqn RAF, Capt AJ Mayo & Lt JW Jones, KIAs.
l. D9589, 201 Sqn RAF, 2/Lt MS Misener, KIA.
m. Escadrille Spa 94, Sgt A Martin, MIA, Spad VII.
n. F5952, 65 Sqn RAF, Lt HE Dempsey, POW.
o. B6502, 6 Sqn RAF, Lt JET Sutcliffe, POW & 2/Lt LA Clack, POW.
p. C8593, 35 Sqn RAF, 2/Lt JM Brown, OK & 2/Lt A Gilchrist, OK.

Losses

Ltn Reinhardt	4	Wounded in action Tinscourt.
Vfw Franz Hemer	6	Wounded in action.
Ltn Egon Patzer	36	Killed in action Montdidier, probably by Capt J Battle, CO of Spa 103, over Etelfay.
Uffz Otto Stockmann	66	Taken POW, La Cuche Fokker DVII 771/18.

10 August 1918

Obltn R v Greim	34	DH9	S Lihons	1000	19	
Vfw P Groll	40	SE5	Swartenbrouck	1010	2	
Ltn F Noltenius	27	Dolphin	N Pussieux	1040	1	a.
Vfw W Neuenhofen	27	Dolphin	Etalon	1040	6	a.
Vfw A Lux	27	Dolphin	Pussieux	1040	3	a.
Ltn F Büchner	13	BF2b	Laon, N Saulchoy	1125	14	
Uffz Lohrmann	42	SE5	Rosières	1125	1	b.
Ltn E Udet	4	Camel	S Marcourt	1130	50	c.
Ltn HJ Borck	15	SE5	N Roye	1200	2	

Obltn E Löwenhardt	10	SE5	Chaulnes	1215	54	d.
Ltn F v Kökeritz	11	SE5		1215	1	
Hptm R Berthold	JGII	DH4	Licourt	1220	43	
Hptm R Berthold	JGII	DH4	Ablaincourt	1230	44	e.
Ltn O v B-Marconnay	15	SE5	NE Chaulnes	1240	–	
Ltn J Veltjens	15	SE5	Arvillers	1245	24	f.
Obltn H Auffarth	29	Camel	Proyart	1310	20	g.
Ltn H Maushake	4	RE8	S Vauvillers	1600	5	h.
Ltn O Creutzmann	46	SE5	NE Albert	1715	7	
Ltn S Büttner	61	DH4	Baugy	1805	5	
Uffz K Pietzsch	58	Balloon	Fismes	1825	1	i.
Ltn J Veltjens	15	Spad 2	Beauvraignes	1830	25	
Ltn E Udet	4	Camel	S Fay	1945	51	j.
Ltn A Hets	37	a/c			6	
Vfw G Dobberke	60	Spad			8	
Vfw A Korff	60	Spad			3	
Ltn A Laumann	66	DH9			21	
Ltn A Laumann	66	DH9			22	
Vfw R Luedecke	81	Spad	S Braisne		3	
Vfw D Averes	81	Spad	S Braisne		4	
Vfw R Luedecke	81	Spad	S Braisne		4	
Ltn H Knappe	81	Spad	Braisne		8	

a.   87 Sqn RAF lost two Dolphins this date: C4176, Lt TT Shipman, POW and D3774, 1Lt GS Harvey USAS, POW.
b.   E1286, 56 Sqn RAF, Lt H Allen, KIA.
c.   B7399, 3 Sqn RAF, Lt VB McIntosh, KIA.
d.   B8429, 56 Sqn RAF, Capt WO Bolger, KIA.
e.   B9344, 49 Sqn RAF, 2/Lt H Hartley & Sgt OD Beetham, POWs.
f.   D6094, 56 Sqn RAF, Lt HT Flintoft, POW.
g.   D1783, 73 Sqn RAF, Lt SA Dawson, KIA.
h.   C5069, 5 Sqn RAF, 2/Lt CF Grant, KIA & 2/Lt WH Webber, KIA.
i.   French 47 Compagnie Aérostières, S/Lt G Fournier, OK.
j.   43 Sqn RAF.

Losses

Obltn Erich Löwenhardt	10	Killed in a collision with Lt Alfred Wenz 1215, Chaulnes, parachute failed.
Ltn Alfred Wenz	11	Collision with Löwenhardt, baled out OK.
Ltn Muhs	12	Taken prisoner Cuvilly, E Bouchir 1150.
Ltn Franz Büchner	13	Motor hit in fight with Spads, forced to land.
Hptm Rudolf Berthold	JGII	Severely wounded in action near Péronne.
Ltn Albert Hets	37	KIA Vendelles Fokker DVII 712/18.
Ltn Paul Billik	52	POW, Vimy-Combles, possibly in a fight with 32 Sqn RAF.
Flg. Georg Lindenberg	52	Injured in a crash.
Flg. Herbert Koch	64	Killed in action Pont-à-Mousson.

11 August 1918

Ltn A Hellwig	79	Spad	NW Bus	0845	4	
Ltn K Plauth	20	DH9	W Lille	0850	3	a.
Ltn L v Richthofen	11	DH12(9)		0930	38	b.
Ltn R Otto	68	Spad	Mourmelon	0930	zlg	
Ltn E Udet	4	DH12(9)	Chaulnes	1000	52	c.
Sgt Beschow	64	Spad	Beney	1050	1	d.
OfStv J Kopka	61	DH4	Grévillers	1105	3	
Vfw K Strünkelberg	9	Spad	S Reims	1130	4	
Vfw E Buder	26	Breguet	Braye	1150	6	

Ltn J Veltjens	15	Caudron	W Roye	1220	26	e.
Ltn J Veltjens	15	Caudron	W Roye	1225	27	f.
OfStv G Dörr	45	Breguet	Braisne	1230	20	
Lth J Klein	15	SE5	W Nesle	1235	13	
Ltn J Veltjens	15	SE5	Nesle, N Roye	1240	28	
Ltn O v B-Marconnay	15	SE5	Gruny	1240	12	
Obltn O v Boenigk	21	Spad	E Arcy	1325	21	
Sgt M Kuhn	21	Breguet	E Arcy	1325	6	
Uffz W Dost	21	Breguet	E Arcy	1325	1	
OfStv W Kühne	18	Balloon	Thiaucourt	1627	5	g.
Ltn H Pippart	19	Balloon	Brély	1700	22	h.
Ltn H Becker	12	Spad	N Roye	1730	12	i.
Ltn U Neckel	13	Spad	Goyencourt	1730	21	j.
Ltn J Grassmann	10	Dolphin	Eclusier	1855	5	k.
Ltn A Heldmann	10	Dolphin	E Frise	1900	10	l.
Ltn F Büchner	13	Camel	Estrées	1908	15	
Ltn F Büchner	13	Camel	Roye, Estrées	1910	16	
Ltn H Schäfer	15	Breguet	SW Noyon	1945	6	
Gefr Felder	19	Breguet	Chauny-Roye	1955	1	m.
Ltn S Büttner	61	DH4	La Bossière	2115	6	
OfStv J Kopka	61	Balloon	1 km SW Piennes	2120	4	
Ltn K Bolle	B	Spad	Fismes		30	n.
OfStv K Thom	21	Spad			–	
Vfw G Fieseler	25	Nieuport	S Trnovo		11	o.
Ltn G Meyer	37	SE5			14	p.
Ltn A Laumann	66	Spad			23	
Ltn Sauermann	70	DH9	Nr Karlsruhe		2	q.
Uffz F Telge	81	Spad	Magneux		1	
Ltn H Knappe	81	Spad	Magneux		9	

a. C2199, 206 Sqn RAF, Lt EHP Bailey & 2/Lt R Milne, KIAs.
b. DH9 D3097, 98 Sqn RAF, 2/Lt BC Geary & 2/Lt EH Edgell, KIAs.
c. DH9 D1721, 98 Sqn RAF, 2/Lt JD Connolly, POW & 2/Lt EH Clayton, POW/DOW.
d. Spad VII 3435 '10', 103rd Aero, 1Lt VW Todd, POW.
e. Escadrille R 239, MdL Fey, WIA, Soldat Martin & Adj Pousse, WIAs.
f. Escadrille R 239, Brig Flamen, Sgt Richer & Soldat Crapel, MIAs.
g. 127, 7 Balloon Co USBS, Lt BT Burt, OK & Sgt HO Nicholls, OK.
h. British Balloon 12-16-5 (SR 92).
i. Escadrille Spa 37, Adj R Martin, MIA, Spad XIII.
j. Escadrille Spa 37, Adj M Coupillaud, MIA, Spad XIII.
k. B7876, 19 Sqn RAF, Lt MS Gregory, KIA.
l. C4043, 19 Sqn RAF, Lt RK Douglas, KIA.
m. Escadrille Br 117, S/Lt Kaciterlin & Adj-Chef Cambray, KIAs.
n. Salmson 2A2, 88th Aero, 1Lt JH McClendon & 2Lt CW Plummer, KIA.
o. Serbian Escadrille 524, Cpl D Pallière, KIA.
p. C8886, 60 Sqn RAF, 2/Lt RK Whitney, WIA.
q. D501, 104 Sqn IAF, 2/Lts JE Parke & W Bradford, POWs.

Losses

Ltn Bodo von der Wense	6	Killed in action Péronne-Herbecourt.
Ltn Paul Wenzel	6	Severely wounded in action Nesle.
Ltn Max Festler	11	Killed in action La Chapellette.
Ltn Hans Joachim Borck	15	Killed in action Rethonvillers near Nesle.
Ltn Hans Pippart	19	KIA Noyon during balloon attack, jumped from 150 ft but 'chute had no time to deploy.
Uffz Bernhard Vollers	20	Killed in a crash Menin airfield, test flight.
OfStv Karl Thom	21	Severely wounded in action.
Obltn Josef Mühlfeldt	23	Severely wounded Bertincourt by Verdun, during Dolphin combat – DOW 12 August.

Uffz Max Bauer	23	Shot down in flames, parachuted safely, in combat with Dolphins.
Uffz Schmid	24	Forced to land after difficult combat 2100.
Ltn Martin	46	Wounded in action S Römerstrasse.
Vfw Paul Völker	60	Severely wounded, DOW 13 August at Eppes.
Ltn Straube	70	Wounded in action near Hagenau.
OfStv Paul Steinbacher	81	Killed in action Reims.

12 August 1918

Ltn Hesse	75	Spad	Olenberg	0810	1	a.
Ltn F Röth	16	SE5	Langemarck	0840	19	b.
Vzflgmstr W Thöne	MFJ1	Camel	Poelkapelle	0845	3	
Ltn W v Richthofen	11	Camel	E Péronne	0930	4	c.
Ltn E Just	11	Camel	E Péronne	0935	5	c.
Ltn L v Richthofen	11	Camel	NW Péronne	0935	39	c.
Ltn L v Richthofen	11	Camel	NW Miséry	0950	40	c.
Vfw A Jühe	8	Spad	by Reims	1055	3	d.
Vfw R Francke	8	Spad	Reims	1055	13	e.
Vfw E Wiehle	43	SE5	Hazebrouck	1115	2	
Flgmt C Kähler	SFS2	Camel	Wenduyne	1129	2	
Ltn E Udet	4	SE5	Péronne	1130	53	f.
Ltn R Schmidt	43	DH9	Lacouture	1130	1	
Ltn R Spies	SFS2	Camel	Middlekerke	1140	3	
Vzflgmstr W Thöne	MFJ1	Camel	Wenduyne	1150	4	
OfStv J Mai	5	Camel	Maricourt	1215	20	g.
Ltn zS G Saschenberg	MFJ1	Camel	Sea off Ostende	1253	20	h.
Ltn zS G Saschenberg	MFJ1	DH4	Sea off Ostende	1255	21	i.
Flgmt G Hubrich	SFS2	Camel	Westende	1310	2	j.
OfStv F Altemeier	24	SE5	NW Roye	1810	16	k.
Ltn O Brandes	24	SE5	NW Roye	1810	1	l.
Vfw K Schlegel	45	Balloon	Droizy	1830	14	
Ltn R Reimer	26	Balloon	Fère-en-Tardenois	1840	3	m.
Vfw K Schlegel	45	Balloon	Loupeigne	1840	15	
Vfw W Seitz	8	Spad/AR2	Jonchéry	1850	9	
Ltn K Romeis	80	Balloon	Laronxe	1850	1	
Ltn zS M Stinsky	SFS2	Camel	Middlekerke	2000	1	
Vfw K Strünkelnberg	9	Breguet	NW Reims	2010	5	
Ltn zS T Osterkamp	MFJ2	Camel	Ramskapelle	2050	21	n.
Ltn zS T Osterkamp	MFJ2	Camel	Dixmuiden	2050	–	
Ltn zS T Osterkamp	MFJ2	G100	...N Ostkerke	2100	–	
Ltn O Könnecke	5	Fighter			29	o.
OfStv R Schleichhardt	18	DH9	Maurmünster		2	p.
Ltn K Monnington	18	DH9	Bühl-St Marie		4	q.
Ltn Kollatz	41	Breguet			1	
Vfw Bochmann	41	Breguet			1	
Ltn K Ritscherle	60	Spad	Braisne		5	

a.   Escadrille Spa 315, Sgt M Bertrou, KIA, Spad VII.
b.   D6875, 85 Sqn RAF, Lt TC Martin, KIA.
c.   209 Sqn RAF lost three Camels this date: B7471, Lt DK Leed, D9657, Lt RM Walker, KIAs and D9668, Capt JK Summers MC, POW.
d.   Escadrille Spa 84, Sgt R Vatta, MIA, Spad XIII.
e.   Escadrille Spa 156, MdL Roque, MIA, Spad VII.
f.   E3984, 40 Sqn RAF, Capt IF Hind, KIA.
g.   209 Sqn RAF ?
h.   D9507, 17th Aero, 1Lt RD Gracie, KIA.

i.   D1691, 218 Sqn RAF, Ens Mosely,OK & Lt MM Lowry, OK.
j.   D9648, 204 Sqn RAF, Lt WA Pomeroy, FTL, OK.
k.   E3949, 41 Sqn RAF, Lt JA Gorden, KIA.
l.   D6193, 40 Sqn RAF, Lt HH Wood, POW.
m.   French 68 Compagnie Aérostières.
n.   17th Aero, 1Lt HB Aldermann, WIA.
o.   SE5 40 Sqn RAF ?
p.   D2931, 104 Sqn IAF, 2/Lt OF Meyer & Sgt AC Wallace, POWs.
q.   D3084, 104 Sqn IAF, Lt GH Patman & 2/Lt JMS Macpherson, POWs.

Losses

Vfw Hermann Benzien	30	Injured in a crash.
Ltn Robert Schmidt	43	Downed in flames, combat with SE5s, parachuted OK, but slightly burned.
OfStv Fritz Blumenthal	53	Taken prisoner in Fokker DVII (Alb) 817/18, 'Nickchem IV' (G/5/20), by Camel of 209 Sqn & SE5 of 41 Sqn RAF.
Uffz Emil Possin	53	Wounded in action.
Uffz Winter	68	Wounded in action by Flak.
Vfw Heinrich Krüger	70	Killed in action Grunstadt.
Gefr Johann Janiszewski	75	KIA Romagny near Fontaine in Allied lines by Spads, 1710, in a Fokker DVII., (G/5/24). But possibly the claim by Br221 at 1620.
Vfw Karl Kallmünzer	78	Wounded, died of wounds, Wasselnheim.

13 August 1918

Uffz P Hüttenrauch	7	Camel	Zuidschoote	0850	3	a
Ltn U Neckel	19	Camel	Le Quesnel	1200	22	b.
Gefr Scheutzel	65	DH4	Arnaville	1400	–	
Ltn G Ungewitter	78	DH9	Halleville	1400	1	
Ltn K Monnington	18	DH9	N Arrich-Thionville	1705	5	c.
Ltn K Monnington	18	DH9	N Arrich	1705	6	d.
Ltn zS P Achilles	SFS2	DH9	Dixmuiden	1715	2	
Flgmt C Kairies	SFS2	DH9	Dixmuiden	1715	3	e.
Obltn B Loerzer	JGIII	SE5	Chaulnes	1720	29	f.
Vfw O Fruhner	26	SE5	Foucheres	1720	15	g.
Ltn H Frommherz	27	SE5	Rouvroy	1730	12	
Ltn R Klimke	27	DH9	Roye	1820	15	h.
Ltn F Röth	16	Balloon	Lampernisse –	1920	20	i.
Ltn F Röth	16	Balloon	–Oudecapelle	1920	21	j.
Ltn F Röth	16	Balloon	"	1920	22	k.
Ltn Elting	69	Spad	Les Petites Loges	1940	1	l.
Uffz Stehling	69	Spad	Les Petites Loges	1940	1	l.
Ltn E Koepsch	4	Breguet	Bilancourt	1945	6	m.
Uffz E Binge	16	BF2b	Armentières	1945	3	
Ltn A Raben	18	DH9	Altdorf, NE Metz		3	n.
OfStv W Kühne	18	DH9	by Wieginger		6	n.
OfStv W Kühne	18	DH9	by Chambrey		7	n.
OfStv W Kühne	18	DH9	Altdorf		–	
Oblt H-H v Bodien	59	DH4	Haynecourt		2	
Vfw J Hohly	65	DH4	Les Eparges		3	
Ltn zS G Saschenberg	MFJ1	Spad			–	
Ltn zS G Saschenberg	MFJ1	a/c			–	

a.   D3917, 41 Sqn RAF, Lt EH Barksdale, OK.
b.   D9642, 201 Sqn RAF, Major CD Booker,DSC, KIA.
c.   D2881, 104 Sqn IAF, 2/Lt FH Beaufort & 2/Lt SO Bryant, KIAs.
d.   D7229, 104 Sqn IAF, 2/Lt HPG Leyden & Sgt AL Windridge, KIAs.

e.   B1701, 211 Sqn RAF?

f.   E1308, 60 Sqn RAF, Lt EJC McCracken, POW.

g.   D6979, 60 Sqn RAF, Lt JR Anderson, KIA.

h.   D3088, 104 Sqn IAF, 2/Lt EO Clarke, KIA & Lt JLC Sutherland, POW.

i.   Belgium Balloon No 3, Adj Herion, OK & Sgt Kaldfleisch, OK.

j.   Belgium Balloon No 6, Adj Brossel, OK & Sgt Doly, OK.

k.   Belgium Balloon No 2, Adj Delaporter, OK & 1/Sgt Tillemans, OK.

l.   Two French Spads lost, Escadrille Spa 98, Sgt P Jolivet near Montbré, Spad XIII and Spa 154, Brig E Brune,Spad VII – both KIA.

m.   Escadrille Br 45, Lt Marinier & Lt Porteau de la Morandière, MIAs.

n.   205 and 206 Sqns RAF lost the following DH4s and DH9s: DH4 A7573, 205 Sqn RAF, Lt T Fattorini & 2/Lt SJ Parkes, KIAs; DH4 D8429, 205 Sqn RAF, Lt FO McDonald, WIA & Sgt FG Manning, KIA; DH9 D5590, 206 Sqn RAF, Lt CS Johnson & 2/Lt AB Sangster, KIAs and DH9, 206 Sqn RAF, 2/Lt E Calvert, (O) DOW.

Losses

Ltn Lothar Freiherr von Richthofen	11	Wounded by American Camels of the 148th Aero.
Ltn Hilmar Schickler	19	Killed in action Roye.
Ltn Erwin Häfner	22	Killed in a collision Balâtre 1100.
Flg Hermann Horstmann	22	Killed in the above collision.
Flg Hoffmann	24	Lightly injured in a crash, remained on unit.
Ltn Gutsche	36	Wounded in action Bussny.
Vfw Stein	45	Lightly wounded in action.
Ltn Dieter Collin	56	Severely wounded Bailleul and later DOW.
Obltn Reinhold Ritter von Benz	78	Killed in action Mondon Wald, 1400, in Fokker DVII 4461/18, combat with DH4s.
Gefr Emil Eitenfelder	79	Wounded in action.
Ltn Rudolf Spies	SFSII	Wounded in action Jabbeke with DH9s.
Flgobmt Klotzsch	MFJ1	Wounded in bomb attack Jabbeke a/f 0650.
Flgmstr Wilhelm Drews	MFJ2 ⎫	
Vzflgmstr Günther Knie	MFJ2 ⎬	All three killed in bombing attack Jabbeke airfield at 0640 hours.
Flgmstr Wilhelm Grabowski	MFJ2 ⎭	

14 August 1918

Ltn H Brünig	50	Spad 2	Besannes	1045	6	a.
Ltn H Leptien	63	Dolphin	SW Bailleul	1105	5	b.
Ltn W Sommer	39	DH9	Bertincourt	1120	2	c.
Uffz G Staudacher	1	BF2b		1150	1	
Ltn H Becker	12	SE5	Villers Carbonnel	1200	13	
Ltn Koch	12	Sopwith	Marchélepot	1200	–	
Ltn U Neckel	19	SE5	Chaulnes	1205	23	d.
Ltn J Klein	15	Breguet	Chaulnes	1215	14	
Ltn W Bastian	MFJ1	Camel	Oostkamp –	1240	1	e.
Flgmt H Hackbusch	MFJ1	Camel	– Zeebrugge	1240	1	e.
Vfw E Buder	26	Breguet	Chaméry	1255	8	
Ltn H-J Rolfes	45	Spad	Branges	1340	9	
Gefr J Schlimpen	45	Spad	Branges	1340	5	
Obltn T Dahlmann	JGIII	SE5	Fresnoy	1625	2	
Ltn F Reimer	26	SE5	Mézières	1630	4	
OfStv J Ledermann	13	1 Seater	Chaulnes	1840	1	f.
Ltn F Büchner	13	Camel	Chaulnes	1840	17	f.
Vfw A Haussmann	13	Camel	Chaulnes	1840	9	f.
Ltn F Büchner	13	Camel	Chaulnes	1840	–	
Ltn E Udet	4	BF2b	S Vermandovillers	1900	54	g.
Ltn Schramm	56	BF2b	Wervicq	1915	1	h.
Vfw Rothe	61	1 Seater	S Tracy le Mont	1950	–	
Ltn G Tschentschel	72	Breguet	Fismes, Lhéry	2035	4	
Vfw K Arnold	72	AR2	Fismes, Lhéry	2035	4	

Ltn O Könnecke	5	BF2b		30
Sgt M Kuhn	21	Balloon	SW Soissons	7
Vfw E Buder	26	SE5	Folies	–
Vfw E Buder	26	Breguet	Harbonnières	–
Obltn B Loerzer	JGIII	SE5		30
Vfw O Fruhner	26	SE5	Quesnil	–
Vfw J Hohly	65	DH4	NE Gaudach	4

a.   Possibly Escadrille Spa 51, Lt Vuillaume & Lt Bouchet, KIAs, their Spad XVI falling in flames near Orne.
b.   E4434, 87 Sqn RAF, Lt RA Hewat, KIA.
c.   D2861, 49 Sqn RAF, 2/Lt JG Andrews, KIA & 2/Lt J Churchill, KIA.
d.   C1888, 92 Sqn FAR, Lt HA O'Shea, POW.
e.   17th Aero lost two Camels this date, D9455, 1Lt LE Case, KIA and F2134, 2Lt WH Shearman, POW/DOW.
f.   46 Sqn RAF lost three Camels: F2086, 2/Lt GAR Hill, POW; F2112, 2/Lt CE Thorpe, POW and D6631, 2/Lt JE Crouch, KIA.
g.   C852, 88 Sqn RAF, Lt AR Stedman & 2/Lt GR Howard, POWs.
h.   C987, 20 Sqn RAF, Lt DE Smith, KIA & 2/Lt J Hills, POW.

Losses

Flg Eickhoff	17	Injured in a crash Vivaise airfield.
Ltn Heinrich Kroll	24	Severely wounded in action Omencourt.
Ltn Kurt Brüninghaus	31	Killed in a collision St Loup airfield with Ltn Emil Meyer, who parachuted safely.
Uffz Karl Klein	37	Killed in action Vendelles.
Gefr Biehl	59	Wounded in action.
OfStv Belitz	69	Injured in a crash.
Uffz Ludwig Wittmann	80	Taken prisoner 1700 in Albatros DVa (OAW) 6831/17, combat with DH9s.
Flgmt Karl Goldenstedt	MFJ1	Killed in action over Oostkamp.

15 August 1918

Ltn K Hetze	13	Spad	Crapeaumesnil	0920	3	
Ltn Schramm	56	Camel	St Julien	0935	2	a.
Ltn E Baumgärtel	56	Camel	St Julien	0935	1	a.
Ltn P Strähle	57	Spad	Tahure	1005	–	
Ltn H Böhning	79	Spad	Chevincourt	1025	13	
Ltn A Merz	28	Breguet	Ambonnay	1125	1	
Vfw G Klaudat	15	Caudron	NE Ribécourt	1220	1	b.
Vfw O Fruhner	26	Sopwith	Parvillers	1625	16	
Ltn E Udet	4	Camel	Herleville	1715	55	c.
Ltn P Lotz	44	Camel	Hallu-Chaulnes	1720	8	
Vfw W Stör	68	Spad	St Rémy Wald	1730	3	
Ltn K Hetze	13	Spad	Liaucourt	1925	4	
Ltn K Plauth	20	Camel	E Passchendaele	1935	4	d.
Sgt M Kuhn	21	Spad			8	
Ltn K Odebrett	42	Caudron	E Compiègne		13	e.
Uffz E Sonneck	66	Spad			6	
Sgt Dittberner	66	Spad			2	
Ltn J Fichter	67	Salmson			5	f.
Vfw Wimmer	80	DH4			–	g.
OfStv Gruenwald	K3	DH4	Courbesseaux		1	g.
Ltn zS T Osterkamp	MFJ2	G100	Ostende		–	

a.   204 Sqn RAF lost two Camels in the am: B7176, Lt JR Robinson, WIA and D9630, Lt CD Darlington, KIA.
b.   Escadrille C 46, Adj Loiler, MdL Anceau, KIA & 2/Lt P Penfield, KIAs.
c.   D1927, 4 Sqn AFC, Lt RG Smallwood, WIA.
d.   E4405, 204 Sqn RAF, Lt DE Culver, POW.

e. Escadrille C 46, Brig Dupart, Sgt WJ McKerness (American), & Sgt Colin, all KIA.
f. 91st Aero, 1Lt JH Lambert, OK & 1Lt HN Morgan, OK.
g. 55 Sqn RAF.

Losses

Sgt Emil Vitzthum	16	Wounded, Ypres, in combat with 204 Sqn RAF; DOW 16 August Linselles
Vfw Fritz Schwarz	33	Killed in a crash St Loup airfield.
Ltn August Wüst	42	Killed in action Bois de Thiescourt.
Vfw Karl Roman	56	Killed in a crash Rumbeke airfield.
Flgmt Friedrich Gröschke	SFS2	Lightly wounded in action 2000, but remained on unit.

16 August 1918

Ltn E Udet	4	Spad	S Foucaucourt	1040	56	a.
Flg L Kormann	79	Spad	Coucy-le Château	1145	1	
Ltn J Veltjens	15	Spad 2	S Noyon	1220	29	
Ltn O v B-Marconnay	15	Spad	SE Tracy le Val	1220	13	
Ltn G v Hantelmann	15	Spad	Carlepont	1220	5	
Ltn E Rolff	6	Camel	Mesnil	1230	3	b.
Ltn J Veltjens	15	Spad	W Lassigny	1930	30	
Vfw G Fieseler	25	AR2	N Negocani		12	
Ltn J Bender	25				-	
Vfw Waldvogel	25				–	
Uffz A Müller	39	BF2b			1	
Ltn S Büttner	61	Balloon			7	
Ltn S Büttner	61	Spad			8	
Ltn S Büttner	61	Balloon			9	
Uffz Henkel	61	Spad			1	
OfStv J Kopka	61	Balloon			5	
Vfw T Boelcke	67	Spad			2	
Vfw Lemke	70	DH4	Dageburg		1	c.
Vfw K Bücher	K1a	DH4			2	c.
OfStv Gruenwald	K3	DH9	Buchsweiler		–	c.
Ltn zS G Saschenberg	MFJ1	Camel	Sea off Zeebrugge		22	d.
Ltn zS G Saschenberg	MFJ1	DH9	Sea off Cadzand		23	e.
Ltn zS T Osterkamp	MFJ2	DH9	Off Blankenberge		22	f.

a. Escadrille Spa 3, S/Lt J Caël, POW, Spad XIII.
b. D9595, 203 Sqn RAF, Sgt PM Fletcher, POW.
c. 55 Sqn IAF, lost three DH4s with two other crews being WIA: A7781, 2/Lt JB McIntyre & 2/Lt HH Bracher,KIAs; A7813, 2/Lt J Campbell, POW & 2/Lt JR Fox, POW/DOW, and D9273, 2/Lt EA Browhill & 2/Lt WT Madge,both KIA.
d. 213 Sqn RAF.
e. B7623, 211 Sqn RAF, 1Lt DR Harris USAS & 2/Lt J Munro, Interned.
f. D1708, 218 Sqn RAF, Lt AC Lloyd & 2/Lt MG Wilson, Interned.

Losses

Vfw Lechner	6	Injured in a crash.
Ltn Ernst Riedel	19	Killed in a crash testing Fokker EV 107/18 Chéry les Pouilly airfield.
Vfw Otto Senff	48	Killed in action Catigny.

17 August 1918

Ltn K Plauth	20	SE5	W Wervik	1000	5	a.
Ltn J Gildmeister	20	SE5	E Wervik	1000	2	b.
Vfw G Klaudat	15	Spad XIII	Beauvraignes	1710	2	
Uffz Vahldieck	50	Spad	Ormes	1715	1	
Ltn J Veltjens	15	Spad	Roye	1720	31	

Ltn G v Hantelmann	15	Spad	Roye	1720	–	

a.   E4014, 41 Sqn RAF, Lt TM Alexander, KIA.
b.   F5910, 41 Sqn RAF, Lt WG Claxton, DSO, DFC, POW.

Losses

Ltn Helmuth Fürstenau	44	Killed in action Berlancourt Fokker DVII.

18 August 1918

Vfw O Hennrich	46	Balloon	Marcelcave	1845	9	
Uffz G Staudacher	1	RE8	Beaumetz	1940	2	a.
Ltn A Lindenberger	B	Breguet	Moulin-Touvent		6	
Ltn E Bormann	B	AR2	Nouvron		3	b.
Ltn S Büttner	61	Balloon			11	

a.   6 Sqn RAF.
b.   Possibly Escadrille AR 268, S/Lt Paquier,KIA & Lt Cournaire,WIA.

Losses

Ltn Wilhelm Gäckstatter	51	Killed in action Fletre 1845.

19 August 1918

OfStv J Mai	5	BF2b	by Lihons	0805	21	a.
OfStv J Mai	5	BF2b	by Lihons	0805	22	b.
OfStv J Mai	5	SE5	by Transloy	0835	23	c.
Ltn A Laumann	10	SE5	Bapaume	0842	25	
Ltn A Heldmann	10	SE5	Aveluy	0900	11	
OfStv P Aue	10	Camel	SW Puisieux	0900	8	
Ltn Matzdorf	6	Camel	E Beauvais	0950	2	
Ltn F Büchner	13	BF2b/DH9	Pertain	1006	18	d.
OfStv R Jörke	39	BF2b/DH9	Arras	1050	11	d.
Ltn A Fleischer	17	Spad	Château Thierry	1750	3	e.
Vfw T Boelcke	67	Balloon	Thierville		3	f.

a.   C926, 48 Sqn RAF, 2/Lt ES Glasse & 2/Lt CW Woodend, collision
b.   with D8027, 48 Sqn RAF, Lt RH Davis & 2/Lt EG Locke,all KIA.
c.   E1348, 56 Sqn RAF, Lt TD Hazen, KIA.
d.   98 and 104 Sqns ?
e.   Escadrille Spa 94, MdL M Gaulier, MIA, Spad XIII.
f.   French 61 Compagnie Aérostières.

Losses

Ltn Emil Rolff	6	Killed in a crash due to wing failure of a Fokker EV at Bernes, 0950 hours.
Flg Anders	45	Injured in a crash.

20 August 1918

Ltn F Noltenius	27	Balloon	N V-Cotterêts	1255	2	a.
Ltn H-J Rolfes	45	Breguet	Chezy au Mont	1325	10	b.
Vfw A Hausmann	13	Breguet	Blérancourt	1600	10	b.
Vfw T Boelcke	67	Balloon	Montzéville	1730	4	
Vfw H Donhauser	17	Breguet		1855	1	b.
Ltn F Anders	73	Voisin	Warmeriville	2335	3	c.
Ltn F Anders	73	Voisin	Châlons	2350	4	d.
Ltn A Lindenberger	B	AR2	W Champs		7	
Ltn F Büchner	13	Spad			19	e.
Ltn F Büchner	13	Breguet			20	b.
Ltn O Steger	53	2 Seater			1	

a.   French 71 Compagnie Aérostières, S/Lt Pujan, OK & 2/Lt E Martinet, OK.
b.   Three French Breguets were lost: Escadrille Br 108, Lt Marques & S/Lt Maguet, MIAs; Br 127, S/Lt

Dufayet, & S/Lt Castets, MIAs and Br 131, Adj Emmanuelli & S/Lt Ulrich, MIAs.
c.   Escadrille VB 222, Lt Poissonnier & MdL G Lepicier, KIAs.
d.   2996, Escadrille VB 25, MdL Cronan, & Sgt E Mangot, MIAs.
e.   Escadrille Spa 155, Lt Castaignet, MIA, Spad XIII.

Losses

OfStv Jakob Ledermann	13	Taken prisoner after combat with Spads.
Ltn Erich Raabe	41	Wounded in action in the foot.
Gefr Johannes Schlimpen	45	Killed in action Fismes.
Vfw Thilo Boelcke	67	Killed in action Montzéville near Fresnil in Albatros DVa (OAW) 6591/17, during balloon attack.

21 August 1918

Ltn Porak	72	Spad	Gueux	1035	1	
OfStv W Beyer	42	Spad	N Gury	1140	4	
Ltn H Böhning	79	Spad 2	Nampsel	1140	14	
OfStv G Dörr	45	Spad XI	Rosnay	1145	21	
Ltn Krayer	45	Spad	Rosnay	1150	1	
Vfw Rüttgers	71	Spad	Diefmatten	1205	1	a.
Ltn W Blume	9	Spad	Missy aux Bois	1228	19	
Ltn U Neckel	19	Spad XIII	Quierzy	1400	24	
Ltn zS T Osterkamp	MFJ2	DH9	Sea off Breedene	1400	23	b.
Feldw K Schmückle	21	Spad	Soissons	1630	4	
Ltn J Keller	21	Spad	Soissons	1630	2	
Ltn F Höhn	21	Breguet	S Soissons	1630	21	
Uffz G Staudacher	1	DH4	Moislains	1645	3	c.
Uffz Weidemann	1	SE5	Longavesnes	1645	1	
Ltn O v B-Marconnay	15	Breguet	Chauny	1650	–	
Ltn J Klein	15	Breguet	Chauny	1650	–	
Vfw G Klaudat	15	Breguet	Chauny	1700	3	
Ltn Siebert	15	Breguet	Chauny	1700	–	
Vfw K Schlegel	45	Balloon	Vic	1715	18	d.
Obltn R v Greim	34	DH9	NE Péronne	1720	20	
Ltn R Otto	68	Breguet	Bezannes	1720	3	
Vfw K Schlegel	45	Balloon	Branges	1745	17	e.
Vfw A Haussmann	13	Breguet	Champs	1800	11	
Ltn E Udet	4	SE5	S Hébuterne	1830	57	
Vfw O Hennrich	46	2 Seater	Ayette	1830	–	
Ltn H Steinbrecher	46	SE5	Ayette	1846		
Ltn E Udet	4	Dolphin	S Courcelles	1915	58	f.
Vfw R Nebel	73	Spad	Vaux Varennes	1950	1	
Ltn F Anders	73	Voisin	Heutrégiville	2350	5	g.
Obltn T Cammann	74	Voisin	Annelles	2350	9	g.
Ltn O Löffler	B	Breguet	W Champs		4	
OfStv G Dörr	45	Spad	Rosnay		22	
Ltn K Brendle	45	a/c			–	
Ltn S Büttner	61	DH4			12	
Vfw Rothe	61	Balloon			2	
Vfw R Rübe	67	Balloon			4	h.
Flgmt C Kairies	SFS2	Camel	off Blankenberghe		4	i.
Flgmt G Hubrich	SFS2	DH4	Westende		3	
Ltn P Becht	SFS2	Camel	Ichteghem		1	i.
Ltn E Krantz	SFS2	DH4	Ichteghem		2	
Flgmt G Hubrich	SFS2	Camel	Zeebrugge		4	i.
Ltn G Saschenberg	MFJ1	DH4	Sea off Zeebrugge		24	

a.   Escadrille Spa 49, Sgt Perrier, WIA.
b.   D8420, 202 Sqn RAF, Lt GR Hurst,OK & Sgt LA Allen, WIA.
c.   F6112, 107 Sqn RAF, Lt HC Curtis & Lt FG Davies, KIAs.
d.   French 83 Compagnie Aérostières, Cpl Gaitz-Hocki, OK.
e.   French 33 Compagnie Aérostières, Lt Cabard, OK.
f.   Camel E1478, 148th Aero, 2Lt TW Imes, WIA.
g.   Escadrille VB 121 lost two Voisin's this date.
h.   French 25 Compagnie Aérostières, Cpl Aboucays & Asp Depoux, OK.
i.   213 Sqn RAF lost two Camels, D3380, Lt J Wooding, POW and D9659, Lt WA Rankin, FTL, OK.

Losses

Ltn Johannes Hentschel	9	Injured in a crash.
Uffz Rudolf Klamt	10	Wounded in action.
Flg Karl Scharrenbroich	39	Killed in a crash Bapaume airfield.
Ltn Hans Joachim Rolfes	45	Lightly wounded 'v' Spads, remained.
Vfw Eichhorn	58	Injured in a crash on take-off.
Vfw Anton Bernhörster	61	Killed in action Montigny Fokker DVII 2184/18 (G/3/12) by Camel of 3 Sqn RAF.
Flgmt Friedrich Gröschke	SFS2	Killed in action in Sea off Blankenberge, Fokker DVII 885/18.

22 August 1918

Ltn E Udet	4	Camel	N Braie	0830	59	a.
Vfw J Pütz	34	BF2b	N Méaulte	0835	7	b.
OfStv E Prime	78	DH9	Mannheim	0900	2	c.
Ltn H Jungwirth	78	DH9	Ingeweiler	0905	1	c.
Ltn W Nebgen	7	BF2b	Westroosebeke	0940	2	d.
Uffz G Staudacher	1	SE5	Courcelles	1100	4	
Vfw Kister	1	BF2b	Courcelles	1100	2	
Uffz G Borm	1	RE8	Courcelles	1100	1	
Vfw H Donhauser	17	Spad	Soissons	1135	2	
Ltn E Udet	4	SE5	W Maricourt	1230	60	
Ltn A Laumann	10	SE5	Becourt-Becordel	1245	25	
Ltn W Peckmann	9	Spad	Queuneviers	1340	2	
Vfw A Haussmann	13	Balloon	Carlepont	1410	12	
Ltn Hinneberg	59	DH9	Ablainville	1410	2	
Ltn F Höhn	21	Balloon	Selens	1430	9	
Ltn W Kohlbach	10	SE5	Cappy-s-Somme	1745	3	e.
Ltn A Laumann	10	SE5	NW Bray	1745	26	
OfStv W Hippert	74	Caudron	NW Soissons	1900	8	
Ltn E Bormann	B	Spad	S Neufheuse		4	
Vfw H Korsch	53	Spad	Coucy le Château		1	
Vfw Knobel	57	RE8	Achiet le Grand		1	
Ltn S Büttner	61	Balloon			13	f.
Ltn H v Hippel	71	Spad	Sennheim		–	
OfStv W Hippert	74	Breguet			–	

a.   F1969, 80 Sqn RAF, 2/Lt AL Tupman, KIA.
b.   Possibly 62 Sqn RAF which had two crews shot up this date.
c.   104 Sqn IAF lost seven DH9s: C2179, Lt GHB Smith & Sgt W Harrop, MM, POWs; C6202, 2/Lt J Valentine & 2/Lt CG Hitchcock, POWs; D1048, 2/Lt RT Seale, POW & 2/Lt CGV Pickard, KIA; D1729, Capt JB Home-Hay, MC, DFC, & Sgt WT Smith DCM, MM, POWs; D2812, Capt EA McKay, MC, DFC & Lt RAC Brie, POWs; D2917, 1/Lt HP Wells & 2/Lt JJ Redfield, POWs, and D5729, Lt E Cartwright & Lt AGL Mullen, KIAs.
d.   D7993, 20 Sqn RAF, Capt D Latimer, MC, DFC, POW & Lt TC Noel, MC, KIA.
e.   E3918, 64 Sqn RAF, Lt KJ Isaac, WIA.
f.   French 87 Compagnie Aérostières.

Losses

Vfw Kister	1	Wounded in action.

Ltn Artur Merz	28	Severely wounded in action Ghislain by Bapaume 0830, DOW 27 August, in Mons.
Obltn Hugo Krauss	32	Killed in crash on take-off Villers-au-Tertre.
Uffz Walter Feibicke	44	Killed in a crash Gussy on practice flight.
Ltn Walter Boldt	52	Forced to land between the lines but got back.
Uffz Bödinghaus	61	Taken prisoner Ribécourt Pfalz DXII 1460/18.
Sgt Starost	61	Taken prisoner Ribécourt.
Obltn Theodor Cammann	74	Wounded in action.

23 August 1918 The Battle of Bapaume

Obltn H Auffarth	29	Camel	NW Gavrelle	0805	21	
Vfw W Seitz	8	Spad	Bouvancourt	0935	10	
Vfw R Francke	8	Spad	Bouvancourt	0935	14	
Ltn W Junck	8	Spad	S Vendeuil	0940	2	
Ltn O Brandes	24	Spad	Blérancourt	1005	2	
Vfw A Schymik	24	Spad	Blérancourt	1005	1	
Ltn zS T Osterkamp	MFJ2	Camel	Pervyse	1210	24	
Vfw G Fieseler	25	Spad	Sivestrena		13	a.
Vfw E Schütze	25	Spad	..... W Vitole		5	
Ltn K v Schönebeck	33	Camel	W Bray, Pys		5	
Uffz W Hofacker	65	Caudron	Gironville Wald		1	
Ltn zS B Heinrich	MFJ1	DH4	Boitshoeke		12	

a. Serbian Escadrille 524, 2/Sgt C Cooran & 2/Sgt R Kakiru, KIAs.

Losses

Ltn Raven Frhr von Barnekow	11	Lightly wounded remained with unit.
OfStv Emil Bergmann	22	DOI from a crash Flavy-le Martel airfield.
Flg Hermann Jander	24	Killed in action Blérancourt 1005 with Spads, probably by Spa 86, a DVII at Blérancourt, pilot POW/DOW.
Uffz Theurer	38	Wounded in action.
Ltn Georg Vieth	61	Collided with Vfw Rothe St Gobain and killed.
Vfw Rothe	61	Lightly injured in the above crash, remained.
Flg Leonard Kormann	79	Killed in action St Martin-sur-Cojeul, near Fismes, 1200, in Fokker DVII 4284/18 (G/3/13).

24 August 1918

Ltn W Blume	9	Spad	N Soissons	1200	20	
OfStv G Dörr	45	AR2	Vizaponin	1330	23	
Obltn R v Greim	34	Camel	NW Bapaume	1800	21	a.
Ltn F Höhn	21	Spad	NW Soissons	1830	10	
Uffz W Dost	21	Spad	NW Soissons	1835	2	
Ltn O Könnecke	5	SE5	N Bapaume	1920	31	b.
Ltn K Plauth	20	AWFK8	Comines-Wervik	2010	6	c.
Ltn E Thuy	28	SE5	Tilloy		26	d.
Vfw G Spadinger	28	SE5	Tilloy		1	d.

a. F5985, 17th Aero, 2Lt GT Wise, POW.
b. D6970, 1 Sqn RAF, 1/Lt RH Ritter, KIA.
c. D5176, 82 Sqn RAF, 2/Lt T McCarthy & 2/Lt CW Sommerville, KIAs.
d. 56 Sqn RAF lost two SE5s: B8414, Lt HJW Roberts, POW and D6121, 2/Lt DC Collier, KIA.

Losses

Obltn Fritz Walter Grosch	4	Lightly wounded in action Guise.
Uffz Ernst Binkenstein	51	Killed in action Ploegsteert Wald.
Gefr Richard Probst	79	Wounded, died 21 October at Schneidemühl.
Ltn Herbert Wilhelm Franz Knappe	81	Severely wounded in action.

25 August 1918

Vfw Knobel	57	Dolphin	NE Martinpuich	1000	2	a.
Flg Hechler	57	Dolphin	SW Bapaume	1000	1	a.
Vfw H Donhauser	17	Breguet	Aubignicourt	1145	3	b.
Vfw O Hennrich	46	Balloon	W Albert	1210	10	c.
Vfw H Donhauser	17	Spad	Vézaponin	1835	4	
Ltn M Kämmerer	35	DH4	Bévillers	1900	2	d.
Ltn E Thuy	28	RE8	Eterpigny		27	e.
Uffz Schaack	28	SE5	Bapaume		1	
Ltn E Thuy	28	Camel	Courcelles		28	f.
Uffz Rosenau	33	SE5	Pelves		2	
Ltn P Strähle	57	Dolphin	Achiet le Grand		–	
Ltn J Jensen	57	Dolphin	Achiet le Grand		–	
Ltn Blum	57	DH9	Haucourt		2	
Flgmt C Kairies	SFS2	Camel	Blankenberge		5	
Flgmt C Kairies	SFS2	Camel	Ichteghem		6	g.

a.   87 Sqn RAF lost two Dolphins this date: D3718, Capt AAND Pentland MC DFC, WIA, and C8109, Lt DC Mangan (American), FTL, OK.
b.   Escadrille Sal 18, Brig Fournillon & Asp Bogey, KIAs.
c.   British Balloon 1-18-3 (AR 7).
d.   DH9 D1075, 49 Sqn RAF, Lt CH Stephens & 2/Lt AB Henderson, POWs.
e.   C2611, 12 Sqn RAF, 2/Lt WJ McLean, WIA & Lt Godson, OK.
f.   C3314, 73 Sqn RAF, Lt HLM Dodson, KIA.
g.   C6358, 213 Sqn RAF, Lt EC Toy, KIA.

Losses

Ltn Friedrich Wilhelm Dieves	45	Taken prisoner Ferme Marigny in a Fokker DVII 4162/18, after hit by French AA fire.
Vfw Siegried Walter	55	Killed in action Tulkern.
Ltn Otto Fitzner	65	Wounded in action.

26 August 1918   The Battle of the Scarpe

Obltn O Schmidt	5	Balloon	S Morcourt	1645	11	a.
Uffz Leicht	5	Balloon	Harbonnières	1700	1	
Ltn H Frommherz	27	Camel	Sapignies	1745	13	b.
Ltn H Frommherz	27	Camel	Vaulx	1800	14	c.
Ltn H Frommherz	27	Camel	NE Beugny	1805	15	d.
Ltn R Klimke	27	Camel	N Beugny	1955	16	e.
Vfw Donhauser	17	Balloon	Carlepont	2000	6	
Vfw Donhauser	17	Spad	N Cuts	2005	5	
Ltn K Bolle	B	Camel	W Beugny		31	f.
Ltn F Heinz	B	Camel	Bourlon Wood		1	g.
Obltn B Loerzer	JGIII	Camel	Beugny		31	h.
Ltn K v Schönebeck	33	Camel	Dury		6	
Ltn W Preuss	66	Spad	Soissons		9	

a.   British Balloon 29-13-5 (SR 81).
b.   D9516, 148th Aero, 1Lt GV Siebold, KIA.
c.   F5951, 17th Aero, 1Lt WD Tipton, POW.
d.   C141, 17th Aero, 1Lt HB Frost, POW/DOW (2 Oct 1918).
e.   D6595, 17th Aero, 2Lt RM Todd, POW.
f.   F1958, 17th Aero, 2Lt HH Jackson,Jr, KIA
g.   B5428, 17th Aero, 1Lt L Roberts, KIA.
h.   F1964, 17th Aero, 2Lt HP Bittinger, KIA.

Losses

Gefr Konrad Becker	48	Killed in action Fins.
Vfw Ludwig Hilz	K4b	Died at Ludwigshafen, Flieger Schule I.

27 August 1918

Ltn M Johns	63	DH9	Henin sur Cojeul	0734	5	
Ltn H v d Marwitz	30	Camel	Tilloy	0740	10	a.
Ltn H Frommherz	27	BF2b	Graincourt	0805	16	b.
Obltn A Gutknecht	43	RE8	St Laurent	0830	–	
Ltn H Lange	26	Sopwith	Croisilles	0840	4	a.
Vfw F Classen	26	SE5	Croisilles	0840	5	a.
Ltn F Riemer	26	Sopwith	Mercatel	0845	5	a.
Ltn P Strähle	57	Camel	W Chérisy	0845	12	a.
Ltn J Jensen	57	Camel	Chérisy	0850	2	a.
Vfw O Fruhner	26	SE5	Ecourt	0905	17	
Vfw Knobel	57	Camel	N Hendecourt	0910	3	c.
Ltn Blum	57	Camel	Bullecourt	0910	3	c.
Ltn T Quandt	36	Camel	Tilloy	1055	9	c.
Flg Möhring	36	Camel	SW Boiry	1105	1	c.
Ltn T Quandt	36	Camel	Marcoing	1105	10	c.
Vfw H Donhauser	17	Spad	NW Terny	1910	7	d.
Ltn H Eder	23	RE8	Cagnicourt	2030	1	
Ltn H Seywald	23	RE8	SE Mercatel	2050	4	
Ltn Blum	57	RE8	Gemelincourt		–	

a. 208 Sqn RAF.
b. E2514, 22 Sqn RAF, Lt FM Sellars, POW & 2/Lt TB Collis, KIA.
c. Combat with 54 and 73 Sqns RAF.
d. Escadrille Spa 93, Adj L Hannebique, MIA, Spad XIII.

Losses

Ltn Wolff	6	Severely wounded in action W of Nesle.
Vfw Michael Sigmann	78	Lightly wounded in action Luneville.

28 August 1918

Ltn O Weisshaar	65	Balloon	Raulecourt, Jouy	1110	1	a.
Ltn O Weisshaar	65	Balloon	Gironville	1112	2	b.
OfStv W Kühne	18	Balloon	NW Trembelcourt	1230	8	c.
OfStv W Kühne	18	Salmson	Trembelcourt	1235	9	d.

a. 5th Balloon Co USBS, 2Lt JW Lane, OK & 2Lt JS Burrell, OK.
b. 9th Balloon Co USBS, 1Lt SV Clarke, OK & Cpl LS Balay, OK.
c. 129, 6th Balloon Co USBS, 1Lt GR Nixon, OK.
d. 12th Aero, 1Lt E Orr, DSC, OK & 1Lt PA Henderson, OK.

Losses

OfStv Wilhelm Kühne	18	Slightly wounded remained with unit.

29 August 1918

OfStv R Jörke	39	BF2b	Beauvraignes	0745	12	
Ltn H v d Marwitz	30	SE5	Haplincourt	0810	11	a.
Vfw G Staudacher	1	DH4	Somain	0845	5	b.
Ltn J Jensen	57	DH9	SW Chérisy	0930	3	
Ltn E Koch	32	Camel	Aniche	0940	7	c.
Ltn H Hager	32	Camel	Monchy-Tilloy	0940	2	c.
Ltn K Brendle	45	Breguet	Soissons	0945	6	
Ltn Vollbracht	5	BF2b	Ligny	1000	1	
Ltn H Böhning	79	Breguet	Pinon	1010	15	
Vfw A Lux	27	BF2b	Wancourt	1040	4	
Vfw H Behrends	61	Balloon		1120	2	d.
Vfw H Behrends	61	Balloon		1120	3	e.
Ltn M Johns	63	DH4	W Lécluse	1120	6	f.

Obltn T Dahlmann	JGIII	Sopwith	Wancourt	1125	3	
Ltn F Reimer	26	Sopwith	Monchy	1125	6	c.
Vfw K Bohnenkamp	22	Balloon	SW Selens	1300	7	g.
Vfw K Bohnenkamp	22	Spad	SE St Paul	1300	8	
Vfw H Donhauser	17	Spad	St Paul aux Bois	1525	8	
Obltn B Loerzer	JGIII	Sopwith	Chérisy		32	
Obltn B Loerzer	JGIII	Sopwith	Chérisy		33	
Ltn K Christ	28	Camel	N Noyelles		3	
Vfw H Gockel	33	Camel	Bugnicourt		2	
Obltn E Friess	34	Camel	E Estrées		1	
Vfw K Schlegel	45	Spad	Fismes		19	
Ltn Berling	45	Spad	Fismes		1	
Ltn H-J Rolfes	45	Spad	Fismes		11	
Ltn K Brendle	45	Spad	Fismes		–	
Ltn P Strähle	57	Camel	Brébières-Chérisy		13	c.
Ltn P Strähle	57	Camel	S Brébières		14	c.
Flg Hechler	57	Camel	N Bourlon Wood		2	c.
Vfw O Wieprich	57	DH9	Epinoy		4	
Obltn H-H v Boddien	59	DH4	Wavrechain		3	h.
Ltn W Preuss	66	Spad	Vénizel		10	
Ltn W Preuss	66	Spad	Missy-aux-Bois		11	
Ltn Kummerfeld	66	Spad	Couvrelles		1	
Gefr O Henschler	66	Spad	Serches		1	

a.   C9061, 64 Sqn RAF, Lt EA Parnell, KIA.
b.   F5825, 57 Sqn RAF, Lt J Caldwell, KIA & Sgt AT Wareing, KIA.
c.   43 Sqn RAF lost five Camels: C8215, Capt LG Loudoun; D1785, Sgt ACT Harbour; D6542, Lt WK MacFarlane; D9470, Lt SE Crookell, all POW, and E1485, 2/Lt W Omerod, KIA.
d.   French 29 Compagnie Aérostières, Lt Petit, WIA.
e.   French 87 Compagnie Aérostières, S/Lt Lecot, WIA.
f.   98 Sqn RAF.
g.   5th Balloon Co USBS, 1Lt F Durrschmidt, OK & 1Lt LG Bowers, OK.
h.   F6167, 57 Sqn RAF, Sgt THC Davies & 2/Lt WTS Lewis, POWs.

Losses

Gefr Peter Peltzer	5	Severely wounded Biaches-Herbercourt, DOW 31 August at Bernes.
Ltn Ewald Siempelkamp	30	Injured in a crash – Fontaine Notre Dame.
Vfw Rudolf Lander	52	Killed in a crash at FEA 13 Bromberg.
Vfw Knobel	57	Severely wounded in action with Camels.

30 August 1918

Ltn A Laumann	10	Camel	Estrées	0955	27	a.
OfStv P Aue	10	Camel	Estrées	0955	9	a.
Ltn A Raben	18	DH4	S Amanweiler	1200	4	b.
Ltn zS T Osterkamp	MFJ2	DH9	Ostende	1440	–	
Flgmt Illig	MFJ2	DH9	Ostende	1440	1	
Vzflgmstr K Scharon	MFJ2	Camel	near Werkem	1440	–	
Vzflgmstr H Goerth	MFJ2	Camel	by Handzame	1440	5	c.
Ltn Lidl	78	Balloon	Parroy Wood	1612	1	d.
Vfw O Fruhner	26	SE5	Inchy	1750	18	e.
Ltn F Noltenius	27	BF2b	S Etang, Boiry	1750	3	f.
Ltn K Bohny	17	Spad	Beugneux	1855	4	
Vfw H Donhauser	17	Breguet	Cuts	2010	9	
Ltn G Büren	18	DH4	Ennerchen		1	b.
Ltn W Frickart	65	DH4	Herméville		7	b.
OfStv Tiedje	65	DH4	Latour		–	b.

| Vfw Christiansen | 67 | DH4 | ...W Mars-la-Tour | 1 | b. |

a.   B9271, 46 Sqn RAF, Lt PH Goodhugh, POW/DOW.
b.   55 Sqn IAF lost 5 DH4s: A7589, 2/Lt WW Tanney & 2/Lt AJC Gormley; A7708, 2/Lt HH Doehler & 2/Lt AS Papworth,all POWs; A7783, 2/Lt PJ Cunningham, KIA & 2/Lt JG Quinton, DOW; A7972, 2/Lt TH Laing & 2/Lt TFL Myring and D8396, 2/Lt RIA Hickes & 2/Lt TA Jones,all KIA.
c.   D9482, 65 Sqn RAF, 2/Lt HG Pike, KIA.
d.   French 89 Compagnie Aérostières, S/Lt Lacaille, OK & S/Lt Veron, OK.
e.   C6456, 64 Sqn RAF, Lt RB Luard, POW.
f.   DH4 D8385, 57 Sqn RAF, Lt LK Devitt, WIA & Sgt AC Loveday, Inj.

Losses

OfStv Wilhelm Kühne	18	Killed in action location unknown combat with DH4s.
Uffz Tegtmeier	57	Shot down Seranvillers, and returned.
Uffz Wilhelm Hofacker	65	Killed in action Herméville,S Etain with DH4s.

31 August 1918

Ltn R Stark	35	Balloon	by Noyelles	0855	–	
Ltn H Steinbrecher	46	RE8	S Fremicourt	1450	4	a.
Ltn F Noltenius	27	SE5	Roeux	1505	4	b.
Ltn E Koepsch	4	Camel	Combles	1620	4	c.
Ltn W Blume	9	Spad	E Juvigny	1840	21	
Ltn Hospelt	9	Spad	E Juvigny	1841	2	
Ltn W Blume	9	Spad	E Pont St Mard	1900	22	
Obltn E v Wedel	11	Dolphin	SE Péronne	1945	10	d.
Ltn J Schulte-Frohlinde	11	Camel	Péronne	1945	1	
Ltn F v Köckeritz	11	Dolphin		1945	2	e.
Ltn A Lindenberger	B	RE8	Honnecourt		8	f.
Ltn O Steger	53	Spad	Fresnes		2	
Ltn W Preuss	66	Spad	Bagneux		12	

a.   C2727, 6 Sqn RAF, 2/Lt GE Herring & Capt WG Shedel, POWs.
b.   E5977, 64 Sqn RAF, Capt TStP Bunbury, KIA.
c.   D6927, 85 Sqn RAF, Capt GD Brewster, MC, OK.
d.   D3687, 23 Sqn RAF, 2/Lt CHA Bridge, POW/DOW.
e.   23 Sqn RAF.
f.   F5886, 5 Sqn RAF, Lt T Killeen, OK & Lt RJ Evans, WIA, FTL.

Losses

Uffz Karl Pabst	50	Killed in action Charleville 1150, Fokker DVII (OAW) 2012/18.
Ltn Hirschfeld	81	Wounded in action.
Ltn Bertram Heinrich	MFJ1	Killed in action Thourout with Camels.
Ltn Werner Bastian	MFJ1	Killed in action Thourout with Camels.

Jasta Armee Assignments as of 1 September 1918

Western Front

1 Armee 8,12,13,15,19,62,68,72s,73,74
2 Armee 4,5,6,10,11,34b,37,46
3 Armee 3,47w,49,54s
4 Armee 7,16b,20,40s,51,56,MFJI,MFJII,MFJIII,MFJIV,MFJV
5 Armee 67
6 Armee 14,29,30,43,52,63
7 Armee 9,21s,41,45,50,60,66,81
9 Armee 17,48,53,61
17 Armee 1,B,23b,26,27,28w,32b,33,35b,36,39,57,58,59

18 Armee 22s,24s,31,42,44s,79b
19 Armee 18,77b,80b
Det 'A' 70,78b,K3
Det 'B' 69,71,75,76b
Det 'C' 64w,65

Other Fronts

11 Armee	25	Macedonia
11 Armee	38	Macedonia
	55	Turkey

1 September 1918

(See also, *"Bloody April... Black September"*, Franks, Guest and Bailey, Grub Street, 1995)

Vfw K Schlegel	45	Balloon	Ouilly	1005	20	a.
Oblt R v Greim	34	Camel	St Pierre-Waast	1100	22	
Ltn E Bormann	B	BF2b	S Lécluse	1345	5	b.
Obltn B Loerzer	JGIII	BF2b		1345	35	c.
Vfw W Skworz	36	DH4	Brunemont	1345	2	d.
Ltn T Quandt	36	SE5	S Pronville	1555	11	e.
Vfw H Gockel	33	Camel	Quéant	1750	3	f.
Uffz H Nülle	39	Camel	Bailleul	1750	1	f.
Ltn W Sommer	39	Balloon	Tilloy	2110	3	g.
Ltn F Kresse	7	RE8			zlg	
Uffz Schaack	28	DH4	Tilloy		2	
Ltn T Quandt	36	SE5	Hamel		–	
Ltn T Quandt	36	SE5	Mercatel		–	
Vfw F Poeschke	53	Voisin	Brétigny		2	h.

a.   French 29 Compagnie Aérostières, Adj Proust, OK.
b.   E2479, 62 Sqn RAF, 2/Lt LB Raymond, POW & 2/Lt DS Hamilton, KIA.
c.   62 Sqn RAF.
d.   F6096, 57 Sqn RAF, 2/Lt JG Dugdale & 2/Lt FB Robinson, POWs.
e.   E5939, 32 Sqn RAF, 2/Lt JO Donaldson, USAS, POW.
f.   209 Sqn RAF lost two Camels: E4388, 2/Lt HV Peeling, and E4393, 2/Lt RL Scharff, both POWs.
g.   British Balloon 28-10-1 (SR 59), Lt Kitcat & Lt Freshney, both OK.
h.   Escadrille V106, Cpl Revolte & Soldat Robin, MIAs.
Losses – Nil

2 September 1918   Battle of the Drocourt-Quenant Line

Ltn K Brendle	45	Balloon	Reims	0810	8	
Ltn T Quandt	36	Camel	Ecourt-St Quentin	0820	12	a.
Uffz O Bieleit	45	Spad	Maizy, Baslieux	0820	1	
Ltn E v Wedel	11	Arm a/c	Fregicourt	0955	11	
Ltn A v Brandenstein	49	Spad	Suippes	1010	5	
Ltn H Lange	26	Camel	Villers	1015	5	b.
Vfw O Fruhner	26	SE5	Villers	1025	19	c.
Ltn H Frommherz	27	BF2b	Hamel	1030	17	
Gefr J Jacob	17	Spad	Savigny	1100	1	
Ltn F Noltenius	27	Camel	Etaing	1100	5	
Ltn Buddeberg	50	Spad	Braise	1100	1	
Vfw O Fruhner	26	SE5	Baralle	1110	20	
OfStv G Dörr	45	Spad	Ormes	1125	24	
Ltn F Noltenius	27	AWFK8	Rumaucourt	1130	6	d.
Ltn Meixner	45	Spad	Château	1130	1	e.

OfStv G Dörr	45	Spad	.... de la Malle	1130	25	e.
Ltn K Brendle	45	Balloon	near Reims	1200	9	
Ltn Christiansen	21	Spad	NW Fismes	1210	1	
Ltn W Sommer	39	RE8	Fampoux	1220	4	f.
Ltn W Nebgen	7	AWFK8	Lomme	1230	3	g.
Vfw Mack	63	AWFK8	Lomme by Lille	1230	1	g.
Obltn T Dahlmann	JGIII	Camel	Haucourt	1240	4	
Vfw C Mesch	26	Camel	Haucourt	1240	7	
Vfw C Mesch	26	Sopwith	Haucourt	1242	8	
Obltn B Loerzer	JGIII	Camel	Dury, NE Baralle	1245	36	
Ltn H Lange	26	Camel	N Baralle	1245	6	
Ltn Ehlers	26	Camel	NE Baralle	1245	1	
Ltn O Löffler	B	Camel	Beugnâtre	1300	5	
Ltn H Habich	49	Breguet	Chalons	1320	2	h.
Ltn M Dehmisch	58	RE8	Vis-en-Artois	1330	5	i.
Obltn G Rassberger	80	Balloon	Brouville	1510	1	j.
Uffz H Nülle	39	Balloon	Tilloy	1515	2	k.
Ltn Krayer	45	Balloon	Reims	1555	2	l.
Ltn H Rolfes	45	Salmson	Magneux	1600	12	m.
Ltn U Könnemann	45	Spad	Magneux	1600	2	
Ltn H Rolfes	45	Salmson	Magneux	1605	13	n.
Ltn J Filbig	80	Balloon	Laronxe	1710	1	
Ltn G Bürck	54	Balloon	Champenoux	1718	3	o.
Ltn Christians	21	Spad	E Fismes	1740	2	
Ltn H Hentzen	9	Spad	W Terny-Serny	1833	2	
Vfw Dünnhaupt	58	DH9	Hamel	1845	1	
Ltn H Brünig	50	Spad	Fismes	1920	7	
Flg F Wolff	17	Spad	Savigny	1930	1	
Vfw H Donhauser	17	Spad	Bagneux	1930	–	
Vfw H Donhauser	17	Breguet	St Marcel	2000	–	
Ltn B Hobein	20	BF2b	Gheluvelt	2000	3	p.
Ltn R v Barnekow	20	BF2b	Gheluvelt	2000	5	p.
Ltn W Sommer	39	Balloon	N Bapaume	2100	5	q.
Ltn E Bormann	B	Camel	Dury-Hennecourt		6	r.
Ltn E Bormann	B	Camel	W Havrincourt		7	r.
Ltn E Bormann	B	Camel	Sauchy-Lestrée		8	r.
Ltn O Löffler	B	Camel	S Pelves		6	r.
Ltn O Löffler	B	Camel	S Palluel		7	r.
Ltn F Heinz	B	Camel	by Boiry		2	
Ltn G v Hantelmann	15	Spad			–	
Obltn E v Schleich	23	RE8	NW Bapaume		31	
Vfw F Classen	26	Sopwith	Palleul		6	
Vfw A Lux	27	RE8	Hamel		5	
Vfw A Lux	27	BF2b	Vis-en-Artois		6	
Ltn Stoltenhoff	27	RE8			2	
Uffz W Kahle	27	Camel	Vis-en-Artois		1	
Vfw E de Ritter	27	Camel	St Quentin		–	
Ltn K v Schönebeck	33	EA			7	
Ltn T Quandt	36	Sopwith	Flesquières		-	
OfStv R Jörke	39	RE8	Bailleul		3	s.
Ltn W Preuss	66	Breguet	Bagneux		13	t.
Flg Eyssler	66	Spad	N Soissons		1	
Ltn H Quartier	67	Balloon			2	u.
Uffz. Baumgarten	67	Balloon			2	v.
Ltn R Otto	68	Breguet	Rémy Wald ...		4	

Uffz Huar	68	Breguet	.... W Compiègne	3	
Ltn G Clausnitzer	72	Balloon		1	w.
Ltn F Höhn	81	Spad	Coucy le Château	11	
Ltn zS G Saschenberg	MFJ1	a/c		25	

a.   E4381, 209 Sqn RAF, Lt WM Wormald, KIA.
b.   D845, 40 Sqn RAF, Lt HW Clarke, DOW.
c.   40 Sqn RAF.
d.   B4174, 35 Sqn RAF, 2/Lt H Nattrass, WIA & Lt FA Lawson, WIA.
e.   Escadrille Spa 20 lost two Spads: Sgt Deglise-Favre & Lt Brasseur, MIAs and Adj Dutrey, OK & Sgt Latapie, KIA.
f.   C2467, 52 Sqn RAF, 2/Lt RG Walton, WIA & 2/Lt G Bradbury, WIA.
g.   82 Sqn RAF only suffered one loss.
h.   Escadrille Br 289, Cpl Fournier, WIA & Lt de Boeuxis, WIA.
i.   F6015, 52 Sqn RAF, 2/Lt JC Garlake, OK & 2/Lt L Sharp, WIA.
j.   130, 3rd Co USBS, 1Lt GC Carroll, OK & 1Lt HP Niebling, OK.
k.   British Balloon 5-10-1 (SR24).
l.   French 27 Compagnie Aérostières, Asp Simondi, OK.
m.   88th Aero, 1Lt RW Hitchcock, KIA & 2Lt FM Moore, KIA.
n.   88th Aero, Capt R Page, OK & 1Lt PF Carl, Jr, FTL, OK.
o.   French 89 Compagnie Aérostières, Lt Hiernot, OK.
p.   48 Sqn RAF lost the following Bristol Fighters: E2214, 2/Lt O O'Connor & 2/Lt JJ Ambler, POWs and E2455, 2/Lt IMB McCulloch, POW & 2/Lt LP Perry, KIA.
q.   British Balloon 43-16-3, Lt H Tallboy, OK.
r.   148th Aero lost the following Camels: D6700, 2Lt JD Kenyon, POW; and D8245, 1Lt FE Kindley, shot up, damaged; E1412, 1Lt LH Foster, KIA; E1414, 2Lt O Mandel, POW; and E1471, 2Lt JE Frobisher, POW/DOW.
s.   C2729, 5 Sqn RAF, Lt L Coleman & 2/Lt CE Garden, KIAs.
t.   Escadrille Spa 34, MdL Verges, KIA & Lt Barat, Injured.
u.   French 52 Compagnie Aérostières, S/Lt Gravier, OK.
v.   French 81 Compagnie Aérostières, S/Lt Lamaud, OK.
w.   French 72 Compagnie Aérostières, S/Lt Brutus, OK.

Losses

Ltn Konrad Brendle	45	Killed in action 0920 Crecy au Mont near Reims in a Fokker DVII, possibly by Spa 91.
Uffz Hennies	49	Wounded in action.
Uffz Karl Pabst	50	Shot down by French AA fire, Fokker DVII 2012/18; POW/DOW.
Ltn Hans Quartier	67	Taken prisoner 0940 Prosnes Fokker DVII; AA fire from 72 Cie Aérostières.
Ltn Gottfried Clausnitzer	72	Killed in action in his balloon attack.
Vfw Michael Sigmann	78	Wounded in action Luneville.
Flg Ludwig Prillwitz	81	Taken prisoner Bouleuse in a Fokker DVII.

3 September 1918

Ltn Schramm	56	BF2b	Morseele	1015	3	
Ltn W Blume	9	Spad	S Fismes	1030	23	
Ltn H Rolle	9	Spad	S Fismes	1030	3	
Gefr E Mix	54	Balloon	Meseltal	1040	2	a.
Ltn T Quandt	36	SE5	Noreuil	1125	13	b.
Uffz H Nülle	39	Balloon	Vis-en-Artois	1515	3	c.
Uffz H Nülle	39	Balloon	Arras-Cambrai	1517	4	d.
Ltn O Löffler	B	DH9	Epéhy	1625	8	e.
Vfw M Hutterer	23	DH9	Arleux	1625	4	f.
Ltn G Wember	61	Balloon	Rückkehr	1700	1	g.
Vfw O Fruhner	26	Camel	Sin-le-Noble	1735	21	
Obltn B Loerzer	JGIII	SE5	Douai	1740	37	h.
Ltn A Lindenberger	B	BF2b	by Combles	1805	9	
Ltn T Quandt	36	BF2b	Eterpigny	1805	14	i.

Ltn Vollbracht	5	BF2b	W Havrincourt	1840	2	j.
Ltn F Rumey	5	SE5	S Péronne	1847	30	k.
OfStv J Mai	5	DH4	N Bertincourt	1850	24	
Obltn H Auffarth	29	SE5	Guémappe	2000	22	
Ltn F Weber	29	SE5	Pelves	2000	2	
Uffz S Westphal	29	SE5	Agny	2000	1	
Uffz P Schönfelder	29	SE5	Agny	2000	1	
Vfw M Hutterer	23	Dolphin	Marcoing	2005	5	l.
Ltn E Hencke	31	Camel	Rony-le-Petit	2010	2	
Vfw O Hennrich	46	SE5	NE Beugnâtre	2035	11	
Ltn zS G Brockhoff	MFJ2	DH4	E Furnes	2050	3	
Rittm H v Brederlow	17	Spad	Soissons		1	
Vfw H Donhauser	17	Spad	Soissons		10	m.
Vfw O Fruhner	26	Camel	W Cantin		zlg	
Ltn H Frommherz	27	RE8	Beugnâtre	am	18	n.
Ltn H Frommherz	27	RE8	Beugny	pm	19	o.
Ltn A Hübner	36	SE5	Aubencheul		3	p.
Vfw W Skworz	36	SE5	Sancourt		3	
Uffz R Neumann	36	SE5			–	
Ltn F Thiede	38	BM1C	Lake Dorian		6	q.
Vfw Mack	60	Spad			1	
Uffz F Engler	62	Balloon			–	r.
Vfw W Stör	68	Balloon	Wald of St Rémy		4	s.
Vfw D Averes	81	Spad	Soissons		5	t.
Vfw D Averes	81	Spad	Soissons		6	t.
Ltn F Höhn	81	Spad	Soissons		12	t.

a.   140, 1st Co USBS, 2Lt WS Anderson, OK.
b.   E6000, 60 Sqn RAF, Lt JFM Kerr,FTL, OK.
c.   British Balloon 37-3-1 (AR 74), Lt Lockwood, OK & Cpl Knights, OK.
d.   British Balloon 5-10-1 (AR 71), Lt Henry, OK & Cpl Banks, OK.
e.   D2963, 98 Sqn RAF, Lt CG Gowing, OK & 2/Lt JGW Halliday, KIA.
f.   98 Sqn RAF.
g.   French 76 Compagnie Aérostières.
h.   32 Sqn RAF (no loss).
i.   B1344, 20 Sqn RAF, Lt WF Washington & 2/Lt K Penrose, KIAs.
j.   20 Sqn RAF, 2/Lt FJ Ralph,DFC (O), KIA.
k.   D7202, 98 Sqn RAF, 2/Lt RT Ingram & 2/Lt KJW Dennitts, KIAs.
l.   C4163, 87 Sqn RAF, Lt FW Ferguson, KIA.
m.   Escadrille Spa 96, Cpl Pradel, MIA.
n.   B7888, 12 Sqn RAF, Lt AW Macnamara & Lt H Jonsson, MC, KIAs.
o.   C6299, 12 Sqn RAF, Lt TS Bulman, WIA & Lt Smith, WIA.
p.   E4064, 56 Sqn RAF, Lt A Vickers, KIA.
q.   C4907, 150 Sqn RAF, Lt JP Cavers, KIA.
r.   French 44 Compagnie Aérostières, Adj Branche, OK.
s.   2nd Balloon Co USBS, 2Lt F Henry, OK & Sgt SC Burnham, OK.
t.   One of these was Escadrille Spa 91, Cpl Dumont, KIA.

Losses

OfStv Josef Mai	5	Lightly wounded in action in upper left leg.
Flg Hermann Wirth	32	Killed in action Douai.
Vfw Wilhelm Skworz	36	Killed in action Abancourt.
Uffz Friedrich Engler	62	Severely wounded in action in the above balloon attack against the 44th Compagnie.

4 September 1918

Ltn Ehlers	26	Camel	Palleul	0910	2
Vfw E Buder	26	Camel	Cantin	0910	9

Obltn T Dahlmann	JGIII	BF2b	Palleul	0910	5	a.
Obltn T Dahlmann	JGIII	Camel	Palleul	0912	6	b.
Vfw O Fruhner	26	SE5	W Cantin	0915	24	b.
Vfw F Classen	26	Camel	Cantin	0918	7	b.
Obltn B Loerzer	JGIII	Camel	Monchecourt	0920	38	b.
Vfw O Fruhner	26	Camel	S Douai	0920	22	b.
Vfw E Buder	26	Camel	Gouy	0925	10	b.
Ltn F Röth	16	RE8	Neuf Berquin	0930	23	
Vfw O Fruhner	26	Camel	Corbehem	0930	23	b.
Uffz A Müller	39	DH9	Chelmes	1010	2	c.
Uffz H Haase	21	Balloon	Sarcy	1015	3	d.
Uffz H Nülle	39	DH4	St Aubert	1015	5	c.
Ltn Spille	58	DH9	Helesmes	1040	2	c.
Vfw Jeep	58	DH9	d'Hivergies Ferme	1045	2	c.
Ltn E Bormann	B	SE5	by Pelves	1100	9	e.
Ltn R Wenzl	6	Camel	Raillencourt	1100	7	f.
Ltn M Dehmisch	58	BF2b	Emerchicourt	1100	6	g.
Vfw G Staudacher	1	Camel	Sailly-Cambrai	1110	6	f.
Ltn G Meyer	37	2 Seater	W Cambrai	1110	15	
Obltn O Schmidt	5	BF2b	Gouzeaucourt	1115	12	
Ltn E Siempelkamp	64	Salmson	N Pont-à-Mousson	1205	4	h.
Ltn Seifert	17	Spad	Soilly	1230	1	
Vfw K Schlegel	45	Balloon	Sarcy	1304	21	i.
Uffz A Bader	64	Balloon	Mandres	1334	1	j.
OfStv G Dörr	45	Spad	N Fismes	1400	26	k.
Ltn H Rolfe	45	Spad	N Fismes	1400	14	k.
Obltn Otto Schmidt	5	Balloon	Loos	1415	–	
Ltn E Just	11	Balloon	Barastre	1715	6	l.
Ltn W Peckmann	9	Spad	Soissons	1815	3	m.
Ltn F Rumey	5	Camel	Quéant	1830	31	
Ltn Berling	45	Balloon	Mont Notre Dame	1930	2	n.
Ltn A Laumann	10	Camel			28	o.
Vfw G Fieseler	25	Spad	Budimirtsa		14	p.
Ltn H Frommherz	27	DH4	Recourt		20	q.
Vfw A Lux	27	Camel	Cantin		7	b.
Vfw A Hübner	36	SE5	Mercatel		4	
Ltn T Quandt	36	SE5	Quéant		15	
Ltn Bleibtraub	45	Breguet	Condé-sur-Aisne		zlg	
Vfw A Korff	60	Spad			4	r.
Ltn W Preuss	66	Breguet	SE Crécy-au-Mont		14	s.
Uffz Baumgarten	67	Balloon	Ansauville		3	t.
Ltn F Jacobsen	73	RE8/AR2			6	

a.   18 Sqn RAF.

b.   70 Sqn RAF suffered eight losses: B9269, Lt J Leveson-Gower, POW; C8239, Capt JH Forman; D1930, Lt R McPhee, all POW; D3406, 2/Lt WM Herriot, DOW; D9416, Lt JA Spilhaus, KIA; D9418, Lt SW Rochford, POW; D9458, 2/Lt KH Wallace and E1472, Lt DHS Gilbertson, both KIA.

c.   107 Sqn RAF suffered three losses: C6169, Lt BE Gammell & 2/Lt F Player, KIAs; D3106, 2/Lt JC Boyle, POW & 2/Lt FCB Eaton, KIA, and F6172, Lt ERL Sproule & 2/Lt GT Coles, POWs.

d.   French 27 Compagnie Aérostières, Sgt Euriburt, OK.

e.   E5979, 64 Sqn RAF, 2/Lt V Harley, POW.

f.   3 Sqn RAF.

g.   D7945, 62 Sqn RAF, Lt WK Swayze & 2/Lt WE Hall, POWs.

h.   5225 '12', 91st Aero, 1Lt F Foster, POW & 1Lt R Sebring, KIA.

i.   French 26 Compagnie Aérostières, Adj Boitard, OK.

j.   10th Balloon Co USBS, 1Lt ER Likens, OK & 1Lt DG Boyd, OK.

k.   One of these was Escadrille Spa 68, Sgt R Trouchaud, KIA.

l.   British Balloon 11-19-3, Lt H Tallboy, OK & 2/Lt J McGilchrist, OK.
m.   Escadrille Spa 92, MdL C Chambaz, MIA.
n.   French 25 Compagnie Aérostières, Sgt Godefroy, WIA.
o.   D9501, 80 Sqn RAF, 2/Lt EO Champagne, FTL, OK.
p.   Serbian Escadrille 524, Sgt LR Sproyelle & Lt EM DeButinier, KIAs.
q.   A7853, 18 Sqn RAF, Lt WB Hogg & 2/Lt AE Stock, KIAs.
r.   Escadrille Spa 83, Capt J de Luppe, POW.
s.   3309, Escadrille Br 19, Sgt Gauthier, WIA & Sgt Mulot, OK.
t.   French 43 Compagnie Aérostières, Cpl Aboucaya, OK & Cpl Guilbert, OK.

Losses

Vfw Kurt Jentsch	B	Wounded in action Emerchicourt 0835.
Uffz Hans Reimers	6	Killed in action Ligny-St Flochel.
Ltn Bernhard Lauscher	31	Injured in a crash.
Uffz Reinhold Neumann	36	Killed in action Abancourt.
Ltn Kurt Waldheim	36	Killed in action Abancourt.
Uffz Tegtmeier	57	Wounded in action Aniche.
Vfw Dünnhaupt	58	Severely wounded in action.
Uffz Alfred Bäder	65	Lightly wounded in action, remained.
Flg Otto Wagner	79	Taken prisoner in Fokker DVII 4503/18, combat with Lt D J Hughes, 3 Sqn RAF.

5 September 1918

Ltn F Rumey	5	SE5	N Bouchain	1005	32	a.
OfStv J Mai	5	SE5	Bugnicourt	1110	25	b.
Ltn G Meyer	37	SE5	Havrincourt	1200	16	c.
Ltn auf der Haar	46	SE5	N Havrincourt	1200	–	c.
Obltn B Loerzer	JGIII	SE5	Inchy	1210	39	c.
Ltn T Himmer	37	SE5	NE Ribécourt	1210	2	c.
Ltn auf der Haar	46	SE5	NE Ribécourt	1210	–	c.
Ltn B Hobein	20	BF2b	Espières	1350	4	
Vfw Kautz	46	Balloon	Beugny	1515	2	d.
Ltn R Wenzl	6	Balloon	Croiselles	1525	8	e.
Ltn F Schliewen	6	Balloon	Croiselles	1525	1	f.
Flgmt Mayer	MFJ2	Camel	Stahlhille	1525	4	g.
Vfw K Schlegel	45	Balloon	Fismes	1730	22	h.
Flgmt K Engelfried	MFJ4	DH9	W Knocke	1750	2	i.
Uffz L Jeckert	56	Camel	Lendelede	1825	2	j.
Ltn L Beckmann	56	Camel	Vorsmohlen	1827	8	j.
Ltn P Bäumer	B	BF2b	S Douai	1840	23	k.
Uffz A Müller	39	DH4	Douai	1845	3	
Vfw F Classen	26	Camel	Hénin-Lietard	1900	8	l.
Ltn H Frommherz	27	Camel	Marquion	1900	21	m.
Vfw C Mesch	26	Camel	Cuiney	1905	9	n.
Vfw A Lux	27	Camel	Marquion, Barelle	1905	8	o.
Uffz Ruppert	39	Balloon	Dury	1910	1	p.
Ltn E Koepsch	4	SE5	Pailencourt	1915	8	q.
Ltn W Ott	16	Camel	Langemarck	2010	1	
Ltn A Fleischer	17	Spad			–	r.
Obltn E v Schleich	23	Camel	Landres		32	
Ltn K Ritscherle	60	Spad	Leury		6	s.
Ltn W Preuss	66	Breguet	Villeneuve		15	t.
VzFlgMstr Zwang	MFJ2	Camel	by Stahlhille		zlg	

a.   C1909, 64 Sqn RAF, Lt WAF Cowgill, POW.
b.   C1876, 60 Sqn RAF, 2/Lt SA Thomson, KIA.
c.   92 Sqn RAF suffered three losses this date: B8428, Capt GA Wells, POW; D372, Lt HB Good, KIA and D6889, Lt EV Holland, POW.

d.   British Balloon 43-16-5, Lt CT Smith, OK.

e.   British Balloon 45-12-3, 2/Lt E Caton, OK.

f.   British Balloon 35-12-3, Sgt AW Woollgas,OK.

g.   D1824, 213 Sqn RAF, 2/Lt CE Francis,POW.

h.   French 47 Compagnie Aérostières, S/Lt G Fournier, OK.

i.   C1294, 218 Sqn RAF, Lt JG Munro, Int & 2/Lt TW Brodie, Int.

j.   210 Sqn RAF Lost two Camels this date: B7280, Capt HA Patey, DSC, and E4390, Lt L Yerex, both POWs.

k.   DH4 57 Sqn RAF.

l.   B778, 4 Sqn AFC, 2/Lt MH Eddie, KIA.

m.   D8136, 4 Sqn AFC, 2/Lt AH Lockley, KIA.

n.   E1407, 4 Sqn AFC, Lt LTE Taplin, DFC, WIA, POW.

o.   E7174, 4 Sqn AFC, Lt DC Carter, KIA.

p.   British Balloon 5-10-1 (SR 134), Lt Birchal, OK & Cpl Kneller, OK.

q.   60 Sqn RAF.

r.   Escadrille Spad 76, Lt Mantcewitch, OK.

s.   Escadrille Spad 164, Lt FC McCormack, WIA.

t.   Cpl Gaillard, OK & Asp Marille, OK.

Losses

Ltn Joachim von Winterfeld	4	Killed in action St Amand 1900, by 60 Sqn RAF, baled out but parachute caught fire; flying Fokker DVII which became G/3/17.
Ltn Schenk	5	Lightly wounded in action.
Ltn Heinrich Hager	32	Severely wounded in action 1200.
Uffz Otto Rösler	37	Killed in action Flesquières.
Gefr Jakob Katzner	43	Killed in action Somme; body found 16 September, possibly G/3/18.

6 September 1918

Ltn W v Richthofen	11	Dolphin	E St Quentin	0945	5	a.
Obltn P Blumenbach	31	Dolphin	St Quentin	0950	3	b.
Ltn H Maushake	4	Camel	SE Aubencheule	1055	6	
Ltn Buddeberg	50	Salmson	S Soissons	1220	2	c.
Ltn M Dehmisch	58	RE8	Monchy	1315	7	d.
Ltn M Dehmisch	58	Balloon	Monchy	1340	8	e.
Vfw O Hennrich	46	Balloon	S Le Mesnil	1455	12	f.
Ltn H Rolfes	45	Salmson	Magneux	1635	15	g.
Ltn Berling	45	Balloon	Magneux	1645	3	h.
Ltn H Rolfes	45	Balloon	Fismes	1645	16	i.
Ltn Krayer	45	Balloon	Magneux	1645	3	
Vfw H Knaak	9	Spad	N Soissons	1820	1	
Ltn M Näther	62	Breguet	Silléry	1842	12	j.
Uffz W Dost	21	Spad	E Braisne	2005	3	k.
Ltn O Löffler	B	BF2b	N Bourlon Wood		9	l.
Ltn E Bormann	B	Camel	NW Bourlon		10	m.
Ltn P Bäumer	B	BF2b	W Cantaing		24	n.
Ltn A Lindenberger	B	Camel	Lagnicourt		10	m.
Vfw Amschl	31	DH9	Noyon		3	
Ltn S Garsztka	31	DH9	St Quentin		–	
Ltn M Hänichen	53	Breguet	Coucy le Château		2	o.
Ltn M Hänichen	53	Spad	Coucy le Château		3	p.

a.   C8166, 23 Sqn RAF, Capt N Howarth, KIA.

b.   23 Sqn RAF.

c.   Escadrille Sal 17, MdL Baillodz,OK & Lt LeFloch, KIA.

d.   C2479, 52 Sqn RAF, Lt J Talbot, WIA & Sgt HJ Sampson, WIA.

e.   British Balloon 8-1-1 (AR20).

f.   British Balloon 14-14-5.

g.   Escadrille Sal 18, Cpl Nal & Soldat Jeandemange, KIAs.

h.   French 83 Compagnie Aérostières, Sgt Gaitz-Hocki, OK.
i.   French 68 Compagnie Aérostières, Lt Charotte, OK.
j.   Escadrille Br 260, Sgt Blovac & Lt Millot, KIAs.
k.   Escadrille Spa 86, MdL Perrot, WIA.
l.   C4745, 11 Sqn RAF, Lt CB Seymour & 2/Lt EG Bugg, KIAs.
m.   208 Sqn RAF had only a single loss, D9484, Lt AH Hiscox, KIA.
n.   D7906, 11 Sqn RAF, Lt EN Underwood, KIA & 2/Lt CM Coleman, KIA.
o.   Escadrille Br 269, Lt Salvetat & S/Lt Descousis, MIAs.
p.   Escadrille Spa 90, Sgt G Florentin, DOW.

Losses

Gefr Pägelow   71   Missing in action.

7 September 1918

Ltn Hofmann	79	Spad	Villequier-Aumont	0810	2	
Ltn F Rumey	5	DH4	St Quentin	1125	33	a.
Ltn F Bornträger	49	Breguet	Aubérive	1130	2	b.
Ltn H Habich	49	Spad	St Hilarie	1135	3	c.
Obltn O Schmidt	5	Balloon	SW Bertincourt	1145	13	d.
Vfw A Haussmann	13	Salmson	Jeandelize	1230	13	e.
Ltn J Schulte-Frohlinde	11	SE5	N Havrincourt	1300	2	
Ltn O v B-Marconnay	19	Salmson	E Montsec	1325	14	f.
Ltn Schulte-Schlutiu	3	DH9	Buchsweiler	1400	–	g.
Uffz H Forstmann	K1a	DH4	Frankenthal	1415	3	g.
Obltn R Nebel	K1a	DH4	Niederbronn	1426	2	g.
Ltn W v Richthofen	11	SE5	W Le Catelet	1940	6	h.
Ltn W v Richthofen	11	SE5	W Le Catelet	1945	7	h.
Obltn E Wedel	11	SE5	Le Catelet	1945	12	h.
Ltn G Weiner	3	DH9	Dassberg	pm	5	g.
Ltn G Weiner	3	DH9	Burscheid	pm	6	g.
Vfw J Hohly	65	Spad	Essey, S Pannes		5	i.
Ltn H Stutz	71	Breguet	W St Ulrich		5	j.
Ltn K Seit	80	DH9		pm	3	g.

a.   A7587, 205 Sqn RAF, Lt DJT Mellor, KIA & 2/Lt JC Walker, POW.
b.   Sgt Malot & S/Lt Morin, FTL, OK.
c.   Escadrille Spa 140, Sgt Thomas & S/Lt Moles, MIAs.
d.   British Balloon 41-12-3 (Balloon not destroyed).
e.   91st Aero, 1Lt AW Lawson & 1Lt HW Verwohlt, POWs.
f.   Escadrille Sal 5, MdL Clerc, KIA & S/Lt Thirion, WIA.
g.   99 Sqn IAF lost D2916, Lt G Broadbent, WIA/POW & 2/Lt MA Dunn, POW and 104 Sqn IAF lost:
B7653, 2/Lt JE Kemp,POW & 2/Lt EB Smailes, DOW; D3268, Sgt E Mellor, KIA & Sgt J Bryden, POW and
D7210, 2/Lt WEL Courtney & 2/Lt AR Sabey, POWs.
h.   84 Sqn RAF had two losses this date: C8895, 2/Lt WB Aldred, DOW and D6917, Lt EC Bateman, KIA.
i.   Spad XIII 49th Aero, 2Lt WT Kent, KIA.
j.   Escadrille Br 221, Adj Chenard & S/Lt Plebert, KIAs.

Losses

FldwLtn Schiller   Kest1a   Severely wounded in action
                              with 104 Sqn IAF.

8 September 1918

Unknown Pilot		MFJ2	Balloon

Losses

Gefr Kurt Blumener   6   Killed in action Beaurevoir, parachute failed.

9 September 1918

Uffz K Treiber	5	BF2b	–

Obltn E v Schleich	23	Camel	W Douai		33
Vfw G Fieseler	25	Nieuport	Orchida		–
Ltn H Frommherz	27	DH9			–

Losses – Nil

10-11 September 1918

No Claims – No Losses

12 September 1918   The St Mihiel Offensive

Ltn K Hetze	12	Breguet	Thiaucourt	1000	5	a.
Ltn K Hetze	12	Breguet	Bois le Pretre	1002	–	b.
Ltn G v Hantelmann	15	Breguet	near Buxieres	1135	7	c.
Vfw R Mossbacher	77	Salmson	Thimmenheim	1235	3	d.
Obltn O v Boenigk	JGII	Salmson	Thiaucourt	1310	22	e.
Ltn G v Hantelmann	15	Spad	Limey	1935	8	f.
Ltn Grimm	13	Breguet	Thiaucourt		2	g.
Ltn F Büchner	13	DH4	Vieville-en-Haye		21	h.
Ltn F Büchner	13	Breguet	Thiaucourt		22	i.
Ltn F Büchner	13	DH4	Hattonville		23	j.
Ltn M Kliefoth	19	Spad	Pont-à-Mousson		1	k.
Gefr C Schmidt	35	RE8	Quéant		1	
Ltn R Stark	35	DH4	Hermies		7	
Sgt Beschow	64	Salmson	Broussey		2	l.
Uffz A Bader	64	Breguet	Friauville		2	m.
Vfw Trautmann	64	Salmson	Broussey		zlg	n.
Obltn E Wenig	80	DH4	Phlyn		4	o.

a.   20th Aero, 1Lt GM Crawford, POW & 96th Aero, 2Lt JA O'Toole, KIA.
b.   12th Aero, 2Lt DH Arthur, OK & 2Lt HT Fleeson, OK.
c.   4495, 96th Aero, 1Lt A Gunderlach & 2Lt PH Way, KIAs.
d.   Escadrille Br 13, Cmdt Rocard & Lt de Loisy, MIAs.
e.   3203 '15', 1st Aero, 1Lt H Aldrich, WIA & 1Lt D Ker, KIA.
f.   Spad XIII 15137 'Ø', 139th Aero, 1Lt DE Putnam, DSC, Ld'H, MM, CdeG, KIA.
g.   Escadrille Br 128, Sgt Cardenne & Cpl Mallet, MIAs.
h.   8th Aero No.32143, 1Lt HW Mitchell & 1Lt JW Artz, POWs.
i.   Escadrille Br 132, Sgt Godin & Sgt Laigros, MIAs.
j.   50th Aero No.32298 '17', 1Lt HL Stevens & 1Lt EH Gardiner, KIAs.
k.   22nd Aero, 2Lt VR McCormick, WIA.
l.   104th Aero No.1143, 1Lt D Johnson, KIA & Cpl AD Johnson, POW.
m.   Escadrille Br 29, Lt Mariage & S/Lt Lavidalie, KIAs.
n.   12th Aero, Major Brereton, OK & Capt Vallois, WIA.
o.   135th Aero No.32114, 1Lt WC Suiter & 2Lt GE Morse, KIAs.

Losses – Nil

13 September 1918

Lt H Müller	18	DH9	W Thiaucourt	0910	7	a.
Ltn R Stark	35	DH4	Recourt	1050	8	
Vfw Hofmann	35	DH4	Recourt	1050	1	
Vfw G Klaudat	15	Spad	Vionville	1355	4	b.
Ltn J Jacobs	7	BF2b	Bailleul-Kemmel	1500	25	
Ltn B Hobein	20	BF2b	Bailleul	1500	–	
Ltn B Hobein	20	BF2b	Bailleul	1500	–	
Ltn O v B-Marconnay	19	Breguet	Charney	1720	15	c.
Ltn Scheller	19	Breguet	Rembercourt	1720	3	d.
Ltn Gewert	19	Spad	Jaulney	1720	1	e.

Vfw H Klose	54	DH9	Serrières	1750	2	f.
Vfw K Delang	54	DH9	St Géneviève	1750	3	f.
Ltn G v Hantelmann	15	Spad XIII	NW Thiaucourt	1805	9	g.
Obltn O v Boenigk	JGII	Spad	S Thiaucourt	1815	23	h.
Vfw G Klaudat	15	Spad	S Mercy	1815	5	i.
Vfw G Klaudat	15	Spad	SE Mercy	1815	6	j.
Ltn H Schäfer	15	DH9	Pont-à-Mousson	1840	–	
Ltn O v B-Marconnay	19	Breguet	Charney, Jaulney	1930	16	k.
Ltn M Kliefoth	19	Spad	Jaulney	1930	2	l.
Ltn M Dehmisch	58	Balloon	Monchy	1940	9	m.
Uffz Seidel	3	DH9			–	
Ltn F Büchner	13	Spad	Allamont		24	
Ltn F Büchner	13	Spad	Allamont		–	
Ltn F Büchner	13	Spad	Allamont		1	
Ltn F Büchner	13	Spad	Allamont		2	
Vfw A Haussmann	13	Spad	Allamont		14	
Vfw G Fieseler	25	Nieuport	Starinstograduta		15	n.
Uffz Bünning	K3	Spad			2	

a   8th Aero, 1Lt HB Rex & 2Lt WF Gallacher, KIAs.
b.   Spad XIII 15142, 213th Aero, 1Lt F Sidler, KIA.
c.   96th Aero No.12006, 1Lt T Farnsworth & 1Lt R Thompson, KIAs.
d.   96th Aero No.4493, 1Lt S Hopkins & 1Lt B Williams, KIAs.
e.   Spad XIII 7577, 93rd Aero, 2Lt CP Nash, POW.
f.   99 Sqn IAF lost two DH9s: D1670, 2/Lt EE Crosby & 2/Lt CP Wogan-Brown, KIAs and D3218, 2Lt FA Wood, USAS & 2/Lt C Bridgett, KIAs.
g.   Spad XIII 15302, 103rd Aero, 1Lt EB Jones, KIA.
h.   Escadrille Spa 155, Cpl Boulard, KIA.
i.   Spad XIII 15206, 28th Aero, 1Lt WS Stephenson, KIA.
j.   139th Aero, 1Lt RO Lindsay, WIA.
k.   Escadrille Br 225, Sgt de Kermal & S/Lt Girard, MIAs.
l.   Spad XIII 4413 '17', 13th Aero, 1Lt RRS Converse, POW.
m.   British Balloon 8-1-1 (SR74).
n.   Serbian Escadrille 508, 2/Lt RG Bonend, KIA.

Losses

Ltn Eugen Kelber	12	Killed in action Longeville, probably by Sgt Montagne of Spa 155.
Ltn Kurt Hetze	13	Wounded while in an automobile.
Ltn Siebert	15	Injured in a crash landing but remained.
Ltn Adolf Rienau	19	Bailed out OK after scrap with 13th Aero 1900 hrs.

14 September 1918

Ltn G v Hantelmann	15	DH4	Conflans	0900	10	a.
Vfw T Weischer	15	DH4	Auconville	0900	2	b.
Ltn H Müller	18	Spad	Thiaucourt	0900	8	c.
Ltn G v Büren	18	Spad	Gorze	0905	2	d.
Ltn H Müller	18	Spad	Thiaucourt	0910	9	e.
Ltn H Müller	18	Spad	SE Thiaucourt	0915	10	f.
Ltn H Künster	18	Spad	Thiaucourt	0915	1	f.
Ltn M Gossner	77	Balloon	Pont-à-Mousson	0940	3	g.
Obltn G Rassberger	80	DH9	Rolters, Pelter	1000	2	h.
Ltn Buddeberg	50	Spad	Kerillour, ...	1020	3	i.
Ltn K Maltezky	50	Spad	... Revillon	1020	1	i.
Ltn F Rumey	5	SE5	S Le Catelet	1110	34	j.
Oblt O v Boenigk	JGII	Spad	NW Lachaussée	1140	25	k.
Ltn J Klein	15	Spad	N Lachaussée	1140	14	l.

Ltn G v Hantelmann	15	Spad	St Benoit	1615	11	m.
Vfw K Schmuckle	15	Spad	St Benoit	1620	5	n.
Obltn H Kohze	3	DH9	Pont-à-Mousson	1150	–	
Ltn W Blume	9	Spad	S Laffaux	1155	24	
Ltn W Blume	9	Spad	Braye	1200	25	
Ltn M Gossner	77	Spad	Bois de Rappes	1245	4	
OfStv B Ultsch	77	Spad	Jaulny	1245	9	
Ltn M Gossner	77	Salmson	Villecey	1320	5	o.
Ltn H Müller	18	Spad	W Pont-à-Mousson	1440	11	p.
Uffz Lohrmann	42	DH9	W Holnon Wald	1532	2	
Ltn G v Hantelmann	15	Spad	Lachausssée	1615	12	
Ltn U Könnemann	45	Salmson	Fismes	1620	3	q.
Ltn Christians	67	Balloon	Clermont, Verdun	1630	2	r.
Uffz H Marwede	67	Balloon	Clermont, Verdun	1630	2	s.
Uffz H Marwede	67	Balloon	Clermont, Verdun	1634	3	t.
Ltn M Näther	62	Balloon	Mailly	1635	13	u.
Uffz H Marwede	67	Balloon	Clermont, Verdun	1638	4	v.
Ltn F Noltenius	27	Balloon	Vis-en-Artois	1740	7	w.
Obltn G Rassberger	80	Spad	Champenoux	1750	3	
Ltn F Bacher	3	Spad	Thiaucourt	1815	2	
Ltn Gewert	19	Salmson	Beney	1920	2	x.
Ltn P Bäumer	B	RE8	Cantaing		25	
Ltn F Kresse	7	RE8	SE Ypres		1	y.
Ltn H Becker	12	Breguet	Lüttlingen/Metz		14	z.
Ltn F Büchner	13	Breguet	Mars la Tour		25	aa.
Ltn F Büchner	13	Breguet	Latour		26	bb.
Ltn Fe Büchner	13	Breguet	Conflans		2	cc.
Ltn Grimm	13	Breguet	Conflans		3	dd.
Ltn W Niethammer	13	Breguet	Puxe		3	ee.
Obltn O v Boenigk	JGII	Spad	N Lachaussée		24	ff.
Ltn R Rienau	19	DH4	Conflans		3	
Ltn O v B-Marconnay	19	Salmson	Conflans, Jonville		17	gg.
Ltn M Kliefoth	19	DH4	Conflans		3	hh.
OfStv G Dörr	45	Salmson	Blanzy		27	ii.
Ltn H Rolfes	45	Spad	Blanzy		–	
Gefr E Mix	54	a/c			3	
Ltn K Ritscherle	60	Spad	NW Fismes		7	
Ltn E Siempelkamp	64	Spad	W Auvillers		–	
Ltn E Siempelkamp	64	Salmson	near Bonzée		5	jj.
Ltn W Frickart	65	Caudron	La Tour		8	kk.
Vfw J Hohly	65	Caudron	St Maurice		6	ll.
Ltn W Preuss	66	Spad			16	mm.
OfStv Hasenpusch	67	Breguet	Doncourt		2	nn.
Vfw Wimmer	80	Spad			-	

a. 11th Aero, 32251, 2Lt FT Shoemaker & 2Lt RM Groner, POWs.
b. 11th Aero, 32615, 2Lt H Schidler, WIA/POW & 2Lt H Sayre, KIA.
c. Spad XIII 4578 '5', 13th Aero, 1Lt CW Drew, WIA/POW.
d. Spad XIII 15145 '12', 13th Aero, 1Lt AA Brody, POW.
e. Spad XIII 4486 '4', 13th Aero, 1Lt HB Freeman, POW.
f. One of these was 4562 '11', 13th Aero, 1Lt GR Kull, KIA.
g. 169, 5th Co USBS, 1Lt MR Smith, OK & 1Lt JM Fox, OK.
h. 99 Sqn RAF.
i. One of these was Escadrille Spa 152, MdL A de Freslon, MIA.
j. D6131, 84 Sqn RAF, Lt JE Reid, POW.
k. 22nd Aero, 2Lt RJ Little, FTL, OK.
l. 95th Aero, 1Lt S Sewell, FTL, OK.

m.   Spad XIII 7580 '23', 22nd Aero, 1Lt PE Hassinger, KIA.
n.   22nd Aero, 1Lt AC Kimber, FTL, OK.
o.   88th Aero, Capt KP Littauer, FTL,OK & 2Lt TE Boyd, WIA.
p.   Escadrille Spa 153, Sgt P de Villeneuve, KIA.
q.   Escadrille Br 287, Sgt Bonnet,OK & S/Lt Jounin, KIA.
r.   French 57 Compagnie Aérostières, (Balloon not destroyed).
s.   French 25 Compagnie Aérostières, S/Lt Boret, OK.
t.   French 30 Compagnie Aérostières, Adj A Lurcat, OK.
u.   French 76 Compagnie Aérostières, Asp Chaudy, OK.
v.   French 31 Compagnie Aérostières, Cpl Guilbert, OK.
w.   British Balloon 5-10-1 (SR 135) – booby-trap with ammonal explosive.
x.   24th Aero, 3325, 1Lt JJ Goodfellow & 1Lt E Durrand, KIAs.
y.   4 Sqn RAF, Lt TO Henderson, WIA & 2/Lt F Butterworth, KIA.
z.   Escadrille Br 132, Lt de Vielle & Cpl Valat, MIAs.
aa   Escadrille Br 132, Lt Calbet & Sgt Destieux, MIAs.
bb   Escadrille Br 132, Cpl Fontaine & Cpl Pillot, MIAs.
cc   Escadrile C 46, Sgt Boeglin, Sold Monfils & Sold Rust, MIAs.
dd   Escadrille Br 132, Cpl Mestre & Asp Grand, MIAs.
ee   Escadrille Br 132, Cpl Jacquet & S/Lt Teilhac, MIAs.
ff   USAS Spad.
gg   USAS machine.
hh   91st Aero, No.3303, Capt K Roper & 1Lt PH Hughey, KIA
ii   Escadrille Sal 280, Adj Giafferi & Lt Arquis, KIAs.
jj   99th Aero, 1Lt J Hayes-Davis, OK & 1Lt CE Spencer, OK, FTL.
kk   Escadrille Sal 46, Cpl Dubuisson, Sold Mantel & Sold Vincent, MIAs.
ll   Escadrille Sal 46, Lt Resel, WIA & Sgt Lacassagne, WIA.
mm   113, Escadrille Spa 160, Sgt G Fuoc, MIA.
nn   Escadrille Br 243, Sgt Landreux & Lt Sabirini, MIAs.

Losses

Gefr Anton Kempa	3	Taken prisoner.
Ltn Paul Wolff	13	Taken prisoner Lake Lachaussée 1510, Fokker DVII.
Ltn Günther von Büren	18	Wounded in action.
Ltn Eugen Siempelkamp	64	Wounded in action in the above combat.

15 September 1918

Uffz H Nülle	39	Balloon	Villers-Dury	0923	6	a.
Uffz H Nülle	39	Balloon	Villers-Dury	0924	7	b.
Uffz H Nülle	39	Balloon	Villers-Dury	0925	8	
Uffz H Nülle	39	Balloon	Villers-Dury	0926	9	
Obltn R v Greim	34	SE5	S Hermies	0930	23	
Uffz de Ray	58	Camel	near Cambrai	1130	1	
Ltn H Seywald	23	Camel	Marquette	1205	5	c.
Ltn H Schäfer	15	DH9	SW Metz	1210	7	d.
Ltn G v Hantelmann	15	DH9	SW Metz	1215	13	e.
Vfw T Weischer	15	DH9	S Metz	1215	3	f.
Obltn H v Wedel	24	BF2b	Nauroy, Estrées	1215	3	
Ltn H Leptien	63	RE8	W Armentières	1230	6	g.
Ltn M Johns	63	RE8	W Armentières	1230	–	
Ltn U Neckel	6	BF2b	Estrées	1235	25	h.
Ltn W Kohlbach	10	Camel	Cantaing	1255	4	i.
Ltn M Gossner	77	Balloon	4 km E Limey	1325	6	j.
Ltn M Gossner	77	Balloon	Lironville	1325	7	k.
Vfw Jeep	58	Balloon	Vitry	1350	3	l.
Uffz K Pietzsch	58	Balloon	Wancourt	1350	2	m.
Ltn Meixner	45	Balloon	Braisnes	1500	2	n.
Ltn H v Freden	50	Balloon	Juvigny	1505	8	o.

Ltn H v Freden	50	Balloon	Juvigny	1507	9	p.
Ltn zS R Poss	MFJ4	Camel	Zeebrugge	1510	6	q.
Vfw O Hennrich	46	Balloon	Bertincourt	1545	13	r.
Ltn G Meyer	37	SE5	Noyelles	1700	17	
VzFlgMstr H Hackbusch	MFJ5	DH9	nr Kokelaere	1705	2	s.
Flgmt K Kutschke	MFJ5	DH9	Walcheren	1705	2	s.
Flgmt K Engelfried	MFJ5	DH9	Walcheren	1710	3	s.
Ltn zS Freymadl	MFJ5	DH9	Middleberg	1720	1	s.
Vfw R Jörke	39	SE5		1745	14	
Uffz K Treiber	5	Balloon	W Fins	1800	1	t.
Gefr B Bartels	44	Balloon	St Simon	1800	1	
Vfw M Hutterer	23	SE5	St Leger	1810	6	u.
Uffz H Kleinschred	23	Camel	Arleux	1815	1	
Flg S Braun	23	Camel	Ecoust, S Menin	1815	1	
Vfw O Fruhner	26	RE8	Palleul	1905	25	v.
Ltn R Stark	35	Dolphin	Cagnicourt	1905	9	
Ltn H Stoer	35	SE5	Cagnicourt	1908	1	
Ltn J Jacobs	7	AWFK8	Passchendaele	1910	26	w.
Ltn F Riemer	26	SE5	Palleul	1920	7	
Vfw C Mesch	26	Balloon	Boiry Notre Dame	1930	10	x.
Vfw Schneck	9	Spad	E Vailly	1940	2	
Ltn F Noltenius	27	BF2b	Bourlon Wood	1940	7	
Ltn G Meyer	37	SE5	Bourlon	1945	18	
Ltn F Büchner	13	Spad	Thiaucourt		27	y.
Ltn F Büchner	13	Spad	Lachaussée		28	z.
Ltn O v B-Marconnay	19	Spad	Petry		18	aa.
Ltn R Rienau	19	Spad	Petry, Pagny		4	bb.
Ltn Scheller	19	Spad	Petry		4	cc.
Obltn E v Schleich	23	AWFK8	Marcoing		34	
Vfw G Fieseler	25	Nieuport	Dedebala		16	dd.
Vfw C Mesch	26	SE5	Rémy		11	
Sgt W Kahle	27	SE5			–	
Ltn E Thuy	28	Camel			29	
Gefr C Schmidt	35	Camel			2	
Ltn F Höhn	60	Balloon	Villersovoye		10	ee.
Vfw A Korff	60	Balloon			5	ff.
Ltn Leibfried	64	Salmson	by Blenod		1	
Vfw J Hohly	65	Spad	St Rémy		7	gg.
Ltn J Fichter	67	Balloon	Douaumont		6	hh.

a. British Balloon 37-10-1 (SR 136).
b. British Balloon 43-10-1, Lt HV Williams, OK & Lt RHW Davidson, OK.
c. F6107, 73 Sqn RAF, 2/Lt JA Matthews, POW.
d. D7205, 104 Sqn IAF, 2/Lt RH Rose & 2/Lt EL Baddeley, POWs.
e. D3263, 104 Sqn IAF, 2/Lt AD Mackenzie & 2/Lt CE Bellard, KIAs.
f. D3245, 104 Sqn IAF, 2/Lt GL Hall & 2/Lt WD Evans, POWs.
g. C2649, 42 Sqn RAF, 2/Lt RM Marshall, WIA & 2/Lt A Mulholland, OK.
h. E2512, 20 Sqn RAF, Lt FE Finch, WIA/POW & 2/Lt CG Russell, POW.
i. E4404, 203 Sqn RAF, Sgt RR Lightbody, KIA.
j. 137, 1st Co USBS, 1Lt FR Burton, OK.
k. 264, 2nd Co USBS, 2Lt HE Dugan, OK.
l. British Balloon 5-10-1 (AR56).
m. British Balloon 20-1-1 (AR68).
n. French 54 Compagnie Aérostières.
o. French 29 Compagnie Aérostières, Sgt Bosc, OK.
p. French 87 Compagnie Aérostières, S/Lt G Lemaitre, OK.
q. E4418, 204 Sqn RAF, Lt RC Pattulo, KIA.

r.   British Balloon 44-19-3, Lt RGA Holbrook, OK.
s.   211 Sqn and 218 Sqn RAF suffered two losses: D3210, 2/Lt JM Payne, OK & Lt CT Linford, WIA (211) and C2158, Lt WS Mars & 2/Lt HE Power both inj/Interned.
t.   British Balloon 14-14-5, Lt GH Adams, OK.
u.   C1875, 1 Sqn RAF, Lt W Newby, FTL, OK.
v.   F5894, 5 Sqn RAF, Lt JM Bright, WIA & 2/Lt EP Eveleigh, WIA.
w.   C8571, 82 Sqn RAF, 2/Lt HT Hempsall & Lt JHM Yeomans, MC, POWs.
x.   British Balloon 8-1-1 (SR152).
y.   Escadrille Spa 92, Sgt Bernon, MIA.
z.   Escadrille Spa 92, Cpl J Rouanet, MIA.
aa   Escadrille Spa 154, S/Lt L Gros, WIA.
bb   Escadrille Spa 150, Adj E Stahl, KIA.
cc   Escadrille Spa 95, Sgt L Fabel, POW.
dd   Serbian Escadrille 505, Sgt EM de la Bastik, KIA.
ee   French 83 Compagnie Aérostières, Adj Dunard, OK.
ff.   French 33 Compagnie Aérostières, S/Lt Aasche, OK.
gg   Spad XIII 15221, 147th Aero, 1Lt EA Love, KIA.
hh   2nd Balloon Co USBS, 1Lt WJR Taylor, OK.

Losses

Ltn Johannes Klein	15	Lightly wounded in action, remained.
Ltn Paul Vogel	23	Killed in action Faubourg d'Amiens, Pfalz DXII 2486/18 by 1 & 62 Sqns RAF (G/HQ/6).
Vfw Ernst de Ritter	27	Severely wounded in action.
Ltn Friedrich Noltenius	27	Lightly wounded in action remained.
Ltn Hilmar Quittenbaum	28	Killed in action Arleux-Douai.
Uffz Ottoweil	33	Lightly wounded in action.
Uffz Kurt Pietzsch	58	Wounded in action Wancourt 1350.
Flgmt Karl Engelfried	MFJ5	Forced to land in Holland, Fokker DVII 5584/18, later returned to unit.

16 September 1918

Sgt Hoffmann	K3	Spad	SE Frescaty	0740	1	a.
Ltn J Jacobs	7	SE5	W Menin	0840	27	b.
Ltn H Böhning	79	DH9	NW Bellenglise	0840	16	c.
Vfw O Fruhner	26	BF2b	Fontaine	0845	26	d.
Uffz Brüngel	31	Scout	Gricourt	0845	1	
Ltn H Lange	26	BF2b	N Quiney	0850	7	e.
Ltn Breidenbach	44	DH4	Roupy	0850	1	
Ltn F Rumey	5	DH9	W Villers Guislain	0900	35	f.
Ltn K Plauth	20	DH9	Armentières	0900	7	g.
Obltn B Loerzer	JG3	BF2b	Dourges	0900	39	
Ltn Holle	31	DH4	NE Douchy	0915	1	
Vzflgmstr H Goerth	MFJ2	Camel	Zerkeghem	0915	6	h.
Vfw G Klaudat	15	Spad	Urvillers	1120	zLg	i.
Ltn G v Hantelmann	15	Spad	SW Conflans	1120	14	j.
Uffz H Kleinschred	23	DH4	Denain	1130	2	
Unknown Pilot	47	Balloon		1130	2	k.
Ltn H Seywald	23	DH4	W Cantin	1155	6	l.
Ltn F Rumey	5	SE5	Marquion	1230	36	
Ltn F Rumey	5	Camel	Marquion	1235	37	
OfStv G Dörr	45	Spad	Blanzy, Fismes	1300	27	
Ltn G Weiner	3	DH9	Alt-Eckendorf	1330	7	m.
OfStv E Prime	78	DH9	"	1330	–	
Ltn G Meyer	37	BF2b	Marquion	1530	19	
Uffz Gengelin	37	BF2b	NW Cambrai	1540	2	
Ltn O v B-Marconnay	19	Breguet	Fleville	1755	19	n.
Ltn O v B-Marconnay	19	Breguet	Brie nr Conflans	1755	–	o.

Gefr Felder	19	Breguet	nr Conflans	1755	2	p.
Ltn R Rienau	19	Breguet	Brie nr Conflans	1755	5	q.
Ltn F Riemer	26	Sopwith	Baralle	1755	–	
Vfw F Classen	26	Sopwith	Recourt	1755	–	
Vfw C Mesch	26	Sopwith	Riencourt	1755	12	
Ltn Marcard	26	SE5	Saucy-Cauchy	1800	2	
Ltn J Jensen	57	RE8	N Sauchy-Cauchy	1915	4	
Ltn J Jacobs	7	Balloon	Poperinghe	1935	28	r.
Ltn P Bäumer	B	BF2b	NE Hénin-Lietard		26	
Ltn O Löffler	B	BF2b	Haveluy		10	
Ltn O Löffler	B	BF2b	NE Arras		11	
Ltn F Hoffmann	B	BF2b	N Bapaume		1	
Vfw Lieber	7	SE5	Menin		1	
Uffz Peisker	7	SE5	Menin		1	
Obltn E v Schleich	JGp8	AWFK 8	Marquion		34	
Obltn B Loerzer	JGIII	SE5			41	
Ltn F Noltenius	27	DH9			8	
Ltn R Klimke	27	DH4/BF2b			17	
Ltn E Thuy	28	SE5			30	s.
Ltn J Korff	60	Spad			6	
Ltn A Stephan	70	DH9	Gemersheim		1	t.
Sgt Metzger	70	DH9	SE Landau		1	t.
Ltn G Frädrich	72	Spad			3	
Ltn H Mahn	72	Spad			2	
Ltn F Anders	73	Farman	Moronvillers		5	u.
Ltn zS T Osterkamp	MFJ2	Camel	Coxyde		24	h.
Ltn zS T Osterkamp	MFJ2	Camel	Coxyde		25	h.
Ltn zS Wilhelm	MFJ4	Camel	Zeebrugge		1	h.

a.   Spad XIII 4506 '14', 13th Aero, 1Lt RM Stiles, KIA.
b.   E6002, 29 Sqn RAF, 2/Lt PJA Fleming, POW.
c.   D9250, 205 Sqn RAF, 2/Lt FF Anslow, POW & Sgt L Murphey, KIA.
d.   C878, 11 Sqn RAF, 2/Lt L Arnott & 2/Lt GL Bryars, KIAs.
e.   C946, 11 Sqn RAF, Lt JC Stanley, USAS, WIA & 2/Lt EJ Norris, POWs.
f.   A7987, 57 Sqn RAF, 2/Lt JP Ferreira & 2/Lt LB Simmonds, KIAs.
g.   103 Sqn RAF.
h.   210 Sqn RAF suffered two losses: B7271, 2/Lt EB Markquick, and D3357, 2/Lt JA Lewis, both KIA.
i.   493, Escadrille Spa 77, Cpl Walk, WIA/POW.
j.   Escadrille Spa 77, S/Lt M Boyau, KIA.
k.   French 50 Compagnie Aérostières, Cpl Leverrier, KIA.
m.   F5712, 2/Lt WE Johns, WIA, POW & 2/Lt AE Amey, KIA.
l.   D3267, 98 Sqn RAF, 2/Lt FJ Keble & 2/Lt CH Senecal, POWs.
n.   14, 96th Aero, 1Lt CP Anderson & 1Lt HS Thompson, KIAs.
o.   96th Aero, 12005 '20', 1Lt CR Codman & 2Lt SA McDowell, POWs.
p.   96th Aero, 4726 '4', 1Lt RC Taylor & 1Lt WA Stuart, KIAs.
q.   96th Aero, 4875 '1', 1Lt NC Rodgers & 2Lt KP Strawn, KIAs.
r.   British Balloon 5-5-2.
s.   B8427, Lt HA Kullberg,DFC, WIA.
t.   110 Sqn IAF lost: E8410, Sgt A Haigh & Sgt J West, KIAs and F997, Lt HV Brisbin & 2/Lt RS Lipsett, POWs.
u   Escadrille F 114, MdL G Ravault, Adj Deaux, POWs, S/Lt Bombezin, KIA.

Losses

Ltn Friedrich Kresse	7	Killed in action Nieppe, Houplines, with 209 Sqn RAF, (G/1/16).
Flg Siegfried Braun	23	Killed in action Cantin 1850 Pfalz DXII.
Gefr Kurt Brandt	51	KIA, Quesnoy by 2 AFC Sqn (G/10/5).
Obltn Hans Schlieter	70	Lightly wounded in action remained.
Vfw Walter Sieg	71	Killed in a crash Habsheim airfield

0725 Pfalz DXII 2675/18.

Flgmt Nake	MFJ1	Lightly wounded in action.			
Vzflgmstr Horst Sawatzki	MFJ1	Lightly wounded in action.			

17 September 1918

Ltn F Rumey	5	SE5	Rumilly	0905	38	a.
Ltn H Boes	34	SE5	N Cambrai	1000	2	
Ltn F Brandt	26	Camel	Hermies	1157	9	
Ltn F Rumey	5	Camel	NW Cambrai	1300	39	
Ltn F Noltenius	27	Balloon		1500	9	b.
Ltn G v Hantelmann	15	Spad	Rembercourt/Metz	1510	15	c.
Flgmt G Hubrich	MFJ4	Camel	Batt Zeppelin	1833	5	
Ltn F Rumey	5	Camel	SW Cambrai	1910	40	d.
OfStv J Mai	5	Camel	SW Hermies	1912	26	d.
Ltn G Weiner	3	Breguet	N Falkenberg		8	e.
Ltn F Büchner	13	Salmson	Dampvitoux	am	29	f.
Vfw G Fieseler	25	Spad	Monastir		17	g.
Ltn H Frommherz	27	DH9			22	
Vfw A Korff	60	Balloon			7	h.
Ltn F Jacobsen	73	DH4 (USA)			–	

a.   E4053, 40 Sqn RAF, 2/Lt FW King, WIA/POW.
b.   British Balloon 20-1-1 (SR151).
c.   95th Aero, 1Lt WH Heinrichs, WIA/POW (Spad 15199?).
d.   46 Sqn RAF lost two Camels: F2130, Lt H Toulmin, MC, KIA and F6226, 2/Lt CE Usher-Sommers, POW.
e.   Escadrille Br 111, S/Lt E de Carnell & Sgt A Puel, MIAs.
f.   24th Aero, 1049, 1Lt WL Bradfield & 1Lt AL Clark, POWs.
g.   Serbian Escadrille 524, Cpl R Niga, KIA.
h.   French 33 Compagnie Aérostières, Adj L Flament, OK.

Losses

Sgt Hans Popp	77	Killed in action Warville-Eply 1655 Fokker DVII, by 74 Sqn RAF (G/2/22).

18 September 1918   Battle of Havrincourt and Epéhy

OfStv O Sowa	52	DH9	Lomme by Lille	1135	4	
Ltn S Garsztka	31	Camel	Lempine	1140	2	a.
Ltn S Garsztka	31	AWFK8	Saulcourt	1150	3	b.
Ltn H Böhning	79	Balloon	Vaux	1440	17	c.
Ltn F Noltenius	27	Balloon		1510	10	d.
Ltn C Degelow	40	Balloon	Poperinghe	1520	14	e.
Uffz K Treiber	5	Balloon	Longavesnes	1540	2	f.
Ltn G v Hantelmann	15	Spad	W Conflans	1630	16	g.
Ltn F Büchner	13	Spad	Chambley	1725	30	h.
Ltn U Neckel	6	DH4	Conflans	1730	26	i.
Ltn H Becker	12	DH4	Conflans	1730	15	j.
Ltn H Becker	12	DH4	Conflans	1730	16	k.
Ltn H Besser	12	DH4	Conflans	1730	1	l.
Ltn A Greven	12	DH4	Conflans	1730	1	m.
Flg Wilke	12	DH4	Conflans	1730	1	n.
Ltn F Büchner	13	Spad	W Chambley	1730	31	o.
Ltn F Büchner	13	Spad	Dampvitoux		32	p.
Vfw G Fieseler	25	Nieuport	E Cerna-Royka		18	q.
Ltn F Thiede	38	AWFK8	Lake Dorian		7	r.

a.   D6971, 92 Sqn RAF, Lt CM Holbrook, POW.
b.   F7395, 35 Sqn RAF, Lt MC Sonnenberg, WIA/DOW & 2/Lt J Clarke, KIA.
c.   British Balloon 22-15-5.

d.   British Balloon 8-1-1- (AR 37).
e.   British Balloon 36-17-2.
f.   British Balloon 14-14-5.
g.   Spad XIII 7555, 27th Aero, 1Lt JH Wehner, DSC, KIA.
h.   Spad XIII 15252, 213th Aero, 1Lt DM McClure, POW.
i.   11th Aero, 1Lt VP Oatis, OK & 1Lt RP Guthrie, FTL, OK.
j.   11th Aero, 1Lt LS Harter & 1Lt M Stephenson, KIAs.
k.   11th Aero, 1Lt JC Tyler & 1Lt HH Strauch, KIAs.
l.   11th Aero, 1Lt EB Comegys & 2Lt AR Carter, KIAs.
m.   11th Aero, 1Lt TD Hooper & 1Lt RR Root, POWs.
n.   11th Aero, 1Lt RF Chapin & 1Lt CB Laird, POWs.
o.   Spad XIII 4600, 28th Aero, 1Lt F Philbrick, KIA.
p.   Spad XIII 4512 '18', 95th Aero, 1Lt WH Taylor, KIA.
q.   Serbian Escadrille 506, Sgt JC Perrau, KIA.
r.   C3590, 47 Sqn RAF, Lt JA Brandt & 2/Lt H Gerhardt, KIAs.
Losses – Nil

19 September 1918

Uffz P Hüttenrauch	7	AWFK8	Voormezeele	0905	4	a.
Ltn J Schulte-Frohlinde	11	RE8	Bellenglise	1600	3	b.
Ltn J Jacobs	7	Camel		1900	29	
Vfw G Fieseler	25	Nieuport	Monastir		–	
Ltn F Thiede	38	Camel	Lake Dorian		8	
Ltn K Maletzky	50	Balloon	Noyon		2	

a.   C2718, 6 Sqn RAF, Lt Owen, OK & Lt Sterling, OK, FTL.
b.   C2490, 3 Sqn AFC, Lt DF Dimsey, OK & Lt RFC Machin, (lost on 18Sep18 ?)
Losses
Ltn Erich Kämpfe   13   Severely WIA, died 20 Sep, Metz.

20 September 1918

Ltn F Noltenius	27	SE5	Marcoing	0745	11	a.
Ltn H Frommherz	27	Camel	Marcoing	0745	23	b.
Ltn W Neuenhofen	27	Camel	Proville	0745	8	b.
Ltn G Meyer	37	SE5	Hermies	0800	20	c.
Ltn zS M Stinsky	MFJ2	Camel	SE Pervyse	1005	2	d.
Vzflgmstr K Scharon	MFJ2	Camel	Pervyse	1005	1	d.
Obltn O Schmidt	5	BF2b	Fresnoy le Grand	1037	14	e.
Uffz Leicht	5	BF2b	Croix Fonsomme	1040	2	e.
Ltn K Odebrett	42	DH9	SE Montigny	1050	14	
Ltn C Degelow	40	BF2b	Roubaix	1055	15	f.
Ltn F Noltenius	27	Camel	Aubigny-au-Bac	1445	12	g.
Ltn F Brandt	26	Camel	Ecourt	1540	10	h.
Vfw O Fruhner	26	Camel	Cagnicourt	1545	27	h.
Ltn P Bäumer	B	Camel	E Rumaucourt	1550	27	h.
Ltn J Jacobs	7	Camel			–	
Vfw G Fieseler	25	Nieuport	Trojviartzi		19	i.
Ltn F Kirchfeld	73	Voisin			2	
OfStv W Schluckebier	73	Voisin			2	j.
Ltn F Anders	73	Voisin			6	
Ltn zS P Becht	MFJ1	Camel	Beerst		2	d.
Ltn zS T Osterkamp	MFJ2	Camel	Praat-Bosch		27	d.

a.   E4072, 24 Sqn RAF, Lt EP Larrabee, US, POW.
b.   60 Sqn RAF lost F5472, Lt GFC Caswell, WIA/POW, and 201 Sqn RAF lost C125, Lt J Mill, KIA in this action.
c.   D6945, 60 Sqn RAF, 2/Lt HFV Battle, WIA.

d.   204 Sqn RAF lost three Camels: B6319, Lt DF Tysoe, WIA; D3387, 2/Lt EG Rolph, POW and D8205, 2/Lt CL Kelly, KIA.

e.   E2158, 20 Sqn RAF, Lt AR Strachan & 2/Lt DM Calderwood,KIAs. Only 20 Sqn loss.

f.   E2260, 48 Sqn RAF, Lt MFJR Mahoney & 2/Lt JN Keir, POWs.

g.   F6192, 148th Aero, 1Lt H Jenkinson, KIA.

h.   203 Sqn RAF lost two Camels: E4377, 2/Lt CG Milne, POW and E4409, Lt MG Cruise, KIA.

i.   Serbian Escadrille 506, 2/Sgt LA Michelle & Pvt E Arnrow, KIAs.

j.   GB 1 lost three Voisins, the only known crew loss was V3348, Escadrille VB 25, MdL E Conan, MIA.

Losses

Vfw Otto Fruhner	26	Lightly wounded 1545 in collision with Camel of 203 Sqn RAF. Parachuted safely, and remained with unit.
Ltn Schneider	26	Shot down by 203 Sqn RAF, OK.
Flg Friedrich Kinzig	55	Killed in action Djenin airfield.
Ltn Helmut Gantz	56	Killed in action Armentières.
Ltn Hans Böhning	79	Wounded in action Fokker DVII(Alb) 747/18.

21 September 1918

Ltn C Degelow	40	RE8	Houthulst Wald	1045	16	a.
Ltn K Plauth	20	DH9	N Houthulst Wald	1200	8	
Ltn J Jacobs	7	DH4	Dixmuiden-Roulers	1222	30	b.
Ltn J Jacobs	7	DH4	Roulers	1230	–	
Ltn Oldenburg	22	AWFK8	Cambrai	1830	1	
Ltn F Noltenius	27	Camel	Gavrelle	1830	zLg	
OfStv J Mai	5	BF2b	E Montecouvax	1840	27	
Uffz S Westphal	29	SE5	E La Bassée	1845	2	c.
OfStv R Schleichhardt	18	Spad	Facq Wald	1900	3	
Ltn H Müller	18	Spad	Combres Höhe	1905	12	
Ltn E Spindler	18	Spad	Combres Wald	1915	2	
Ltn P Bäumer	B	DH9	E Bourlon Wood		28	d.
Ltn P Bäumer	B	DH9	E Lagnicourt		29	e.
Ltn P Bäumer	B	DH9	E Morchies		30	e.
Ltn R Klimke	27	Camel			–	

a.   F5976, 7 Sqn RAF, Lt WG Allanson & 2/Lt WL Anderson, MC, KIAs.

b.   D3092, 108 Sqn RAF, 2/Lt DA Shanks & Sgt RJ Sear, KIAs.

c.   D6958, 74 Sqn RAF, Capt S Carlin MC, DFC, DCM, POW.

d.   F5827, 57 Sqn RAF, 2/Lt OMcI Turnbull & Lt DFV Page, KIAs.

e.   205 Sqn RAF suffered only one loss – A8089, Lt AN Hyde & 2/Lt WW Harrison, KIA, although 2/Lt Tunstall was WIA.

Losses

Ltn Rudolf Klimke	27	Severely wounded in action.
Ltn Schmitt	27	Severely wounded in action.

22 September 1918

Vfw K Bohnenkamp	22	Camel	N Epéhy	0750	9	
Vfw K Bohnenkamp	22	Camel	Epéhy	0750	10	
Ltn H v d Marwitz	30	Camel	S Neuve Eglise	0815	12	a.
Ltn F Bieling	30	Camel	Ploegsteert Wald	0820	1	a.
Ltn F Riemer	26	Camel	W Sauchy	0850	8	b.
Ltn W Neuenhofen	27	Camel	near Albert	0850	9	c.
Vfw Belz	1	RE8	Cambrai	0855	2	
Ltn F Brandt	26	Camel	W Sains	0858	–	d.
Ltn K Odebrett	42	Breguet	S Flavy le Martel	0956	15	e.
Obltn O v Boenigk	JGII	DH4/Salm	Utcourt		26	
Obltn B Loerzer	JGIII	Camel			42	d.

Ltn H Frommherz	27	Camel			24	f.
Ltn E Thuy	28	SE5	Vitry		31	g.
OfStv H Hünninghaus	66	Spad	Pont Arcy		3	

a. 4 Sqn AFC lost two Camels, one downed in allied lines and E7191, 2/Lt TH Barkell, FTL, OK.
b. F5969, 17th Aero, 2Lt GP Thomas, KIA.
c. F6034, 17th Aero, 1Lt GA Vaughn,Jr, FTL, OK.
d. 17th Aero.
e. Escadrille Br 123, 1Lt EM Powell,(O) USAS, WIA.
f. F2157, 17th Aero, 1Lt TE Tillinghast, POW.
g. C8864, 56 Sqn RAF, 2/Lt JC Gunn, POW.

Losses

Ltn Karl Barenfeind	34b	Killed in action Demicourt by 17th Aero.

23 September 1918

Ltn O v B-Marconnay	19	Breguet	Pont-à-Mousson	1030	20	a.
Ltn G v Hantelmann	15	DH4	S Metz	1120	17	
Ltn Oldenburg	22	Balloon	Atilly	1620	2	b.
Oblt H v Wedel	24	SE5	Villers Outreux	1620	4	
Ltn H Leptien	63	RE8	S Fleurbaix	1710	7	c.
Vfw K Ungewitter	24	BF2b	Levergies	1725	4	d.
OfStv F Altemeier	24	BF2b	Levergies	1725	–	
Ltn F Rumey	5	Dolphin	Bussy-Baralle	1815	41	e.
Ltn B Hobein	20	FB2b			–	

a. Escadrille Sal 28, Cpl Latil & Sgt Saloman, MIAs.
b. 7th Balloon Co USBS, Ltn L Ferrenback, OK & Lt H Sapiro, WIA.
c. C2300, 42 Sqn RAF, 2/Ls DA Newson & 2/Lt GEM Browne, KIAs.
d. E2562, 20 Sqn RAF, Lt J Nicolson & 2/Lt BW Wilson, KIAs.
e. D3741, 87 Sqn RAF, Lt FW Goodman, WIA.

Losses

Vzfw Paul Färber	22	Killed in action Sailly, combat 87 Sqn RAF ?
Ltn Krayer	45	Injured in a crash landing.
FlgzgObMt Karl Schiffmann	MFJ4	KIA, Ichteghem, combat 213 Sqn RAF.

24 September 1918

Ltn M Dehmisch	58	SE5	Abancourt	0730	10	a.
Ltn F Rumey	5	SE5	S Bussy	0820	42	
Vfw R Wirth	37	BE2b	S Beauvois	0820	4	b.
Obltn O Schmidt	5	SE5	Rumaucourt	0830	15	
Uffz Leicht	5	SE5	Bellone, N Hamel	0830	3	
Ltn G Wember	61	Balloon		0905	2	c.
OfStv Bansmer	44	Spad	SW Attigny	1030	2	
Ltn K Plauth	20	DH9	La Bassée	1040	9	d.
Vfw K Bohnenkamp	22	AWFK8	Vermand	1040	11	
Ltn J v Busse	20	DH9	Longies	1050	8	d.
Ltn J Gildemeister	20	DH9	Longies	1050	3	d.
Vfw F Poeschke	53	Spad	Bésine	1100	3	e.
Vfw O Hennrich	46	Balloon	NE Manancourt	1120	14	
Uffz H Haase	21	Balloon	S Braisne	1350	4	f.
Ltn zS Wilhelm	MFJ4	Camel	Pervyse	1415	2	g.
Vfw O Hennrich	46	Balloon	Fins	1610	15	h.
Vfw O Hennrich	46	Balloon	Fins	1612	16	i.
Ltn auf der Haar	46	Balloon	Fins	1612	1	
Ltn J Klein	15	Spad	Lachaussée	1615	16	
Ltn P Achilles	MFJ5	DH9	Werckem	1620	3	j.
Vfw Becker	44	BF2b	Metz-en-Couture	1725	3	

OfStv J Mai	5	DH9	1 km S Beauvois	1730	28	k.
Vfw Mack	63	SE5	S Ypres	1800	2	
Sgt M Kuhn	21	Balloon	SW Fismes	1815	9	l.
Ltn J Jacobs	7	Camel	Moorslede	1835	31	m.
Ltn C Degelow	40	SE5	Zillebeker See	1900	17	n.
OfStv G Dörr	45	Spad	Soissons	1900	29	o.
Ltn P Bäumer	B	Camel	Sailly	am	31	p.
Ltn P Bäumer	B	DH9	SW Clary		32	k.
Ltn O Löffler	B	DH9	W Cambrai		12	k.
Obltn H-H v Boddien	59	SE5	Anneux		4	
Obltn F Krafft	59	SE5	Inchy		2	
Obltn H-H v Boddien	59	DH4	La Pave		5	
Ltn Lehmann	59	BF2b	Boursies		1	q.
Ltn H Jebens	59	BF2b	Bantouzelle		1	q.
Ltn G Wember	61	Balloon			2	r.

a.   E4054, 40 Sqn RAF, Capt GJ Strange, KIA.
b.   E2515, 62 Sqn RAF, Lt NN Coope & 2/Lt HS Mantle, both WIA/POW.
c.   French 29 Compagnie Aérostières, Asp Bixiaux, OK.
d.   103 Sqn RAF lost 2 DH9s: D2877, Lt CH Heebner & 2/Lt D Davenport, KIAs and F5842, Lt HC Noel, KIA & Sgt LC Ovens, POW.
e.   Escadrille Sal 263, Sgt Delporte & S/Lt Burfin, KIAs.
f.   French 75 Compagnie Aérostières, S/Lt Briere, OK.
g.   D8147, 210 Sqn RAF, Capt SC Joseph, DSC, WIA.
h.   British Balloon 31-18-3, Cpl R Stewart, OK & 2/Lt A Hopkins, OK.
i.   British Balloon 1-18-3, Lt J King, OK & 1/AM A Hopkins, OK.
j.   D7208, 108 Sqn RAF, 2/Lt JM Dandy & Sgt CP Crites, POWs.
k.   49 Sqn RAF lost: E658, Lt HJ Bennett, DOW & 2/Lt RH Armstrong, POW; E8869, Capt ED Asbury & 2/Lt BT Gillman, KIAs and F6098, Lt CC Conover, POW & 2/Lt HJ Pretty, WIA/POW, along with three other DH9s shot up.
l.   French 43 Compagnie Aérostières, Adj Coupillard, OK.
m.   204 Sqn RAF.
n.   E4074, 41 Sqn RAF, Capt C Crawford, POW.
o.   49th Aero, 1Lt EL Moore, WIA.
p.   4 Sqn AFC, Capt EJ Kingston-McCloughry, WIA.
q.   62 Sqn RAF ?
r.   French 45 Compagnie Aérostières, Adj A Renard, OK.

Losses

Vfw Peter Stenzel	4	Killed in action Fort d'Englos, 88 Sqn RAF.
Ltn Bruno Hobein	20	Wounded in action.
Vfw Schmidt	27	Lightly WIA, remained, 17th Aero combat.
Sgt Karl Rau	40	Died in hospital Locquignol.
Ltn Wilhelm Meyer	47	Taken prisoner Suippes 1630, during balloon attack in Fokker DVII 4522/18 – ground fire from 45 Cie Aérostières.
Ltn Martin Demisch	58	Severely wounded in action Abancourt, DOW 25 September.

25 September 1918

Ltn R Fuchs	77	Spad	Arnaville/Verdun	0805	1	a.
Ltn J Grassmann	10	Balloon	Pont-à-Mousson	0950	6	b.
Gefr Meyer	3	DH9	Saaralben	1115	1	
Ltn R Schmidt	78	DH9	Zabern	1430	1	
Ltn Keisze	K1b	DH4	Mannheim	1430	1	
Unknown Pilot	K3	DH4	Zabern	1430		
Vfw Gott	K9	DH4	Darmstadt	1430	–	
OfStv E Prime	78	DH4	Bühl Airfield	1500	–	
Ltn zS P Achilles	MFJ5	Camel	Hooglede	1750	4	c.

Uffz K Treiber	5	Spad	SW Le Bosquet	1800	3	d.
Ltn S Garsztka	31	DH9	Fresnoy le Petit	1800	4	e.
Vflgmstr A Zenses	MFJ2	Camel	Wynendaele	1800	8	c.
Uffz Brüngel	31	DH9	Busigny	1805	2	e.
Ltn zS P Achilles	MFJ5	Camel	NW Roulers	1805	5	c.
Obltn R v Greim	34	DH9	S Escaufort	1815	24	e.
Ltn F v Braun	79	BF2b	Villers-Guislain	1825	2	
Ltn F Piechulek	56	Camel	Kortemarck	1850	11	f.
Ltn F Noltenius	27	Camel	Cambrai		13	
Ltn F Hengst	64	Salmson	by Waville		3	g.
Ltn A Stephan	70	DH4	S Alberschweiler		2	h.
Vfw Lemke	70	DH4	Bergzabern		2	h.
Vfw T Krist	70	DH4	Brumath		1	h
Ltn F Anders	73	Farman	Moronvillers		7	i.

a.   Escadrille Spa 88, Cpl P Abebes, MIA.
b.   247, 10th Balloon Co USBS, 1Lt JW Lavers, OK.
c.   213 Sqn RAF lost the following Camels: B7252, Lt CP Sparks, POW; D3360, 2/Lt JC Sorley, KIA and D8216, Lt LC Scroggie, KIA.
d.   Escadrille Br ?, Adj Fabiani & S/Lt Lormail, MIAs.
e.   27 Sqn RAF lost two: D3163, 2/Lt CB Sanderson, POW/DOW & Sgt J Wilding, WIA/POW and E8857, 2/Lt AV Cosgrove & 2/Lt SC Read, KIAs.
f.   C66, 204 Sqn RAF, 2/Lt T Warburton, POW.
g.   Escadrille Sal 47, Sgt Chauffeur & MdL Alby, KIAs.
h.   55 Sqn IAF lost 4 DH4s, one to Flak: D8356, 2/Lt JB Dunn & 2/Lt HS Orange, KIAs; D8388, 2/Lt RC Pretty & 2/Lt GR Bartlett, POWs; D8413, 2/Lt AJ Robinson & 2/Lt HR Burnett, KIAs and F5714, 2/Lt GB Dunlop & 2/Lt AC Heyes, POWs; in addition, D8392 was badly shot up and the observer, 2/Lt JTL Attwood, KIA.
i.   Escadrille F 114, Lt Bizard, Capt Garnier & Asp Rives, all MIA.

Losses

Uffz Janzen	17	Injured in crash.
Gefr Franz Wagner	79	Killed in action Ferme-Preselles, Fokker DVII(OAW) 4631/18 'Lot', during 22/25 Sqns RAF action.

---

26 September 1918   The Battle of the Meuse-Argonne

Ltn M Näther	62	Spad	Bezonvaux	0710	14	a.
Vfw W Seitz	8	Spad	Etain	0810	11	b.
Ltn F Höhn	60	Spad	Somme-Py	0830	12	
Gefr Röhr	50	Breguet	SE Perthes	0831	1	
Uffz K Hofmann	60	Spad	Massiges	0900	1	
Vfw K Bohnenkamp	22	Camel	NW Roussoy	1025	12	
Flgmt K Engelfried	MFJ5	Camel	Wenduyne	1030	4	c.
Flgmt C Kairies	MFJ5	Camel	Neumünster	1030	7	c.
Uffz Ernst	49	Breguet	Tahure	1050	1	
Ltn zS Freymadl	MFJ1	DH4	Ostende	1115	2	d.
Vzflgmstr H Sawatzki	MFJ1	Camel	Ostende	1115	1	e.
Ltn W Blume	9	Spad 2	Tahure	1215	26	
Ltn G v Hantelmann	15	Spad	by Etain	1215	17	f.
Ltn H Schäfer	15	Spad	SW Etain	1215	9	g.
Ltn F Höhn	60	Balloon	Minaucourt	1215	11	h.
OfStv G Dörr	45	Spad XI	Fismes	1300	30	
Vfw R Francke	8	Spad	Etain	1350	15	i.
Ltn F Rumey	5	BF2b	Grugies	1410	43	j.
Ltn Hebler	68	Balloon	Aubreville	1415	2	k.
Ltn Hebler	68	Balloon	Aubreville	1415	3	l.

Vfw C Mesch	26	Camel	St Quentin	1430	13	m.
Ltn M Näther	62	Balloon	Thienville	1535	15	n.
Ltn Breidenbach	62	Balloon	Thienville	1535	1	o.
Ltn H Habich	49	Balloon	Minaucourt	1540	4	p.
Ltn M Näther	62	Spad	Abancourt	1545	16	q.
Vfw A Jühe	8	Spad	Etain	1600	4	
Ltn H v Gluczewski	4	DH9	SE Kemnat	1615	2	
Obltn G Rassberger	80	Spad	Athienville	1630	zLg	
Vfw O Hennrich	46	Balloon	Liéramont	1645	17	r.
Sgt Fröhlich	46	Balloon	Liéramont	1645	1	s.
Obltn E Udet	4	DH9	Monteningen	1710	61	t.
Ltn F Bacher	3	DH9	Buch by Metz	1715	–	
Vfw Glasemann	3	DH9	Selzeck	1715	1	
Uffz Seidel	3	DH9	SE Frescaty	1715	1	
Ltn R Kraut	4	DH9	S Metz	1715	1	
Obltn E Udet	4	DH9	Buch by Metz	1720	62	t.
Ltn J Klein	15	DH9	Vern, S Metz	1720	17	
Ltn M Gossner	77	DH9	Manningen	1725	8	t.
OfStv B Ultsch	77	DH9	Kubern	1727	10	t.
Vfw Schäflien	77	DH9	Pullingen	1730	1	t.
Vfw O Agne	77	DH9	Grossprunach	1730	1	t.
Ltn J v Ziegesar	15	DH4	Pont-à-Mousson	1740	2	u.
Ltn S Garsztka	31	SE5/Camel	Fresnoy le Petit	1740	5	v.
Ltn H v Freden	50	Balloon	Perthes	1755	10	w.
Ltn K Maletzky	50	Spad	Perthes	1800	3	
Ltn F Rumey	5	DH4	Cambrai	1805	44	x.
Uffz K Treiber	5	DH4	2 km E Le Pavé	1805	4	x.
Ltn K Maletzky	50	Spad	Le Mesnil	1810	4	y.
Ltn E Bormann	B	Camel	N Cambrai		11	
Ltn H Becker	12	DH4	Longuyon-Landres		17	z.
Ltn H Becker	12	DH4	Longuyon-Landres		18	aa.
Ltn H Besser	12	DH4	Longuyon-Landres		2	bb.
Vfw O Klaiber	12	DH4	Longuyon-Landres		2	cc.
Ltn A Greven	12	DH4	Giraumont		2	dd.
Ltn F Büchner	13	Spad	Consenvoye		33	ee.
Ltn F Büchner	13	Salmson	Charpentrie		34	ff.
Ltn F Büchner	13	Spad	Gercourt		35	gg.
Ltn F Büchner	13	Spad	Etreillers		36	hh.
Vfw A Haussmann	13	Spad	Bertincourt		15	ii.
Obltn B Loerzer	JGIII	Camel			43	
Obltn B Loerzer	JGIII	Camel			44	
Ltn H v Freden	50	Salmson	Ville sur Tourbe		11	jj.
Ltn W Frickart	65	Spad	S Delut		9	kk.
Ltn H Mahn	72	?			3	
Ltn H Mahn	72	Spad			4	
Ltn G Tschentschel	72	?			5	
Ltn G Frädrich	72	?			4	
Ltn E Schulz	72	?			1	
Vfw A Nagler	81	Spad	Suippes		6	ll.
Vfw D Averes	81	Breguet	N Tahure		7	

a.   Spad XIII 15195 '22', 13th Aero, 1Lt TP Evans, POW.
b.   Spad XIII 15102 '8', 13th Aero, 2Lt VH Burgin, POW.
c.   204 Sqn RAF lost two Camels this date: C75, 2/Lt GEC Howard, and D3374, Lt WB Craig, both KIA.
d.   A7632, 202 Sqn RAF, Lt FAB Gasson & 2/Lt S King, KIAs.
e.   E1552, 65 Sqn RAF, 2/Lt WR Thornton, POW.

f.   Spad XIII 15129 '8', 139th Aero, 1Lt HR Sumner, POW.

g.   Spad XIII 15153 '1', 139th Aero, 1Lt HA Petree, KIA.

h.   French 21 Compagnie Aérostières.

i.   Spad XIII 7660 '3', 49th Aero, 1Lt IJ Roth, KIA.

j.   E2163, 'L' Flight, 2/Lt CA Harrison & Lt JA Parkinson, POWs.

k.   French 39 Compagnie Aérostières.

l.   244, 8th Balloon Co USBS, 1Lt CJ Ross, KIA & 2Lt HD Hudnut, OK.

m.   D8168, 208 Sqn RAF, Capt A Storey, WIA.

n.   228, 9th Balloon Co USBS, 1Lt SV Clarke, OK & 2Lt SE White, OK.

o.   167, 3rd Balloon Co USBS, 1Lt HP Neibling, OK & 1Lt GC Carroll, OK.

p.   French 19 Compagnie Aérostières, S/Lt Vallier, OK & S/Lt Defleury, OK.

q.   50th Aero, 2Lt DC Beebe, OK & 2Lt MK Lockwood, FTL, OK.

r.   British Balloon 6-15-5.

s.   British Balloon 14-14-5.

t.   99 Sqn IAF suffered six losses: B9347, Capt PE Welchman, MC, DFC, WIA/POW & 2/Lt TH Swann, WIA/POW; B9366, 2/Lt S McKeever, WIA & Lt Boniface, OK, FTL; C6272, 2/Lt CRG Abrahams & 2/Lt CH Sharp, KIAs; D3213, 2/Lt WHC Gillett & 2/Lt H Crossley, both WIA/POW; D5573, 2/Lt LG Stern & Lt FO Cook, KIAs; E632, Lt SC Gilbert & 2/Lt R Buckby, KIAs and D544, Lt HD West, OK & 2/Lt JW Howard, KIA, was badly shot up but returned.

u.   D7232, 104 Sqn IAF, Lt OL Malcolm & 2/Lt GV Harper, KIAs.

v.   F1975, 80 Sqn RAF, 2/Lt H Walker, KIA.

w.   French 30 Compagnie Aérostières.

x.   57 Sqn RAF lost two DH4s: D8419, Lt PWJ Timson & Lt AN Eyre, KIAs and F6187, Lt FG Pym, WIA/POW & Sgt WCE Mason, POW/DOW.

y.   Escadrille Spa 26, Capt JMX Sevin, FLT, OK.

z.   32915, 20th Aero, 1Lt PN Rhinelander & 1Lt HC Preston, KIAs.

aa   32819, 20th Aero, 1Lt RP Matthews & 2Lt EA Taylor, KIAs.

bb   32792, 20th Aero, 2Lt DB Harris & 2Lt E Forbes, KIAs.

cc   32492, 20th Aero, 1Lt MC Cooper & 1Lt EC Leonard, POWs.

dd   32286, 20th Aero, 2Lt GB Wiser & 1Lt G Richardson, POWs.

ee   Spad XIII 7519, 27th Aero, 2Lt IA Roberts, KIA.

ff   1st Aero, No.5229, 1Lt JF Richards II & 2Lt AF Hanscom, KIAs.

gg   Spad XIII 4505 '4', 94th Aero, 2Lt A Nutt, KIA.

hh   94th Aero, 1Lt AB Sherry, FTL, OK.

ii   Spad XIII 7515 '24', 139th Aero, 1Lt HA Garvie, POW.

jj   Escadrille Sal 16, Sgt Lemaire, WIA & Lt Champagnet, OK.

kk   Escadrille Spa 315, Cpl Boutin, WIA.

ll   Escadrille Spa 89, Sgt R Caillet, KIA.

Losses

Obltn Ernst Udet	4	Wounded in action shot in the thigh.
Vfw Robert Wirth	37	Severely wounded in action.
Ltn Mappes	37	Lightly wounded in action remained on unit.
Vfw Karl Weinmann	50	Taken prisoner location unknown.
Vfw Huar	68	Wounded in action.
Vfw Robert Mossbacher	77	Wounded in action.

27 September 1918   The Battle of the Canal du Nord

Vfw H Juhnke	52	BF2b	W Armentières	0755	–	
Obltn R v Greim	34	Camel	S Masnières	0815	25	
Ltn R v Barnekow	1	SE5	Bourlon Wood	0930	6	a.
Uffz G Borm	1	SE5	St Olle-Cambrai	0940	2	a.
OfStv F Altemeir	24	BF2b	Marcy, Fontaine	1020	17	b.
Ltn R Rückle	33	BF2b	Busigny	1130	2	c.
Ltn F Rumey	5	Camel	E Marquion	1205	45	d.
OfStv J Mai	5	Camel	Sauchy-Cauchy	1210	29	d.
Ltn E Thuy	28	SE5	Sauchy-Cauchy	1210	–	
Uffz K Treiber	5	SE5	W Cambrai	1250	5	
Ltn F Piechulek	56	Camel	NW Torhout	1250	12	e.

Ltn R v Barnekow	1	DH4	Sailly	1300	7	f.
Uffz G Borm	1	Dolphin	Bourlon Wood	1300	3	g.
Vfw F Classen	26	BF2b	S Brunemont	1403	9	h.
Obltn O Schmidt	5	BF2b	Cattenières	1550	16	i.
Vfw O Hennrich	46	BF2b	Neuvilly	1600	18	i.
Ltn H Körner	19	Spad	Pagny	1655	4	
Ltn H v Freden	50	Balloon	Minaucourt	1655	12	j.
OfStv E Prime	78	Spad	Herbeviller	1700	3	
Gefr Meyer	3	Spad	Champenoux	1730	2	
Ltn G Bassenge	B	SE5	Noyelles	1735	4	
Vfw F Classen	26	SE5	Sailly, W Cambrai	1735	10	
Vfw A Korff	60	Spad	N Tahure	1810	8	
Ltn F Höhn	60	Spad	Marfaux	1820	13	k.
Vfw Zimmermann	60	Spad	Tahure	1820	1	
Vfw H Pfaffenritter	60	Spad	Tahure	1820	3	
Uffz K Fervers	B	Snipe	by Aubenscheul		1	
Ltn E Bormann	B	Snipe	N Ecoust		12	
Ltn E Bormann	B	Snipe	E Epinoy		13	
Ltn P Bäumer	B	Snipe	S Oisy		33	
Ltn P Bäumer	B	DH4	W Cambrai	am	34	l.
Ltn P Bäumer	B	SE5	W Cambrai	am	35	m.
Ltn H Vallendor	B	Camel	N Bourlon Wood	am	3	n.
Ltn H Vallendor	B	Camel	by Marquion		4	
Obltn B Loerzer	JGIII	a/c			43	
Obltn B Loerzer	JGIII	a/c			44	
Ltn H Frommherz	27	SE5			25	a.
Ltn H Frommherz	27	SE5			26	a.
Ltn C Degelow	40	BF2b	W Valenciennes		18	
Ltn J Jensen	57	DH9	Fechain	pm	5	
Vfw F Senf	59	DH9	Goeilzin	am	1	
Ltn M Näther	62	Spad	Montzéville		17	o.
Vfw A Nagler	81	Breguet	N Tahure		7	p.
Vfw D Averes	81	Spad	Ville		8	q.

a.   40 Sqn RAF lost four SE5s: B8442, Lt ND Willis, POW; C9135, 2/Lt PB Myers, KIA; E1345, 1Lt R Mooney, USAS, WIA/POW and E1350, 2/Lt GMJ Morton, KIA.
b.   E2566, 20 Sqn RAF, Lt FE Turner & 2/Lt CE Clarke, KIAs.
c.   C944, 62 Sqn RAF, 2/Lt PS Manley & Sgt GF Hines, POWs.
d.   54 Sqn RAF, only loss was B6421, Lt P McCaig, KIA.
e.   E1549, 65 Sqn RAF, 2/Lt RO Campbell, American, KIA.
f.   A7899, 18 Sqn RAF, Lt RC Bennett,DFC & Lt NW Helwig, DFC, POWs.
g.   E4501, 19 Sqn RAF, Capt CV Gardiner, DOW.
h.   E2153, 88 Sqn RAF, Lt C Foster & Sgt T Proctor, KIAs.
i.   22 Sqn RAF lost three BF2bs: D8089, 2/Lt GJ Smith & Lt GB Shum, POWs; E2243, Lt JR Drummond, KIA & 2/Lt CH Wilcox, POW, and E2477, Capt SFH Thompson & 2/Lt CJ Tolman, KIAs.
j.   French 31 Compagnie Aérostières.
k.   Escadrille Br 111, Sgt-Maj Leteneur & Asp Etchberry, WIAs.
l.   A8031, 25 Sqn RAF, Lt DH Hazell & 2/Lt DB Robertson, KIAs.
m.   F5495, 56 Sqn RAF, Lt GO Mackenzie, KIA.
n.   D9472, 73 Sqn RAF, 2/Lt WA Brett, KIA.
o.   Escadrille Spa 77, MdL J Thévenod, KIA.
p.   Escadrille Br 108, Lt Metayer & Asp Mullet,both WIA.
q.   Escadrille Spa 100, Sgt Gantois, WIA.

Losses

Ltn Fritz Heinz	B	Killed in action Awoingt, SE Cambrai.
Ltn Fritz Rumey	5	Shot down in a fight with an SE5, baled out but parachute failed.

Ltn Steiling	19	Severely injured in a crash on take off.
Ltn Holle	31	Severely wounded in action.
Ltn Paul Strähle	57	Wounded in action Aniche, with 18 & 22 Sqns RAF.
Oblt Hans-Helmut von Boddien	59	Severely wounded in action.
Ltn Hans Jebens	59	Killed Bouchin Fokker DVII, parachute failed.
Ltn Max Näther	62	Lightly wounded 'v' 27 Sqn, remained.

28 September 1918   The Battles in Flanders

Name	Unit	Type	Place	Time	No.	Ref
Uffz L Jeckert	56	RE8	Moorslede	0800	3	a.
Ltn F Höhn	60	Balloon	Tahure-Perthes	0810	14	b.
Ltn F Höhn	60	Balloon	Bethélainville	0830	15	c.
Ltn G Bassenge	B	SE5/Camel	Ham-Lenglet	0835	5	d.
Ltn O v B-Marconnay	19	DH4	Dannevoux	1035	21	e.
Vfw F Poeschke	53	Spad	Somme-Py	1145	4	f.
Uffz K Boness	53	Spad	Somme-Py	1150	1	g.
Ltn zS T Osterkamp	MFJ2	Camel	Woumen	1230	27	h.
Vfflgmstr A Zenses	MFJ2	Camel	Woumen	1230	9	h.
Ltn E Baumgärtel	56	SE5	Ypres	1240	2	
Ltn Wolff	60	Spad	Vienne-le Château	1315	1	i.
Flgmt Nake	MFJ1	DH9	Leke	1430	1	j.
Ltn A v Brandenstein	49	Spad	Cernay	1545	6	
Ltn K Plauth	20	Camel	S Roulers	1740	10	
Ltn zS R Poss	MFJ4	Dolphin	W Roulers	1745	7	k.
Flgmstr A Bühl	MFJ4	Dolphin	Roulers	1745	4	k.
Ltn J Raesch	43	Camel	SE Ypres	1750	2	l.
Ltn zS T Osterkamp	MFJ2	Breguet	Pierkenshoek	1810	28	m.
Ltn zS H Bargmann	MFJ2	DH9	Beerst	1815	1	
Flgmt Pfeiffer	MFJ2	Camel	Woumen	1815	1	n.
Uffz K Fervers	B	Camel	Epinoy	am	2	o.
Ltn O Löffler	B	Salmson	Epinoy-Marcoing		13	
Ltn J Jacobs	7	SE5	Moorslede		32	p.
Ltn J Jacobs	7	SE5	Moorslede		33	
Ltn F Büchner	13	Salmson	Nantillois		37	q.
Ltn W Niethammer	13	Salmson	Pagny		4	r.
Uffz E Binge	16	SE5			4	
Ltn C Degelow	40	Camel	Armentières		19	
Obltn H-E Gandert	51	RE8			8	
Ltn F Piechulek	56	DH4	Wervicq		13	s.
Vfw Krebs	56	SE5	Kastelhoek		1	
Vzfw R Rübe	67	Balloon			–	
Ltn G Frädrich	72	AR2	Mauré		5	t.
Vfw K Arnold	72	AR2	Mauré		4	u.
Ltn E Schulz	72	Spad	Ardeuil		2	v.
Ltn H Mahn	72	Spad	Ardeuil		5	w.

a. C2530, 7 Sqn RAF, 2/Lt HM Matthews, WIA & 2/Lt C Fletcher, DOW.
b. French 67 Compagnie Aérostières, Lt R Weiss, OK.
c. 176, 6th Balloon Co USBS, 1Lt HF Gossett, OK & 1Lt GR Nixon, OK.
d. F3220, 203 Sqn RAF, Sgt WN Mayger, MM, KIA.
e. 9th Aero, 2Lt LD Warrender, WIA & 1Lt HC Crumb, DOW.
f. Escadrille Sal 252, Sgt Ball & S/Lt Nouvellon, KIAs.
g. Escadrille Spa 62, Cpl Gérard, MIA.
h. 204 Sqn, only one loss, D8186, Lt RMcI Gordon, WIA.
i. Escadrille Spa 62, Cpl Gaulhiac, MIA.
j. A8025, 202 Sqn RAF, Capt AV Bowater & Lt DL Melvin, POWs.

k.   79 Sqn RAF 1 loss, F6020, Lt RJ Morgan, American, POW.
l.   C1914, 29 Sqn RAF, Capt EC Hoy, DFC, POW.
m.   A2, 2 Belgium Escadrille, W/O RJMM Cajot & Lt ATM Bricoult, POWs.
n.   D8187, 204 Sqn RAF, Lt RM Bennett, KIA.
o.   F5937, 209 Sqn RAF, Lt JA Fenton, KIA.
p.   41 Sqn RAF ?
q.   88th Aero, 2Lt HW Loud, KIA & Capt CT Trickey, POW.
r.   9th Aero, 2Lt HA Dolan, OK & 2Lt BD Woom, OK.
s.   A7849, 202 Sqn RAF, Lt AM Stevens & 2/Lt WHL Halford, KIAs.
t.   Escadrille Br 9, Cpl Moser & S/Lt Le Comte des Floris, MIAs.
u.   Escadrille Br 123, Adj Montez & Sgt Pautrat, MIAs.
v.   Escadrille Spa 65, Sgt Milhau, MIA.
w.   Escadrille Spa 65, Sgt Bourgeois, WIA.

Losses

| Uffz Heinrich Brobowski | 53 | Taken prisoner near Somme-Py. |
| Uffz Karl Hofmann | 60 | Killed in action Argonne Forest. |

29 September 1918   Battle for The Hindenburg Line

Vfw Krebs	56	SE5	Westroosebeke	0815	2	
Vzflgmstr H Hackbusch	MFJ1	Camel	SE Oostkamp	0820	3	
Ltn zS Freymadl	MFJ1	Camel	SW Oostkamp	0820	3	
Flgmt Riess	MFJ1	Camel	SW Oostkamp	0820	1	
Uffz L Jeckert	56	RE8	Zonnebeke	0830	4	
Uffz K Treiber	5	DH9	NE Caudry	0845	6	a.
Ltn J Mai	5	BF2b	E Caudry	0850	30	b.
Ltn K Odebrett	42	SE5	Bohain	0940	16	c.
Ltn H v Freden	50	Spad	Somme-Py	1000	13	d.
Obltn H v Wedel	24	SE5	Hesdins	1020	5	
Vfw O Hennrich	46	SE5	Villers Outreaux	1020	19	e.
Ltn auf der Haar	46	SE5	Villers Outreaux	1020	2	
OfStv F Altemeier	24	BF2b	Montbrehain	1040	18	f.
Ltn A Lenz	22	SE5	Bellenglise	1050	6	
Flgmt E Blaass	MFJ2	Camel	Oudekapelle	1205	3	
Ltn Kohlpoth	56	DH9	Beythen	1230	1	g.
Ltn W Rosenstein	40	DH9		1240	5	g.
Ltn H Henkel	37	Balloon	Graincourt	1400	4	h.
Uffz A Bader	64	Spad	SW Chambley	1720	3	i.
Ltn R Rienau	19	Spad	Brieulles	1855	6	j.
Ltn H Rolfes	45	BF2b	Masnières	1900	18	
Uffz K Fervers	B	BF2b	Cagnoncles		3	k.
Vfw P Keusen	B	BF2b	E Irony		1	k.
Ltn P Bäumer	B	RE8/BF2b	Marcoing		36	k.
Ltn P Bäumer	B	Camel	Bourlon Wood		37	l.
Ltn P Bäumer	B	Camel	S Sailly		38	l.
Obltn H-E Gandert	51	Balloon	Langemarck		–	
OfStv H Hünninghaus	66	Spad	N Jouy		4	m.
Uffz O Bieleit	66	Breguet	N Jouy		2	n.
Ltn zS T Osterkamp	MFJ2	Breguet	W Zarren		29	o.

a.   D3172, 27 Sqn RAF, 2/Lt HS Thomas & 2/Lt T Brown, KIAs.
b.   F5814, 11 Sqn RAF, 2/Lt TT Smith & Lt JL Bromley, KIAs.
c.   C8841, 1 Sqn RAF, Lt LN Elworthy, POW.
d.   Escadrille Spa 31, Capt P Reverchon, MIA.
e.   C9293, 84 Sqn RAF, 2/Lt DC Rees, KIA.
f.   E2561, 20 Sqn RAF, 2/Lt NS Boulton & 2/Lt CH Case, KIAs.
g.   218 Sqn RAF suffered two losses: D3272, 2/Lt JC Pritchard & 2/Lt AE Smith, KIA, and E8883, Lt HP Brummell & Sgt RS Joysey, POWs.

h.   British Balloon 12-16-3 (Badly damaged but not destroyed).
i.   4638, 93rd, 1Lt RH Fuller, KIA.
j.   Spad XIII 95th Aero, 2Lt GO Woodard, POW.
k.   22 Sqn RAF had two losses: E2266, 1Lt E Adams (USAS) & Sgt GH Bissell, KIAs, and E2517, Lt CWM Thompson & Lt LR James, POWs.
l.   46 Sqn RAF suffered two losses: D6572, 2/Lt NF Moxon and F5960, 2/Lt AM Allan, both POW.
m.   Spad XIII 7642 '13', 49th Aero, 1Lt TA Gabel, KIA.
n.   Escadrille Spa 42, Sgt Kalley & Lt Kervadoe, MIAs.
o.   Escadrille Spa 34, MdL de Bellencourt & Lt de Bussy,both WIA.

Losses

Ltn Fritz Hoffmann	B	KIA, W of Cambrai by 64 Sqn RAF.
Obltn Hans-Eberhard Gandert	51	Wounded in action and taken prisoner during a balloon attack.
Ltn Gerold Tschentschel	72	Wounded in action.

30 September 1918

Vfw W Schmelter	42	SE5	Bohain	0900	2	
Vfw F Nüsch	22	Camel	Omisy	1025	2	
Ltn H Henkel	37	BF2b	Crevecoeur	1700	5	a.
Ltn S Garsztka	31	SE5	Lehaucourt	1800	6	b.
Ltn H Habich	49	Salmson	Mauré	1820	5	c.
Ltn F Ray	49	Breguet	Somme-Py	1820	17	d.
Ltn A Wunsch	67	Salmson			–	
Vfw A Nagler	81	Spad	Ville		8	e.

a.   C2442, 12 Sqn RAF, 2/Lt TH Jacques & Lt FN Billington, KIAs.
b.   C9298, 92 Sqn RAF, 2/Lt L S Davis KIA.
c.   Escadrille Sal 106, Adj Coudère & S/Lt Zuber, FLT, OK.
d.   Escadrille Br 123, Adj A Montel & Sgt M Pollet, MIAs.
e.   Escadrille Spa 164, Cpl S Heine, KIA.

Losses

Vfw Hermann Bernemann	29	Killed taking-off from Marckebeke.
Ltn Georg Schlenker	41	Severely wounded in action.

JASTA ARMEE ASSIGNMENTS AS OF 1 OCTOBER 1918

Western Front

1 Armee 72s,73
2 Armee 5,34b,37,46
3 Armee 17,41,47w,48,49,50,53,60,61,81
4 Armee 7,16b,20,29,40s,51,56,MFJ1,MFJ1I,MFJ3,MFJ1V,MFJV
5 Armee 8,12,13,15,19,62,65,67,68,74,77b
6 Armee 14,30,43,52,63
7 Armee 9,21s,45,66
17 Armee 1,B,26,27,28w,33,36,57,58,59
18 Armee 22s,24s,31,42,44s,79b
19 Armee 3,18,54s,80b,K3
Det 'A' 23b,32b,35b,39,70,78b
Det 'B' 69,71,75,76b
Det 'C' 4,6,10,11,64w

Other Fronts

11 Armee 25	Macedonia	
11 Armee 38	Macedonia	

1 October 1918

Vfw W Schmelter	42	RE8	N St Quentin	0900	3	a.
Ltn Körner	37	BF2b	Haussy	0915	1	b.
Ltn F Blume	37	BF2b	Haussy-Solesmes	0915	1	b.
Vfw K Bohnenkamp	22	DH9	NW St Quentin	1015	13	c.
Ltn U Fischer	22	Spad	Cérisy	1040	4	
Ltn O Brandes	24	SE5	N St Quentin	1125	–	
Uffz Schneider	1	Camel	Proville	1300	1	
Ltn auf der Haar	46	Balloon	Gouzeaucourt	1610	3	d.
Vfw O Hennrich	46	Balloon	Gouzeaucourt	1620	20	e.
Obltn E v Schleich	23	Breguet	Fôret de Menden	1620	35	
Ltn J Veltjens	15	Spad	SE Buzancy	1640	32	
Ltn G v Hantelmann	15	Spad	SE Buzancy	1640	20	
Vfw G Klaudat	15	Spad	SE Buzancy	1640	7	
Flgmt E Blaas	MFJ3	DH9	E Houthulst	1720	4	f.
Vzflgmstr H Goerth	MFJ3	DH9	S Houthulst	1725	7	f.
Ltn zS R Poss	MFJ4	DH9	SE Roulers	1725	8	f.
Uffz Schneider	1	RE8	Haynecourt	1730	2	a.
Flgmt E Blaas	MFJ3	Camel	E Houthulst	1730	5	g.
Flgmt G Hubrich	MFJ4	DH9	SE Roulers	1730	6	
Vzflgmstr H Goerth	MFJ3	Camel	S Handzeeme	1750	8	g.
Obltn O Schmidt	5	SE5	Ferme de Pavillon	1755	17	h.
Sgt M Kuhn	21	Balloon	W Fismes	1810	10	i.
Sgt M Kuhn	21	Balloon	W Fismes	1815	11	j.
Ltn J Jacobs	7	DH9			37	
Ltn F Büchner	13	Salmson			38	k.
Ltn H Müller	18	Spad			13	l.
Ltn H Künster	18	Spad			2	m.
Ltn W Neuenhofen	27				10	
Ltn Stoltenhoff	27				–	
Vfw E Schäpe	33				6	
Ltn C Degelow	40	SE5	Menin		20	n.
Ltn K Plauth	51	DH9	Roulers		11	f.
Ltn W Preuss	66	a/c			17	
Flgmt K Kutschke	MFJV	DH9	Roulers		3	
Ltn zS P Achilles	MFJ5	Camel	Dixmuiden		6	
Ltn Fischer	MFJ3	Camel	Klerkem		1	

a. 5 Sqn RAF ?
b. 11 Sqn RAF.
c. D9269, 57 Sqn RAF, 2/Lt AH Mills-Adam & Lt P Sherek, KIAs.
d. British Balloon 41-12-3.
e. British Balloon 43-16-3.
f. 108 Sqn RAF lost three DH9s: D5835, Lt F Hopkins & Lt JW Firth, KIAs; D5847, Lt AM Matheson & 2/Lt FR Everleigh, POWs; D7342, Lt GA Featherstone & 2/Lt F Owen, KIAs, and in addition F5847, 2/Lt CS Whellock & 2/Lt JW White, WIAs, was badly shot up.
g. 210 Sqn RAF lost two Camels: D1883, Major RDG Sibley and F3235, 2/Lt RW Johnson, both KIA.
h. B8427, 1 Sqn RAF, Lt W Joffe, DSO, KIA.
i. French 83 Compagnie Aérostières.
j. 7th Balloon Co USBS, 1Lt BT Burt, OK & Sgt HO Nicholls, OK.
k. 1st Aero, No.867 '1',1Lt RF Fox & 1Lt WA Phillips, KIAs.
l. Spad XIII 7558 '26',13th Aero, 1Lt CA Brodie, KIA.
m. Spad XIII 7890 '1', 13th Aero, 1Lt GD Strivers, KIA.
n. F5464, 74 Sqn RAF, Lt AM Sanderson, KIA.

Losses:

Flg Kurt Marocke	5	Killed in action at Bernot by Origny.
Vfw Friedrich Nüsch	22	Killed in action.

Ltn zS Freymadl	MFJ1	Wounded in action.
Flgmt Berndt	MFJ1	Wounded in action.
Flgmt Christian Kairies	MFJ5	Taken prisoner, DOW 2 October 1918 Zeebrügge.

2 October 1918

Ltn Schneider	26	BF2b	Avesnes	0830	–	
Ltn E Meyer	31	Camel	SE Homblières	0950	1	
Ltn W Blume	9	Spad	Gueux	1015	27	a.
Ltn J Jacobs	7	Spad	NE Houthulst Wood	1032	36	
Rittm K-B v Döring	1	Camel	Cambrai	1125	10	b.
Ltn R v Barnekow	1	Camel	Cambrai	1130	8	b.
Uffz G Borm	1	SE5	Cambrai	1130	4	
Ltn O v B-Marconnay	19	Breguet	Brabant, N Neuvilly	1130	22	
Uffz B Barthels	44	Camel	Croix Fonsomme	1200	2	c.
Vfw F Poeschke	53	AR2	Liry	1435	5	
Vfw F Poeschke	53	Spad XI	Liry	1435	6	
Ltn F Klausenberg	53	AR2	Liry	1435	1	
Ltn J Jensen	57	Balloon	Beuvry	1550	6	d.
Ltn A v Brandenstein	49	Breguet	Somme-Py	1745	7	
Ltn A v Brandenstein	49	Breguet	Liry	1815	8	
Ltn J Jacobs	7	DH9	Stadenberghe		35	e.
Vfw E Schäpe	33	DH9			7	f.
Vfw E Schäpe	33	?			8	
Ltn C Degelow	40	Camel	Roulers	am	21	g.
Ltn F Höhn	41	Balloon			21	h.
Ltn K Plauth	51	RE8	Gheluvelt		11	i.
Uffz A Bäder	65	Salmson	Gercourt		1	j.
Vfw D Averes	81	Spad	Somme-Py		9	k.
Vfw A Nagler	81	Spad	Somme-Py		9	l.

a.   Escadrille Spa 150, Sgt H Durand, MIA, Spad VII.
b.   F5926, 54 Sqn RAF, 2/Lt WJ Densham, KIA, only loss.
c.   F1977, 46 Sqn RAF, 2/Lt JK Shook, POW.
d.   British Balloon 5-10-1.
e.   D1080, 108 Sqn RAF, 2/Lt ATW Boswell & 2/Lt RP Gundill, KIAs.
f.   57 Sqn DH4 ?
g.   F3121, 213 Sqn RAF, Capt ML Cooper, OK, FTL.
h.   French 31 Compagnie Aérostières.
i.   C2742, 53 Sqn RAF, 2/Lt MW Wakeman & Lt JB Pierce, KIAs.
j.   99th Aero, 1Lt CC Kahle KIA & 1Lt CE Spencer, WIA.
k.   Spad XIII 3597, Escadrille Spa 165, S/Lt R Decugis, collision.
l.   Spad XIII 11133, Escadrille Spa 165, Sgt Louison, collision.

Losses:

Ltn Raven v Barnekow	1	Lightly wounded in action, remained with unit.
Vfw Belz	1	Taken prisoner at Tilloy, Fokker DVII 5301/18, after combat with 54 Sqn RAF (G/1/17).
Ltn Max Kliefoth	19	Injured in a collision with Ltn Seibert of Jasta 15.
Ltn Sylvester Garsztka	31	Wounded in action.
Ltn Bachem	44	Wounded in action.
Vfw Josef Hohly	65	Wounded in action by ground fire.
Flg Franz Neumann	79	Severely wounded in action.

3 October 1918

Vfw K Ungewitter	24	SE5	Seboncourt	0900	5	a.
Uffz W Dost	21	Spad	S Pontavert	0920	4	
Ltn J Veltjens	15	Breguet	Brieulles	0955	34	b.
Ltn K Bohny	17	Spad	Mauré	0955	5	

Vfw K Arnold	72	Spad	St Souplet	1015	5	
Ltn F Kirchfeld	73	Breguet	S Machault	1040	4	b.
Ltn v Melle	50	Spad	Liry	1045	1	c.
Ltn J v Busse	20	a/c		1050	9	
Vfw M Kiep	43	DH9	SW Carvin	1235	3	
Ltn K W Ritscherle	60	Balloon	Somme-Py	1255	8	d.
Ltn R v Barnekow	1	BF2b	Cambrai	1430	9	
Ltn P Bäumer	B	BF2b	Rumilly	1430	39	
Uffz H Marwede	67	Balloon	Montfaucon	1430	5	e.
Ltn H Becker	12	Spad	NW Aincreville	1630	19	f.
Ltn O v B-Marconnay	19	Spad	Limey	1630	23	g.
Ltn F Kirchfeld	73	Spad	Aubérive	1640	4	h.
Uffz H Haase	21	Balloon	W Fismes	1730	5	
Ltn J Jacobs	7	SE5/Camel	Ste Marguerite		37	
Ltn J Jacobs	7	SE5/Camel	Ste Marguerite		38	
Ltn J v Busse	20	a/c			10	
Ltn J v Busse	20	a/c			11	
Ltn A Burkard	29	DH4			2	
Ltn C Degelow	40	Spad	Roulers		22	i.
Ltn W Rosenstein	40	Spad	Roulers		6	i.
Ltn H Gilly	40	Spad	Roulers		5	i.
Vfw P Groll	40	Spad	Roulers		3	i.
OfStv G Dörr	45	Salmson	Coucy le Château		30	j.
Gefr. Tracinski	57	Camel			1	
Vfw E Hanzog	57	Dolphin			1	k.
Ltn W Preuss	66	Breguet	Jouy		18	b.
Uffz O Bieleit	66	Breguet	Jouy		3	b.
Vfw R Rübe	67	Balloon			5	l.
Vfw D Averes	81	Spad	St Hilaire		10	m.
Vzflgmstr A Zenses	MFJ2	DH9	N Roulers		10	n.
Vzflgmstr A Zenses	MFJ2	DH9	Roulers		11	n.
Flgmstr C Kuring	MFJ2	DH9	Roulers		4	n.

a. E1268, 24 Sqn RAF, Lt E Carpenter, KIA.
b. Three French Breguets lost: Escadrille Br 282, MdL Maindron & Brig Billet, KIAs; Br 128, Cpl Puyaubert & Asp Goyot, MIAs; Br 214, Cpl Guy & S/Lt Dhers, MIAs.
c. Escadrille Spa 85, Lt H Dumont, WIA, FTL N of Somme-Py.
d. French 67 Compagnie Aérostières, Lt R Weiss, WIA.
e. 135, 6th Co USBS, 1Lt WJR Taylor, OK.
f. 94th Aero, 1Lt ER Scroggie, POW.
g. 95th Aero, 1Lt WL Avery, WIA/POW.
h. Escadrille Spa 156, Brig Bourgoin, KIA.
i. Escadrille Spa 82 lost Cpl L Rolland, Cpl H Flourieux, and Brig E Pirolley, all MIA.
j. Escadrille Sal 106, Adj Lieudonne & Lt Hamon, MIAs.
k. D3769, 19 Sqn RAF, 2/Lt ES Farrand, POW.
l. French 51 Compagnie Aérostières.
m. Escadrille Spa 159, Cpl F Desouches, KIA, Spad VII.
n. F1159, 206 Sqn RAF, Sgt R Walker, WIA/POW & Cpl AF Bailey, KIA, only loss.

Losses:

Ltn Paul Hasselmann	28	Killed in action over Douai.
Obltn Erich Friess	34	Shot down in flames but landed unharmed.
Ltn Fritz Höhn	41	Killed in action at St Martin l'Heureux, shot down by S/Lt M de Cordou, Spa 94 (probable).
Uffz Hans Marwede	67	Taken prisoner 1430 hours NE Montfaucon, shot down by defensive fire from the 6th USBC.
Ltn Hermann Meyer	MFJ4	Killed in action Flanders.

4 October 1918

Ltn W Frickart	65	Spad 2	Montfaucon	0700	10	a.
Ltn F Piechulek	56	Hanriot	Beveren	0730	14	b.
Ltn H Becker	12	Spad	W Villers-levant-Dun	0915	20	c.
Vfw K Schmückle	15	Spad	Maastal	0915	6	d.
Ltn J Veltjens	15	Spad	NE Brieulles	0955	34	e.
Ltn H v Freden	50	Spad	St Morell	0955	15	
Ltn J Jacobs	7	Spad	Roulers	1031	39	
Ltn R v Barnekow	1	Camel	Cambrai	1130	10	f.
Rittm K-B v Döring	1	Camel	Anvillers	1130	11	f.
Uffz G Borm	1	Camel	Cambrai	1130	5	f.
OfStv P Aue	10	Spad	Montfaucon	1130	10	
Ltn F Liebig	1	Camel	Cambrai	1150	1	
Ltn P Bäumer	B	BF2b	Cambrai	1430	40	
OfStv Tiedje	65	Spad	Oussel	1710	3	
Ltn H Körner	19	Salmson	Vilosnes	1745	5	
Ltn G Bassenge	B	SE5	Joncourt		6	g.
Ltn P Bäumer	B	SE5	Montbréhain		41	
Ltn K Bohny	17	Spad	St Morel		6	
Ltn Kaiser	17	Spad	St Morel		1	
Ltn A Fleischer	17	Spad	St Morel		4	
Vfw A Hübner	36	SE5	Le Châtelet		5	
Ltn C Degelow	40	Camel	Vif St Bauf	am	23	h.
Ltn W Rosenstein	40	Camel	Vif St Bauf	am	7	h.
Uffz Stehling	69	Caudron	S Montreaux		2	i.
Ltn F Kirchfeld	73	Balloon	Chambrecy, W Reims		–	j.

a.   Escadrille Spa 265, Sgt Wolff & Lt Jourdain, MIAs, Spad XI.
b.   11e Escadrille Belgium, Sgt Max Martin, KIA, Nieuport XVII.
c.   Spad XIII 7624, 13th Aero, 1Lt HG Armstrong, KIA
d.   Spad XIII 7625 '17', 28th Aero, 1Lt JF Merrill, KIA.
e.   Spad XIII 15132, 49th Aero, 1Lt CA Kinney, KIA.
f.   80 Sqn RAF lost two Camels: F1990, Lt JW Andrews, and F5954, 2/Lt TW Whitman, American, both KIA.
g.   F5520, 85 Sqn RAF, Lt CW Davison, KIA.
h.   213 Sqn RAF lost two Camels: D3341, Lt WG Upton, and D9601, 2/Lt KG Ibison, both KIA.
i.   Escadrille R 242, S/Lt Gérard, OK, Sgt Fortin, WIA & Cpl Ravaux, WIA, shot down near Fossemange in the Muhlhouse area, only Caudron loss.
j.   British Balloon 9-6-2.

Losses:

Ltn Kurt Schibilsky	10	Taken prisoner.
Ltn Oliver von Beaulieu-Marconnay	19	Lightly wounded in action, remained with unit.
Ltn Hermann Silberschmidt	22	Killed in action at Flavigny le Grand.
Uffz Paul Podbiol	40	Killed in action Menin, Wervik.
Ltn Schulze	51	Wounded in action.
Ltn Ernst Baumgärtel	56	Killed in action Gheluvelt.
Ltn Hermann Tölke	79	Wounded in action 1045 hours Lehaucourt

5 October 1918

Ltn A Burkard	29	DH9	Marke	0830	3	a.
Uffz S Westphal	29	DH9	Aelbeeke	0830	3	a.
Obltn H Auffarth	29	DH9	Aelbeeke	0830	21	b.
Offz K Gregor	29	DH9	Aelbeeke	0830	4	
Ltn G Wember	61	Balloon		1100	3	c.
Ltn H Habich	49	Spad	Somme-Py	1106	6	d.

Sgt M Kuhn	21	Balloon	Braisne	1217	12	e.
Vfw H Donhauser	17	Spad		1310	11	
Ltn P Lotz	44	SE5	N Levergies	1555	9	f.
Uffz Lohrmann	42	SE5	Magny la Fosse	1600	3	
Ltn P Lotz	44	SE5	Ramicourt	1600	-	f.
Ltn R Schneider	79	BF2b	Honnecourt	1600	5	
Ltn H Schäfer	15	Spad	Nantillois	1605	10	g.
Vfw T Weischer	15	Spad	Montfaucon	1605	4	h.
Ltn K Bohny	17	AR2		1710	7	
Ltn J Buckler	17	AR2		1715	34	
Sgt Vetter	21	Spad	S Orainville	1810	1	
Ltn G Bassenge	B	Camel	Crevecouer		7	
Ltn G Weiner	3	DH9	Heimbach		9	i.
Ltn F Bacher	3	DH9	Leitzweiler		3	i.
Uffz R Kühne	3	DH9	Enkenbach		1	i.
Ltn E Thuy	28				33	
Vfw K Gregor	29	DH9			4	a.
Ltn C Degelow	40	DH9	Gent		24	j.
OfStv G Dörr	45	AR2	Brimont		31	
Vfw A Nagler	81	Spad	Sechault		10	k.
Sgt Hoffmann	Kest3	DH9a	Trippstadt		2	i.

a.　206 Sqn RAF one DH9 and one FTL: B7678, 2/Lt HL Prime, POW/DOW & 2/Lt C Hancock, POW, and C2193, Sgt G Packman,Inj & 2/Lt JW Kennedy, OK, FTL as well as 'b'.
b.　D560, 206 Sqn RAF, Lt CJ Knight & 2/Lt JH Perring,POWs. (See also 'a'.).
c.　51 Compagnie Aérostières.
d.　Two Spads lost: Escadrille Spa 26, S/Lt R Garros, KIA Spad XIII, and Spa 168, Sgt L Costes, MIA, Spad XIII.
e.　54 Compagnie Aérostières.
f.　56 Sqn RAF lost two SE5s: E5708, Lt JA Pouchot, DCM, and H7253, Lt FE Bond, POWs.
g.　Spad XIII 8519 '16', 22nd Aero, 1Lt JA Sperry, POW.
h.　Spad XIII 7618 '14', 22nd Aero, 1Lt HB Hudson, KIA.
i.　110 Sqn IAF lost three DH9as: E8439, 2/Lt DP Davies & 2/Lt HMD Speagell,
　　POWs; F980, 2/Lt A Brandrick, POW & 2/Lt HC Eyre, KIA, and F1010, Capt AG Inglis & 2/Lt WGL Bodley, POWs.
j.　E8872, 211 Sqn RAF, 2/Lt VGH Phillips & 2/Lt AF Taylor,both WIA.
k.　Escadrille Sal 264, Sgt Capelet, WIA & S/Lt Lagarde, OK, FTL near Brimont.
Losses:
Ltn Arno Benzler　60　Lightly wounded in action, remained with unit.

6 October 1918

Ltn Thiel	49	Breguet	Orfeuil	0830	1	a.
Ltn H Habich	49	Breguet	Somme-Py	0830	7	a.
Vfw W Seitz	68	2 Seater	Davennes	0925	12	
Ltn F Noltenius	6	Balloon	Puvenell Wood	1115	14	b.
Obltn O Schmidt	5	RE8	E Esnes	1225	18	
Ltn W Leusch	19	Balloon	Cuisy	1810	3	c.
Ltn G Wember	61	Spad			4	
Uffz Langjahr	61	Spad			1	
Flgmt K Kutschke	MFJ5	DH9	Blankenberghe		4	d.

a.　Two Breguets lost: Escadrille Br 208, Sgt Dupuy,KIA & Lt Guinet,WIA and Br 267, S/Lt Vicario & S/Lt Cardey,KIAs, N Pont-Faverger.
b.　10th Co USBS, 1Lt ER Likens, OK.
c.　11th Co USBS, 1Lt JA McDevitt,OK & 2Lt GD Armstrong,OK.
d.　E8934, 108 Sqn RAF, 2/Lt W Freer,KIA & 2/Lt JW Neil,KIA ?
Losses:
OfStv Hans Knaak　9　Killed in action, 1000 hours Soissons.

7 October 1918

Uffz C Elfers	69	Balloon	Miécourt, Switzerland	0941	–	a.
Ltn Spille	58	Camel	Saucourt	1035	3	
Ltn C Degelow	40	Camel	Gent	1130	25	b.
Ltn R v Barnekow	1	BF2b	Avesnes-le-Sec	1210	11	c.
Vfw H Donhauser	17	Breguet	Montheis	1225	12	
Vfw P Groll	40	Camel	Gent	1715	4	b.
Ltn H Gilly	40	Camel	Gent	1715	6	b.
Ltn W Rosenstein	40	Camel	Gent	1715	8	b.
Ltn J Jacobs	7	Camel			40	
Ltn H Stutz	71	Spad	Hindlingen		6	
Vzflgmstr K Scharon	MFJ2	Camel	S Blankenberg		2	
Vzflgmstr K Scharon	MFJ2	DH9	Roulers		3	d.

a.　Swiss Balloon D.8, 2nd Sec, Lt W Flury, KIA. Elfers was court martialled for this act. (See *Over The Front Vol. 9, No. 1*, page 81.)
b.　65 Sqn RAF and 70 Sqn RAF lost three Camels: E1537, 2/Lt B Lockey, interned ; H7001, 2/Lt LSR Jones, KIA (65 Sqn) and E7176, 2/Lt HD Lackey, KIA (70 Sqn).
c.　E2591, 11 Sqn RAF, Sgt AL Cridlan & Sgt GE Fuller, KIAs.
d.　Possibly 211 Sqn RAF, no loss.

Losses:

Flg Schade	5	Severely injured on a practice flight.
Ltn Herbert Boy	14	Taken prisoner, downed by 29 Sqn RAF, baled out, injured on landing.
Vfw Paul Groll	40	Killed in action Gent with Camels.

8 October 1918　　　The Second Battle of Le Cateau

Obltn O Schmidt	5	RE8	N Honcourt	0750	16	a.
Vfw M Schnell	58	SE5	Cambrai	0840	1	
Vfw K Ungewitter	24	SE5	Bohain	0945	6	
Obltn A Gutknecht	43	SE5	S Cambrai	1500	zlg	b.
Ltn H-G v d Marwitz	30	SE5	Gouzeaucourt	1515	13	c.
Ltn W Junck	8	Spad	Bricquenay	1630	3	
Ltn W Blume	9	Dolphin	N Remaucourt	1640	28	d.
OfStv F Altemeier	24	BF2b	Brancourt	1730	19	e.
Ltn W Preuss	66	Fr 2 Str	Pinon	1800	19	f.
Uffz K Fevers	B	Camel	Cambrai, Cagnoncles		4	
Ltn P Bäumer	B	Camel	Bautigny		42	
Ltn J Jacobs	7	Balloon	Kemmelberg		41	
Uffz A Eigenbrodt	7	Dolphin			3	
Ltn F v Röth	16	BF2b	Gheluvelt		24	g.
Ltn Willisch	27				1	
Uffz S Westphal	29	Spad XVI			4	
Ltn C Degelow	40	Camel	Ypres	am	26	h.
Ltn K Plauth	51	Camel	Roulers	am	13	i.
Ltn C Berr	51	Camel	Roulers	am	1	
Ltn Kohlpoth	56	Camel	Ingelmünster		2	

a.　E229, 59 Sqn RAF, 2/Lt JCG Drummond & 2/Lt P Chavasse, KIAs.
b.　D3992, 40 Sqn RAF, Lt WV Trubshawe, WIA.
c.　C1133, 29 Sqn RAF, Lt JP Murphy, POW.
d.　E4378, 209 Sqn RAF Camel, 2/Lt F Cornwell, POW.
e.　E2420, 20 Sqn RAF, Lt FW Ely & 2/Lt JG McBride, KIAs.
f.　Possibly Escadrille Sal 24, MdL Couturier & Adj Guinard, MIAs.
g.　C2894, 7 Sqn RAF RE8, 2/Lt J Graham & Lt MA O'Callaghan, both WIA.
h.　D3382, 210 Sqn RAF, 2/Lt RW Hopper, POW.
i.　N6376, 213 Sqn RAF, 2/Lt EB Holden, FTL, OK.

Losses:

Uffz August Eigenbrodt	7	Lightly wounded in action.
Flg Kurt Oertel	20	Killed in action Roulers.
Ltn Carl Berr	51	Lightly wounded in action, parachuted, but severely injured on landing.

9 October 1918

Uffz F Ulm	34	Camel	N Maretz	0800	1	
Ltn R Otto	68	Spad	Billy	0910	5	
Ltn O Löffler	B	DH9	Thulin, Sebourg	1440	14	a.
Ltn H Vallendor	B	DH9	Sebourg	1440	5	a.
Sgt Fröhlich	46	DH9	Sebourg	1440	–	
Ltn H Steinbrecher	46	DH9	Sebourg, Roisin	1440	–	
Ltn G v Hantelmann	15	Spad	E Montfaucon	1615	21	
Ltn H Schäfer	15	Spad	Montfaucon	1615	11	
Uffz Dannemann	56	Breguet	Ardoye	1615	2	b.
Vfw Krebs	56	Breguet	Ardoye	1617	3	b.
Ltn Gröpler	8	a/c		1700	1	
Ltn O v B-Marconnay	19	Spad	Crépion	1730	24	
Vfw W Seitz	68	2 Seater	Etain	1730	13	
Ltn M Näther	62	Balloon	Montfaucon	1740	18	c.
Ltn M Näther	62	Spad	Montfaucon	1745	19	d.
Ltn P Bäumer	B	BF2b	Preseau		43	e.
Ltn J Jacobs	7	Balloon	SW Dixmuiden		42	
Ltn J Jacobs	7	Balloon	SW Dixmuiden		43	
Ltn J Jacobs	7	Camel			–	
Ltn W Niethammer	13	Salmson			5	
Obltn H Auffarth	29	BF2b			22	
Obltn H Auffarth	29	Camel			23	f.
OfStv G Dörr	45	Breguet	Coucy le Château		32	b.
Ltn K Plauth	51	Salmson	Iseghem		14	
Gefr Tracinski	57	BF2b	Beuvry		2	
Flgmt G Hubrich	MFJ4	Dolphin	Zarren		7	

a.   107 Sqn RAF lost two DH9s: D1107, 2/Lt DE Webb & 2/Lt JH Thompson, KIAs, and F5846, 2/Lt C Houlgrave, POW & 2/Lt WM Thompson, KIA.
b.   Three Breguets lost: Escadrille Br 29, Cpl Daladier & Sol Corbisier,; Br 238, Sgt Le Mercier & Cpl Charles and Br 238, Cpl Ballou & Cpl Feignier, all MIA.
c.   151, 7th Co USBS, 1Lt DM Reeves, OK & Sgt HO Nicholls, OK.
d.   213th Aero, 1Lt R Phelan, OK.
e.   E2256, 62 Sqn RAF, Capt L Campbell, KIA & 2/Lt W Hodgkinson, KIA.
f.   Belgian Escadrille 10e, Spad VII, Lt J Goethals KIA.

Losses:

Obltn Waldemar von Dazur	20	Lightly wounded in action, remained with unit.
Ltn Hans Braun	34	Collided with Uffz Franz Ulm at 1100 hours, and killed in the crash at Croix Fonsomme.
Ltn Gerhard Hoffmann	68	Killed in action Preutin.
Uffz Paul Dyrbusch	68	Killed in action Preutin.

10 October 1918

Ltn H v Freden	50	Spad	Liry	1000	16	a.
Vfw A Niemz	11	Spad	near Aure River	1200	3	
Ltn M Näther	62	Breguet	Haumont	1203	20	
Ltn M Näther	62	Spad	near Haumont	1223	21	
Ltn Hagen	62	DH4	Haumont	1324	2	
Flg O Müller	62	DH4	Haumont	1324	1	

Ltn K Monnington	18	DH4	Onville	1400	7	b.
Ltn F Noltenius	6	Spad	Fontaine	1500	15	
Ltn G Meyer	37	Balloon	Bevillers, N Cambrai	1645	21	c.
Ltn F Blume	37	Balloon	N Cambrai	1645	2	d.
Ltn A Heldmann	10	Spad	Dannevoux	1650	12	
Ltn J Grassmann	10	Spad	Fontaine	1650	7	
Ltn W Kohlbach	10	Spad	Lihou-Fontaine	1650	5	e.
Ltn O v B-Marconnay	19	Spad	Landres	1700	25	
Ltn Mappes	37	Engl a/c	NE Denain	1700	1	
Ltn H Becker	12	Spad	Beauvessaire	1730	21	f.
Vfw O Klaiber	12	DH4	La Croix	1730	3	g.
Vfw O Klaiber	12	DH4	La Croix	1730	4	h.
Obltn F v Röth	16	Balloon	Ypres-Stade	1730	25	i.
Obltn F v Röth	16	Balloon	Ypres-Stade	1730	26	j.
Obltn F v Röth	16	Balloon	Ypres-Stade	1730	27	k.
Ltn J Schäfer	16	RE8	W Ypres	1730	3	
Uffz H Haase	21	Balloon	E Soissons	1740	6	l.
Ltn Leibfried	64	DH4	Wald by Fey-en-Hay		2	
Vfw Trautmann	64	DH4	Montauville		1	m.
Ltn P Schwirzke	68	Balloon	Maasknie		2	n.
Ltn H Mahn	72	Spad			6	
Obltn T Cammann	74	Spad			10	

a. Spad VII 11281, Escadrille Spa 57, Cpl Le Bescou, KIA.
b. American machine.
c. British Balloon 8-1-1.
d. British Balloon 20-1-1.
e. Spad XIII 7588, 147th Aero, 2Lt WW White,Jr, DSC, KIA.
f. Spad XIII 4640 '7', 49th Aero, 1Lt GO West, KIA.
g. 32904, 20th Aero, 1Lt WC Potter & 1Lt HW Wilmer, KIAs.
h. 8th Aero, 1Lt CS Garrett & 1Lt RJ Cochran, KIAs.
i. British Balloon 38-7-2.
j. French 25 Compagnie Aérostières, Adj R André, OK.
k. French 91 Compagnie Aérostières, S/Lt E Patry, OK.
l. French 75 Compagnie Aérostières.
m. 31062, 20th Aero, 1Lt HE Turner & 1Lt JH Weimer, KIAs.
n. French 81 Compagnie Aérostières, S/Lt G Delmas, OK.

Losses:
Ltn Johann Schäfer	16	Killed in action Flanders by Spa 161 pilot.
Uffz Heinrich Haase	21	Wounded in action in a balloon attack.
Vfw Tschierschke	24	Lightly wounded in action.
Vfw Heinrich Pfaffenritter	60	Killed in a collision at St Juvin.
Sgt Karl Bohnenberger	60	Killed in a collision at St Juvin.
Vfw Heinrich Forstmann	K1a	Killed in action Meunzein.

11 October 1918

No Claims

Losses:
Ltn Josef Keller	43	Injured in crash during a test flight.
Ltn Otto Hofmeister	79	Killed in a crash at La Flamengrie Pfalz DXII 2581/18.

12 October 1918

Ltn. H v Freden	50	Balloon	Orfeuil	17	a.

a. French 28 Compagnie Aérostières, S/Lt Millet, OK.
Losses – Nil

13 October 1918

Vfw H Donhauser	17	Breguet		1805	13	

Losses:

Ltn Fritz G Anders	73	Wounded in action.				

14 October 1918

Ltn F Blume	37	Sopwith	N Bevillers, Neuville	0930	3	
Ltn G Meyer	37	Balloon	Bevillers	1510	22	a.
Ltn X Dannhuber	79	Dolphin	Bohain	1710	11	
Ltn J Jacobs	7	Balloon	Dixmuiden		44	
Oblt F v Röth	16	DH9	Ledeghem		28	
Ltn W Neuenhofen	27	?			11	
Sgt W Kahle	27	SE5			2	
Ltn Stoltenhoff	27	a/c			3	
Ltn E Thuy	28	a/c			34	
Ltn E Thuy	28	a/c			35	
Ltn K Christ	28	?			4	
Ltn K Christ	28	?			5	
Uffz S Westphal	29	SE5			5	
Uffz S Westphal	29	SE5			6	
Ltn A Burkard	29	RE8			4	
Ltn A Burkard	29	SE5			5	
Obltn H Auffarth	29	Breguet	NW Roulers		24	
Obltn H Auffarth	29	SE5			25	
Obltn H Auffarth	29	RE8			26	b.
Obltn A Gutknecht	43	SE5	Ypres	pm	6	c.
Ltn G Schobinger	43	SE5	Ypres	pm	1	c.
Vfw K Buberg	43	SE5	Ypres	pm	1	c.
Ltn K Plauth	51	Camel	Eeghem		15	d.
Ltn M Johns	63	SE5	Ypres		7	
Ltn W Preuss	66	Caudron	S Soissons		20	
Vfw O Bieleit	66	Spad	Coucy-les-Eppes		4	e.
Uffz Goerner	66	Breguet	S Laon		1	
Vzflgmstr A Zenses	MFJ2	Dolphin	Roulers		12	
Vzflgmstr A Zenses	MFJ2	Camel	Roulers		13	
Vzflgmstr A Zenses	MFJ2	Balloon	Staden		14	
Vzflgmstr K Scharon	MFJ2	Camel	Roulers, Courtemark		4	
Ltn zS R Poss	MFJ4	Camel	Zarren		9	f.
Flgmstr A Bühl	MFJ4	Dolphin	Roulers		5	g.
OfStv Hoffknecht	MFJ4	Dolphin	Iseghem		1	g.
Flgmt G Hubrich	MFJ4	Dolphin	SW Roulers		8	g,
Ltn zS R Poss	MFJ4	Balloon	Houthulsterwald		10	
Ltn zS R Poss	MFJ4	Camel	Houthulsterwald		11	f.
Flgmt G Hubrich	MFJ4	Camel	Iseghem		9	f.

a.   British Balloon 43-16-3.

b.   E33, 7 Sqn RAF, Capt SW Cowper-Coles, KIA & 2/Lt RW Davidson, KIA.

c.   2 Sqn AFC lost two SE5s: D6968, Lt JAH McKeown, KIA, and E5989, Capt EW Cornish, POW.

d.   F3116, 210 Sqn RAF, 2/Lt CC Fountain, KIA.

e.   Escadrille Spa 82, Sgt G Vercouter, MIA.

f.   213 Sqn RAF lost six aircraft during the day: D3378, 2/Lt WT Owen; D3409, Capt JE Greene, DFC; D8177, 2/Lt FRL Allen; D9673, 1Lt K MacLeish, USNRF; F3120, 2/Lt JCJ McDonald, and F5987, 2/Lt EB McMurty, all KIA.

g.   87 Sqn RAF lost one Dolphin and one forced to land: E4636, Lt RJ Farquharson, POW, and E4493, Lt CA Bryant, OK, FTL.

Losses:

Obltn Fritz Ritter von Röth	16	Wounded in action, shot in the foot.
Ltn Willisch	27	Wounded in action.
Ltn Emil Meyer	31	Wounded in action.
Ltn Georg Meyer	37	Lightly wounded in action, remained with unit.
Uffz Tracinski	57	Injured in a crash.
Flg Max Thomas	73	Killed in action Liart.
Uffz Johann Spannkupt	79 ·	Wounded in action Moulain Ferme, N Wassigny.
Ltn zS Max Stinsky	MFJ4	Killed in action Snelleghem.

15 October 1918

Vfw K Arnold	72	Breguet	Avancon	0950	6
Ltn J Jacobs	7	DH9	N Wervicq		47
Vzflgmstr A Zenses	MFJ2	Dolphin	Roulers		15
Vzflgmstr K Scharon	MFJ2	Dolphin	Roulers		5
Ltn zS G Sachsenberg	MFJ1	Camel	Hooglede		– a.

a.   11e Belgian Escadrille, Capt Hiernaux FTL, OK.

Losses:

Ltn Günther Dobberke	60	Injured in a crash collecting a new Fokker DVII at Armee Flug Park Nr3.
Ltn zS Reinhold Poss	MFJ4	Taken prisoner.
FlgObMt Schönbaum	MFJ5	Wounded in action.
Flgmt Baum	MFJ5	Interned in Holland.

16 October 1918

Ltn A Burkard	29	SE5		6
Vfw E Schäpe	33			–
Ltn K Plauth	51	Camel		–

Losses:

Vfw Albert Haussmann	13	Killed near Romagne; shot down and baled out but his neck was broken.

17 October 1918

Obltn T Cammann	74	?		11
Ltn Richter	74	?		1

Losses – Nil

18 October 1918

Ltn M Näther	62	Spad	Gercourt	1425	22	
Vfw H Donhauser	17	Spad		1530	14	
Vfw H Donhauser	17	Spad		1540	14	
Ltn G v Hantelmann	15	DH4	S Grandpré	1625	22	a.
Ltn J Veltjens	15	DH4	Argonne, S Grandpré	1630	35	a.
Ltn O Könnecke	5	SE5	1 km SE Le Cateau	1745	32	
Ltn H Henkel	37	RE8	W Solesmes	1745	6	b.
Ltn H Jeschonneck	40	Spad	Roulers near Gent		2	c.
Ltn H Gilly	40	Spad	Roulers near Gent		7	c.
Ltn H Gilly	40	Spad	near Gent		8	c.
Obltn A Gutknecht	43	BE2b	Tournai		–	
Ltn J Raesch	43	BF2b	Tournai		–	
Vfw W Seitz	68	1 Seater	Romagne		14	
Ltn Dangers	74	DH4	Esnes		1	

a.   Possibly Salmsons of 12th Aero who had two observers WIA, 1Lt AL Hopkins and 2Lt HS Bean.
b.   D4909, 59 Sqn RAF, Lt TH Upfill & 2/Lt JC Walker, KIAs.

c.   Escadrille Spa 82 lost Lt H Changine & Cpl P Trepp, MIAs.

Losses:

Ltn Gustav Boehren	10	Wounded in action and taken prisoner Sommerance.
Ltn Oliver Frhr von B-Marconnay	19	Severely wounded in action Gouzeaucourt, died of wounds on October 26, 1918 at Avion.
Ltn Stein	56	Wounded in action.
Sgt Albert Karsten	48	Killed in action Valenciennes.
Ltn Erich Klink	68	Killed in action Bantheville.

19 October 1918

Ltn J Jacobs	7	Camel	Wyndendaele	1130	46
Ltn J Jacobs	7	Spad			47

Losses:

Ltn Reinhold Maier	30	Killed in action Ellignies.
Vfw Ludwig Zacher	79	Killed in action Chimay.

20 October 1918

No Claims – No Losses

21 October 1918

Ltn K Seit	80	Balloon	Grand Mont	1530	4	
Ltn G v Hantelmann	15	Spad	Remonville	1615	23	a.
Ltn F Büchner	13	a/c	Argonne		39	
Ltn W Preuss	66	Spad	Missy		21	b.
Uffz Goerner	66	Breguet	Itancourt		2	
Obltn W Karjus	75	DH4	Ensslingen		1	c.

a.   Escadrille Spa 159, MdL Granger, KIA.
b.   Spad XIII 14560, Escadrille Spa 154, Sgt L Kremer, MIA.
c.   110 Sqn IAF lost seven DH9as on a raid to Frankfurt: E8484, 2/Lt AWR Evans & Lt RWL Thomson F984, Lt SL Mucklow & 2/Lt R Riffkin; F985, Major LGS Reynolds & 2/Lt MW Dunn, all POW; F986, 2/Lt JORS Saunders & 2/Lt WY Brain, KIAs; F1005, Capt WE Windover & 2/Lt JA Simpson, POWs; F1021, 2/Lt P King, POW & 2/Lt RG Vernon, POW/DOW and F1029, Lt J McLaren-Pearson & Sgt TW Harman, POWs.
Losses – Nil

22 October 1918

Ltn G v Hantelmann	15	Spad	Brieulles	1700	24	a.
Vfw Mühlhausen	3	DH9	Dudweiler		1	
Unknown pilot	7	Dolphin			–	
Ltn F Büchner	13	2 Seater			40	
Ltn W Neithammer	13	2 Seater			6	
Ltn K Plauth	51	Breguet	N Deinze		16	b.
Ltn zS P Achilles	MFJ5	DH9	N Bellem		7	c.

a.   Spad XIII 7708, 94th Aero, 1Lt RJ Saunders, KIA.
b.   Escadrille Br 234, MdL Raynaud & S/Lt Stofft, MIAs.
c.   D1110, 108 Sqn RAF, Lt CF Cave & 2/Lt H McNish, KIAs.
Losses:

Ltn Willi Nebgen	7	Killed in action Lemberge, Gontrode.

23 October 1918

Ltn H Boes	34	RE8		0900	3	
Ltn U Neckel	6	AR2		1255	27	
Ltn F Noltenius	11	Balloon	Château-Cheherry	1255	16	a.
Vfw H Donhauser	17	Spad	Vrizy	1255	16	b.
Vfw Trautmann	64	DH9	Metz-Sallon, N Ars	1305	2	

Ltn Prahlow	Kest3	DH9	Frescaty	1305	–	
Ltn K Monnington	18	DH9	Fourasse Wood	1315	8	c.
Ltn M Näther	62	Balloon	Cierges	1340	23	d.
Ltn F Noltenius	11	Spad	Aure River	1605	17	e.
Ltn F Noltenius	11	Balloon	Baulny	1700	18	f.
Ltn J Hentschel	7	DH9	W Guise	1710	1	
Obltn R v Greim	34	SE5	SW Neuville	1800	26	
Obltn R v Greim	34	SE5	Boursies	1800	27	
Uffz Leicht	5	BF2b			4	
Ltn A Auer	40	BF2b	near Dutch Border		1	
Ltn K Plauth	51	DH9	Vosselaere		17	g.
Ltn J Jensen	57	BF2b			–	
Ltn Leibfried	64	Breguet	Pagny/Pont-à-Mousson		3	
Ltn zS G Sachsenberg	MFJ1	DH9	Bellen-Ursel		26	g.
Ltn zS G Sachsenberg	MFJ1	Camel	Bellen-Ursel		27	h.
Ltn zS G Sachsenberg	MFJ1	Camel			28	h.
Vzflgmstr A Zenses	MFJ2	Camel	Merendrée		16	h.
Vzflgmstr A Zenses	MFJ2	Camel	Ostwinkel		17	h.
Vzflgmstr A Zenses	MFJ2	Camel	Rousele		18	h.
Ltn zS Merz	MFJ2	Camel			1	h.
Vzflgmstr K Scharon	MFJ2	Camel	Rousele		7	h.

a.   555, 5th Balloon Co USBS, 1Lt CL Furber, OK & 2Lt JW Lane,OK.
b.   Escadrille Spa 164, S/Lt M Robert, FTL, OK.
c.   D2932, 104 Sqn IAF, 2/Lt BS Case, WIA, POW, DOW & 2/Lt H Bridger, WIA, POW.
d.   312, 7th Balloon Co USBS, 1Lt DM Reeves, OK & 2Lt GE Quisenberry, OK.
e.   Escadrille Spa 159, Sgt EB Fairchild, WIA.
f.   2nd Balloon Co USBS, 1Lt RM Batten,OK & Major Wallace, OK.
g.   108 Sqn RAF only lost C6314, Capt GC Hayes, KIA & 2/Lt G Brown, KIA.
h.   204 Sqn RAF lost five Camels: D8223, Sgt CMA Mahon, and D9608, Capt T W Nash, DFC, D9613, Lt
OJ Orr; E4420, Lt FG Bayley and F3101, 2/Lt G Sutcliffe, US, all KIA.

Losses:

Vfw Gustav Klaudat	15	Severely wounded in action Bois de Money.
Ltn Paul Lotz	44	Killed in a crash at Donstiennes, wing failed at 1000 meters during a practice flight.
Vfw Emil Hanzog	57	Killed in action Bantigny.
Vfw Alfred Nauwerk	57	Killed in action Bantigny.
Ltn Hermann Bargmann	MFJ2	Killed in action.

24 October 1918

Vfw Schneck	9	Breguet	Asfeld-la-Ville	1210	3	a.
Ltn J Buckler	17	Breguet	Méry		35	
Ltn Hübner	73	Salmson	Asfeld		1	

a.   Escadrille Br 44, Lt Bérard & Lt Seyller, KIAs.

Losses:

Ltn Emil Koch	32	Severely wounded in action.
Ltn Karl Jerratsch	Kest7	Killed in action Düsseldorf.

25 October 1918

Vfw K Treiber	5	SE5	N Mourmelon	1055	7	a.
Obltn R v Greim	34	SE5	Fellaries	1200	28	a.

a.   E1276, 60 Sqn RAF, Lt LH Smith, POW – only loss.

Losses:

Uffz Gustav Praclik	5	Wounded in action 1105 Mormal Wood, parachuted from his Fokker DVII safely.
Ltn Otto Brandes	24	Wounded in action 1225 hours.

Ltn Gerhard Wohlgemuth	26	Killed in Action, location unknown.

26 October 1918

Ltn F Klausenberg	53	Breguet	Höhe 167 near Attigny	1240	2	
Ltn W Leusch	19	Spad	Dannevoux	1704	4	a.
Sgt W Kahle	27				3	
Vfw E Schäpe	33				11	
Vfw E Schäpe	33				12	
Ltn C Degelow	40	Spad	Gent		27	b.
Vfw E Wiehle	43	SE5	Velennes		3	
Uffz P Rüggeberg	43	SE5	Velennes		1	
Ltn J Raesch	43	SE5	Velennes		5	c.
Ltn zS G Sachsenberg	MFJ1	Camel	Essenghem		29	
Ltn zS P Becht	MFJ1	Balloon	W Deinze		3	d.
Ltn zS G Brockhoff	MFJ3	Balloon	Deinze		4	d.
Ltn zS P Achilles	MFJ5	Balloon	N Deinze		8	d.
Flgmt K Engelfried	MFJ5	Balloon	NW Deinze		6	d.

a.   Spad XIII 147th Aero, 2Lt ML Dowd, KIA.
b.   Escadrille Spa 161, MdL A Noulet, MIA.
c.   F900, 29 Sqn RAF, 2/Lt RSG MacLean, US, KIA.
d.   In the Flanders Sector, four French balloons were attacked and two were flamed, those of the 85 and 74 Compagnie Aérostières; the observers, S/Lt Beruardi, S/Lt Ragué, & Asp Martin made safe jumps; the two not flamed were riddled by bullets, the obs, S/Lt Bruyère & Sgt Monteaux, also made safe descents.
Losses:
Uffz Fritz Zogmann   26   Killed in action Saultain.

27 October 1918

Ltn A Scheicher	34	Camel		1000	6	a.
Ltn G Dörr	45	Spad	La Malmaison	1000	–	b.
Ltn J Raesch	43	SE5	Mont St Auber	1030	6	c.
OfStv F Altemeier	24	BF2b	Le Quesnoy	1105	–	
Pilot Unknown	41	BF2b	Le Quesnoy	1105	–	
Vfw K Bohnenkamp	22	Dolphin	Bories	1120	14	d.
Ltn G Dörr	45	Spad	Amifontaine	1540	34	
OfStv L Prime	78	Spad	Herbéviller	1700	zlg	
Vfw K Schlegel	45	Fr Art a/c	La Malmaison		–	
Ltn J Jacobs	7	BF2b			48	
Ltn W Neuenhofen	27	?			12	
Ltn H-G v d Marwitz	30	a/c			14	
Ltn C Degelow	40	Camel	Wynghene		28	e.
Ltn W Rosenstein	40	Camel	Wynghene		9	e.
Vfw K Schlegel	45	Fr Art a/c	La Malmaison		–	
Ltn O Scherf	59	Dolphin	Douai		1	f.
Vfw F Senf	59	Dolphin			2	
Ltn O Scherf	59	Dolphin			–	
Uffz O Bieleit	66	Spad	Nizy-le-Comte		5	
Gefr Schubert	69	Spad	Velescot		1	
Uffz C Elfers	69	Balloon	St Cosman		1	g.
Ltn H v Hippel	71	Spad	Hartsmannweiler Kopf		2	
Ltn W Schwartz	73	Spad	Aisnetel		7	h.
Vfw Harbers	73	Spad	Aisnetel		1	
Vfw Harling	73	Spad	Aisnetel		1	i.
OfStv W Schluckebier	73	Breguet	Aisnetel		3	
Vfw Hermann	73	Breguet	Aisnetel		1	

Ltn F Kirchfeld	73	Spad	Aisnetel		6	
Vzflgmstr A Zenses	MFJ2	Camel	S Deinze		19	e.
Vzflgmstr K Scharon	MFJ2	Camel	Deinze		8	e.

a.   E1587, 70 Sqn RAF, 2/Lt CA Critchton, WIA/POW.
b.   Escadrille Sal 22, Lt Borda, KIA.
c.   H676, 29 Sqn RAF, Capt GW Wareing, DFC, KIA.
d.   D5236, 19 Sqn RAF, 2/Lt WJ Nesbitt, KIA.
e.   204 Sqn RAF lost four Camels: C144, 2/Lt N Smith, POW; E4387, 2/Lt PF Cormack; F3112, 2/Lt AJF Ross, and F3940, 2/Lt HG Murray, all KIA.
f.   B7984, 23 Sqn RAF, 2/Lt AR Pratt, POW.
g.   42 Compagnie Aérostières, Lt Linkenheyl, OK & S/Lt Dessarp, OK.
h.   Escadrille Spa 112, MdL de Freslon, WIA.
i.   Escadrille Spa 112, MdL E. Lengrand, MIA.

Losses:

Ltn Erich Schaarschmidt	9	Taken prisoner.
Ltn Max Kliefoth	19	Taken prisoner 1640 hours Exermont.
Ltn Hinky	44	Wounded in action.
Vfw Karl Paul Schlegel	45	Killed in action La Malmaison 1540 hours.
Vfw August Scheffler	81	Killed in action Fontaines.

28 October 1918

OfStv F Altemeier	24	RE8	W Happengarbes	0920	20	
Uffz Baumert	58	DH9	Mons	1245	1	a.
Ltn E Schulz	72	Spad	Château-Porcien	1510	3	b.
Ltn E Schulz	72	Spad	Château-Porcien	1510	4	c.
Vfw Schlemmel	9	SE5	SE Vervins	1535	2	
Vfw K Bohnenkamp	22	DH9	Wassignies	1620	15	
Vfw F Poeschke	53	Spad	Chuffilly	1640	7	
Vfw H Korsch	53	Spad	Vaubourg	1655	2	
Ltn F Noltenius	11	Balloon	Eglisfontaine	1700	19	d.
Ltn H Frommherz	27	Camel			27	
Ltn H Frommherz	27	BF2b			28	
Ltn Grönig	27				1	
Sgt W Kahle	27				4	
Uffz Jahnke	27				1	
Vfw M Kiep	43	SE5			–	
Vfw E Wiehle	43	SE5			4	
Ltn G Frädrich	72	Spad			6	
Ltn zS G Sachsenberg	MFJ1	DH9	Deinze		30	

a.   D535, 27 Sqn RAF, 2/Lt CM Allan & 2/Lt JP Coleman, POWs.
b.   Escadrille Spa 154, S/Lt M Coiffard, DOW.
c.   Escadrille Spa 154, S/Lt H Condemine, OK.
d.   314, 8th Balloon Co USBS, 2Lt AR Stubbs, OK.

Losses:

Vfw Alfons Schymik	24	Killed in action Happengrabes by Pommereuil 0925 hours, in Fokker DVII 329/18.
OfStv Alfred Jäschke	30	Taken prisoner Cordes near Tournai in a DVII (G/2/28).
Ltn Adolf Auer	40	Wounded in action and taken prisoner Ooteghem near Sterhoek, Fokker DVII 4043/18, combat with 41 Sqn RAF (G/2/27).
Vfw Max Hermann Kiep	43	Killed in action St Auber.
Vfw Max Schnell	58	Killed in action 1230 hours Wasmuel.
Gefr Ludwig Hugel	65	Killed in action 1300 hours Pagny, Pont-à-Mousson.
Uffz Heinrich Scharl	79	Killed in action Floyon.
Vfw Andreas Emele	80	Killed in action Fremerchen.

29 October 1918

Ltn R Wenzl	6	Spad	Sommerance	1100	9	
Vfw R Schneider	19	Breguet	Champigneulle	1250	3	
Ltn W Junck	8	Spad		1500	4	
Ltn H v Freden	50	SE5	Cattillon	1540	18	a.
Oblt T Dahlmann	JGIII	Camel	W Valenciennes	1605	7	
Ltn F Schliewen	6	Spad		1625	2	
Ltn Rieth	6	Spad		1630	1	
Obltn R Hildebrandt	53	Spad	Château-Porcien	1630	6	
Ltn J Grassmann	10	Spad	Cierges	1655	8	
Ltn W Schwartz	73	Balloon	Germaincourt	1720	8	b.
Ltn E Bormann	B	Camel	E Valenciennes		14	
Ltn P Blunck	B	Camel	Marly Presea		2	
Vfw P Rothe	14	Balloon			4	c.
Vfw P Rothe	14	Balloon			5	
Ltn J v Ziegesar	15	Salmson	Champigneulle		3	d.
Ltn H Frommherz	27	RE8			29	e.
Uffz Rosenau	33	?			3	
Vfw E Schäpe	33	?			13	
Ltn G Meyer	37	DH9			23	f.
Vfw E Wiehle	43	SE5			5	
Uffz B Barthels	44	Balloon	Villers-le-Sec		3	
Ltn M Näther	62	Spad	Exermont		24	g.
Ltn M Näther	62	DH9	Sivry		25	h.
Ltn M Näther	62	DH4	Montfaucon		26	h.
Uffz Rozmiarek	62	DH4	W Sivry		1	h.
Uffz R Lochner	64	Salmson	St Benoit		1	
Ltn W Preuss	66	Salmson	Fay-le-Sec Ferme		22	
Ltn Selzer	74	?			1	
Sgt Weidner	74	?			1	
Obltn T Cammann	74	?	Near Vilosnes		12	
Ltn Dangers	74	?	Near Vilosnes		2	
Ltn zS G Sachsenberg	MFJ1	a/c			31	

a. F5476, 1 Sqn RAF, Lt W Newby, KIA.
b. French 86 Compagnie Aérostières.
c. British Balloon 13-8-2.
d. 12th Aero No.1180 '15', 1Lt SW Beauclerk, KIA & 1Lt AR Patterson, POW.
e. C2695, 42 Sqn RAF, Capt GW Glasson & Lt WJ Hagen, WIAs.
f. E8978, 104 Sqn IAF, 2/Lt HD Arnott & 2/Lt B Johnson, KIAs.
g. Spad XIII 8884, 94th Aero, 1Lt EG Garnsey, KIA.
h. 135th Aero had a DH4 FTL, 1Lt EC Landon, OK & 1Lt PH Aldrich, DSC, KIA.

Losses:

Ltn Martin Fischer	6	Killed in action Montfaucon.
Uffz Hans Haslbeck	32	Killed in action Erquelinnes.

30 October 1918

Obltn H Auffarth	29	SE5	Dottenigs	1010	27	
Vfw A Hübner	36	BF2b	Tournai	1010	6	a.
Ltn G Dörr	45	AR2	Missy	1100	35	
Ltn U Könnemann	45	AR2	Froidmont	1105	4	
Ltn H Frommherz	27	Dolphin	near Mons	1120	30	b.
Vfw W Seitz	68	Spad	Chémy	1140	15	
Vfw O Klaiber	12	Spad	Champigneulle	1200	5	
Ltn H Becker	12	Spad	NE Landres	1220	22	

Vfw M Hutterer	23	Snipe	Seebourg	1220	7
Ltn W Neuenhofen	27	Dolphin	Mons	1220	13 b.
Sgt W Kahle	27	Dolphin	Mons	1220	5 b.
Vfw Wittchen	12	Spad	Verpel	1230	1
Ltn H Lange	26	DH9	Crespin	1235	8 c.
Vfw F Classen	26	DH9	Slolin	1235	– d.
Gefr Pissowotzky	54	Balloon	Bois de Monsard	1540	1 e.
Vfw O Klaiber	12	Spad		1630	6
Ltn U Neckel	6	Spad		1645	28 f.
Ltn A Heldmann	10	Spad	S Damvillers	1700	13
Obltn G Rasberger	80	Spad	Bulmont	1700	4
Ltn K Bohny	17	Balloon	Avancon	1730	8 h.
Ltn J Grassmann	10	Camel	Briere Ferme	1735	9 i.
Ltn O Löffler	B	DH9	N Quieuvain		15 j.
Ltn A Lindenberger	B	SE5	Harchies		11 k.
Ltn E Bormann	B	SE5	N Neuville		15 k.
Obltn K v Griesheim	B	SE5	Fresnes		1 k.
Ltn P Blunck	B	Dolphin	Fayet		3 j.
Ltn Schlack	B	DH9	Blaton		1 j.
Ltn Bertling	12	Spad			1 g.
Ltn G v Hantelmann	15	Salmson	Buzancy		25 l.
Ltn G v Hantelmann	15	Spad			26
Uffz Jahnke	27	Dolphin			2 b.
Obltn H Auffarth	29	SE5	Wervicq		28
Obltn H Auffarth	29	BF2b			29
Uffz Marchner	32	?			2
Vfw E Schäpe	33	?			16
Vfw E Schäpe	33	?			17
Ltn F Blume	37	a/c			4
Ltn H Henkel	37	a/c			7
Ltn C Degelow	40	SE5	Courtrai		29 k.
Ltn J Raesch	43	a/c			7
Ltn H Steinbrecher	46	a/c			5
Uffz E Mix	54	Balloon	W Pont-à-Mousson		–
Uffz Hösrich	62	Spad	Romagne		1
Ltn Adomeit	62	Spad	Brieulles		1
Obltn Grosse	72	Spad	Château-Porcien		2
Ltn H Mahn	72	Spad	Château-Porcien		7
Ltn F Kirchfeld	73	Spad			7
Ltn Dumler	76	DH9	Carspach		1
Flgmt Wasserthal	MFJ4	DH9	Deinze		1

a.   E2451, 88 Sqn RAF, Lt GF Anderson,DFC & 2/Lt CMW Elliot, WIAs.
b.   19 Sqn RAF lost five Dolphins: E4511, 2/Lt F Lynn,and E4552, 2/Lt CN Boyd; E4637, 2/Lt RB Murray D3768. 2/Lt RW Duff, all POWs, and B7855, Capt JW Crane, KIA.
c.   D7325, 98 Sqn RAF, Lt DW Holmes & Lt JE Prosser, KIAs.
d.   98 Sqn RAF.
e.   250, 69th Balloon Co USBS, 2Lt JA Allen, OK & 2Lt FM Morgan, OK.
f.   Spad XII 7812 '14', 22nd Aero, 1Lt JD Beane, KIA.
g.   Spad XIII 15266 '15', 22nd Aero, 1Lt R de B Vernam, DSC, POW.
h.   French 4 Compagnie Aérostières, Lt R Collas, WIA.
i.   F1430, 185th Aero, 1Lt EH Kelton, Inj, POW.
j.   49 Sqn RAF had one loss: D502, 2/Lt BW Cotterell & Sgt WH Gumbley, KIAs.
k.   32 Sqn RAF suffered three losses: E6010, Capt AA Callender, US, DOW; D3440, 2/Lt W Amory, POW and D6132, Lt RW Farquhar, KIA.
l.   12th Aero, 1Lt HD Muller & 2Lt JM Foy, POWs.

Losses:
Uffz Josef Nebl   23   Killed in action.

31 October 1918

Ltn U Neckel	6	Spad		1250	29	a.
Ltn Bertling	12	Spad	Villers-levant-Dun	1630	2	
Ltn A Greven	12	Spad	Villers-levant-Dun	1630	3	
Ltn K-A v Schönebeck	33	2 Seater			8	
Vfw E Schäpe	33	2 Seater			18	
Ltn H Henkel	37	a/c			8	
Uffz P Rüggeberg	43	SE5			2	
Ltn Sarginhausen	69	Spad	Niedersept		1	b.
Ltn F Kirchfeld	73	Spad	Château-Porcien		8	

a.   27th Aero, 1Lt SW White, KIA.
b.   Escadrille Spa 315, Brig J Catton, KIA.
Losses – Nil

JASTA ARMEE ASSIGNMENTS AS OF 1 NOVEMBER 1918

Western Front

1 Armee 72s,73
2 Armee 5,23b,32b,34b,35b,37,46
3 Armee 17,48,53,61
4 Armee 7,14,16b,20,29,40s,51,56,MFJI,MFJII,MFJIII,MFJIV,MFJV
5 Armee 4,6,8,10,11,12,13,15,19,62,67,68,74,77b
6 Armee 28w,30,33,43,52,63
7 Armee 9,21s,45,66
17 Armee 1,B,26,27,36,57,58,59
18 Armee 22s,24s,31,41,42,44s,47w,49,50,60,76b,81
19 Armee 3,18,54s,80b,K3
Det 'A' 39,70,78b
Det 'B' 69,71,75,76b
Det 'C' 64w,65

Other Fronts

11 Armee 25   Macedonia
11 Armee 38   Macedonia

1 November 1918

Ltn H Mahn	72	Spad	Château-Porcien	1138	8	a.
Obltn K Bolle	B	SE5	W Harchies		32	b.
Ltn A Lindenberger	B	SE5	SE Harchies		12	b.
Ltn H Vallendor	B	SE5	Fresnes		6	b.
Ltn O Könnecke	5	DH4			33	c.
Vfw M Hutterer	23	SE5	SW Valenciennes		8	d.
Vfw O Stadter	32	?			4	
Ltn H Mahn	72	Spad	Château-Porcien		9	e.
Vfw M Meinberg	75	Breguet	Obersulzbach		2	f.
Ltn P Brecht	MFJ1	2 Seater	E Deinze		4	
Flgmt Wasserthal	MFJ2	Camel	SE Deinze		2	
Flgmstr G Hubrich	MFJ4	Camel	N Deinze		10	

a.   Escadrille Spa 152, Adj E Manson, KIA.
b.   32 Sqn RAF lost three SE5s: E4004, 2/Lt SE Burden, KIA; E5811, Lt H Wilson, KIA and E5662, Capt CL Veitch, shot up, damaged, OK.
c.   F1068, 25 Sqn RAF, 2/Lt RG Dobeson & 2/Lt FG Mills, POWs.
d.   C1150, 64 Sqn RAF, 2/Lt GW Graham, MM, KIA.
e.   Escadrille Spa 15, Sgt H Fourcade, MIA.
f.   Salmson 2A2, 258th Aero, 2Lt A Miller, OK & 1Lt JA Logan, OK.

Losses:
Ltn Stier   MFJ5   Shot down in flames, parachuted, landed OK.

2 November 1918

Vfw F Poeschke	53	Spad	Terrore	0845	8
Vfw A Bader	64	Spad	Amanweiler		1	a.

a.   213th Aero, 1Lt RT Aldworth, POW
Losses: nil

3 November 1918

Vfw L Reimann	78	Spad	Marainville	1300	2	
Ltn K Romeis	80	Camel	Gerden	1300	2	
Ltn W Junck	8	Spad	Le Chesne	1400	5	a.
Vfw E Buder	26	RE8	Onnaing	1450	11	
Ltn R Wenzl	6	Spad	Montfaucon	1455	10	b.
Ltn R Wenzl	6	Spad	Montfaucon	1455	11	c.
Ltn F Noltenius	11	DH4	Barricourt	1515	20	d.
Ltn F v Köckeritz	11	Spad		1550	3	
Ltn S Gussmann	11	AR2		1605	5	
Ltn H Becker	12	Spad	E Joncq	1620	23	e.
Ltn H Körner	19	Spad	Stenay	1620	6	e.
Ltn Telge	12	Spad	Beaumont	1621	1	e.
Ltn A Greven	12	Spad	Pouilly	1622	4	e.
Ltn Bertling	12	Spad	Beaumont	1623	3	e.
Vfw Wittchen	12	Spad	Sommauthe	1624	2	e.
Flg Rossbach	12	Spad	Sommauthe	1625	1	e.
Ltn W Leusch	19	Breguet	Beaumont	1625	5	
Ltn A Hildebrandt	4	Spad	Woevrewald	1650	1	
Ltn Geppert	4	Spad	Stenay	1650	1	
Ltn Reinhardt	4	Spad	Andevanne	1650	1	
Vfw Schumann	17	2 Seater			1	
Ltn A Fleischer	17	2 Seater			5	
Ltn A Fleischer	17	2 Seater			6	
Gefr Viktor	71	Balloon	St Cosmann		1	f.

a.   Escadrille Spa 95, Adj E LeGros, MIA.
b.   Escadrille Spa 88, MdL Bilbault, MIA.
c.   Escadrille Spa 88, MdL L Barré, MIA.
d.   32440, 20th Aero, Lt D MacWirter, OK & Lt WS Holt, OK.
e.   Spad XIII 15254 '3', 22nd Aero lost 2Lt EB Gibson, WIA/DOW; 18757 '14', 2Lt G Tiffany, POW, and 16508, 1Lt HR Clapp, KIA.
f.   French 33 Compagnie Aérostières, Lt Van Hache,OK & Adj Chevallier, OK.

Losses:
Ltn Heinrich Maushake   4   Severely wounded in action with the 103rd Aero.

4 November 1918

Ltn H Lange	26	BF2b	Vieux-Rengts	1015	–	
Flgmstr G Hubrich	MFJ4	Camel	S Deinze	1058	11	a.
Flgmstr G Hubrich	MFJ4	Camel	Gent	1103	12	a.

Flg Hoffmann	24	BF2b	Mormal Wood	1140	–
Ltn O Könnecke	5	DH4	Mormal Wood	1145	34
Obltn O Schmidt	5	a/c		1145	20
Vfw K Ungewitter	24	Dolphin	W Berlaincourt	1207	7	b.
Ltn E Bormann	B	Snipe	E Renaix	1320	16	c.
Vfw P Keusen	B	BF2b	Villereau	1430	2
Ltn E Koepsch	4	DH9		1450	9	d.
Vfw E Buder	26	DH9	Blangries	1530	12
Vfw F Ehmann	47	Spad	N Touly	1530	8
Vfw A Niemz	11	DH4		1645	4	d.
Ltn F Noltenius	4	DH9	Carrigan	1650	21	d.
Ltn J Schulte-Frohlinde	11	DH9		1700	4	d.
Obltn K Bolle	B	Snipe	Englefontaine	pm	33	c.
Obltn K Bolle	B	Snipe	Englefontaine	pm	34	c.
Obltn K Bolle	B	Snipe	Tournai		35	c.
Obltn K Bolle	B	Snipe	Escanaffles	pm	36	c.
Ltn O Könnecke	5	?			35
Ltn G v Hantelmann	15	DH4	near Stenay		27	e.
Ltn H Frommherz	27	BF2b			31	f.
Ltn H Frommherz	27	BF2b			32	f.
Ltn W Neuenhofen	27				14
Ltn W Neuenhofen	27				15
Sgt W Kahle	27				6
Ltn Holthusen	29	Camel			3	a.
Vfw B Brunecker	29	Camel			3	a.
Vfw H Kluth	29	Camel			1	a.
Uffz H Plum	29	Camel			2	a.
Vfw H Weibelzahl	29	Camel			2	a.
Ltn O Steger	36	BF2b	Tournai		3
Ltn G Meyer	37	a/c			24
Ltn C Degelow	40	DH9	near Dutch Border	pm	30	g.
Uffz B Barthels	44	Balloon			4
Ltn K-W Ritscherle	60	Spad	E Reims		–	h.
Vfw K Gerster	62	Breguet	Brieulles		2
Ltn P Schwirzke	68	Balloon	Dannevoux		3	i.
Vfw W Seitz	68	Breguet	Dannevoux		16
Flgmstr A Bühl	MFJ4	Dolphin	S Scheldewindeke	am	6

a.   65 and 204 Sqns RAF lost the following Camels: E7193, Lt J Reid, US KIA; F1936, 2/Lt HG Luther, WIA, POW; F6355, 2/Lt FR Pemberton, US, WIA (all 65 Sqn); E4384, Lt JR Chisman, FTL OK, and F6257, 2/Lt JD Lightbody, KIA, (of 204 Sqn).
b.   C8165, 87 Sqn RAF, 2/Lt HJ Curtis, KIA.
c.   4 Sqn AFC lost five Sopwith Snipes: E8038, Lt PW Symons; E8062, Capt TCR Baker, MM; E8064, Lt AJ Palliser, all KIA; E8072, Lt EJ Goodson and E8073, Lt CW Rhodes, both POW.
d.   27 Sqn RAF lost two DH9s plus one FTL: D7355, 2/Lt JG Symonds & Lt WG Lacey, MC, KIAs; D7356, 2/Lt WJ Potts & Sgt CW Metcalfe, POWs and D572, 2/Lt HD Williams, OK & 2/Lt HB Smith, OK, FTL.
e.   11th Aero, 32905, 1Lt DE Coates & 2Lt RA Thrall, KIAs.
f.   62 Sqn RAF lost two BF2bs: D7948, Lt FCD Scott & 2/Lt C Rigby, KIAs and E2513, Lt F Sumsion & Capt WG Walford, KIAs.
g.   C2224, 103 Sqn RAF, Lt JG Carey & 2/Lt DC McDonald, POWs.
h.   Escadrille Spa 170, MdL A Recoques, MIA.
i.   French 61 Compagnie Aérostières.

Losses:

Vfw Paul Keusen	B	Killed in action Monbray.
Uffz Paul Schönfelder	29	Killed in action Oosterzeele, Belgium.
Uffz Otto Hägele	32	Killed in action Le Quesnoy.

5 November 1918

Ltn R Wenzl	6	DH9	Stenay, Malmy	1010	12	a.
Ltn W v Richthofen	11	DH4	S Montmedy	1030	8	b.
Ltn H Bahlmann	4	DH4	Dun-sur-Meuse	1035	1	c.
Ltn A Heldmann	10	Spad	Sivry	1035	14	d.
Obltn E v Wedel	11	Spad		1035	13	d.
Ltn O Fitzner	65	DH4	Beney	1220	8	
Vfw Glasemann	3	DH4	Morsberg	1600	2	
Ltn K Seit	80	Breguet	Kambrich	1600	5	
Ltn O Fitzner	65	Balloon	Monsard	1640	9	e.
Sgt G Albrecht	64	Breguet	Champlon		1	
Ltn F Hengst	64	Breguet	Mesnil		4	

a.   DH4 32910, 20th Aero, 1Lt SP Mandell, KIA & 2Lt RB Fulton, POW.
b.   32941, 20th Aero, 1Lt LB Edwards & 1Lt KC Payne, POWs.
c.   20th Aero, 32940 '2', 1Lt KG West & 1Lt WF Frank, KIAs.
d.   One of these was Escadrille Spa 88, Sgt J André, POW, the other was from the 93rd Aero, 1Lt LL Carruthers, POW.
e.   15th Balloon Co USBS, 1Lt RL Davis, OK & 1Lt RE Butcher, OK.

Losses:

Ltn Richard Kirst	10	Killed in action Loupoy.
Ltn Fritz Leicht	31	Killed in action Beney.
Sgt Gustav Albrecht	64	Killed in collision with above Breguet over Marcheville near Champlon. Also claimed by Sal 277 crew.

6 November 1918

Ltn U Neckel	6	Spad	Fôret de Woevre	1130	30	a.
Ltn J Grassmann	10	Spad	NE Sivry	1130	10	
Ltn A Heldmann	10	Spad	NE Sivry	1130	15	
Vfw H Nülle	39	DH9	Ibingen, St Georg	1500	10	b.
Vfw H Nülle	39	DH9	Bühl	1500	11	b.
Uffz Krüchelsdorf	39	DH9	Bühl	1500	1	b.
Vfw Brüchner	78	DH4	Ibingen, St Georg	1500	–	c.
Vfw R Schneider	19	Spad	Stenay	1625	4	
Ltn W Leusch	19	Spad	Stenay	1625	–	

a.   Spad XIII 7528 '4', 28th Aero, 1Lt BE Brown, POW.
b.   C3040, 99 Sqn, 2/Lt CE Thresher & 2/Lt W Glew, MIAs; and 104 Sqn IAF lost: D1050, 2/Lt HL Wren & 2/Lt WH Tresham, POWs and D3101, 2/Lt Hemingway & Sgt GA Smith, KIAs.
c.   D8384, 55 Sqn IAF, Lt G Richardson & 2/Lt JB Ward, MIAs.

Losses – Nil

7 November 1918

No Claims – No Losses

8 November 1918

Ltn J Buckler	17	RE8			–
Uffz A Bäder	65	Salmson	Buzy		2

Losses – Nil

9 November 1918

Ltn H v Freden	50	DH9	Beaumont	1135	–	
Ltn R Stark	35	SE5	E Bavai Wood		10	a.

a.   E5795, 56 Sqn RAF, 2/Lt JC Crawford, KIA.

Losses:

Ltn Karl Thom	21	Severely injured in a crash landing.
Ltn Heinz Frhr von B-Marconnay	65	Taken prisoner near Verdun Fokker DVII 4635/18 marked 'U10'.

10 November 1918

Ltn P Schwirzke	68	Balloon	Haudainville, Verdun	1014	4	a.
OfStv F Altemeier	24	RE8	by Solre	1050	21	b.
Ltn H Holthusen	29	SE5			4	
Uffz B Barthels	44	Balloon	Salon-le-Château		5	c.
Ltn H V Freden	50	BF2b	Froid Chapelle		–	d.

a.   3rd Balloon Co USBS, 1Lt GC Carroll, OK & 1Lt FD Cummings, OK.
b.   C2691, 12 Sqn RAF, Lt DB Agnew & 2/Lt S Coates, POWs.
c.   5th Balloon Co USBS, 1Lt LG Bowers, OK & 1Lt G Phelps, OK.
d.   F4421, 20 Sqn RAF, 2/Lt EAC Britton, POW & Sgt RJ Dodds, KIA.
Losses – Nil

11 November 1918

Waffenstillstand

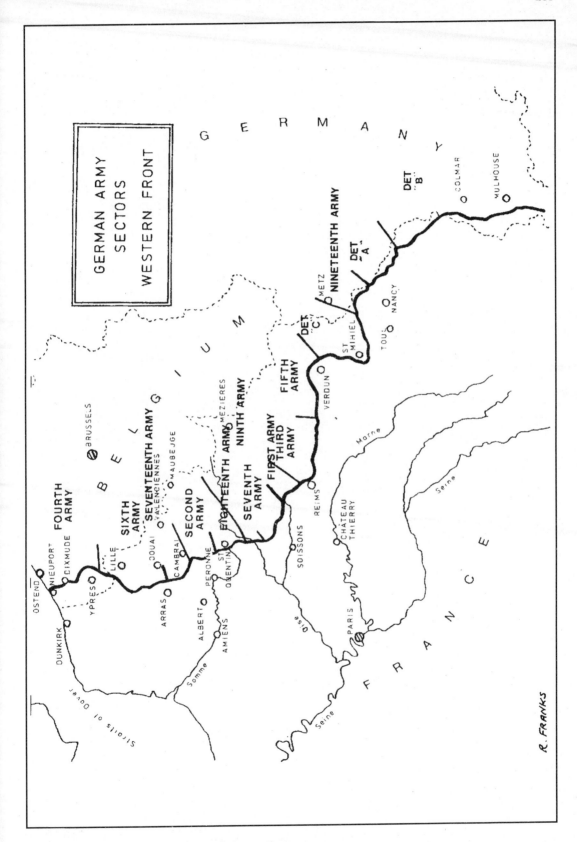

GERMAN ARMY
SECTORS
WESTERN FRONT

GERMANY

DET "B"

COLMAR

MULHOUSE

NINETEENTH ARMY

DET "A"

METZ

DET "C"

NANCY

TOUL

ST MIHIEL

VERDUN

MÉZIÈRES

FIFTH ARMY

SEVENTEENTH ARMY

NINTH ARMY

EIGHTEENTH ARMY

FIRST ARMY
THIRD ARMY

SECOND ARMY

SEVENTH ARMY

B E L G I U M

BRUSSELS

MAUBEUGE

VALENCIENNES

REIMS

Marne

Seine

FOURTH ARMY

SIXTH ARMY

NIEUPORT

DIXMUDE

LILLE

DOUAI

CAMBRAI

PERONNE

ST QUENTIN

SOISSONS

CHÂTEAU THIERRY

OSTEND

YPRES

ARRAS

ALBERT

AMIENS

Somme

Oise

Seine

PARIS

F R A N C E

DUNKIRK

Straits of Dover

R. FRANKS

NOTES

NOTES